The Björling Sound

The Björling Sound

A Recorded Legacy

Stephen Hastings

University of Rochester Press

First published 2012

University of Rochester Press
668 Mt. Hope Avenue, Rochester, NY 14620, USA
www.urpress.com
and Boydell & Brewer Limited
PO Box 9, Woodbridge, Suffolk IP12 3DF, UK
www.boydellandbrewer.com

ISBN-13: 978-1-58046-406-2

Library of Congress Cataloging-in-Publication Data

Hastings, Stephen, 1957– author.
The Björling sound : a recorded legacy / Stephen Hastings.
pages cm
Includes bibliographical references, discography, and index.
ISBN 978-1-58046-406-2 (hardcover : alkaline paper)
1. Björling, Jussi, 1911–1960—Performances. 2. Vocal music—Performances. 3. Tenors (Singers)—Biography. I. Title.
ML420.B6H37 2012
782.1092—dc23

2011049720

A catalogue record for this title is available from the British Library.

This publication is printed on acid-free paper.
Printed in the United States of America.

I dedicate this book to Robert von Bahr, another noble Swede deeply engrossed in music and recordings.

CONTENTS

ILLUSTRATIONS

PREFACE

This book was written in response to living sounds rather than printed words, but it would never have been written had it not been preceded by two other books: Harald Henrysson's *A Jussi Björling Phonography*, the second edition of which was published in 1993, and Anna-Lisa Björling and Andrew Farkas's *Jussi*, which appeared three years later. The former, offering a scrupulously researched and richly annotated listing (recently updated in an online version)[1] of all published and unpublished recordings featuring Jussi Björling as a child and adult, is a primary resource for the present volume, providing most of the factual information about the recordings included here. The writer is equally indebted to Henrysson's translations of many of the Swedish songs sung by Björling and reviews commenting on his early performances. No less invaluable is his complete chronology of the tenor's appearances in opera, recital and concert, which is included in the *Phonography* and has since been expanded further.[2] *Jussi*—which has proved an equally inspiring work of reference—is a biography combining the uniquely close perspective offered by the memories of Björling's wife (who heard her husband sing, onstage and off, more than any other person) with the broader scope and historical accuracy guaranteed by Farkas's interviewing and fact-checking. Although she is reticent about the exact circumstances of his death in September 1960,[3] Anna-Lisa's experience as a trained singer makes her an unusually credible commentator on the tenor's artistic progress.

The present book is also indebted to a very specific place: the Jussi Björling Museum in the tenor's home town of Borlänge in central Sweden, where a very complete archive of books, press cuttings, and recordings has been presided over by Henrysson and more recently by Jan-Olof Damberg, both of them untiring in their assistance to this writer. With so much material so easily accessible, this project began as an attempt to analyze all the tenor's recordings listed in *A Jussi Björling Phonography*. Over the years, however, it has become clear that a certain amount of selection was necessary if I wished to present the tenor within the context of ongoing performing traditions. It is only through comparison with other singers working within the same repertoire that relative values can be established, terminology clarified, and influences brought to light. I have thus limited the range of recordings covered, excluding for example Björling's discs of dance music, some of which were recorded under the pseudonym of Erik Odde. The recordings I do deal with—which cover almost his entire classical repertoire—are listed in chronological order at the beginning of each chapter or section. The releases referred to are those I consider best, and have listened to while writing this book. If no record label and catalogue number are mentioned, then the recording is unpublished.

Critical analysis of recordings is a not unexacting discipline, but it has yet to achieve universal recognition as an expression of musical scholarship. For this reason I have tried to be as precise as possible in describing what is happening musically in each performance (I refer generally to the original version of the score when Björling sings in Swedish translation), while at the same time giving a clear assessment of the aesthetic results of that performance. Listening is an art, not a science, but since ears (and memories) can easily be deceived I have used a few simple instruments to check pitch and duration. I am most grateful to Professor Johann Sundberg of the Royal Institute of Technology in Stockholm for providing some objective evidence to support my subjective impressions concerning the frequency range of Björling's singing. I have not included his spectrograms here,[4] but hope that he will soon publish the results of his own research on Björling.

I provide relatively little nonmusical information on the tens of tenors who are compared with Björling in the chapters that follow, but readers will find biographical sketches of many of them in John Potter's *Tenor: History of a Voice*, and in the two volumes of Michael Scott's *The Record of Singing*. Catalogue numbers of early twentieth-century recordings listed in the notes generally refer to the original release on shellac discs.

I owe a debt of gratitude to Stefan Johansson of the Royal Swedish Opera and the Malmö Opera for sharing his vast knowledge of Swedish operatic traditions; to Helena Iggander and her staff in the archive of the Royal Swedish Opera for letting me examine scores and cast listings; to John Pennino for allowing me generous access to the Metropolitan Opera's photographic archive; to Dan Shea and Sue Flaster of the American Jussi Björling Society for giving me the opportunity to speak about the tenor's recordings in a series of well-organized conferences worldwide; to Emily Kilpatrick for her scrupulous and adept editing of the manuscript; to Marianne Flach Turnbull for her translation of the tenor's autobiography; to Michael Aspinall for teaching me so much about the art of singing and sending me copies of his rare shellac discs; to Franca, my life's companion, for firing me with the ambition to see this project through to the end; and above all to the municipality of Borlänge for helping make this publication financially feasible.

Figure 1. Björling sings in his Met dressing room, 1940. Courtesy of the Jussi Björling Museum.

A BIOGRAPHICAL NOTE

Jussi Björling's life was relatively brief by twentieth-century standards: he was born in Borlänge, in the province of Dalarna in central Sweden, on February 5, 1911, and died forty-nine years later (September 9, 1960) on the island of Siarö in the archipelago north of Stockholm. Yet it was an intense, if unostentatious, life: immensely gratifying for the many who heard him perform in public between the ages of four and forty-nine; perplexing at times for the performer himself, a reserved, stubborn, but likeable man of changing moods, who intermittently abused the body he had transformed into the mellowest of musical instruments. His compulsive drinking bouts were a largely private affair, a source of secret anguish for his much-loved family and himself (although the secret was sufficiently well-known to taint his otherwise glowing public reputation). Accompanist Frederick Schauwecker's recollection of Jussi accidentally smashing a chandelier at a postrecital reception at the Swedish Embassy in Washington[1] is a rare example of alcohol-fuelled exuberance in public. Although the ill-health that heavy drinking generated in the 1950s did not make the work of entrepreneurs, general managers, and record companies any easier (there were quite a few cancellations), it rarely affected the singer's efficiency on the multiple occasions he did perform. It is probable, indeed, that the tenor's stark familiarity with the darker side of his own nature deepened his understanding of the multifaceted characters he played on stage. And his professionalism and need to communicate through music were such that even in the last year of his life—when his heart was sending him constant warning signals—he sang twenty-nine times in public and made two major studio recordings.

The brevity of Björling's life was amply counterbalanced by the number of experiences he managed to cram into those five decades. He did not have much formal schooling, but by the age of ten he had performed widely as a singer in the Björling Quartet[2] in Sweden and the United States, had made his first recordings, and had sung at his mother's graveside in Stora Tuna. By the time he was twenty his father too had died and he himself had fathered a son (Rolf), submitted himself to the rigorous training of the veteran baritone John Forsell, and made his debuts as a solo singer on the radio, in the recording studio, and at the Royal Swedish Opera. By the age of thirty he had already performed fifty-three roles, had been married (to Anna-Lisa Berg) for six years, had acquired two more sons, Anders and Lars (plus a daughter—Birgitta—out of wedlock), had performed at the principal opera houses in Vienna, Prague, Dresden, Budapest, London, San Francisco, Chicago, and New York, and had given recitals at the Konzerthaus in Vienna, London's Queen's Hall, and New York's Town Hall and Carnegie Hall. By thirty-five he had fathered another daughter (Ann-Charlotte), was a household name in his native land—where he had acquired a cherished summer retreat on Siarö—and had written an engagingly humorous autobiography. Its title, *My Voice Is My Luggage*, speaks of the wanderer's life Björling had always led, and would continue to lead until a month before he died.

Björling's career took him from Helsinki to San Francisco, from Saskatoon to Cape Town, from modest parish churches and open-air amusement parks to the world's most prestigious concert halls and opera houses. Two venues in particular, however, played a fundamental role in moulding him as an artist and consolidating his world-wide fame. His artistic home was the Royal Opera in Stockholm, where he sang all but one (Don Carlo) of his fifty-five stage roles, totalling 659 complete opera performances in a thirty-year time-span. He ceased to be a permanent member of the company in 1939, but returned regularly as a guest artist in the decades that followed. Although his first operatic engagement outside Sweden (a *Don Giovanni* in Helsinki) occurred as early as May 1931, fewer than 30 percent of his theatrical performances (272 out of a total of 931) took place outside the Swedish capital.

Figure 2. Preparing for a performance of *La bohème*. Courtesy of the Jussi Björling Museum.

The Metropolitan Opera was the American company for which Björling sang longest (1938–59) and most often: 121 performances (including those on tour) of eleven works. The collaboration was interrupted during World War II, and was later tarnished by Jussi's difficult relationship with general manager Rudolf Bing. Sometimes he was surrounded by even better casts in Chicago and San Francisco (where he also sang regularly for many years). Yet it was at the Met that he was broadcast ten times in seven operas and recorded privately in another two, and it was partly the enthusiasm of New York audiences that turned a publicity-shy man—who would have chosen to be a fisherman if a singing career had not been possible—into a living legend.

Björling was genuinely proud of his achievements, but how truly contented his legendary status made him is uncertain. His friend of many decades, Björn Forsell, contrasted the "optimistic, exuberantly happy" Björling in his twenties with the "more subdued" singer in his forties, "weighed down with the responsibility"[3] of being a tenor of worldwide fame. There is surely much truth in Forsell's words (which could however be applied to many middle-aged men of conspicuous achievement), yet it is probable that without the disciplined existence that a high-profile career (combined with family commitments) imposed, the self-destructive strain in the tenor's personality might have undermined his artistic standing. In his music-making, which was perhaps the truest mirror of the singer's soul, the contrasting moods of ebullience and melancholy remained poised in remarkable balance until about a year before Björling's death.

INTRODUCTION

The most haunting Nordic voices of the past two centuries—particularly those belonging to the tenor and soprano registers—have often seemed to reflect not only the distinctive vowels of the languages spoken in Sweden, Norway, and Finland but also the colors and textures of the landscapes in which they were created: the luminescence of fir-framed expanses of water on summer nights, the chromatic absoluteness—encompassing the entire color spectrum—of the snow and ice that transform those landscapes in winter. These are voices that shine without becoming dry, combining an unmasking purity of timbre with an all-embracing range of overtones.

It was qualities such as these that made a legend of the "Swedish Nightingale" Jenny Lind in the Victorian age and that enabled the Norwegian singer Kirsten Flagstad to achieve a unique status among the great sopranos of the twentieth century. An analogous combination of disarming purity and rainbow richness sets the Swede Jussi Björling apart from all other tenors documented on disc.

The Björling sound was not however entirely unique to Jussi: his father David (1873–1926) trained as a tenor in New York and Vienna, sang three operas with some success, and provided his sons with a vocal technique that enabled them to perform professionally as children and stood them in good stead throughout their adult careers. Jussi's brothers Olle (1909–65) and Gösta (1912–57) both had appealing tenor voices, as did his eldest son Rolf (1928–93), and the recordings of these three singers reveal the imprint of a characteristic Björling sound. Those same recordings, however, make it clear that it was Jussi who possessed the purest, most powerful, and most individual instrument, employed with unfailing musical sensibility and a communicative urgency that was deceptively understated.

In his autobiography, published when he was just thirty-four, Björling wrote, "even if I wasn't around during the beginnings of the gramophone, I can truly say that the gramophone was around during my beginnings."[1] He was in fact barely nine years old when his voice was first immortalized, along with Olle's and Gösta's, on six 78 sides. And he was just eighteen—and still a student at Stockholm's Royal Music Academy—when he made his first test recordings as a tenor.

The gramophone remained "around" Björling for the rest of his life. Rarely during his adult career did more than a year pass by without his entering a recording studio. He is one of the very few operatic artists—others include fellow Scandinavians Flagstad and Lauritz Melchior—whose voices can be heard both on acoustic discs, which were phased out in the mid 1920s, and on stereo recordings, which first became readily available in the latter half of the 1950s. Even though twenty-six of the roles he sang in the first decade of his adult career (half his entire operatic repertoire) are not even partially documented in sound, and although Ivan Kozlovsky (1900–93) covered a wider-ranging repertory, no other tenor born before 1915 was so extensively recorded—live and in the studio—in complete operas: thirty-five recordings survive, of a total of fifteen works.

As an instrument Björling's voice was, from the very beginning, exceptionally phonogenic. As mellow as a Cremona violin, it was capable of investing a melodic line with the lingering melancholy of a clarinet or cor anglais, and of rising above the staff with a bell-like peal or a trumpety *squillo.* The manner in which it was used, moreover, has not dated over the past five decades: the technique of the singer is as much a model today for aspiring tenors as it was during his lifetime.

Although Björling might have been surprised by his lasting popularity, he was well aware of the permanence of recordings. Indeed he was ahead of his time in proposing, in 1945, the institution of a "State Phonograph Record Archive" where "the performance of many outstanding musicians and singers would be preserved for the future."[2] He himself acknowledged that recordings had taught him "to smooth out imperfections and observe the development" of his own voice. Moreover, he had certainly drawn equally valuable lessons from the discs of Enrico Caruso (1873–1921), unquestionably the tenor whose critical reputation places him above all others in the twentieth century. Caruso's artistic personality proved decisive in establishing the gramophone as a genuine musical instrument. In spite of the technical limitations of acoustic recordings, no other male voice on record has matched the splendor of that timbre. The Neapolitan quickly became one of the dominant musical personalities of his age, influencing the sound worlds of several composers and innumerable singers.

Yet Caruso's phrasing rarely approaches the dynamic, coloristic, and rhythmic subtlety that one hears in the recordings of the finest instrumentalists of the period, such as the cellist Pablo Casals (though the tenor consciously emulated the sound of the cello) or the pianists Alfred Cortot, Josef Hofmann, and Sergei Rachmaninoff. To encounter a similar range of inflection one usually has to seek out less generously endowed tenors, such as Caruso's fellow Neapolitan Fernando De Lucia, unequalled in the fantasy and grace of his embellishments, or the vocal charmers (and composers) Tito Schipa and Richard Tauber. Other twentieth century models of technical mastery combined with musical imagination included Kozlovsky and Alfredo Kraus, while more recently Juan Diego Flórez has proved capable of phrasing with the technical virtuosity and expressive freedom of a great instrumentalist. If on the other hand we seek—in the tenor range—a combination of life-enhancing musicality and rare vocal splendor, then Björling stands alone. Neither Caruso, nor Beniamino Gigli, nor Luciano Pavarotti (uniquely popular in their respective eras) offer such consistent, intense, and varied musical pleasure in the way they use their voices. Even Placido Domingo, who in recent decades has won enormous admiration for both his sensual timbre and solid musicianship, arguably commands too limited a range of dynamics and color (he has never cultivated the use of head tones) for him to be able to phrase with consistent individuality.

In Björling voice, technique, and musical instincts were integrated to a degree that is only possible when vocal training begins at a very early age. For this reason it is difficult to separate the qualities of the musician from those of the singer. Whereas De Lucia, Tauber, Kraus, and Flórez require a certain degree of melodic, rhythmic, and harmonic complication to express their musical personalities (De Lucia even modifies the opening line of "Che gelida manina" in his recording of Puccini's aria),[3] Björling can transfix the listener just by singing two adjacent notes in the middle register. The much-admired Scottish tenor Joseph Hislop, who taught Jussi how to sing a top C, likened his pupil's phrasing to that of the Russian violinist Jascha Heifetz.[4]

If this were the whole story, Björling would have had no rivals among the great tenors of the twentieth century. However, operatic singing—and even Lieder singing, in a more limited sense—is as much about theater as it is about music; about verbal eloquence as well as beautiful sounds. Björling understood this, but his virtues as a man of the theater were relatively passive ones. Although the very purity of his emission favored clear diction, even in languages he did not speak with ease, sung words still need to be delivered with something more than clarity. In this respect Björling—although he could be strikingly eloquent at times, particularly when singing in his mother tongue—was less consistently inspired than a number of his tenor colleagues, all of whom were also at their best when singing in their native languages: De Lucia, Tauber, and Schipa once again spring to mind, along with Charles Friant and Georges Thill, Sergei Lemeshev and Kozlovsky, Giuseppe di Stefano, and Carlo Bergonzi. As the English critic John Steane put it, "with Björling, the thrill of his resonance is never emotionally neutral, but it remains essentially as pure song rather than the musical reshaping of an actor's declamation."[5] The same was true in recital: there is no attempt, for example, to distinguish between the different voices in Sibelius's dialogic "Flickan kom," even though the singer's involvement in the story he is telling is never in question.

In an operatic context, Björling's ability, or inclination, to grasp a musical phrase and transform it into a theatrical gesture was less integral to his artistic personality than has been the case with many Latin tenors (Franco

Corelli seemed to live for such moments), although it came spontaneously to the fore in operas that brought out the more flamboyant side of his nature. Nevertheless, he was perfectly aware of the viscerally spectacular effect of sustained top notes, and was better equipped than most to produce those notes to musically pleasing effect.

As an actor Björling's primary quality was perhaps his stillness on stage, an eschewing of superfluous agitation, and the employment of gestures that were naturally integrated with the production of the voice. The harmonization of body and sound is one of the secrets of operatic acting, and when a vocal technique is as effortless as Björling's this can produce a deep sense of well-being in an audience. Yet a convincing stage portrayal equally depends on facial expression and the ability to adapt gestures and gait in such a way as to lay bare the soul of a character—and nothing suggests that the Swedish tenor was particularly versatile in these respects.

He could, however, darken or lighten his voice at will to mirror the emotional content of the music he was singing. And the soprano Elisabeth Söderström (who knew what she was talking about) recalled that the expression in Björling's eyes when performing an opera was always that of the character he was playing, never that of the singer.[6] This ability to identify with a specific role reminds us of an important aspect of this tenor's art: the immediacy of his musical response, even at the hundredth performance of a particular song or aria. Although in the recording studio he can occasionally sound emotionally blank, like all great artists he was almost incapable of delivering a routine performance—and this was true right to the end, when his serious heart condition meant that public appearances were often accompanied by unnerving physical symptoms.

If one compares the video recordings of Björling with those of Roberto Alagna (b. 1963), one of his most talented successors in the *lirico-spinto* repertoire who, like the Swede, has sung roles ranging from Nemorino, Roméo, and Rodolfo to Canio, Manrico, and Radamès, then there is little doubt that it is the Frenchman who generally offers the more completely integrated theatrical interpretations. If, on the other hand, one bases the comparison purely on aural evidence, then it is often the Swede who emerges as the more varied, interesting, and musically satisfying performer. Alagna undeniably reveals a special sensitivity to the expressive nuances of the two languages (French and Italian) he speaks to perfection, but Björling can command a greater brilliance and gentleness of sound and a more subtle control of vibrato, while his chiaroscuro effects emerge as entirely free musical choices, unhampered by technical limitations. The perfect poise of his voice on the breath at all times means that he can derive inspiration from his idol Caruso without sounding like a mere imitation, as is sometimes the case when Alagna adopts a Pavarotti or Corelli-like color. The Björling sound—with its melancholy hue that tends to make itself felt even in the brightest music—is recognizable after one or two notes. The Alagna sound—like that of a number of contemporary tenors who have learnt to sing largely through listening to recordings—is less immediately identifiable.

Listening to the discs of all the tenors mentioned above reminds us that sound recordings, though infinitely varied, offer a fuller realisation of a composer's vision than a score alone. A score needs to be decoded in order to become music, inevitably leaving much to chance and to the sensibility of the performer. This is particularly true of opera, where alternating voices in a leading role can radically modify our perception of the character portrayed, however scrupulously each singer may respect the notation. Yet although the first vocal recordings of real interest (those made on Edison cylinders by Julius Block in Russia)[7] date back to 1890, only recently have musicologists started taking sound documentation seriously.[8] A traditionally book-based culture—with academics writing texts about other texts, sometimes bypassing sounds entirely—often failed in the past to consider recordings as serious musical documents. Therefore, although we have fairly complete documentation on disc of the performance histories of a number of operas that featured prominently in Björling's repertoire—*Cavalleria rusticana, I pagliacci, Manon Lescaut, La bohème,* and *Tosca*—no exhaustive studies exist of these histories.

A number of partial attempts at such performance histories have, however, been made, usually by music critics specialized in reviewing opera recordings. Record reviewers who combine a firm grasp of the score with an untiring interest in comparative listening are often able to explore fundamental dimensions of musical experience that have been relatively neglected by musicologists. These elements, which may be decisive in determining the emotional response of the average listener to the composer's creative gestures, often cannot be encoded within a score: subtle variations of color, dynamics, vibrato, pitch, and duration that emerge within a musical paragraph; the unwritten ornaments that sometimes embellish that paragraph, the continuity and strength of the legato that gives it shape, and the ever-varying stresses and accents that bring words to life.

It is these dimensions that this book inhabits with particular relish, for it is here that we can discover what made Johan Jonatan Björling—as he was was christened in Stora Tuna church, not far from his birthplace in Borlänge, on March 18, 1911—a unique interpretative artist, remarkable not only for his repertory choices (the multiple roles that were thrust upon him in the first decade of his career), but above all for his ability to approach familiar songs and well-practiced parts with renewed creativity every time he sang them.

Björling's theatrical repertoire—fifty-five roles in all—was ampler than that of most leading tenors (although this figure pales alongside Nicolai Gedda's sixty-five parts and Placido Domingo's mind-boggling one hundred thirty), and when he was in his twenties his career was truly a voyage of discovery, outrageously daring in its juxtaposition of some of the most difficult parts ever conceived. No other leading tenor of the twentieth century attempted the role of Arnold in *Guillaume Tell* at the age of nineteen, or alternated performances in *La fanciulla del West, La bohème, Die Entführung aus dem Serail, La traviata, Faust, Sadko, Tosca, Prince Igor, Cavalleria rusticana, Il barbiere di Siviglia,* and *Fidelio* within a three-month period, when he was just twenty-four.[9]

This phenomenal precociousness is, however, only very partially documented on disc. The voice of Björling as immortalized in the studio between 1929 and 1935 possesses a quite enchanting freshness, but the music he sings is rarely very demanding in its complexity. In those early years, moreover, he recorded arias from only nine of the forty-five roles he performed on stage during the same period. His recording projects became more ambitious when he started making discs for the international market in 1936, but after he ceased to be a permanent member of the Royal Swedish Opera three years later his stage roles were pared down to a mere twelve (only two of which were added after 1940). His concert work—which from the World War II onward was more intense than his theatrical activity—was similarly based on a consolidated collection of songs and arias, although in this case the repertoire was much wider-ranging.

The twelve operatic roles on which Björling focused during his international career—the Duke of Mantua, Manrico, Riccardo, Don Carlo, Radamès, Faust, Roméo, Canio, Turiddu, Des Grieux, Rodolfo, and Cavaradossi—all survive in complete recordings, as do his interpretations of Alfredo in *La traviata,* Pinkerton in *Madama Butterfly,* and Calaf in *Turandot* (the last of these never attempted on stage), while a substantial part of his recital and concert repertoire in that same period was captured both live and in the studio. Indeed, a feature of his legacy in sound is the existence of more than one version of the great majority of the arias and songs that he recorded. These multiple versions were partly motivated by evolving technology (after the first twenty years of his career 78s were largely replaced by LPs) and partly by the increasing number of live recordings that were preserved, the first one as early as 1934.

Any comprehensive analysis of the Swedish tenor's recordings will thus unfold as a series of variations on a number of largely familiar themes. They are familiar because Björling was in some ways (even considering the Nordic emphasis of his recital programs) very much a mainstream international tenor, focusing on some of the most popular art songs and operatic titles of all time. A substantial proportion of his recorded legacy can therefore be viewed as part of a wide-ranging and ongoing performing tradition, and compared with the output of all the other major tenors of the twentieth century. Of all Nordic tenors who emerged in the course of that century—including his more linguistically versatile fellow-countryman Nicolai

Gedda—it was Björling whose voice most closely rivalled the great Italian and Spanish singers in their warmth of timbre and expansiveness of phrasing. Nevertheless, even his most extrovert assumptions tend to maintain a quality of otherness—a melancholy underlay—that sets them apart and allows for a different perspective on the character who is singing. This book attempts to view afresh the characters Björling portrayed through the sound-perspective of his interpretations on record. This leads in turn to a clearer perception of the singer as a human being. Like all great theatrical artists he was capable of revealing on stage layers of accumulated experience that remained largely hidden in everyday life. Music enabled him to lay bare his emotions—interconnecting with the imaginative life of the composers and poets of other ages—in a way that compels the sensitive listener to respond both to the singer and the song.

This communicative directness naturally explains why Björling—or rather Jussi, as he was first called by his Finnish grandmother at a very early age—was able to "sing straight to the national soul of Sweden"[10] (Nicolai Gedda), winning the hearts of his countrymen more than any other classical singer of the past century.[11] His recorded output of patriotic songs and haunting ballads from the far North is as central to his identity as an artist as any aria or Lied. While from the 1920s onward an increasingly sharp divide developed between classical and popular musicians, Björling—like Caruso and Gigli before him and Di Stefano and Pavarotti later in the century—was more inclined to break down barriers than to erect them. In the 1930s he recorded popular dance tunes on 78s, while in the 1940s and 1950s he regularly performed before mass audiences every summer at Stockholm's Tivoli amusement park, and was a frequent guest on decidedly middlebrow radio and TV shows in the United States.

In preparing this book I have done my best to listen to every recording made of Björling's singing voice between 1920 and 1960. The chapters that follow focus mainly on the classical repertoire that he recorded most memorably, with the composers presented in alphabetical order and their compositions arranged chronologically. In these chapters each recording is analyzed within the context both of Björling's career and of the whole history of tenor singing in the twentieth century. Chapter 25 deals more briefly with his most outstanding performances of a wider range of music.

Just as a singer can reveal or conceal his inner nature through song, so can a writer either expose himself or cover up his tracks when unfolding his narrative. Since Björling was such an honest performer I have attempted to follow his example here, without any diplomatic adjustments of tone or content. This is very much one man's account of a great singer's music-making, inspired by the hope that at least some of my responses to the Björling sound will mesh creatively with the reader's own.

ADAM

"Cantique de Noël"

December 22, 1945: New York, Rockefeller Center
Unknown pianist

December 21, 1946: New York, Rockefeller Center
Unknown pianist

December 20, 1954: Stockholm, Södersjukhuset
Harry Ebert, pf.
WHRA-6036

February 8, 1959: Stockholm, Concert Hall
Royal Court Orchestra, cond. Nils Grevillius
EMI 5 75900 2

The "Cantique de Noël"—"Julsång" in Augustin Kock's Swedish translation—is as good a place to start as any, not only because the names of the composer, Adolphe Adam, begin with an A, but also because his Christmas song deals joyfully with the theme of birth. This song, which sets a text by Placide Cappeau de Roquemaure and was first performed on December 24, 1847, has long been part of the repertoire in Swedish churches at Christmas. Although Björling's first recording was made half-way through his adult career, he had probably performed the "Julsång" since childhood. The song's popularity in the early twentieth century is demonstrated by the fact that it was included in the world's first audio radio broadcast of music, relayed on December 24, 1906, from Brant Rock in Massachusetts. Björling's first three recordings of the "Julsång" were also Christmas broadcasts. And although two of them were made in New York, he stuck to the Swedish translation—singing the first and third verses, with unchanging words in the refrain—as if to underline the fact that he associated this music with Yuletide in his own land (both performances were relayed shortwave to Sweden). If one excepts his father David, who probably taught him the song, there is no reason to believe that Björling's interpretation was influenced by any other singer. He may, however, have heard Enrico Caruso's 1916 recording,[1] in the original French: a masterful performance, striking in its contrast between the *mezza voce* delivery of the two verses and the amplitude of the refrain, where the Neapolitan pulls out all the stops on the high Gs and climactic B-flat of "Noël." Caruso's rendition is stylish, too: in the second verse he introduces couple of melodic variants, entirely appropriate to vocal music from the first half of the nineteenth century.

Björling's first recording—in relatively poor sound—is less openly demonstrative of the singer's skill. Like Caruso he opts for Adam's original key of E-flat major, but he eschews the optional B-flat at the climax, sings the last verse as written, and is less varied in dynamics. It is indeed a performance of great simplicity—and herein lies its strength. The voice is so free from any trace of self-regard or sentimentality that it seems uniquely equipped to convey both the humility and wonder of the first verse, and the religious fervor that invests the refrain. It not only suggests the openness of the singer to spiritual experience, but makes that experience accessible to the listener too. The sounds are so well supported that a sense of continuity and flow is maintained even when Björling doesn't make explicit use of legato. The breath support lends vitality to the words, while the singer spontaneously regulates the intensity of every attack so that each phrase smoothly follows the preceding one. There is never any sense of weakness when the line dips to the bottom of the staff, for the sound is as perfectly focused in the baritone register as in the tenor range. The basic tempo adopted (♩ = 65) respects Adam's *Andante maestoso* marking, but is sufficiently flexible for the music to sound like an outpouring of feeling rather than something learnt by rote.

This first recording, however, is easily surpassed by the one Björling made a year later. This time the song is transposed up a half-tone, with an effortless B-natural at the climax, and the phrasing is much more nuanced, with a softly plaintive quality to "dödens smärta led" in the first verse and "stilla grav" in the second. Even the refrain—where the singer exhorts listeners to fall on their knees—is remarkable for its spiritual inwardness.

The 1954 performance was broadcast from a hospital in Stockholm, with Harry Ebert, Björling's most frequent accompanist (they gave approximately three hundred recitals between 1936 and 1959), at the keyboard. The physical presence of an audience seems to galvanize the singer: after a brief introduction (where his speaking voice proves a musical delight in itself), he offers an interpretation that is much more heroic in emphasis, reminiscent at times of Georges Thill's 1932 recording (in the original French),[2] although the tempo is less precipitous and the culminating B-flat more impressive in its balance of head and chest resonance. Björling regularly varies the intensity of the more sustained notes, most of which are reinforced after the attack.

Björling's only commercial version of the "Julsång" was recorded in 1959 at Stockholm's Concert Hall,[3] where he had made the great majority of his discs of single songs and arias. Seven other songs were recorded on that day, reminding us of the professionalism of a tenor who rarely needed to repeat anything when performing in front of a microphone, and never resorted to "dubbing" single notes (a practice that became widespead among star tenors in the decades that followed). The conductor, undertaking his final studio recording with Björling, was the Stockholm-born Nils Grevillius (1893–1970). Having taken up a position as violinist at the Royal Opera in the year of Björling's birth (1911), Grevillius had first mounted the podium in the same house in 1917. Assuming the post of principal conductor from 1932 to 1953, he led7 275 of the tenor's 659 performances with the company. Grevillius had also enjoyed a long association with the Swedish Broadcasting Corporation: present at Björling's first audition for the radio in 1928, he had subsequently worked with him on innumerable broadcasts, while also conducting most of the tenor's studio recordings. No other leading tenor of the twentieth century enjoyed such an intense relationship with one conductor. The scrupulous but flexible "Grillet" posthumously praised Björling for his "beautiful control over his voice, like a Kreisler on the violin, a Casals on the cello."[4]

On this occasion Grevillius provides Björling with an orchestral accompaniment complete with bells and other festive instruments, an arrangement that could seem tinselly if the voice were not so unerring in its truthfulness. The tenor sings in E major once again, and the performance emerges as an ideal compromise between the inwardness of the 1946 broadcast and the ringing thrust of the 1954 recording. As in the earlier broadcasts, the embellishments—acciaccaturas and turns—are executed with a precision that was rare in mid-twentieth century tenors, with the final *gruppetto* elaborated for added effect. This last recording was for many years Björling's most popular disc in his native Sweden.

ALFVÉN

If Björling had been born a hundred years earlier, leading composers would surely have seized the opportunity to write for a voice of such rare beauty. In the central decades of the twentieth century, however, beauty of tone was often considered to be irrelevant to the expressive ethos of the age. Benjamin Britten once claimed to "loathe what people normally call a beautiful voice":[1] it was the much less generously endowed English tenor Peter Pears (born eight months before Björling) who, thanks to his close association with Britten, would leave the greatest mark on mid-century classical music. Yet not all composers of merit were deaf to the potential of the Björling sound. It is probable that Hugo Alfvén, now recognized as one of the finest Swedish composers of the twentieth century, had that voice in mind when he wrote one of his most memorable love songs in 1946. The composer was an unassuming man, but in June 1957 he found the courage to write to the tenor:

> A few days ago I sent you my latest song: "Så tag mit hjerte." It's the most wonderful, heartfelt poem I have ever set to music, so unspeakably tender that I can never read it without tears coming to my my eyes. Naturally my thoughts have gone to you and your interpretation of "Skogen sover"; but I simply have not dared send my latest song to you, for that would have seemed like an implicit request—would you like to record this song also?—and I didn't want to take the risk of receiving a negative answer. But now I feel that I have to take the risk.[2]

It was a risk well worth taking, for Björling's recording of the song, made twenty months later, has never been surpassed. The other three Alfvén songs he recorded reveal an equally rare imaginative identification with the composer's expressive idiom.

"Jag längtar dig"

February 8, 1959: Stockholm, Concert Hall
Royal Court Orchestra, cond. Nils Grevillius
Swedish Society Discofil SCD 1100
August 5, 1960: Gothenburg, Concert Hall

Gothenburg Symphony Orchestra, cond. Nils Grevillius
Bluebell ABCD 092; WHRA-6036

"I long for you" is one of seven poems by Ernest Thiel, which Alfvén set to music in 1908. It is an obsessive love song (the first-person pronoun "Jag" recurs eight times in fourteen measures), sung by a Björling in his late forties with a rare combination of youthful ardor and adult awareness, introspective melancholy and tenorial exuberance. The single verse is repeated, with a modified, lower ending the first time, while in the final measures of the repeat Björling omits the mordent that embellishes the top A-sharp.

The two performances offer different perspectives on the song, for Björling almost never sang the same music in exactly the same way. The studio recording is more impulsive and determined in tone, with a sonorous low ending to the opening section and an exultant climax (the A-sharp is held for six seconds) in the repeat. The Gothenburg performance—recorded just over a month before he died—maintains a similar profile, but offers a softer close to the first verse and a magical half-voice on the words "ditt skönhets rike," suggesting a closer identification with the object of desire.

"Skogen sover"

March 1, 1940: New York, Manhattan Center
Harry Ebert, pf.
Bluebell ABCD 050

April 11, 1949: New York, Carnegie Hall
James W. Quillian, pf.
WHRA-6036

June 1954: Bergen, Concert Palace
Bergen Philharmonic Orchestra, cond. Carl Garaguly
Bluebell ABCD 006

March 2, 1958: New York, Carnegie Hall
Frederick Schauwecker, pf.
RCA 60520-2-RG

April 13, 1959: Atlanta, Glenn Memorial Auditorium
Frederick Schauwecker, pf.
Bluebell ABCD 020

August 5, 1960: Gothenburg, Concert Hall
Gothenburg Symphony Orchestra, cond. Nils Grevillius
Bluebell ABCD 092

In "The Forest Asleep," inspired by another Thiel poem, the atmosphere of the still summer night in the forest where two lovers are resting is as important as the feelings explicitly conveyed: the forest itself seems impregnated with unexpressed emotion. Björling's interpretation of this song—which was encored and captivated the composer when he performed it at the Théâtre des Champs Elysées in June 1937—has never been equalled on disc, and never fails to work its enchantment. This is particularly true of his first recording, in the original key of D-flat major, made three years after the Paris concert. It demostrates how imaginative his phrasing was when singing the music of his own land (a repertoire in which he never felt the need to model his sound on anyone else's), and how easily he could command the purest of head voices, exemplified here by the suspended *pianissimo* attack on the initial high F. The terminology used to describe such sounds has often aroused controversy. "Head voice," however, seems appropriate here: it involves a higher placement and more crystalline sound than a straightforward *mezza voce*, without suggesting the distinct separation from the main body of the voice that is implied by falsetto. Indeed with Björling there is no separation of registers, here or on in any later recordings.

Although the first recording is hard to beat, there is much to treasure in the subsequent versions. The close miking at the 1949 Carnegie Hall concert enables us to "observe" the workings of that head voice at even closer quarters, and it proves a fascinating experience. In Bergen five years later the orchestral accompaniment interacts with the voice in a more complex manner, making it sound, on certain vowels, like a wind instrument. At the Carnegie Hall in 1958 the contrast is stronger than ever between the hushed opening and the darker sounds in the lower octave, while the more distant microphone placement in Atlanta gives us a sense of how magically the voice travelled through space. In Gothenburg—with an orchestra once more—the voice sounds (in comparison with Bergen) warmer and more caressing, less instrumental in effect but no less beautiful.

Grevillius's recollections of that concert—their very last together—demonstrate how musically painstaking Björling remained to the end:

> During the first rehearsal he made a trifling error in one of the final measures of Alfvén's "Skogen sover," a mistake which the audience would barely have noticed. But Jussi was annoyed with himself. "Such damned carelessness with those eighth notes!" he said and assured me that he would go back to the hotel and look over the passage again. The next day he came over to me before the rehearsal and said triumphantly: "I can do it now!" That was the way he was always with his work—dedicated and extremely particular.

This recollection admittedly contrasts with the pianist Ivor Newton's memories of how strongly the tenor disliked rehearsing,[3] yet what Björling seems to have objected to most in later years was wasting his time and increasingly precious energies on practising music he had already mastered.

Rarely does one come across any recorded performance in which he sounds underrehearsed.[4]

"Endräkt"

June 6, 1953: Stockholm, Stadion
Band of the Royal Svea Life Guards, cond. Ille Gustafsson
VAIA 1189

Patriotic feeling ran deep in Björling, as is clear from this four-square E-flat major hymn entitled "Concord," sung in a lusty *forte* during an open-air flag day broadcast from the stadium in Stockholm. The recording is not free from distortion, but the two verses, which sit largely in the singer's middle and lower registers, are delivered without bluster, the fervor of the declamation reinforced by his manner of attacking each note right in the middle and by the solid breath support that informs the phrasing, making every syllable resonate tellingly. The almost baritonal sound he makes here reminds us of the widely varying colors that Björling could draw on when needed, and how naturally he adapted those colors to the accompaniment (in this case the brass and timpani).

"Så tag mit hjerte"

February 8, 1959: Stockholm, Concert Hall
Royal Court Orchestra, cond. Nils Grevillius
Swedish Society Discofil SCD 1100

This song, composed in 1946 to a text in Danish by Tove Ditlevsen, reveals the vulnerability of a lover who hands over his heart to the loved one. Björling captures this sense of emotional exposure, combining a timbre still pristine in its youthful glow with a capacity for feeling heightened by long and often painful experience. In his voice the poem acquires stratified meanings, for the tenor's heart was itself by then—quite literally—extremely vulnerable. Although the song is hardly daring harmonically by mid-twentieth-century standards, the exactness of the tenor's intonation makes every modulation tell. Alfvén keeps the listener in a state of suspension at the end of the first three verses (the song has an AABA structure), returning to the tonic—a G-flat sustained on a thread of tone—only at the end of the fourth and final verse, "nu kan det knuses / men kun av dig." This conclusive phrase was the only section that Björling asked to repeat during the recording session:[5] in his second attempt he offers us the most prolonged of all his pianissimos on record. Since the only dynamic marking in the score here is a *piano* in the orchestral accompaniment, this is an example of how an imaginatively engaged singer can complete an expressive gesture barely hinted at by the composer.

ATTERBERG

Fanal
"I männer över lag och rätt"

March 4, 1935: Stockholm
Unspecified orchestra, cond. Nils Grevillius
Naxos 8.110722

Act 3: Finale
January 29, 1934: Stockholm, Royal Opera House
Jussi Björling (Martin Skarp), Helga Görlin (Rosamund) Joel Berglund (Jost), Gösta Bäckelin (Vassal), Leon Björker (Duke); Royal Swedish Opera Chorus, Royal Court Orchestra, cond. Nils Grevillius
Bluebell ABCD 103

In the first decade of his operatic career Björling sang five contemporary Swedish theatrical works: Edvin Znieder's *Bellman,* Natanael Berg's *Engelbrekt,* Hilding Rosenberg's *Resa till Amerika,* Ture Rangström's *Kronbruden,* and Kurt Atterberg's *Fanal.* The last of these, a ballad-style drama based on an old Rhenish legend as retold by Heinrich Heine (*Der Schelm von Bergen*), proved popular with 1930s audiences: after the the world premiere in Stockholm on January 27, 1934, Björling performed it on twenty-two other occasions over the subsequent five seasons. Atterberg, who was forty-seven in 1934 and a well-established figure in Swedish musical life (active also as a critic and conductor), had set to music a German libretto by Ignaz Michael Welleminsky and Oscar Ritter. The world premiere, however, was given in Swedish, as were all operas in Stockholm at that time (although guest artists from abroad often sang their parts in the original language).

Fanal had been written between 1929 and 1932. One wonders whether the composer had Björling's voice already in mind when shaping the music assigned to Martin Skarp, who saves the Duke's daughter during a peasant uprising in sixteenth-century Germany and thereby wins her hand, liberating himself from the despised role of public executioner that he has

Figure 3. Martin Skarp and Rosamund (Helga Görlin) in *Fanal*, Stockholm, 1934. Photograph by Almberg and Preinitz. Courtesy of the Royal Swedish Opera Archive.

inherited from his father. In vocal terms the role is punishingly difficult: the act 1 monologue—a declamatory *Andante* in 3/4 time, in which Martin pleads in court to be freed from his obligation to inherit his father's profession—has an uncomfortably high tessitura, requiring a full-throated emission with repeated ascents to B-flat. In his studio recording made with Nils Grevillius (who had conducted the world premiere) in 1935, the tenor overcomes these hurdles as if they did not exist. His singing here is quite remarkable for its clarion beauty of tone, crispness of articulation and underlying humanity. He makes the best possible case for music of limited inspiration, and we can easily imagine the audience being swept away by his phrasing. When talking about technique, Björling preferred not to reason in terms of registers,[1] and this attitude seems entirely justified here: we have the impression that the multiple Fs and Gs at the top of the staff (where most tenors have to switch to a more carefully "covered" tone) require no adjustment whatsoever.

The other recording of Björling's Skarp was made just two days after the world premiere. The earliest live documentation of his singing, it includes the entire finale of the third act, beginning with another solo for the tenor ("Nu bröder, ändas våra strider") which contrasts markedly with Martin's earlier monologue. The tessitura is lower here and the melodic line more solidly anchored to a single key (C major). This, combined with the reassuring 4/4 rhythm, makes for a suitably rousing happy ending: the melody is in fact repeated at the close of the opera where the tenor is joined by the chorus and other principal singers. Before this final ensemble, the solo develops first into a quartet (with Helga Görlin, Leon Björker and Gösta Bäkelin joining Björling) and then a quintet, incorporating Joel Berglund. The overall effect of this concerted episode is unfortunately disappointing, for Atterberg's writing is not only unduly complicated in relation to his expressive intent, but also markedly unvocal. Throughout the scene, however, one is struck by Björling's ability to dominate the stage, even alongside singers of considerable personality. These two extracts from *Fanal* were the only "creator" recordings he ever made, but their importance lies decidedly in the singing rather than the song.

BEETHOVEN

"Adelaide" (op. 46)

July 15, 1939: Stockholm, Concert Hall
Harry Ebert, pf.
EMI 5 75900 2; Naxos 8.11078

August 23, 1949: Los Angeles, Hollywood Bowl
Hollywood Bowl Symphony Orchestra, cond. Izler Solomon
Standing Room Only SRO-845-1

September 24, 1955: New York, Carnegie Hall
Frederick Schauwecker, pf.
RCA 88697748922

March 2, 1958: New York, Carnegie Hall
Frederick Schauwecker, pf.
RCA 60520-2-RG

When Beethoven found the courage to write to Friedrich von Matthisson in 1800, telling him he had set the poet's "Adelaide" to music several years earlier, he claimed that the song had come "warm from" his heart.[1] Some fifteen years later, the composer performed "Adelaide" with the tenor Fritz Wild as part of a concert for the Empress of Russia, a choice that suggests an abiding affection for the song. It was the composer's last public appearance as a pianist, although he accompanied Wild once again in "Adelaide" at a private concert in the home of a Viennese music-lover in the spring of 1816.

Björling's first known performance of "Adelaide" also took place in a private house, that of the Swedish Liberal politician Sven Theodor Palme, in Stockholm in February 1931. He continued to include the song in his recital programs until the final years of his life. "Adelaide" was both the longest German song in his repertoire and the piece that, more than any other, attested to his special qualities as a singer of Lieder. These qualities can be heard at their best in his 1939 studio recording. Although Björling was then barely twenty-eight, his sensitivity as an artist was at a peak, as was his technical ability to transform that sensitivity into phrasing of surpassing finesse. Described by John Steane as "something of a wonder,"[2] this is probably the recording that has won Björling the most generous praise from critics over the decades.

That 1939 session was the first occasion on which the Swedish tenor recorded Lieder, or indeed anything in German. He had studied the language briefly with John Forsell (director of the Royal Swedish Opera from 1923 until 1939) earlier in the decade, and had practised during his stays in Vienna, Nuremberg, Berlin and Dresden in 1936–37 (these visits included a well-received recital at Vienna's Konzerthaus in March 1936). Björling began his career as a solo recitalist at a very young age, but in the early years only had time for a few recitals every season. From this point of view the July 1939 recording session represented a turning point, for he had recently terminated his full-time contract with the Royal Swedish Opera and would thereafter spend more time performing on the recital platform than on the operatic stage.

The unique aura created in this recording makes itself felt right from the opening measures, where Harry Ebert's introduction (in the original key of B-flat major) is a model of legato and singing tone. As the pianist is assigned what proves to be an embellished version of the tenor's opening line, the singer must immediately match the piano sound if he does not want to sound earthbound by comparison. Björling not only duplicates the liquescent tone of the keyboard in the opening measures (marked *dolce e piano*), but also exploits the extra closeness of the voice to the microphone to create an atmosphere of real intimacy. The poet here is addressing his beloved Adelaide, but his use of the second person singular—"*dein* Freund"—creates the illusion of a direct bond with the listener, which makes it easier for us to enter his imaginative world, infused with the "magical light" of a "spring garden." The luminosity of the tone makes the images come alive, and time seems to stand still for an instant when Björling switches to head voice for the upper Gs of "Zauberlicht" and "wankende."

This pure tone suggests the right degree of freedom from emotional constraint, but has none of the breathiness or contrivance of the typical falsetto. When Björling was questioned eleven years later by readers of the magazine the *Etude* on the use of falsetto, he replied:

> Falsetto in Italian means false tone. The difference between a falsetto and a *pianissimo* is that the first shows more escape of breath and lacks the overtone and floating quality of the *pianissimo*. I am not one of those who believes that a falsetto should be acquired or is a necessity in developing or using the voice.[3]

This explanation is clear enough, but when we apply these terminological distinctions to the tenor's own singing they sound like an over-simplification, for the disembodied head voice heard in this recording (which many would define as a well-sustained falsetto) clearly differs in color from a simple *piano* tone produced by the same voice in the same phrase in later recordings. Yet it is hard to deny the "floating quality" of these sounds—especially when the tenor ascends to the high A of "dein Bildniss"—and their entirely unbreathy integration into the line: indeed, it is the unearthly quality of the soft singing that sets this recording apart from those by other tenors. Nicolai Gedda[4] also proves a master in blending head and chest resonance in those opening phrases, but the relatively hurried tempo in his 1969 recording prevents those sounds from making their full effect, while Fritz Wunderlich's *piano* tone in his final recital[5] is insufficiently supported for the phrasing to prove truly evocative.

The second verse has a different melodic line but maintains the ever-varying triplet accompaniment. Here the poet's focus shifts from the garden to the wider world beyond: Adelaide's image is reflected in water, snow, clouds, and stars, and the voice takes on at times a more forthright, portentous tone. A feature of Björling's singing here is a discreet use of portamento, which reinforces our sense of an imagination in full flight. The poet's visions, however vivid, are nevertheless unaccompanied by any real chance of erotic fulfilment; this explains why the underlying melancholy of the tenor's timbre—which comes to the fore in the descending sixteenth notes of "den Tages Goldenwölken"—proves so apt. One of the unique features of Björling's voice was its ability to communicate sadness and optimism at the same time, and in this Lied—where joy and desperation are constantly mingled—the complexity of the feelings expressed is conveyed through the quality of the tone rather than through verbal inflection. The text is delivered with clarity but without extra stresses, for the real meaning of the Lied lies partly in what is left unsaid.

The third verse, which begins in D-flat major, evokes sounds rather than sights. Björling's voice is at its most evocative here, particularly in observing the sudden contrast between the *forte* of "Wellen rauschen" and the *piano* of "Nachtigallen flöten," where he suggests better than any other singer on disc the heartbreaking purity of the bird's song.

The cabaletta-like *Allegro molto* does not bring with it an unequivocally happy ending, but rather a stark vision of the future: the poet imagines the flowers on his grave, springing from the ashes of his heart, with the name of Adelaide shining from each purple petal. While this is seen as a wondrous manifestation of life after death, it was nevertheless daring of Beethoven to set these apparently morbid words to such a breathlessly affirmative melody. Björling eases us gently at first into the opening measures of the *Allegro*—respecting Beethoven's *piano* marking in the accompaniment—but in the repeats of "deutlich schimmert auf jedem Purpurblättchen" his phrasing acquires an increasingly feverish quality, as if the poet were aware that his imagination has got slightly out of control. But by the time he reaches the final, soft, "Adelaide"—rising gently from the dominant (F) up to the tonic (B-flat)—we sense that the emotional crisis has passed and that the vision of death is now one of calm—and, for the listener, deeply soothing—acceptance.

Only through comparison with other singers do we become fully aware of the miracle Björling achieved in this recording. The baritone Heinrich Schlusnus, singing in A-flat major in 1930,[6] comes close to rivalling the Swede in his fusion of pellucid diction with a suave legato, but the tone is too blasé; the voice lacks the innocence manifest in the words and music. Peter Anders, in a 1942 recording,[7] offers equally solid tone production and sharper dynamic contrasts in the *Larghetto,* but the absence of a genuine head voice limits the evocative force of the music, and the German tenor's tendency to employ portamentos only when Beethoven specifically requests them reduces the flow of his phrasing.

At least one critic, David Hamilton, prefers Anders's performance to Björling's, lamenting the latter's lack of "emotional commitment."[8] On a first hearing it might indeed seem that Björling, in comparison with Gedda or Anders, is simply trying to phrase as smoothly as possible without focusing sufficiently on verbal meanings. It is important, however, to distinguish between the emotional emphasis with which a singer pronounces a word, and his ability to conjure up a visual image that corresponds to that word. While these two skills sometimes coincide, they are not identical, and it is the latter in which Björling excels: his singing here has less "face" to it than Wunderlich's or Anders's (in other words it is harder to imagine the physiognomy of the man who is singing), but it transports us more effortlessly into his imaginative world. Words in his voice become colors, sounds, and sensations rather than remaining simply words.

Björling never succeeded in matching the studio recording in his later broadcasts. At the Hollywood Bowl in 1949 he is accompanied by an orchestra and we are strongly aware of his desire to project the song into the largest natural amphitheater in the United States, sacrificing the dialectic between *piano* and *forte* in order to achieve an operatic amplitude of phrasing (this is also the slowest of his four recordings of the Lied). The relatively poor recording reduces our perception of the voice's mellow beauty, as it picks up the melody from the solo clarinet in the opening measures, and Izler Solomon occasionally has difficulty in responding to the singer's rubato. This is a rather literal performance, even though Björling's German pronunciation has gained in confidence: he had studied in the meantime with Wilhelm Freund, who taught Lieder at the Royal Music Academy in Stockholm.

At the Carnegie Hall in 1955 the voice is much better recorded, and Frederick Schauwecker's accompaniment is more prominent than was Ebert's in the Stockholm studio. The singing is graceful, with greater intimacy of feeling than in Los Angeles and a well placed *mezza voce* (as opposed to a pure head voice) on the top A of "dein Bildniss." Björling, however, is not on his best form and the lack of bloom on his tone is conspicuous. The best part of the performance is the *Allegro molto,* where the play of rubato is more imaginative than in the earlier recordings, and words are communicated with greater crispness.

When Björling returned to the Carnegie Hall in March 1958 the voice was darker and the phrasing revealed a stronger degree of imaginative engagement, with more freedom in the upper register and a wider range of dynamics. The top A is attacked *mezzo forte* this time and then tapered away, and the final cries of "Adelaide!" in the *Larghetto* ring out more penetratingly than before. The *Allegro* is slower than in 1955, generating a deeper sense of thrust. However, Björling no longer achieves a truly telling contrast between "Wellen rauschen" and "Nachtigallen flöten," and one misses the singular radiance and melancholy of the studio reading, for this is the song of a young man's longing, which requires a young man's voice to unveil its multifaceted meanings.

"Die Ehre Gottes aus der Natur" (op. 48 no. 4)

February 8, 1959: Stockholm, Concert Hall
Royal Court Orchestra, cond. Nils Grevillius
Swedish Society Discofil SCD 1100

Björling's sole recording of the fourth of the six Gellert settings (op. 48) confirms his distinguished status as a Beethoven singer. This recording nevertheless occupies a more peripheral position in the composer's discography than the 1939 "Adelaide" because the text is sung in Jacob Axel Josephson's very free Swedish translation, which weakens the philosophical overtones of the poem, turning it into a straightforwardly affirmative hymn.

Björling probably learned this song as a hymn in his childhood (it was in his father's repertoire), and that is how he delivers it here. Hymn-singing, however, is an art, and a challenging one at that when the vocal writing is as awkward as it proves in this case (Beethoven is ever unheeding of the limitations of the human voice). Few tenors or baritones can produce equally firm, resonant tone on the C below the treble staff and on the G above it, and Björling is not alone in transposing the music.

One singer who does perform it in the original key of C major is Heinrich Schlusnus, the finest German baritone of his generation, whose 1930 recording[9] demonstrates a perfect union of words and tone throughout the range and at all dynamic levels.

Björling takes the Lied up a tone and the result is even more rousing. His singing is on the grandest scale: true to Beethoven's indication *Majestätisch und erhaben,* the notes roll out as if produced by a fine organ, with each pitch savored for its full range of overtones. The precision and decisiveness of the tenor's declamation lend an extra degree of poignancy to the line as it modulates first to A minor (in "vernimm, o Mensch") and then to F major in the questioning "Wer trägt der Himmel unzählbare Sterne?" Here Björling chooses to sing the repeated Fs at the top of the staff in a candid *mezzo piano,* against the accompaniment's *pianissimo,* so as not to compromise the imposing scale of the phrasing. Other singers opt for a *mezza voce*: Dietrich Fischer-Dieskau, singing a tone below the original key in his 1966 recording,[10] here suggests a genuine spirit of philosophical enquiry. This is one of his most inspired performances on disc and represents an ideal alternative to Björling's more straightforward delivery. The Swedish tenor, however, stirs the blood in the final measures, rising to the G and A with resplendent ease and linking the last two notes with a resolutory portamento.

Missa Solemnis (op. 123)

December 28, 1940: New York, Carnegie Hall
Jussi Björling (tenor), Zinka Milanov (soprano), Bruna Castagna (contralto), Alexander Kipnis (bass); Westminster Chorus, NBC Symphony Orchestra, cond. Arturo Toscanini
Music & Arts CD 4259

Only a handful of the thirty-nine recordings of full-scale operas and religious works with Björling can be considered close to definitive in their all-round excellence. One of these is this live performance of Beethoven's *Missa Solemnis,* broadcast in 1940. The four soloists are arguably the finest group of singers ever recorded in the Mass and Toscanini conducts like one possessed, driving the performers to the limits of their abilities. This very striving after the impossible arguably represents the essence of the Beethoven style, particularly in the great masterpieces written in the final years of the composer's life. The sense of exaltation with which the soloists overcome the multiple hurdles placed before them proves a source of awe on every hearing: it is hard not to agree with John Steane when he concludes—at the end of a stringently argued survey of complete recordings—that this is the finest of them all, containing "the widest range of emotions and the most deeply felt."[11]

As Björling recalls in his autobiography, this achievement was the result of an intense rehearsal schedule, which he had to fit in between Met performances of *Un ballo in maschera* and *Faust.* This schedule generated a serious conflict between Toscanini and the NBC Orchestra that was only resolved many months later.[12] Björling's recollection of the experience, however, was untroubled in its enthusiasm: "Everyone participated throughout with their hearts and souls. No one stood around saving his energies. As a result, the evening performance was brilliant. I did not feel at all tired until the whole thing was over; then I was entirely exhausted."[13]

This was the ninth time Björling had performed Beethoven's Mass. It had become something of a tradition for him to sing it in Stockholm under the leadership of Tullio Voghera (a friend of Toscanini's who had settled in Sweden and who coached Björling in many an operatic role) in the period leading up to Easter every year. His very first performance had taken place on Easter Sunday 1931 (April 5), while in March 1935, astonishingly, he had sung it the day before his debut as Florestan in *Fidelio* (a role which remains undocumented in disc). The Carnegie Hall performance, which took place between Christmas and the New Year, turned out to be Björling's last. His decision not to return to the work is understandable, for it would have been almost impossible to surpass the experience of singing it with Toscanini. Although the tenor part in the *Missa Solemnis* is often no more than a rich golden thread running through a great tapestry, there are moments in which Beethoven allows the soloist to take the initiative, becoming for a few brief seconds the focal point of the whole sacred rite. Björling's is the first solo voice we hear in the opening "Kyrie eleison," with a sustained D on the first syllable of "Kyrie" that emerges from nowhere. It is not the voice of an operatic tenor removed from his habitual context of midnight trysts and pacts with the devil, but that of an unmasked human being, inwardly disposed to converse with the transcendent. A similarly exposed tenor entry introduces the solo section of the second "Kyrie eleison" toward the end of the movement. This time the voice rings out on a top G before descending by means of a portamento to the E immediately below. In the intermediate "Christe eleison" the tenor is less prominent, but the listener cannot but appreciate the smooth regularity of the flowing lines of conjunct quarter notes on "eleison," where the voice intertwines with those of Bruna Castagna, Alexander Kipnis, and Zinka Milanov: the four remarkable instruments maintain their distinctive flavor while fulfilling their contrapuntal function.

Both the "Gloria" and the "Credo" are remarkable for the way in which the composer lends specific musical expression to almost every line of the Latin text (pronounced by Björling with caressingly Italianate diction). In both movements the tenor rewards listeners with a number of unforgettable details. In the "Gloria" he makes the most of the tender melody of "Gratias agimum tibi," the voice floating limpidly above the serenade-like accompaniment of clarinets, bassoons, horns, and basses, while later we note the expressive urgency of "Domine figli unigenite" (attacked together with Kipnis), the pleading solo line of "suscipe deprecationem," the noble humanity of "ah, miserere nobis," and the melismatic fluency of "in gloria Dei patris." In the "Credo" Björling's *mezza voce* captures perhaps better than that of any other tenor on record (not excepting Fritz Wunderlich in the 1966 Karajan recording)[14] the mystical stillness of the Doric melody in "Et incarnatus est," which here becomes the spiritual centerpoint not only of the movement but of the whole Mass. No less impressive are his stirringly heroic delivery of the D major "et homo factus est" and the sense of awe and pity conveyed in the D minor "Crucifixus etiamo pro nobis." The listener receives the impression that it is the tenor who is speaking for all humanity throughout the central section of the "Credo," while in the passagework of the conclusive Amens his execution, like that of the other soloists, is bold and vehement.

In the final two movements Björling has fewer opportunities to shine individually. It is rare, however, to hear a tenor sustain the low tessitura in the opening section of the "Sanctus" with such smooth and solid tone. In the "Benedictus" his legato matches that of concertmaster Mischa Mischakoff, and his prodigious technique is further demonstrated by the sustained *piano* G above the staff on "venit." Equally remarkable is his entry in "Agnus Dei," where the opening E is attacked softly and then wells up from within, while his delivery of the word "miserere" conveys a total comprehension of sorrow. This is particularly true in the dramatic recitative "Agnus Dei, miserere nobis": an episode that Toscanini invests with a genuine sense of drama, with the soloists responding whole-heartedly.

BIZET

The only Bizet work in which Björling appeared on stage was *Djamileh,* a charming *opéra comique* (with spoken dialogue), first performed in 1872. In the 1933 revival in Stockholm he played the role of Haroun, a rich, bored young Egyptian whose emotional fickleness is cured by the resourceful and seductive Djamileh. It is a typical French lyric tenor role with a relatively high tessitura; the twenty-two-year-old Björling was praised for his tasteful singing, "brilliant in the big numbers," but was taken to task for his unripe acting: "The spoken scenes sounded frightful," wrote Kurt Atterberg.[1]

These critical reservations help us understand why Björling never sang Don José on stage,[2] even though *Carmen* clocked up more performances than any other work at the Royal Opera during his career. In the 1930s his voice may have been considered too lightweight for a role often associated in Sweden with Wagnerian tenors,[3] while in the 1950s Bizet's masterpiece was performed there as an *opéra comique* (without Guiraud's accompanied recitatives), which would have obliged Björling to deal once again with spoken dialogue. At the Met too *Carmen* was a repertory staple, but the role tended to be reserved for skilful singing actors of striking presence.

During the same period *Les pêcheurs de perles* was absent from the repertoire of both houses, which explains why Björling never attempted the more static role of Nadir, a part that in any case requires more nuanced phrasing than he was able to achieve in his two attempts at the *romance* "Je crois d'entendre encore."

Les pêcheurs de perles
"Au fond du temple saint"

January 3, 1951: New York, Manhattan Center
Jussi Björling (Nadir), Robert Merrill (Zurga); RCA Victor Symphony, cond. Renato Cellini
RCA 88697748922; Naxos 8.110788

"Je crois entendre encore"

September 7, 1945: Stockholm, Concert Hall
Royal Court Orchestra, cond. Nils Grevillius
Testament SBT 1427

September 28, 1945: Stockholm, Concert Hall
Stockholm Philharmonic Orchestra, cond. Tor Mann
Bluebell ABCD 036

Björling's only recording of the famous duo "Au fond du temple saint" was the last of the four duets that he recorded with Robert Merrill on January 3, 1950. It was initially coupled, on a 78 disc, with the contrasting "Sì, pel ciel marmoreo giuro" from Verdi's *Otello*. The tenor had been interested in these two duets for some time—in 1948 he had let RCA know that he wished to record them with Leonard Warren[4]—and his instinct proved right, for no other recording by Björling has proved as universally popular as the *Pearl Fishers* duet. He never performed this music on any other occasion, but the expressive balance of the two male voices, with Merrill's sturdy, grainier tone setting off the shimmering beauty of the tenor's sound, lends the duet a heart-warming vitality that transcends the original dramatic context. Both singers felt later that this was the most artistically successful of their duet recordings.[5]

This music had enjoyed considerable popularity long before Björling and Merrill got round to recording it: over forty versions already existed on 78s. All of them are cut—the piece was too long to fit onto one side of a 78 disc—and none of them end in the manner devised by Bizet when he composed the work in the summer of 1863. His original *Allegro moderato* conclusion, "Amitié sainte," is more psychologically coherent than the 1885 posthumous version (reelaborated by an anonymous composer) heard here, with its reprise of "Oui, c'est elle, c'est la déesse." The cut in the Björling-Merrill recording involves the dramatic recitative beginning "Mais dans mon âme soudain," where Nadir and Zurga recall how their love for Léïla brought a temporary end to their friendship. Björling's brother Gösta—who had an attractive voice with a more prominent vibrato and less expansive top than Jussi—recorded this recitative in a 1952 broadcast with baritone Erik Saedón;[6] it can also be heard in some earlier recordings—notably the urgent rendition with José Luccioni and Pierre Deldi (1935)[7]—as can some of the dialogue that precedes the duet.

A number of those early discs, however, adopt the same cuts as Björling and Merrill. This is true of Edmond Clément and Marcel Journet's 1912 acoustic recording,[8] in which two highly tuned instruments intermingle with musical elegance and telling diction. Their phrasing is subtly nuanced and Clément, unlike Björling, attacks the top B-flat of "Son voile" softly, as Bizet prescribes. Still more eloquent are Alain Vanzo and Gabriel Bacquier in their complete broadcast of the opera under Manuel Rosenthal in 1959.[9] In no other version of this music are the words brought so sensitively to life and with such variety of phrasing, with the tenor's easy head voice employed to breathtaking effect. But although this performance is unsurpassed among complete recordings of the duet, Vanzo lacks the oneiric beauty of the Björling sound, with its combination of warm overtones and timbral translucency in the opening half of the duet in particular. The lulling smoothness of the Swedish tenor's legato, his ability to echo the purity and candor of the solo flute that first introduces the E-flat major refrain ("Oui, c'est elle, C'est la déesse"), and his lingering just long enough on the crest of every phrase, all captivate the listener right from the opening measures.

The performing tradition of *Les pêcheurs de perles* was not exclusively French-speaking, for the work had been popularized the world over in Italian translation. Although the translation inevitably banalizes the music, neither the 1908 recording by Enrico Caruso and Mario Ancona[10] (where the baritone indulges in languorous portamentos and the Neapolitan tenor evokes an atmosphere of sultry sensuality), nor the 1927 disc by Beniamino Gigli and Giuseppe De Luca[11] (where the tenor inflects the line with characteristic sentimentality) are inferior in tonal luster to the Björling and Merrill version. And while in the duet the Swedish tenor remains uniquely persuasive in his combination of musical sensitivity and vocal beauty, the critical balance shifts in favor of the Italians when we consider Nadir's act 1 *romance* "Je crois entendre encore." Here Björling cannot match the intoxicating abandon of Gigli's classic 1929 interpretation[12] (sung in Italian in A-flat minor), where the sweetest of head voices, abetted by a caressing legato, draws us into an atmosphere of reverie on a tropical night. Nor can he equal the baritonal allure of Caruso's 1916 rendition in French,[13] striking in its erotic urgency.

Björling's two September 1945 recordings sound buttoned-up by comparison. He takes the aria down a tone, to G minor (as Caruso had done), but sings it in good French, adding the traditional unwritten cadence at the end with an interpolated top B-flat. In the studio version, however, Bizet's *piano* markings are ignored at the opening of each verse, as well as in the upper register, where the top notes are sung in full voice. Only the very last note is produced in a pure head voice. It is a pity Björling chose to imitate Caruso rather than Gigli in this aria, for there is little doubt that Bizet expected the highest notes to be sung in a *voix de tête.*

We hear a more attractive performance from Björling in the live radio recording made later the same month. The beginning of each verse is more hushed this time, and Tor Mann's flexible tempo allows more expressive verbal inflection. The timbre, however, sounds drier than before, the top notes are over-muscular in attack, and the final note is less haunting.

In this aria Björling is easily surpassed by a number of more recent tenors, including Nicolai Gedda, who in his complete recording under Pierre Dervaux[14] sings with enormous suavity in truly idiomatic fashion.

Carmen
"La fleur que tu m'avais jetée"

August 10, 1938: Stockholm, Concert Hall
Unspecified orchestra, cond. Nils Grevillius
Naxos 8.110701

June 8, 1939, Hilversum
Hilversum Radio Orchestra, cond. Frieder Weissmann
Bluebell ABCD 006

April 8, 1941: Stockholm, Concert Hall
Swedish Radio Orchestra, cond. Nils Grevillius
Bluebell ABCD 066

November 15, 1948: New York, Rockefeller Center
Bell Telephone Orchestra, cond. Donald Voorhees
Eklipse EKR CD29

September 19, 1950: Stockholm, Royal Academy of Music
Swedish Radio Orchestra, cond. Nils Grevillius
Naxos 8.110788

October 1, 1950: Berlin, Titania Palast
RIAS Orchestra, cond. Kurt Gaebel
Urania 22.165

November 20, 1950: New York, Rockefeller Center
Firestone Orchestra, cond. Howard Barlow
Kultur DVD D2424

September 24, 1955: New York, Carnegie Hall
Frederick Schauwecker, pf.
RCA 88697748922

December 14, 1955: New Orleans, Municipal Auditorium
Frederick Schauwecker, pf.
Premiere CD 122-1

June 26, 1958: Stockholm, Gröna Lund
Bertil Bokstedt, pf.
Bluebell ABCD 114

July 18, 1958: Stockholm, Concert Hall
Stockholm Philharmonic Orchestra, cond. Georg Ludwig Jochum
Bluebell ABCD 036

April 13, 1959: Atlanta, Glenn Memorial Auditorium
Frederick Schauwecker, pf.
Bluebell ABCD 020

In concert and recital Björling regularly sang a number of arias from operas he never performed complete. Of these Don José's flower song from *Carmen* was his favorite—hardly surprising, as it is superbly crafted for a well-schooled voice and provides listeners with a telling psychological portrait. Even in concert a skillful singer can draw us into the atmosphere of Bizet's drama, revealing not only the tenderness of an infatuated young man but also the obsessive nature of his feelings, the seeds of violence that will lead José to kill "the thing he loves."

Though unusually urgent in its expressive impact, the flower song maintains a classical symmetry underlined by the harmonic structure, the soft dynamics in the opening and final measures, and the regular ebb and flow of tension created by the alternation of crescendos and decrescendos, and by the carefully regulated balance between free declamation (*colla voce*) and more strictly rhythmical passages (*a tempo*). Some tenors, encouraged by Bizet's indications of *stringendo, ritardando,* and *rallentando,* and by the potent emotionalism of Meilhac and Halévy's text, overindulge in rubato here, but this was never true of Björling. He first recorded the piece in Stockholm in August 1938, together with his only studio rendition of Des Grieux's "En fermant les yeux" from *Manon*; they were his first-ever recordings in French. At that time Björling had made only two brief visits to France and had never sung an entire French opera in the original language, but he had performed quite a number of nineteenth-century French roles in Swedish translation and had thus had ample opportunity to familiarize himself with the style. Although neither his consonants nor his vowels have the crisp exactitude of the best French tenors, his pronunciation maintains an excellent balance between verbal clarity and beauty of sound. Björling may well have been helped by his regular accompanist Harry Ebert, who had spent twenty years in Paris. Ebert had first accompanied Björling in recital in July 1936, and they performed the flower song together on many occasions.

The 1938 recording, however, was made with full orchestral accompaniment. The *Andantino* marking is respected, although the tempo is slightly slower than Bizet's metronome indication. Björling unhestitatingly attacks the opening high F, a note that coincides awkwardly with the tenor's register break. Bizet of course was entirely aware of this; his intention was to make the tenor sound emotionally exposed right from the beginning. This is emphasized by the *piano* marking, as well as by the very length of the note, and its pairing with the definite article "La." While Björling's attack is admirably pure, he sings the F rather too loudly and fails to caress the key word "fleur" (marked *con amore* in the score) that represents the semantic starting point of the narrative that follows. He does, however, shape this phrase with a tenderness that was uniquely his own. His interpretative approach derives strength from the musical line rather than from the words: the bitter recollection in B-flat minor ("Je me prenais à te maudire, à te détester") lacks the biting accents that Charles Dalmorès (1912)[15] and Charles Friant (1927)[16] bring to it, but the subsequent transition to A-flat major is handled with unusual suavity. Björling uses the rest after "détester" to create a sense of suspension; the listener feels that José is recalling emotions as if they had been experienced in a dream. The next harmonic shift, to the F major of the *fortissimo* climax on "te revoir, ô Carmen," is superbly managed: Björling employs a wide dynamic range to convey the dangerously obsessive nature of José's infatuation, binding the phrases with rhythmic urgency and a melting legato that nevertheless respects the written rests. Although he eschews the written diminuendo in the ascent to the top B-flat—a note that once again exposes José's emotional vulnerability—his *forte* high note is of such concentrated beauty that the emotional tension is released without breaking the continuity of line. The final four measures are sung as notated, with a shapely *messa di voce* on the C of "t'aime."

His next recording, a 1939 broadcast from Holland, is even more nuanced. Björling respects the *piano* marking on the opening note this time and lingers briefly on "fleur." His phrasing is finished in every detail, with expressive balances perfectly judged, and in the closing measures he introduces a diminuendo on the top B-flat, attacking the note *mezzo forte* and then paring it down to a whisper. The ability to make such a diminuendo in the upper register was a recently acquired technical feat that Björling was happy to show off on this occasion. The only thing one regrets about this conclusion is the rather rushed ascent to the top note: this is always a temptation for tenors, but it is not what Bizet wanted: Charles Friant's leisurely, almost hesitant, upward progress proves much more psychologically revealing (he also sings a *pianissimo* B-flat).

While it is unlikely that Björling ever heard Friant's recording, he was probably familiar with Caruso's 1909 disc, in which the Italian tenor offers a stylish performance in rather good French. And his subsequent rendition, a broadcast with Grevillius, is closer to Caruso in richness of sound (the timbre is much darker and denser here). This time, however, the Swedish tenor is less scrupulous than the Italian in his respect for the score. He seems to have rethought the phrasing of the aria: for the first time he introduces a portamento joining the F of "un seul espoir" to the top A-flat of "te revoir, ô Carmen." This typically Italianate device can be heard in the 1923 disc (in Italian translation) by Miguel Fleta, but not in Caruso's recording.[18] Björling also suppresses the rest in "à te détéster, à me dire," diminishing our perception of the hesitant nature of Don José's discourse: the originality of this aria derives, after all, from our realization that in every phrase the character is seeking the exact words to convey what he feels. Björling compensates however for the loss of this tentative quality by projecting the words themselves with greater urgency than ever before. In the latter half of the aria we can almost believe that this is the voice of a killer (in Mérimée's novel we discover that Carmen is not Don José's first victim). The ascent to the B-flat—not too hurried this time—is managed much as in the 1938 recording, and the top note is sung *mezzo forte* with disarming purity of tone. The conclusion, on the other hand, is rather overweighted.

A performance on *The Bell Telephone Hour* in 1948 confirms Björling's decision to eliminate some of the rests (including the one in the phrase "que le destin l'ait mise là sur mon chemin"), to attack "te revoir, ô Carmen" by means of a portamento, and to sustain the climactic B-flat *forte.* He holds to these choices in all later recordings, which do not reveal any particular evolution in his interpretation of the aria, although they vary according to the mood of the moment and his ever-changing physical condition. The coloring of the voice is sometimes darker and thicker, sometimes brighter and more transparent, and the tenor invariably adapts his approach to the character of his instrument.

The most exciting of his later orchestral recordings is the one recorded in Berlin, where the voice is somber in coloring but in peak condition, with a notably ringing top A-flat on "m'enivrais" and all the words vibrantly alive. The second studio recording, made eleven days earlier, is less vivid, and the tempo is rather slower than in 1938 (as befits a now larger voice). Nevertheless, there has been little loss of tonal beauty in the intervening twelve years; in particular the handsome playing of the English horn in the orchestral introduction is beautifully matched in Björling's mellifluous entry. It is equally gratifying to observe Björling's performance of the aria in *The Voice of Firestone* telecast in November 1950. In a drawing room setting we see him standing in evening dress before a painted scene from the opera, holding a carnation in his hand. In many ways this stylized image sums up Björling's interpretative approach to the aria here: he mesmerizes us with his singing rather than stirring us with his emotional engagement. Yet there is nothing superficial or false in what he does: his facial expression and gestures are unostentatiously natural. The phrasing is decidedly lyrical (the final measure is beautifully intoned), and although his voice production seems effortless, we notice when he relaxes at the end of the aria just how much physical energy has gone into producing that liquid tone.

The most impressive of the recital performances is the 1959 Atlanta recording. Here the relatively distant microphone placement, as well as the stereo recording, perfectly capture the mellow beauty of Björling's sound. The tempo adopted, as in all these later recordings, is closer to an *Andante* than to Bizet's *Andantino* (although it is nothing like as slow as the version by Fleta), but the singing is as focused as ever.

BORODIN

Prince Igor
"Medlenno den' ugasal" ("Dagen gick långsamt till ro")

March 1933: Stockholm, Concert Hall
Unspecified orchestra, cond. Nils Grevillius
Bluebell ABCD 016 (take 1); Naxos 8.110722 (take 2)

January 23, 1957: Stockholm, Concert Hall
Royal Court Orchestra, cond. Nils Grevillius
RCA 88697748922

July 28, 1960: Stockholm, Gröna Lund
Bertil Bokstedt, pf.
Bluebell ABCD 114

Eight appearances as Lensky in *Eugene Onegin*, eleven as the Hindu Guest in *Sadko* and thirty-six as Vladimir Igorevich in *Prince Igor*: Björling's record in Russian opera was a respectable one. The Borodin role comes eighth in the list of the parts he sang most often—after Rodolfo (114 performances), Faust (71), Manrico (67), the Duke of Mantua (56), Cavaradossi (51), Roméo (44), and Riccardo (38)—yet is easily forgotten, for Björling neither recorded the opera complete nor sang it in any language other than Swedish. The opera was not in the Met's repertoire during the central decades of the twentieth century. Even if the tenor had sung it in America he would probably have been expected to perform it in translation. And Anna-Lisa Björling makes it quite clear in her biography how thoroughly her husband disliked relearning parts in English: he put up strong resistance before agreeing to sing *Fidelio* in that language for a concert performance in 1948.[1]

Vladimir's Recitative and Cavatina were recorded in March 1933, the month in which Björling made his role-debut at the Swedish premiere of Borodin's masterpiece. Nils Grevillius conducted, both in the theater and in

Figure 4. Björling as Vladimir in *Prince Igor*, Stockholm, 1934. Photograph by Almberg and Preinitz. Courtesy of the Royal Swedish Opera Archive.

the recording studio. The first take differs quite markedly from the second, being much more intimate in character and respectful of Borodin's hushed dynamics. The vocal line in this A-flat major *Andante* is inspired by the *bel canto* aesthetic, as becomes clear when we listen to Dmitri Smirnov's 1923 recording.[2] Although the tempo is somewhat rushed in order to fit the music onto one side of a 78 disc, the Russian tenor's singing is of great refinement, displaying a fine legato and a formidable control of dynamics in the upper register, where he observes the diminuendo markings on the top A-flats in the recitative and at the end of the aria.

The twenty-two-year-old Björling cannot yet match the forty-one-year-old Russian in technical finish: while this is a more sophisticated performance than his earlier operatic recordings, the legato is not truly binding in effect and he respects none of Borodin's diminuendo markings. He does however make his first attempt at sustained soft singing on disc. And although he has difficulty in projecting some of the *piano* Gs and Fs at the bottom of the staff, the recording displays two important qualities: the rounded beauty of his tone, which highlights the attractiveness of the youthful Vladimir in this nocturnal love song, and his instinctive feeling for portamento, an intrinsic part of the expressive *bel canto* vocabulary, which partly compensates for the less than solid legato.

This first recording by Björling is similar in some ways to the one made by the thirty-four-year-old Sergei Lemeshev three years later:[3] the Russian tenor was as expert a technician as Smirnov, but the display of technique is subordinated to the presentation of a dreamily ingenuous lover, whose vulnerability is accentuated by the intensity of his longing for Konchakovna. Björling himself creates a similarly touching impression, yet if we listen carefully to this first take we can understand why he wanted to have a second attempt at the aria: the final A-flat—though projected in a head voice that approaches the effect Borodin sought with his diminuendo marking—is slightly hesitant.

The new take reveals that Björling still felt more comfortable with a full-throated production in that early phase of his career. His tone is both richer and more limpid, qualities that pay particular dividends in the opening phrase of the Cavatina, which descends from and then returns to the C in the middle of the staff. Here the amber warmth of the lower-middle register and the sense of lift created by the rising interval of a sixth (typical of this aria), spanned by a rare slide, draws the listener into the character's imaginative world.

In all his recordings Björling performs only the second verse of the Cavatina. This cut was common at the time, for it made it possible to fit the scene (recitative included) onto one side of a shellac disc without rushing. But we lose something too, for the first verse is not identical to the second and the full psychological potential of the scene is left unexplored.

In the 1957 recording Björling's voice has lost some of its youthful sheen but gained in consistency throughout the range. Although here too he generally favors louder dynamics, we now have the impression that the voice will do exactly what is asked of it. In the opening phrases of the recitative the single notes are bound together in a more expert fashion and with a more interesting play of rubato. Every transition is smoothly managed and dynamic contrasts are thrown into relief; the lower middle register has filled out, and the *forte* top notes (culminating in a B-flat) are totally controlled in their brilliance. This time the spirit of the performance is reminiscent less of the vulnerable Lemeshev than of the supremely confident Ivan Kozlovsky,[4] who conveys a comparable degree of vocal mastery in his 1941 soundtrack recording, and who, like Björling here, ends the aria with a captivatingly ethereal A-flat. Although the Ukrainian tenor better conveys the intimate rapture of the music (singing both verses without hurrying), it is the Swede who, thanks to the sheer beauty of his tone, suggests a more dashing figure, reflecting in his range of colors the rich poetic imagination of the young lover.

The 1960 recital performance is also well worth hearing, for although the voice is darker than ever Björling recaptures much of the intimacy of his first 1933 take, and takes advantage of the less restrictive piano accompaniment to phrase with greater freedom. As in all previous performances he conveys the melancholy of the love-sick Vladimir to a striking degree, but this time the veil of sadness is all-enveloping and more strongly mingled with erotic yearning. For much of his career Björling's voice was one of innocence rather than knowing sensuality, but toward the end of his life the increasingly baritonal richness of his lower-middle register lent a potent new dimension to his love songs. This does not prevent him, however, from vaulting by means of a featherweight portamento to a *pianissimo* A-flat in the final measures.

BRAHMS

"Die Mainacht" (op. 43 no. 2)

April 11, 1952: New York, Manhattan Center
Frederick Schauwecker, pf.
Testament SBT 1427; Naxos 8.110789

Sehr langsam and ausdrucksvoll (very slow and full of expression) is the indication Brahms gives performers at the beginning of this 1864 setting of Ludwig Hölty's poem. Although most singers attempt in different ways to do justice to the song's expressiveness, a surprising number fail to respect the tempo indication. In his 1974 recording Dietrich Fischer-Dieskau dispatches the three strophes in just 3:34,[1] often preferring to peck at the notes rather than facilitating the legato flow of the music. Fritz Wunderlich, singing in his own home,[2] also takes it rapidly, but his sustained *mezza voce* (which draws inspiration from the *piano* markings in the accompaniment) generates an appropriately nocturnal atmosphere of hushed tension. The song is uncomfortably low for a tenor in the original key of E-flat major, so Wunderlich takes it up to G-flat major. John McCormack does the same in a 1924 recording,[3] whose relatively rapid pace can be justified by the time limits imposed by the 78 side. His legato is smoother than that of the two German singers and his diction no less clear (though his Irish accent is conspicuous).

Heard after these performances Björling's recording (also in G-flat major) comes as something of a revelation: he respects the tempo indication (the duration is 4:17), heightening the tension of a melodic line that avoids settling on the tonic until the end of the third verse. The slow unfolding of the melody also points up the continuity of Björling's legato, characteristically strengthened by portamentos. Equally remarkable are the smoothness and amplitude of his dynamic contrasts and the musicality of his diction, in which consonants are never over-stressed. In this melancholy song of unfulfilled love, which finds little consolation in the moonlight and birdsong of a May night, the easy pace gives him time to impregnate words such as "traurig" and "Träne" with a mournful coloring. At the same time there is something strangely comforting in the beauty of Björling's tone. Although the poem is written in the present tense, the expression suggests emotion recollected at a certain distance. We can believe in the "scalding" tear mentioned in the final line, but don't really feel its intensity.

Listening to this performance one suspects that Brahms himself is distancing himself from the full emotional implications of the words, yet in truth it is possible—and possibly desirable—to suggest intense unhappiness in every phrase. We hear this in Emmi Leisner's recording,[4] made a decade before Björling's, where the wider expressive range of a female voice is brought into play. The tone and line are no less well-sustained and the pace is even more leisurely, but every note is delivered with an emotional explicitness that suggests tears may break out at any moment.

"Ständchen" (op. 106 no. 1)

September 24, 1955: New York, Carnegie Hall
Frederick Schauwecker, pf.
RCA 88697748922

March 2, 1958: New York, Carnegie Hall
Frederick Schauwecker, pf.
RCA 60520-2-RG

In terms of facial expression Björling, like many Swedes, tended toward understatement. Nevertheless, video recordings demonstrate that his delivery, though sometimes deadpan, was by no means po-faced, for a delightful half-smile breaks out at times (the tenor himself marked his scores with smiles wherever the expression was upbeat). Listening to his playful rendition of the opening verse of "Ständchen," recorded during his 1955 New York recital, we can surely hear that smile although the effect is slightly marred by a verbal slip in the opening line, which muddles the word order in "so recht für verliebte Leut!" This error is repeated in the same hall three years later, when a darker, fuller tone robs the music of some of its charm.

Unlike the songs with this title by Schubert and Strauss, "Ständchen"—inspired by a poem by Franz Kugler—is not itself a serenade, but a lighthearted depiction of three students serenading a beautiful girl. It is very much a man's song, which Björling sings in the original tenor key of G major. As in "Die Mainacht," each verse differs in character and expression. In both these performances the second verse is delightfully crisp, building up to a big crescendo, with the tenor and accompanist rhythmically together at all times. The final verse, which tells of how the serenade invades the dreams of the sleeping girl, is sung softly and sweetly (observing the composer's markings in the piano accompaniment), with a delicious head voice on the high G-sharp of "Geliebten." Other singers, however, have delivered these final lines more arrestingly. In particular the tenor Leo Slezak—who began his career when Brahms was still alive—slows the pace much more markedly in his 1928 recording,[5] making a sustained use of head voice when penetrating the girl's subconscious. And he introduces another big rallentando, also accompanied by head tones, toward the end of the first verse. As a result, each of the three sections of the song is relished more fully for its distinctive flavor and there is no risk (as there is with Björling) of the song passing by agreeably without really engaging the imagination of the listener.

DONIZETTI

L'elisir d'amore
"Una furtiva lagrima"

November 10, 1944: Stockholm, Concert Hall
Swedish Radio Symphony Orchestra, cond. Tor Mann
Bluebell ABCD 078

September 7, 1945: Stockholm, Concert Hall
Royal Court Orchestra, cond. Nils Grevillius
Naxos 8.110788

September 28, 1945: Stockholm, Concert Hall
Swedish Radio Symphony Orchestra, cond. Tor Mann
Bluebell ABCD 036

October 3, 1952: Stockholm, Concert Hall
Swedish Radio Orchestra conductor Sten Frykberg
Naxos 8.111083-85

January 23, 1957: Stockholm, Concert Hall
Royal Court Orchestra, cond. Nils Grevillius
RCA 5934-2; Profil Hänssler PH 08009 (alternative take)

Perhaps more than most arias, "Una furtiva lagrima" is best heard in context. This *Larghetto* in 6/8 time describes a state of unadulterated happiness, yet it begins in B-flat minor with talk of tears, and ends in B-flat major with Nemorino's realization that he would be happy to die after achieving a single moment of communion with Adina. This simple character gains access here to a less earthbound dimension of experience, which lifts the whole opera onto a higher expressive plane. The ecstasy of emotional fulfilment brings with it an almost dislocating perception of eternity: reality is almost too good to be true and time seems to stop while the music flows.

Figure 5. Nemorino and Adina (Helga Görlin) in *L'elisir d'amore*, Stockholm, 1933. Photograph by Almberg and Preinitz. Courtesy of the Royal Swedish Opera Archive.

Yet how exactly should it flow? Probably in such a manner as to reinforce the "effect of suspension" that John Steane identifies as defining the artistry of the Neapolitan tenor Fernando De Lucia: the ability to make us savor "experience as *present*, not (as we usually meet it) as a point where the music drama moves from past to future."[1] This effect—which is one of the defining features of *bel canto*—is determined partly by the floating quality of the voice production and partly by a constant play of rubato, reinforced by a taste for extemporary ornamentation, freeing the music from any sense of metronomic predictability. De Lucia's own recording of the Romanza,[2] made when he was fifty-seven, is masterly in the way it keeps the listener alert in every measure; the same is true of acoustic recordings by Enrico Caruso,[3] Giuseppe Anselmi, John McCormack, and Alessandro Bonci.[4] While from the 1920s onwards even the more imaginative tenors tended to adopt a more literal approach, confining rallentandos to the ends of the two verses and eschewing the traditional ornament on "invidiar."

Jussi Björling, who was first recorded in this aria some eleven years after he last sang Nemorino on stage,[5] was no exception. His voice in 1944 was still engagingly youthful and the iridescence of his line (thrown into relief by the delicate harp accompaniment), the precision of his *abbellimenti*, and the clarity of his diction (he makes just one slip—si puo*i* morir"—that is not repeated in this or in later performances) are all worthy of a master of *bel canto*. But if we compare this reading with Caruso's 1904 disc, we realize how much better the latter captures the aria's intimacy of mood, savoring the full expressive potential of each phrase through a constant play of rhythmic and dynamic contrasts. Giuseppe di Stefano's 1944 recording[6] also has a unique sweetness and eloquence, with a lingering close to each verse, although the Sicilian tenor cannot equal Caruso's and Björling's *souplesse* in the cadenza. The two Italian tenors perform the traditionally elaborated version of this cadenza, but employ slightly different words: Di Stefano sings the now conventional "di più non chiedo, si può morir d'amor" and Caruso a less coherent "di più non chiedo, a(h) non morir d'amor," while Björling sings "di più non chiedo che morir d'amor." This latter solution works well semantically, although the plainer musical setting adopted (with one rather than two ascents to the high A) may disappoint.[7] Bonci's and De Lucia's recordings remind us that in the nineteenth century the cadenza was much less standardized than is now the case.

Ten months later the Swede made his first studio recording of the aria, with very similar results. The cadenza incorporates the extra top A this time and more is made of the *smorzando* on "per poco i suoi sospir," but otherwise the performance is once again rather square in its phrasing. Another radio recording, made three weeks later, reveals a greater stillness of mood, in spite of the relatively rushed tempo. Björling begins both verses in a genuine *piano*, which enables him to make a more moving crescendo on

"M'ama," where the switch from B-flat minor to D-flat major invests the line with an overwhelming warmth of feeling. The cadenza is identical to that of the 1944 performance, while the 1952 broadcast—once again from Stockholm—duplicates the version heard in the earlier of the two 1945 renditions, but with a more impressive crescendo on the first top A. The voice has gained in body here, but the phrasing is still limited in its imaginative scope.

Björling came close to conveying the true spirit of this Romanza in his second studio recording, made in Stockholm in 1957. The voice is even richer in overtones than in 1952, but he manages a strikingly gentle attack in the opening verse, where his sound seems to echo that of the solo bassoon in the orchestral introduction. This performance is less musingly inward in tone than those by Tito Schipa,[8] Di Stefano, and Juan Diego Flórez,[9] but tellingly exploits—like the recordings by Caruso, Carlo Bergonzi,[10] and Luciano Pavarotti[11]—the full dynamic range of a spinto tenor. The climax of "M'ama" is his most heart-warming ever, and the dying close of the first verse more lovingly managed. Björling had clearly been listening to Caruso's recordings, for he imitates the echo effect on "si può morir" in the second verse. In the cadenza he now adopts the traditional formula (as published by Luigi Ricci);[12] the final return to the tonic is also available in an alternative soft version,[13] which sets the seal on a very fine performance.

GOUNOD

Gounod's two great operatic masterworks, *Faust* and *Roméo et Juliette,* tell stories that have long been an integral part of Western culture. What matters is not the outcome of the story, but the manner of its telling. The absorbing quality of both narratives depends as much on stillness as on movement, on time suspended as on forward momentum, on the singers' ability to mesmerize the listener as on the conductor's sense of direction.

The roles of Faust and Roméo were fundamental in establishing Björling's international reputation as a great singer of French music, for they were the only two of the eight French roles he sang that were performed in the original language and recorded complete. When he studied the parts in translation in the early 1930s he would have felt himself very much part of an ongoing performing tradition: Gounod—who in 1865 became, as Björling would ninety-one years later, a member of the Royal Swedish Academy of Music—was one of the most popular operatic composers in Sweden between 1870 and 1950. Although casts in Stockholm were less illustrious than those at the Paris Opéra or the Met, Nordic voices proved well suited to the composer's style, which requires a consistently limpid tone and an elegantly drawn line. Björling assimilated this style above all from his fellow Swedes, and in particular from John Forsell, the distinguished baritone and director of the Royal Opera, who in the early 1930s went over the entire role of Roméo with him on the island of Stenungsön, near Gothenburg, where star pupils were given extra summer training. Björling never made any formal study of the French language, and his stays in France and Belgium were too short for him to pick it up there (he was booked to sing Roméo and Faust at the Paris Opéra in the spring of 1953, but a bout of bronchitis forced him to cancel). His musical ear was nevertheless so sensitive that he was able to assimilate the correct pronunciation (in a manner that rarely offends French ears today) without any real difficulty. Björling was aided in this by his accompanist Harry Ebert, who taught him the French text of *Roméo et Juliette* in the summer of 1945.

It wasn't, however, until the 1950s that he had the opportunity of working on *Faust* with French conductors. And he never seems to have been much influenced by the recordings of French tenors, although he spoke admiringly of Lucien Muratore in one of his interviews.[1] Moreover in thirty years of performing Gounod's music—he first sang the role of Tybalt in *Roméo et Juliette* as early as August 1931 and last sang Faust in April 1960—Björling never shared the stage with a French Juliette or Marguerite. This reminds us of the decline in the native French school of singing from the 1930s onward, which in turn affected the theatrical fortunes of Gounod's most popular operas during the final decade of the tenor's career, when both *Faust* and *Roméo et Juliette* lost their central places in the repertoire. Their fall from grace surely also owes something to their failure to conform to a typically twentieth-century aesthetic (itself now outdated), based on the conviction that life is fundamentally meaningless and that the more realistically one presents that meaninglessness, the better a work of art, or performance, is likely to be. If, however, Gounod's strong religious beliefs were irreconcilable with such an aesthetic, to enjoy these operas we don't need to adhere to the specifics of his faith. It is sufficient to accept the idea that the cathartic effect of tragic events on the operatic stage can derive not only from uncompromising realism but also from the power of music to transform the apparent ugliness of suffering and death into an experience of transcendent beauty (which is exactly what happens in the last act of *Roméo et Juliette*). It is enough to acknowledge the capacity of great operatic performers to transfix the audience not only through total identification with the role they are playing, but also through the mesmeric power of subtly-inflected song.

Messe Solennelle de Sainte Cécile
"Sanctus"

November 13, 1938: Detroit, Masonic Temple Auditorium
Ford Motor Symphony Chorus and Orchestra, cond. José Iturbi
VAIA 1189

April 15, 1946: New York, Rockefeller Center
Firestone Chorus and Orchestra, cond. Howard Barlow
Radio Years RY 15

It is hardly surprising that Björling never sang any complete performances of Gounod's 1855 *Messe Solennelle*, for the work offers little gratification for a tenor of his range and skill. Even the "Sanctus," with its gently melismatic solo passages, is hardly challenging in its scope, and the latter part of it is assigned exclusively to the chorus. Yet the firmness of line and frankness of diction—an English translation is used—displayed in what was possibly Björling's first performance of this music, on the *Ford Sunday Evening Hour* in 1938, are by no means to be despised, even though he fails to respect a number of the dynamic markings indicated in the score and gets into a muddle in the second solo. First of all he forgets the words; then, clearly unnerved, he elaborates on the melodic line and entirely omits a repeat of "full of thy glory." It seems likely that he was either sight-reading the music after limited rehearsal or had not been expecting to have to sing it in English. The blandness of the choral singing and the generic accompaniment remind us, moreover, of the pitfalls of presenting classical music to the masses in a "popular" packaging: Theodor Adorno's critique of the "radio voice,"[2] with its flattened sonorities and banalization of meaning, is perfectly applicable here.

Yet while it is true that Björling himself was seldom at his most committed as an interpreter when performing in this sort of context, these radio shows often recorded music which he never performed elsewhere: his only repeat performance of the "Sanctus" took place on the *The Voice of Firestone* eight years later. This time he sings the original Latin text and has clearly studied the score carefully, adopting a soft, prayerful tone for the opening measures and respecting the *piano* and *forte* attacks on the top As of "Plenisunt" in the second solo. Even more than in 1938, Björling's singing is delectably smooth in both legato and registral balance, yet also strikingly sincere. The words are movingly delivered, in a manner that the German tenor Gerhard Stolze, in Igor Markevitch's 1966 recording of the Mass,[3] cannot even remotely approach. The latter's relatively squeezed, undersupported tone and pretentious phrasing are worth comparing with Björling's performance because they remind us that what seems effortlessly natural in the 1946 broadcast is in fact entirely exceptional.

Faust
Complete Recordings

December 23, 1950: New York, Metropolitan Opera House
Jussi Björling (Faust), Dorothy Kirsten (Marguerite), Cesare Siepi (Méphistophélès), Frank Guarrera (Valentin), Thelma Votipka (Marthe); Metropolitan Opera Chorus and Orchestra, cond. Fausto Cleva
Naxos 8.111083-85

December 19, 1959: New York, Metropolitan Opera House
Jussi Björling (Faust), Elisabeth Söderström (Marguerite), Cesare Siepi (Méphistophélès), Robert Merrill (Valentin), Thelma Votipka (Marthe); Metropolitan Opera Chorus and Orchestra, cond. Jean Morel
Myto 906.33

Extracts from act 1
January 4, 1936: Stockholm, Royal Opera
Jussi Björling (Faust), Joel Berglund (Méphistophélès); Royal Court Orchestra, Royal Swedish Opera Chorus, cond. Nils Grevillius

Extracts from acts 1–3 and 5
March 7, 1937: Vienna, Staatsoper
Jussi Björling (Faust), Esther Réthy (Marguerite), Alexander Kipnis (Méphistophélès), Alexander Svéd (Valentin); Vienna State Opera Chorus and Orchestra, cond. Josef Krips
Koch Schwann 3-1454-2 (selection from acts 2 and 5 only)

"Salut! demeure chaste et pure"

November 13, 1938: Detroit, Masonic Temple Auditorium
Ford Motor Symphony Orchestra, cond. José Iturbi
VAIA 1189

June 8, 1939: Hilversum, AVRO Studio
AVRO Hilversum Orchestra, cond. Frieder Weissmann
Bluebell ABCD 006

July 14, 1939: Stockholm, Concert Hall
Unspecified orchestra, cond. Nils Grevillius
EMI CDH 7610532

September 25, 1944: Stockholm, Royal Opera House
Royal Court Orchestra, cond. Nils Grevillius
Bluebell ABCD 103

May 12, 1946: Detroit, Masonic Temple
Ford Symphony Orchestra, cond. Fritz Reiner
WHRA-6036

March 6, 1950: New York, Rockefeller Center
Firestone Orchestra, cond. Howard Barlow
Kultur DVD D2424

March 19, 1951: New York, Manhattan Center
RCA Victor Orchestra, cond. Renato Cellini
RCA 88697748922

"Anges pures"

December 5, 1937: New York, Carnegie Hall
Jussi Björling (Faust), Grace Moore (Marguerite), Donald Dickson (Méphistophélès); General Motors Symphony Orchestra, cond. Erno Rapee
WHRA-6036

The last time Björling donned a theatrical costume was on April 1, 1960. The setting was the War Memorial Opera House in San Francisco (in a performance staged by the Cosmopolitan Opera) and the opera was Gounod's *Faust*, a work which, more than any other in the Swedish tenor's international repertoire, focuses on those processes of transformation and transcendence that are an integral part of the craft of any great singer. It is an opera that delights in its capacity for theatrical illusion, exploiting vocal prowess as skillfully as it deploys makeup, costume and stage machinery. Björling sang *Faust* more than any other theatrical work except *La bohème*, and one cannot help feeling that it came to represent his own capacity to transform himself before an audience, regenerating the legend of a voice that never aged significantly either in sound or spirit.

He had made his debut as Faust twenty-six years earlier (August 25, 1934), at the Royal Swedish Opera, and had sung the work fairly regularly throughout his career. The longest interval between performances occurred when Gounod's opera was dropped from the repertoire in Stockholm in the late fifties. That was a sign of the times, reflecting the general fall from favor of a work that can seem an ambiguous product of very nineteenth-century obsessions: the tale of Marguerite's seduction and repudiation is related with almost voyeuristic relish, and Faust himself—though largely responsible for her suffering and insanity—never faces up to the full implications of his behavior. Yet although as the acts progress the focus of our emotional engagement is increasingly deflected from Faust to Marguerite, the potency of the music is such that a few eloquent lines of recitative at the beginning of the prison scene ("Mon cœur est pénétré d'épouvante") are sufficient to sway us temporarily back in his favor. Some singers have found little psychological substance in the role, but Björling never seems to have tired of it: indeed, he sang it more often than such specialists in the French repertoire as Georges Thill, Nicolai Gedda and Alfredo Kraus.

Unlike Gedda, Björling never made a studio recording of the complete opera, but his two official versions of the Cavatine ("Salut! demeure chaste et pure") have long been considered paragons of excellence, while live recordings give us a pretty good idea of the standards he set in the rest of the opera. The first of these is the radio broadcast (in Swedish) of extracts from the opening act of a Stockholm performance in 1936. It was the tenor's twentieth attempt at the role and he was accompanied—as he had been sixteen months earlier—by Nils Grevillius on the podium and the bass-baritone Joel Berglund as Méphistophélès. Berglund tends toward understatement as an interpreter, but his smooth vocalism gives pleasure, while the conducting is a little too smooth, lacking in the crisp rhythmic articulation the music demands. The recording begins fairly early in the scene, with Faust's "Ô coupe des aïeux," and although the twenty-four-year-old tenor cannot

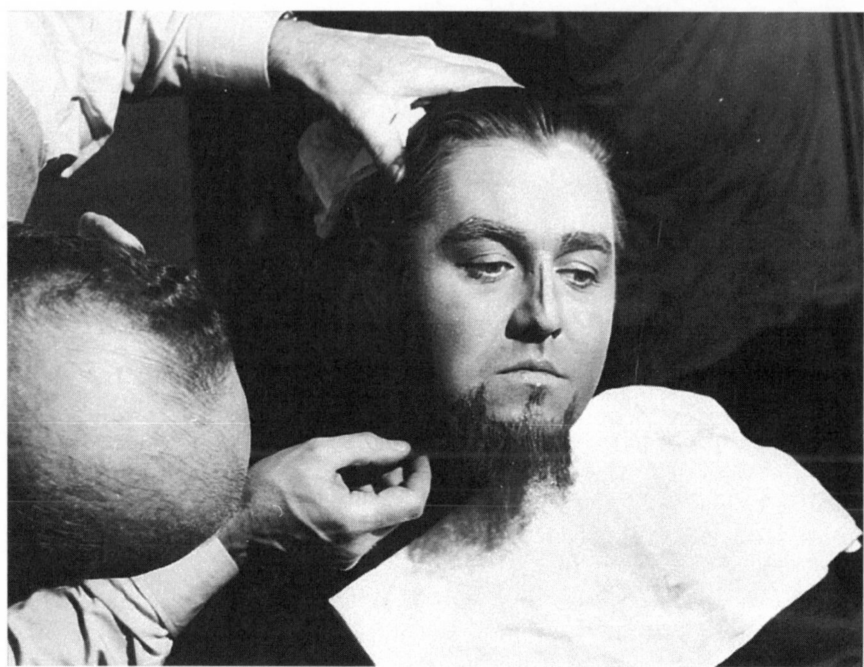

Figure 6. Preparing for the first act of *Faust*, Stockholm, 1940. Courtesy of the Jussi Björling Museum.

conceal the youthfulness of his voice, his somber coloring of the words (which never muddies diction) lends plausibility to his portrayal of the ageing philosopher. There is arguably not much "face" to his singing here—it was only toward the end of his career that the tenor succeeded in suggesting the character's age by means of vocal inflection as well as make-up—but he brings real urgency to "Maudites soyez-vous, ô voluptés humaines!" Shortly after Méphistophélès's entrance the recording skips forward to the first statement of "À moi les plaisirs," the G major *Allegro ben marcato* that encapsulates the ageing Faust's hedonistic vision of eternal youth. The elasticity with which the voice dominates the rhythm here—with a welcome bloom on the prolonged notes—makes this vision come alive before our eyes, even though the character himself remains elusive. A similar effect is created in "Ô merveille!" where Björling negotiates the tricky F-sharps on the register break with a liquid loveliness of sound that reminds us of Reynaldo Hahn's comments on the "hallucinatory" capacity of beautiful singing to summon up images:[4] here Björling evokes not only Faust's sense of wonder but also the breathtaking vision—Marguerite at the spinning-wheel—that arouses that wonder.

That exclamation is the last we hear of Björling's 1936 Faust, but fourteen months later the tenor was recorded in extracts from a Viennese performance, where he sang once again in Swedish while the rest of the cast performed in German. There is a lot of distortion in the recording, made by the Staatsoper's engineer Hermann May with a microphone hung above the stage, but the sound is sometimes vivid and Josef Krips's leadership more inspiring than Grevillius's. He fully exploits the singing tone of the Viennese strings and his flexibility in rubato enables Alexander Svéd to nail home Valentin's "Avant de quitter ces lieux" to overwhelming effect. This was the only opera performance in which the famous bass Alexander Kipnis (Méphistophélès) sang with Björling, but he was clearly struck by his young colleague, for he later declared that of all the tenors he had known it was the Swede who possessed "the greatest voice for most of the Italian and French roles."[5]

Although the Cavatine has not survived, it was the tenor's voice that was most extensively recorded during the evening, starting from "Eh bien! puisque la mort me fuit" in the first act. This time the character seems more arrestingly individual in outline: there is a crazed compulsiveness to "Salut! ô mon dernier matin," and "Ô coupe des aïeux" is thrown into relief by the vividness of the accompaniment, with the ***fp*** chords strongly underpinning the melody, while Faust's invocation of Satan acquires a more weighty momentousness. The initial statement of "À moi les plaisirs" is less bright and buoyant this time, as if Björling consciously wished to suggest a character weighed down by the pessimism of age (though this impression may have something to do with the murky recording), while the A major reprise at the end of the act has the unmistakable energy of youth, although here too distortion limits the aural delight.

We get a close-up of Björling's pristine voice during Faust's first exchange with Marguerite in act 2. The conversational "Ne permettrez-vous pas" (here spoilt slightly by the fact that the two characters are using different languages) is delivered with rare radiance, ending with a beguiling diminuendo on the F-sharp of "chemin." The subsequent declaration of love, where the tenor vaults to a top B on the words "Je t'aime," is stunning, although Björling takes the liberty of singing the note in a brilliant *forte* rather than respecting Gounod's *pianissimo.* This infidelity can be partly justified by the purity of the sound itself, with its very high placement, and by the fact that audiences in the mid-twentieth century were increasingly reluctant to warm to the sort of reinforced falsetto that the composer asks for here: it may be heard suavely employed by the American tenor Richard Crooks, whom Björling had heard in recital in Stockholm when he was still a student, in a 1940 Met broadcast from Boston.[6]

Crooks, who sang the work in the original language with idiomatic phrasing, is also a formidable rival in the garden scene, particularly in an ethereal "Ô nuit d'amour," sung with such daring softness that we feel irresistibly drawn into the hushed nocturnal atmosphere. Björling, partnered by the Hungarian soprano Esther Réthy, commands a denser beauty of tone, encompassing a wider range of dynamics in the phrase that opens the duet, "Quoi! je t'implore en vain!" and proving truly melting in "Laisse-moi contempler ton visage," where the voice passes from *piano* to *forte* and back again with bewitching smoothness of legato. The sound remains liquid in the repeated "Éternelle!" while "Ô nuit d'amour" is begun almost as softly as in Crooks's rendition, without resort to falsetto. Björling's later recordings would never surpass the combination of tonal beauty and intimacy of expression achieved on this occasion. We are deprived, however, of Réthy's reply, for the recording jumps forward to the very end of the act, where Faust rushes forward to embrace Marguerite at her window, joining her on a sustained top C ("Marguerite!") that in the score is written only for the soprano. The effect is suitably exultant, but would not be attempted again in Björling's complete recordings of the opera.

There is less of interest in the extract from the final scene, where the trio is launched by Réthy in tones that are tremulously vulnerable rather than hopeful. Although Björling's singing is firm and bright, it is not especially favored by microphone placement, while the cut of eight measures in the middle of the trio further reduces his opportunities to shine. What does impress is the boldness of Krips's big ritardandos, introduced to broaden the sweep of the soprano's soaring line. The final measures of the trio are sung here as written, with no added top Bs, but in the tense exchange that follows Réthy deviates rather wildly from the score.

Although the context—a General Motors concert—is more prosaic, we get a fuller sense of Björling's potential in this scene in the recording made nine months later at the Carnegie Hall. Here the voices are more evenly balanced, and the baritone Donald Dickson—who had sung Valentin at the Met in May that year—proves incisive in the relatively high tessitura of Méphistophélès's part, while Grace Moore and Björling, though they perform in different languages (she, like Dickson, in French, he in Swedish) are well matched in tonal luster and musical intensity. Although it is a concert performance, Erno Rapee's excellent command of rubato seems to justify Owen Lee's claim that this is "one of the most effective pieces ever written for the stage."[7] The soprano's voice is firmer and more striking in its beauty than Réthy's, and the French language lends it a markedly emotional coloring. The tenor's sound is at once pleading and penetrating, and the brilliant pair of B-naturals (sung together with the soprano) that he interpolates at the climax give us the impression that Faust here is much closer in spirit to Marguerite than to Méphistophélès.

While Björling had only one further opportunity to perform with Moore, he did not lack other distinguished partners in his early years in this opera.

Fifteen months before the 1937 recording with Kipnis he had sung Faust in Stockholm alongside the Méphistophélès of Fyodor Chaliapin, the most remarkable operatic bass of the twentieth century, while his first French Faust, conducted by Wilfrid Pelletier at the Met in December 1939, signed away his soul to the savvy Méphistophélès of Ezio Pinza.

The tenor's earliest surviving recording of "Salut! demeure" was made a year before that performance, during a *Ford Hour* concert conducted by the piano virtuoso José Iturbi. These Sunday broadcasts attracted millions of listeners, which makes it the more surprising that the opening words of the Cavatine emerge as "Var hälsad, dygdens kyska boning." Evidently Björling did not yet feel ready to sing the aria in French, even though he used that language in a later number in the program, Des Grieux's "En fermant les yeux" from Massenet's *Manon.* As is often the case, the Swedish translation brings out the inherent melancholy in Björling's tone, as well as a clarinet-like resonance on certain vowels that blends suggestively with the playing of the orchestra. This sort of instrumental purity is well-suited to an aria designed to generate an aura of mystery and "worshipful stillness."[8] Falling in love for Faust is not only a call to action but also a cause for contemplation, and if the tenor invests too much erotic urgency in the Cavatine the words end up sounding irrelevant: why would a sexually impatient lover take the trouble to extol Marguerite's "chaste and pure" dwelling?

In a 2004 Covent Garden production by David McVicar,[9] Roberto Alagna, wearing nineteenth-century attire, managed to reconcile this contradictory situation by delivering the aria with a self-indulgent smile and decadent phrasing, suggesting that Faust's rhapsodical style of address was no more than a cynical form of play-acting. This ironical perspective tends, however, to distance us from the composer's inspiration, intellectualizing our relationship with the music. It does not really help us understand the aria any better if we wish to return to it again and again and succumb—when it is phrased with a refinement and finish that Alagna could no longer quite muster in 2004—to its genuine enchantment.

Written in A-flat major, "Salut, demeure" has an ABA^1 structure and a melody embellished with an obbligato for solo violin that seems to express, in Gérard Condé's words, "ce que les mots ne disent qu'à demi" (that which the words only half express).[10] The aria's hypnotic effect partly depends on the tenor's ability to spin the line with nuanced elegance and flexibility of pulse, lending flavor to the words without loosening the legato. This is a matter of musical sensibility but also of technique, for the words should seem to float on a regular flow of breath, so unerring in its slow momentum as to give the impression of continuing uninterrupted even during the rests. It is this sort of illusion that Björling achieves in his first (1938) recording, with the added bonus of a rare beauty of tone, enriched with a natural vibrancy that draws attention to itself only when the expression requires it:

the opening phrase of the E-flat major recitative, where the voice intones "Quel trouble inconnu" over a tremolo in the lowest register of the accompanying strings, offers one such moment. The sensual awakening of Faust is intensified here by Björling's use of an ample vibrato on the sustained notes, while the high G-natural of "Ô Marguerite" vibrates more discreetly, preparing us for the purity of sentiment that imbues the subsequent aria.

Vocal technicians might raise their eyebrows at the notion of a singer controlling the degree of vibrato he uses, for this could potentially lead to a tightening of the muscles in the mouth or throat and a consequent hardening or constriction of the sound. What Björling does here—as in all the music he sang—is in fact entirely instinctive: his vibrato is indeed variable in intensity, but it is regulated spontaneously by the breath flow and the emotional response of the singer to the words and musical setting.

While the recitative is sensual in tone, the Cavatine emerges a romantic dream, the opening measures are traversed as if in a trance. The iridescence of his tone is such that the voice is never upstaged by the solo violin. It is perhaps the enveloping legato of that instrumental solo that prompts the tenor to make relatively generous use of portamentos. Examples include the rising interval of "innocente" and the descent on "divine" in the A section and the first octave drop to the low E-flat on "innocente et divine" in the reprise. The fact that most tenors ignore Gounod's explicit portamento marking in the latter case reminds us of how difficult it is to execute neatly if the voice lacks a solid lower register.

"Salut! demeure" is one of the three arias in the Swedish tenor's international repertoire that climax on an exposed and traditionally prolonged high C (in the score it is a quarter note capped by a fermata).[11] Here he takes a breath during the phrase leading up to that note, but the sound itself is free and well integrated. There is no conspicuous variation of volume on the top note, but the tone is a well-regulated blend of head and chest resonance. This balance of registers distinguishes Björling's voice production throughout the aria, for he often tempers an unmistakably "adult" sound with soft overtones, even in the more propulsive central section. He combines the head and chest voices with such ease that we tend to take this skill for granted, yet comparison of this performance with one by Placido Domingo, who never really developed his head voice,[12] makes us realize how rare a quality it is.

Björling sang the Cavatine in Swedish again in his 1939 Hilversum broadcast. The voice is less closely recorded here and sounds even more engagingly youthful. He doesn't perform the recitative this time and the slightly faster pace adopted by conductor Frieder Weissmann leads to a more *marcato* approach—with less dynamic variety—and to the suppression of a number of portamentos. Yet there are ample compensations, such as the transitional passage of repeated Cs in the middle register ("C'est là! oui!"), underpinned by changing orchestral harmonies (C major, F minor), which diminish progressively in volume and lead imperceptibly, without any pause for breath, to the reprise of "Salut! demeure" (A-flat major). This linking effect is not prescribed in the score, where two eighth-note rests precede the reprise, but it represents the sort of refined vocal gesture that Gounod's writing clearly encourages, and which would become a feature of Alain Vanzo's performances in later decades. A similar approach can be heard in the live performance from Covent Garden in 1928[13] with Joseph Hislop (who was heard in this role by Björling in Stockholm in 1937), in Sergei Lemeshev's refined 1933[14] version in Russian, and in Helge Rosvænge's 1938 German language recording,[15] which includes extra ornaments that can be found in the German edition of the score.[16]

Björling had clearly been listening intently to Caruso's superb 1906 version,[17] for he reproduces here the Neapolitan's prodigious crescendo (after a *mezza voce* attack) on the top C. In Hilversum the effect is slightly less spectacular, but one can only marvel that it was risked in live performance. This note of course can be dealt with in a variety of ways. Some singers—Giuseppe di Stefano, Vanzo, Giuseppe Sabbatini—opt for a strikingly diminished sound, while others—John McCormack, Crooks, Thill, Jonas Kaufmann—employ a reinforced falsetto of considerable beauty. The important thing is that the note should seem neither blaringly loud (in Gounod's original manuscript the voice was accompanied by an oboe) or lacking in body (the preceding measures are marked by a crescendo). Björling succeeds here in arousing a sense of wonder without giving the impression of showing off. Comparison with Caruso highlights the superiority of his legato: witness his smooth delivery of the slow descent from F to C on "pure" in the reprise, where the Neapolitan eases the sound forward with the aid of an aspirate.

Perhaps it would be more pertinent, however, to compare Caruso's disc with Björling's 1939 studio recording in French. Once again there is no recitative, but his command of Barbier's original text is in no way inferior to the Italian singer's (though less eloquent than Thill's),[18] and the words are articulated with unostentatious intimacy of expression. (Björling's fellow tenor and friend Set Svanholm commented on his colleague's "natural and almost unaccented handling" of French, even though he had received "no tuition whatsoever in that language.")[19] The hushed delivery of "pauvreté" and "félicité" in the first verse reveals genuine sensitivity of feeling: here again Björling seems to echo Hislop, with whom he studied during the 1930s. The B section is also more varied in shading than before and "où se devine la présence" is sung in one breath, again with a crescendo on the top C (though the attack is louder this time). All in all this is a performance of great restraint and beauty, of art that conceals art.

Once Björling had made his debut in the Met's production of *Faust*, he preferred to sing the role in French, even in his native Sweden, as a bilingual

1944 recording from the Royal Opera (which includes most of the Cavatine, preceded by Faust's recitative and Siebel's couplets) demonstrates. The voice is darker and fuller-bodied here, and Barbier's text sounds more alive than in the EMI recording; the singer seems to be focusing intently on the meaning of every word. He is aided in this by Grevillius's expansive tempo, which also gives him time to reinstate the portamentos heard in 1938, and to mould a tapered close to the opening verse, with greater emphasis on the attack of the reprise. It is a pity that the recording fades way into silence before the climax, for in some ways this is his finest performance of the aria so far: the fact that it is sung in a theatrical context makes all the difference.

The 1946 recording from Detroit is by contrast decidedly out of context: it derives from another *Ford Hour* (with Fritz Reiner this time) and is transposed down a semitone, which explains the relative weakness of "me voici" (descending here to a low D) at the end of the recitative. The expressive balance of the scene is nevertheless maintained, if with less idiomatic diction than usual.

Four years later Björling sang "Salut! demeure" on TV for *The Voice of Firestone*, this time in the original key. No other aria he performed on television exposes the tenor's style and technique so fully across a wide range, and there are no stage trappings here to distract the viewer from his voice, face and gestures: he stands before a curtain in his white tie and tails and draws us into the atmosphere of the garden scene using all the expressive resources at his disposal. It is a tribute to those resources that the slight nervousness initially apparent in the singer's eyes is transformed, as soon as he opens his mouth, into the trepidation of the aspiring lover. The relative intimacy of the television studio encourages Björling to adopt a markedly lyrical approach. Faust appears here as a morally untainted romantic lover, whose function is simply to enrapture the audience with his singing.

Björling's delivery of both the words and music is undemonstratively natural. We notice how he contrasts the outer sections (the repeated phrases are delivered more extrovertly the second time): as in all his performances, he varies the reprise according to the mood of the moment. On the notes around the top of the staff we can perceive him creating extra space for gentle overtones by raising the soft palate, while in other moments his lingering half-smile seems to facilitate the ease and ring of the louder notes. Yet such is the union between sound and countenance that every technical maneuver is turned into a manifestation of feeling. The mixed head resonance on "que de richesse en cette pauvreté" in the opening *Larghetto* naturally results in a facial expression of heightened sensitivity; the characteristic oval-shaped opening of the mouth conveys a sense of almost mystic raptness, while the baring of the upper teeth on the propulsive ascent to A-flat in the reprise ("Salut!") suggests exultant happiness. Björling keeps his chest raised and his lungs well-stocked with air throughout the aria and this lends his body an almost weightless quality that belies his portly figure. One notes both the rapidity and efficiency of his intakes of breath—never interfering with the solid emission of tone and the shaping of phrases—and the persuasiveness of his gestures. The arms move forward and upward as if accompanying the curves of the melody, sometimes with the hands almost touching: the singer seems to be reaching out emotionally both to the invisible Marguerite and to the listener. As in most of his recordings of the aria, Björling steals a breath before "la présence," but the line is in no way broken (either aurally or visually) and the top C—though less prolonged than in other performances—emerges as a release of pent up tension, without disturbing the continuity of the concluding phrase.

Many of these qualities—ease of emission, sensitivity of feeling and elegance of phrasing—were shared by Björling's most worthy successor in the role of Faust, Alfredo Kraus, whose interpretation of this aria can be observed in a 1971 video recording of the opera from Tokyo,[20] made when the Spanish tenor was forty-three. Kraus too was capable of mesmerising his audience in this Cavatine with his poised legato, and of offering listeners a salutary shock with his razor-sharp top C. Yet in purely musical terms the relatively dry and astringent quality of his tone, which weakens somewhat in the lower register, makes his performance less gratifying than Björling's. The sounds Kraus makes are never ugly, but they are not capable in themselves of generating an illusion of youth and beauty (an effect the Spaniard achieves by means of his ever-graceful stage presence). While this is partly a matter of natural endowment (just listening to the speaking voices of Kraus and Björling[21] brings home the superior musicality of the latter's instrument), it is also arguably a matter of technique. Watching Björling one senses that he can draw on a range of overtones that depend not only on the ample proportions of his facial resonators (his cheeks for example are much fuller than Kraus's), but also on the bone structure of his entire body. The bones in our bodies are interconnected and when those in the head resonate intensely it is possible to make the rest of the skeleton vibrate in sympathy. This, according to P. Mario Marafioti,[22] was the secret of Caruso's exceptional richness of tone; it perhaps explains how Björling—although initially no more than a lyric tenor—could draw at will on extra reserves of deeply-rooted sound, and make his debut in the vocally challenging role of Faust when he was just twenty-three. Kraus's technique—though it enables the singer to exercise a rare degree of control over the sounds produced—tends to limit the expressive range and tonal beauty of the voice by its tight focus on facial resonance. In Björling the whole body of the singer is brought into play, and while this makes the technique more vulnerable—particularly if the body itself is not in good health—it also leaves it more open to inspiration, to the sort of emotional expression that cannot be controlled by the brain.

This helps us understand why Björling's single performances vary much more than Kraus's in their coloring and expressive emphasis, and why sometimes it seems as if his body is dictating the sound he should make and influencing—for better or worse—his emotional response to the melodic line. This is the impression we receive from his first complete recording of *Faust*, a Met broadcast first heard in December 1950. Björling had recently opened the season with a new production of Verdi's *Don Carlo*, and was in many respects at the apex of his career. His voice had almost fully matured, gaining extra weight and body in the lower register, and few other tenors could challenge his supremacy in the roles he sang best. During this Saturday afternoon performance his voice is in magnificent shape: if one excepts Caruso, no other Faust extensively recorded during the twentieth century can equal his combination of tonal beauty throughout the range and elegance of phrasing. Both the baritonal lower register, particularly important in the opening act, and the top C function perfectly, his legato is impeccable in its breadth and finish, and his rhythmic sense so electric that at times—as in the *Allegro ben marcato* that brings the first act to a close—it seems as if the tenor himself is conducting the performance.

In spite of this, Paul Jackson is surely right in stating that Björling seems to be "in a state of disconnect" during this performance, doing "little to lend individuality and grace to his phrases."[23] This impression is confirmed if we compare "Salut! demeure"—louder and more automatic in phrasing than usual—with his earlier recordings of the aria. His relative lack of sensitivity seems to affect Dorothy Kirsten's Marguerite, whose responses in the garden scene are less spontaneous than they had been a year earlier in another Met broadcast,[24] with Di Stefano as Faust. What is lacking here is not musical alertness—one notices, for example, how naturally Björling's timbre assimilates the sound of the clarinet that accompanies the opening word ("Rien!") in act 1, while a few measures later it mirrors the coloring of the bassoon—but an ability to share the feelings of the character. The tenor's first brief melody, "J'ai langui, triste et solitaire," unfolds in the lower middle register of his voice with impressive sonority but limited eloquence. If we compare the Swede's phrasing with Hislop's we notice how varied the dynamics of the Scottish tenor are, how crisply he projects the words, and how skillful he proves in suggesting the frailty of old age without compromising the elegance of the melody. His pupil sounds monotonous by contrast: although he renders effectively enough the transfixed quality of "Le ciel pâlit," he does not exploit the heightened intensity of the words set to single pitches, in order to capture the psychological torment of a philosopher who has reached a turning point in his existence. Gounod's characterization is masterly throughout this act, but Björling seems unwilling to unlock his imagination, even though the voice does its duty magnificently: witness the sonorous descent to D-flat, when Faust asks death to take him under its wing.

The character's second brief solo, the F major "Salut! ô mon dernier matin!," where he expresses his resolve to commit suicide, seems to suit the tenor's mood much better; his phrasing here suggests a reckless despair that surpasses the Viennese performance. While he proves less successful in conveying Faust's vacillation when he raises the cup of poison to his lips, his rageful cursing of human pleasures and invocation of Satan are delivered with real vehemence, if not with the sort of verbal incisiveness displayed by César Vezzani in his complete recording[25] (where the expert conducting of Henri Büsser proves much more telling than Fausto Cleva's routine effort at the Met) or by the Belgian Fernand Ansseau[26] (who, like Vezzani, is partnered with Marcel Journet's Méphistophélès). Björling, however, is every bit as buoyant as Ansseau and Vezzani in the 6/8 rhythm of "À moi les plaisirs," which is delivered with a compelling elasticity. Unlike Domingo in his complete recording with Georges Prêtre he does not consciously attempt to make Faust sound like an old man here, but his timbre in the middle register is sufficiently mature, while the grand scale of the singing gives us the impression that the philosopher is a personality to be reckoned with even in old age.

After an ecstatic *mezza voce* "Ô merveille!" the reprise of "À moi les plaisirs," sung by a rejuvenated protagonist, is even more brilliant in its impact than in the Viennese performance. The change of key (to A major) lends an extra lift to the melody, which is further enhanced by the underpinning of the bass voice. There is no risk here of the tenor being eclipsed by Méphistophélès (sung here by Cesare Siepi), as almost happened in Stockholm in 1935, when Chaliapin attempted to suppress the tenor's exuberance by smothering him with his cloak.[27] Björling's voice rings out with as much generosity as Vezzani's and Ansseau's, but with an extra refinement of glowing tone that tells us how handsome Faust has become after his transformation.

Faust's role in the second act is more limited: from this point onward the character can risk appearing a mere cypher in the hands of the ever-resourceful Méphistophélès if the tenor fails to take full advantage of the expressive opportunities offered him. The first of these is the brief encounter between Faust and Marguerite. Björling initially addresses Kirsten with caressing legato, but no longer makes a diminuendo on "chemin," and his subsequent declaration of love is too muscular: the top B is not only attacked *forte* but resounds thickly. The best approach to this exposed high note is arguably to attack it *pianissimo,* as indicated, and then make a crescendo; the French tenor Georges Noré, in Sir Thomas Beecham's 1948 studio recording,[28] shows how it should be done. Even more striking is Ivan Kozlovsky[29] in his complete 1948 Russian-language version: he attacks the B *mezzo piano* and then builds up to an impressive *forte* before fining away the sound again. This is a remarkable demonstration of the expressive potential of the *messa di voce,* for no other singer on record has crammed so much meaning into this single note.

The third act arouses mixed feelings, partly because Kirsten's girlishly open tone sounds artificial to modern ears, and partly because her tenor partner proves unwilling to modulate his phrasing and inflect words with real sensitivity. The limited imaginative scope of Björling's singing is made clear by comparison with the Met broadcast featuring Di Stefano in the leading role. The Italian tenor makes the words come alive and his dynamic shading is much more sensitive. His diminuendo on the top C at the climax of "Salut! demeure" is truly ravishing, as is the *mezza voce* (verging on falsetto) displayed in "Laisse-moi contempler ton visage" and "Ô nuit d'amour." It must be admitted, however, that in the aria Björling continues to offer formidable competition, for although a number of phrases are less nuanced here than on *The Voice of Firestone*, the dense flow of his legato draws attention to the shallower support of Di Stefano's voice, with its less balanced blending of words and tone. The latter sounds at times almost as if he is speaking on the prescribed pitches, an approach that may make the character seem more likeable, but diminishes his aura of mystery.

Björling brings little conviction to Faust's comment on Marguerite's dead sister ("C'était un ange! oui, je le crois!"), and in the ensemble that follows he fails to employ the full range of dynamics (from *pianissimo* to *forte*) indicated by Gounod. Although "Laisse-moi contempler ton visage," an F major melody of rare loveliness, displays his voice at its most magnificent, the very concentration of his sound renders his manner of address too public. This lack of intimacy—even in comparison with Caruso's famous recording,[30] notable for its baritonal richness—affects not only the cantabile but also the snatches of conversation, such as "Que dit ta bouche à voix basse?" Nevertheless, Björling makes much of the etherial *pianissimo* "Éternelle!" (these tricky notes, poised on the register break, have a more liquid quality than Di Stefano can muster) and invests the timeless "Ô nuit d'amour" with truly gorgeous tone. In this case the relative detachment of his phrasing is better suited to the words, which transport the souls of the two lovers into a context of all-embracing nature. Once again, however, the Swede is less imaginatively engaged than in his 1937 performance, and one misses the caressing head voice employed not only by Crooks and Di Stefano but also by Beniamino Gigli in his 1919 recording (in Italian) with Maria Zamboni.[31]

In the *Allegro* that follows, truncated by a thirty-measure cut, the solidity of Björling's tone contrasts markedly with Kirsten's artful breathiness. The *Andante* "Divine pureté" offers the tenor a further opportunity to display the sculpted beauty of his middle register, while the phrase that follows Marguerite's "Adieu" culminates in a dazzling A-natural above the staff ("Ah! Fuyons!").

Eighty-odd pages of score separate Faust's last appearance in act 2, as he rushes forward to embrace Marguerite at her window (there are no top Cs this time), from his next entrance with Méphistophélès. In the Met production the scene of Marguerite at the spinning wheel is omitted, but the course of events has become quite clear by the time Faust reappears. While the philosopher's sense of shame is evident ("j'ai peur de rapporter ici la honte et le malheur"), Gounod and his librettists allow us only brief glimpses of the character's remorse: it is up to the tenor to exploit them to the full. Björling fails to do this, either in the short dialogue with Méphistophélès or in the duel trio that follows shortly afterward, where Faust expresses his horror at the prospect of spilling the blood of Marguerite's brother. In the latter case the problem lies largely in Cleva's inability to shape the ensemble in such a way as to enable each of the three singers to achieve maximum emotional impact. Björling spends his voice unsparingly, but his first two ascents to the top B-flat are cut short by the conductor's reluctance to observe the *ritardando molto* indicated in the score. This is a pity, for both Siepi and Frank Guarrera—a theatrically incisive Valentin—are fully engaged in their roles here.

This is the only recording of *Faust* with Björling that includes a selection from the Walpurgis Night scene in act 5. This episode does not, however, seem to have stimulated his theatrical instincts—Faust's comments are resonantly, but neutrally, voiced—and the ebullient "Chant bachique" (for tenor and chorus) is cut. The prison scene is much more gratifying for the tenor, and once Faust has been left alone we hear Björling at his inspired best. In "Ô torture! Ô source de regrets et d'éternels remords" the words are uttered with the depth of feeling the musical setting deserves, and the voice synthesizes the blended timbres of the flutes, oboes, clarinets, and bassoons, creating an atmosphere of genuine spiritual desolation. Even here there is not much dynamic variety in Björling's phrasing, but the words are so crisply enunciated—with the sonorous low C of "tué par elle" approached by means of a neat portamento—that it is hard not to be stirred by his song. Caruso's cello-like 1910 recording[32] seems to be a model for his phrasing throughout this scene. The Swede's tone becomes more neutral again during the duet with Marguerite, where Kirsten's coy emoting was possibly as alienating for him as it is for most listeners today. It is difficult in fact to believe this Faust when he repeats Marguerite's "Oui, c'est moi, je t'aime," and the ringingly declamatory "Elle ne m'entend pas!" at the end of the duet sounds impersonal. The final trio is also less than overwhelming, partly because Cleva seems to have little sense of how the piece should go. His rhythmic inflexibility prevents the voices from blooming, even on the traditional added high Bs.

Just three months after the Met broadcast, the tenor made his second studio recording of "Salut! demeure," a much more lyrical performance than the one at the Met. He rarely takes his voice beyond a *mezzo piano* in the opening passage, while the contrasting central section—where Faust's thoughts about Marguerite range more widely and less obsessively, reminding us of his philosophical cast of mind—provides the necessary variety of rhythm and dynamics without breaking the ecstatic mood. As in the Hilversum performance, the transition to the reprise of the opening section is managed without pause for breath, as is the climactic phrase, "où se devine la presence," capped by a superb C (slightly steelier than in 1939). Renato Cellini's tempo is ideal, giving the tenor time to include most of portamentos we hear in his earliest recording. In this performance we are more than ever aware of a melancholy substratum to the phrasing, suggesting that Faust subconsciously regrets the fact that he is about to destroy the aura of chaste beauty that surrounds Marguerite's dwelling. This stratified meaning surely explains the sense of mystery that is generated by the fusion of words and music. At the same the time, the excellent recording brings the unnamed solo violinist to the fore, perfectly blending his tones with those of the tenor. We have the impression here of two fine musicians drawing inspiration from each other, and are reminded of the artistically fruitful partnerships linking Fritz Kreisler with John McCormack and Misha Elman with Enrico Caruso on recordings made in the second decade of the twentieth century. Björling himself was never partnered on disc by a celebrated violinist, but, as earlier chapters have noted, Nils Grevillius and Joseph Hislop compared him with Kreisler and Heifetz. This recording reminds us how responsive his voice was to the beauty of accompanying instruments, to a degree that has arguably never been equalled by any other tenor documented in sound.

In November 1953 Björling inaugurated the Met season by taking the leading role in Peter Brook's new production of *Faust*, conducted by Pierre Monteux. When he next sang the role at the Met, during his final season there in December 1959, it was in the same production (set in nineteenth-century Paris). The conductor this time was the fifty-six-year-old Jean Morel, who had replaced Monteux as chief conductor of the Orchestre Symphonique de Paris in 1938. From the opening measures of the Introduction, Morel's *Faust* is more elegant and wide-ranging in feeling than Cleva's reading. Although Björling's voice takes longer to warm up than in 1950, he appears infinitely more responsive to character and situation. His initial "Rien!" is no longer a sonorous tenorial calling-card, but the troubled statement of a vacillating soul (to the extent that the very placement of the voice sounds uncertain), bringing home the emotional nakedness of what is perhaps the most desolate opening of any nineteenth-century opera. In "J'ai langui, triste et solitaire" the voice not only sounds older—as is quite appropriate here—but also more sensitive. The phrases are modulated with real understanding of what it means to survive in an enfeebled body, for Björling's own strong physical frame was by then seriously undermined. "Salut! ô mon dernier matin" confirms this impression of fragility, though the upper register rings out securely; and Faust's lengthy curse is less thrilling but more inwardly felt than before. After Méphistophélès's entrance, where Siepi's articulation is notably enlivened by Morel's accompaniment,

Björling turns the hedonistic "À moi, les plaisirs" into the crazed dream of an old man, sung mostly *mezzo piano.* His *mezza voce* "Ô merveille!" is as lovely as ever and the reprise of the *Allegro* at the end of the act, while less brilliant than in 1950, is unfaltering in rhythm and tone.

Faust's exchange with Marguerite during the Kermesse introduces us to the soprano Elisabeth Söderström, the finest Swedish singing actress of her generation, heard here in her only recording with Björling. She responds to the tenor's very public address (his vibrato is rather prominent) with affecting simplicity of tone. The top B of Björling's "Je t'aime," though attacked from below, opens up more winningly this time before the line descends seamlessly to the lower G.

In act 2 we hear another splendid B—approached with exemplary cleanness and held so generously as to resonate in every corner of the old Met—at the climax of "Salut! Demeure." Here, as in the Detroit concert in 1946, the tenor transposes downward, although this time the transposition involves only the final section of the Cavatine. As was traditional at the Met, the modulation takes place on the words "tu fis" toward the end of the middle section, where the half note on the second word is transformed from a B into a B-flat. To tinker in this manner with the harmonic scheme of an aria so that the reprise is in a different key (G major) to the opening statement (A-flat major) might seem sacrilegious, but in truth the well-tried expedient works well; and it would in any case be churlish to complain when the performance is as finished as Björling's. This is indeed one of his most sensitive accounts of the aria. The pace is leisurely, giving him time to fine away the phrases in the *Larghetto* and to reinstate all the portamentos heard in the 1937 performance, including the one spanning the tricky octave drop in the reprise, descending here to a low D. Morel ensures that the B section is *un poco più mosso* and no more than that, enabling the tenor to bring extra eloquence to Faust's vision of Marguerite as a child of Nature.

In the quartet—where Siepi and Thelma Votipka (Marthe) also phrase with greater subtlety than in 1950—Björling's delivery of recitative is much more alert, and during the ensemble he employs a broader range of dynamics, observing the *pianissimo* of "Mon cœur parle." In "Laisse-moi contempler ton visage" every word is caressed and the phrases, as in the Viennese performance, are built on a *messa di voce* rather than being sculpted in a solid *mezzo forte.* One appreciates his *piano* attack on the G-flat of "silencieux" in "Ô nuit d'amour," and the rare portamento linking the D-flat of "nuit" to the F of "d'amour." At forty-eight Björling can still summon up a melting beauty of tone that makes the twenty-eight-year-old Gedda (who in his 1953 studio recording phrases similarly to his fellow Swede)[33] sound ordinary by comparison. The subsequent *Allegro* is more compelling this time, thanks to Söderström's sincere emotional engagement, although once again the episode is considerably abbreviated and the tenor refrains from joining Marguerite on the A-flat.

When Faust returns to the stage in act 4 Björling sounds completely attuned to the character's anguish and shame in "J'ai peur de rapporter ici la honte et le malheur," and his voice rings out to splendid effect at the climaxes of the duel trio, where Morel respects Gounod's ritardandos. It is true that the tenor cannot match the magnificence of Caruso on the B-flats, but the overall musical balance is much better here than in the Neapolitan's cramped Victor recording with Marcel Journet and Antonio Scotti.[34] This trio was the very last occasion on which Björling's voice mingled with that of his friend Robert Merrill (Valentin). It was their twentieth theatrical performance together, on the same stage and in the same opera that had occasioned their first collaboration thirteen years earlier.

The Walpurgis Night scenes had been included when Brook's production was first unveiled in 1953, but they are omitted in this afternoon broadcast. In the dialogue at the beginning of the prison scene, Björling dismisses Méphistophélès with a "Laisse-moi" rather than a "Laisse-nous." This, along with other details of phrasing, suggests that he may have restudied the score since the Cleva broadcast, possibly during rehearsals with Monteux in 1953. When Méphistophélès obeys the order, Björling demonstrates his remarkable command of French recitative in "Mon cœur est pénétré d'épouvante," sung *mezza voce* this time, creating a truly introspective mood. The subsequent duet "Elle ne m'entend pas!" is achingly delivered, and the final trio comes across much more thrillingly than in 1950, thanks to Morel's sure play of rubato. Although the audience breaks in with applause at the climax, the tenor maintains his concentration for Faust's final pleading cries of "Marguerite!"

His pleas of course are chillingly rejected by the woman he loves, who achieves salvation partly through a full recognition of Faust's role in her moral downfall. And this *dénouemnent* tends to be somewhat jarring for listeners, for although in the final trio the words make it clear that Faust and Marguerite are on different wavelengths (he orders her to flee with him while she is begging for heavenly intervention), the increasingly parallel course of their melodic lines—augmented by the tenor's traditional interpolations—gives us the impression that they are once again united in spirit, for the expressive potency of the music is such that the meaning of the words is effectively neutralized.

Sir Thomas Beecham seemed however untroubled by such paradoxes when, in 1943, he defined *Faust* as one of the dozen operas that represent "the quintessence of lyrical charm and beauty,"[35] reminding us that it is the unfathomable magic of Gounod's melodies that transfixes audiences and keeps the opera on the world's stages. And if we want to understand the mysteriously hypnotic quality of those melodies, then we can do little better than listen to Björling sing them. In his final recording of *Faust,* where the voice seems connected at every level to the sensibility of the man and musician, there is no doubting the emotional import of any phrase he sings, nor the charisma of the character who is singing. Gounod's Faust does not philosophize like

Goethe's—or go through the motions like Berlioz's or Boito's (two roles that Björling sang in Stockholm alone)—but manifests his genius through the beauty of his song. The more beautiful the singing, the more persuasive that genius becomes.

The only video recording we have of Björling performing Gounod's music demonstrates how harmoniously this singer combined effortless emission of tone with simple gestures and effective facial expression. This was partly an inborn gift, but it also owed something to the advice given to the tenor by the legendary Swedish actor Gösta Ekman—whose own potency of gesture was immortalized when he played the leading role in Friedrich Wilhelm Murnau's silent film *Faust* made in 1926—after a performance of Gounod's opera at the Royal Swedish Opera in 1937. Björling (who possessed a remarkable visual memory) instantly absorbed a rapid lesson on how to move on stage and use his hands,[36] and put it into practice without delay. In his autobiography he tells us that 1937 represented a turning point in his artistic progress.[37]

Roméo et Juliette
Complete Recordings

March 27, 1940: Stockholm, Royal Opera House
Jussi Björling (Roméo), Hjördis Schymberg (Juliette), Sven Herdenberg (Mercutio), Simon Edwardsen (Tybalt), Benna Lemon-Brundin (Stéphano), Olle Strandberg (Paris), Sigurd Björling (Capulet), Leon Björker (Frère Laurent); Royal Swedish Opera Chorus, Royal Court Orchestra, cond. Nils Grevillius
Bluebell ABCD 088

February 1, 1947: New York, Metropolitan Opera House
Jussi Björling (Roméo), Bidú Sayão (Juliette), John Brownlee (Mercutio), Thomas Hayward (Tybalt), Mimi Benzell (Stéphano), George Cehanovsky (Paris), Kenneth Schon (Capulet), Nicola Moscona (Frère Laurent); Metropolitan Opera Chorus and Orchestra, cond. Emil Cooper
Immortal Performances IPCD 1003-2

Act 2
May 13, 1943: Stockholm, Royal Opera House
Jussi Björling (Roméo), Hjördis Schymberg (Juliette), Göta Allard (Gertrude); Royal Court Orchestra, cond. Nils Grevillius
Bluebell ABCD 103

"Ah! lève toi, soleil!"

September 29, 1930: Stockholm, Concert Hall

Unspecified orchestra, cond. Nils Grevillius
Naxos 8.110722

September 6, 1945: Stockholm, Concert Hall
Royal Court Orchestra, cond. Nils Grevillius
Bluebell ABCD O16 (take 1); EMI 5 75900 2 (take 2)

"Ange adorable"

April 8, 1941: Stockholm, Concert Hall
Jussi Björling (Roméo), Hjördis Schymberg (Juliette); Stockholm Radio Orchestra, cond. Nils Grevillius
Bluebell ABCD 066

August 10, 1949: Stockholm, Concert Hall
Jussi Björling (Roméo), Anna-Lisa Björling (Juliette); Stockholm Concert Association Orchestra, cond. Nils Grevillius
EMI 5 75900 2

August 23, 1949: Los Angeles, Hollywood Bowl
Jussi Björling (Roméo), Anna-Lisa Björling (Juliette); Hollywood Bowl Symphony Orchestra, cond. Izler Solomon
Standing Room Only SRO 845-1

September 30, 1951: San Francisco, War Memorial Opera House
Jussi Björling (Roméo), Bidú Sayão (Juliette); San Francisco Opera Orchestra, cond. Gaetano Merola
WHRA-6036

November 11, 1951: Los Angeles, CBS Radio Studio
Jussi Björling (Roméo), Anna-Lisa Björling (Juliette); Ray Noble and his Orchestra

"Nuit d'hyménée"

August 23, 1949: Los Angeles, Hollywood Bowl
Jussi Björling (Roméo), Anna-Lisa Björling (Juliette); Hollywood Bowl Symphony Orchestra, cond. Izler Solomon
Standing Room Only SRO 845-1

October 23, 1949: San Francisco, War Memorial Opera House
Jussi Björling (Roméo), Anna-Lisa Björling (Juliette), San Francisco Opera Orchestra, cond. Gaetano Merola
WHRA-6036

September 30, 1951: San Francisco, War Memorial Opera House
Jussi Björling (Roméo), Bidú Sayão (Juliette); San Francisco Opera Orchestra, cond. Gaetano Merola
WHRA-6036

In a 1960 tribute to Björling, Björn Forsell recalled the voice of the tenor when he was starting his studies at the Royal Music Academy in 1928: "How he sang, even then! Perhaps even more beautifully, more naturally, more lyrically than he did later when he acquired technique with all its pluses and minuses."[38] There is nothing self-serving in this recollection, for the technique that Jussi went on to acquire was at least partly attributable to the teaching of Björn's father, John Forsell. If we listen to Björling's first operatic disc—recorded in September 1930, when he had just sung his first major role (Don Ottavio in *Don Giovanni*)—we can understand exactly what he meant. That recording, of Gounod's "Ah! lève-toi, soleil!," sung in Swedish translation as "Höj dig, du klara sol," reveals an artist whose ingenuousness of technique is mated to a dewiness of tone that enchants the ear.

No other major tenor documented on disc has demonstrated his precocity so early and so engagingly (although McCormack was almost equally young when first recorded). Since Roméo is such a quintessentially youthful character, there is something singularly appropriate in the uncalculating buoyancy of this early traversal of one of opera's headiest love-songs, where the sound has little to do with any concept as sophisticated as "interpretation." The phrases indeed are not yet shaped with any real sense of direction and the notes are not truly bound together (suggesting that legato was an acquired art for this tenor), although a couple of portamento-like gestures are made in the opening measures. Björling's only significant attempt at dynamic modulation—an appropriate softening of tone on "Qui vient caresser sa joue"—is but shyly hinted at. The ABA[1] structure of this Cavatine, not dissimilar to that of "Salut! demeure chaste et pure" in *Faust*, leaves him somewhat rudderless in the freer declamation of the B section, where his inexperience in singing with an orchestra is evident; and the three top B-flats, though arrow-like in their attack and star-like in brilliance, are not yet milked for maximum effect or fully integrated into the melody.

Yet all these limitations are counterbalanced by the sheer radiance of Björling's tone, which has a transfiguring effect in an aria that likens Juliette to the rising sun: "astre pur et charmant." Björling had learnt from early childhood how to achieve the right balance between ear, larynx, diaphragm and resonance chambers so as to guarantee the maximum brilliance of sound with the minimum physical effort, and any subsequent training was simply a matter of regulating that skill to deal with the entire range of music he had to perform.

"Ah! lève-toi, soleil!" was well-suited to Björling's voice when he started his training at the Academy, for initially his upper range did not extend above a B-flat (the highest note in the Cavatine). Across the opera as a whole the part extends half a tone higher to a B-natural, which was probably the upper limit of the veteran tenor Pierre Michot, who created the role at the Théâtre-Lyrique Impérial in Paris in 1867. Another factor in the choice of this aria was the work's lasting popularity at the Royal Swedish Opera, where it had been given its premiere as early as 1868 and had become a firm favorite by the turn of the century, particularly when the much-loved tenor Arvid Ödmann was singing Roméo. Gounod's masterpiece—which had in fact been dedicated to "sa Majesté Charles XV, Roi de Suède et de Norvège"—was featured in twenty-two seasons at the Royal Opera between 1920 and 1950; Björling would no doubt have seen performances of the work as early as 1928–29, when he was studying in Stockholm (Hislop sang the opera that season). He was personally coached in the role of Roméo by Forsell, who was particularly fond of this score and who served as a father figure for Jussi in those early years. There is no doubt that the young tenor assimilated much from the distinguished baritone, then in his sixties, who was still capable of singing splendidly, and whose career had taken him to Berlin, London, New York, and Vienna. Forsell did a lot to improve Björling's musical discipline, stylistic poise and stage deportment and the tenor was forever grateful for this training, although he was not alone in occasionally resenting the military-style authoritarianism with which it was imparted.

Before he was allowed to make his debut in the leading role, Björling was assigned the part of Tybalt—opposite the Roméos of David Stockman and Einar Beyron—in three performances of Gounod's opera between August 1931 and February 1932, a useful apprenticeship in a role requiring strong declamation, a secure upper register and agility on stage. He did not have to wait long, however, before he was given a chance to reveal his potential as the romantic lead, making his debut in August 1933 opposite the English soprano Stella Andreva, in a performance conducted by Hilding Rosenberg. He was only twenty-two, an ideal age for Shakespeare's youngest tragic hero, and the consensus of critical opinion was highly favorable.

Björling made a point of quoting in his autobiography the review by critic Moses Pergament, who suggested that the tenor sang with a greater range of dynamic nuance than ever before:

> In contrast to earlier occasions, this evening he impressed more with his warm, softly changing *piano* than with his sonorous *forte*. This does not mean that the voice was lacking in its usual high notes, only that the beauty of the pleasantly surprising, soulfully phrased *piano* singing attracted the most attention. The duet in the second act—the balcony scene—was from the musical standpoint a real experience: less because of the music than because of the performance.[39]

This review suggests that Björling made more limited use of his *mezza voce* in the early years of his career, an impression reinforced by his 1930 recording of "Ah! lève-toi, soleil!" and explained perhaps by David Björling's pamphlet *How to Sing*, which advises against children singing *pianissimo* "because it contracts the throat."[40] It seems likely that Jussi, following his father's advice, had avoided sustained soft singing until he became a student at the Royal Music Academy, where he also perfected his legato and extended his upper register. He may even have adjusted the placement of his voice (Set Svanholm, who was a fellow student, suggests that he was afflicted with "a certain throatiness" when he first auditioned for Forsell, adding that this defect was "quickly corrected").[41] In any case, Björling achieved complete ease in the *messa di voce* when he was in his mid-twenties, and his recordings of that period abound in hairpin dynamics. Other tenors, such as Giuseppe Anselmi, Miguel Fleta and Di Stefano possessed a remarkable facility in *filature* from the very beginning, but their abuse of this natural gift seems partly to have undermined the overall solidity of their techniques, whereas Björling's command of a properly supported diminuendo remained unfaltering to the end of his life.

Although Pergament's comment on the balcony scene may suggest a limited admiration on his part for Gounod's music, it highlights a fundamental truth about many works in the operatic repertory, whose success is as dependent on the creative contribution of the singers as on that of the composer. This in turn reminds us that the best way of renewing the vitality of an opera at each performance is to allow singers to give full expression to their creative instincts.

Björling performed the role of Roméo four more times in 1933 and continued to sing it regularly in Stockholm until the opera was dropped from the repertoire there in the early fifties. He was thus already something of a veteran in the part (with twenty-three performances under his belt) when *Romeo och Julia* was broadcast under Grevillius's direction in 1940. His Juliette was the Swedish soprano Hjördis Schymberg (1909–2008), who was his most frequent stage partner for over a quarter of a century, joining him in thirty-two of his forty-four appearances in this role. Schymberg was essentially a company singer, versatile, technically secure and at ease on stage. If her voice was not especially phonogenic, she undoubtedly had a real feeling for Juliette's music, and the four extended duets for soprano and tenor spotlight the spontaneity of her interaction with Björling (she was always the more extrovert of the two) and her skill in blending her voice with his. Although her timbre was less rich and varied than the tenor's, she could match his Nordic purity in soft passages. From 1936 onward Björling never performed this opera with any other soprano in Sweden. And he continued to sing his part in Swedish at the Royal Opera, even after learning the role in French in 1945.

Most twentieth-century performances of *Roméo et Juliette* were based on the 1888 score prepared by Gounod for the work's debut at the Paris Opéra. The 1940 Stockholm performance includes some of that version's ballet music (culminating in the *Danse bohèmienne*), which is inserted not in the fourth act but during the party scene in act 1, at the end of the choral refrain to Capulet's "Allons! jeunes gens!" A more significant variant—affecting the tenor role this time—is the omission of Roméo's arioso (and related chorus), "Ah! jour de deuil," at the climax of the third act. In Stockholm the scene ends much less spectacularly, with the Duke simply ordering Roméo into exile and the hero immediately expressing his reaction in declaimed recitative, a solution drawn from an earlier version of the score that seems to have been first heard at the Opéra-Comique in 1873. Scores in the Royal Swedish Opera archive suggest that during Björling's career the 1888 edition was used, but with cuts reflecting earlier versions of the score. Acts 4 and 5 are also substantially abridged, with the last act consisting simply of the orchestral interlude ("Le sommeil de Juliette") and the final duet, but this was standard practice in the first half of the twentieth century and can be at least partly justified by the fact that the familiarity of the story makes it unnecessary to fill in every link in the narrative.

Grevillius is not particularly electrifying in his narrative skills, but musically cogent and responsive to the expressive needs of the singers. Björling thrives on this flexibility, from the moment of Roméo's masked entry during the Capulets' party in act 1. In the dialogue with Mercutio the limpid texture of the voice suggests a rare degree of emotional vulnerability, and the words are articulated with unstudied clarity. It is the sound of youth devoid of cynicism, rendered more interesting by a complex range of feelings (as is immediately evident in the mysterious shading of "J'ai fait un rêve!"). A stronger contrast comes after Mercutio's Queen Mab ballad, where Björling distinguishes markedly between the initially lighthearted tone of Roméo's reply and the somber legato that accompanies his admission to being troubled by "un noir pressentiment." His *piano* attack in "Ô trésor digne des cieux," where Roméo (echoing the *thème d'amour* heard in the opera's Prologue) expresses his emotion on first catching sight of Juliette, is melting in effect.

Björling's manner of addressing his loved-one in Swedish was much more restrained than it would be when he sang the same music in the original language. His initial approach, "De grâce, demeurez!" has a hushed charm that is maintained in the F major Madrigal that follows. In the twenty-three-measure opening statement of this duet, built on a slow waltz rhythm, he sustains the melody with striking transparency, poised between *mezzo piano* and *mezzo forte*, with a dying close on "par un baiser." The grace of his phrasing—which almost equals Gigli's[42] in its heady beauty of tone, and surpasses it in smoothness of legato—is demonstrated by the elasticity of the turn on "droit d'approcher," where he only has to make a minimal ritardando in order to fit in all the notes. He may seem impassive here in his inflexion of the words (one is reminded of the first act of his Swedish *Traviata* recorded the year before), but this decidedly instrumental approach pays dividends when the voices unite—witness the tersely beautiful ascents to top A on "rendrez-le moi!" first *forte* and then *piano*—and suits the rarefied atmosphere of the whole piece, in which two souls express their complete affinity. Even when interrupted by the entrance of Tybalt, Björling avoids any excess of emphasis. His cry of surprise, "Dieu!" when he discovers Juliette's identity, is both piercing and intimate, as befits an aside.

The opening of the second act, set in Juliette's garden, is in some ways similar in its expressive mood to the garden scene in *Faust*. In "Ô nuit! sous tes ailes obscures / Abrite moi!" the voice, as if charged by the orchestral introduction, takes on the mysterious quality of the night itself. The atmosphere is intensified during the recitative preceding the Cavatine, where Björling once again matches the luxuriance of the orchestral accompaniment as he breathes life into the phrases.

Björling's approach to "Ah! lève-toi, soleil!" has been greatly refined since the 1930 recording. The voice here is more distant from the microphone and therefore less startling in its immediacy, but the key difference is the sense of flow granted by the fluidity of the legato. The Swedish translation ("fördunkla") impedes the traditional downward portamentos on "étoiles," but the the tenor creates an impression of continuity by means of the even regulation of his breath. In this opening section he starts relatively softly and builds up gradually to the climax on "Parais!" In the B section he uses his *mezza voce* more generously than in any of his other recordings of this aria. The softening effect on "Qui vient caresser sa joue" is particularly expressive this time, not only because the tenor now has total control over volume but also because he introduces a slight pause before the second word (in this case "sakta"), throwing the dynamic contrast into greater relief. An early score conserved in the Royal Opera archive includes a handwritten ***pp*** marking here, suggesting that Björling was following a well-established performing tradition. Another addition to that score is the fermata on the F of the final "astre pur et charmant," and this too is respected.

Even though a number of phrases are lingered over delightfully here, the ascending momentum that characterizes the whole aria never falters, and is thrillingly confirmed by the conclusive B-flat—once more on "Parais!" ("träd fram")—where the dead-center attack releases a stunningly projected sound, sustained for a good nine seconds.

All in all, this is a remarkable performance for the way in which Björling conveys both the extreme sensitivity of the man who is singing and the potency of the desire that draws him like a magnet toward his beloved, combined with a luminosity of timbre that evokes perhaps better than any other voice the "astre pur et charmant" that inspires the song. Gigli, singing in

Italian,[43] admittedly brings a more sun-like warmth to the music, but Björling's sound (and style) are better suited to the nocturnal setting and the elegance of the French idiom.

The duet that follows the Cavatine is a high point of the performance. The opening recitative, "Ô nuit divine!" ("O ljuva natt"), is one of those moments that Björling made uniquely his own, thanks to the singularly instrumental quality of his *mezza voce* when he was singing in his native tongue. The sound is imbued with light, yet free from any suspicion of dryness, precise in its definition of pitch, and apparently weightless, yet unusually dense in texture.

An idyllic lightness of touch is maintained in the *Allegretto* ("Ah! ne fuis pas encore"), where the opening phrase is built on a *messa di voce* and the rhythm is at once urgent and unhurried. When the two voices unite, the singers underplay Gounod's brief *forte* markings in order not to break the atmosphere of shared intimacy, their instruments complementing each other as the tenor circles above and below the soprano line. They equal here the rare aural pleasure of the 1923 disc (in French) with Gigli and Lucrezia Bori,[44] where the Spanish soprano phrases with pointed eloquence and the tenor delights with his inimitable *morbidezza*, although the time limits imposed by the acoustic recording give him little time to linger. In both performances the second strophe of the *Allegretto* is cut.

In Roméo's berceuse-like monologue ("Va! repose en paix") the tenor articulates the twenty-one consecutive Cs in the middle register with such binding legato and pregnant diction that the line gathers tension irresistibly. One can fully understand the effect this singing had on Forsell during his pupil's first performance of the role in 1933. As the stage director Ragnar Hyltén Cavallius recalled:

> Jussi sang the beautiful phrases which end the act with such abandon and such harmony that Forsell, with his usual dramatic energy, squeezed my arm and called out, "Cavallius, did you hear that?" And he rushed to the stage and wrapped Jussi in his arms.[45]

The marriage scene in Frère Laurent's cell at the beginning of act 2 confirms Björling's and Schymberg's close rapport. The unison passages are charmingly intoned, and at the climax of the quartet (where they are joined by Leon Björker's imposingly humane Friar and Göta Allard's Gertrude) they negotiate thrillingly the harmonic progressions on "Sois béni!" (rising by a tone each time): a *trouvaille* (repeated in the fifth act) that proves no less overwhelming here than in the final trio of *Faust*.

The unusually ample dynamic range employed by Björling sharpens our awareness of the character's tendency to oscillate between emotional extremes. The voice is so freely produced that it is easy for him to convey the emotional tension of Roméo's attempt to prevent Mercutio and Tybalt from fighting ("des haines le temps est passé!!"); while the solidity of breath support lends an extra depth of sonority to the explosion of anger that follows the fatal injury to his friend. His invective here is so impassioned that he not only prolongs the top B of "Sois de mon cœur l'unique loi!" but sharpens the note by almost half a tone. Such pitch variations may, however, be seen as part of a singer's expressive armory, no less than subtle variations in rhythm: Björling's *fortissimo* top notes often drew this sharpened intonation, and although it can seem jarring, the extra excitement generated by the dissonance is undeniable here. A similarly sharpened, interpolated top C brings the act to an end on "Mais je veux la revoir!" a note so resoundingly sustained that it does much to compensate for the somewhat skeletal conclusion to the finale in this performance.

Act 4 is dominated by another duet, "Nuit d'hyménée," in which the couple celebrate their wedding night before Roméo departs. The romantic idyll sustained in the initial *Andante* is compromised by a forty-two-measure cut, which gives listeners insufficient opportunity to sense the passing of time before the first unwelcome signs of dawn are perceived. Björling's music-making is memorable throughout the duet, and he applies his legato lavishly to "reste encor en mes bras enlacés," binding the phrase together as if he were literally tying Juliette to himself. In no other recorded opera performance is he so consistently willing to sing *piano* in the upper register (witness the crystalline A-flat on the final "reste encor").

The *Allegretto agitato* that follows ("Il faut partir hélas") reveals Gounod's skill in mingling the two voices in a variety of ways, as they alternate between ecstasy and unease. Björling's strong rhythmic sense enables him to phrase here with the right combination of flexibility and precision; once again he extends the upper range of the part, by joining Schymberg on the top C of "ivresse."

In this recording little more than eleven minutes of music separate the fourth-act duet from the couple's final encounter, a somewhat excessive compression of events if one considers everything that happens (and the time that passes) in the meantime. This does not, however, diminish the credibility of the two scenes in themselves. Roméo's opening recitative in the final act ("Salut! tombeau!") suggests the readiness for death of a genuine tragic hero, and the atmosphere is more hushed and emotionally revealing than on any other recording except Kozlovsky's 1947 Russian performance,[46] where the Ukrainian tenor conveys even better than his much younger Swedish colleague a sense of muted dismay in the opening "C'est là!" Kozlovsky's legato suggests the fine-spun quality of a violin here, while Björling's evokes the more haunting quality of a woodwind instrument. We hear this in "Ô ma femme," where the Swede takes his cue from the somber tones of the clarinet in the preceding measures. For all the real sadness expressed by the music, there is something strangely consoling in his song here.

For Björling, as for Kozlovsky, Roméo's suicide is a private gesture (both underplay Gounod's *fortissimo* on "À toi, ma Juliette!") that only becomes public because of Juliette's sudden reawakening, which leads, in "Viens! fuyons au bout du monde," to the brief, feverish illusion that the two lovers can escape from their predestined fate. When the illusion passes, Björling makes us aware of death encroaching upon the body of Roméo in a slow *Larghetto* ("Console-toi, pauvre âme") of great poignancy. Once again his voice responds to every challenge of the score, ascending *piano* to the top A of "flamme" and *forte* the top B of "lumière" with equal ease and beauty. When he joins Schymberg in the final prayer ("Seigneur, pardonnez-nous") we have the impression of having lived more intensely ourselves while sharing our lives with these two lovers.

The success of the Björling-Schymberg partnership is confirmed by their concert performance of the act 1 Madrigal, broadcast in 1941. Their phrasing—encouraged perhaps by closer miking—is, if anything, tenderer and more intimate than in 1940: even the first ascent to the top A is a restrained *mezzo forte*. All in all this is a cherishable performance, which Björling never surpassed.

A couple of years later the second act of the opera was broadcast from the Royal Opera, once again with Schymberg as "Julia." The tenor's performance is singularly expansive in spirit right from the opening recitative, perhaps because he felt he could give more than usual when performing just a single act. We are reminded that *Roméo et Juliette*, for all its apparent intimacy, became a *grand opéra* in its definitive version. In the Cavatine the phrasing, though more varied than ever in the B section, conveys a stronger sense of direction and is warmer and more ecstatic in tone. This Roméo is more adult and erotically aware, and once again the upper register is generously deployed, although it is less ringing this time. The duet is even better, capturing the genuine communion of the two lovers to a rare degree (especially in "Ah! ne fuis pas encore"), while Roméo's lullaby-like solo at the end of the act, with a *messa di voce* on the final F, is no less mesmeric than before.

At the end of the war the tenor wrote in his autobiography that the "opera role which is closest to me right now is Roméo."[47] However, he had still to face the challenge of singing the role in the original language. In the summer of 1945 he studied the part in French, and on September 6—a few weeks before returning to America for the first time in four and a half years—he made his second studio recording of the Cavatine, destined this time for the international market.

Two takes of the aria survive, supremely confident interpretations in which the formidable ring of the upper register is caught more convincingly than was sometimes the case with studio microphones. His delivery of the French text is accurate and the original words lend greater fluidity to the phrasing: a number of extra portamentos are heard here for the first time, notably in the descending interval of "étoiles" in the A sections (although

Björling never indulges in the exaggerated sliding we hear from Franco Corelli).[48] The two takes are so similar that it is difficult to understand why he bothered to repeat the aria. The answer probably lies in the more compelling attack he achieves on the B-flat of "Parais!" at the end of the second take (the one chosen for publication). The brilliance of this note undoubtedly has a decisive influence on the success of the aria in the opera house and Björling guarantees the effect here by adding an extra D a sixth below from which to kick up to the high note. This well-worn tenorial expedient fulfils its function, although on a recording the slight extra resonance achieved does not compensate for the loss of elegance in comparison with the classically smooth attack in the first take.

This almost obsessive focus on ringing sound calls to mind John Steane's remark on the Björling of the mid-forties, "when records kept appearing, solidly (almost deafeningly) resonant, and stolidly uninteresting."[49] This complaint might seem justified if we compare this second studio recording with Björling's live performances of the same aria, which are rather more varied in dynamics and rhythm (particularly in the B section). We might extend the comparison to the classic 1927 disc[50] by Thill (engaged as Roméo at the Paris Opéra in the late twenties, at the Met in the early thirties and at the Royal Swedish Opera in 1939), whose eloquence is such that one feels that it is the words, as much as the music, that carry the expressive weight of the piece. Yet in terms of rhythm and dynamics the French tenor is no more varied than Björling, and his top B-flats, though vibrant, hardly equal the dazzling thrust of the Swede's. Another legendary French tenor, Edmond Clément, sounds somewhat uncomfortable in the upper register (although he actually attacks the final "Parais!" on the B-flat itself),[51] and even the very fine Émile Scaremberg, in his 1905 disc,[52] hardens as he ascends. Yet Scaremberg, who performed the role at the Paris Opéra that very same year, does offer a combination of colorful diction and nuanced phrasing that arguably clings to the memory longer than Björling's expansive single-mindedness.

The most striking of all interpretations of this aria, however, is that in the complete recording with Kozlovsky. The timbre is unremarkable in itself, but the technical skill and musical imagination of the singer make for compelling listening. Kozlovsky is alone among the tenors mentioned so far in genuinely respecting Gounod's *Adagio* indication in the A sections (though Muratore does the same in his much-abbreviated disc)[53] and this leisurely approach allows for much finer nuancing. The first two B-flats are sustained at considerable length and then suddenly diminished, while the final top note is sung in a reinforced falsetto of disarming beauty, a solution that might seem arbitrary if we fail to notice the *pianissimo* marking in the orchestra at this point and forget how extensively nineteenth-century tenors of the French school employed their *voix de tête.*

Kozlovsky's version of the aria is equally unsurpassed by more recent original-language performances, including the recordings of Gedda (whose 1954 version[54] closely echoes Björling's), Kraus[55] and Alagna.[56] Taken as a whole, however, his complete recording (conducted by Alexander Orlov) cannot equal Björling's second broadcast of the entire opera, relayed from the Met in the same year (1947). The conductor in New York was the Russian emigré Emil Cooper, who leads a performance of appreciable dramatic tension in which the orchestra seems impressively involved in what is happening on stage. This was only Björling's third performance of the role in French (the first had taken place in Los Angeles the preceding November), but his phrasing is no less superbly assured than in 1940. We immediately notice, however, that while the shape of his phrases is largely unchanged, their texture is very different: at the Met his priority is to project Roméo's emotions out into the large auditorium, rather than drawing the audience into a dimension of intimate feeling. As a consequence, his dynamics—which formerly favored *piano* over *forte*—are now inverted. While his insistence on volume is not as unvarying as in the *Faust* broadcast three seasons later—his singing is still finely nuanced and his capacity for feeling is never in question here—we perceive the change in expressive emphasis right from the opening scene, when Roméo first catches sight of Juliette. "Cette beauté celeste" is much more outgoing, and the tenor digs more deeply into "Ô trésor." Nevertheless, the line is undisturbed by any emotional overspill, and the rich beauty of tone displayed throughout the performance has never been equalled on a complete recording of this opera. In a 1984 review, the critic Conrad Osborne defined the experience of listening to the voice as "the equivalent of peering deep into a crystal of perfect form and beauty that is turning in the light, so that it is a prism that flashes to us the spectrum in all its variety, yet always in harmony."[57] This quality emerges strikingly in the act 1 finale, where Roméo's recitative ("Ô douleur!") reveals both the stark dignity of the tragic actor and the ringing overtones of his voice, not only on the high A-flat and G, but also on the D below ("je l'aime").

In the Cavatine Björling manages to surpass the 1945 studio recordings in brilliance of tone while offering a broader and more sensitive range of inflection: he makes much here of the *piano* delivery of "Qui vient caresser sa joue" in the B section and his nuanced phrasing in the coda throws the final B-flat into bolder relief. In the duets with Bidú Sayão the voices do not blend as meltingly as was the case with Schymberg, but we become aware of two strongly defined personalities interacting in a theatrically creative fashion. The Brazilian soprano, who was the pupil of a legendary Roméo, Jean De Reszke (whom Gounod himself had conducted in the role at the Paris Opéra in 1888–89), phrases with greater sophistication than Schymberg and inflects the French text with a subtlety that eludes her tenor partner. This special eloquence adds a degree of charm to her Juliette which compensates for an occasional coyness of manner. Notwithstanding a decidedly lightweight voice, she reveals a genuine instinct for tragedy in the final scenes, and the climaxes of the duets in both the fourth and fifth acts emanate a feverish glow that was largely absent in Stockholm.

Like the Royal Opera, the Met used the 1888 score. This time we hear Björling in the definitive version of the act 2 finale, where the concentrated legato and doleful tone with which he opens the great ensemble, "Ah! jour de deuil," generate a feeling of intense pathos combined with grandiosity of gesture. The interpolated top C with which he ends the act—held for eight seconds and once again astonishing in its puissance—is even more exciting this time: it is sustained above the final measures of the chorus, which highlight the all-surmounting brilliance of the sound. This note was not attempted by Charles Hackett, recorded at the Met as Roméo twelve years earlier:[58] he sticks to the written G, and compensatingly emotionalizes the line "Ah! jour de deuil," a rare stylistic lapse in an otherwise idiomatic performance. Half a century after Björling, Roberto Alagna sought to match the Swede in his 1998 recording of this finale, offering an intense display of noble phrasing. Yet in spite of his effortless top C, the French tenor fails to equal the dynamic range, tonal richness, and overall sense of daring that the Swede conveys in a recording Conrad Osborne described as containing "the finest singing of a complete romantic tenor role, beginning to end, I've ever heard."[59] As for the final act, we may note Michael Scott's comparison of Björling's 1947 "Salut! tombeau!" with Alagna's commercial recording of the same monologue:

> Alagna interpolates into his line an affecting catch in his voice; Björling is content to colour his tone, and make an effect through the music. This is typical of the difference. Like Alagna's, Björling's voice was not big but, because his tone was so limpid, he colours each vowel spontaneously. Alagna may be French, but his diction is not as clear as Björling's, and the vowels are not as pellucid.[60]

After the Met broadcast Björling only sang *Roméo et Juliette* five more times, twice in Stockholm, twice in San Francisco, and once in Los Angeles. The final duet recordings he made with his wife Anna-Lisa and Bidú Sayão could be seen as souvenirs of these occasions, for the two sopranos shared the role of Juliette during the tenor's last performances as Roméo in California in 1951. His wife, who had studied singing with Julia Claussen in Stockholm in the early thirties (the couple had met at the Royal Music Academy) and who performed forty-one times with Björling in public between 1945 and 1955, seems to find the Gounod role more congenial than Puccini's Mimì (the other part she sang on stage). Although her voice and phrasing rarely sound totally relaxed, she reveals an unexpected range of expression in the 1949 Hollywood Bowl performance of "Nuit d'hyménée," and her pure head tone blends agreeably with her husband's in the two versions of "Ange adorable" recorded the same year.

Figure 7. Björling sings Gounod, Massenet, and Puccini on NBC's *Standard Hour*, San Francisco, 1949. Courtesy of the Jussi Björling Museum.

Björling's phrasing in all these selections is closer to the gentle lyricism of the 1940 performance, suggesting that his extrovert portrayal at the Met was not so much the result of a changed perception of the character as a response to the clarion condition of his voice on that afternoon. His interaction with Sayão is delightfully spontaneous in their two 1951 duets (and she retains all her charm). In their final "Nuit d'hyménée," however, the tenor's timbre seems to have lost some of its youthful luster. The same is true of his last performance of the Madrigal with Anna-Lisa on CBS's *Edgar Bergen-Charlie McCarthy Show*, where husband and wife join in the comic banter, delivering carefully scripted quips. This abbreviated performance is nevertheless worth hearing for the relative poise and beauty of Anna-Lisa Björling's tone production. She had clearly benefitted from singing this music so frequently over the previous two years, although the regular joint performances as well as her husband's alcoholism had undoubtedly generated considerable psychological strain. A month after this light-hearted radio appearance Anna-Lisa was recovering in hospital from a nervous breakdown and seriously considering divorce:

> I realized that the vicious circle of sobriety, drinking, remorse, recovery and fresh promises of restraint—only to be broken—would never change. It was like sitting on a powder keg, never knowing when the dangling fuse might ignite. My nerves were frayed and my endurance depleted.[61]

In the end she reconsidered her decision, and continued for another decade to provide the necessary support to an artist whose ability to enchant remained largely intact, even while his body was signalling imminent collapse.

"Repentir"

April 15, 1946: New York, Rockefeller Center
Firestone Chorus and Orchestra, cond. Howard Barlow
VAI VAIA 1189

Gounod's "Repentir," conceived for a mezzo-soprano in the final years of the composer's life and published posthumously, is a dramatic "scène sous forme de prière" that alternates pleading recitatives with a reassuring C major refrain. This refrain, translated (by Gounod's business partner Alfred William Philips) as "O Divine Redeemer," became for several decades a standard repertory piece in the English-speaking world, sung in churches and taught in musical academies. The vocal part is more comfortable for a soprano or mezzo (Jessye Norman, who lies somewhere in between, has offered the most thrilling account of it in recent years) than for a tenor, who needs to possess not only a ringing top A, but also a sonorous C below the staff, an attribute that eludes even some baritones. Björling is one of the few tenors capable of projecting both notes easily and his recording has never been surpassed by other male voices (including the tenors Domingo and Alagna, both of whom sing in the original French).

The Swede—who uses Phillips's translation—makes everything seem easy, yet such a combination of transparent diction and smooth legato throughout the range is rare indeed, as is the singular candor of his phrasing. While Björling was naturally used to singing religious music, and churches had been among the most frequent venues for the Björling Quartet in his childhood, this only partly accounts for the disarming directness of expression he achieves here. In the recitatives we feel he is communicating his own human fallibility, while in the refrain—where the singer begs the redeemer to "remember not" his sins—the profoundly consoling tone leaves no doubt that pardon will be granted. By the time we reach the end of the conclusive recitative we cannot help feeling that if this performance were better recorded, accompanied in a less routine manner and more widely known, it could renew the popularity of a *scène* too often dismissed as *démodée.*

GRIEG

"Jeg elsker dig"

October 7, 1945: Detroit, Masonic Temple Auditorium
Ford Symphony Orchestra, cond. Dimitri Mitropoulos

March 25, 1946: New York, Rockefeller Center
Firestone Orchestra, cond. Howard Barlow
WHRA-6036

June 9, 1954: Bergen, Concert Palace
Bergen Philharmonic Orchestra, cond. Carl Garaguly
Bluebell ABCD 006

October 20, 1955: Seattle, Civic Auditorium
Frederick Schauwecker, pf.
VRCS-2001

"Jeg elsker dig" is perhaps the most famous of all Scandinavian songs, and since Hans Christian Andersen's text—sung here in the original Danish, but with Norwegian pronunciation—is clearly suited to a handsome male voice, it may seem surprising that Björling never recorded it in the studio. Yet these four live performances suggest that this open-hearted declaration of love—dedicated by Grieg to his future wife Nina Hagerup—did not entirely suit him. This is immediately evident in the broadcast with Mitropoulos, where he is heard singing the single stanza in D major (the key usually chosen by tenors). In spite of the melting legato and scrupulous attention to the composer's dynamic markings, which range from *pianissimo* to *fortissimo*, the overall effect is too inward-looking and melancholy to sweep the listener off his (or her) feet. Even when he repeats the stanza, as he does in the other three recordings, and even in the B major performance recorded in Grieg's home town of Bergen, where he sings the repeat more softly, Björling fails to convey the message conclusively. This is one of those songs in which the melody serves above all to heighten the immediacy of the text, as Lauritz Melchior proves in his irresistible 1937 recording.[1] Richard Crooks, singing in the now-dated English translation ("I love thee"),[2] and Richard Tauber, recorded in German,[3] also offer a keener emotional response than Björling, whose diction lacks vitality by comparison.

"En Svane"

April 11, 1952: New York, Manhattan Center
Frederick Schauwecker, pf.
Testament SBT 1427

June 9, 1954: Bergen, Concert Palace
Bergen Philharmonic Orchestra, cond. Carl Garaguly
Bluebell ABCD 006

January 18, 1955: Helsinki, B-Messuhalli
Harry Ebert, pf.

September 24, 1955: New York, Carnegie Hall
Frederick Schauwecker, pf.
RCA 88697748922

April 13, 1959: Atlanta, Glenn Memorial Auditorium
Frederick Schauwecker, pf.
Bluebell ABCD 020

While Björling's delivery of "Jeg elsker dig" sounds reticent, he comes into his own in the allusive "En Svane," an inspired setting of a densely alliterative Ibsen poem evoking the most silently mysterious of all birds, which sings only "in death." The evocative quality of the tenor's voice—his ability to make us forget the medium and focus entirely on the message—is brought fully into play here. The silvery transparency of his timbre (which never becomes merely evanescent) and the sense of repose generated by the firm breath support work their magic in all these performances, demonstrating how well music can reveal meanings that words leave unarticulated.

In the 1952 studio recording (in G-flat major), the closeness of the microphone highlights the purity of Björling's middle register and creates extra excitement in the *fortissimo* climax on "Ja da, da lød det!" The Bergen performance—the only one in the original key of F—is more limited in dynamics but acquires a greater range of colors in response to Grieg's superb orchestral accompaniment. Later recordings reveal Björling's increasing expertise in producing a pure head voice on the G-flat of "var" in the final measures.

In Atlanta everything seems poised in perfect balance, the voice responding in each measure to the singer's imaginative vision with a ductility that rivals the iridescent stillness achieved by Kirsten Flagstad in her farewell concert in 1957.[4] And although Nicolai Gedda, in a 1971 London recital,[5] proves even more virtuosic than his fellow Scandinavians in the use of head tone (developing a *messa di voce* on the second top G-flat), he tends to draw attention to the singer rather than the swan, leaving our visual imagination relatively unengaged.

"En Drøm"

April 11, 1952: New York, Manhattan Center
Frederick Schauwecker, pf.
Testament SBT 1427

January 18, 1955: Helsinki, B-Messuhalli
Harry Ebert, pf.

September 24, 1955: New York, Carnegie Hall
Frederick Schauwecker, pf.
RCA 88697748922

December 14, 1955: New Orleans, Municipal Auditorium
Frederick Schauwecker, pf.
Premiere Opera 122

February 8, 1958: Stockholm, Cirkus
Bertil Bokstedt, pf.
Bluebell ABCD 050

March 2, 1958: New York, Carnegie Hall
Frederick Schauwecker, pf.
RCA 60520-2-RG

April 13, 1959: Atlanta, Glenn Memorial Auditorium
Frederick Schauwecker, pf.
Bluebell ABCD 020

Friedrich von Bodenstedt's poem (translated into Norwegian by Nordahl Rolfsen) describes a dream of love that actually comes true. Grieg's song captures the spirit of the text winningly, building up from a soft *Andante* opening to an overwhelming *Allegro* conclusion: only at the end do we discover that the fair maid met in an arbor in spring was no mere dream but a living woman to whom the poet still clings.

Björling's recordings all transpose the song half a tone down from the original key of D major. In his 1952 studio version he phrases too loudly right from the beginning, using the upward leaps in the opening measures as a means of gathering momentum rather than drawing us into the character's "Drømmesyn." He sings with healthy, well-equalized tone at both ends of the range (from the C below the staff to the A-flat above it), but fails to respect many of the composer's dynamic markings. This proves a recurrent problem, for we hear similarly automatic phrasing in the Stockholm TV broadcast (of which no video survives) in February 1958 and the Carnegie Hall recital a month later. Comparison with the German-language recording made by Tauber in 1920[6] reveals how much more imagination can be invested in this music, for the Austrian tenor (whom Björling heard live in Stockholm while still a student at the Royal Music Academy) evokes the "schöner Traum" with dreamy softness, matching the rhythm so subtly to the dynamics as to make the Swede sound staidly metronomic by comparison.

Björling was, however, capable of singing this song with real flair and understanding. In Helsinki in 1955 he employs a head voice on the upper Fs in the opening measures and prepares the climax with playful deliberation: one notes the hushed delivery of "Det var i skovens lyse Bryn" and the combination of inwardness and buoyancy with which he exploits the stringendo effect of "Og Elven sprang." The New Orleans performance later that year is no less varied, with a more exciting crescendo on the climactic A-flat, partly facilitated by a barely perceptible attack from below. This kick-up effect is heard more distinctly in later performances, including the sensitively-shaped rendition in Atlanta, where it detracts somewhat from the stylistic purity of the singing.

HANDEL

Serse
"Ombra mai fu"

August 23, 1949: Los Angeles, Hollywood Bowl
Hollywood Bowl Symphony Orchestra, cond. Izler Solomon
Standing Room Only SRO 845-1

June 9, 1954: Bergen, Concert Palace
Bergen Philharmonic Orchestra, cond. Carl Garaguly
Bluebell ABCD 006

December 14, 1955: New Orleans, Municipal Auditorium
Frederick Schauwecker, pf.
Premiere Opera 122

April 13, 1959: Atlanta, Glenn Memorial Auditorium
Frederick Schauwecker, pf.
Bluebell ABCD 020

Björling sang Handel's *Messiah* eight times in the 1930s, but the only Baroque music he ever recorded was this opening scene from the opera *Serse* (*Xerxes*), written in the contralto register for the famed castrato Cafarelli. Like most tenors, Björling transposes it up a tone (to G major), and although he offers little in the way of embellishment he sings most expressively, with the words poised on the lips in true *bel canto* style. This music has at times been transposed to a religious context—some tenors have recorded the *Larghetto* to the Italian words "O mio Signor"[1]—and understandably so, for the recitative is indeed a sort of prayer and the aria that follows a hymn of praise. The fact that the objects of the prayer and hymn are a plane tree and the shade it projects should not induce us to suspect an ironical perspective, but rather to share Serse's understanding of Nature as a potent manifestation of divinity. This is possible when the singing itself is a thing of wonder: Enrico Caruso's 1920 recording,[2] for example, has proved a source of inspiration for many tenors. We know that Björling listened to this recording carefully because he clearly imitates the verbal stresses in the recitative (where both tenors include all the appropriate appoggiaturas), the swelling crescendo on the opening note of the *Larghetto* and in the ascending portamento (from A to F-sharp) on the word "soave" in the closing phrase. Beniamino Gigli, who himself imitates Caruso in his 1933 recording,[3] lacks the skill (or the will) to reproduce this portamento, although he does—like Placido Domingo[4] after him—make a sketchy attempt at the trill on the D-sharp of "amabile," which is such a striking feature of the Neapolitan's version. Björling prefers to embellish this word with a graceful turn.

What Caruso, Gigli and Björling have in common is a real feeling for the Arcadian innocence of the setting (something that eludes the more knowing Domingo) and the deep seriousness of the text, as well as an ability to produce a rounded, mellow tone on every note, binding the sounds together while leaving the words free to float on the breath. In his 1949 Hollywood Bowl performance, Björling's imitation of Caruso in the recitative does not disturb the flow of the music or the vitality of his diction: he avoids darkening the voice artificially and can easily produce the sort of imposing volume that is needed to capture the audience's attention in the first scene of the opera—or in the opening number of a concert, as this aria proves to be in each of the recordings listed above. His seamless phrasing contrasts with that of Mario Del Monaco,[5] who also took Caruso as his model but typically adopts a more muscular, lowered-larynx emission: impressive in terms of pure sound, this limits the smoothness of the legato and expressiveness of the words.

In terms of equalization of sound and elegance of phrasing Björling actually surpasses his predecessors in some respects. He avoids any hint of aspiration, and the opening "O" of "Ombra mai fu" is less open than Caruso's, suiting the meaning of the word itself. The attack on the top G of "di vegetabile" is generally cleaner and nobler than Gigli's, although in his 1954 recording Björling is less refined here: he is in poor health and betrays both a certain fragility in the recitative (where "Tuoni" is weakly enunciated) and a loss of roundness at the top of the range (for once one is aware of a register break). His singing remains masterly, however, and one appreciates the *messa di voce* that replaces the simple crescendo on the opening note of the *Larghetto* (an effect that is more fully developed in Tito Schipa's elegant rendition).[6]

The other two recordings, made during recitals, both show the singer in excellent voice, but the full beauty of his timbre is properly caught only in Atlanta, where Björling offers his finest-ever version of the recitative and his most cello-like sculpting of the aria that follows.

LEONCAVALLO

Pagliacci
Complete Recordings

January 10, 1953: New York, Manhattan Center
Jussi Björling (Canio), Victoria de los Angeles (Nedda), Leonard Warren (Tonio), Robert Merrill (Silvio), Paul Franke (Beppe); Robert Shaw Chorale, Columbus Boy Choir, RCA Victor Orchestra, cond. Renato Cellini
EMI 5 66778 2

December 8, 1954: Stockholm, Royal Opera House
Jussi Björling (Canio), Ruth Moberg (Nedda), Erik Sundquist (Tonio), Carl-Axel Hallgren (Silvio), Arne Ohlson (Beppe); Royal Swedish Opera Chorus and Royal Court Orchestra, cond. Lamberto Gardelli
Bluebell ABCD 085

Excerpts
March 12, 1937: Vienna, Staatsoper
Jussi Björling (Canio), Margit Bokor (Nedda), Friedrich Ginrod (Silvio); Vienna State Opera Chorus and Orchestra, cond. Karl Alwin
Koch Schwann 3-1454-2

"Il Prologo"

September 4, 1950: Virum, Denmark
unaccompanied party performance

"Vesti la giubba"

December 20, 1933: Stockholm, Concert Hall
Unspecified orchestra, cond. Nils Grevillius
Naxos 8.110722

March 27–30, 1944: Stockholm, Concert Hall
Unspecified orchestra, cond. Nils Grevillius
Naxos 8.110701

February 16, 1951: New York, NBC Studio
Unspecified orchestra and conductor
WHRA-6036

March 9, 1951: New York, Manhattan Center
RCA Victor Orchestra, cond. Renato Cellini
RCA 88697748922

March 12, 1951: New York, Carnegie Hall
Bell Telephone Orchestra, cond. Donald Voorhees
WHRA-6036

November 19, 1951: New York, Carnegie Hall
Firestone Chorus and Orchestra, cond. Howard Barlow
Kultur DVD D2424

"O Colombina"

July 6, 1950: Stockholm, Gröna Lund
Harry Ebert, pf.
Bluebell ABCD 114

Pagliacci was the only opera in Björling's repertoire that required him to play the role of a performing artist. Since Canio is a clown working within the commedia dell'arte tradition, this enabled the tenor conceal his everyday persona behind layers of makeup and motley. *Pagliacci* was also the only opera in which Björling had to commit murder in full view of the audience. As Nedda's murder takes place in the context of a play within the opera, the theatrical mask of Pagliaccio perhaps made it easier for him to liberate the violence from within. Not all singing actors respond creatively to make-up, but for the Swede it seems to have had an emancipating effect, reinforced in this case by the emotional directness of the music itself, with the vocal line modelled on the syllabic structure of speech.

In truth Leoncavallo's score does not simply exploit the explosive impact of the *parola cantata*, but encourages the tenor to add bitter laughter and tears to his aria and to deliver his final words (addressed to Silvio) on unspecified pitches. It was indications such as these that led—in a work conceived as a manifesto of theatrical realism—to the development of a *verismo* style of singing. This style is best illustrated perhaps not in the surviving discs of the first generation of Canios (born mainly in the 1860s and 1870s), but in extracts from the opera recorded by Aureliano Pertile in 1927[1] and in the complete recording made by Beniamino Gigli in 1934.[2] What these two tenors have in common is their willingness to sacrifice the smoothness and continuity of line in order to highlight the singer's emotional involvement. Later recordings by Mario Del Monaco[3] and José Cura[4] take this a stage further by subordinating the very shape of the melodies to the physiological needs of pure declamation. Yet although Pertile and Cura at least manage to convey, in their very different ways, a genuine sense of tragic awareness, in many singers this extra-musical dimension serves simply to disguise a lack of deep feeling. The (very well-documented) history of this opera on record suggests that the most moving performances are often those which succeed in making Leoncavallo's expressive markings function in purely musical terms, conveying tears through the coloring of the melodies. It is no coincidence that the tenors who contributed most to the opera's success in the early years, Fernando De Lucia and Enrico Caruso, brought to this score the expressive resources of the *bel canto* tradition, with phases densely bound together (the former attacks "Sperai tanto il delirio"[5] with a shimmering upward portamento) and enriched by a repeated rise and fall in volume (the classical *messa di voce*). They did not exclude the laughter and tears requested by the composer, but did not allow them to interfere with the cumulative momentum of the vocal line.

In later generations it was often outside Italy—where the *verismo* style was less all-prevailing in the first half of the twentieth century—that the musical potential of Leoncavallo's opera was more fully realized. In France, for example, Georges Thill (a De Lucia pupil) proved a memorable Canio, as did Helge Rosvænge in German-speaking countries. In Sweden, meanwhile, no one would have been surprised by the lack of laughter and sobs in the twenty-two-year-old Björling's recording of "Vesti la giubba" ("Pudra ditt anlet"). This 1933 disc is the most moving of all the tenor's early operatic recordings: his technique is entirely sufficient to deal with the difficulties of the score and he phrases with rare nobility of tone. This quality is particularly fitting here as Canio's solo is motivated not simply by self-pity and anger but by a more complex awareness of how painful it is to conceal such emotions on stage or expose them to public ridicule. He seems to observe his predicament—in a brief moment of relative stillness—with some of the detachment we associate with tragic heroes of earlier eras, and the audience inevitably shares his suffering, even if it sympathizes with Nedda's desire to elope.

Björling shapes the melody in this *Arioso Adagio* (which moves from an E minor opening to an E major climax) with admirable purity and creates a number of effects that are unique to him. In the recitative his strikingly muted delivery of "Tu sei Pagliaccio" seems to echo the blended timbres of the bassoons and clarinets in the preceding chord. This, combined with the inwardness of mood sustained in the opening measures of the aria and the deeply-felt delivery of the words, enriches both the musical and psychological interest of a solo that can easily seem a facile assemblage of applause-grabbing gestures. The tempo, though enlivened by a constant play of rubato, is respectful of Leoncavallo's metronome marking (♩ = 46). Björling does not embellish the climactic phrase (rising twice to A natural), nor are his breath-spans as long as they will be in later recordings, but the voice already commands both the high placement and the maturity of tone that the music requires (this is after all a decidedly adult aria) and the simple humanity of his diction in the two final measures makes for a more persuasive conclusion than the sobbing requested by the composer. This is a request that does not have to be interpreted literally, but serves to indicate the degree of emotional involvement required.

Björling made his stage debut as Canio in Stockholm in January 1936 and would sing the role another nineteen times over the two successive decades. The live extracts from a bilingual (Swedish-German) performance in Vienna fourteen months after that debut demonstrate how completely at ease he felt in this part, and display his voice at its very best. We first hear him in the final repeat of "A ventitré ore" in the opening scene, where he makes the traditional transposition to the upper octave (employed by the most famous Italian Canios of the previous generation: Pertile, Gigli, and Giovanni Martinelli) with a laser-like projection that captures the character's volcanic temperament. The creator of the role, Fiorello Giraud, who probably did not make this transposition, was nevertheless known for the ease of his high notes, which can be sampled in his 1904 G&T recordings of music by Bizet, Wagner and Verdi that also reveal a well-schooled technique and a complete absence of veristic overplay.

At the Staatsoper the recitative to "Vesti la giubba" is once again singular in its coloring, but flows more naturally and incorporates a bitter laugh. Superbly accompanied by Karl Alwin, the *Adagio* then unfolds as a gigantic *messa di voce*, beautiful both as a musical artefact and as an emotional statament. In the first sixteen measures Björling does not push the volume beyond a *mezzo forte*, suggesting a flow of feelings rather than a flourish of theatrical declamation; an impression of a character thinking aloud that is reinforced by the all-embracing legato (including the rising portamentos on "quà" and "Pagliaccio") and the hauntingly reedy tone of the tenor's half-voice. The introspective atmosphere is maintained in the final seventeen measures. His phrasing in "Tramuta in lazzi lo spasmo e il pianto" is not *violento*, as Leoncavallo prescribes, but conveys a sad awareness of the inevitability of the clown's destiny. The subsequent climax above the staff is intensified not only by the amplitude of the breath-spans and the concentration of the tone but also by the added mordent on the top G of "amore," a device that was probably inspired by Caruso's finest recording of the aria, made in 1907.[6] The sliding descent of "Ridi del duol," affecting in hue, also owes

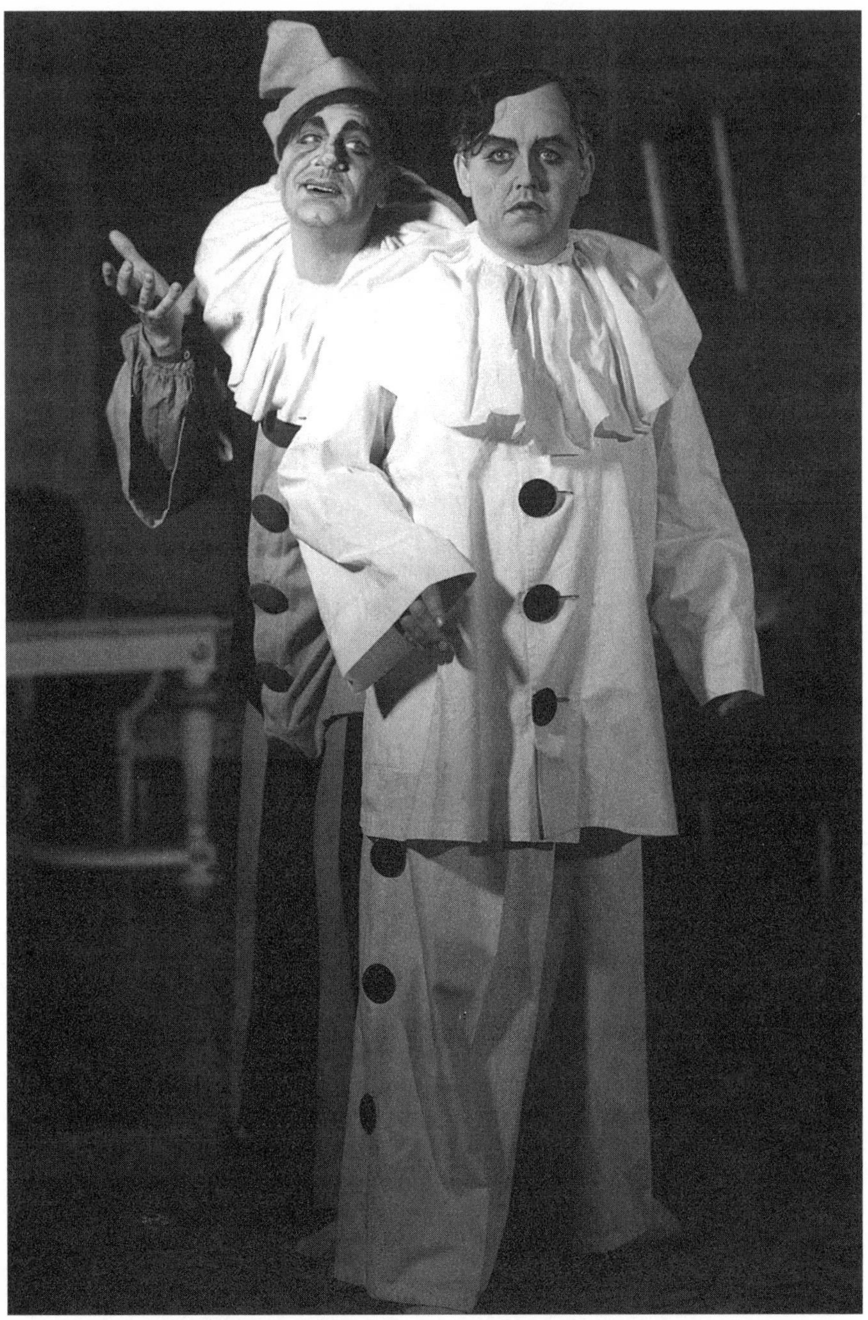

Figure 8. Canio and Tonio (Einar Larson) in *Pagliacci*, Stockholm, 1937. Photograph by Edlund. Courtesy of the Jussi Björling Museum.

something to Caruso, although unlike the Neapolitan Björling again avoids any overt emotionalism in the final measures.

The third extract from the opera is Canio's last extended solo, "No! Pagliaccio non son" ("Jag är ej Pajazzo"), sung on the theatrical troupe's makeshift stage. In the opening *Allegro moderato* Björling has no difficulty with the tessitura of a melodic line that hovers around the top of the staff, and his voice has a searing focus that lends extra bite to the words. At this point in the opera the balance between seething violence (conveyed by the freedom and vehemence of the declamation) and formal constraint (suggested by the rhythmic and harmonic regularity of the aria's structure) is still precariously maintained; we cannot tell which will dominate in the end. For a brief moment—when Canio switches to the major mode for "Sperai tanto il delirio"—we can hope that the verbal outburst will preempt physical violence. Björling shapes this melancholy *Cantabile espressivo* with tones of the utmost beauty, and inserts the traditional gleaming B-flat on "fidente credeva." At the same time he can only produce a moderate volume in the lower-lying "Ma il vizio alberga sol nell'alma tua negletta," reminding us that he could dominate this role with his lyric voice only in smaller theaters or with the aid of a sympathetic conductor (as Alwin proves to be here). As if to compensate for this slight weakness he greatly prolongs the B-flat on "abbietta" and, like most tenors, takes the final words of the solo up an octave for greater impact. Both the variants heard here are also featured in the 1907 complete recording with the resourceful Puerto Rican tenor Antonio Paoli, supervised by the composer himself.[7]

Seven years later Björling recorded "Vesti la giubba" in Italian for the first time. It is a fine performance, free from linguistic errors (though a slight foreign accent is perceptible), displaying a ringing top and a well-honed legato. He includes the laugh but once again there are no sobs at the end; for those who wish to hear the aria sung cleanly and musically in the original language there are few better performances. Björling repeats, as in nearly all his later recordings, the embellishment on "amore" and adds an acciaccatura on the top G of "Ridi Pagliaccio." These grace notes are a special feature of Caruso's 1907 recording and were adopted also by Gigli and Martinelli, while more recent tenors have tended to eschew them. Yet although there is no doubting the sincerity of feeling expressed by the Swede, the words are less alive than in the finest performances of the Italian tenors. De Lucia (who transposes down a semitone)[8] colors the phrases, here as in the other extracts from this opera, with a freedom that can only be achieved by a voice free from undue pressure from the breath, while Giuseppe Anselmi[9] savors every word with an impromptu eloquence that is rivalled by his fellow Sicilian Giuseppe di Stefano. It is almost inevitable that Björling should seem relatively bland by comparison, particularly since he employs a more limited dynamic range when singing in Italian ("Tu sei Pagliaccio!" is delivered *mezzo forte* this time). The rolled *r* of "Ridi del duol"—which the Swede probably picked up from Martinelli's 1927 disc[10] that was later imitated (to much more exaggerated effect) by Richard Tucker—adds little to the emotional impact of his phrasing.

The next time Björling's voice was recorded in music from *Pagliacci* was during a party in Denmark six years later where we hear him singing, unaccompanied and in Swedish translation, the final part of the opera's Prologue (from the *Andante cantabile* "E voi piuttosto" to the end). Björling was not the only tenor to appropriate this music—Gigli, Tauber and Del Monaco recorded it in the studio—although the high-spirited context and the fact that he sings the part a tone down (Gigli, by contrast, transposes up a tone)[11] and rises at the end to a teasingly incongruous B-flat makes this rendition very much a party-piece. His phrasing is nevertheless expressive (there are plenty of portamentos) and the timbre has the oaken quality of a genuine baritone. Although the pace is sluggish and he occasionally takes breaths in odd places, the low B-flats of "è svolto" are less problematic for him than the equivalent Cs are for Del Monaco.[12] It is interesting to note, moreover, that after singing the piece as a baritone (the center of gravity of Björling's voice tended to shift downward when he had had a few drinks), he switches into a decidedly tenorial register for the final B-flat.

Pagliacci is the only opera from which Björling recorded music assigned to three different characters, for he can also be heard singing Arlecchino's Serenade, during an open-air concert in 1950. There was nothing new in this exploit: when De Lucia performed the role of Canio he sometimes appropriated this music (sung offstage) for himself, and Caruso once did the same, incognito, at the Metropolitan. De Lucia was also one of the many leading tenors who chose to record the Serenade in the first half of the twentieth century. His transposed version, which includes extra embellishments, demonstrates his skill in both reinforcing and dimishing sustained tones above the staff, while that of another famous Canio, Pertile, though airy in spirit, is weighed down somewhat by the metallic impurity of the voice itself.

Björling's performance, in Swedish translation, is not particularly well-accompanied; Ebert's playing in the introductory measures does little to suggest the tuning of a guitar. The voice, however, is both luxuriant in coloration and rhythmically buoyant, with a delightful "ping" to the sound throughout the range. The prevailing dynamic is *mezzo forte* (as would be appropriate if he were singing the Serenade backstage), but Björling varies the second verse with an echo effect in "di te chiamando." This being a concert performance, he allows himself to prolong the final A (transposed up an octave) for a good five seconds, to brilliant effect. Tito Schipa takes a similar liberty in his caressingly modulated 1916 performance,[13] as does Ivan Kozlovsky in a Russian-language version,[14] rhythmically as free as De

Lucia's, and including an astonishing *messa di voce* on the first top A. Gigli's 1934 recording is much more adherent to the letter of the score, and even more charming in its playful alternation of head and chest voice. He proves a cuddlier, but less youthfully desirable Arlecchino than the Swede.

The fact that Björling was recorded four times singing "Vesti la giubba" in New York in 1951 suggests that he was considering performing the role at the Met. In the end, however, he never sang Canio on stage in Italian, aware perhaps that he could not match the combination of sheer volume and beauty of tone that Martinelli had guaranteed right up to the early 1940s (Björling may well have seen him in the role in 1941) and that Del Monaco would offer Met audiences between 1953[15] and 1959. Björling seems to have been listening to Martinelli again before the NBC broadcast in February 1951, for he rolls his *r*s conspicuously in the recitative. Caruso, however, was his main focus here: the performance was preceded by an exchange with the Neapolitan's widow, Dorothy, who presented him with one of her husband's costumes and declared that he was the only singer worthy of bearing "Rico's crown."[16] The performance of "Vesti la giubba" is in fact over-conditioned by Björling's desire to make a Caruso-like sound, and proves less expressively revealing than his recordings of the 1930s. The studio recording made a few weeks later is more gratifyingly lyrical in inspiration and avoids the mispronunciation of "singhiozzo" that mars Björling's other performances of the aria that year, but otherwise offers nothing new. The same can be said of the *Bell Telephone Hour* broadcast three days later, but the televised *Voice of Firestone* performance relayed in November is naturally more interesting: this is the only surviving aria in this series sung by Björling in costume, with the scene acted out as if he were on stage. It cannot have been easy for him to enter into the spirit of this highly dramatic solo in a New York studio, but his acting is never less than plausible, if hardly compelling. The camera, in combination with the microphone, however, does expose his less than entirely idiomatic delivery of the text (sometimes our eyes help us hear things better). Björling's Italian pronunciation was in fact unusually good for a Scandinavian tenor of that era (to get the measure of his linguistic achievement it is sufficient to compare this performance with the grotesque effort of Lauritz Melchior, who sang Leoncavallo's aria on the same program in April 1950),[17] but in music whose every melodic inflection is clearly dictated by the words a less than impeccable delivery inevitably arouses a certain unease. To understand what is lacking it is sufficient to compare this performance with Di Stefano's televised interpretation filmed in 1958,[18] notable for the rare clarity with which he articulates the key word "infranto," which awkwardly straddles the register break. The Sicilian tenor achieves this at the expense of the very open tone that was eventually to prove his undoing, but in an aria rooted in verbal immediacy even the most radical solutions can seem justifiable. Still more moving is Roberto Alagna's performance of the aria within the context of the whole opera:[19] he too projects words eloquently—including the difficult "Bah!" in the recitative—and sings with a rare cohesion of gesture and phrasing that is musically as well as theatrically satisfying. Cura's portrayal of a drunken Canio reminds us how easy it is to transform this melody into heightened speech, subordinating musical details to the naturalistic pace of the declamation (which is here very rapid). His is a magnificent theatrical portrayal of degradation and latent violence, but the sounds he makes are quite alien to the *bel canto* aesthetic that still informed the art of the earliest Canios and was unfailingly upheld by Björling. Perhaps only Carlo Bergonzi,[20] after the Swede, has phrased this aria in such a gratifyingly musical fashion.

The complete studio recording made in New York in 1953 was the only occasion on which Björling sang the whole opera in Italian. Although his performance is less completely satisfying than his Turiddu in *Cavalleria rusticana,* it nevertheless withstands the test of time. Although the voice is less ample in volume than Martinelli's or Del Monaco's, Caruso's, or Cura's, we have no difficulty in hearing him in the initial phrases sung "offstage" (the recording was made in the Manhattan Center). When the crowd is finally silenced, Björling lends an appropriately comic inflection to "Mi accordan di parlar?" He is not as naturally eloquent as the Tuscan tenor Galliano Masini in this opening scene,[21] in which Canio illustrates the plot of the play, but his phrasing draws inspiration from the rhythms and textures of the orchestral accompaniment as well as from the meanings of the words. His voice spontaneously assimilates the airy brilliance of the woodwinds in "Un grande spettacolo a ventitré ore," while the graceful humanity of his delivery (as the voice moves effortlessly from the upper G to the tricky lower D) is such that we immediately feel a certain liking for a character who needs to maintain the empathy of the audience right to the end of the opera if the tragedy is to have its full impact. The limpidity of his emission enables him to color the words expressively without resorting to exaggerated emphasis (such as Pertile's wide vibrato or the emotionally charged attacks inserted by Gigli). The character's cordiality is confirmed in the exchange with the Contadini, and one notes how effortlessly he reinforces the C on "Vi pare?!" darkening the sound in an ominous manner. In "Un tal gioco," where the opening *Adagio molto* is taken at a very leisurely pace, we appreciate the ease with which Björling switches in tone from the lighthearted to the deadly serious. In the contrasting *Andante sostenuto assai* Björling exploits the archaic formality of the rhythm without adopting the affected diction that Gigli employs here. He builds up to a threatening top A on "parlo," where the crescendo—much broader than Gigli's—suggests for the first time a real potential for violence, while the melting legato of "Adoro la mia sposa" keeps the different facets of the character in appropriate balance. In the final repeat of "A ventitré ore" the top B is less dazzling than in the Viennese performance, but he compensates by adding a mordent to the A below it, as Pertile and Gigli do in their recordings, a reminder that even *verismo* tenors employed *bel canto* flourishes when they felt it appropriate.

In his next appearance Björling brings us face to face with the potential murderer. The homicidal intensity of the confrontation with Nedda after her plans to elope have been overheard is unlike anything else we hear from this tenor on disc (with the exception of the duet with Jago from *Otello*). Although the convulsive movement of the vocal line brings his foreign accent occasionally to the fore, his ability to reinforce and darken any sound at will proves a formidable expressive weapon, used so unsparingly that the final cry of "il nome!" betrays a degree of rawness that is unusual for him.

"Vesti la giubba" is similar in shape, texture and volume to the 1951 performances, but there are no superfluous rolled *r*s this time, "singhiozzi" is pronounced correctly and the strings of the RCA Victor Orchestra offer a truly singing accompaniment that sets off the tenor's tensile line. All this very orthodox performance lacks is genuine individuality of expression. The same could be said of Canio's first appearance as Pagliaccio in the Commedia. The problem lies not so much in the limited volume he employs in the dialogue beginning "Un uomo era con te" (marked *forte* in the score) as in his failure to convey the tension that underlies Canio's delivery of his well-rehearsed stage routine; the intense sarcasm that informs every inflection of a theatrical dialogue which has suddenly become frighteningly true to life. Galliano Masini is outstanding here, with every word revealing a rare degree of imaginative identification, while Björling comes into his own only toward the end of the dialogue, at "Per la morte!" (addressed to the stage audience), where he opens up the volume to convey an increasing loss of control. "No! Pagliaccio non son" is both noble and fearsome, with the blind fury of the first verse as telling as the deep melancholy of the second, where Canio recalls rescuing Nedda from poverty. Like many other interpreters of the role, Björling models his phrasing on Caruso's 1910 recording. With Caruso, he is perhaps the only tenor who succeeds in combining a rare nobility of spirit with the mounting desire to annihilate the object of his jealousy. In both their recordings we sense a deep feeling of nostalgia when Canio sings of an "amor che era febbre e follia," while in the *Cantabile espressivo* that follows Björling arguably surpasses Caruso in his ability to generate a mood of all-enveloping sadness. At the same time his middle register is now robust enough to project the full bitterness of "Ma il vizio alberga sol nell'alma tua negletta" (where Canio justifies to himself the murder he is about to commit) and the final measures of the solo surpass his Viennese achievement for resonance and amplitude of phrasing.

Since World War II, a number of other tenors have displayed impressively sonorous instruments in this scene, but—in comparison with Caruso and

Björling—Del Monaco has difficulty in shaping the legato phrases with real nobility and Franco Corelli[22] spoils the grand scale of his phrasing with lachrymose inflections (nothing is more alienating than a sentimental killer), while Placido Domingo lacks the technical means to reinforce the sound to truly ringing effect in the upper register. Björling maintains the tension during the final exchange with Nedda (in spite of a certain reticence on the part of Victoria de los Angeles) and his direct attack on the top A-flat of "Ah! tu mi sfidi" is chilling. Canio's final words, "Di morte negli spasmi lo dirai!" and "Ah! sei tu? Ben venga!" offer conclusive evidence of the tenor's bravura as a tragic actor when his emotions are fully engaged. The ending of the opera, capped by Leonard Warren's persuasive delivery of Tonio's "La commedia è finita," is truly lacerating in effect, for we identify simultaneously here with both the murderer and his principal victim.

Just over a year after recording *Pagliacci* in Italian, Björling was broadcast in a complete Swedish-language performance from Stockholm. The opera was coupled that evening with *Cavalleria rusticana* and the tenor played the leading role in both works, as he did on nine other occasions between 1936 and 1955. This particular double-act reveals his interpretative craft in a new stage of its evolution: the voice he employs for Canio is quite unlike the one he uses for Turiddu, a difference not simply determined by the different vowel-sounds of two languages (he sang *Cavalleria* in Italian), but by a conscious desire to make full use of the voice's coloristic potential as a means of revealing character.

The tenor's entrance in the opening scene reminds us the Björling's voice was never that of a dramatic tenor. The sound is penetrating rather than overwhelming, even in this relatively small theater (1200 seats), but his diction displays a variety of inflection that goes beyond his achievement in the studio and brings the character attractively to life. Although the Swedish translation inevitably adheres to the vocal line less snugly than the original Italian, in Björling's performance the melody seems to spring more spontaneously from the words. A curiosity, reflecting local performing traditions, is the single note on the bass drum (rather than the full orchestral chord) that introduces Canio's "Un grande spettacolo" ("Välkomna mitt herrskap"). At the end of this solo the chorus joins him on his conclusive "a ventitré ore," after which there is a seventeen-measure cut, eliminating the tenor's repeat of that phrase.

"Un tal gioco" ("Sådant gyckel") further demonstrates how much more relaxed Björling is when singing in his native language. Once again the shaping of this solo is masterly, and although we cannot see him, we sense the vivid participation of the actor as well as the singer: witness the laughter that coincides with Leoncavallo's *rallentando scherzoso* on "ai colpi di bastone" and the clapping that accompanies "ridendo allegramente." The gradual crescendo up to the reinforced top A of "vi parlo" is as impressively developed as in the studio, and the final phrase of the solo sounds—again—sad and serious rather than sarcastic. The final high-lying repeat of "A ventitré ore" is more exhilarating than ever in its freedom.

The relatively compact sound displayed by the tenor in the opening scene contrasts with his full-throated emission during Canio's next appearance, a confrontation with Nedda that conveys a frightening loss of control combined with a clearly murderous intent. "Vesti la giubba" has an inwardness of expression that recalls Björling's performances of the 1930s—"Tu sei Pagliaccio" is now sung *piano* once again—but this time the extra musical sensitivity is combined with an emotional maturity that brings home the full import of every word.

When singing in his own language Björling has no difficulty in establishing the right degree of tension during the duet with Nedda in the Commedia. Ruth Moberg is more theatrically alive than Victoria de los Angeles, and once again the tenor is at his most inspired in "No! Pagliaccio non son," where he adds a mordent on the E-flat of "più che in Dio stesso in te!" His voice conveys here the unyielding bitterness of the man about to commit murder, rather than the melancholy of the betrayed husband, sounding closer on this occasion to Martinelli than to Caruso. The final lines of the drama are uttered with such bleak resolve that the tenor sounds ripe here to play a role he never got around to singing: Verdi's Otello.

After Björling's debut in *Pagliacci* in 1936 the critic Sven Lindström noted the theatrical potential of a performance that simply need to be freed from constraint. "Come on, let it go, Mr Björling!" he appealed, "and trust your own judgement and your own power."[23] By the time the tenor made his final appearances in the role in 1954–55, he was fully capable of doing this: it is significant that the person who saw him perform more than anyone else, his wife Anna-Lisa, stated that this was the role she "came to love most. His was a deeply moving interpretation, very human and dramatically overwhelming in the climactic moments."[24]

"Mattinata"

September 4, 1929: Stockholm, Concert Hall
Unspecified orchestra, cond. Nils Grevillius
Testament SBT 1427

September 29, 1930: Stockholm, Concert Hall
Unspecified orchestra, cond. Nils Grevillius
Naxos 8.110740

March 27–30, 1944: Stockholm, Concert Hall
Unspecified orchestra, cond. Nils Grevillius
EMI 5 75900 2

October 7, 1945: Detroit, Masonic Temple Auditorium
Ford Symphony Orchestra, cond. Dimitri Mitropoulos

March 15, 1948: New York, Rockefeller Center
Bell Telephone Orchestra, cond. Donald Voorhees
WHRA-6036

November 29, 1950: New York, Rockefeller Center
Firestone Chorus and Orchestra, cond. Howard Barlow
Kultur DVD D2424

July 5, 1951: Stockholm, Gröna Lund
Harry Ebert, pf.
Bluebell ABCD 114

This aubade, in which the singer hails the beauty of the dawn before inviting his beloved to wake up, put on her white dress and open the door to him, was specifically conceived for the gramophone and was first published by the Gramophone Company in 1904, along with the disc featuring Leoncavallo himself accompanying Enrico Caruso on the piano.[25] Sung in E major (a tone above score pitch), it is one of the Neapolitan tenor's most successful early recordings, fervent in delivery and caressing in detail. This first recording served as a model for all later tenors, including Björling, who sang this music in public as early as 1926 and chose it for his HMV test recording in September 1929, when he was eighteen years old. This piano-accompanied performance in Swedish translation represents, along with Geehl's "For You Alone," the earliest documentation of his tenor voice. It records extraordinarily well, revealing a glistening fullness on the As above the staff (as with Caruso, the key is E major) and a remarkable *morbidezza* on the D-sharp below it. What we hear is the quintessential voice of youth, so energizing in its auroral overtones that it fits to perfection the images evoked in Leoncavallo's text. Although Björling has clearly listened to Caruso's recording—he imitates the *messa di voce* on "stuol" (marked in the score by a simple crescendo) and the rising portamento joining the F-sharp of "cantor!" to the A of "Ove"—he does not seem to be consciously interpreting the music here but simply applying his unique voice to the written notes.

A year later Björling recorded the song in Swedish again, this time with an orchestral accompaniment in E-flat major. Here his legato is firmer and his high notes more securely grounded, and he phrases with a real sense of direction, lending a seductive lift to "Metti anche tu." This is already an expert serenader, who exploits the song for its full effect.

The Italian-language recording made fourteen years later is even better. Björling sings with real individuality here (in E major, as in all later recordings), relishing the opportunities for rubato and making this time a simple crescendo on the D-sharp of "stuol," which is then linked by means of a portamento to the B of "Commosso." Although words are not as caressingly poised on the lips as they are in readings by Di Stefano[26] and Luciano Pavarotti,[27] the liquid quality of Björling's timbre interacts with the poetic imagery to telling effect. He also adds an extra flourish to the final cadence, rising to a generously-held top B (which loosens slightly toward the end) before returning to the tonic by means of an acciaccatura.

None of Björling's later recordings include this interpolation and none of them equal this performance. The 1945 version with Mitropoulos is similar in approach but afflicted by poor sound, as is the 1951 outdoor recital. The *Bell Telephone* performance is overloud, transforming a fragrant drawing-room song (as De Lucia reminds us in his exquisite 1911 disc)[28] into a full-blown operatic aria. In the *Voice of Firestone* telecast two years later Björling's approach is more lyrical but the accompaniment of the mixed chorus (in evening dress) makes the song seem like a number from a musical. The tenor's performance is charming, particularly when he smilingly delivers the concluding phrases with his arms round two of the chorus ladies, but as in the *Firestone* "Vesti la giubba," the video reminds us that he is singing in what for him is a foreign language.

MASCAGNI

Cavalleria rusticana
Complete Recordings

January 7–February 1, 1953: New York, Manhattan Center
Jussi Björling (Turiddu), Zinka Milanov (Santuzza), Robert Merrill (Alfio), Carol Smith (Lola), Margaret Roggero (Lucia); Robert Shaw Chorale, RCA Victor Orchestra, cond. Renato Cellini
RCA 6510-2

December 8, 1954: Stockholm, Royal Opera House
Jussi Björling (Turiddu), Aase Nordmo-Løvberg (Santuzza), Georg Svedenbrant (Alfio), Bette Björling (Lola), Margit Sehlmark (Lucia); Royal Swedish Opera Chorus, Royal Court Orchestra, cond. Kurt Bendix
Bluebell ABCD 085

September 1–7, 1957: Florence, Teatro Comunale
Jussi Björling (Turiddu), Renata Tebaldi (Santuzza), Ettore Bastianini (Alfio), Lucia Danieli (Lola), Rina Corsi (Lucia); Chorus and Orchestra of the Maggio Musicale Fiorentino, cond. Albert Erede
Decca 458 224-2

November 16, 1959: New York, Metropolitan Opera House
Jussi Björling (Turiddu), Giulietta Simionato (Santuzza), Walter Cassel (Alfio), Rosalind Elias (Lola), Thelma Votipka (Lucia); Metropolitan Opera Chorus and Orchestra, cond. Nino Verchi
House of Opera CD7263

"Siciliana"

March 3, 1934: Stockholm
Unspecified orchestra, cond. Nils Grevillius
Naxos 8.110722

April 8, 1937: Stockholm, Concert Hall
Swedish Radio Orchestra, cond. Nils Grevillius
Bluebell ABCD 103

September 15, 1948: Stockholm, Concert Hall
Royal Court Orchestra, cond. Nils Grevillius
Naxos 8.110701

"Bada, Santuzza"

November 28, 1937: New York, Carnegie Hall
Jussi Björling (Turiddu), Maria Jeritza (Santuzza); General Motors Symphony Orchestra, cond. Erno Rapee

"Addio alla madre"

March 27–30, 1944: Stockholm, Concert Hall
Unspecified orchestra, cond. Nils Grevillius
Naxos 8.110701

November 10, 1944: Stockholm, Concert Hall
Swedish Radio Symphony Orchestra, cond. Tor Mann
Bluebell ABCD 103

January 1, 1945: Stockholm, Concert Hall
Stockholm Radio Orchestra, cond. Tor Mann
Bluebell ABCD 092

January 13, 1946: Detroit, Masonic Temple Auditorium
Ford Symphony Orchestra, cond. Eugene Ormandy

April 4, 1949: New York, Rockefeller Center
Bell Telephone Orchestra, cond. Donald Voorhees
WHRA-6036

September 19, 1950: Stockholm, Royal Academy of Music
Swedish Radio Orchestra, cond. Nils Grevillius
Naxos 8.110788

October 1, 1950: Berlin, Titania Palast
RIAS Orchestra, cond. Kurt Gaebel
Urania URN 22.165

July 5, 1951: Stockholm, Gröna Lund
Harry Ebert, pf.
Bluebell 114

October 3, 1952: Stockholm, Concert Hall
Swedish Radio Orchestra, cond. Sten Frykberg
Naxos 8.111083-85

January 18, 1955: Helsinki, B-Messuhalli
Harry Ebert, pf.

September 24, 1955: New York, Carnegie Hall
Frederick Schauwecker, pf.
RCA 88697748922

August 5, 1957: Stockholm, Gröna Lund
pianist Bertil Boksted
Bluebell ABCD 114

October 5, 1957: Stockholm, Concert Hall
Stockholm Philharmonic Orchestra, cond. Stig Westerberg
Bluebell ABCD 066

July 18, 1958: Stockholm, Concert Hall
Stockholm Philharmonic Orchestra, cond. Georg Ludwig Jochum
Bluebell ABCD 036

January 4, 1959: London, Palladium
Ivor Newton, pf.

"Because so much was demanded of him, in this *Cavalleria* he was as great a tenor actor as any I have sung with."[1] "This *Cavalleria*," as recalled by Regina Resnik (Santuzza) was a New Year's Eve performance at the Metropolitan Opera House in 1947. The demands made on Björling, who was performing the role for the first time in the original language, were partly those of an uncompromising singing actress, who expected constant give and take on stage. Yet they were also those of the music itself, so direct in its emotional punch that the tenor had no difficulty in abandoning his reserve in the heat of live performance. Turiddu was the role in which Björling's acting was most consistently praised in every phase of his career. As in other *verismo* works, the music had an emancipating effect on the singer: his vocal acting in the two surviving live recordings of the opera makes it easy to imagine the electricity he generated on stage.

In Verga's original novella (1880) we observe Turiddu Macca's philandering with a certain detachment. In the stage play, written four years later, we receive more detailed evidence of his impulsiveness, but feel closer to his mother and to Santa. In Mascagni's opera the dominant point of view is still that of Santuzza, but Turiddu, however irresponsible, behaves with such exuberant spontaneity that he cannot help winning us over (if the voice is an attractive one). In the end he demonstrates such frank awareness of the calamity he has brought upon himself and others as to emerge finally as a tragic figure. The role has a higher tessitura than that of Canio in *Pagliacci* and the character is much younger (the equivalent of Silvio in the traditional companion work). The fact that Björling sang both roles in the same evening on ten occasions is a tribute to his physical resistance, versatility and command of vocal coloring.

The sounds required for Turiddu are brilliant and open, right from the insolent and premonitary aubade sung before the curtain rises. The transgressive freshness of this F minor *Andantino* owes much to its rhythmic insouciance and teasing tessitura, which seems to challenge the tenor to abandon technical orthodoxy and open the vowels on the *passaggio*, so as to highlight the characteristic coloration of the Sicilian dialect (the first Turiddu, Roberto Stagno, was a native of Palermo).

The "Siciliana" was the first excerpt from *Cavalleria rusticana* that Björling recorded (in Swedish translation, as "O Lola bort till dig"), a year before he made his debut in the role. In this 1934 recording his "covering" of the notes at the top of the staff is barely noticeable, but enables him nonetheless to ascend to the A-flats without strain. The casual ease with which he achieves this is highlighted by comparison with another scrupulously musical tenor, Julius Patzak, who makes heavy weather of these passages in his German-language version.[2] As in many of Björling's early recordings, there is an ingenuous simplicity to the phrasing that charms the listener. The underlying sadness in his liquid silver timbre proves well-suited to the fatalism of a young Sicilian who, without knowing it, has reached the last day of his life.

If we move forward to the 1937 broadcast (also in Swedish), we realize what Björling meant in his autobiography when he described that year as a turning point in his career. This time he phrases the music with conscious artistry, swelling and fining away the voice to haunting effect. The repeated A-flats are both reinforced and sung legato, a real feat. The *perdendosi* in the final measures is achieved not by distancing himself from the microphone (as happened in 1934) but by technical control of the voice: few tenors of similar vocal weight—Patzak and Alfred Piccaver[3] are among the exceptions—contrive such a chiselled diminuendo here. All in all this is a unique performance, conveying an extemporary freedom of expression that the tenor never entirely recaptured in his original-language recrodings. Serenades were traditionally delivered with an extra degree of *sprezzatura* in the nineteenth century; the added embellishments we hear in the recordings made by Fernando De Lucia,[4] Enrico Caruso,[5] Edoardo Garbin,[6] Fernando Valero,[7] and Tito Schipa[8] were probably introduced by Stagno himself. Björling adopts a more literal approach and even omits a couple of the written mordents in his two earliest recordings, but the ones he does include are beautifully executed in the live broadcast.

The duet ("Bada, Santuzza") broadcast later that year with the fifty-year-old Maria Jeritza, a legendary singer of an earlier generation, proves more exciting on paper than in sound: Björling's voice is often distorted and the use of two languages, Swedish and Italian, compromises the immediacy of the interaction, although there is no doubting his emotional engagement. We don't get to hear Santuzza's curse, but can appreciate the beauty and freedom of the Czech soprano's middle register. Björling never had any other opportunity to sing with her.

We next hear the tenor in a studio recording of Turiddu's farewell to his mother. This is the noblest scene in the opera, for the character displays a rare generosity of spirit when about to risk his life in a duel with Alfio. Whereas in the rest of the opera the potency of the music lies in its explicitness of expression, here the phrasing draws strength from what is left verbally unexpressed: Turiddu's fear of losing his life. Björling's pronunciation is fallible in what was probably his first attempt at the scene in the original Italian, but the voice conveys all the character's vulnerability. The gentle solemnity of tone adopted when asking for his mother's blessing is infinitely touching, while the impassioned melody of the *Andante con moto* (with its modulation from A-flat minor to A-flat major) is both searingly brilliant and filled with fear. The closing phrases are all the more moving for their absence of sobbing, for here the music says all.

When Björling was broadcast singing this same scene some eight months later he did allow himself a hint of a sob (which he maintained in later performances) in attacking the final "mamma," but overall he reveals not only a firmer grasp of the text but also a deepening of emotional responses. The voice—allowed to expand completely in Tor Mann's spacious setting (the climactic B-flat is held for seven seconds)—acquires an extra resonance and beauty when caught live. If one excepts the opening *Allegro giusto,* Mann's tempos are consistently slower than the metronome markings in the score; however, in this they conform with Mascagni's own two recordings of the opera, made in 1938 and 1940.[9] Björling himself shows no sign here of having learnt from Beniamino Gigli's performance in the composer's 1940 studio recording, but he has clearly listened to Caruso's 1913 Victor disc[10] of the "Addio alla madre." He makes much less than Caruso of the *poco calando* repeat of "un altro bacio," but echoes him in his overall nobility of conception and use of portamento. Both include a rising slide (from E-flat to A-flat) on "Santa" which is not indicated in the score but had long been traditional, and is authorized by Mascagni in the 1938 live recording with Antonio Melandri. It would however be wrong to consider Björling simply as an imitator of Caruso: he exposes himself emotionally in a manner that is entirely his own, and which makes its effect even when the tempos are much brisker than Mann's, as is the case in the 1946 broadcast under Eugene Ormandy.

Two years later the tenor rerecorded the "Siciliana," not in the original (Sicilian) dialect but in the rather insipid Italian translation ("O Lola, bianca come fior di spino") which can also be heard in Piccaver's disc. Unlike the English tenor, he sings the words beautifully and for the first time we hear all the written mordents, but the phrasing is not as deliciously inflected as in 1937, nor is the upper register as brilliant.

Björling was recorded five times in the "Addio alla madre" over the next five years. The studio version and the Gröna Lund recital don't show him at his best, but the other performances are outstanding. The 1952 Stockholm radio broadcast in particular reveals an extra energy of attack on the top A-flats of "S'io non tornassi" and "ch'io le aveva giurato," together with a new maturity of tone. His is by now a truly adult Turiddu, and the music acquires greater tragic depth.

The power in reserve which Björling nearly always has on tap in the upper register is one of the qualities distinguishing his Turiddu from the almost equally persuasive interpretation by Giuseppe di Stefano, whose open production in the upper register made it difficult for him to modulate the sound. Both tenors recorded the opera complete in 1953 and although it is Di Stefano's Serafin set[11] that better withstands the test of time (thanks largely to the compelling presence of Maria Callas) Björling more than holds his own against the young Sicilian tenor, demonstrating in the "Siciliana" how to give the impression of open vowels without compromising the fullness of the upper register. Although he does not bring home the meaning of every word as Di Stefano does, his delivery of the Sicilian text is no less convincing than his pronunciation of the Italian words in 1948: what counts here is above all the clarity of the vowels, and from this point of view Björling was hard to beat.

The duet with Santuzza—interrupted briefly by Lola's appearance—is theatrically masterful (far surpassing the equivalent scene in Verga's play), but it still requires vocal acting of considerable psychological intelligence if it is to make its full impact. Björling and Zinka Milanov had plenty of experience in their respective roles (the tenor had already sung Turiddu twenty-four times) and they have no difficulty, under the competent if unimaginative leadership of Renato Cellini, in maintaining the necessary continuity of line throughout the scene. They also sing their parts wholeheartedly, trusting in the expressive power of the music. Turiddu is constantly on the defensive in this scene and Björling conveys very well the character's attempt to bluff his way out of a tight corner by taking umbrage at Santuzza's entirely justified accusations. He captures the arrogance and emotional ambiguity of the young man, but such is the virile beauty of his tone in the self-defensive displays of temperament that we can understand why women find him so attractive. Only his gruff denial that he loves Lola ("No!") sounds awkward here. He matches Milanov in volume at all times and his tone integrates well with hers when the voices join, but nothing suggests he found her an emotionally stimulating partner in this opera (which they had yet to perform together on stage): her phrasing captures little of Santuzza's vulnerability, and the expansive "No, no Turiddu" is conceived as a vocal showcase rather than as an opportunity for impassioned utterance.

The "Brindisi" reveals Turiddu at his most ebullient. The tension generated is naturally augmented by the audience's knowledge of Santuzza's betrayal, which makes the high spirits seem tragically untimely. When Björling performs this song it is hard to forget the double-edged influence of alcohol—both disinhibiting and enslaving—on his own life. No doubt he too was conscious of this, for there is an electric tension to his singing that makes his performances of this music unique in the history of recording. This distinctiveness derives not simply from his ingratiating timbre, his vivid rhythmic sense, and an ability to invest the cadential phrases with an extra ring that far surpasses the efforts of similarly-endowed tenors such as Di Stefano and José Carreras,[12] but from the way he combines all these qualities to make us share the thrill of living dangerously. Gigli sounds almost staid by comparison, although Mascagni's slower tempo reminds us that the "Brindisi" is marked *Larghetto.* The first recordings, by Caruso,[13] Fernando Valero,[14] and Edoardo Garbin,[15] adopt a similar tempo and demonstrate how freely this music was sung in the early years, with an abundance of rubato and embellishments (Caruso even added a head voice top C at the end of the solo). Björling's singing is relatively literal by comparison, but he makes the most of the indicated rallentandos—often regulated by portamentos—and inserts an acciaccatura on the final "Viva." He also interpolates a top A at the end of the solo (a traditional liberty, taken also by Melandri with the composer's permission in 1938) and an extra B on the final "Beviam!"

The dialogue with Alfio that follows marks a turning point in the drama, for Turiddu is forced finally to be honest with himself and others. The *Largo,* "Lo so che il torto è mio," confirms Björling's ability to express both disarming candor (in admitting his guilt) and deep sorrow (for Santuzza). Only Gigli achieves a similar freshness of expression here, but with a degree of self-pity that lessens the tragic stature of the character. Björling, on the other hand, manages to sound both childlike in the opening "Compar Alfio" and capable of murder in the fiercely conclusive "Vi saprò in core il ferro mio piantar!"

The farewell to Mamma Lucia is as moving as ever. Once again, Björling's Turiddu appears more psychologically complex than Caruso's and less mother-fixated than Gigli's, and reconciles a deep need to be comforted with the desire to protect the women for whom he feels responsible. The purity of the tenor's vowels brings disarming credibility to every word, and the beautifully sculpted line—even in the convulsive final *Allegro*—lends the character a rare dignity.

As mentioned in chapter 12, the 1954 live recording from Stockholm is a bilingual performance (with Björling singing in Italian) coupled with the Swedish-language *Pagliacci.* For the first time we hear the "Siciliana" sung at a proper distance, and for this reason Björling is careful to project it forthrightly, with less dynamic nuance than before but with impressive resonance on the top A-flats.

As in the 1937 broadcast, the constant switching between languages impedes the flow of the duet, where Aase Nordmo-Løvberg, a sincere but uninteresting Santuzza, seldom cultivates a true legato and is not always well-coordinated with her tenor partner, who sings with great declamatory force but fluffs some of the lines.

The prize of this recording is the "Brindisi," a rendition Björling never surpassed (in spite of a mispronunciation of the *g* in "giubilo"). The approach is similar to that of the Cellini recording, but with the extra *chutzpah* one would expect from a live performance. Every rhythmic nuance is relished and the voice seems electrically charged in both the middle and upper registers. Although the tempo is once again much faster than Mascagni's, the constant play of rubato lends the music an improvisatory daring that transcends time.

In the encounter with Alfio, "A piacer vostro" creates an illusion of *parlato* without abandoning the prescribed pitches. The tone production is even more concentrated this time and one notes how much intensity is invested in the single top A of "Povera Santa." In the "Addio alla madre" we hear, for the first time, a tearful inflection on the first "Mamma." During the rest of the scene we can sense the tenor living the part with all his being, forging the phrases with greater incisiveness than ever before, and proving more generous with portamento than in the complete studio recording. His nearest rival in this scene is Di Stefano, who equals Björling in the dialogue with Alfio thanks to the exceptional eloquence of his diction, but whose shallower tones in the farewell that follows deprive the episode of some of its ritual inexorability.

The finest of the thee recital performances of the "Addio alla madre" recorded over the next three years is the Gröna Lund reading, with Bertil Bokstedt offering strong support. Björling's voice is in peak condition, his dramatic instincts as unerring as in the versions with orchestral accompaniment. A month after that recital he made a second studio recording of the opera in Florence, a stereo version that confirms the tenor's unrivalled status in the part at that time and presents the voice in a more flattering ambience than the over-dry sound-stage offered by RCA. The opening "Siciliana"—sung at an appropriate distance—unfolds in rounded tones, making this his finest performance of the original text. For this recording Decca engaged what were arguably the world's three most beautiful voices in the Italian repertoire: Ettore Bastianini surpasses Merrill's achievement as Alfio and Renata Tebaldi proves a more sympathetic Santuzza than Milanov, although she too seems more focused on sound than substance in her duet with Turiddu. This however is Björling's best version of the scene so far (Lucia Danieli is an excellent Lola), and he proves ideally nonchalant in the departing "Dell'ira tua non mi curo!" The "Brindisi" is once again replete with energy, if lacking the extra frisson of the Stockholm broadcast. Björling's Italian is at its most idiomatic throughout the recording, and after a strikingly candid exchange with Alfio he brings plangent lyricism to the *Andante moderato* during Turiddu's farewell ("Ma prima voglio che mi benedici"), with every word stressed for telling impact. If one compares this performance with the very fine recording—in a more resonant acoustic—featuring the young Placido Domingo,[16] one notices how the Spanish tenor's more restricted coloristic range and the less forward focus of his high notes limit his ability to convey the emotional acuity of the situation.

This scene worked magnificently for Björling right to the end of his career. The 1958 Stockholm concert performance is as deeply felt as any, while in the 1959 London recital the richly sensual coloring of the voice lends a new dimension to Turiddu's readiness for death.

Ten months later Björling made his triumphant return to the Met—a standing ovation greets his first appearance on stage—in Mascagni's opera. With his health already precarious, he transposes the "Siciliana" down to E minor for the first time, a transposition adopted with the composer's permission by some of the earliest interpreters of the role, including De Lucia and Valero. The Swede's voice is handsomely poised on the breath, but flows less liltingly than in earlier recordings. The duet with Santuzza, on the other hand, is his finest ever, although—surprised perhaps by the ovation (or by the prompter's repetition)—he repeats the phrase "A Francofonte" near the beginning. Giulietta Simionato's voice has a baleful, coruscating intensity throughout, temperamentally matching her Turiddu in every phrase. There is strong support also from Rosalind Elias's Lola, and the ensemble is capably directed from the pit by Nino Verchi. What emerges is one of the most lacerating versions of this duet ever captured in sound, with the tension increasing implacably right up to the final curse (after which the audience erupts), without any musical compromises.

None of what follows is quite on this level, but there is never any slackening of narrative tension. The "Brindisi" is slightly less electric than before, with no interpolated A at the end of the solo, while in the "Addio alla madre" Björling is unusually explicit in his emotionalism. In a less heated context the tearfulness of "fate da madre a Santa" might sound sentimental, but the tenor only made use of such extra-musical devices when he had sufficient psychological experience to fully feel their expressive truthfulness. And understanding the need to be truthful to himself and others is the very lesson that Turiddu has to learn (the hard way) on the last day of his life.

MASSENET

"Élégie"

September 28, 1945: Stockholm, Concert Hall
Swedish Radio Symphony Orchestra, cond. Tor Mann
Bluebell ABCD 036

Massenet first forged this F minor melody when still a student at the Paris Conservatoire and only adapted it to Louis Gallet's poem some ten years later (in 1869). The melody itself speaks to us with such eloquent inflections that the nostalgic words of the abandoned lover can seem almost superfluous—although this is hardly the case when they are sung by Georges Thill, whose 1932 recording[1] brings those words nobly alive within phrases of rare rhythmic freedom. Even more audacious in this respect is Feodor Chaliapin, whose Russian-language disc in D minor[2] was made a year earlier. No other interpreter of this song translates the composer's indication in the opening measures (*très expressif et avec accablement*) so imaginatively into sound, or renders with such specificity of feeling the *avec douleur* marking in "Comme en mon cœur tout est somber et glacé." Chaliapin's dynamic range is greater than any other on disc, and his phrasing surpasses that of the accompanying cello in its silky legato.

This song is a true test-piece and the finest recordings (at least by male voices) tend to be those by the greatest singers of any era. In the 1910s no one surpassed Enrico Caruso's version in French with Mischa Elman on the violin,[3] and it was this disc that served as a model for Björling. His Swedish-language recording ("O min ungdoms saliga vår") was made in G minor (the same key adopted by Richard Tauber[4] and Alfredo Kraus[5]), using the arrangement with piano and violin accompaniment. This version opens with a long violin introduction, and although Björling's sound production was often more reminiscent of a wind instrument, on his entrance here the tenor traces the melody with a sweetness of tone, exactness of intonation and continuity of line that challenge the anonymous violinist. In addition, we hear a wide range of dynamics (almost as impressive as Chaliapin's), a constant play of portamentos (as classically poised as Caruso's), and a meltingly nostalgic coloring of the words (the voice retains its *morbidezza* even at *fortissimo*) that is unique to Björling. Although he proves less audacious in his rubato than Thill, he does not make the mistake of banalizing the song (Massenet's tempo indication is *très lent*) by singing it too fast, as Kraus does. He has closer competition from Tauber, who—like Chaliapin and Björling himself—sings the final "toujours" (an F at the top of the staff) in a desolate *pianissimo.*

Manon
"Le rêve"

August 10, 1938: Stockholm, Concert Hall
Unspecified orchestra, cond. Nils Grevillius
EMI 5 75900 2

June 8, 1939: Hilversum, AVRO Studio
AVRO Hilversum Orchestra, cond. Frieder Weissmann
Bluebell ABCD 006

November 19, 1945: New York, Rockefeller Center
Firestone Orchestra, cond. Howard Barlow
WHRA-6036

January 8, 1951: New York, Rockefeller Center
Bell Telephone Orchestra, cond. Donald Voorhees
WHRA-6036

September 24, 1955: New York, Carnegie Hall
Frederick Schauwecker, pf.
RCA 88697748922

Massenet's Des Grieux would have been an ideal role for Björling in the first decade of his adult career, but as *Manon* was absent from the repertoire of the Royal Swedish Opera in the 1930s we must make do with his recordings of the two arias (he also sang "Pourquoi me réveiller" from *Werther* in recital, but never committed it to disc). "Make do" is hardly the right term, however, for the 1938 version of "Le rêve" is one of Björling's most evocative, showing the interpreter at the peak of his powers. It also represents what was then a rare synthesis of the mellifluous, but stylistically overheated, Italian performing tradition (well represented by Beniamino Gigli and Miguel Fleta)[6] and the more restrained and verbally pointed French school, whose nasal emphasis perhaps limits its appeal to a broader audience (recordings by Edmond Clément[7] and David Devriès[8] are typical of this tradition at its best). Björling was the first tenor to record the aria combining plausible French with a honeyed yet limpid tone. His example would be followed in later decades by Nicolai Gedda,[9] Cesare Valletti[10] and Roberto Alagna,[11] all of whom sang the role on stage and projected the text more tellingly than Björling. The abiding fascination of his version derives—as is the case with Gigli and Julius Patzak,[12] both of whom sing the aria in translation—not from the specific psychological inflections of the phrasing but from the genuinely dreamlike atmosphere that the voice conjures right from the introductory recitative (which is omitted only in the Hilversum broadcast). The singer draws us into Des Grieux's world of romantic (or bourgeois) fantasy, weakening our desire to ponder the irony of the situation (at this point in the opera Manon has already decided to abandon her lover). The means he employs to achieve this are those of a classical *bel canto* technique, based on a seamless legato and *messa di voce*. In truth, Björling does not execute the full crescendo and fading away indicated by Massenet on the top A of "faut" (a feat demonstrated by Leon Campagnola),[13] but his drawn-out diminuendo (where he passes from a *voix mixte* to a pure head tone) is hardly less impressive, and a genuine *messa di voce* can be perceived on the E of "ô Manon" in the final measures.

From 1945 onward the tenor simplifies the A-natural climax by attacking it in a straightforward (but well-integrated) head voice, but otherwise there is little change in his phrasing across the eighteen-year span of his recordings. The 1955 performance does, however, convey an extra degree of intimacy, making it one of the highlights of this otherwise rather disappointing Carnegie Hall recital.

"Ah! fuyez, douce image"

September 6, 1945: Stockholm, Concert Hall
Unspecified orchestra, cond. Nils Grevillius
EMI 5 75900 2

September 28, 1945: Stockholm, Concert Hall
Swedish Radio Symphony Orchestra, cond. Tor Mann
Bluebell ABCD 036

January 13, 1946: Detroit, Masonic Temple Auditorium
Ford Symphony Orchestra, cond. Eugene Ormandy

March 15, 1948: New York, Rockefeller Center
Bell Telephone Orchestra, cond. Donald Voorhees
WHRA-6036

October 23, 1949: San Francisco, War Memorial Opera House
San Francisco Opera Orchestra, cond. Gaetano Merola
Urania 22.120

Like "Le rêve," this aria reveals Des Grieux's capacity for self-illusion, but in vocal terms it requires a wider spectrum of dynamics and an ability to sustain full-throated top B-flats with ease. Björling possessed both the necessary range and power in reserve, and his five recordings of this music (including the recitative) are clearly influenced by Caruso's 1911 disc[14] (also in the original French), which has never been surpassed in terms of sonic magnificence and is almost equally remarkable for its seamless legato and intensity of expression. In spite of his overwhelmingly rich baritonal sound, the Neapolitan tenor attacks the *sostenuto cantabile* softly (Massenet's marking is ***pp***), building up slowly to a *fortissimo* climax in both verses. In his studio recording, Björling's range of dynamics is less spectacularly ample (he attacks the aria *mezzo forte*), but he too guarantees a binding legato (important in a scene which can easily lose cohesion), a broad spectrum of colors and an upper register that functions as a genuine emotional release, without the unsteadiness that weakens Roberto Alagna's otherwise fine recording,[15] or the strain that afflicts many light-voiced tenors here. Most striking of all is a singular humanity of accent that encourages us to share Des Grieux's desire to free himself from Manon's influence, rather than observing his predicament from a distance. There is something touchingly guileless in the way Björling lays bare the soul of the character: we sense a total sincerity, for example, in the G major prayer that divides the two verses of the aria, while the harmonic instability of "Entre le monde et moi" betrays through his voice the character's underlying insecurity. Björling proves here that a limpid articulation of the text (free from nasal emphasis) on a well-supported flow of breath is all that is needed to bring us intimately into contact with the character. The psychological acuity of his singing is even more evident in the broadcast later that month, where Tor Mann's more leisurely tempo results in a slight loss of forward momentum but gives the tenor the chance to explore the character thoroughly from within (starting with a softer attack on "Ah! fuyez"). Much of this insight is maintained in the concert with Eugene Ormandy four months later—where the voice sounds singularly boyish—while subsequent performances, though still elegant and impassioned, are overloud and less sensitive to nuance.

MEYERBEER

L'Africaine
"Ô paradis" ("O paradiso")

September 4, 1937: Stockholm, Concert Hall
Unspecified orchestra, cond. Nils Grevillius
Naxos 8.110701

December 5, 1937: New York, Carnegie Hall
General Motors Symphony Orchestra, cond. Erno Rapee
WHRA-6036

June 8, 1939: Hilversum, AVRO Studio
AVRO Hilversum Orchestra, cond. Frieder Weissmann
Bluebell ABCD 006

July 6, 1950: Stockholm, Gröna Lund
Harry Ebert, pf.
Bluebell ABCD 114

October 23, 1950: New York, Rockefeller Center
Bell Telephone Orchestra, cond. Donald Voorhees
WHRA-6036

March 9, 1951: New York, Manhattan Center
RCA Victor Orchestra, cond. Renato Cellini
RCA 88697748922

May 25, 1952: Stockholm, Skansen
Harry Ebert, pf.
Bluebell ABCD 1001

On several occasions Björling recorded arias from operas he was yet to perform on stage, but only once did he sing an aria in Italian on disc before interpreting the whole role in Swedish. That role was Vasco de Gama in Meyerbeer's *L'Africaine*, the last opera in which he debuted at the Royal Opera in Stockholm (October 1938). Both the Italian and Swedish texts were translations from the original French, but for much of the twentieth century tenors generally preferred to record the G-flat major *Andantino* (in which the explorer marvels at the beauty of his exotic surroundings) in Marco Marcelliano Marcello's Italian version, which involves a number of modifications to the melodic line. The Swede's first recording immediately stands out as one of the best ever made, for the unalloyed lyricism of his sound mirrors the uncontaminated luxuriance of the setting. He establishes an effective contrast between the contemplative spaciousness of the first twenty-six measures, where the high strings and woodwinds dominate in the accompaniment, and the brassier colonial possessiveness of the section beginning "Nostro è questo terreno fecondo." At the same time he shapes the music with unerring legato, thus preventing this through-composed *grand air* from emerging as a patchwork of recitative and arioso. Equally, he distinguishes between the two top B-flats, expanding from *mezzo piano* to *forte* on the first ("Tu m'appartieni") and delivering the second in a ringing *fortissimo*, after which he returns to the tonic, prolongs and repeats the A-flat and embellishes the final G-flat.

Björling was here working within a well-established performing tradition: the crescendo on the first B-flat and the embellished conclusion to the aria can both be heard in Enrico Caruso's 1907 recording,[1] made at the time of his Met debut in the role. Although the coloring of the Neapolitan's voice is already decidedly dark, this is one of his recordings that reveals the best balance between head and chest voices: the ethereal attack on the opening G-flat of "O paradiso" is as exemplary as the full-throated conclusion. That opening however is slightly spoilt by a conspicuous aspirate ("pa-ha-radiso"), echoed by Beniamino Gigli in his 1928 recording.[2] In many ways the latter is unrivalled as a sensuous embrace of the tropical setting (his blend of head and chest resonance is even more seductive than Caruso's), yet he is capable also of a trumpety flourish in "Nostro è questo terreno fecondo." Both Gigli and Caruso reveal a perfect command of the text, while Björling smudges some details and muddles (as in "Celeste Aida"; see chapter 23) the elements of earth and fire ("suol" and "sol"). The Swede follows Gigli's example in elaborating the embellishment of the sustained top G-flat of "m'appartieni"; he may also have drawn inspiration from the German-language recording made in 1926 by an exact contemporary of Gigli's, Lauritz Melchior, a performance quite unique in its combination of epic breadth and tonal density.[3]

Björling himself constructed the music on a larger scale in his later recordings, making the aria longer and louder but also less evocative in its musical balance (and without correcting all the verbal errors), whereas the Carnegie Hall and Hilversum recordings maintain a luminosity of tone that is close to ideal and that has been rivalled (but not equalled) in more recent decades by Carlo Bergonzi[4] (who aspirates like Caruso and Gigli) and Gianni Raimondi[5] (who doesn't).

In most of Björling's performances, particularly the rather hurried *Bell Telephone Hour* version, the transitional passage "Spettacolo divin! / In te rapito io son!" (marked *doux* in the score) is lacking in flavor because he dispatches it too rapidly. A more leisurely and persuasive solution is to be found in Fernando De Lucia's transposed version, recorded in 1917[6] at the end of a stage career that never included Meyerbeer's work. The Neapolitan had nevertheless sung "O paradiso" in concert as early as 1885, just twenty years after the work's world premiere, and his favoring of softer dynamics (which dominate in the score) and a more majestic pace bring to mind the phrasing of another golden-age tenor, Jean de Reszke, who was captured live in two excerpts from this solo, sung in French, at the Met in 1901.[7] The sound quality is abysmal, but the recording nevertheless reveals a more leisurely unfolding of the aria, with abundant use of the head voice, which is quite distinct from the Italian performing tradition. A similar approach informs Lucien Muratore's recording,[8] while the most celebrated Vasco de Gama in recent decades, Placido Domingo, favors acquisitive imperialism over pure contemplation, confining his head voice to the aria's opening.[9]

MOZART

Don Giovanni
"Il mio tesoro"

September 24, 1955: New York, Carnegie Hall
Frederick Schauwecker, pf.
RCA 88697748922

"Of all the styles of opera singing I think Mozart's suits me best" Björling wrote in his autobiography, recalling that "Dalla sua pace" from *Don Giovanni* was the first aria he was allowed to study formally at the Royal Music Academy, after spending the first semester working on his vowels ("I had to learn to articulate with my mouth and not my throat") and on vocalizes by Concone and Panofka ("You had to know these by heart—if you didn't, you were in trouble").[1] His fondness for the aria was reinforced by the fact that Don Ottavio was the first full-scale role he sang on stage (in August 1930, alongside John Forsell as protagonist); it is surprising that he never recorded it.

Although "Il mio tesoro" seems not to have featured in the Stockholm performances (which presumably stuck to the "Viennese" version of the score) we do have a recital recording of this aria, the most challengingly florid in his concert repertoire.[2] While the tenor was not in his best voice for the Carnegie Hall recital (a few notes around the top of the staff slip slightly back into the throat), his rendition is quite unlike any other on record. This unique quality is perhaps best explained by a point made by Björling in an article for the *Etude*: "The vocal passage from the lowest to the highest tones must be accomplished as evenly as on a piano."[3] After Frederick Schauwecker's graceful piano introduction, the tenor's voice seems indeed to assimilate the instrument's pearly articulation, maintaining the rounded beauty of individual notes (without sacrificing legato) even in the fastest passagework. The voice also displays an all-comprehending humanity of tone that lends appropriate dignity to Don Ottavio as a genuine antagonist of Don Giovanni, closer in spirit to the tenor heroes of Mozart's *opere serie* than to Ferrando in *Così fan tutte*.

Figure 9. Björling's debut role in 1930: Don Ottavio in a Stockholm *Don Giovanni*. Courtesy of the Royal Swedish Opera Archive.

Nevertheless, this concert performance does not fully explore the dramatic potential of the aria. Tito Schipa, in a 1934 Met performance under Tullio Serafin,[4] makes much more of the expressive contrasts between the two verses (both of which are repeated), in particular the G minor section beginning "Ditele che i suoi torti." Yet in that performance, as Paul Jackson pointed out, "the famous test phrase [the long melisma on "tornar," leading back to the B-flat major reprise] is badly mangled."[5] Björling's execution of this passage, if one excepts a momentary loss of rhythmic aplomb in the first two measures of sixteenth notes, is shaped with a musicality that has few rivals on disc, even though he snatches a couple of breaths on the way. Other tenors, such as John McCormack,[6] Peter Anders,[7] and Cesare Valletti,[8] have sung it in one breath; the Irish tenor's 1916 recording is still unsurpassed for regularity and smoothness, while Anders (who sings in German), like Placido Domingo in more recent years,[9] brings a denser dramatic coloring to the *Andante* that proves equally intriguing. Only Valletti's performance, however, caresses the ear as consistently as Björling's; in spite of the Swede's unstylish omission of a couple of appoggiaturas, hearing him sing this music is as gratifying an experience as listening to Edwin Fischer perform a Mozart piano concerto.

Die Zauberflöte
"Dies Bildnis ist bezaubernd schön" ("Ack, detta är en ängels bild")

June 26, 1958: Stockholm, Gröna Lund
Bertil Bokstedt, pf.
Bluebell ABCD 114

June 16, 1959: Stockholm, Gröna Lund
Harry Ebert, pf.
Bluebell ABCD 114

Between 1930 and 1937 Björling sang nineteen performances of the three Mozart operas in his repertoire (*Die Entführung aus dem Serail, Don Giovanni* and *Die Zauberflöte*), plus two performances of the Requiem. His credentials as a Mozart singer were thus entirely respectable, even though he performed all the operas in translation. Swedish is again the language of these open-air performances of Tamino's E-flat major aria ("Ack, detta är en ängels bild"), recorded over twenty years after his last appearances in the role. The two performances are very similar in phrasing, but the voice is more ringing and beautiful in 1958 (in spite of the fact that the tenor repeatedly clears his throat[10] before attacking the aria).

In this first performance it is the aristocratic poise and virile tone of Mozart's prince that strike the listener. The tempo has the unhurried pace of a true *Larghetto* and the sculpted melody has a three-dimensional fullness and nobility of coloring that induce awe rather than identification: the temporal and spiritual status of the young man in love is as important, we feel, as the emotional impulses to which he is giving voice. While that voice has less "face" to it than Fritz Wunderlich's,[11] it is much steadier and more focused throughout the range, with extra resonance brought impressively into play in the final measures (where Björling reinforces the volume on nearly all the prolonged notes). Listening to this performance we are reminded how much Mozart disliked a prominent vibrato in singers, and how instinctively the tenor adapted his emission to the needs of specific composers.

The overall character of Björling's performances is reminiscent of the 1911 recording by the Dutch tenor Jacques Urlus[12] (who made a name for himself in heroic roles) rather than the more strongly inflected (but relatively plebeian) versions by Richard Tauber[13] and Helge Rosvænge.[14] Although the Swede employs fewer dynamic contrasts than most, he introduces a number of echo effects that suit the sonata-like structure of the aria to perfection.

PUCCINI

When Björling was born on February 5, 1911, Puccini was resting at his lakeside retreat in Torre del Lago in Tuscany. Five days earlier the composer had written to Arturo Toscanini recalling their collaboration in New York the previous December, when *La fanciulla del West* had been given its world premiere at the Metropolitan with Enrico Caruso as Ramerrez. Björling would have the honor of "creating" this role in Swedish twenty-three years later.

When Puccini died on November 29, 1924, Björling was already an experienced performer, who had been singing in public for nine years. On that day he gave a recital with his brothers Olle and Gösta and their father David in a church in Skutskar, on the Baltic coast near Gävle. It is not known whether he had sung any of Puccini's music at that age, but he was probably familiar with a number of arias—from *La bohème*, *Tosca*, and *La fanciulla del West*—that were in his father's concert repertoire, and would soon start singing them himself as his voice moved down into the tenor range. By the time *Turandot* (the last opera he would record complete) was staged at La Scala on April 25, 1926, Björling was beginning to sound like a tenor. He performed that day in Skurup Church in the south of Sweden with Gösta and Olle.

In subsequent years Björling was to come into close contact with a number of musicians who had collaborated with Puccini, not only Toscanini—who had conducted the world premieres of *La bohème*, *La fanciulla del West*, and *Turandot*, as well as important productions of *Manon Lescaut* and *Tosca*—but also Tullio Serafin, Vittorio Gui, Victor de Sabata, and Ettore Panizza (all of whom are mentioned in the composer's correspondence). He also worked with the assistant conductor Luigi Ricci, who had collaborated with the composer and published a book entitled *Puccini interprete di se stesso* in 1954—the year in which Björling made his Rome recording of *Manon Lescaut*, for which Ricci was hired as assistant conductor.

If composer and tenor had been active before Edison invented the phonograph, historians may have been tempted to deduce from all this that the Swede was an authoritative exponent of an "authentic" Puccini tradition.

Within a twentieth century context, however, the extensive documentation of singers who were performing Puccini's operas while the composer was still alive makes us much more wary of the concept of authenticity, for the expressive formulas adopted by those early interpreters vary enormously. While there is clearly a difference between the first generation of Puccini singers (including Fernando De Lucia and Enrico Caruso, still strongly influenced by their nineteenth century schooling) and the generation that followed (including Beniamino Gigli and Aureliano Pertile, more overtly "realistic" in their expressive vocabulary) it is not easy, or perhaps even useful, to decide which of these singers are closer to the composer in spirit. Puccini spent most of his life (and wrote some of his best music) in the nineteenth century, and a number of his most popular operas are set in the past. Yet unlike Rossini, Bellini, and Donizetti, he rarely seems to have composed with specific singers in mind,[1] and while he never stated (as Verdi did) that he was writing for the singers of the future, he did point out, in a letter concerning the casting of *Turandot*, that "in past times, the right singers emerged with the operas themselves, and it will happen again."[2]

Turandot was Puccini's final work, left unfinished at his death and performed posthumously, and it marked the end of an era for Italian opera. Puccini was the last composer to exploit to the full the finely-honed legato technique traditionally associated with his native school of singing, and there is no doubt that a rich, easily modulated, middle register and a ringing top are prime requisites for his leading tenor roles. Perhaps only *Il tabarro*, the most grittily veristic of his scores, can be approached with equal success in a more expressionistic manner, neglecting beauty of tone for its own sake. Curiously Luigi was Björling's only major Puccini role that was never recorded (although EMI was planning a recording around the time of the tenor's death). He did, however, perform the opera four times between October and December 1934 (the same three-month period in which he made his debuts in *La bohème* and *La fanciulla del West*); after the first night Kurt Atterberg commented, "The auditorium is flooded with beautiful sound as soon as he opens his mouth in a Puccini work."[3]

In the first fifteen years of Björling's adult career, the most widely-admired tenor in this repertoire was Gigli, who performed five Puccini roles in all, and recorded *La bohème*, *Madama Butterfly*, and *Tosca* in the studio in 1938–39. Björling was familiar with Gigli's discs from an early age and first heard him on stage in Chicago in 1937, but his recordings reveal no significant traces of the Italian tenor, whose musical sensibility was much less refined than the Swede's in all matters except rhythm and basic tone production, of which he was a master. A more likely model was Björling's mentor Joseph Hislop, whom he almost certainly heard singing Des Grieux, Rodolfo, and Cavaradossi in Stockholm, and whose Puccini recordings reveal an admirable combination of musicality and technical ease. The deepest influence however was surely that of Caruso, who, like Hislop, sang Puccini with the seamless legato that was no longer considered indispensable by tenors such as Gigli and Pertile. Björling could not match the sensual richness of the Neapolitan's sound—and erotic desire motivates Puccini's leading tenors more than any other single impulse—but the musical sensitivity of his phrasing and coloring of words, and his ever-developing capacity for feeling cast a nobler light than usual on the student Des Grieux, the poet Rodolfo, and the painter Cavaradossi (all of whom acquire an extra dimension of humanity through suffering), and make it harder for us to despise even the caddish Pinkerton and the self-centered Calaf. Björling sang in almost precisely the same number of performances of Puccini's operas as Verdi's (221 Puccini appearances, 222 Verdi ones), but explored a greater range of Puccini's roles and a much more representative selection of his operas. His sole omissions were *Le villi, Edgar, La rondine* and *Gianni Schicchi,* and only the last of these was regularly staged in the three decades that separated Björling's stage debut from his untimely death.

Manon Lescaut
Complete Recordings

December 10, 1949: New York, Metropolitan Opera House
Jussi Björling (Des Grieux), Dorothy Kirsten (Manon), Giuseppe Valdengo (Lescaut), Salvatore Baccaloni (Geronte), Thomas Hayward (Edmondo), Jean Madeira (Un Musico); Metropolitan Opera Chorus and Orchestra, cond. Giuseppe Antonicelli
Myto 011 H056

July 11–17, 1954: Rome, Teatro dell'Opera
Jussi Björling (Des Grieux), Licia Albanese (Manon), Robert Merrill (Lescaut), Franco Calabrese (Geronte), Mario Carlin (Edmondo), Anna Maria Rota (Un Musico); Rome Opera Chorus and Orchestra, cond. Jonel Perlea
Naxos 8.111030-31

March 31, 1956: New York, Metropolitan Opera House
Jussi Björling (Des Grieux), Licia Albanese (Manon), Frank Guarrera (Lescaut), Fernando Corena (Geronte), Thomas Hayward (Edmondo), Rosalind Elias (Un Musico); Metropolitan Opera Chorus and Orchestra, cond. Dimitri Mitropoulos
WHRA-6020

November 1, 1959: Stockholm, The Royal Opera
Jussi Björling (Des Grieux), Hjördis Schymberg (Manon), Hugo Hasslo (Lescaut), Arne Tyrén (Geronte), Lars Billengren (Edmondo), Margareta Bergström (Un Musico); Royal Swedish Opera Chorus, Royal Court Orchestra, cond. Nils Grevillius

Opera Depot OD 10190-2; Caprice CAP 22051 (excerpts)

"Tra voi, belle, brune e bionde"

September 1957: Florence, Teatro Comunale
Orchestra of the Maggio Musicale, cond. Albert Erede
Decca 443 930-2

"Donna non vidi mai"

September 7, 1948: Stockholm, Concert Hall
Royal Court Orchestra, cond. Nils Grevillius
Bluebell ABCD 016 (take 1); EMI 5 75900 2 (take 2)

January 8, 1951: New York, Rockefeller Center
Bell Telephone Orchestra, cond. Donald Voorhees
WHRA-6036

October 5, 1957: Stockholm, Concert Hall
Stockholm Philharmonic Orchestra, cond. Stig Westerberg
Bluebell ABCD 066

July 18, 1958: Stockholm, Concert Hall
Stockholm Philharmonic Orchestra, cond. Georg Ludwig Jochum
Bluebell ABCD 036

August 5, 1960: Gothenburg, Concert Hall
Gothenburg Symphony Orchestra, cond. Nils Grevillius
Bluebell ABCD 092

Manon Lescaut, which premiered in Turin in 1893 with Giuseppe Cremonini as Des Grieux, was the first complete opera in which Björling appeared. On July 21, 1930, the tenor made his debut at the Royal Opera in Stockholm as the Lamponaio under the leadership of Nils Grevillius. He was only nineteen (and was there on a scholarship contract with a minimal stipend), but one can imagine the haunting effect of his rainbow-fresh instrument in the Lamplighter's G minor melody in the second act. Just four weeks later he would take on the challenging role of Don Ottavio in Mozart's *Don Giovanni* and from that point he never looked back, although company discipline required him to sing occasional *comprimario* parts until 1936. Puccini's score had been given its Swedish premiere in the production by Ragnar Hyltén-Cavallius in 1929, with Hislop in the leading role of Des Grieux; in the summer of 1930 that part was taken by the twenty-nine-year-old Einar Beyron.

Figure 10. Des Grieux in *Manon Lescaut*, New York, 1949. Photograph by Louis Melançon. Courtesy of the Metropolitan Opera Archive.

Björling himself did not sing the role in Stockholm until 1951, but eighteen months earlier, in the fall of 1949, he was involved in major revivals at the War Memorial Opera House in San Francisco and at the Metropolitan, the opera having been absent from the repertoires of both houses for a couple of decades. This was the first opera in which Björling made an American role-debut, and the productions were so successful that they contributed significantly to the work's popularity in the United States over the following decades. He sang Des Grieux just twenty-five times in all, but in vocal terms at least was unrivalled in the part during the final decade of his life: no other tenor of that era captured so movingly the youthful impetuousness and aching sadness of Prévost's *chevalier* as he binds his destiny to that of the caprice-driven woman he loves.

Thirteen months before his debut as Des Grieux Björling recorded the first act Romanza in B-flat major, "Donna non vidi mai." This is the only Puccini aria that conveys what it feels like to fall in love in the very moment it happens. The opening echoes a line from Ariosto's *Orlando Furioso* ("ch'altra non vidi mai simile a questa")[4] and the music develops from themes introduced during the preceding duet with Manon. It is an aria of considerable dynamic contrasts (the accompaniment begins *pianissimo* and ends *fortissimo*), which works well in a variety of interpretations, ranging from the extrovert delivery of Gigli[5] and Giuseppe di Stefano[6] to the introspective musings of Giuseppe Anselmi[7] and the *bel canto* grace (with added embellishments) of De Lucia[8] and Edoardo Garbin.[9] Björling generally seeks (like Caruso before him) a middle way, establishing a fine balance between reflective lyricism and rising passion. His phrasing in this first recording is impressive on its own terms, but less detailed in dynamics and inflection than that of Pertile in an early disc (1923).[10] The Italian tenor, whom the composer described in a letter as the "finest Des Grieux I could possibly desire,"[11] lingers over words (linked by effects of assonance and consonance that were typical of the madrigal tradition in Italian poetry) with keen imaginative identification, building up slowly to the climax, while Björling moves through the music more rapidly, creating a relatively generalized impression, although his less intrusive vibrato guarantees a clearer definition of line and the golden splendor of his timbre makes the listener warm to the character immediately. There is no lack of ardor in his delivery, although he makes a couple of pronunciation errors in the first take (originally unpublished) that are promptly corrected in the retake.

This second take is more detailed in expression: the acciaccatura on the E-flat of "cessar!" is better finished, the words are projected with greater freedom, and, as before, the performance is adorned with unobtrusive portamentos that enhance the impression that the whole aria is conceived in a single melodic arc. As in the first version, although the top As and B-flats are elegantly bound within the melody they have an exciting ring, particularly the climactic B-flat on "deh! non," sung *con slancio* as Puccini prescribes and approached by means of an impulsive portamento from the dominant a fourth below. Björling really drives home this climax, just as Caruso does in the 1913 recording[12] that the Swedish tenor had listened to carefully: he also imitates the repeat of the D in the penultimate measure ("*no-on* cessar!"), an elegant way of highlighting the mediant so as to confirm the definitiveness of this final return to the tonic. The decorative use of *suoni ribattuti* in cadences is believed to have been introduced by Giovanni Battista Rubini in the first half of the nineteenth century, and this was a feature of Caruso's style that Björling employed sparingly. Another Italian tenor, Giovanni Martinelli, who recorded the aria for Victor a year after Caruso and clearly took him as a model for his phrasing, eschewed this embellishment, perhaps considering it archaic.[13] Like most of his colleagues he simply prolongs the D without repeating it, a less graceful way of achieving the same end.

In spite of similarities in phrasing, Caruso's version of this *Andante Lento* lasts a full thirty seconds longer than Björling's. Although the latter's tempo is closer to Puccini's metronome marking (♩. = 63), comparative listening suggests that this music requires a little more space if the tenor is to savor the meaning of what he is saying. Hislop's fine Swedish-language recording with Grevillius[14] is also much more leisurely than Björling's, while Pertile's is even slower than Caruso's. Pertile made this disc just a few months after he had sung the role with Toscanini at La Scala, while Caruso had performed the role under Toscanini and Puccini's supervision in June 1910, when the Met staged six works at the Paris Opéra during its first-ever tour abroad.

Björling took his bow in Herbert Graf's new production at the Met in November 1949, under Giuseppe Antonicelli's baton. The electric rhythmic pulse established by the Italian maestro in the opening pages will not surprise those familiar with his 1948 *Bohème* broadcast, and Thomas Hayward's excellent Edmondo sometimes has difficulty in keeping up with his beat. When Björling enters we can appreciate his rhythmic exactness, but he fails to catch the light-hearted tone of the opening "L'amor?!" and in the successive banter the voice sounds bottled up. The lingering caress of "E tosto!!" nevertheless prepares us for a madrigal of unusual grace. "Tra voi belle" (marked *con grazia*) is sung with a generous display of rhythmic, dynamic, and verbal nuance and with idiomatic diction: Björling's only error is his mispronunciation of "giovinetta" (sounding the *g* as a *y*) in the second verse. He captures well the pseudo-archaic elegance of the *canzonetta* (with its elaborate play of rhyme and alliteration) and Antonicelli allows him plenty of scope for rubato. The tenor omits the mordent on "vegga," but makes a feature of the one on "eterna," rising cleanly to the top A on "m'aspetta?": all in all a delightful performance, which seems to echo Hislop's Swedish recording[15] made shortly after the Stockholm premiere of the opera.

The transformation of the teasingly gallant Des Grieux of the opening scene into the awe-struck lover of the first encounter with Manon is totally convincing. The tenor addresses the unknown girl in tones that, while conserving an eighteenth-century elegance of manner, suggest a young man who is only gradually coming to terms with his own feelings. The pristine beauty of his timbre, with its constant alternation of light and shade, contrasts with Kirsten's "girlish" sounds, which don't stand the test of time. As the dialogue develops and Des Grieux gains confidence, Björling's delivery of certain metaphorical flights (such as "E in voi l'aprile nel volto si palesa") sounds slightly stilted, and while we appreciate the luminosity of the soft E-sharps on the register break in "riluce un'altra stella," we notice the uncharacteristic constriction on the optional high B that precedes them. "Donna non vidi mai" is taken at a more leisurely pace than in the 1948 recordings and the phrasing acquires a breadth that makes it easier for us to share the feelings of the character. Although Björling's *mezza voce* isn't as dreamy as Pertile's (or Francesco Merli's in the first complete recording of the opera, made in Milan in 1931),[16] the timbre is still lovely. He eliminates on this occasion the *nota ribattuta* on the final "non cessar," no doubt at Antonicelli's bidding; it would be reinstated in all subsequent recordings. However, the sounds above the staff are not as free and ringing as in the 78 discs, and this impression of an instrument slightly below par is confirmed by Cecil Smith's review of the first night for *Musical America*: he observed that the tenor's voice "was not in its most resonant condition"[17] until the end of the third act.

Although Smith is dismissive of Björling's stage deportment as Des Grieux—"the art of acting does not fall within his purview"—the tenor was often praised for his vocal acting in this opera: a month earlier Alfred Frankenstein wrote in the *San Francisco Chronicle* that he had exhibited "histrionic resources" he "had never shown before."[18] Frankenstein was probably referring to the dramatic outburst at the end of the third act, where Des Grieux implores the ship's captain to take him on board as a hired hand, a moment in which the potency of the singing seemed to transform the whole body of the singer. It is probably true, however, that Björling never entirely possessed the range of facial expression and gestures needed to project visually the disdain, ecstasy and despair felt by Des Grieux during the second act.

An occasional expressive blankness is evident even on disc in this 1949 recording: in the dialogue with Edmondo words such as "Davvero?!" and "Salvami!" don't register with sufficient urgency. Much better is the second duet with Manon, where the melody rises and falls through his voice to seductive effect, culminating in a truly ardent declaration of love ("V'amo! . . . v'amo!"), although it is the concentration of tone rather than the vividness of the words that generates tension here. The final measures sung together with Kirsten terminate in a lusty joint B-flat, and Björling rises to the same note again in the unaccompanied imploration ("Manon v'imploro. Ah!

fuggiam!") that finally convinces her to accompany him to Paris. He sings securely here, but lacks the emotional abandon revealed in later broadcasts.

While in the first act Renato Des Grieux is the dominant and (with the help of Edmondo) apparently the most dynamic character, in the rest of the opera his actions are largely dependent on the woman to whom he has bound his fate. The character's realization of what is happening as the two of them spiral downward is what makes the final acts so cathartic in effect. Love in this late-romantic opera emerges as a form of "human bondage," but Puccini's hero is aware of what is happening to him, no less than the narrator in Prévost's novel, who recalls his amorous fixation with sobering hindsight.

The music devised for the tenor in the second act is so expressively charged that few singers with the right vocal equipment fail to make an impression here (although this scene is difficult to act out convincingly on stage). Björling sounds tensed-up at the beginning, as if more intent on making a muscular sound than on laying bare the feelings of the character, but he relaxes in time to capture the sad bitterness of "taci, tu il cor mi frangi" with a degree of nobility that saves this Des Grieux from the demeaning effect of self-pity. Even in Des Grieux's most all-embracing declaration of love, "Nell'occhio tuo profondo io leggo il mio destin," the tenor makes us understand that the character is in no way blinded by his emotions. It is precisely this clear-headedness that distinguishes Björling's interpretation from those of tenors—Di Stefano comes immediately to mind—whose entire focus seems to be on immediate erotic fulfillment. He nevertheless conveys as well as anyone the almost postcoital huskiness of "Dolcissimo soffrir." The delivery of "Senti, di qui partiamo" sounds noncommital, but Des Grieux's bitterly honest "Ah! Manon, mi tradisce il tuo folle pensiero," which had been recorded on 78s by over twenty tenors (including Hislop and the then general manager of the Met Edward Johnson), is imbued with a stark melancholy that clings to the memory. Björling sings "d'un tratta" instead of "d'un tratto" (a mistake that recurs in later recordings), but captures the sense of degradation in "Fango nel fango io sono."

In the rapid conclusion to the act he is too distant from the microphone to make much impact in the hectic fugal trio with Manon and Lescaut. However, he releases a brilliant B-natural in "Con te portar dei solo il cor," and his final cries of "Manon!" bring the act to a wrenching conclusion.

The opening exchanges with Lescaut in act 3 find the tenor superbly responsive to the music's moods: again his voice seems to echo the orchestral colors (such as the desolate low D sustained for nine measures by the bass clarinet), lending a singular beauty to the simplest phrases, while in "Dietro al destino mi traggo livido" his phrasing adheres to the music with rare poetic freedom. The slower pace of this act makes it easier for him to savor every word, and Des Grieux's deep love for Manon emerges all the more convincingly in the duet with the soprano. Few tenors have sung "fu perché fede mi regnava in core" as candidly as Björling: his voice has a quality of all-comprending compassion that once again gives the impression of a character rising, rather than sinking, to the challenges laid before him by destiny. After the great ensemble that occupies much of the act, in which the tenor's voice emerges only intermittently (he was possibly saving it for what follows), we come to the most sustained heroic piece of singing in the entire opera: Des Grieux's gesture of defiance that then turns into a desperate plea to the captain to let him board ship with Manon—"Ah! non v'avvicinate!" In many ways this could be seen as a typical example of veristic bluster, for here the syllabic declamation needs to be delivered with a sustained vehemence that seems closer to the dynamics of speech than of song. Yet although Björling adds some sobs (curtailed in later performances), he conveys the unhinged quality of the character's utterances through largely musical means, welding the legato with searing continuity and precision (in spite of his mispronunciation of "mestiere") and sustaining the climactic B with a concentrated beauty of tone that compels the captain to submission. Many singers have made much of this moment (it was recorded as a solo by almost thirty tenors before Björling sung it), but arguably none of them manages to combine such free and potent declamation with such a variety of color and purity of tone. Giacomo Lauri Volpi, for example, achieves a similar nobility of expression in his 1934 disc,[19] but the rhetoric sounds stiff and formal by comparison. There is less humanity in the Italian tenor's supplication, less contrast between the imploringly hopeful "io verrò felice" and the sheer desperation of "io piango," and his legato is more fragmentary.

In the fourth act the Tristanesque sense of weariness conveyed by the orchestral introduction suggests the right vocal coloring for Des Grieux's opening line, "Tutta su me ti posa, o mia stanca diletta." Here the chamber-like accompaniment highlights the perfect focus of the voice, allowing each interval and every syllable to tell within the ebb and flow of the legato line: Björling, like all great singers, binds phrases together on the breath even when there are no specific legato markings in the score. As the music opens up in the duet that follows, the voice continues to shape the melody with an unerring command of rhythm and dynamics. Even though he makes a muddle of the words in "vedi, son io che piango," he proves truly moving in the soaring phrases that follow and when the voices unite, he ascends with Kirsten (who is at her best in this act) to an effortless high C. More eloquent still are his desperate cry "E nulla! nulla!" and the mighty plea to the heavens that follows. In the rest of the act Kirsten sings a shortened version of "Sola, perduta abbandonata" (Puccini modified this aria a number of times during his lifetime) and several measures are cut both immediately after the aria and after Des Grieux's passionate "Un funesto delirio ti percuote, ti offende," where Björling sings (as in subsequent recordings) a thrilling, higher variant of the melodic line (also adopted by Merli in the 1931 recording and by a number of other tenors).

He performed Puccini's opera again during Bing's first season at the Met, and two days after a performance on January 6, 1951, he was recorded singing "Donna non vidi mai" on the radio (including "En fermant les yeux" from Massenet's *Manon* in the same program). The microphone picks up more vibrato than one hears in earlier recordings, but the vocal quality is splendid, his emission freer than in the first Met broadcast. As is always the case, no two performances by Björling are entirely alike: in this case he introduces, in one of the repeats of "deh! non cessare," an acciaccatura on the top A rather than on the lower E-flat.

When the tenor made his official recording of *Manon Lescaut* in 1954 he hadn't sung the opera on stage for almost three years. The first recording he ever made in Italy, this interpretation has won considerable critical acclaim over the years. When the recording date arrived, however, Björling was unwilling to leave his island retreat on Siarö (north-east of Stockholm) and ended up flying to Rome a day late. This reluctance to respect such an important contract suggests that part of him wanted to rebel against the stressful lifestyle of a world-class tenor. Indeed, his body had been showing signs of rebellion for some time: he had suffered from persistent laryngitis during the preceding winter and early spring, his immune system weakened by twenty-five years of heavy alcohol consumption. His most recent recording, a recital broadcast from Bergen just four weeks earlier, revealed clear signs of vocal unease. The same cannot be said of the Puccini recording, even though Philip Hope-Wallace, in his review for the *Gramophone*,[20] claimed he had heard Björling's voice "in better condition" on other occasions, unfavorably comparing the climax of "Donna non vidi mai" with the 1948 HMV recording. A more obviously strained moment is the culminating B-natural in "Ah! non v'avvicinate!" in act 2: the tone has a grainy quality to it at first and only gradually regains its habitual purity. It must be stressed, however, that RCA's microphones failed to capture the full splendor of the tenor's upper register even when the voice was functioning perfectly.

Studio conditions make it possible, however, to appreciate the surpassing subtlety of Puccini's scoring, and although the playing of the Rome Opera Orchestra is hardly virtuosic, conductor Jonel Perlea offers a refined reading, if less emotionally charged than Tullio Serafin's recording made at La Scala three years later. Björling's vocal partner, Licia Albanese, was two years younger than him (she was forty-one at the time), but this was to be her last commercial recording of a complete opera. Although her artistry was widely admired—Toscanini had chosen her for his complete radio broadcasts of *La bohème* and *La traviata* in the 1940s—and she would remain a much-loved star of the Met for another decade, the loss of freshness in her voice is all too evident here. While the upper register retains its impetuous luster and a good range of dynamics, the lower octave has a cindery quality that is hard to reconcile with the youth and beauty of Manon. Her projection of the words, on the other hand, is so absolute in its conviction, her phrasing so rhythmically alive and emotionally pregnant, that the singer compels us to believe in the character. The Italian soprano sang a number of times in the opera house with Björling (fifteen performances of *Bohème, Manon Lescaut,* and *Tosca* between 1946 and 1959) and although one could hardly claim that the two voices were perfectly matched, theirs was a theatrically-alive attraction of opposites. Albanese drew inspiration above all from textual values, while Björling expressed his emotional response in a more purely musical fashion, coloring his voice and moulding phrases in such a way as to echo the orchestral timbres and highlight the harmonic structure.

This sensitivity is evident right from Des Grieux's entrance: the transparency of Perlea's accompaniment—less hurried than Antonicelli's—is immediately reflected in Björling's tone. The opening lines are delivered in a more relaxed, colloquial manner, with a hint of a smile, and "Tra voi, belle" is more respectful of Puccini's *piano* markings, although the alliterative effects are less engaging and the climactic A is attacked from an added note below. Des Grieux's first vision of Manon, "Dio, quant'è bella," which was blurted out at the Met, is presented more congruously as an aside. When he addresses her directly he conveys an attractive shyness of manner that renders his wooing ("O come siete bella!") no less persuasive, although this time he makes less sense of the rapid—and for a Swede slightly tongue-twisting—"non è un convento che sterile vi brama!" and once again the high B of "sul vostro destino" sounds pinched. The dryness of Albanese's voice is most conspicuous in this duet, but her ability to feel the full import of the words she is singing is immediately clear and together with Björling she conjurs up an atmosphere of suspended time. Falling in love is like a dream, Puccini seems to be telling us with his shifting harmonies and subtle orchestration (muted strings and horns), and it is the singers' ability to make their voices float on the breath that transforms the composer's intuition into persuasive reality.

"Donna non vidi mai" is Björling's most lyrical performance of this music so far, musingly tender rather than searingly impassioned. We are reminded here of the romantic innocence of the seventeen-year-old *chevalier* at the beginning of Prévost's novel. The tenor's greater experience in the role pays dividends in the dialogue with Edmondo that precedes the second encounter with Manon and the duet itself is more caressing. The unaccompanied solo "Ah! Manon," which brings the duet to a convulsive close, is now thrown into greater relief: the phrase is truly savored, and although the ascents above the staff are slightly arid by Björling's standards, they are notably richer in overtones than the open sounds of Giuseppe di Stefano (Björling's most formidable rival in the role in the 1950s) in the Serafin recording.

The second-act duet with Albanese finds the tenor less stiff in the opening measures, and the richly contrasting personalities of the two singers lend extra interest to the drama. In a way this performance parellels the Serafin recording: there it is the soprano (Maria Callas) who sings the duet with the musical sensitivity of a great instrumentalist; here the tenor (Björling) makes music in every phrase. Their partners, Di Stefano and Albanese, are more emotionally explicit and verbally incisive, but less elegant in expression. With Björling, we again sense both Des Grieux's psychological dependence on Manon and his tragic awareness of how morally compromising that bondage is: the characteristic melancholy of his sound makes it impossible for us to distance ourselves from his point of view, however rationally aware we may be of his weakness.

As at the Met, the effectiveness of the second act is augmented by the presence of a responsive Lescaut (Robert Merrill) and a convincing Geronte, although Franco Calabrese's phrasing is less startlingly vivid than Baccaloni's. The close microphone placement and the precision of the ensemble, allow us to feel the presence of Des Grieux more vividly in the fugal *Allegro* that follows Lescaut's breathless arrival, but Björling's upper register lacks freedom in the desperate plea "Con te portar dei solo il cor!"

In the fifth chapter of Prévost's novel, Des Grieux describes himself as one of those men "of a finer cast" who "are accessible to ideas and sensations which far exceed the ordinary faculties of human nature."[21] Björling consistently conveys that extra dimension of sensitivity in act 3: no other singer delivers "L'attesa m'accora" in such a plaintive half-voice. The tenor's lines in the duet with Manon and the great ensemble that follows are shaped with exquisite feeling, and in "Guardate, pazzo son" he makes a real climax of "piango e imploro," reinforcing the second top A to moving effect.

The Perlea recording is the only one that features Björling in an uncut version of Puccini's fourth act, which was recorded in a single take on the first day of the sessions, and this is in some respects the tenor's most lyrical reading of this music. In the repeat of "su me ti posa," near the begining of the act, his voice speaks eloquently both of Des Grieux's tenderness for the ailing Manon and of the sheer isolation of the two lovers in a hostile territory, while at the same time preparing us musically for the strings' eerie evocation of the rising wind immediately afterward. Although the expressive contrast with Albanese's palpitatingly realistic Manon is never less than striking, one feels that his ideal partner here would have been Callas, who was also capable of blending and contrasting alchemically with the orchestra and who at the end of the opera seems to transcend death while staring it in the face, just as Björling's Des Grieux transcends the mere pathos of the impotent onlooker.

The tenor's next recording of *Manon Lescaut*, the live broadcast from the Met in March 1956, brings Björling closer to Albanese, however: under the influence of Dmitri Mitropoulos—who had conducted Puccini's opera for the first time just two weeks earlier—he reveals more than ever the compulsive underside of Des Grieux's character, his willingness to abase himself in order to regain the undivided attention of a woman of proven capriciousness and venality. The sixty-year-old Mitropoulos was not only a musician of genius but also a formidable man of the theater. His constant ebb and flow of rubato sometimes leads to uncertain ensemble in choral passages, but he was ever-inspired in his accompaniment of the soloists, turning the orchestra into an expressive voice that shares the emotional life of the characters, without ever drowning them out.

In this afternoon performance we sense we are in the presence of a character who lives dangerously because he feels compelled to do so; because that is the only way he can feel alive. The same quality of feeling that we perceive in the tenor's performances as Turiddu and Riccardo. The voice here is darker, thicker and more dramatic than in the two earlier complete performances, and although this leads to an occasional loss of musical refinement, the expressive range of the character is broadened. Björling's top register is unconstricted, and the extra relish with which he delivers the words makes up for a slight loss of dynamic variety. The opening dialogue with Edmondo is less airy than in 1954, but more earthily humorous (we hear a knowing chuckle). "Tra voi belle" has an infectiously broad freedom, and the climactic A is attacked more cleanly than with Perlea. In the first encounter with Manon, Björling sings less softly and not at all shyly but maintains the dreamy atmosphere, while Mitropoulos's tempo variations allow him space to articulate—for the first time in a recording—the grace notes on "perdonate al dir mio." He also projects with impressive ease the high B-natural in "Sul vostro destino riluce un'altra stella." "Donna non vidi mai" is almost Caruso-like in its warm-hearted expansiveness, although less varied than previously in its dynamic contrasts. In the second encounter with Manon the intensity of the accompaniment turns the brief joint climax ("Ah! mio sospir infinito") into an experience of passionate union that helps us understand why the characters subsequently feel so deeply bound to each other. Des Grieux's plea to Manon to flee with him to Paris is overwhelming, winning him a spontaneous round of applause.

Even more compelling is the climax of the second-act duet "Nelle tue braccia care v'è l'ebbrezza, l'oblio!" where Mitropoulos encourages the singers to relish the sense of orgasmic release, far surpassing the effect achieved in the Rome recording. Björling digs deeply into every phrase, and while this highlights the occasional verbal slip, it also makes the character's emotions register more directly than ever. "Nell'occhio tuo profondo" rings out as a singularly defiant gesture in the face of destiny (without the overblown rhetoric of Mario Del Monaco in his 1954 recording)[22] and as the scene develops Björling explores the chevalier's conflicting feelings with uncommon emotional honesty and sensual explicitness. We feel that this honesty is rooted in self-knowledge, for in spite of the tenor's instinctive reserve and unostentatious, family-grounded existence he had himself experienced physical and mental degradation on many occasions, every time his dark, restless *alter ego* came to the surface. It is during the solo "Ah! Manon, mi tradisce il tuo folle pensiero" that the character's complexity emerges most devastatingly. Here Des Grieux is accusing himself, as much as the woman he loves, laying bare his feelings with rueful self-awareness. The breathless pace of the scene that follows leads to a momentary disorientation in the tarantella-like trio (Björling delivers a question, "Il vecchio?" several measures too late), but the tenor makes up for this with his most heart-aching delivery of "Con te portar dei solo il cor," capped by a stunning top B.

Throughout the third act the extra degree of narrative tension Mitropolous generates is clearly felt, even though in the great ensemble Guarrera is much closer to the microphone than the soprano and tenor. At the beginning of the act we notice the contrast between the plangent low As of "Ansia eterna crudel" and the vulnerably open Es in "L'attesa m'accora!" a few measures later, a fine example of the tenor's expressive command of chiaroscuro. Throughout the duet with Manon Björling conveys a special ripeness of sound and meaning, and in the interval between the two verses of the Lamplighter's song (rendered in robust tones by James McCracken, himself soon to become a *primo tenore*), his voice blends fascinatingly with the low tremolo of the string accompaniment (and distant bell) as he gives instructions to Manon. At the same time, he is unstinting in expressing the "intense passion" that Puccini asks for in "disperato è il mio prego," achieving a degree of truthfulness unequalled in earlier recordings. In the great plea "Guardate, pazzo son!" the eloquence of the orchestra inspires him to achieve a rare fusion of declamation and song, although he breaks the line for a breath after the culminating B-natural, sustained with daring vibrancy.

The fourth act also builds, with heightened realism and intensity of feeling, on what was achieved in the RCA recording. Mitropoulos, who had offered a richly articulated reading of the Intermezzo before the beginning of the third act, here inspires Björling to exploit the full emotional potency of the melody that derives from that symphonic interlude, "Vedi, vedi, son io che piango." Although the tenor was singing fewer high Cs in public by 1956, the note pours out generously here when he joins Albanese at the climax of the duet. In the subsequent *Allegro* the expression becomes increasingly convulsive: "E nulla! nulla!" is as stirring as in 1949, and this time the Met orchestra emotes as strongly as the singer, who then calls on the heavens ("O immoto ciel!") with a pathos unsurpassed in any of his recordings. Albanese observes the same cut as Kirsten in "Sola, perduta, abbandonata," but otherwise the act is performed complete.

Björling's next performances as Des Grieux took place at the Lyric Opera in Chicago in October 1957, and judging from Seymour Raven's review in the *Chicago Tribune*—"a slim and youthful looking Björling . . . tore loose with the most emancipated physical performance I have ever seen him sing"[23]—the role continued to engage him totally. The Lescaut of that production, Cornell MacNeil, recalled that "in the scene where he sings 'No! Pazzo son!' I forgot to sing my responses. I was just astounded watching him, both as a singer and actor."[24] This was the only opportunity Björling had to work on this score with a maestro who had known Puccini well, the veteran Serafin, who had first conducted *Manon Lescaut* in Genoa in 1916. Björling's Manon was Renata Tebaldi, who in purely vocal terms was unrivalled in the role on stage in the 1950s. The two singers had just made their complete *Cavalleria rusticana* for Decca at Florence's Teatro Comunale, and in the same week Björling had recorded a number of arias with Alberto Erede, including "Tra voi belle." His phrasing is lighter than with Mitropoulos but no less vivid: words are relished and every detail shines. Less imagination goes into his performance of "Donna non vidi mai" broadcast in July 1958, more lyrical than in 1956 but slightly labored on top.

Björling's final performance of *Manon Lescaut*, which took place in Stockholm on November 1, 1959 (just ten months before his death), was broadcast live.[25] He had recently suffered a collapse while recording *Madama Butterfly* in Rome, and his wife Anna-Lisa recalled that "his colleagues on stage were quite alarmed by his physical condition."[26] Yet although the tenor limited his range of movement on stage, vocally this is possibly his finest performance of all: the voice is as freely produced as at the Met in 1956, but more translucent in texture. The performance is bilingual, with only Björling singing in Italian, but this doesn't faze him and the rest of the cast is impressively involved. Arne Tyrén's sonorous bass—free from any *buffo* inflections—makes the part of Geronte more musically gratifying (and sinister) than usual, and the tenor Kolbjörn Höiseth captures the melancholy of the Lamplighter's song to a rare degree, perhaps offering some idea of the effect Björling himself may have made when he sang the role in the same production twenty-nine years earlier. Hjördis Schymberg's Manon is more problematic, for her *spinto* phrasing, though technically efficient, is achieved by sacrificing legato, and her tone mirrors the beauty of the character only, intermittently, in the last two acts, where she spins some exceptional pianissimos.

Björling is at his best right from the beginning, interacting with Edmondo (an excellent Lars Billengren) more spontaneously than ever. "Tra voi belle" is similar in shape to the 1956 performance but delivered with an extra degree of rubato, dynamic shading and exuberance. Grevillius tends to favor faster tempos than Mitropoulos, but he allows plenty of space for his leading tenor to phrase with ease, and in the first duet with Manon Björling brings a number of details into finer focus than ever before. "Donna non vidi mai" is as lyrical as in 1958, but more improvisatory in character, with greater freedom above the staff.[27] In the second encounter with Manon a number of phrases—such as "l'età gentil che v'infiora il viso"—are delivered with rare poetic sensibility and "Manon v'imploro" is as exciting as at the Met, again winning a round of applause.

Grevillius cannot equal Mitropoulos in the second-act duet, where Schymberg's jerky phrasing dampens the erotic tension of the climax, but Björling offers many moments to treasure, particularly in the lingering attack in "Nell'occhio tuo profondo." The Swedish conductor comes into his own in the trio later in the act, highlighting the tarantella rhythm. The *Intermezzo* is shifted to the beginning of the fourth act, an incongruous decision if one recalls that this symphonic interlude is designed to evoke Manon's imprisonment and journey to Le Havre. This was presumably a standard feature of Hyltén-Cavallius's production, which had been conducted by Grevillius since its debut thirty years earlier. Another surprise at the beginning of the third act is the use of a wind machine in the opening measures (up to the entrance of Manon), which rather distracts us from Björling's eloquent phrasing, but the tenor's voice is heard more distinctly than usual in the great ensemble and his plea to the captain is as thrilling as ever, the phrases bound together with warm portamentos and the top register impressively expansive. Since he is in Sweden[28] Björling eschews the traditional sobs entirely, and this further highlights the tensile strength of the line.

The fourth act in Stockholm fails to match the tragic intensity Mitropoulos achieved, but Björling sings with his customary compassion and generosity of spirit, rising easily to the top C (this was the last time he sang this note in public). The desperate cry "E nulla! nulla!" is as eloquent as ever. The final pages of the opera are heavily cut: twenty-four measures are omitted after Des Grieux's "Un soccorso," "Sola, perduta abbandonata" is even shorter than at the Met, and at the end of the aria there is a twenty-measure cut which leads us directly from "sguardo invano" to "gelo di morte!"

Des Grieux's "Donna non vidi mai" was the last piece of music by Puccini that Björling recorded, at his Gothenburg concert on August 6, 1960: a performance of distilled lyricism, suggesting a purity of inspiration that seems to belie the long bouts of depression[29] that afflicted him during those last weeks of his life.

When reviewing one of the revivals of Graf's production at the Met in 1975, Andrew Porter wrote that "in a serious, dramatic, balanced performance of *Manon Lescaut*, the emotional weight of the piece is carried by Des Grieux."[30] Not only does the tenor have "most of the numbers" (four strongly contrasting solos in acts 1, 2, and 3), but, as in the novel, it is largely from his point of view that we observe the downward spiral of Manon, and our ability to be moved by her fate will depend partly on the tenor's own capacity for feeling. The same is true of Rodolfo in *La bohème*, who watches Mimì gradually succumb to illness in the second half of the opera, but the Parisian poet's love is a less obsessive, all-embracing and morally compromising experience.

The role of Des Grieux was in Björling's repertoire for a mere ten years, yet it is the best documented of his Puccini parts. It is arguably also the role that best enabled him to explore his own identity through the music, encompassing a range of expression that is rivalled on disc only by his Riccardo in *Un ballo in maschera*, another character whose melodic profile evokes at times the graceful manners of an earlier age.

La bohème
Complete Recordings

December 25, 1948: New York, Metropolitan Opera House
Jussi Björling (Rodolfo), Bidú Sayão (Mimì), Frank Valentino (Marcello), Mimì Benzell (Musetta), George Cehanovsky (Schaunard), Nicola Moscona (Colline), Salvatore Baccaloni (Benoit, Alcindoro); Metropolitan Opera Chorus and Orchestra, cond. Giuseppe Antonicelli
WHRA 6020

March 16–April 6, 1956: New York, Manhattan Center
Jussi Björling (Rodolfo), Victoria de los Angeles (Mimì), Robert Merrill (Marcello), Lucine Amara (Musetta), John Reardon (Schaunard), Giorgio Tozzi (Colline), Fernando Corena (Benoit, Alcindoro); RCA Victor Chorus and Orchestra, cond. Sir Thomas Beecham
EMI CDS 7 47235 8

Act 1
March 21, 1940: Stockholm, Royal Opera House
Jussi Björling (Rodolfo), Hjördis Schymberg (Mimì), Sven Herdenberg (Marcello), Carl Richter (Schaunard), Leon Björker (Colline), Folke Cambraeus (Benoit); Royal Court Orchestra,
conductor Nils Grevillius
Bluebell 013

Final scene from act 1
September 25, 1949: San Francisco, War Memorial Opera House
Jussi Björling (Rodolfo), Licia Albanese (Mimì); San Francisco Opera Orchestra, cond. Karl Kritz
WHRA-6036

January 30, 1956: New York, Long Island, NBC Studio
Jussi Björling (Rodolfo), Renata Tebaldi (Mimì); Symphony of the Air, cond. Max Rudolf
WHRA-6036 (CD); VAI 4244 8 (DVD)

Acts 1 and 3–4
September 30, 1957: Malmö, Stadsteater
Jussi Björling (Rodolfo), Ethel Mårtensson (Mimì), Nils Bäckström (Marcello), Astri Herseth (Musetta), Arne Hasselbad (Schaunard), Bengt von Knorring (Colline); Malmö Symphony Orchestra, cond. Sten Åke Axelson
Bluebell ABCD 078

"Che gelida manina"

December 1936: Stockholm, Concert Hall
Unspecified orchestra, cond. Nils Grevillius
Naxos 8.119701

April 8, 1937: Stockholm, Concert Hall,
Swedish Radio Symphony Orchestra, cond. Nils Grevillius
Bluebell ABCD 103

November 28, 1937: New York, Carnegie Hall
General Motors Symphony Orchestra, cond. Erno Rapee

June 8, 1939: Hilversum, AVRO Studio
AVRO Hilversum Orchestra, cond. Frieder Weissmann
Bluebell 006

December 8, 1940: Detroit, Masonic Temple Auditorium
Ford Symphony Orchestra, cond. Eugene Ormandy

April 8, 1941: Stockholm, Concert Hall
Stockholm Radio Orchestra, cond. Nils Grevillius
Bluebell ABCD 066

January 1, 1945: Stockholm, Concert Hall
Stockholm Radio Orchestra, cond. Tor Mann
Bluebell ABCD 092

August 23, 1949: Los Angeles, Hollywood Bowl
Hollywood Bowl Symphony Orchestra, cond. Izler Solomon
Naxos 8.111083

October 23, 1949: San Francisco, War Memorial Opera House
San Francisco Opera Orchestra, cond. Gaetano Merola
Urania 22.120

November 7, 1949: New York, Rockefeller Center
Bell Telephone Hour Orchestra, cond. Donald Voorhees
WHRA-6036

January 13, 1951: New York, Manhattan Center
RCA Victor Orchestra, cond. Renato Cellini
RCA 88697748922

April 17, 1951: Stockholm, Royal Academy of Music
Swedish Radio Orchestra, cond. Sten Frykberg
Bluebell ABCD 103

September 24, 1955: New York, Carnegie Hall
Frederick Schauwecker, pf.
RCA 88697748922

July 19, 1956: Stockholm, Gröna Lund
Harry Ebert, pf.
Bluebell ABCD 114

April 13, 1958: Atlanta, Glenn Memorial Auditorium
Frederick Schauwecker, pf.
Bluebell ABCD 020

"O soave fanciulla"

June 17, 1941: Stockholm, Concert Hall
Jussi Björling (Rodolfo), Hyördis Schymberg (Mimì); unspecified orchestra, cond. Nils Grevillius
EMI CDH 761053 2

January 1, 1945: Stockholm, Concert Hall
Jussi Björling (Rodolfo), Hyördis Schymberg (Mimì); Stockholm Radio Orchestra, cond. Tor Mann
Bluebell ABCD 092

August 10, 1949: Stockholm, Concert Hall
Jussi Björling (Rodolfo), Anna-Lisa Björling (Mimì); Stockholm Concert Association Orchestra, cond. Nils Grevillius
EMI 5 66306 2

August 23, 1949: Los Angeles, Hollywood Bowl
Jussi Björling (Rodolfo), Anna-Lisa Björling (Mimì); Hollywood Bowl Symphony Orchestra, cond. Izler Solomon
Naxos 8.111083-85

October 23, 1949: San Francisco, War Memorial Opera House
Jussi Björling (Rodolfo), Anna-Lisa Björling (Mimì); San Francisco Opera Orchestra, cond. Gaetano Merola
Urania 22.120

March 6, 1950: New York, Rockefeller Center
Jussi Björling (Rodolfo), Anna-Lisa Björling (Mimì); Firestone Orchestra, cond. Howard Barlow
Kultur DVD D2424

"In un coupe?"

January 3, 1951: New York, Manhattan Center
Jussi Björling (Rodolfo), Robert Merrill (Marcello); RCA Victor Orchestra, cond. Renato Cellini
RCA 88697748922; Naxos 8.110788

Jussi Björling's enduring popularity as a singer owes much to his recordings of this most popular of Puccini's operas, which was staged almost every season in Stockholm and New York during his adult career and which he performed more than any other theatrical work. *La bohème* had been premiered in Turin in 1896 with Evan Gorga in the tenor role, but it was De Lucia and Caruso who revealed the full expressive potential of Rodolfo, the acutely sensitive, convention-defying and usually penniless young poet who is in many ways the protagonist of this singularly poetic score. Apart from the opening scene of act 3, we tend to follow the action from his point of view: it is no coincidence that the journalist Rodolphe in Murger's *Scènes de la vie de Bohème* (the literary source of the libretto) was a largely autobiographical figure. In the opera too (although it is Schaunard who is the musician) Rodolfo seems to reflect some aspects of his creator's (in this case Puccini's) personality: no other male figure in his works reveals such a whimsically humorous spirit, such quickness of imagination.

A number of twentieth century tenors—notably Caruso himself, Gigli, Gianni Raimondi and Luciano Pavarotti—sang Rodolfo more often than Björling, but the Swede left his own very individual mark on the role, with which he had probably been familiar since childhood (his father David had sung the part in 1912). Although reviews of both his first performance in Stockholm in 1934 (when Moses Pergament complained that "dramatically, the role wasn't worked through")[31] and his final appearances at Covent Garden in 1960 (when Desmond Shawe-Taylor likened his Rodolfo to "a frock coated Victorian solicitor interviewing a young lady in distress")[32] suggest that his acting sometimes required a conscious suspension of disbelief, his singing has stood the test of time supremely well. The complete studio recording under Sir Thomas Beecham is still widely considered a touchstone of excellence.

As an all-round performance the Beecham *Bohème* is arguably the finest studio version of any complete opera with Björling, and a number of the tenor's separate recordings of "Che gelida manina" come close to perfection, yet what survives in sound is but a small sample of his wide-ranging theatrical experience in this opera. He clocked up a total of one hundred and fourteen performances as Rodolfo in ten different countries (eleven if we include the first act staged at the Théâtre de la Cité Universitaire in Paris in 1936),[33] but only one of these has been preserved entirely in sound.

He first recorded "Che gelida manina" in December 1936, two years after his debut in the opera. It was his first disc in Italian and marked the launching of his career as an international recording artist. The competition was formidable: Rodolfo's *racconto* had already been committed to disc by about a hundred and thirty tenors, including all the finest exponents of the role in the early twentieth century. Yet Björling's first version, recorded when he was just twenty-four, immediately stands out for its youthful radiance. The opening phrase is introduced by a sustained A-flat for clarinet and harp, and his mirroring of these blended timbres truly gives the impression of the "voice full of emotion" that Puccini demands. He sings this phrase *piano* rather than the indicated *pianissimo* (in a letter to his publisher Giulio Ricordi of October 1895, Puccini—echoing Verdi—wrote that "when one wants *piano* one puts ***pppp***"),[34] but his tone is both *dolcissimo* and *affettuoso*, as required, and his phrasing as *ben legato* as the muted strings that accompany him from the second measure onward. It is singular how musically varied he makes the opening A-flats, the single pitch of the first three measures, thanks to his pellucid vowels and attention to note values. His head voice attack on the top A-flat of "Cercar che giova?" is disarming in its purity, and one cannot help noting the substratum of melancholy that underlies this conversational opening. Björling's inner melancholy tends to surface even when wooing a "bella bambina": a secret sadness adds to the fascination of the wooer. As the voice opens up in the second phrase one appreciates how seamlessly the line passes from *piano* to *forte*, a quality that is much less evident in Gigli's 1931 recording,[35] where the head tones are clearly detached from the main body of the voice. The sounds the Italian tenor makes are mellifluous and his interpretation is a charming, if dated, mixture of humor and sentimentality, but the contrast between the two types of voice production undermines to a certain extent the credibility of the character. Björling's voice is better integrated as an instrument and flows more smoothly and nobly, without however passing over details: the mordents on "notte" and "vicina" (elegant touches which remind us that Rodolfo is not a contemporary of Puccini's but someone living in an earlier, more gracious, era); the *stentando* that highlights the melodic curve of "qui la luna," and the constant tempo variations. Like the majority of tenors, however, he fails to observe the tricky diminuendo on the high B-flat of "chi son," although he does bind the note persuasively to the A-flat of "e che faccio."

A more questionable departure from the score comes in the transitional *Andante Lento* section beginning "In povertà mia lieta," which is here sung considerably faster than the opening *Andantino affettuoso.* The informally conversational quality of Puccini's melodic writing means that such liberties—albeit in contrast with the metronome markings—are less structurally compromising than they would be in an aria by Verdi, but Björling makes things more difficult for himself by his impulsive pace here, for he trips up over the key word "chimere" (Roberto Alagna demonstrates by contrast how expressive Puccini's tempo can be when every word is relished).[36] The crescendo on "l'anima ho milionaria" is truly expansive, however, and the broad melody of "Talor dal mio forziere" (Rodolfo's leitmotif) is sustained with ideal warmth and concentrated tone, starting with a handsome upward portamento on "Talor." This embellishment is not exhibited self-consciously—like the featherweight *pianissimo* slide De Lucia introduces in his 1917 recording[37]—but simply serves to bind the phrase together more compellingly while highlighting the harmonic structure. In semantic terms this phrase is elaborate metaphor, an expression of both Rodolfo's literary imagination and his desire to deploy every available resource in his attempt to seduce Mimì. The poet's strategy is partly undermined, however, by Björling's uncertain grasp of the text: "forziere" becomes "forzieri," "gioielli" is sung with a a softened Swedish *g,* and "furto" is transformed into "fortu." These errors inevitably weaken the credibility of the self-confident Rodolfo, who makes an (admittedly meager) living out of his communicative skills. But to use these slips, as Nigel Douglas does, as a excuse to castigate Björling as "a sloppy linguist"[38] is unfair: Douglas not only fails to take the tenor's later recordings into account, but also underestimates the expressive impact of Björling's sensitive blending of words and tone in the rest of the aria. Even when he mispronounces words, his coloring of the phrases is always appropriate: having already performed Puccini's opera in Swedish eighteen times, he understands exactly the import of what he is singing. While it is true that Björling never learned to speak Italian in a more than rudimentary fashion, a good command of the spoken language—while always valuable—doesn't inevitably guarantee more expressive diction when singing, particularly if the emission itself is lacking in limpidity.

The climax of "Che gelida manina" is the ascent to the top C (a mere eighth note in the score) on the word "speranza!": an exultant note, accompanied by an orchestral *allargando* and *fortissimo,* which leaves us with little doubt that Rodolfo will succeed in winning Mimì's love. The traditional (unwritten) fermata on this C provides Björling with an unmatched opportunity to show off the beauty and freedom of his upper register. The duration of the note—rarely less than generous—naturally varies in each performance, but the sound he makes seldom disappoints in its radiant purity and ringing projection. This first recording is no exception, although one regrets the tenor's rushed approach to the note. His nervousness here could be explained by the fact that this was the first time he produced a top C on record (Giuseppe Lugo, singing in French in 1932,[39] is a model here, approaching the C by means of an elegant portamento).

The final phrase—in spite of a Swedish sounding vowel on the opening syllable—is sung with the soft, sweet urgency Puccini requires. As in the opening measures, one is struck by Björling's ability to make his tone reflect the amalgam of the accompanying instruments. He also makes much of the fermata on the D-flat of "piaccia," never ceasing to make music even when Rodolfo seems simply to be speaking on preestablished pitches.

However remarkable the first recording of "Che gelida manina" may be, the tenor's next version, recorded in Swedish during a concert four months later, is in some ways even more striking. It is an introverted reading: over the years we will notice how Björling alternates two rather different approaches to this aria depending on the musical context and the language. Although the opening phrase is sung slightly louder this time, the Swedish vowels immediately lend his voice a more inward, clarinet-like coloring, and a number of phrases taper away gracefully. He achieves a fine diminuendo this time on the B-flat of "chi son," although he makes less a feature of it than Miguel Fleta (1927)[40] or Carlo Bergonzi (1957).[41] He still speeds up at the beginning of the *Andante Lento* ("In povertà mia lieta"), but this only throws the *allargando* of "l'anima ho milionaria" into greater relief. His phrasing as a whole is less overtly emotional: portamentos for example are largely eschewed, reminding us of what Elisabeth Söderström admitted once to the British broadcaster John Amis: "If I sang songs as warmly in Sweden as I would here or in countries south of here they would all say I was too sobby."[42] Like Caruso (1906)[43] and Tito Schipa (1913)[44] in their excellent interpretations of the aria (and Jan Peerce in the 1946 Toscanini recording)[45] Björling omits here the slide joining the first two notes of "Talor dal mio forziere," a choice that is dictated by the fact that in the very free Swedish translation ("Jag strålas av ett ögonpar") those notes no longer correspond to the syllables of a single word. In any case, none of his colleagues can rival the laser-like exactness of his exposed attack on the top A-flat, and the underlying portamento of the breath is so clearly felt that the line maintains its conversational fluidity. The most striking feature of this reading, however, is the concentrated, forward placement of Björling's tone, which blooms startlingly in the upper register: every time the voice ascends above the staff it acquires an extra degree of resonance and purity. This Rodolfo is not particularly humorous or charming, but in a sense he transcends mere charm, singing like an archangel inspired by the unlimited luster of the instrument at his disposal. The top C is completely unforced, attacked with unusual cleanness and energy, and when descending the tenor lends greater emphasis to the downbeat by repeating the top B-flat and adding an acciaccatura, a traditional embellishment that can be heard in Caruso's recording of the aria (transposed down half a tone) and which Björling would be maintain in later performances.

Although many of the musical qualities heard over the radio in Sweden in April 1937 remain intact in his next recording of "Che gelida manina" (the *General Motors* broadcast in November of the same year), the expressive balance shifts decisively, favoring this time the warm immediacy of direct communication rather than the restrained purity of poetic inspiration. This is particularly evident in his extrovert delivery of the recitative-like "Chi son? Son un poeta." Björling sings the Italian text in a much more idiomatic fashion this time, demonstrating that he has worked hard since making the HMV recording eleven months earlier. The improvement was doubly necessary because he was due to sing the entire role of Rodolfo for the first time in Italian in Chicago two weeks later. The recording lacks depth, but there is never any doubting the youthful glow of the voice and the performance as a whole is exuberant and affectionate, soaring and reflective, entirely spontaneous yet musically satisfying in every detail. The tenor lingers longer this time on the top A-flat of "luna" in the opening *Andante* and the high C climax is once again thrilling in its roundess and ease. It would be hard to imagine a more auspicious New York debut for the twenty-six-year-old singer.

Once Björling had mastered the words and music of an aria, there was nothing cerebral in his approach to performing it: we must not therefore expect the eighteen subsequent traversals of Rodolfo's Romanza to reveal a systematic deepening of his understanding of the music. The two 1937 performances are already remarkably complete in their expressive grasp, and Björling's interpretative approach was at all times largely instinctive: new insights tend to arrive as if by chance, when the singer is completely possessed by the music he is singing. What his subsequent performances do reveal is an uncommon sensitivity to the context in which he was working—the rhythmic pulse of the conductor and the specific timbres of the accompanying instruments—and a straightforward desire to respond to the mood of the moment. Although he was often described by critics as a singer of cool temperament, recordings reveal that Björling's moods varied much more than those of the average tenor. These moods were naturally connected with the physical quality of the voice itself, which not only changed gradually in weight and range over the years but varied from day to day in its coloration, although it remained remarkably consistent in its technical reliability. The extemporary quality of the Romanza itself—where Rodolfo introduces himself in a combination of urgent recitative and soaring arioso, without any musical repeats—is quite unique in Puccini's output. "Che gelida manina" has been described as "a love poem in search of its own inspiration,"[46] and we have the impression that Rodolfo is making up the words and music as he goes along. Through this role Puccini succeeds in saying some important things about the nature of inspiration itself, which languishes when Rodolfo has to write a leading article for *Il Castoro* but then suddenly burgeons when he finds himself thrown into close physical contact with a beautiful woman. In his multiple recordings of the aria Björling demonstrates how rich and varied his own access to inspiration was.

The next recording (Hilversum, 1939) comes after the tenor's highly successful Met debut in the role (Anna-Lisa Björling remembered his leg "shaking violently" as he sang the aria during that first performance)[47] and shows him inhabiting the part with commendable ease. The opening is his softest yet and truly *piena d'emozione*: for the first time we hear an unwritten mordent on the D-flat of "non si trova" (a grace-note employed by Caruso that subtly expresses Rodolfo's psychological need to add an embellishment when hiding the truth from Mimì, for he has of course already found her key). Another ornament that Björling probably derived from the Neapolitan tenor—whose singing in this aria has a classical poise that has rarely been equalled—is the upward portamento to the E-flat of "dir" in the final measure: both features were maintained in his subsequent Italian-language performances of the aria. This ending is particularly magical in effect, with *messe di voce* on the two most extended notes. The rest of the aria is very fine indeed, with no conspicuous pronunciation errors and a perfect balance between poised cantabile and impromptu recitative. The top register is not as astonishingly vivid as in April 1937 and the high C is attacked less cleanly this time, but the note itself is generously sustained and the transition from the *forte* climax to the soft ending is masterly.

Björling's first extended extract from *La bohème* is the broadcast in Swedish of the first act from the Royal Opera in March 1940, his fortieth performance as Rodolfo. As at his debut six years earlier, the Mimì was Hjördis Schymberg, who partnered him on stage more than any other soprano, singing thirty-three joint performances of *La bohème* over twenty-three years. The intimacy of atmosphere established during the opening act reminds us of the advantages of performing this opera in a relatively small house. In Swedish the humor in the opening scene sounds understated, but the interaction is verbally alert and musically subtle, and one has the impression that the accompanying instruments are active participants in the drama. In none of his later recordings of this music is Björling's voice so impregnated with youth. Rodolfo's opening phrases soar heart-warmingly and contrast deliciously with the *pianissimo* rendition of "L'amore è un caminetto che sciupa troppo," a dynamic echoed in Marcello's response. The tenor's fellow Bohemians are all fresh-voiced and quick-minded, but the Swedish language does not always facilitate the sort of legato singing that is essential in Italian opera and even Björling delivers some lines—such as "In quell'azzurro guizzo languente sfuma un'ardente scena d'amor"—in a less flowing manner than we are used to. He nevertheless conveys a real sense of enjoyment here, without ever being rushed off his feet, and the spontaneity of the interaction is enhanced by the singers' close attention to the score.

The selection published in CD begins with Mimì's entrance: here the muted accompanying strings establish a mood of romantic expectation which contrasts with the boisterous comedy of the preceding scene. Most tenors take their cue here from the libretto, underlining the immediate attraction Rodolfo feels for this unknown woman. Björling takes his cue from the music: he sings softly in tones that sometimes mirror, sometimes complement the instrumental textures, revealing Rodolfo's emotional transformation through the clarity of the vowels and the razor-sharp definition of line. As is appropriate, "Che bella bambina!" is sung as a genuine aside. Schymberg's more outgoing personality provides a perfect foil for the unusually soft-spoken Rodolfo, whose strength of feeling is revealed in the very delicacy of his phrasing.

The aria itself is understandably closer in spirit to the 1937 Swedish-language recording than to the more recent performances in Italian. Owing possibly to a more distant microphone placement, Björling's upper register is less vivid this time, although the C—attacked in characteristically impetuous fashion—is once again gloriously free. This climax is thrown into relief by the wide range of dynamics employed throughout the Romanza, which is based on a series of ample *messe di voce,* suggesting a continual ebb and flow of tension. Few performances of this aria are at once so intimate and so exciting.

The short but emotionally charged duet that brings act 1 to a close was always a highlight of Björling's performances, partly because of his skill in blending his voice with that of the soprano. He attacks "O soave fanciulla" *dolcissimo* and *piano,* as the composer requires, and captures to a rare degree the ecstatically contemplative quality of "o dolce viso di mite circonfuso alba lunar." Mimì's pale, beautiful face inspires fanciful imagery in the poet, and Björling's voice acquires a correspondingly moon-like radiance here. The crescendo that begins on "in te ravviso" is built up very slowly so that the final syllable on "sognar" (an F-sharp at the top of the staff) can expand thrillingly before the brilliantly precise attack on the top A of "Fremon già nell'anima." Unlike most tenors, he then repeats "Fremon nell'anima" in a poised *pianissimo.* Both singers combine here a sense of timeless rapture and colloquial piquancy (Björling is gently insinuating in "Sarebbe così bello restar qui"), and the final offstage measures are magical: Björling sings the written E while Schymberg ascends to a secure top C, and both notes register harmoniously as part of a dying close.

Nine months later the tenor was back in the United States, performing in an Ormandy-led *Ford Sunday Evening Hour.* Once again he is in an extrovert mood in the act 1 *racconto* (naturally sung in Italian). This time however the impetuous approach to the climactic word "speranza" doesn't produce the expected effect, for a crack opens up on the top C, which is abandoned fairly quickly. The throaty attack on the opening E flat of "Or che mi conoscete" surely speaks of the singer's own surprise at what has happened, although he masks his unease by delivering the final measures with greater than usual emphasis.

In April 1941 Björling sang the aria in the original language on Swedish radio for the first time. His voice during this broadcast sounds darker and more dramatic than usual, and this, combined with Grevillius's spacious tempo affects the interpretative approach (the aria lasts thirty seconds longer than the 1936 recording, demonstrating how flexibly the conductor breathed with the singer he was accompanying). Although he does not transpose downward, in no other performance does Björling come so close to the baritonal coloring of the Caruso recording. With the more leisurely pace, the section beginning "In povertà mia lieta" (where Rodolfo expounds his philosophy of life) acquires real incisiveness for the first time, thanks also to the ease with which the voice projects in the relatively low tessitura. No less telling is the caress on "occhi belli," the point in the aria where the poet makes it clear that his figurative language is inspired entirely by Mimì. This compensates in part for the rather deliberate opening (sung *mezzo forte*, as if thinking aloud rather than addressing a young woman). The top C is on the same grand scale as the rest of the aria, and the note is again attacked directly, without any link from the preceding A-flat. The abruptness of the attack—a feature of many of Björling's recordings—can probably be explained by the tenor's desire to generate the greatest possible brilliance of tone, and that is certainly what he achieves here. Yet the overall impression created by this performance is rather unsmiling. By cultivating a resolutely dark tone this Rodolfo sounds preoccupied with some inner sorrow: the words "tosto si dileguar!" bear a weight of sadness that would surely have surprised Puccini.

Three months later Björling returned to the Stockholm Concert Hall to record "O soave fanciulla" in the original language. This time his voice is more typically lyrical in its alternation of light and shade, but although Schymberg is once again his partner and Grevillius is on the podium, the performance is quite different from the 1940 broadcast. Not for the first time, the Italian language encourages the tenor to favor *mezzo forte* over *piano*, but both singers phrase with a certain charm and the joint attack of "Fremon già nell'anima" is tingling in its precision. The traditional portamentos are all in place and one notes again the musical effect created by Björling when singing phrases on a single pitch (the contrasting vowels of "che freddo fuori"). One nevertheless regrets his failure to respect Puccini's *pianissimo* in "Che m'ami dì" (which proves more captivating in the Swedish-language recording) and the lack of a distancing effect in the final measures.

The tenor's next *Bohème* recording, in early 1945, was also broadcast from the Stockholm Concert Hall. Tor Mann's liking for leisurely tempos lends the Romanza an almost record-breaking expansiveness. At 5:26 it lasts more than a minute longer than the 1936 recording, calling to mind the eccentric but fascinating disc (lasting 5:16) made by De Lucia, the first great Rodolfo, in 1917. The ease with which Björling adapts to this tempo is a tribute to his breath control and musical flexibility, and although the aria loses some of the light-heartedness heard in the 1937 New York broadcast, and the drawn-out tempo exposes occasional oddities of pronunciation, a number of details (the grace notes in particular) are more elegantly finished than ever before and the continuity of the tenor's legato ensures that the narrative loses none of its cohesion. The opening measures are particularly poetic, and as in 1941 one notices the singular melancholy of "e i bei sogni miei . . . tosto si dileguar!" with a languorous slide linking the C of "miei" to the E-flat of "tosto." The culminating high note is less forward than in 1941, but is impressively prolonged—closer to seven seconds in duration than to the usual four—without upsetting the balance of the phrase.

Immediately after the aria Schymberg joins her favorite tenor partner in an equally spacious reading in Italian of "O soave fanciulla," which combines the virtues of their two previous recorded performances. The crescendo in the opening measures is built up slowly and Puccini's dynamic markings are largely respected, except in "Che m'ami dì," which is sung with a fervor that seems well suited to the more sensual character of the soprano's phrasing here. The conclusive paragraph is lingered over dreamily, and the distancing effect helps Schymberg's voice soar sweetly above the staff.

It would be hard to imagine a greater contrast between the poetic inwardness of those final measures and the cracklingly colloquial opening to the Met performance of Puccini's opera conducted by Giuseppe Antonicelli at the Met four years later, a spirited Christmas Day broadcast of an opera whose first two tableaux unfold on Christmas Eve. Such contrasts are in many ways an integral part of a work in which movement and stillness, comedy and tragedy are held in subtle balance throughout. "Vie charmante et vie terrible!" wrote Murger in the preface to his novel, and it is undoubtedly true that if the charm and high spirits are lacking then the tragedy too will lose its impact.

This certainly seems to have been the conviction of Antonicelli, who was born in the year of the opera's premiere and whose *bohémiens* are depicted in primary colors, consuming their existences at a breathless pace. This approach owes much to Toscanini, who had conducted the world premiere and had recorded his own version of *La bohème* in New York a couple of years earlier. In the opening scene of act 1 Antonicelli keeps the music moving even more rapidly than the seventy-nine-year-old maestro in his NBC broadcasts in February 1946, although he slows down notably for the first encounter between Rodolfo and Mimì. The two conductors share four cast members—Frank

Valentino as Marcello, George Cehanovsky as Schaunard, Nicola Moscona as Colline and Salvatore Baccaloni doubling as Benoit and Alcindoro—and only the Italian bass functions better in the earlier recording, for Toscanini persuades him to stick to the score, making the landlord less of a caricature. The Met Orchestra, though not as virtuosic as the NBC Symphony, benefits from the more natural opera house acoustic and certainly knows how to accompany the singers in this most popular of Italian operas (this was the thirteenth Met broadcast of Puccini's masterpiece since 1932).

The real difference however is the Rodolfo: with Toscanini, Jan Peerce sings with scrupulous musicality but sounds his age (forty-two), making a committed but ultimately dull figure of the romantic lead; with Antonicelli, the thirty-seven-year-old Björling—a decade after his Metropolitan debut in the role—still sounds astonishingly youthful, his voice golden in timbre and brimming with energy. Beauty of timbre is one of the prime requisites of the role of Rodolfo, who should appear as immediately attractive to Mimì as she does to him, and it is fairer perhaps to compare the Swedish tenor's portrayal to that of the equally golden-voiced Gigli in the complete 1938 recording under Umberto Berrettoni.[48] The Italian tenor avoids abusing his falsetto in this performance and sings with a sunny tone, but much of the time sounds excessively avuncular. He is careful at first not to overstretch his upper register (at forty-eight his voice doesn't bloom as spontaneously as Björling's above the staff) and although diction is always clear, it is often mannered: his emphasis on the words tends to punctuate the legato, lending a slightly jerky quality to even the most expansive melodic arcs. Although Gigli has been lauded for his chuckling humor, this gives the impression of a middle-aged singer contemplating the wit of the character he is playing at a comfortable distance. Björling too chuckles at one point—to underline the mock-concern of "Colline, sei morto?"—and even laughs openly (in perfect tune) at Schaunard's imitation of Milord's English accent, but his humor generally, and rightly, has the bittersweet tang of youth. In the opening duet with Marcello he doesn't inflect the phrases with the whimsical irony of Pavarotti at his best (with Karajan),[49] but his high spirits are contagious and his willingness to add fermatas in the upper register lends credibility to Rodolfo's poetic fancy while adding extra springiness to the snatches of melody. He delivers "L'amore è un caminetto che sciupa troppo" in pointed fashion and he never sounds fazed by Antonicelli's rapid momentum: we always have the impression that it is the singers who set the pace.

After the entrance of Mimì, there is none of the hushed atmosphere conveyed in the 1940 Stockholm broadcast: Björling's phrasing is extrovert and full-bodied. The empathy expressed in "Che viso d'ammalata" registers less strongly and "Che bella bambina!" is more of a public statement. The character is ever-engaging, but less freshly original in conception. We appreciate, however, the appropriately ambiguous coloring of Rodolfo's "No!" when he denies having found Mimi's key, while five measures later we notice the harmonic modulation that permits a downward transposition, enabling the tenor to begin the Romanza in C major. This transposition (then standard practice at the Met: only Jan Peerce, in the surviving pre-1950 *Bohème* broadcasts, sticks to the original key)[50] is surprising, for at this point in his career Björling still had effortless access to the top C, as he demonstrates in this performance, for the climactic B-natural is attacked sharp (practically a C) before settling on the right pitch. Never before, however, has he seemed so warmly and single-mindedly intent on seducing Mimì (there is no trace of melancholy here), and the colorful accompaniment of the Met Orchestra (which included a number of Italian players) contributes to the expressive cogency of the performance. The tenor's pronunciation is more idiomatic than ever and each word is relished, although it is a pity he sings "In povertà mia lieta"—marked *dolce e legato*—in such a declamatory fashion.

In a Juilliard master class on this aria in 1971, Maria Callas suggested:

> Don't give undue importance to this aria either in voice or in tempo. It is simple; Rodolfo and Mimì are simple people. What you must give importance to is the words. He is telling her precious lies, flirting with this girl he likes—but lightly, not seriously."[51]

This 1948 performance is the one in which Björling comes closest to approaching that playful spirit (captured to perfection in a 1944 Radio Lausanne recording by Callas's frequent tenor partner Giuseppe di Stefano).[52] Yet the enduring fascination of the Swede's recorded performances of this music derive from a less cynical view of the Romanza's dramatic function; a sense that Rodolfo—while flirting with Mimì in a casually manipulative fashion—reveals genuine emotional sensitivity and depth of imagination.

The object of Rodolfo's autobiographical presentation, Bidú Sayão, was nine years older than Björling, yet she was still capable of investing legato phrases with an autumnal beauty. At the same time she was compelled (owing to the limitations of her lightweight instrument) to accept a number of vocal compromises in order to project the personality of Mimì, opening the vowels in the lower-middle register so as to make the words register in the large auditorium. As a result she sounds childlike or petulant in some phrases, in spite of her excellent command of Italian, which compromises the very adult mood of the duet. Björling attacks "O soave fanciulla" with genuine emotional abandon, albeit without the refinement heard in the 1940 Swedish broadcast. As was traditional at the Met, Rodolfo joins Mimì on the final top note, a B on this occasion (Sayão modulates into a lower key in the phrase "V'aspettano gli amici," here sung entirely on the F-sharp), a musically coarser ending in comparison with Puccini's original conception. A partial renovation of the very old Met production (which dated back to the beginning of the century) had shifted the attic stairs to the front left of the stage (as Milton Cross informs us in his radio commentary), meaning that the none-too-airy ascent to the top B is decidedly audible, as is the applause that breaks out before the joint high note has terminated.

Rodolfo has a less prominent role in the second act of the opera, but Björling—whose voice, now fully warmed-up, has seldom sounded so handsome—seizes every opportunity to shine. His exchanges with Mimì, revealing the poet's tenderness and incipient jealousy (one notices the painful vehemence of "Chi guardi?"), are well captured by the radio microphone and in the brief solo in which he introduces her to his friends the minimal accompaniment enables us to enjoy the perfect intonation and equalization of the sounds he makes, together with the impetuous buoyancy of the phrases, delivered with the sort of impromptu exuberance typical of the character. The arioso "Dal mio cervel sbocciano i canti" speaks as much of Puccini's creative imagination as of Rodolfo's, and the composer could hardly have found a better spokesman than Björling. This solo is a highlight of Gigli's complete recording too, but the sentimental cast of his phrasing compromises the purity of the melodic line, suggesting a rather inferior level of poetic inspiration. While Marcello, Schaunard and Colline poke fun at Rodolfo's high-flown language, their deflating irony serves more to maintain the right expressive balance within this festive act than to undermine the sincerity of the poet, who further expounds his philosophy of art and life in the brief episode commenting on the purchase of Mimì's bonnet (which Puccini added for the Palermo production two months after the 1896 premiere). Here too Björling sings with total conviction, while his jealous warning to Mimì ("Sappi, per il tuo governo, che non darei perdono in sempiterno") is understated, partly because Antonicelli fails to bring this phrase into sufficient relief. Rodolfo's light-hearted comments in the rest of the act are largely absorbed into the ensemble, which moves forward with engaging vivacity.

The opening scene of act 3 is the only episode in the opera during which Rodolfo remains off-stage (asleep on a bench in the adjacent cabaret), but after his entrance Puccini assigns him some of the most expressive music ever penned for tenor voice. Once one has heard Björling perform this music it can be difficult to associate it with any other singer. This effect is partly attributable to the extraordinarily limpid quality of his instrument (purer in emission than Pavarotti's, stylistically unsullied in comparison with Gigli's, richer in overtones than Di Stefano's,[53] more musically responsive than Raimondi's[54]), which enables the words—bitter and sarcastic at first—to register vividly within a perfectly drawn legato line. No less extraordinary here is the tenor's ability to identify with the complex personality of the character he is playing. The dialogue with Marcello shows Rodolfo being gradually compelled to lay bare his soul to his friend. The candor and beauty of Björling's timbre in "Invan, invan nascondo"—where the music shifts from the ambivalent minor mode to an open-hearted major—stir the listener deeply, while "Mimì è tanto malata" reveals the sorrowful compassion felt by Rodolfo for the woman he loves, and his ascents above the staff have a ringing intensity that clings to the memory. Perhaps a little too much of this full-bodied sound is heard in the opening section of the concluding quartet, which is not sung with the full range of nuance of which he was capable. Few tenors, however, have matched the quality of the *mezza voce* he releases as if by magic on the top As of "carezze" and "fior."

Act 4 opens with Puccini's only real duet for tenor and baritone, a bittersweet scene in which Rodolfo and Marcello reveal the emotional discomfort caused by the infidelity of Mimì and Musetta. The tenor also gives expression to composer's own nostalgia for the passing of youth ("mia breve gioventù"). "O Mimì, tu più non torni," an elegiac *Andantino mosso,* consists of simultaneous asides by voices that sing increasingly in unison. It is well-suited to Björling, who had performed this duet in concerts with the Swedish baritone Einar Larson in April 1935. Both he and Valentino are here rather over-generous in volume, however: their phrasing is lusty (the two very different timbres blend well), but lacking in chiaroscuro. It is a pity that the tenor sings "odorossi" instead of "odorosi," and that the baritone takes the penultimate note of the *Andantino* (an E above the staff) down an octave, thus breaking the effect of the unison. The first part of the duet, an *Allegro vivo,* is very much alive, and Björling captures the depth of feeling masked behind Rodolfo's feigned indifference to Marcello's taunts.

This playfulness returns to the fore in the scherzo-like scene in which the four Bohemians exorcise their poverty through play-acting: a mock banquet followed by a parodic dance sequence that rapidly "degenerates" into a mock duel. Rodolfo's imitation of an elderly gallant ("vezzosa damigella") draws a hilariously senile timbre from Björling, a reminder of how responsive his voice was to the most varied coloristic requirements. He responds with equal flexibility to the emotional demands of the final scene. One is struck in particular by the melting desperation with which he attempts to warm Mimì's hands ("Qui nelle mie!"); by his ability to make even a simple descending interval of a third ("No! No!") into a thing of beauty, and by the gentle stillness with which he shares with Sayão the recollections of their first encounter. Björling's capacity for stillness on stage—making gestures only when indispensable—was one of his strengths as an actor. This quality, perceptible in the voice as well as the body, is particularly necessary in the final scene of *La bohème,* where the attention is rightly focused on the dying woman and the feelings of the poet are conveyed as much through the orchestra as through the vocal line.

Four months before the Met broadcast Björling had performed the opera for the first time with his wife. The performance—a Red Cross gala at the

Royal Opera—went well and encouraged the couple to perform together on a number of other occasions over the next few years, in both opera and concert. The first of these occasions was a studio recording of "O soave fanciulla" made with Grevillius in August 1949. Anna-Lisa sings with correct diction and commands an appreciable purity of tone in the upper octave, but her phrasing as Mimì is stiff and Björling is not at his most imaginative. He joins his wife on the top C at the end of the scene, probably in order to support her in that highly exposed phrase, and his very fine *mezzo piano* note—no less beautiful than the C sung in *falsettone* by Gigli in his 1919 recording[55] with Maria Zamboni—blends ideally with hers. Later that month they performed the duet in public at the Hollywood Bowl. Anna-Lisa is tremulous at times but her husband phrases more sensitively here, with a *piano* attack on "Fremon nell'anima," and they both cope well with the final note. This duet was preceded by a satisfyingly virile performance of Rodolfo's Romanza in the original key, much sunnier in tone than the 1941 or 1945 recordings.

A month later, Björling was recorded in the act 1 finale of a complete performance of *La bohème* at the War Memorial Opera House in San Francisco, conducted by Karl Kritz. It is the only time he can be heard in an extract from this opera with the soprano who was most strongly identified with the role of Mimì in America at that time, Licia Albanese. Her voice is notably fresher here than in her later recordings of *Manon Lescaut* and her interpretation, though in some respects dated, is more compelling than Sayão's. Björling interacts with Mimì more gently than in the Met broadcast, but he again transposes the Romanza downward (sharpening the top B). In "O soave fanciulla," on the other hand, they both ascend effortlessly to the top C and Björling's phrasing is caressing in tone and subtle in dynamics. Only this final part of the scene has so far been released.[56]

After his last opera performance in San Francisco, he was again broadcast from the War Memorial Opera House in a *Standard Hour* concert, which included another winningly Italianate rendition of the Romanza. His top C is not only more thrilling than the B sung in the same house a month earlier, but also bound more evenly than usual into the arching phrase. In the duet that follows, though Björling is less sensitive to dynamic markings than he was with Albanese, Anna-Lisa offers her most relaxed and persuasive performance so far.

After the tenor's return to New York, the Romanza featured in another radio broadcast, which must surely rate as one of his finest ever: the *Bell Telephone Hour* conducted by Donald Voorhees on November 7. Once again the phrasing is theatrically compelling (crowned by a resplendent, six-second top C).

Five months later the husband and wife team performed Puccini's duet on television for *The Voice of Firestone*. Both of them are in evening dress—with his tails, pursed lips, and brillantined hair, Björling looks like the caddish leading man in a drawing-room drama—and the scene is acted out in a stylized fashion: the two singers face each other at first as they gradually close in for a kiss, and then turn embracing toward the camera. Anna-Lisa looks uncomfortable most of the time, but begins to relax in the second half of the scene, where the higher tessitura shows off her voice to better effect. Björling sings with rare delicacy, capturing the intimacy of the emotional atmosphere, although he truncates the top C before his wife does. His facial expression and movements are completely at one with the music and the physical production of the voice: it is striking how much sensual abandon he manages to convey here, even though he makes no real attempt to render the specific character of Rodolfo.

At the beginning of 1951 the tenor recorded two selections from *La bohème* for RCA in New York. On January 3 he performed the C major duet from the fourth act with Merrill. It is smoothly delivered, with more dynamic variety in the *Andantino mosso* than one hears in the live Met recording with Valentino, but the opening dialogue is lacking in theatrical vitality (Merrill is a bit of a stick and Björling slips up on a couple of words). Although the voices blend and there are some euphonious moments, such as the joint descending portamento to the tonic at the end of the duet, this performance is inferior to the scenes from *Otello, La forza del destino* and *Les pêcheurs de perles* recorded on the same day.

Björling's second studio recording of "Che gelida manina," made on January 13, is a more interesting performance, one of his most richly humane so far in its balance between Italian fervor and Swedish inwardness. The opening phrase is sensitively voiced and the rest of the aria unfolds persuasively, although the high C resonates less spectacularly than in recent live performances and the conclusion is not ideally intimate. Better still is the concert rendition relayed from the Royal Academy in Stockholm three months later. Although the sheer beauty of his tone production is dulled by the slightly scratchy recording and the portamento on "Talor" ascends with less grace than usual, the expressive balance archieved in the New York studio is maintained and the upper register rings out more frankly. Overall one notes a greater variety of phrasing and a more impromptu delivery of the text.

More than four years were to pass before another recording was made of Björling's Rodolfo. During this period the tenor began to feel increasingly comfortable with the semitone transposition in the Romanza. There is nothing scandalous about this—as already noted, it was very much part of the Met's performing tradition, while Puccini himself transposed Rodolfo's music for the creator of the role in Turin, Evan Gorga, and both De Lucia and Caruso followed suit—although it obviously means that when Mimì repeats the opening line of "Che gelida manina" in the final scene of the opera the musical reminiscence is no longer in the same key. The aria is the final encore in Björling's 1955 Carnegie Hall recital. Although RCA released most of this recital on LP in the 1950s, "Che gelida manina" was first published as recently as 2003, and it is immediately clear why the tenor originally rejected it. Schauwecker's accompaniment is routine, and while the voice functions fairly well at softer dynamics, it tends to tighten up whenever extra volume is required. This is one of the rare Björling recordings in which the break that separates the chest from the head register is clearly perceptible. The culminating top B functions better than the other high notes and the phrasing maintains its musical dignity, but the interpretation has never sounded so lackluster.

The voice is better integrated in a 1956 televised staging of the act 1 finale, using a set provided by the Metropolitan Opera House. The program was the ninety-minute *Producer's Showcase: A Festival of Music,* promoted by Sol Hurok. It featured some of the leading classical artists of the 1950s accompanied by the Symphony of the Air under the baton of Max Rudolf, who remembers the show being mounted in a "barn" of a studio on Long Island.[57] The scene from *Bohème* is the longest of all the excerpts and the highlight of the program. Björling is partnered here by Renata Tebaldi, but the telecast proves more revealing as a documentation of their individual approaches to roles they had made their own, rather than as a souvenir of a stimulating artistic partnership. A number of things limit the credibility of their interaction. The scene begins logically enough with the trilling flute of the orchestral *Allegretto* accompanying Rodolfo's attempt to write an article for *Il Castoro,* but the knock on the door is followed incongruously by a forty-eight-measure cut to Mimì's "Oh! sventata, sventata!": we thus miss the poetry of the initial encounter between the two *bohémiens* and it understandably takes the singers some time to create the right atmosphere of intimacy. It is immediately evident, moreover, that the thirty-three-year-old Tebaldi looks not only much younger than the forty-four-year-old Björling, as one might expect, but also much healthier: she towers almost imperiously over the tenor while he is groping for the key and delivers all her music on a decidedly grand scale, singing her aria more to an imagined gallery than to the young poet with whom Mimì is supposed to be gradually falling in love. The tenor has aged considerably since we last saw him in an extract from *Bohème* six years earlier: his movements are now those of a portly middle-aged man and when he allows his body to relax after finishing the Romanza we can read a certain weariness on his face, as well as the desire to show interest in Mimì's narrative. Nevertheless, "Che gelida manina" is much more winning than at the Carnegie Hall in 1955 and the orchestral accompaniment naturally brings out richer overtones in the voice. Björling starts it in a kneeling position, but stands for most of the narration: after inviting Mimì to take a seat (very much the nineteenth-century gentleman), he picks up a copy of *Il Castoro* when he reveals his profession, draws close to Mimì for "due ladri: gli occhi belli," and puts a shawl round her shoulders when she has a brief coughing fit. Since the voice hardly shows signs of age—Björling offers a fine, manly execution of the Romanza, which begins very gently, ends with particularly urgency and crests on a generous B—the performance works well on its own terms, particularly if we focus as much (as the cameras invite us to do) on Tebaldi's often radiantly smiling reaction as on the tenor's face and gestures. In "O soave fanciulla," attacked immediately after Mimì's aria, Björling seems newly energized (he approaches Mimì much as he did in the *Firestone* broadcast), bracing himself to measure up to the rich outpouring of the soprano's voice. None of his soprano partners heard thus far in this music can equal the enveloping sensuality of the Tebaldi sound, particularly in "Tu sol comandi, amore." The two voices are well matched in their evenness of tone, clarity of diction and generous use of portamento, and throughout the duet one delights in the sheer luxuriance of the blending timbres, even though the dynamics do not always tally with Puccini's markings. The interaction of the two singers conveys a degree of ceremony and reserve that is no longer fashionable with modern directors (unlike Anna-Lisa, Tebaldi withdraws her lips just as Jussi is about to kiss her), but their gestures never contradict the spirit of the music (suspension of disbelief is required only when Rodolfo addresses this rather tall Mimì as "mia piccina"), and one senses the two singers feeling increasingly comfortable in each other's company.

After viewing the NBC telecast, we might not anticipate any new insights from Björling's subsequent performances as Rodolfo, so it is a joy to discover that his most satisfying interpretation of the role is the one immortalized in the Beecham recording made just two months later. The sessions were arranged at the last minute (there were no piano rehearsals) and some had to be sandwiched between Björling's performances of *Manon Lescaut* and *Tosca* at the Metropolitan. Beecham's vision of the Puccini score—which he had conducted more than three hundred times in the early decades of his career—was colored by his conversations with the composer, who had visited London in 1920 to check on a new production of *Il trittico* at Covent Garden. As Beecham told Irving Kolodin, "What I have undertaken to do in this recording represents—as Puccini indicated in my own score—his view of this earlier work not many years before he died."[58]

One of the most immediately striking aspects of this *Bohème*, particularly if one compares it to performances led by Italian conductors in the preceding decades, is the leisurely pace at which the opera unfolds (the recording is fourteen minutes longer than Toscanini's)—a pace that does indeed suggest an older man's savoring of a score written in his youth. Both Björling and his Mimì, Victoria de los Angeles, succeed in impregnating Illica's and Giacosa's drama of youthful high spirits and tragic loss with a deep glow of nostalgia. *La bohème* is indeed a deeply nostalgic work, in which Puccini mingles the gritty realism and all-too-fallible characters of Murger's novel with the idealized memories of his own youth as a struggling composer in Milan. In the third act Marcello accuses Rodolfo of being "geloso, colerico, lunatico, imbevuto di pregiudizi, noioso, cocciuto," but only the first of these defects finds resonant expression in Puccini's music, just as Mimì's relationships with other men are never brought to the fore. There is always a risk that the principal characters may become over-sentimentalized, and this was surely what obsessed Toscanini in his urgently narrated yet drily monochromatic NBC recording. The English conductor, by contrast, avoids sentimentality by working with singers of rare refinement: it would be hard to imagine two more consumate musicians than Björling and de los Angeles in the principal roles, and the other members of the cast compensate with their musical suavity and vocal accomplishment for what they lack in idiomatic ease (there were no Italians in the cast). Only the Swiss bass Corena disappoints with his self-indulgent deviations from the written notes in the roles of Benoit and Alcindoro.

Beecham's opening *Allegro vivace* lacks the fizzy ebullience of Antonicelli's attack, but the orchestral playing has a sheen and buoyancy typical of Beecham's work and although Björling's voice sounds less rich and ringing in the studio ambience than in the Met eight years earlier, the spacious tempo enables him to capture better than ever the imaginative flair of the poet. Rodolfo's exchanges with Marcello are less sharply ironical, but gain in whimsical lyricism (although the slow tempo exposes an egregious error of gender when he silences Colline with "zitta" rather than "zitto"). Merrill is not at first as vivid a partner as Valentino, and it is not hard to find recorded performances that sound more crisply colloquial than this one in the opening scene (Pavarotti and Rolando Panerai are splendid here in their Decca recording). Few, however, are as musically beguiling: even the tale of Milord and his parrot (John Reardon offers a well-drawn Schaunard) unfolds here to charming effect.

In a studio recording it is possible to spotlight instrumental details that pass almost unnoticed in live performance, and the poetic intensity of Björling's singing in the second half of the act is inspired not only by Beecham's willingness to let the music breathe, but also by the often exquisite accompaniment. The sweetness of the solo violin (played by concertmaster Oscar Shumsky) that accompanies him in "io resto per terminar l'articolo di fondo del *Castoro*" encourages the tenor to spin out the phrase in honeyed tones. In the scene that follows Björling succeeds in articulating the Italian text with the lyrical inwardness that more typically characterized his interpretations in his mother tongue, with the advantage of being able to respect the original sonorities and note values. This is the first recording in which he encounters a Mimì who not only understands what he is doing expressively, but is able to respond with equal sensitivity. De los Angeles enters wholeheartedly into Puccini's atmosphere of magical intimacy, combining a striking purity of diction with a breathtaking loveliness of timbre that constantly reflects the orchestral colorings. The soprano often mirrors the radiant string tone while the tenor picks up the plaintive sound of the wind instruments: a sustained B for the oboe, for example, is echoed immediately in "Ed ora come faccio?" The harmonically telling phrase that follows, "Che viso d'ammalata," has rarely sounded at once so moving and so instrumentally pure. Björling achieves exactly the right expressive balance in "Che bella bambina!" conveying the exclamatory warmth of feeling without betraying the aside, and this atmosphere is maintained in the second part of the dialogue, in spite of the brisker pace and wider dynamic range.

Beecham and his orchestra envelop Rodolfo's Romanza in a dreamily romantic aura, with the harp and flute more prominent than usual, encouraging the tenor to exploit his head resonance to lend an extra degree of airiness of the poet's flights of fancy. This is the only Italian language recording in which Björling observes the diminuendo on the top B-flat of "chi son," and immediately afterward he pronounces "Son un poeta" with a modest caress, lending extra credibility to a statement that often sounds matter-of-fact. Never before has he expounded Rodolfo's philosophy of life with such unforced lyricism ("In povertà mia lieta"), his *dolce e legato* singing appearing a natural response to the dulcet caress of the accompanying strings. The soft dynamics in the opening part of the aria make "Talor dal mio forziere" even more heartwarming by contrast, and the subsequent ascent to top C is graceful and luminous, if less dazzling and prolonged than in some earlier performances. It was clearly Beecham's decision to keep the music moving here (he was aware of Puccini's dislike of self-indulgent fermatas): in the theater such displays may be justified by the special physical tension they generate, but on disc the extra duration counts for little; it is more important that the note itself should be of fine quality and bound elegantly within the phrase. Björling is also at his best in the final measures (sung much more softly than in the 1951 Cellini recording), bringing to a graceful conclusion one of his most memorable interpretations of Rodolfo's *racconto.* This performance has few rivals even when compared to the finest postwar recordings by Italian tenors. Di Stefano (who recorded the opera with Antonino Votto that very year), Raimondi (who is best heard in a 1962 studio version of the aria),[59] and Pavarotti (who is characteristically engaging in the Karajan recording) combine considerable beauty of timbre with an idiomatic immediacy of expression that Björling could never quite equal. Roberto Alagna, the finest Rodolfo of recent years, is as emotionally sensitive as any of these in his 1999 recording, though his voice, however beautiful, is less solidly supported on the breath and less instantly recognizable. Arguably none of them, however, can rival the Swedish tenor in terms of musical refinement or poetic inwardness of expression. The only Italian tenor of recent decades who does phrase with comparable finish, Carlo Bergonzi (superb in his 1957 recital), sounds emotionally reserved and almost formal in approach: the beginning of the aria is exquisitely hushed, but the vowel sounds are more covered than Björling's and the character, rather than speaking with emotional frankness, seems to be consciously maintaining a certain distance from Mimì.

"O soave fanciulla" is another highlight of the Beecham recording. The tenor and soprano combine delicacy of phrasing and tonal iridescence, and the conductor seems intent on bringing out the finest qualities of the singers, who listen to each other intently. When Rodolfo sings "In te ravviso il sogno che vorrei sempre sognare!" we sense an impressive verbal eloquence, drawing inspiration from the deepest of feelings. The conclusion of the act is as atmospheric as in any of Björling's recordings of this music, with the tenor settling quietly on the mediant while the soprano ascends to the tonic.

In the second act, Björling's voice displays a silvery aura that is markedly melancholy, in contrast with the golden-hued extroversion of eight years earlier. It is almost as if Rodolfo has sensed from the start that the relationship with Mimì cannot last, and this lends greater logic to phrases such as "Sappi per il tuo governo," which are further thrown into relief by the close microphone placement and spacious tempo. Rodolfo's presentation of Mimì to his friends is less exciting but more lyrically expansive than before. In the same way the skirmishes between Marcello and Musetta are less colorful than with Valentino and Benzell, but clearer in meaning because the conductor allows more time for the words to register.

Other conductors, such as the elderly Gavazzeni, have proved more sensitive than Beecham to the bleak wintry atmosphere of the third-act opening, but Björling once again reveals an exceptional depth of feeling in the duet with Marcello and subsequent trio. Even though he cannot quite equal the sheer intensity of tone and utterance achieved with Antonicelli, he brings a singularly mournful quality to "Mimì è tanto malata," thanks to Beecham's chilling rendering of the *Lento triste* 2/4 rhythm. No less telling is the intensity of the cellos' *messa di voce* accompanying "Essa canta e sorride," and the inwardness of expression (as if Rodolfo were thinking aloud) conveyed in "Mimì di serra è fiore." The tender self-deceptions of the duet between Rodolfo and Mimì, which unfolds as if time has been suspended, beguile the listener too (the interchanges of Marcello and Musetta are not allowed to destroy the mood of harmony created). The beauty of de los Angeles's phrasing and the wistful accompaniment encourage Björling to surpass himself here.

Merrill's Marcello improves as the opera moves forward and his fourth-act duet is much more lively than in 1951, although he still cannot equal Valentino's caustic humor in the opening *Allegro vivo*. The subsequent *Andantino mosso* is comparable in beauty with the Di Stefano-Panerai performance in their 1956 recording, although the Sicilian's diction is more telling than Björling's, who nevertheless avoids his former pronunciation errors. The play-acting episode that follows works very well and Björling's "vezzosa damigella" is again genuinely funny, while in the final scene Beecham's well-judged tempos highlight the exceptional musicality of Björling's phrasing, the secret sadness of "Zitta, riposa," and the yearning quality of "sempre, sempre." The only disappointment is his inconclusive conducting of the interlude that precedes "Sono andati?" during which the orchestra should tell us clearly what Rodolfo is feeling, even though the character remains silent (Karajan makes much more of this moment). The rest of the act however is movingly accompanied and as beautifully sung as any performance on disc, and after the death of Mimì one is struck (as in the 1948 broadcast) by Björling's unrhetorical directness of expression. We may recall at this point that the tenor's mother, Ester Sund, had died of tuberculosis when he was still a boy, and that the six-year-old Jussi had sung at her graveside during the funeral service in Stora Tuna, on April 30, 1917. Although his memories of his mother were understandably faint, that was not the sort of experience he could easily forget.

Three months after finishing the Beecham recording, the tenor sang "Che gelida manina" during an open recital in Gröna Lund. The Romanza is once again taken down a semitone (Björling never performed it again in public in the original key) and at the lower pitch the voice sounds darker, with a hint of muscularity in the upper register, but much healthier than in the 1955 Carnegie Hall recital.

More musically revealing is the recording of Puccini's opera made in the Stadsteater in Malmö fourteen months later. It was the only time Björling sang a complete opera in this house, which had been inaugurated in 1944, and the new production was presented as part of a Swedish-Italian music week. It was thus perhaps appropriate that the performance should be bilingual, with the star tenor singing in Italian and the rest of the cast in Swedish. This alternation certainly didn't dampen the enthusiasm of the critic Sten Broman, who considered this *Bohème* "the most grandiose opera performance ever given here," praising Björling both for his acting and for his "*bel canto* singing" that "poured forth with a previously seldom heard richness and suggestivity, also in half-voice and in the finest pianissimo, and the most intense parts had a magnetic fire and at the same time a fascinating refinement."[60] Broman's words are borne out by the in-house recording (the microphone was placed by the prompter's box) of three of the four acts, which demonstrates how incapable Björling was of delivering a routine interpretation in this opera, even after he had performed it in public more than a hundred times, and how flexible he still was in adapting to the tempos of different conductors. Sten Åke Axelson takes some scenes even slower than Beecham: "Che gelida manina"—a pensively melancholy reading—lasts almost as long as the 1945 performance under Tor Mann, while "Mimì di serra è fiore" registers as a desolate lament that transcends its dramatic context. Throughout this third act, where the climaxes above the staff are as vibrantly sustained as ever, one is struck by the sheer humanity of Björling's portrayal, by that capacity for feeling that is the secret of every great interpretative artist. This quality is much more important than mere musical correctness, which is why the tenor's rare slip below the indicated pitches at the end of the (rather awkward) phrase "Me, cagion del fatale mal che l'uccide!" passes almost unnoticed. Another deviation from the score comes at the very end of the opera, where the second cry of "Mimì!" is transformed into an anguished sob that speaks eloquently of the involvement of the singer. Björling had watched his father die three decades earlier, and he shared this knowedge with the audience every time he sang this opera.

The opening scene of the opera is omitted on the CD release and indeed we find nothing new in Björling's performance here: the constant switching between languages tends to dampen the comedy (Axelson's pace is rather too ponderous). But the initial dialogue with Mimì (a luminous and sensitive Ethel Mårtensson) is treasurable, similar in atmosphere to the Beecham recording.

Björling sang the role of Rodolfo on stage almost every year from his 1934 debut until his death twenty-six years later. The sole exception was 1959, but even that year he continued to sing "Che gelida manina" in concert: his last recording of music from this opera is the Romanza performed as an encore during his Atlanta recital in April. As one might expect, the mood conveyed by Rodolfo on this occasion is a buoyant one. We hear the audience laughing heartily before the tenor announces the aria, and this good humor is reflected in the amber elegance of his unhurried phrasing, warmly building to a splendid climax.

Rumor has it that someone may have taped one of Björling's final performances in *Bohème* at Covent Garden in 1960, but no recording has surfaced. It seems in any case appropriate to end this survey in the cheerful atmosphere of Atlanta rather than in the chill of an English winter, six months before the tenor's death. Björling was a very sick man in London—on March 15 he heroically sang the entire opera after suffering what now seems to have been an severe attack of atrial fibrillation—and sickness is antithetical to Rodolfo. The poet is very much a survivor (Murger's novel includes a postlude which hints at his comfortable apartment and the success of a book he has written): the horror he experiences is that of a healthy man watching helplessly as the woman he loves succumbs to a fatal disease. Yet despite Björling's fragility in this final London season, critic Philip Hope-Wallace's review of the first night described the "riding strength" of the climax of the Romanza, with the tenor "turning his head and as it were spinning the note right out round the house."[61] This sort of effect is associated with some of the great *fin de siècle* singers such as Mattia Battistini, but has rarely been attempted in recent decades, as critic Robert Baxter certified in his recollection of a Björling *Bohème* in San Francisco in October 1958:

> Lingering lovingly on the high note, he slowly turned his face from one side of the stage to the other. When he aimed his voice directly at where I was sitting, a golden beam of sound shot through the dark and lit up the house with its incandescent glow. Four decades and countless *Bohèmes* later, I have still not felt the same physical sensation Björling's voice caused. No other tenor I've heard sing Rodolfo—not Tucker, nor Di Stefano, not Gedda, not Corelli, not Pavarotti, Domingo, or Carreras, not Alagna—has matched that magical moment.[62]

This sort of experience cannot really be conveyed on disc—although we have ample recorded evidence of Björling lingering generously on that top note—but it reminds us that great operatic singing is not simply a matter of interpreting the music codified in the score. It is also about exploiting the full potential of the human body as a musical instrument and projecting sounds that vibrate in the air, producing specific physical sensations when they are absorbed (not only through the ears) by those who are listening. An experience that is at once more elemental, and more spiritually rarefied, than straightforward "musical appreciation."

Tosca
Complete Recordings

July 2–18, 1957: Rome, Teatro dell'Opera
Jussi Björling (Cavaradossi), Zinka Milanov (Tosca), Leonard Warren (Scarpia), Fernando Corena (Sagrestano), Leonardo Monreale (Angelotti); Rome Opera Chorus and Orchestra, cond. Erich Leinsdorf
RCA 09026-63305-2

November 21, 1959: New York, Metropolitan Opera House
Jussi Björling (Cavaradossi), Mary Curtis-Verna (Tosca), Cornell MacNeil (Scarpia), Lawrence Davidson (Sagrestano), Norman Scott (Angelotti); Metropolitan Opera Chorus and Orchestra, cond. Dimitri Mitropoulos
House of Opera CD9175

Acts 1–2
April 4, 1956: New York, Metropolitan Opera House
Jussi Björling (Cavaradossi), Zinka Milanov (Tosca), Walter Cassel (Scarpia), Gerhard Pechner (Sagrestano), Clifford Harvuot (Angelotti); Metropolitan Opera Chorus and Orchestra, cond. Dimitri Mitropoulos
House of Opera CD9167

Acts 2–3
February 12, 1959: Stockholm, Royal Opera House
Jussi Björling (Cavaradossi), Kjerstin Dellert (Tosca), Arne Wirén (Scarpia); Royal Swedish Opera Chorus and Royal Court Orchestra, cond. Nils Grevillius
Bluebell 078; Caprice CAP 22063

"Recondita armonia"

November 13, 1933: Stockholm, Concert Hall
Unspecified orchestra, cond. Nils Grevillius
Naxos 8.110722

December 3, 1936: Stockholm
Unspecified orchestra, cond. Nils Grevillius
Naxos 8.110701

December 5, 1937: New York, Carnegie Hall
General Motors Symphony Orchestra, cond. Erno Rapee
WHRA-6036

September 12, 1950: Stockholm, Royal Academy of Music
Swedish Radio Orchestra, cond. Nils Grevillius
EMI 5 75900 2

"E lucevan le stelle"

November 13, 1933: Stockholm, Concert Hall
Unspecified orchestra, cond. Nils Grevillius
Naxos 8.110722

September 4, 1937: Stockholm, Concert Hall
Unspecified orchestra, cond. Nils Grevillius
Naxos 8.110701

July 10, 1943: Stockholm, Royal Academy of Music
Stockholm Radio Orchestra, cond. Sixten Ehrling
Bluebell ABCD 103

September 12, 1950: Stockholm, Royal Academy of Music
Swedish Radio Orchestra, cond. Nils Grevillius
EMI 5 75900 2

October 1, 1950: Berlin, Titania Palast
RIAS-Orchestra, cond. Kurt Gaebel
Urania 22.165

September 30, 1951: San Francisco, War Memorial Opera House
San Francisco Opera Orchestra, cond. Gaetano Merola
WHRA-6036

September 24, 1955: New York, Carnegie Hall
Frederick Schauwecker, pf.
RCA 88697748922

December 14, 1955: New Orleans, Municipal Auditorium
Frederick Schauwecker, pf.
VRCS-2007

March 2, 1958: New York, Carnegie Hall
Frederick Schauwecker, pf.
RCA 60520-2-RG

January 4, 1959: London, Palladium
Ivor Newton, pf.

The French playwright Victorien Sardou was impressed when Luigi Illica visited him in Paris in 1894 and showed him the compact three-act Italian libretto he had derived from Sardou's five-act drama, *La Tosca*, which had first been staged at the Théâtre de la Porte-Saint-Martin (with Camille Dumény as Cavaradossi) seven years earlier. The revised version of that libretto (with some serious rewriting by Giuseppe Giacosa), set to music by Puccini in 1898–99, is indeed an ably crafted piece of theater in which—if one excepts the emptily rhetorical close to the third-act duet—every detail is calculated to heighten narrative tension. The plot is melodramatic rather than tragic because it is the thrill of the murder (Scarpia), two suicides (Angelotti and Tosca), interrogation, torture, and execution (Cavaradossi) that transfix the spectator, rather than any catharsis-inducing pity for the characters involved. Indeed the action in the opera is so rapid and character-development reduced to such a minimum (Cavaradossi is not even given time to apologize for cursing Tosca after her betrayal, as he is in Sardou's play) that those who see the opera numerous times tend to seek extra stimuli to compensate for the loss of suspense. The performance history of *Tosca* tells us that these stimuli are often of a fetishistic nature: vocal exploits—the tenor's sustained cry of victory in the face of Scarpia in act 2; the soprano's prolonged top C followed by an unwritten plunge into the chest voice during her third-act narrative—and sweeping gestures that tend to bring to the fore the unmistakable personalities of the performers more than the characters portrayed. This explains why Puccini's fifth opera has been widely parodied and often treated with critical disdain. Yet when musically inspired singing actors collaborate with a conductor who believes in the drama, those same characters can acquire a credibility that extends (in our imagination) beyond the duration of their presence on stage.

"Singing actor" is not a term one would usually apply to Björling, particularly at the beginning of his career when his minimal stagecraft was often censured by Stockholm critics. As his wife put it, "He had an intuitive feeling for acting, but the emotions reflected in his face were effective only at a short range: they were too subtle to communicate beyond the footlights, and he couldn't project them through posture and movement."[63] Nevertheless, when the tenor first sang Cavaradossi at the Royal Opera in October 1933 (his first major Puccini role), his acting was praised as well as his singing. Teddy Nyblom opined that the "top notes had a splendor reminiscent of Caruso and there was an Italian verve to his singing and acting: one would have to go very far back in our opera's annals to find a performance comparable to this one."[64]

Less than a month later, the tenor recorded both of Cavaradossi's arias with Grevillius (who had conducted the debut performance) and it is immediately clear how congenial he found the role. The singing, in Swedish translation, has in truth relatively little in common with Caruso's (the Neapolitan recorded "Recondita armonia" twice and "E lucevan le stelle" five times in the first decade of the twentieth century), but displays to impressive effect the qualities that were unique to Björling. In particular one is struck, in the F major "Recondita armonia" (which Björling had sung on the radio as early as as March 1928), by the singular coloring of the reflective opening statement, graced with an Arcadian beauty that seems to draw inspiration from the flutes and clarinets in the orchestral introduction (which themselves evoke the brushstrokes of Cavaradossi upon the canvas). Björling is less daringly introspective here than De Lucia[65]—who floats the opening phrase in a *mezza voce* that respects Puccini's *piano* indication—but as pure song this beginning, assisted by a leisurely tempo, is hard to beat. He attacks the phrase *mezzo piano* and tapers away to a *pianissimo* (as the composer requests) in "l'ardente amante mia," a dynamic that heightens rather than reduces the tension because it reveals a genuine intimacy of feeling when Cavaradossi alludes to the woman he loves. Unlike the fifty-seven-year-old De Lucia, the voice of the twenty-two-year-old Björling releases sounds of crystalline beauty that truly evoke the "armonia" of the "bellezze diverse" that the artist observes while glancing from the small portrait of Tosca to his painting of Mary Magdalen. The expansive brilliance of his ascent to the top A in "e te baltade ignota" is however at variance with the composer's *piano* marking, investing the "unknown beauty" who inspired his painting with undue importance. Those tenors who follow the score more closely here (De Lucia, Giuseppe Anselmi,[66] and Jon Vickers[67]) deserve particular respect, for the aria gains enormously if it builds up slowly to the climax. The great majority of performers ascend to the top A in a full throated *forte,* but few of these can match the purely musical effect that Björling creates here, augmented by the abundance of dynamic shading in the rest of the phrase. Equally admirable is the pensive simplicity with which he delivers the recitative-like "l'arte nel suo mistero le diverse bellezze insiem confonde": the repeated Bs and As in the middle register highlight the purity of his vowels. At the same time the Swedish language accentuates the inherent melancholy in Björling's tone, which contrasts somewhat with the serene affirmation of Cavaradossi's mood and the hint of comedy suggested by the grumbling of the Sacristan (here omitted) that accompanies the aria. The ending, moreover, is slightly perfunctory. The attack on the top A of "ah! il mio solo pensier" is not entirely clean and the climactic B-flat is arguably held too briefly (although Björling is faithful here to Puccini's notation: the B-flat is only an eighth note and Puccini indicates an *allargando* rather than the fermata tradition would suggest).

The musical refinement of this performance nevertheless lends an appropriate dignity to Puccini's lover, who was educated in Paris and cultivates a courageous republicanism. This aspect of the character, which is of considerable significance in Sardou's play (where the painter's progressive political beliefs contrast markedly with Tosca's instinctive royalism) is in truth understated in the libretto, but the opera gains in dramatic cogency if Cavaradossi reveals from the start a nobility of sentiment that makes him seem capable of acts of self-sacrificing generosity.

The other dominant trait of the character is his strong erotic imagination, which is already implicit in "Recondita armonia" and becomes explicit in "E lucevan le stelle" in act 2. Sensuality is not easy to define in vocal terms (partly because different listeners perceive it in different ways), but it is an essential component of Cavaradossi's farewell to love and life, in which the artist recalls an amorous encounter with Tosca in his villa on the outskirts of Rome. The words naturally establish the erotic tension of the aria and from this point of view Björling was at an advantage, for his unclouded tone—which echoes the soulful sound of the solo clarinet that introduces the aria—makes every syllable tell. The opening lines are sung in a caressing *mezza voce* with colors that vary in response to the changing pitches of the phrases and the increasing closeness of the object of desire. Yet if we compare the texture of his voice to that of Caruso in his final recording made in 1909[68] or to that of Domingo in his 1980 *Tosca*[69] led by James Levine, we become aware of what is lacking: a rich, sultry density of sound that conveys full sensual awareness of the experience recalled. This was a quality that Björling never possessed to an overwhelming degree (his voice was fundamentally an innocent one), but came close to achieving in some later recordings of the aria. Here he can only offer an ingenuous approximation of that very adult sound. He may, however, have already heard Caruso's final recording of the aria, for the dynamics of his phrasing are in some ways similar, and would remain so until the early 1950s. Particularly notable in this regard is the ascent to the first A-natural (on "disciogliea") in a gleaming *forte*, with no hint of the diminuendo that singers such as De Lucia (1920)[70] and Fleta (1924)[71] had rendered traditional, and which is also hinted at in Caruso's 1904[72] rendition of the aria. In this earlier recording Caruso's voice is more supple and the style conserves some of the graces of an earlier era. Like De

Lucia, he embellishes the word "languide," an ornament that he eliminated five years later and is eschewed by more recent tenors, including Björling, who may never have heard this early disc with piano accompaniment.

As the focus of the character shifts from past to present ("muoio disperato!") Björling's singing, doleful in tone and meticulous in its observation of Puccini's tenuto markings, retains its instrumental purity and he opens up the sound on the culminating top A ("amato") to thrilling effect. There is no hint here of the sobbing that Puccini asks for at the end of the aria and that Caruso includes in his earlier recordings in a manner that proves disconcerting when removed from a theatrical context, but the emotional sincerity of the Swedish tenor's phasing is never in doubt.

Although *Tosca* was performed every season in Stockholm during the thirties, forties and fifties (and was a staple work at the Met too), Björling only sang Cavaradossi fifty-one times in all, mostly in the final fifteen years of his life. The probable reason for this is that the role is a relatively easy one and opera managers felt that the tenor's exceptional skills could be better exploited elsewhere. The three live performances of Björling's *Tosca* that are at least partially documented on disc were made during the last five years of his career, when his health was waning and he was no doubt happy to have fewer vocal challenges (but no less applause) ahead of him at the beginning of an evening.

Björling did not sing the whole role in Italian until December 1945, when he performed the opera at the Met for the first time, opposite Grace Moore. As early as October 1934, however, he had taken part in a bilingual performance in Stockholm with the Italo-American Dusolina Giannini, a very fine spinto soprano who sang the role of Tosca in the original language. Two years later, as his international career was taking off, he recorded "Recondita armonia" in Italian. The voice sounds more distant from the microphone, but the interpretative approach remains the same, although the Italian language invests the tone with a warmer hue, with little trace of melancholy and fewer echoes of the accompanying wind instruments. The tempo is slightly slower than in 1933 and this lends a wistful pensiveness to "Tosca ha l'occhio nero!" giving the impression of someone thinking aloud. "A te beltade ignota" is once again sung *forte* (as in all subsequent performances), but in the final measures Björling builds the crescendo slowly, releasing the tension on a B-flat that is sustained more generously than before, without any loss of aplomb. In later recordings the tenor would deliver the words with even greater confidence, but there are no pronunciation errors here, as there are in the recording of "E lucevan le stelle" made nine months later, where he stresses the wrong syllables—"*lu*cevan," "o*lez*zava"—in the opening recitative. His shaping of these lines is again musically delightful but lacking in sensuality. In the rest of the aria the phrasing is even more handsomely moulded than before, with similar dynamics but longer breath-spans (this is the only time on disc that Björling sings "le belle forme disciogliea dai veli" in one breath).

Figure 11. Cavaradossi and the Sacristan (Salvatore Baccaloni) during "Recondita armonia" in *Tosca*. Photograph by Louis Melançon. Courtesy of the Metropolitan Opera Archive.

His first live recording of an aria from this opera was made in December 1937 during a *General Motors* broadcast. "Recondita armonia" was the opening number, and the tenor uses it to show off his voice rather than to draw us into the character's imaginative world. The first measures are overloud and he fails to distinguish properly between the simple legato of "Recondita armonia" and the *tenuto* accents of "di bellezze diverse." His phrasing, however, does convey an extra degree of spontaneity, and the softer dynamics of the central section of the aria contrast effectively with the soaring climax, where he kicks up to the B-flat in typically tenorial fashion.

Björling did not perform *Tosca* on stage over the next four seasons, but his broadcast from the Royal Academy of Music in Stockholm in July 1943—the opening number of *Sweden Calling America*—reveals a more mature conception of "E lucevan le stelle," reflecting the greater experience of the man and artist and the increasingly adult solidity of his voice. He gets the stresses right in the opening recitative and above all delivers them in a markedly ardent manner. The vocal coach Luigi Ricci, who would later work with Björling on his RCA recording of *Tosca*, recalled the composer's insistence[73] on the need to invent specific vocal colors for the memories involving the senses of sight ("lucevan"), smell ("olezzava," "fragrante"), and sound ("stridea"), and to capture the inebriating effect of direct physical contact ("mi cadea fra le braccia . . ."). Björling goes quite a long way toward achieving this variety of expression here, making up in vividness of diction and instrumental finish (the echo of the clarinet) what he lacks in sheer sensuality of tone. What he fails to do is register clearly the contrast between erotic memories and the anguished sense of time running out, for both climaxes—with their differently articulated ascents to the A-natural—are still sung *forte*. The ascents are also broken in order to enable the tenor to snatch a breath before releasing the high note. While the breath before "disciogliea" is not in itself reprehensible (though here it is somewhat intrusive), the one before "amato" is syntactically (and musically) distracting, as it separates the auxiliary ("have") from the past participle ("loved"). Here too, however, Björling seems to have gained in emotional understanding of the full import of the words he is singing—he sounds truly desperate rather than simply rueful—and this sets the seal on his most expressively mature rendition of the lament so far.

In September 1950 the tenor returned to the studio to record Cavaradossi's two arias again with Grevillius. "Recondita armonia" is very fine indeed, with plenty of dynamic variety (although the tenor does not observe the *pianissimo* in "l'ardente amante mia") and a resounding conclusion: the phrasing is spacious and lovingly finished. "E lucevan le stelle" is similarly satisfying, although it is disappointing to hear a mispronunciation of "stridea" in the recitative, with the stress on the final rather than the second syllable (a recurrent error he probably picked up from Caruso's 1909 recording). The breath before "disciogliea" is not at all conspicuous this time and in the second climax Björling breathes only after "amato," lending greater shape to a phrase that is further enhanced by a more legato approach to the ascent with its *tenuto* markings on the rising eighth notes (in contrast with the *sforzando* requested during the subsequent descent). He also applies a vibrantly emotional coloring to the closing measures, suggesting barely suppressed tears without breaking the line; this solution would be maintained in future performances. It is interesting to compare this rendition with the interpretation by Di Stefano in his complete recording of the opera with Victor de Sabata (1953).[74] The Italian tenor's voice sounds much more lyrical but is no less beautiful than Björling's here, and his word stresses in the opening recitative are naturally eloquent in a manner that the Swede couldn't quite match. At the same time the younger tenor offers a less vivid timbral contrast between the low Fs of "E lucevan le stelle" and the Bs a third above ("e olezzava la terra") and he deviates unnecessarily from the written notes in "mi cadea fra le braccia . . ." Di Stefano's tone is strikingly intimate—though less well supported than Björling's—in "Oh! dolci baci," and on the top A of "disciogliea" he employs the traditional diminuendo to seductive effect. This device is not specifically prescribed in the score (where dynamic indications are vague), nor is it anticipated in the two orchestral statements of the melody (the second of which is assigned to the solo clarinet) that precede the sung version. Yet this very lack of specific indication is an extra reason for introducing an element of variety the third time round, while the meaning of the word "disciogliea," which helps us visualize Tosca slipping off her clothes while embracing Cavaradossi, itself suggests a diminuendo effect. The other advantage is that the dynamic modulations enable Di Stefano to emphasize the change in mood in the final section of the aria, where his "muoio disperato" (words penned by Puccini himself) rings with uncommon conviction and "e non ho amato mai tanto la vita" is encompassed within a single breath (a feat never attempted by Björling but matched by Placido Domingo and surpassed by Carlo Bergonzi, who introduces a crescendo on the top A).[75] As pure vocalism Di Stefano's version is less impeccable than Björling's, but as an interpretation it conveys a more vivid realization of the intensity and continually evolving nature of Cavaradossi's feelings, with equal elegance of phrasing.

Björling was possibly aware by 1950 that there was more to be got out of this music, for in a radio broadcast from Berlin a month later he attempts for the first time a slight diminuendo on the A-natural of "disciogliea." Unfortunately he breathes both before and after this key word and does the same with "amato" at the conclusion of the aria. No diminuendo is heard on the other hand in the 1951 San Francisco reading, but here the tenor seems to capture to a special degree the emotional fragility of the political prisoner in the face of death.

The next recording of the lament was made during the 1955 Carnegie Hall recital, and is strikingly different in approach. This may be motivated by replacement of the intoxicating sonorities of Puccini's orchestra with Schauwecker's piano accompaniment. As a result the listener focuses intently on every inflection of the vocal line, and since Björling's voice is not in its most luxuriant condition, he sensibly adopts a more lyrical approach. His half-voice remains effortless even though his full voice is not at its most resonant. Tell-tale signs of vocal unease do occasionally emerge—the *pianissimo* F-sharp at the top of the staff on "baci" only gradually gains its customary limpidity and the *fortissimo* climax on the A of "amato" sounds clenched—but in many ways this is a winning performance, closer in phrasing to Di Stefano than to Caruso (perhaps Björling had listened to his younger colleague's recording, for he expressed admiration for him on a number of occasions)[76] and all the more fascinating for that. The freedom granted by the piano accompaniment enables him to draw out the poetry of the recitative (he savors "Mi cadea fra le braccia" with particular fervor) and for the first time he attacks "disciogliea" *mezzo forte* and then fines it down to a diaphanous *pianissimo,* lingering both on the top A and on the subsequent G. In the final measures he compensates for the lack of ring with an extra degree of emotionalism, suggesting a tearful sound without becoming mawkish. The effect was almost identical when he sang "E lucevan le stelle" (as an encore once more) in his New Orleans recital. Here his emission is freer and more biting at the climax, and the diminuendo as magical as before.

The first recording of Björling singing Cavaradossi in the opera house was made just a few months later at the Met and immortalizes—in admittedly abysmal sound and with an over-prominent prompter—most of the first two acts of what was evidently an electrifying performance under Mitropoulos. This was an in-house recording (the first ever attempted at the Met), made in the same period in which Björling was broadcast in *Manon Lescaut* under Mitropoulos's leadership, and was putting the finishing touches to his recording of *La bohème* with Beecham. It is a pity that the quality of his phrasing in *Tosca* is sensed rather than heard in detail, for the performance set a new record for curtain calls at the Met, with Björling and Milanov (this was their first *Tosca* together) coming out to acknowledge applause twenty-five times in all.[77]

The surviving recording starts with the final measures of the *Angelus,* covered in part by the applause greeting Björling's entrance. During the opening exchanges with Gerhard Pechner's Sacristan, we are immediately aware of the tenor's excellent vocal condition and—in spite of the distortion—Mitropoulos's masterful narration. The conductor gives the impression throughout that he and the orchestra are sharing the emotional life of Cavaradossi, Tosca and Scarpia, while at the same time investing every phrase with a strong sense of dramatic momentum. As in *Manon Lescaut,* his beat varies in almost every measure, and he is instinctively aware of how much space each singer needs to bring out the essence of the character portrayed. Björling had always taken "Recondita armonia" fairly slowly (Puccini qualifies the *Andante lento* with a *più lento* at the beginning of the solo) and Mitropoulos encourages him here to give his most spacious reading so far, enabling the audience to get the measure not only of the singer but also of the character. Too often this aria is used by tenors as an opportunity to warm up their voices, but here Björling savors every phrase (with Pechner commenting in a lively fashion), maintaining the structural stability of the solo by reinforcing the legato with unobtrusive portamentos (he does this instinctively when a conductor stretches the tempo). The singing is on a grand scale and there are fewer dynamic nuances than in his first recording of this music made twenty-three years earlier, but the beauty of the voice is no less striking than before. Its texture is now amber-toned and decidedly adult: the low Fs of "amante mia" reveal a baritonal strength that speaks of genuine sensual awareness, while the prolonged and ringing B-flat at the climax demonstrates Björling's healthy desire to give the audience something to get excited about at the beginning of a performance. Interaction between the stage and the audience is an integral part of the dramaturgy of Italian opera, for an electrified audience transmits energy back to the singers on stage, helping them meet the challenges that follow with even greater expressive tension.

The tenor was suffering from a bad back on this occasion and this limited his range of movement: he was walked, rather than dragged, offstage after Cavaradossi's outburst in the second act and was tied to a stake for the execution in act 3, so that he wouldn't have to fall when shot. Yet nothing in his singing suggests that his mind was on anything but the feelings of Cavaradossi; in the first exchange with Angelotti he is rhythmically alert, and his words are delivered with striking urgency. There had been no rehearsals before the performance and Milanov remembered much later that Björling had been physically unresponsive during the long duet with Tosca in act 1—"He didn't want to be in love with me on the stage!"[78] Vocally, however, the two were well matched. The soprano is in luxuriant voice and here she captures not only the domineering character of the primadonna but also some of the spontaneous femininity of the woman in love. Although the microphone rarely conveyed the full magnificence of her sound, the voice projects easily in the large auditorium throughout this scene, without hardening or spreading. Björling responds in an equally generous manner, ably defusing Tosca's jealousy (his laughter is typically musical) and conveying the spontaneity of banter typical of Puccini's conversation scenes while shaping the line as firmly as ever. His verbal inflections are notably varied and idiomatic, which compensates in part for his occasional neglect of dynamic nuance. A high point is Cavaradossi's warm declaration of love, "Qual occhio al mondo," where the climactic phrase, "Occhio all'amor soave," rising from G-flat to B-flat above the staff, displays the tenor's ability to achieve an extra dimension of resonance when entering the top register. This is the kind of effect that the almost equally musical Carlo Bergonzi, who offers a wealth of expressive detail in his 1959 Met broadcast,[79] is unable to duplicate.

Even more stunning is the ascent to the B-natural (the highest note in this role) at the climax of Cavaradossi's denunciation of Scarpia in the subsequent dialogue with Angelotti: the note is held for a good six seconds and beams out into the auditorium. This second exchange with the escaped prisoner is initially as absorbing as the first, and when describing the chief of police Björling clearly conveys his moral disdain for the character without making the mistake (as Gigli does in the 1938 HMV recording)[80] of imitating a Scarpia sound. Di Stefano too fails to match Björling here: although the words carry conviction, the climax lacks heroic heft. Franco Corelli, in his London performance with Milanov in 1957,[81] proves a more formidable rival (and he possessed a perfect *physique du rôle*), but there is something narcisistic about his hanging on to the B that undermines the heroism of the sound itself. Corelli and Di Stefano excel on the other hand in the rapid instructions to Angelotti immediately afterward ("La cappella mette a un orto mal chiuso"), where Björling sounds noncommittal. This dialogue provides not only Angelotti but also the audience with valuable information, so the words must be delivered with a crispness that is not apparent here.

The recording of the second act begins just as Scarpia is starting to interrogate Cavaradossi. The tenor's voice is not always clearly audible during this scene, but he gives us some idea of the stoical courage of Puccini's hero, and this impression is reinforced during the torture scene offstage: the exceptionally musical rendering of his gestures of defiance ("Vi sfido!") and even of his cries of agony heightens our awareness of how nobly Cavaradossi resists torture. Only the very final cry—described by Puccini as a *straziante grido acuto*—is not sung on easily identifiable pitches: it is indeed a fearful, strangulated sound that makes Tosca's decision to reveal Angelotti's hiding place entirely comprehensible. This whole scene is magnificently sustained by Mitropoulos and boldly conceived by Milanov, although the top C—which came to her easily during the Cantata—proves a strain here. Walter Cassell, a solid American baritone, is robust of voice and projects words well as Scarpia, although he doesn't offer a particularly developed portrayal.

Cavaradossi's only solo in the second act is "Vittoria! Vittoria!," the exultant reaction to the news of the defeat of Melas in the battle against the Napoleonic troops at Marengo. Most tenors who attempt this part can manage three ringing high A-sharps on the second "Vittoria!" but it is rare to find one like Björling who, after sustaining those notes with theatrical bravado, drops down to the lower octave for "L'alba vindice appare" without any sense of anticlimax and then rises again with unflagging energy above the staff. The words are delivered with admirable vehemence in every register of the voice: rarely has Cavaradossi seemed such a formidable opponent to Scarpia, all the more courageous in that he is clearly signing his own death sentence with this impulsive political outburst and personal denunciation. The equalization of Björling's voice here enables us to perceive the character with a clarity that is often blurred by mere tenorial bluster (witness Corelli's crass oversinging in London). We can compare the Swede here with the very first Cavaradossi, Emilio De Marchi, who was recorded at the Met in this scene fifty-three years earlier alongside Emma Eames and Antonio Scotti.[82] Although the Italian tenor—who attacks the second "Vittoria!" on the top A-sharp rather than on the F below it—was clearly a resourceful interpreter, he cannot equal the combined puissance and splendor of Björling at his best. It should be recalled, however, that Puccini greatly disliked[83] this tenorial habit of hanging on to the three final syllables of the second "Vittoria!" It is indeed one of those moments when opera is transformed into a collective rite in which vocal athleticism is celebrated as much as dramatic truth. Yet the origin of this vocal overplay lies in the excessive concision of Puccini's dramatic scheme, where Cavaradossi's heroism risks becoming simply an element functional to the needs of an exciting plot. It was perhaps natural that tenors—including De Marchi himself—should rebel against the subordinacy of this function, taking the opportunity here to stretch the barlines and affirm the vitality of the character. Credit should be given to Björling for following this tradition without vulgarizing the music.

Just six days later the Met on tour presented Puccini's opera in Baltimore, where Milanov and Björling were joined for the first time by Leonard Warren as Scarpia. This celebrated trio—who had already collaborated in recordings of *Il trovatore* and *Aida*—met again in the studio in July 1957 to make a complete *Tosca* for RCA. The studio in question was in fact the Teatro dell'Opera in Rome, where the work had been given its world premiere (with only moderate success) on January 14, 1900. None of the three artists had sung any live performances on that stage (although this was Björling's fourth recording there) and the *genius loci* doesn't seem to have worked its magic on this occasion. The weather was stifling, personal relations were strained, and the relative sophistication of the recording technique (a three-track tape was used and a stereo edition later released) hardly compensates for the lack of dramatic momentum in the finished product. Conductor Erich Leinsdorf draws accurate playing and impressive sonorities from the orchestra, but at no point does he approach the fiery excitement conveyed by Mitropoulos at the Met and as a result the drama unfolds in a stilted fashion, in spite of the considerable experience of the leading singers in their respective roles: although Warren had been singing Scarpia for only a couple of seasons, Milanov had first performed the work in 1928 and Björling in 1933. The latter was apparently not always sober during the recording sessions[84] and

Milanov was especially disgruntled about having to rerecord the act 1 love duet because the tenor had been musically imprecise during the first take. As Conrad Osborne puts it, "There is a great deal of quality performing on this set, but as a totality it does not quite jell. The very best of it is from Björling, and most of all in the last act, where he sounds very close to his prime—than which there is no primer."[85]

After straining to hear through the distortion and sonic overlay of the Met performance, it is a joy to listen to every nuance of the Björling's Cavaradossi in excellent sound, although what we hear sometimes arouses more admiration than enthusiasm. The opening dialogue with the Sacristan is less engagingly spontaneous because Corena overplays his role. Leinsdorf more or less duplicates Mitropoulos's spacious tempo for "Recondita armonia," in a musically superb rendition. The duet with Leonardo Monreale's Angelotti lacks urgency when compared not only with the live Met recording but also with De Sabata's classic reading with Di Stefano and Franco Calabrese. The extended scene of love and jealousy with Tosca also proves intermittently disappointing: it is hard to believe Milanov when she sings "arde in Tosca un folle amor!" for she sounds detached here, the voice well-integrated but without much luster. Throughout the duet the nervy primadonna prevails over the woman in love. Bruce Burroughs offers detailed explanations not only for Milanov's disappointing vocal condition here but also for her mixed success when she sang this opera at La Scala in 1950.[86] It is probable, however, that her limited impact on Italian-speaking audiences—in spite of superb vocal equipment and accurate pronunciation—is due above all to a fixed "placement" that guarantees reliable resonance while making it difficult to mirror a wide range of emotions through the inflection of words. Her Italian vowels are in truth less distorted (but also less alive) than those of a number of great Latin sopranos in the early twentieth century (including the legendary Claudia Muzio) whose theatrical diction now seems markedly mannered, but they never sound as natural and as sensitive to psychological nuance as they do in the voices of Renata Tebaldi and Maria Callas (the other leading Toscas of the 1950s and 1960s). Milanov has no difficulty in sounding haughty and imperious, but seldom conveys vocally the girlish spontaneity and generosity of spirit that represent the other side of Tosca's personality—even though these attributes were apparently by no means absent in her stage portrayal of the role. By contrast, Björling (whose command of spoken Italian was greatly inferior to Milanov's) possessed a much freer technique that enabled him to brighten and darken, soften and harden those sounds at will and thus easily juxtapose the carefree young artist and lover with the committed political idealist.

Björling's upper register nevertheless sounds tighter and less expansive here than it usually does in live performance. As a result we can't enjoy to the same extent the soaring effect of "Occhio all'amor soave" heard at the Met in 1956. His ascent to the B-flat of "l'alma acquieta" is warm and easy, however, and this time we can better appreciate how smoothly he passes from *forte* to *pianissimo* in the phrase "Ah! M'avvinci nei tuoi lacci, mia serena," one of many felicitous touches in the duet with Tosca. The subsequent dialogue with Angelotti begins well enough—one notices how Björling assimilates the timbre of the horn that sounds when Cavaradossi first mentions Scarpia—but develops less excitingly than with Mitropoulos ("La vita mi costasse" reveals a hint of strain) and once again ends inconclusively.

In the second act, Björling disappoints in the initial interrogation: "Tal violenza!" is excessively subdued and during the cantata Leinsdorf accelerates unduly, so that words cannot register clearly (the off-stage choral singing is also too prominent). Leonard Warren—who in silky legato passages is appropriately insinuating—tends to make a meal of rapid exchanges, although he certainly understands the import of what he is singing and the voice in itself is imposing in its weightiness. As the tension rises, Björling sings his final "Non so" a third above the written notes, for extra effect, but in truth his defiance of Scarpia sounds more convincing once he is offstage. His clearly pitched cries during the torture are even more impressive than at the Met and his final *straziante grido acuto* is unsurpassed on disc. Leinsdorf's unusually slow rendition of the *Andante sostenuto* that accompanies Cavaradossi back on stage allows Milanov to exploit her famous *piano* tones to the full, and for a brief moment we sense a genuine tenderness of feeling uniting the two lovers. This doesn't, however, diminish the vehemence with which Cavaradossi denounces Tosca's betrayal, and "Vittoria! Vittoria!" is once again stalwart and rhythmically electric, although the voice seems stretched almost to the limit here.

Our first encounter with Björling's Cavaradossi at the beginning of the third act (the brief dialogue with the jailer) is an unforgettable one. The limpid *mezza voce*, impeccable legato and nobility of diction are all unrivalled here, while "E lucevan le stelle"—taken at a luxuriantly slow pace—is his best yet, both emotionally alive and remarkable in its instrumental poise as it gradually builds in intensity from a very soft opening. The dreamy sensuousness of "O dolci baci" (sung in a melting half-voice) is enhanced by the singing tone of the accompanying strings, and in the first ascent to the A-natural Björling makes less of a crescendo this time, attacking "disciogliea" in a pure head voice and then fining it away. Interestingly his dynamics are almost identical to those reproduced in *Puccini interprete di se stesso* by Luigi Ricci,[87] who is credited as assistant conductor in this recording (a similar approach is adopted by Bergonzi, who recorded the aria that same year). The concluding phrases are excitingly delivered, but without hurrying. Puccini's markings are scrupulously respected and the second "e muoio disperato" emerges suggestively as a weary echo of the first. The very slow tempo proves emotionally compelling but forces Björling to breathe before the top A of "amato" (as he also does in subsequent recordings).

In the agitated final scene of the opera Milanov's tone tends toward sourness, and this impedes the full involvement of the listener in the amorous exchanges. But the tenor reacts to Tosca's joyous news with tellingly adult scepticism—the low Es of "Scarpia che cede" have an almost baritonal resonance—and then goes on, after Milanov's rather alienating narrative (the words are insufficiently alive), to deliver the most melting rendition of "O dolci mani" ever committed to disc. Leinsdorf gives him plenty of time to spin out his *mezza voce*, with a delightful ascending portamento in "a car*ezz*ar fanciulli." Exceptionally, Björling maintains the *piano* dynamic right up to the top A of "giunte" (marked by a slight crescendo in the score), creating an atmosphere of rare intimacy. He is superior here not only to Di Stefano (whose *mezza voce* is less well supported) but also to Gigli, whose complete *Tosca* recording—made in Rome, like Björling's, some nineteen years earlier—reveals a certain coarsening of the tenor's sensibility in comparison with his early acoustic discs of the same music. Björling however had great respect for his elderly Italian colleague (who was by then seriously ill) and made a point of visiting him during his stay in Rome.

The final section of the duet is not memorable. Björling cannot summon up much emotion in "Amaro sol per te m'era il morire," where he sings "splendori" instead of "splendore" (spoiling the rhyme), and he sounds inert in comparison with Di Stefano, who invests each phrase with specific meaning. His responses to Tosca's instructions on how to fall are admirably natural, however, and after a winning "Parlami ancora come dianzi parlavi" (warmed by portamentos at the close) he executes the culminating "Trionfal" (arguably the weakest passage in the entire score, for the words are simply too banal to sustain the music) with admirable finish, if without much of the *entusiasmo* requested by Puccini.

1958 marked the twenty-fifth anniversary of Björling's debut in *Tosca*, but his only scheduled performances of the opera that year, at the Royal Opera in Stockholm opposite Birgit Nilsson on May 20, proved to be the unhappiest night of his career. He had developed a sore throat after attending his son Lars's school graduation ceremony a few days earlier and rapidly lost his voice during the opening scene, ending up speaking his part until the curtain was mercifully lowered and he was replaced by Einar Andersson. Later that night the tenor gave vent to his unhappiness in a phone call to Grevillius (who had conducted), "crying like a child."[88]

Björling's only 1958 recording of music from *Tosca* documents a much happier occasion: his Carnegie Hall recital two and a half months earlier, where "E lucevan le stelle" was presented as one of the final encores. The sound here is much darker than in the 1955 recital—in the recitative some phrases sound weightier than ever before—and the dynamic range is much wider. The first climax is once again capped by a dreamy *mezza voce*, the first "e muoio disperato" is really nailed home, and the second climax culminates in a ringing *fortissimo*, with no trace of the constriction heard three years earlier. As in his other recitals with piano accompaniment, the ascent to "amato" is rapid and impulsive.

In early 1959 Björling made a brief trip to London for a television appearance on the popular *Sunday Night at the London Palladium*, where he delivered another warmly-sculpted performance of "E lucevan le stelle," displaying an almost baritonal richness in the lower-middle register. Although we hear the usual wrong stresses in the recitative, the performance as a whole is perhaps his most deeply-felt in terms of sensual awareness and tragic forboding.

After this concert the tenor returned to Stockholm for what would prove to be his final performance of *Tosca* at the Royal Opera. It was obviously necessary for him to exorcise the memory of the previous year's debacle and the selection from the second and third acts shows him in secure voice, although the sound is less fresh than in the complete recording and his phrasing less impetuous. This is partly due to the rather slow tempos adopted by Grevillius, who was then in his sixty-seventh year and had retired as musical director of the Royal Opera some six years earlier. He was a respected guest artist, however, particularly in the Puccini repertoire (he had conducted Björling's debut performances as Cavaradossi, Rodolfo, Pinkerton and Luigi in *Il tabarro*). In the second act his leadership throws new light on character and situation and it is regrettable that the performance is not complete: the Scarpia of Arne Wirén—who like Björling was a pupil of John Forsell, the chief of police in the first Stockholm *Tosca* in 1903—is more declaimed than sung, but he manages some chilling effects all the same. While Wirén cannot really compete with Warren, the thirty-four-year-old Kjerstin Dellert—who possessed the looks as well as the voice for the diva—is a more immediately likeable Floria Tosca than the fifty-one-year-old Milanov, in spite of the Swedish translation (adopted by all the singers except Björling).

The first extract from the second act starts toward the end of the torture scene, where Björling's offstage "Ahimé"—particularly prolonged owing to the slow tempo—is more strikingly musical than ever, assuming the color of the accompanying cor anglais. When Cavaradossi is brought on stage he manages to sound both worn out and infinitely tender, spinning a featherweight upward portamento in "Sei tu?" The subsequent exchanges with Dellert are psychologically telling: there is far more sense of genuine interaction than in the studio recording. "Vittoria! Vittoria!" is freer and purer in sound than in 1957, although the rest of the outburst is charted with a degree of caution not previously noticeable before (Björling had been hospitalized a couple of weeks earlier because his heart was playing up).

Act 3 is in particularly good sound: it was recorded in stereo by a member of the Royal Opera staff who sat with a microphone in the auditorium.

Cavaradossi's dialogue with the jailer is as dulcet-toned as ever and "E lucevan le stelle" begins in an atmosphere that combines erotic retrospection with a feeling of world-weariness. Björling sings the recitative so freely that he fails to keep up with the orchestra on the four final notes ("fra le braccia . . .") and has to attack "O dolci baci" almost without a pause for breath. The first ascent to the top A hardly exceeds a *mezzo piano* and once again the repeat of "e muoio disperato" is softer and more resigned in expression.

After Tosca's entrance and narrative Björling takes his time before attacking "O dolci mani." He sticks closer to the score on this occasion, making a slight crescendo on "giunte," but the effect is less buoyant. We clearly get the impression here that Cavaradossi is just humoring Tosca by pretending to believe that they will succeed in escaping ("Liberi!" and "Via pel mar" are notably neutral in expression). Dellert creates an atmosphere of genuine sensual abandon and Björling responds well most of the time, but again fails to make much of "Amaro sol per te m'era il morire": Grevillius's plodding tempo only highlights the lack of vitality in the tenor's diction.

Nine months later Björling's health was no better than before (he had less than ten months to live), but in the first of three *Toscas* at the Met with Mitropoulos—who would also be dead within a year—he gives everything he has, both vocally and emotionally, in an interpretation that continues to develop. The conductor's dramatic pacing, though it never loses its sense of direction and emotional involvement, is more relaxed than before, and the orchestra sounds more distant in relation to the voices. The microphone seems to have been hidden in the prompter's box, and his decidedly sonorous interventions make it difficult at times to focus exclusively on the music. Mary Curtis Verna has the best top register of all Björling's Toscas on record and—although she gets briefly into a muddle in the third act—her command of the Italian text is excellent. As with Milanov, however, her vowels are not entirely pure and this limits the emotional impact of her phrasing. She nevertheless gives an honest performance, as does Cornell MacNeil as Scarpia, a portrayal that is more imposing than Cassel's and more linguistically fluent than Warren's, without approaching the psychological subtlety of Tito Gobbi, who sang the role alongside Björling in Chicago in 1956–57.

The tenor himself is in less lustrous condition than in his earlier Met recording, but the voice is warm and responsive at all dynamic levels, with a commanding ring on top. The character of Cavaradossi comes immediately alive in the opening dialogue with Lawrence Davidson's Sacristan, and "Recondita armonia" is spun out more lyrically this time, with renewed intimacy of expression in "L'ardente amante mia" and "Tosca ha l'occhio nero." The timbre is decidedly Italianate, but with an underlay of sadness that, while never intrusive, lends an extra expressive dimension to the sound. We can relish the broad, clean articulation of "Ah! il mio sol pensier sei tu!" followed by an easy ascent to a resounding B-flat, greeted with prolonged cheering (since Björling's appearances at the Met were by this stage relatively rare, they were all the more appreciated).

The first dialogue with Angelotti unfolds spontaneously and the duet with Tosca derives its cogency from a real sense of psychological interaction. "Qual occhio al mondo" is once again a moment to cherish, thanks to the consistent beauty of the tenor's voice across an octave and a half, although one notes a prominent vibrato in the middle register. The gradual diminuendo on "Ah! M'avvinci ne' tuoi lacci" is less effective than in the studio recording because Björling inopportunely breathes between "ne'" and "tuoi," rather than after "lacci," as the score suggests. Curtis-Verna phrases convincingly throughout, although her cautious use of intermediate vowel sounds (to facilitate the placing of the voice) in the imperative "Giura!!" is immediately shown up by the limpidity of Björling's response: "Giuro!"

The second exchange with Angelotti, apart from a mistaken stress on the final syllable of "avean" (a recurrent error), works better than ever before. The denunciation of Scarpia is utterly electrifying: there is nothing emptily rhetorical in the sustained B-natural of "La vita mi costasse," for Cavaradossi will indeed lose his life as a result of his attempt to save Angelotti, and Björling makes us feel that the character is half aware of this. The lengthy instructions that follow are more urgent than in the two earlier performances, although his delivery is less idiomatic than that of most Italian tenors. On the other hand very few of his colleagues' voices blend so atmospherically with the oboes and bassoons when Cavaradossi describes the secret refuge in the garden of his villa.

The interrogation scene in act 2 also works better this time, with Björling delivering Cavaradossi's first statament *con impeto* as Puccini prescribes. The tenor is at some distance from the microphone here, but the balance with the offstage chorus is more realistic than in the studio recording. During the torture scene Cavaradossi's reply to Tosca ("No—coraggio—Taci, taci! Sprezzo il dolor!") reflects the sonorities of the accompanying oboes and clarinets. This time we clearly hear Cavaradossi's defiant laughter when he learns of Malas's flight and "Vittoria! Vittoria!" is as spine-tingling as in 1956, with the benefit of better sound this time.

In act 3 the dialogue with the jailer is once again exquisite and the Romanza embraces a wider range of dynamics in "le belle forme disciogliea dai veli," passing from *mezzo forte* to *pianissimo,* while "E muoio disperato" once again resounds first outwardly (as a cry of desperation) and then inwardly (as a hushed lament). The tenor reinforces the A-natural at the climax and introduces a tearful raised pitch on the word "vita" in the final measure. This blatant emotionalism that would have been quite foreign to the singer when he made his debut in the role twenty-six years earlier, but it works in this context because his ability to embrace different modes of feeling had expanded greatly over the decades.

Mitropoulos prepares us overwhelmingly for the reunion of the two lovers after the aria and Björling responds with an extra degree of enthusiasm in "Franchigia a Flora Tosca." After the soprano's narration he makes something special of "Tu?! Di tua man l'uccidesti?!" conveying horror, surprise and tenderness all at once. "O dolci mani" is phrased much as it was in Stockholm earlier in the year, with a bigger crescendo on the A-natural above the staff, and "Amaro sol per te m'era il morir"—sung softly and rapidly so as to throw the climax into greater relief—sounds more affectionate this time. The same touching simplicity of feeling lends credibility to the final pages of the duet, in spite of the rhetorical bluster thrust upon the singers by the poet Giacosa.

Right from the beginning of his career, Björling had sung this role with the refinement of a born musician. Listening to his recordings, it is easy to believe that Cavaradossi possesses the sensitivity of spirit of a true artist and political idealist. Perhaps only in the last years of his life, however, did the tenor come to savor certain theatrical moments with full psychological awareness: he knew by then, more than most people realized, that *his* time—like Cavaradossi's—was nearly up and that each performance could be his last.

Madama Butterfly
Complete Recording

September 25–26, October 11, 1959: Rome, Teatro dell'Opera
Jussi Björling (Pinkerton), Victoria de los Angeles (Madama Butterfly), Miriam Pirazzini (Suzuki), Mario Sereni (Sharpless); Rome Opera Chorus and Orchestra, cond. Gabriele Santini
EMI 7 63634 2

Although undeniably the least-lovable of Puccini's tenor leads, the part of Pinkerton needs to be strongly cast, as the composer made clear by assigning it to Giovanni Zenatello at both the Milan and Brescia premieres in 1904. His revision of the score for the production at the Teatro Grande in Brescia, including the addition of the remorseful solo "Addio fiorito asil," contributed notably to the definitive success of an opera that had fallen victim to partisan protests at La Scala. A few years later the Veronese tenor recorded the love duet with the soprano Linda Cannetti, while Caruso made recordings of three extracts from the opera after the success of his performances in London and New York with Emmy Destinn and Geraldine Farrar. Since then many eminent tenors have sung the role on stage or in the studio (or both), and Björling was no exception. He performed the part twelve times in Swedish translation at the Royal Opera in Stockholm (where he made his debut in the work in September 1935) and the Vienna Staatsoper. In Vienna his Butterfly was the fascinating Jarmila Novotná (who also sang Mimì to his Rodolfo in both Austria and the United States), while in Sweden his first

Cio-Cio San was Helga Görlin, one of his most frequent soprano partners in the 1930s and 1940s in roles such as Mimì, Minnie, and Marguerite (in the *Fausts* of Berlioz, Gounod and Boito), Pamina, Aida, and Juliette. They sang the love duet from *Butterfly* together one final time at a charity concert in Stockholm in February 1945. Björling's last complete performance as Pinkerton, however, took place at the Royal Opera in April 1939 alongside Teiko Kiwa (daughter of a Dutch chemist and a Japanese mother).

Björling never recorded any extracts from the opera on 78s, but twenty years after his final stage performances he had an opportunity to record it complete (in stereo) alongside Victoria de los Angeles, the most musical of his soprano partners on disc. This partnership was inspired by the success of the *Bohème* made three and a half years earlier in New York. In this case the choice of conductor—the seventy-three-year-old Gabriele Santini rather than the octogenarian Sir Thomas Beecham—was less felicitous, but there was a strong all-round cast and EMI's producer Victor Olof proved more successful in capturing the resonance of Björling's upper register in the Teatro dell'Opera than RCA's Richard Mohr had been.

Madama Butterfly was in fact Björling's last studio recording of a complete opera and the precariousness of the tenor's health became all too clear when he collapsed while singing the love duet on September 26 (this explains why the recording was completed only a couple of weeks later). In spite of this, he was in remarkably good voice. The sound he makes in the middle register is less incandescent than it would have been twenty years earlier, but the forty-eight-year-old (and very sick) Swede compares well with the much healthier forty-nine-year-old Gigli, who had made a complete recording of Puccini's opera in the same theater twenty years earlier, alongside Toti Dal Monte.[89] Anders Björling recalls that his father listened almost obsessively to that recording as preparation for the role. His aim was probably not so much to freshen his musical memory—which by all accounts was exceptionally retentive—as to assimilate the original Italian text, which he would be singing for the first time.

From this point of view Gigli proved an excellent model, for—apart from the lazy articulation of a couple of consonants—Björling's Italian diction is generally idiomatic in this recording. Although Gigli proves more successful in projecting Pinkerton's sense of humor (in the love duet Butterfly reveals her appreciation of his open-hearted laughter: "ridete con modi sì palesi"), he is less convincing in his attempts to evoke a man who is tall, strong ("alto, forte"), and sexually attractive. In the conversational exchanges with Goro and Sharpless, Gigli's Pinkerton sounds decidedly middle-aged and sometimes relatively dry in timbre. Although the beauty of the voice emerges potently in the lyricism of the love duet and "Addio fiorito asil," the sentimentalism of the singer turns out to be an expressive liability.

Pinkerton is a difficult role to bring off on disc. In the opening act, where we view the action from his point of view rather than Butterfly's—even when we realize how unthinkingly he enters into marriage—Björling portrays a straightforwardly light-hearted, yet manly, figure: superficial but never unsympathetic. The beauty of his voice, combined with impeccable musical instincts, is in many ways his greatest asset: although it has sometimes been fashionable to portray the American naval officer as a distinctly unpleasant character, this interpretative stance inevitably undermines the credibility of Butterfly's intense attachment to him and the overwhelming momentum of the great love duet at the end of the first act. This is the most sensually-charged stretch of music Puccini ever composed, making us identify simultaneously with both the soprano's romantic imagination ("Dolce notte! Quante stelle!") and the tenor's erotic urgency ("Vieni, vieni"). The orgasmic climax in the final measures of the duet suggest how close the composer came to simulating the rhythms of sexual intercourse: it is of vital importance that the two singers should be be emotionally and vocally on the same wavelength (as they are here), giving the impression that it is they—and not the conductor—who are setting the pace. This is hard to achieve in a sterile studio setting (in his 1974 recording Karajan[90] fails markedly to get the balance right) but Santini accompanies the two singers expertly here. This version of the duet is one of the slowest ever recorded—it lasts over a minute longer than earlier recordings by Oliviero de Fabritiis (with Dal Monte and Gigli) and Gianandrea Gavazzeni (with de los Angeles and Di Stefano)[91]—but it is also one of the most stirring and sensuously rapt. De los Angeles sings more beautifully here than she does for Gavazzeni because she is never forced to rush, and Björling surpasses any other tenor on record in beauty of tone. His timbre is more lyrically poised than Caruso's (in his 1908 recording with Farrar),[92] less petulant than Gigli's, more luminous in overtones than Bergonzi's (with Renata Scotto),[93] and more refined in texture than Pavarotti's (whose tight vibrato afflicts a number of phrases in the above-mentioned Karajan version). Like all these singers he commands both a seductive *mezza voce* ("Bimba dagli occhi pieni di malia" is breathtaking) and a refulgent top (only the final top C is slightly labored). He also demonstrates a smooth mellowness in every dynamic transition between those extremes, displaying his consummate skill in slowly building up the tension throughout the scene without giving way to the sort of overheated phrasing exhibited at times by Di Stefano. Björling keeps Pinkerton's libidinous impulse lucidly at the centre of his focus while responding ever-sensitively to de los Angeles's tenderly imaginative Butterfly. The character drawn by Puccini may indeed be a cad but he certainly knows how to make love, and at the end of the duet we hope in spite of everything that he will remain faithful to Cio-Cio-San.

This duet, although it was recorded in rather dramatic circumstances, proves a genuine highpoint of the performance. Björling's Pinkerton nevertheless proves convincing right from the beginning, thanks in part to the conversational responsiveness of Piero De Palma and Mario Sereni who, though not always vividly sustained by the orchestra, offer detailed character portraits as Goro and Sharpless. "Dovunque al mondo" is vocally ideal (although Di Stefano beats him in eloquence if not in the splendor of his top B-flat) and "Amore o grillo" is warm and fluent if rather lacking in nuance: one misses the airy *mezza voce* (requested by Puccini) that Gedda[94] employs in describing Butterfly ("Lieve qual tenue vetro soffiato"), and Di Stefano's vivid verbal articulation ("alla statura, al portamento") on the twenty consecutive B-flats in the middle register. The Sicilian tenor is equally memorable in "Addio fiorito asil" (as is Bergonzi), but the richness of Björling's voice throughout the range, the density of his legato and the natural sincerity of his diction duly make their effect in this solo. In a singer for whom feelings of remorse and self-loathing were by no means unfamiliar, the sense of shame Puccini expresses so potently in this solo clearly struck a deep chord. It is a tribute indeed to Puccini's (and Björling's) humanity that we can feel so close to Pinkerton here, even while understanding his total inadequacy in dealing with the unhappiness he has generated.

La fanciulla del West
"Ch'ella mi creda libero e lontano"

March 4, 1935: Stockholm, Concert Hall
Unspecified orchestra, cond. Nils Grevillius
Naxos 8.110722

September 3, 1937: Stockholm, Concert Hall
Unspecified orchestra, cond. Nils Grevillius
EMI 5 66306 2

September 1957: Florence, Teatro Comunale
Orchestra del Maggio Musicale Fiorentino, cond. Alberto Erede
Decca 433 930-2

Shortly after Björling's debut as Ramerrez on December 29, 1934—the Swedish premiere of *La fanciulla del West*—he was featured on the cover of the magazine *Svensk Damtidning* alongside the soprano Helga Görlin as Minnie, in a photo taken during the final scene of the opera. He was only twenty-three at the time, by any normal standards an absurdly young age for him to be taking on such a heavy role—although David Belasco, author of the play (later turned into a short novel) on which Puccini's opera was based and director of the world premiere production at the Metropolitan in

Figure 12. Ramerrez, Minnie (Helga Görlin) and Rance (Joel Berglund) in the Swedish première of *La fanciulla del West*, December 1934. Photograph by Almberg and Preinitz. Courtesy of the Jussi Björling Museum.

December 1910, repeatedly stressed the youth of the Mexican bandit and his physical resemblance to his American mother. There is little doubt that Björling was chosen partly for his strong body and attractive face which, combined of course with a virile voice, helped audiences understand the irresistible attraction Minnie feels for an outlaw who in the end proves worthy of her trust and generosity.

"Ch'ella mi creda libero e lontano," the tenor's two-minute solo in the last act—twenty-one measures in G-flat major to be sung at a fairly slow pace (*Andante molto lento*) "with deep feeling, growing excited and almost smiling" as the melody rises—is Ramerrez's only extended opportunity to lay bare his feelings. Earlier in the opera (when he is disguised initially as Dick Johnson) we observe him largely through the eyes of Minnie or Rance, and if it weren't for this aria—in which the character reveals his nobility of spirit in the face of death—he would remain little more than the projection of the heroine's romantic fantasies and the goldminers' racial prejudices.

The fact that this is the only memorable aria in the score may well explain why it took so long for *La fanciulla del West*—translated as *Flickan från Vilda Västern*—to reach Stockholm. The aria itself had long been popular out of its original context, however: Björling's father had sung it on a number of occasions, and he himself had performed it during a broadcast with cellist Carl Christiansen as early as April 1930, and included it in his first recital at New York's Town Hall in January 1938 (Edward Johnson, then general manager of the Metropolitan, mouthed the words as he watched his newly-engaged tenor perform).[95] Its brave, stoical, tender message of love, set to a tune that is strangely comforting in its lulling 4/4 rhythm was adopted by Italian troops in World War I to give voice to their feelings of nostalgia and despair. The aria had been recorded by about thirty tenors before Björling committed it to disc in March 1935, just a couple of days before his final performance as Ramerrez in Stockholm and a day after he had sung Almaviva in *Il barbiere di Siviglia*. As it was sung in Swedish translation ("Låt henne tro") under Grevillius's baton, Björling's first "Ch'ella mi creda" can be considered an authentic souvenir of his debut in this role. And a rather thrilling souvenir it is, surpassing all earlier recordings of this aria for sheer purity of sound and classical poise. The sound floats freely on the breath, making it easy for the tenor to modulate dynamics throughout the range and open up on the top B-flats, as he does (in a different way each time) at the two climaxes.

Puccini's first Ramerrez, Caruso—though greatly admired in the part—never recorded the aria (the publisher Ricordi was opposed to the idea, fearing the recording would diminish sales of sheet music), so Björling did not have an opportunity to learn directly from his idol in this role. Unlike the first two tenors who did record the aria—Amedeo Bassi (1912),[96] who sang at the Rome premiere under Toscanini, and Giovanni Zenatello (1911)[97]—he adopted a consistently dark, Caruso-like timbre in the aria, varying his vibrato as instinctively as a cellist, in accordance with the expressive needs of the music. This is particularly noticeable in the final phrase, lying in the lower-middle register, where he vibrates the B-flat of "mio *solo* fior" (marked by a fermata) as well as the conclusive G-flat in order to lend emotional emphasis to the return to the tonic. This is a more musical solution than the self-indulgent sobbing of Pertile's 1924[98] recording (which also adopts much vibrato and a notably dark tone). Compared to Pertile, or Bassi, Björling is rather sparing in his use of portamentos, but his phrasing is much purer in legato than that of Zenatello—who creates an expressive effect through intensity of diction rather than a beautifully-sustained line—and much more Italianate in quality than that of Julius Patzak, whose 1931 recording in German[99] is too rapid and *marcato,* with an excess of head voice at the climaxes. The tempo adopted is less expansive than was then usual, respecting Puccini's metronome marking (♩ = 40) only in the opening measure, but—unlike Patzak—Björling never sounds hurried: the quickened pace reflects the character's expressive urgency, and proves well-suited to the compact dimensions of his voice at that time. Puccini told the conductor Serafin that this aria should become Ramerrez's "testamento morale,"[100] and that is exactly the impression that Björling conveys here.

Two and a half years later the tenor and conductor returned to the studios in Stockholm to record the aria in Italian. The tempo adopted is slightly slower this time and the Italian language brightens the coloring of the voice, making this Ramerrez sound excessively ingenuous. Probably Björling felt less confident, at this early stage, in his use of chiaroscuro when singing in a foreign language, although his Italian sounds more idiomatic than that of his early mentor, the senior tenor Martin Öhman, who was broadcast singing the aria in 1935.[101] His only conspicuous verbal slip here concerns the name Minnie, which he had pronounced correctly, in the American fashion, in his earlier recording; here he seems to want to Italianize it. Luigi Ricci, who worked closely with Puccini, underlines the correct pronunciation in *Puccini interprete di se stesso,*[102] and it is strange that Björling should have persisted in his error even when he made his final recording of the aria in Italy twenty years later. Overall the 1937 recording is rather generalized in expression: although Björling adds a few extra portamentos this time (no bad thing in such emotionally pregnant music), there is less tension to his phrasing, particularly in the final measures.

"Ch'ella mi creda" is one of the relatively few operatic arias[103] that Björling recorded three times in the studio as a separate number, though no live recordings survive of his concert performances. At Florence's Teatro Comunale in 1957 the voice is more distant from the microphone than in 1937 but clearly has more body to it and this time he sings the Italian text with an appropriately dark coloring. The pace is considerably slower than before (the sung part lasts twenty seconds longer than in the 1935 recording), yet phrases are welded together more solidly, thanks to the ample breath spans and a more generous use of portamento, and the words are uttered with a more touching, manly dignity than in 1937. The two ascents to the top B-flat are drier in sound than in the earlier recordings, but the notes themselves have a bitingly Italianate quality to them that well-suits the mood of this impressively idiomatic reading.

Although he only sang eight performances early in his career, Björling clearly cared about the role of Ramerrez, and his first and last recordings of "Ch'ella mi creda" are among the finest ever made of this aria. He cannot match the bronze-like density of sound produced by Del Monaco in his complete Decca recording of the opera (1958),[104] the combination of doom-laden drama and uncommon sensitivity offered by Giuseppe Giacomini in a heavyweight 1989 rendition,[105] or the rare verbal eloquence of Di Stefano who, in a 1955 recital,[106] conveys better than any other tenor the tenderness of Ramerrez's love for Minnie. Nevertheless, the deep melancholy that impregnates this music (the character believes he has only a few minutes to live) acquires a unique resonance in Björling's timbre, and it is easy to imagine the psychological closeness he felt to this taciturn character who initially hides the darker side of his life from the woman he loves.

Turandot
Complete Recording

July 3–11, 1959: Rome, Teatro Dell'Opera
Jussi Björling (Calaf), Birgit Nilsson (Turandot), Renata Tebaldi (Liù), Giorgio Tozzi (Timur), Piero De Palma (Pang), Tommaso Frascati (Pong), Mario Sereni (Ping), Alessio de Paolis (Altoum); Rome Opera Chorus and Orchestra, cond. Erich Leinsdorf
RCA 09026-62687-2

"Nessun dorma!"

July 10, 1943: Stockholm, Royal Academy of Music
Stockholm Radio Orchestra, cond. Sixten Ehrling
Bluebell ABCD 103

March 27–30, 1944: Stockholm, Concert Hall
Unspecified orchestra, cond. Nils Grevillius
Naxos 8.110701

November 10, 1944: Stockholm, Concert Hall
Swedish Radio Symphony Orchestra, cond. Tor Mann
Bluebell ABCD 078

August 23, 1949: Los Angeles, Hollywood Bowl
Hollywood Bowl Symphony Orchestra, cond. Izler Solomon
Standing Room Only SRO 845-1

April 17, 1951: Stockholm, Royal Academy of Music
Swedish Radio Orchestra, cond. Sten Frykberg

July 5, 1951: Stockholm, Gröna Lund
Harry Ebert, pf.
Bluebell ABCD 114

March 10, 1952: New York, Rockefeller Center
Firestone Orchestra, cond. Howard Barlow
Verona 27022

March 2, 1958: New York, Carnegie Hall
Frederick Schauwecker, pf.
RCA 60520-2-RG

April 13, 1959: Atlanta, Glenn Memorial Auditorium
Frederick Schauwecker, pf.
Bluebell ABCD 020

With its soaring vocal line rising thrice to top A (capped on the third occasion with a B natural); with its exceptionally delicate yet all-enveloping orchestral accompaniment; with its shifting harmonies (hovering between G major and D major) and spatial depth (suggested by the offstage female chorus), "Nessun dorma!" is one of the most evocative arias ever conceived for the tenor voice. A nocturnal love song sung beneath a starry sky on the steps of a pavilion in the gardens of the royal palace, it starts in an almost passive, introspective manner, taking its cue from the heralds' offstage warning: "Questa notte nessun dorma in Pekino!" Calaf, however, is utterly focused on his objective. His challenge to Turandot is keeping the entire population of Peking awake, but he has no fear of his secret being discovered and has a clear vision of the events that will unfold the next morning, when he will reveal his name at dawn and conquer the princess's heart. In Calaf the dreamer and the man of action are integrated to a degree that is rarely achieved in real life. His ability to influence the course of destiny is underlined at the very end of the opera (as completed by Alfano), when the main theme of his aria is repeated by the entire chorus. Although the behavior of the prince (who is after all a creature of legend) can hardly withstand any close moral scrutiny, it is all too easy to identify with this born winner in the atmosphere of suspended time Puccini creates at the beginning of the third act.

In the final years of his life, the composer considered several tenors for the role of Calaf. He seems to have actually auditioned Martinelli in the aria "Nessun dorma!" as early as 1921, expressing the desire that he should create the role.[107] After Puccini's death Toscanini tried to engage the tenor for the world premiere at La Scala but was prevented from doing so by Giulio Gatti Casazza, who refused to free him from his Metropolitan contract. One of the opera's two librettists, Giuseppe Adami, claimed[108] that the composer had modelled Calaf's music to fit the voice of Giacomo Lauri Volpi, but this tenor's candidacy for the premiere was apparently vetoed by Toscanini, which may explain why Puccini—in September 1924, just two months before he died—sent a telegram to Gigli asking *him* to sing *Turandot* at La Scala the following April.[109] In the end none of these tenors took part in the premiere (Toscanini assigned the part to the Spaniard Fleta, who never made discs of any of Calaf's music)[110] but all three were later recorded in "Nessun dorma!": Martinelli was captured live at Covent Garden in 1937, Lauri Volpi and Gigli in the studio in 1942 and 1949 respectively. Although they were vocally in decline when the recordings were made, their interpretations of the aria fully justify Puccini's confidence in their abilities.

Of the three tenors only Lauri Volpi sang the role frequently on stage, right up to the final years of his career in the late fifties, and in theory Björling could have listened to his disc (and may have heard Martinelli over the radio) before he himself was first broadcast singing "Nessun dorma!" from the Royal Academy of Music in July 1943. If he had heard the two Italians, however, there is little indication that he was influenced by them, or by any other of the two dozen or so tenors who had been recorded in the aria since the opera's 1926 premiere. The performance under Sixten Ehrling's baton is nevertheless masterly, marred only by a verbal slip in the seventh measure, where this Calaf sings of stars that, rather than trembling with love ("tremano d'amore"), devise schemes of love ("tramano d'amore").

Semantics apart, one is struck by the breadth and beauty of a performance that unfolds with contemplative ease. The score indicates an *Andante sostenuto* for this aria, but Björling always preferred a slower pace, exploiting every phrase for maximum effect rather than favoring the forward momentum generated, for example, by Lauri Volpi. This is the case right from the opening "Nessun dorma!," and although Björling is not the only tenor on record to possess a solid low D for the repeated phrase (in his 1926 recording Hipólito Lázaro produces a decidedly baritonal sound),[111] perhaps no other interpreter sculpts this opening with such perfectly equalized tone: the upper and lower D in his voice are both ideally steady and well-integrated. This homogeneity of sound is naturally not appropriate in all contexts—some operatic music (particularly for the wider ranging female voices) calls for the different registers to be thrown into sharp contrast—but it was a quality prized by all the great *bel canto* theorists of the eighteenth and nineteenth centuries and proves a genuine virtue in the opening of this Romanza, where Calaf's second "nessun dorma!" echoes the first just as the first echoes the distant cries of the offstage chorus.

Throughout the aria Björling adopts the ardently lyrical tone of a young man in love: there is caress, not scorn, in his voice as he imagines Turandot in her "fredda stanza." No other tenor who recorded the piece in those early years—not even Antonio Cortis (1929)[112] or Lauri Volpi—shapes the music with such pristine beauty. A feature of this and later recordings by Björling is his tendency to linger on the dotted quavers of "*fre*dda stanza," "*lo* dirò" and "tramon*ta*te stelle," augmenting our awarness of how intensely Calaf savors his nocturnal vigil. He also prolongs—more than most of his colleagues do in early recordings—the top B-natural that in the score is simply an accented eighth note leaning on the sustained final A (a whole note). Most discs made in the 1920s—by singers as eminent as Pertile (1927) and Thill (1927), Cortis (1929), Lázaro, and Richard Tauber (1926)—reproduce the closing measures more or less as written, but as early as 1927 Alessandro Valente[113] prolongs the B to exciting effect, a gesture adopted by all major tenors in recent decades. Björling's ascents above the staff are electric in tension (the voice gains in intensity as it rises), and the attack on the final top A is embellished by an acciaccatura, an effect that can also be heard in Martinelli's recording, and which would be maintained by the Swedish tenor in future performances.

In March 1944 Björling recorded the aria for HMV, and this proved to be one of his most successful discs both commercially and artistically. As ever, studio microphones capture the voice differently, smoothing out edges but also lessening the impact of the upper register. What one appreciates here is the tenor's respect for Puccini's *piano* dynamic, indicated in the first measure of the vocal line and justified by the refined accompaniment in the opening section of the aria. This Calaf phrases with even greater sensitivity of feeling than before, the clarity of the words—Björling's diction is quite faultless this time—set off by the natural vibrancy of the voice production, which is rendered more evident by the close miking. This effect never degenerates into the pronounced vibrato heard in the recordings of Pertile,[114] Thill,[115] and Merli,[116] a vibrato that can be exciting in other contexts but that ill-suits the transparency of Puccini's instrumental setting. The sustained A, E and D of "la luce splenderà" represent a test case in this respect, for a voice cannot shine here if it is vibrating too strongly. Björling passes this test with surpassing ease. The HMV reading also compares favorably with the performance by the thirty-seven-year-old Pavarotti in his complete 1972 recording.[117] This performance—along with later versions by the Italian tenor—has supplanted Björling's in the popularity stakes, but proves less consistently satisfying in detail. An example of this is the phrase "Ed il mio bacio scioglierà il silenzio che ti fa mia," which Pavarotti delivers in a somewhat perfunctory fashion, while Björling daringly inverts Puccini's dynamics, making a diminuendo rather than a crescendo in the middle of the phrase and fining away the voice on the upper F of "scioglierà." This effect reduces the erotic urgency of Calaf's musings, but lends greater scope to his emotional imagination.

Seven and a half months after making the HMV recording, Björling sang "Nessun dorma!" on Swedish radio again, this time accompanied by Tor Mann, who offers the tenor a luxuriantly spacious setting for his long-breathed phrasing. The aria lasts 3:51—surely a record among performances by singers of real merit—and is crowned by a phenomenal eight-second top B. Björling adds the occasional extra portamento: the one linking the lower G of "stanza" with the upper F of "guardi" is as graceful as it is rare. Puccini's music sounds even dreamier here: it is the quality of the prince's imagination that emerges rather than his desire to conquer. We only realize that there may be some other dimension to this music when we compare this interpretation to the recordings by Martinelli[118] and Lauri Volpi, both of whom project the words with an inexorable resolve that reminds us of the compulsive nature of Calaf's behavior, his need to transform his desires immediately into action, whatever the consequences may be, and the strong sense of predestination and inviolability that surfaces in the proud "Ma il mio mistero è chiuso in me." In Martinelli this single-mindedness has a more noble urgency to it; in Lauri Volpi one perceives the haughty decadence of the proto-fascist hero. This tenor's "Nessun dorma!" is both fascinating and repellant: less musically enriching than Björling's, but arguably more convincing within the dramatic context of the third act.

1944 was the year in which Björling bought his complete score of *Turandot*, enabling him to read through the whole part and get the full measure of an opera that he had probably already seen on stage during the Royal Opera's 1936–37 season. That he liked what he read is demonstrated by the fact that he accepted Gaetano Merola's offer to perform the work in San Francisco in the autumn of 1950 (the tenor's wife was slated to sing the role of Liù). This engagement never came to fruition because the dates overlapped with the all-important inauguration of the Bing era at the Metropolitan, a televised production of *Don Carlo* with Björling in the title role. Meanwhile, the tenor did perform "Nessun dorma!" at the Hollywood Bowl in the summer of 1949. One can imagine the impact of this aria performed on a starlit summer night, and this is indeed a wonderful performance. Although he employs a narrower range of dynamics than in 1944, never has his Calaf seemed so sure of himself and his destiny: "tramontate stelle!" is cosmic in its breadth and, in spite of the shallow recording, the climactic B is electrifying. For the first time we hear Björling kick up to this note from the lower D, but the ascension is rocket-like and sparks off an immense ovation.

Just a few weeks after Björling's Californian concert a fifty-nine-year-old Gigli finally got around to recording "Nessun dorma!" in the studio.[119] The voice shows signs of wear and some sustained notes oscillate a little, but it is a commanding performance all the same, marked by the entirely appropriate extra emphasis on key phrases ("chiuso in me," "nessun saprà," "che ti fa mia") that generally distinguish mother-tongue singers.

In May 1951 Björling gave another stirring performance of the aria at the Swedish Royal Academy of Music, more intimate in tone this time but no less resplendent above the staff, although he sings a nonsensical "sulla tua bocca, tramontate stelle!" in the final measures. His only recording of the aria for *The Voice of Firestone*, in March 1952 (no video survives), is another spacious reading—indeed, so spacious that it almost loses momentum, owing to Howard Barlow's lackluster accompaniment.

In the 1950s Björling was recorded three times singing Calaf's Romanza in recital. As in Verdi's "Celeste Aida," this involves a considerable sacrifice in the quality of the accompaniment, for no pianist can hope to approximate the coloristic range and dynamic refinement of Puccini's instrumental setting. Björling's sense of line is so formidable that the aria still enchants and enthralls, even when—as in Gröna Lund in 1951—he adopts a strikingly intimate approach, employing his head voice to an unusual extent. This may be because he was not on his best form, but if that was the case it simply demonstrates how skillful he was in using the limited resonance of his upper register as a pretext to invest the aria with a more inward-looking lyricism.

At the Carnegie Hall in 1958 the voice sounds fuller and darker (partly because the aria is transposed down a semitone) and is well recorded. This is one of Björling's more thrusting readings, but he still maintains a handsome diminuendo in "scioglierà il silenzio." In Atlanta a year later he again adopts the transposition: the phrasing is mellower and more introspective and his voice sounds as beautiful as ever.

Just three months later Björling found himself in Rome, recording the aria for RCA within the context of the complete opera. This final "Nessun dorma!" is in one sense the most satisfactory of all his versions, for his phrasing is as refined as ever and for the first time the offstage chorus is not replaced by the orchestra (or piano), enabling us to savor Puccini's panoply of sound effects. These effects are very important in this Living Stereo recording, which tends, however, to recess the solo singers in relation to the orchestra, an unfortunate arrangement that was favored increasingly by record companies (and conductors) in the years that followed. It could be argued that the balances reproduced here are similar to those heard normally in a large opera house, where the orchestra often vies with the leading singers for the audience's attention. In a theater, however, our perception

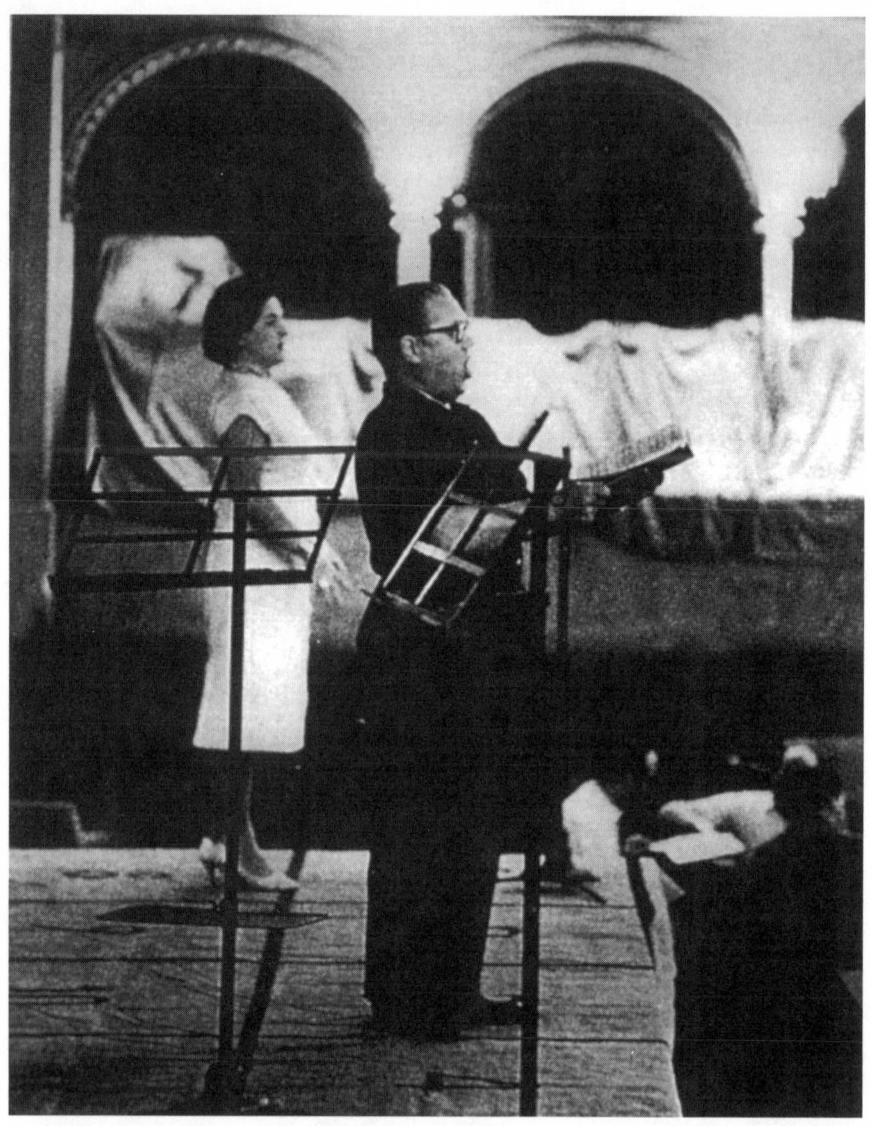

Figure 13. Recording *Turandot* with Birgit Nilsson at the Rome Opera, July 1959. Courtesy of the Jussi Björling Museum.

of the sounds emitted by the singers is heightened by our ability to read the words on their lips and the emotions on their faces. On disc singers require greater prominence: compare the vividness of Piero De Palma's Pang in the 1957 Serafin recording[120] with the comparatively subdued effect he makes here. Another problem concerns the relative tightness of Björling's upper register as heard over the studio microphones. This is a feature of all his recordings supervised by Mohr and the engineer Lewis Layton, and although it doesn't unduly dim the brilliance of the B-natural in "Nessun dorma!" it does reduce the overall impact of his first and only complete Calaf. A certain dryness of tone may have been caused by the heat of the Roman summer (in her memoirs, Birgit Nilsson recalls it being swelteringly hot),[121] but it is significant that when the tenor returned to Rome two months later to record *Madama Butterfly* for EMI, the voice was captured in much freer form in the upper octave, as it was in various live recordings made that year.

Calaf is a formidably heroic role for a medium-sized voice and Björling was in redoutable company here, having to match the generous outpourings of both Nilsson (Turandot) and Tebaldi (Liù). As we have seen in other contexts, the need to show his muscle sometimes leads him to tense up vocally, inhibiting the free flow of words on the breath. For sheer eloquence he cannot match the phrasing of Di Stefano in a live recording in Vienna in 1961.[122] The Italian's upper register is blaringly open and unreliable in pitch, but he never lets the vocal difficulties distract him from the business of phrasing as expressively as possible. His finest moments coincide with Björling's best, with the difference that the latter is more introspective, while the former relates more strongly to the singers who are sharing the stage with him. Di Stefano had a fair degree of experience in the role on stage, while Björling had never sung it in the theater; here he interacts with a Tebaldi who had also only performed Liù in the recording studio and a conductor, Erich Leinsdorf, who arouses greater admiration for his technical efficiency than for his ability to involve the orchestra emotionally in the unfolding drama.

Calaf is the most important character to emerge in the first act of the opera, yet the leading tenor's opportunities to convey the charisma of the "unknown prince" are relatively few and need to be exploited to the full. First impressions are all important, and any sort of understatement here tends to register simply as blandness, particularly when some key phrases sink into inaudibility. Björling's entrance is unmemorable: he doesn't command the declamatory strength needed to project the low E-flats of "Non c'è esilio per noi, padre, nel mondo!" and although his characteristic timbre, "heavy with unshed tears,"[123] is appropriate for "T'ho pianto padre," Calaf's music requires a rhetorical urgency—and an expansive resonance in the upper register—that are lacking here. Throughout this scene both Corelli (at his best in a broadcast from La Scala)[124] and Pavarotti (outstanding in a

1977 live recording from San Francisco)[125] sing with greater expressive freedom, the latter demonstrating how intensely vibrant diction can help even a lyric voice to project in low-lying passages.

One of the turning points in the opera—when Calaf's hatred for Turandot is transformed into love the very moment he catches sight of her—also registers blandly in this recording (partly because the voices are too recessed). Björling curses the princess effectively enough, but when he suddenly changes track, overwhelmed by her beauty, his tone is too melancholy to convey the prince's erotic excitement, which registers intoxicatingly in recordings by Di Stefano, Corelli, and Pavarotti. While his voice has the necessary sweetness for "il suo profumo è nell'aria," he fails to capture the decadence of feeling that is evoked here. Everything Calaf says in this first act highlights the fanatical absoluteness of his emotions and each syllable needs to be milked for full meaning. Examples of this—and of Björling's difficulty in achieving the right sort of febrile intensity—are "io soffro, padre, soffro," "No! No! Io solo l'amo!" and "Son tutto una febbre, son tutto un delirio! Ogni senso è un martirio feroce!"

The short aria "Non piangere Liù" is a different matter: this emotionally ambivalent but beautifully crafted melody acquires in Björling's voice a weight of sadness that justifies the unusually slow tempo adopted here (Puccini prescribed an *Andante lento sostenuto*). This recording would be worth acquiring just for these two and a half minutes of prodigious music-making, where we get the mysterious feeling—beyond the literal meaning of the words—that Calaf is expressing his sorrow (and Puccini's) for what will happen to Liù later in the opera. This tenderness is heightened not by sentimentality (as is suggested by Corelli) but by a bleak awareness of the inexorability of human destiny.

Björling's firm line and pellucid diction serve him well when addressing Alessio De Paoli's Emperor at the end of the first act, while in the opening scene of the second act he creates a more mixed impression. In this penultimate year of his life he can still nail a respectable top C when Calaf joins Turandot in the conclusive phrase of her aria, "Gli enigmi sono tre, una è la vita!" Initially his voice is covered by Nilsson's, but he then reinforces the sound to make his presence felt. This reflects not just the pride of the veteran performer determined to show his worth alongside the emerging diva (although Nilsson was only seven years younger than her fellow Swede, her international career began in a much later phase of her life), but also the technical awareness that it is better to attack exposed high notes *mezzo forte* and then make a crescendo on them rather than attempting to take them by storm. This prudent approach, however, rather undermines Calaf's relish in living dangerously during this scene: both Corelli and Pavarotti face the vocal challenges with greater insolence, rising to a second top C (an optional note that Björling eschews) in "Ti voglio tutta ardente d'amor!"

In the rest of the opera Björling alternates moments in which he seems underpowered or insufficiently incisive—"Quest'incubo dissolvi," "Sconterete le sue lacrime," "Principessa di morte"—and others of truly melting lyricism: "Il tuo nome non sai," "Nessun dorma!," "tu sei morta, o mia piccola Liù!," and "Oh! Mio fiore mattutino." This last arioso—sung to the accompaniment of an offstage female chorus after Calaf has finally conquered Turandot with a kiss—has the airy fragrance of a Tosti song, and although Di Stefano makes more of the words, Björling moulds the melody with a suavity of tone that frees us for one delightful moment from the rather oppressive atmosphere of this final scene (Alfano's ending, as reproduced in the standard Ricordi score, is performed here uncut, as is the rest of the opera).

Turandot is a problematic work that can prove electrifying in the theater but is difficult to bring off in the studio. Although tempers were sometimes frayed during the Rome sessions, this does not seem to have heightened the tension of the music-making. We would be poorer without Björling's complete Calaf, but the recording serves as a reminder that he was probably right to avoid interpreting this part on stage. "Nessun dorma!" of course is another matter: it was the most recently composed operatic aria that he performed regularly in concert and recital, and no other tenor has sung it with greater refinement of tone and elegance of phrasing.

RANGSTRÖM

Tre Ballader ("En ballad om Lameks söner," "En ballad om narren och döden," "En ballad om god sömm")

January 31, 1942: Stockholm, Concert Hall
Stockholm Radio Orchestra, cond. Sixten Ehrling
Bluebell ABCD 050

Björling was not one of those rare vocal actors who can assume a specific physiognomy for every score they sing, but his voice was an exceptionally flexible instrument and when challenged—as in these three ballads, composed in 1938–41—he could vary its coloration to a considerable degree, delivering the texts by Frans G. Bengtsson (still living at the time of the songs' composition) with uncommon vividness. The 1942 radio broadcast (no audience was present) was the world premiere of these quirky ballads. Rangström had been familiar with the tenor's voice for over a decade, having formerly worked for the press department of the Royal Swedish Opera, where Björling had made a strong impression as Mats in the Strindbergian opera *Kronbruden*, performed on the composer's fiftieth birthday in November 1934.

Rangström presented the singer with some freshly-cooked lobsters after this broadcast performance,[1] and while listening to the recording we can well understand his delight. Yet the first of the ballads in particular—a tongue-in-cheek tale of Lamech's three sons, inspired by the Book of Genesis—is very different in style from most of the music the tenor sang, being an example of Rangström's experimental "speech-melody," in which the highly characterful vocal line seems to spring directly from the words themselves. In no other recording does Björling—splendidly supported here by a twenty-four-year-old Sixten Ehrling—project the text with such pointed irony, subordinating his vocal palette to verbal meanings. Rangström instructs the singer to perform the music "med godt humör" and "ad libitum," and that is exactly what the tenor does, sticking to the original key of E major in spite of the baritonal tessitura.[2]

In the somber and sinister ballad about Death and the Jester his voice takes on a quite different hue, responding once again both to the meaning of the words and to the distinctive textures of the accompanying orchestra. The third ballad, about "good sleep," boasts a more traditionally beautiful melody, for which the voice becomes onces again its silvery, melancholy self. The melancholy is enriched here with oriental overtones, while the transparency of the timbre lends the pessimism of the words ("He is best off who sleeps for good") an enigmatic yet numbing candor.

"Tristans död"

April 11, 1949: New York, Carnegie Hall
James W. Quillian, pf.
WHRA-6036

October 5, 1957: Stockholm, Concert Hall
Stockholm Philharmonic Orchestra, cond. Stig Westerberg
Bluebell ABCD 092

The hallucinatory quality of this highly dramatic "Death of Tristan," during which the character observes the ship bringing Isolde as it approaches the coast of Brittany, was composed in the mid-1930s and sung by Björling over a rather longer period of time than the *Tre Ballader*. He is very responsive in these performances both to the music and to Bo Bergman's verse (which he switches around in the fifth and eighth measures), but the heroic scale of his singing in the opening and conclusive sections of the scene sounds over-muscular in recital and functions much better with the full orchestral support provided in the Stockholm performance, where a number of details are better integrated into the whole. Both the fermata on the top G-sharp of "O min amur"—which obviously can be better sustained by the strings than by the piano—and the climactic top A-sharp on "står" (which the tenor further sharpens in New York, as if to compensate for the lack of an orchestra), prove more telling in Stockholm. In both performances, however, it is the softer legato singing in the central *Andante* ("Jag hör som ett svall från Cornwalls kust") that draws the listener most persuasively into the inner life of the dying hero.

ROSSINI

"La danza"

August–November 1937: Stockholm
Svensk Filmindustri Orchestra, cond. Nils Grevillius
Bluebell ABCD 092

December 8, 1940: Detroit, Masonic Temple Auditorium
Ford Symphony Orchestra, cond. Eugene Ormandy
VAIA 1189

Rossini played a central role in Björling's early career. The tenor was applauded in eleven performances as Arnold in *Guillaume Tell* (one of the most challenging parts in the standard repertoire) and scored a big success as Almaviva in *Il barbiere di Siviglia,* which he performed twenty-six times between 1931 and 1937. It is a pity that he was never recorded in "Ecco ridente in cielo," which he embellished with an interpolated top C (replacing the written E of "mio"),[1] for it would have shown off the coloratura singing in which he considered himself a virtuoso at that time.[2] His friend Gösta Kjellertz described Björling's florid divisions as being comparable to those of "violinists or pianists with great technical ability. You heard every note in his scales. . . . Everything sat perfectly for him and he did it with the greatest ease."[3]

Björling also played the part of Rossini, opposite Helga Görlin as Isabella Colbran, in Bernhard Paumgartner's *Rossini in Neapel,* a lightweight work that received its Swedish premiere in Stockholm in November 1936 and incorporates the Italian composer's famous tarantella, "La Danza" (composed to a text by Carlo Pepoli in the early 1830s). Although the melody of this rhythmically infectious song is relatively unembellished, it does require a brilliantly focused emission and the ability to articulate words and notes with great rapidity. It is marked *Allegro con brio,* with the metronome of ♩ = 152, and both Björling's recordings sustain a dizzying pace from beginning to end. In the first of these the tenor performs just one verse (as he did in

Figure 14. Marcello (Folke Cembraeus) and Rossini in Paumgartner's *Rossini in Neapel*, Stockholm, 1936. Courtesy of the Royal Swedish Opera Archive.

the Paumgartner opera) and maintains a perfect balance between a ringing tone on every note and well-oiled fluidity of movement. The recording is part of the soundtrack of his first movie, *Fram för framgång* (Head for success), a rather pedestrian comedy directed by Gunnar Skoglund in which Björling's delivery of the Rossini song is a decided highlight. It is presented as an impromptu performance by the tenor Tore Nilsson, who interrupts a tedious educational program on the radio to demonstrate what he's worth to the director of the station (the actor Harry Roesck Hansen), much to the delight of the schoolchildren who are dutifully listening to the broadcast. It is indeed the sunniest performance imaginable, ending on a shining top A (a traditional octave transposition), and although the camera cuts tiresomely to other less interesting faces, it returns fleetingly to the tenor's smiling countenance in the final measures.

Both verses can be heard (plus most of the orchestral introduction, which is missing in the film) in the Ormandy-led performance on the *Ford Sunday Evening Hour* three years later. The phrasing is as dazzling as before, with top As at the end of both verses (sung to an identical Swedish text), the final high note being sustained until the orchestra falls silent.

In spite of the translated text, these performances are no less exhilarating than Luciano Pavarotti's live rendition (1988)[4]—uniquely crisp in its delivery of the Italian text—and the dark-voiced version by Enrico Caruso (1912),[5] which captures the "Neapolitan" spirit of the music better than any other. Beniamino Gigli's 1938 recording,[6] perhaps the closest to Björling's in juiciness of tone, simplifies the line somewhat and omits the tricky acciaccaturas (spanning upward intervals of a fourth) on the high As, which the Swede executes as winningly as anyone.

Although Björling admitted in his 1945 autobiography that his voice was by then heavier and less well suited to "coloratura à la Rossini,"[7] he never lost his vocal flexibility, thanks to regular practice of vocalizes by Concone and Panofka. It was this virtuoso training that made it easy for him not only to execute the long melismas "Il mio tesoro" and the big cadenza at the end of "La donna è mobile," but also to pass slowly from one note to another with the utmost grace and simplicity.

Stabat Mater
"Cujus animam"

October 12, 1938: Stockholm, Concert Hall
Unspecified orchestra, cond. Nils Grevillius
Bluebell ABCD 016 (take 1); EMI 5 75900 2 (take 3)

The tenor aria from Rossini's *Stabat Mater* was composed in 1841 and has long been favored as something of a showpiece by singers with an extensive upper range. Being rather too long to fit comfortably onto one side of a shellac disc, relatively few recordings of it were made in the first half of the twentieth century. Those that were made inevitably included a number of cuts, especially in the orchestral introduction and postlude and in the third and final verse of the aria. Björling's cuts are practically identical to those heard in Caruso's 1913 recording,[8] although his decision to start the third verse with "et tremebat cum videbat" suggests that he may have listened to Gigli's 1932[9] record as well.

The Neapolitan's disc is well worth hearing, for he is one of the few tenors whose dark tone matches the sorrowful density of the Jacopone da Todi's Latin text (which many composers set to music), and whose weighty phrasing lends an appropriately majestic quality to Rossini's *Allegretto maestoso.* Björling does not attempt to imitate the baritonal coloring of that reading, but his singing has the same sort of dignity and he too makes much of the repeated "Mater" in the second verse, the syllables united by sighing portamentos. He also repeats an error of pronunciation made by his predecessor (who like Björling himself had a sketchy formal education), singing "constristantem" rather than "contristatam." Unlike Caruso, Björling does not use the fermata in the penultimate measure of the aria to launch an extra cadenza, but he executes the written cadenza with greater panache, opening up the sound on the top D-flat where Caruso produces a rather pinched tone (quickly abandoned). Throughout the aria indeed Björling negotiates the upward leaps—which sometimes span an octave—with greater elegance than either Caruso or Gigli, who banalizes the music with his aspirated vocalization and heart-on-sleeve emotionalism, and replaces the culminating D-flat with an easily accessible B-flat.

The Swede has more formidable competition from Pavarotti, particularly in a live 1967 performance with Carlo Maria Giulini,[10] which is free from cuts and exceptionally expressive in diction and radiant in the upper register, although Rossini would not have expected (or wanted) tenors to approach the D-flat with such a chesty weighting of the tone. Vittorio Grigolo, in a live recording made in Rome in 2004,[11] has offered a more stylish solution, attacking the note in a pure head voice and then reinforcing it, but his quivering diction in the rest of the aria sometimes sounds like a parody of Pavarotti. By contrast, Björling's more evenly-produced vibrato lends excitement to the melody while not interfering with his ability (in both takes, which are practically identical) to vary the coloring of individual words, investing the music with a somber hue that aptly tempers the effect of the jaunty rhythm.

SCHUBERT

"He is no Lieder singer" declared the *Gramophone* reviewer in 1958,[1] commenting on the recently released recording of Björling's 1955 Carnegie Hall recital. It would be easier to overlook this dismissive comment were its author not one of the most respected critics of the twentieth century, Andrew Porter, whose remarks were based not only on that specific recording, but also on recollections of live recitals in London. Björling regularly sang Lieder during the last twenty years of his career and in many recitals a number of songs by Schubert and other German composers were featured early in the evening. At the Carnegie Hall Schubert is in fact the most fully represented composer: four Lieder, sung consecutively. Porter was well aware of this, which makes his comment all the more damning, implying that the singer devoted a substantial amount of time to performing music which he was ill-suited to interpret. The critic justifies his reservations by stating that the tenor "has no trace of intimacy" and that the "Björling of the recital platform delights me for a few songs or arias by his well-produced stream of fine tone, but then monotony sets in."

The majority of Björling's surviving Schubert performances were recorded live. The condition of the voice varies somewhat, but it is immediately clear how well-chosen the Lieder are, for they are all conceived for a male singer (usually a tenor) and benefit considerably from a voice of great beauty spun out on an even flow of breath. Björling doesn't generally embellish the melodic line, as some recent tenors (such as Christian Prégardien) have quite legitimately done, but he adopts a classical *bel canto* approach to the music that is not only historically appropriate—Schubert after all was a contemporary of Donizetti's and Italian opera was immensely popular in Vienna throughout his lifetime—but also sounds naturally right, at least in the songs he chose to sing.

A *bel canto* technique, involving a perfect fusion of words, portamento-enriched legato and beautiful tone, was not however a priority for most eminent male Lieder singers of the 1950s (when most of Björling's Schubert recordings were made). The most celebrated of these was Dietrich Fischer-Dieskau, who arguably gave of his best in the darker, more pessimistic songs, well attuned to the cultural climate of postwar Germany.[2] The German baritone applied intense intellectual concentration to his recitals and recordings, which explore the entire catalogue of Schubert's Lieder. The musical intelligence and poetic sensibility of this new generation of Lieder singers made critics (who often respond more willingly to mental than to emotional stimuli) suspicious of the apparently casual approach to this repertoire adopted by older singers like Björling, who repeatedly sang the same very popular Lieder in almost every recital and never felt the need to extensively explore *Die schöne Müllerin* or *Winterreise* (he recorded just one song, "Die böse Farbe," from the former cycle).

Recordings demonstrate, however, that there was rarely anything routine about the performances of the ten Schubert Lieder Björling did sing. Although he was not, as Porter reminds us, one of those rare singers capable of transforming a large auditorium into an intimate drawing room, his liquid projection of glowing tone, the words poised on the breath, can arguably reach out to a contemporary audience more movingly than the contrivedly hushed and undernourished tone of some recent tenors specializing in this repertoire.

"Die Forelle" (D. 550)

April 11, 1952: New York, Manhattan Center
Frederick Schauwecker, pf.
Testament SBT 1427

September 24, 1955: New York, Carnegie Hall
Frederick Schauwecker, pf.
RCA 88697748922

December 24, 1955: New Orleans, Municipal Auditorium
Frederick Schauwecker, pf.
Premiere Opera 122

March 2, 1958: New York, Carnegie Hall
Frederick Schauwecker, pf.
RCA 60520-2-RG

April 13, 1959: Atlanta, Glenn Memorial Auditorium
Frederick Schauwecker, pf.
Bluebell ABCD 020

Jussi Björling was himself a fisherman—specializing in pike rather than trout—and spent many a tranquil hour in his boat on Siarö sound every

Figure 15. Before a recital at the Civic Auditorium in Pasadena in 1940. Courtesy of the Jussi Björling Museum.

summer. But he was not a cold-hearted one (when he caught more fish than were needed for dinner he would let some of the catch loose)[3] and thus had no difficulty in sharing the poet's pain when the angler resorts to muddying the waters in order to trap the trout. This famous Lied, which Schubert revised a number of times over the years, is limited in range (just over an octave), deceptively similar to a folk song in its rhythmic patterns, and quickly over: Björling's recorded performances all last less than two minutes. If we read the final verse (which the composer chose not to set) of Christian Friedrich Schubart's poem, where young girls are advised to beware of men with rods if they don't want to bleed too late ("Sonst Blutet ihr zu spät"), the allegorical meaning becomes clear. Schubert and his circle habitually used a code language when referring to sexual themes and if we listen to Heinrich Schlusnus's 1943 recording,[4] where the German baritone takes the music (transposed down to B major) at a much slower pace than usual, the implicit meaning becomes almost menacingly evident.

It is not necessary, however, for the interpreter to be aware of these hidden meanings. In Björling's 1952 studio recording, in some ways his best, he approaches the words and music (sung in the original key of D-flat major) with absolute simplicity of feeling, capturing the ingenuousness that Schubert simulates in his initially strophic setting. His narrator relates what he observes with keen interest but without imposing his own personality on the narration as Fritz Wunderlich does, for example, in his Edinburgh recital,[5] finessing the line in a manner that is ultimately self-regarding. With Björling the focus is on the tale rather than the teller. This is enhanced by the purely evocative qualities of his voice, whose silvery overtones, fluidity of movement, and buoyancy of emission help us visualize the sparkling stream and happy, playful trout, while the liquid beauty of his vowels reinforces the play of assonance that characterizes each verse. The sixteenth notes, used above all to vary melodic repeats, are always clearly articulated but never impede the steady flow of the line or the cumulative energy of the 2/4 rhythm. The harmonic tensions of the third verse, where the melody is suddenly alive with the drama of the trout writhing on the line, are conveyed vividly but without exaggeration. Although Björling does not adopt a hushed tone for his narration, he has plenty of power in reserve for the crescendo on "Er macht das Bächlein tükkisch trübe," accompanied by a sudden acceleration in tempo. This speeding up (not indicated in the score) is faithful to what we know of nineteenth-century performance practice,[6] and is achieved here with rare rhythmic dexterity and admirable synchronization of singer and accompanist.

Schauwecker's playing sounds slightly sluggish in the 1955 Carnegie Hall recital, where the singing maintains much of its variety even though the more distant microphone placement makes the luminous timbre less tangibly present. The same is true of the New Orleans concert, but here the voice is fresher, the performance more spontaneous than ever and the drama of the trapped trout seems more deeply felt. Similar qualities distinguish the 1958 performance, where a decidedly baritonal coloring lends a more adult seriousness to the narration without sacrificing the flexibility of the phrasing. The final note of the Lied (a D-flat) is prolonged greatly beyond its notated value (as in earlier performances) and tapered away gracefully. This effect is duplicated in the Atlanta recital, where the tone is dappled with light and shade, but the phrasing betrays less involvement.

"Frühlingsglaube" (D. 686)

January 30, 1940: New York, Manhattan Centre
Harry Ebert, pf.
Bluebell ABCD 050

September 24, 1955: New York, Carnegie Hall
Frederick Schauwecker, pf.
RCA 88697748922

December 14, 1955: New Orleans, Municipal Auditorium
Frederich Schauwecker, pf.
Premiere Opera 122

March 2, 1958: New York, Carnegie Hall
Frederick Schauwecker, pf.
RCA 60520-2-RG

April 13, 1959, Atlanta, Glenn Memorial Auditorium
Frederick Schauwecker, pf.
Bluebell ABCD 020

The words and music of this Lied—in which the coming of spring, with its gentle breeze and fresh fragrances, is seen as a reason for renewed hope—are in many ways ideally suited to Björling's voice and temperament. In the original key of A-flat major the vocal line sits comfortably in his middle register, which in 1940 conserves a dewy freshness that predisposes us to believe that "Die Welt wird schöner mit jedem Tag." In this early performance Björling makes the melody float: his tones are perfectly supported on the breath and the *gruppetti* are executed exquisitely. Words are clearly articulated and one is aware, to a certain extent, that the singer thinking about the meaning of what he is singing (he lightens the tone appropriately for "nun muss sich alles, alles wenden"). Overall, however, the phrasing is short on specific meaning. The fact that he attacks the opening phrase *mezzo piano* rather than taking his cue from the *pianissimo* marking in the accompaniment is indicative of his failure to achieve genuine intimacy of expression in a song that is not a public statement of optimism, as it becomes here, but a private message addressed by the poet to his "armes Herz" (poor heart). Schlusnus, who recorded the Lied in the same key in 1938,[7] is more varied in both dynamics and tempo, more daring in his desire to highlight verbal meanings. Wunderlich achieves an even greater intimacy,[8] and his voice at its best approaches Björling's in beauty of tone.

Fifteen years later, at the Carnegie Hall, the tenor's sound is drier but still luminous and the phrasing is more specific in detail, with a stronger emphasis on the optimistic "O frischer Duft, o neuer Klang." A still greater precision can be sensed in the New Orleans recital three months later, while at the Carnegie Hall in 1958 the dramatic coloring of the voice turns the Lied into an openly public statement: not exactly what Schubert had in mind, perhaps, but more appreciable in its frankness than the relative indeterminacy of the studio version. The tenor's finest performance of "Frühlingsglaube," however, is to be heard in the 1959 Atlanta recital: the voice is as mellifluous as ever and although the phrasing is largely unchanged in its overall contours, the expression is more deeply felt and personal. The singer really seems to love the music he is singing on this occasion, and this naturally enhances our understanding of the words.

"An die Leier" (D. 737)

January 30, 1940: New York, Manhattan Centre
Harry Ebert, pf.
Bluebell ABCD 050

March 2, 1958: New York, Carnegie Hall
Frederick Schauwecker, pf.
RCA 60520-2-RG

"To the Lyre" is the only Lied sung by Björling in which the poet (in this case Franz von Bruchmann, who offers a free translation of Greek verses by Anacreon) presents himself as a singer frustrated with the expressive means at his disposal. He aspires to sing of the heroic exploits of Atreus's son or of Cadmus or of Alcidis, but his lyre refuses to submit to his will and only plays songs of love. In the original Greek poem the singer's frustration is a rhetorical device veined with irony; in Schubert's Lied it suggests a genuinely divided soul, for there is a strong contrast between the expansive (*langsamer*) E-flat major melody that represents the lyre's most congenial form of expression and the rapid (*Geschwind*) heroic recitative in the relative minor that precedes it and recurs at the beginning of the second verse.

In Björling's voice this conflict seems to reflect contrasting impulses in his own artistic nature: we often hear him assume a heroic stance which—however convincingly sustained in vocal terms—sounds less moving and sincere than his purely lyrical singing. This is exactly what happens in this Lied, which is transposed up a third for the 1940 studio recording. The recitative sections are certainly not lacking in volume, ring, and thrust, but these qualities are achieved by sacrificing eloquence of diction. The words are pronounced clearly and correctly, but they sound compressed rather than liberated by the concentrated energy needed to produce a heroic tone. When Björling passes into the major mode, on the other hand, his phrasing becomes uniquely persuasive: not only does he shape the melody with caressing sweetness (twice adding a brief shake on "Erklingen"), but he also brings the words spontaneously to life. The purity of the *ö* in "tönen" is a delight, and the key word "Liebe," repeated six times during the course of the song, glows with inspiration, particularly when he ascends in a melting head voice to the top A, where Harry Ebert allows him an ample *allargando.* His soft singing, sustained on a cushion of air, is much richer in overtones than that of Fischer-Dieskau, who is rather too brisk in cantabile and whose voice, though agreeable, lacks Björling's sheen and lift.[9] Björling is no less attentive than the German baritone to Schubert's notation: the mordents in the recitative passages are well executed and all the appoggiaturas are respected except for the very first one (on "singen"), where he introduces an acciaccatura instead (possibly a misreading of the score), thus providing the declamatory opening with a more biting close.

The only other recording of this Lied was made during Björling's Carnegie Hall recital in 1958. The tenor performs it in D minor/F major this time, and although the darker coloring of the voice and the extra power available arguably add tension to the recitatives, the melody is less entrancingly beautiful in shape and texture.

"Wandrers Nachtlied" II (D. 768)

January 30, 1940: New York, Manhattan Center
Harry Ebert, pf.
Grammofono 2000 AB 78719

March 1, 1940: New York, Manhattan Center
Harry Ebert, pf.
Bluebell ABCD 050

April 11, 1952: New York, Manhattan Center
Frederick Schauwecker, pf.
Testament SBT 1427

The text of this brief yet all-encompassing Wayfarer's Nightsong was first written out on the wall of a hunting chalet in the Thuringian hills, where the thirty-one-year-old Goethe had climbed to view the sunset. It was set to music of almost equal concision (there are a couple of repetitions, but the whole Lied fits easily onto one page) and surpassing spiritual understanding by a twenty-four-year-old Schubert in 1822. The first recording listed here—never officially released by HMV—was made by a twenty-eight-year-old Björling, who captures from the opening phrase the transfixed wakefulness of the observer. In describing the stillness of the mountain peaks, treetops, and birds in the forest, he embraces the natural world before turning his attention to man. The tenor prefers a *mezzo piano* opening to the *pianissimo* adopted by some colleagues (and indicated in the accompaniment), which this enables him to suggest the firmly-grounded point of view of a mature human being, while the purity of his sound lends philosophical dignity to the deceptively simple words. Here, as in later recordings, Björling takes a pensive but questionable breath before the first verb ("ist ruh"), but elsewhere consolidates his legato with neat upward portamentos, joining "in" to "allen" in the fourth measure and "du" to "auch" in the eleventh and thirteenth measures. The evenness of his scale and steadiness of the tone lend a degree of solemnity to the crescendo on "Warte nur" (where the key shifts briefly from B-flat major to G minor) before rising to the sustained F at the top of the staff on "balde," where the note is fined away to the purest of head tones. In the repetition of the phrase, where the wayfarer addresses himself ("Soon you too will be at rest"), the F is floated still longer and more airily, perhaps suggesting that death should be perceived not as a threat but as a doorway to another dimension.

Björling recorded this Lied again just over a month later in the same studio, and this disc too was never published by HMV. The performance made available through Bluebell is so similar in phrasing, timing and inflection to the earlier one that it might seem simply a different transfer of the earlier recording (or vice-versa). The texture of the voice appears to be brighter and sweeter here, however, sounding more distant from the microphone, and the qualities that make the earlier version so striking emerge all the more persuasively.

The reading of the Lied that EMI finally published demonstrates how consistent the tenor's approach to this music remained. This recording lasts twelve seconds longer than the earlier ones (partly because Schauwecker shapes the two introductory measures more expansively), but there are no significant differences in phrasing. The voice of the forty-one-year-old Björling is naturally more mature and his moulding of the opening phrase more authoritative. There is less imaginative caress to the words "die Vöglein schweigen," however, and the head voice on "balde" is not as effortless this time, although the second ascent is sweeter and almost as prolonged as in 1940.

Overall, however, the vision of the Wayfarer seems bleaker and less optimistic here, making the performance arguably less cherishable.

"Die böse Farbe" (*Die schöne Müllerin*, D. 795)

January 30, 1940: New York, Manhattan Centre
Harry Ebert, pf.
Bluebell ABCD 050

July 6, 1950: Stockholm, Gröna Lund
Harry Ebert, pf.
Bluebell 114

April 11, 1952: New York, Manhattan Center
Frederick Schauwecker, pf.
Testament SBT 1427

September 24, 1955: New York, Carnegie Hall
Frederick Schauwecker, pf.
RCA 88697748922

One cannot help regretting that Björling never attempted a complete Schubert song-cycle. *Die schöne Müllerin* in particular would have been ideally suited to his voice and temperament, as "Die böse Farbe," the seventeenth of the cycle, makes clear. In spite of the springiness of the melody and the apparently jaunty rhythm (the tempo indication is *ziemlich geschwind*) this is one of the most deeply unhappy—indeed, furious—songs in Björling's repertoire: the miller's animation reflects his increasing madness and despair.

The sheer humanity of the tenor's voice in January 1940 (a disc never issued on shellac) partly compensates for the decontextualization of a song that can be fully understood only within the cycle. The crispness of Björling's diction, his respect for Schubert's dynamics and subtle command of rhythm nevertheless bring the miller's emotional state into sharp focus. The only licence is the traditional (and highly effective) rallentando every time the line rises to the G-natural above the staff, which offers the listener time to assimilate the intensity of the feelings expressed. At the same time this is one Schubert Lied in which Porter's accusation that Björling revealed "no trace of intimacy" in recital seems pertinent. If we compare his first recording with the interpretation of Axsel Schiøtz—who had studied, like Björling, with John Forsell, and who committed the whole cycle to disc in 1945—we notice how much more delicately the Danish tenor explores the deep pain of the character.[10]

The Swede however equals him—in urgency of feeling if not in psychological inwardness—in his 1950 recording of the Lied, which is also his best.

Accompanied once again by Ebert, this is his only Schubert recording made in Sweden, in an apparently incongruous outdoor setting. Both the pianist and the singer are exceptionally alive to the manic quality of the music this time, the voice sounding so forward that the words and rhythms register with electric clarity. The pace adopted is precipitous, yet there is never any sense of rushing and the tenor finds time to insert a number of deft portamentos and to lighten his voice to touching effect in the fourth verse, "Und singen ganz leise bei Tag und Nacht / Das eine Wörtchen: Ade!"

A couple of years earlier, the eminent critic-composer Virgil Thomson—who, as Joseph Horowitz put it, "delighted in not even acknowledging the conventional wisdom that revered what he debunked"[11]—had singled out this Lied for praise after a Carnegie Hall recital by Björling in 1948, in such a way as to highlight what he described as the tenor's "poor basic training":

> The placement of his voice just misses a maximum exploitation of its possibilities of beauty by a slight throatiness. He vibrates just behind the masque, or upper part of the face, rather than squarely in it. Occasionally a happy vowel, usually an ah, in the upper middle register will come out full and correctly focused. In Schubert's "Die böse Farbe" the whole piece stayed forward, because its active movement did not give him time to swallow the vowels which his loyalty to consonants, pronounced always trippingly on the tongue, had opened favorably. But his slow work was invariably less lovely than one wished, and his high loud work (the heroic tenor effects) were regularly a little forced."[12]

This is one of the most articulate negative statements ever made about Björling's technique and although hindsight suggests that it may be exaggerated, it does pinpoint a problem that sometimes emerged when the tenor was not on top form. Björling's basic technique was established when he was still a child and he seems not to have developed a method for maintaining the voice fully forward in the mask when his energy level was sagging. His solution to this problem—as one can hear in the 1955 Carnegie Hall recital, where he is clearly out of sorts—is usually to increase the breath pressure (which sometimes works, but often causes the sound to bottle up) or to resort to a head voice (which rarely fails him in its beauty and ease). We have an example of this in his final recording of "Die böse Farbe," where the soft top G of "ade" in the fourth verse is sung more exquisitely than ever, while when he attacks the same note *forte* (particularly on a covered vowel like the *u* of "zum") the sound slips back into the throat. This tendency is less marked in the 1952 studio version, where Björling is in better form, although the voice sounds drier and darker than in earlier recordings and the slower tempo adopted by Schauwecker seems almost ponderous at times.

"Die Allmacht" (D. 852)

April 15, 1946: New York, Rockefeller Center
Firestone Orchestra, cond. Howard Barlow
VRCS 2000

April 11, 1952: New York, Manhattan Center
Frederick Schauwecker, pf.
Testament SBT 1427

March 2, 1958: New York, Carnegie Hall
Frederick Schauwecker, pf.
RCA 60520-2-RG

The inspiration for this Lied derived not only from the lines penned by Johann Ladislaus Pyrker in his religious epic poem *Elisa* but also from the setting in which Schubert met the poet in the summer of 1825 and put his words to music: the Austrian resort of Bad Gastein, with its towering mountain scenery that seemed to speak of an omnipotent creative force. Few pieces of vocal music convey so genuine a feeling of wonder, and considering Björling's easy access to the sublime here, it is regrettable that he was never recorded in Berlioz's "Invocation à la Nature" from *La damnation de Faust*, an opera that he sang ten times at the Royal Opera in 1936.

His first recording of "Die Allmacht" was made ten years later on *The Voice of Firestone*, where the singer shares his song with the Firestone Chorus and the orchestral arrangement lends a jaunty falsity to music that should prove almost numbing in its honesty. In this case it is the mixed chorus that is charged with evoking the more terrifying manifestations of "Ominpotence" (an English translation is used), while the tenor enters with a gentle "It's heard in the rustling of leaves in the forest," observing Schubert's *piano* marking in the vocal part to melting effect. Björling's voice, though marred by a catch in the throat in one attack, emerges so convincingly here as a reassuring medium of belief that he transcends the banality of the setting: the sound he makes is unequivocally trusting, transparent both in sound and expression, yet suitably rousing when joining the chorus in the final phrase, where Schubert moves strikingly from G-flat major to C major.

This C major affirmation becomes almost too much of a good thing in Björling's studio recording of the Lied, made in 1952. The tenor proves formidable in sustaining the vocal line across an almost two octave range: even the low Cs acquire impressive resonance. This heroic sculpting of the sound is achieved, however, at the cost of a muscular "placement" that also affects his lyrical singing (his *piano* is still beautiful, but less melting than in 1946). The tenor seems somehow tensed up to meet the vocal hurdles, and our awareness of his striving after effect gets in the way of the direct expression of the song. It is a performance that arouses admiration, but proves less moving than the radio broadcast made by Nicolai Gedda in 1964,[13] where the low Cs are barely audible but the upper register resonates more freely (if not more ringingly), enabling the words to project with greater feeling. In Gedda's voice—here at its most beautiful—the Lied becomes a vehicle for truly personal expression, as it does to an even greater extent in Hilde Scheppan's wartime rendition:[14] technically the German soprano sounds almost amateurish alongside Björling (and we cannot but note, in Hitler's Germany, the censorship of the word "Jehovah"), yet she conveys the full fragility of the individual human soul facing up to the omnipotent, making Björling's singing sound strangely impersonal by comparison.

In the tenor's final recording, made at the Carnegie Hall in 1958, the phrasing is less adamantine and finished in detail—he makes a muddle of the words at "In des Waldstroms laut aufrauschendem Ruf"—but the overall expressive balance is better. The *piano* and *forte* sections are equally persuasive, and although the focus remains on the "might" of Jehovah rather than the "beating heart" that gazes upward in "prayer and hope," the omnipotent force evoked no longer seems so monolithic and remote.

"An Sylvia" (D. 891)

January 30, 1940: New York, Manhattan Center
Harry Ebert, pf.
Naxos 8.110789

November 19, 1945: New York, Rockefeller Center
Firestone Orchestra, cond. Howard Barlow
WHRA-6036

November 20, 1950: New York, Rockefeller Center
Firestone Orchestra, cond. Howard Barlow
Kultur DVD D2424

March 2, 1958: New York, Carnegie Hall
Frederick Schauwecker, pf.
RCA 60520-2-RG

"Who is Silvia, what is she / That all our swains commend her?" The answer of course is that she is the intelligent, honest and attractive daughter of the sometimes despotic Duke of Milan. She is courted, in Shakespeare's early comedy *The Two Gentlemen of Verona*, by the wealthy but foolish Thurio as well as by the 'two gentlemen,' fickle Proteus and Valentine; the latter, her true love, naturally ends up winning her hand. It is Proteus and Thurio, however, who arrange for Silvia (Sylvia) to be serenaded in the fourth act of the play with the song that Schubert set to music in July 1826, using his friend Eduard von Barenfeld's translation, which had been published in 1825. The setting is masterly in its directness, but manages to combine the ardor typical of the tenor voice with humorous commentary from the left hand of the piano accompaniment, which prevents the high-flown praise of this much-favored young lady from spilling over into sentimentality. The tempo indication is *Mässig* and many singers favor a brisk pace and an urgent, sometimes arch, delivery. Björling lets the music unfold unhurriedly, allowing for full enjoyment every phrase. No other male singer on disc projects the words and music so caressingly: this is as true of the Carnegie Hall recital in 1958 as of the official HMV recording made just a few blocks away in the same city eighteen years earlier.

It is this early version that most captures the imagination. When he recorded it, Björling had been singing the Lied in public for at least nine years. It was featured in his Copenhagen recital in July 1931, the first occasion on which he sang German Lieder before a large audience. If one excepts the spacious tempo, his interpretative approach follows tradition (and semantic logic) in lending a more forthright emphasis to the first and third verses, while delivering the second in softer tones. Yet the manner of his execution is anything but ordinary, for every note is steady and luminous in its resonance, and every phrase is shaped with surpassing grace, thanks to the underlying portamento of the breath. The vowels of Barenfeld's text are cherished for their purity more than by any other singer, while the consonants are never shirked but help propel the melody forward without impeding its flow. Dynamics are varied as a spontaneous result of refined musical instincts playing upon a tone that can be modulated with ease. Most of the more prolonged sounds (the dotted half notes) are either slightly reinforced or slightly diminished, and the final measures of each verse are particularly rich in dynamic contrasts, ending with a hushed return to the tonic (the key is A major). This is especially true of the second verse, where Björling takes his cue from the words "süsser Ruh." In the last two verses he employs a barely perceptible portamento to span the octave leap up to the E at the top of the staff on "und verweilt" and "Kränze." Other portamentos coincide logically enough with Schubert's slur markings joining consecutive notes, further contributing to a singularly stylish performance.

In November 1945 Björling sang the song on *The Voice of Firestone*, his first public appearance in New York after the end of World War II. This time he performs just the first and third verses, using the original Shakespearian text, which fits the music well, although the word-order is inverted in a couple of lines. This is the only occasion on which he sings words by Shakespeare in the original language and once again we can cannot but delight in the purity of his diction, even if he pronounces the word "mortal" as if it were the Italian "mortale." He makes us feel the difference between Barenfeld's "Schöne" and Shakespeare's "Holy" in the third line, and the spirit of the song remains intact in spite of the cut and an orchestral setting that is blander than Schubert's original piano accompaniment.

Five years later he sang the Lied again on the same program, which by then was televised. In this broadcast the tenor—impeccable in his white tie and tails—is seen singing in German (the second verse is cut, as in 1945) at the end of a Thanksgiving Dinner. This convivial situation is in a way typically Schubertian, though the quality of the music-making is once again compromised by the generic accompaniment. It is a pleasure, however, to be able to observe his voice production functioning so naturally, lending an easy sincerity to his stance and facial expression. Some vocal technicians might frown at his shoulders rising with every intake of the breath, but in Björling's case this speaks not of shallow breathing but of the need to maintain the chest in a raised position. In his pamphlet on singing, David Björling insisted on the importance of keeping "the chest high and the back straight,"[15] thereby facilitating an open throat and augmenting the resonance of the voice. Björling's chest is always well expanded here and during the first verse his arms float at a slight distance from his flanks, lending a surprising buoyancy to his solid stance. For the second verse he stands at the head of the table, wine glass in hand, as if about to propose a toast. The facial expression is unsmiling and totally concentrated, yet serene: the singer understands that there is no need for extra gestures to underline the flowery rhetoric of the words.

"An Sylvia" was also featured in Björling's Carnegie Hall recital in 1958. The tone here is darker and fuller and the vibrato a little more prominent. Words are less deliciously pellucid than before, although the timbre remains youthful. This performance does not reveal Björling at his very best, yet it compares well with renditions by other tenors, including the live recording of Wunderlich during his final recital in Edinburgh in September 1966.[16] The German singer has been praised by critics almost as often as the Swede for his beauty of tone, but in this case comparison makes it clear how relatively cloudy and unsteady his emission was, particularly in soft singing. Neither the words nor the notes are as clearly articulated as in Björling's recordings, and the line is not sufficiently supported for a genuine legato to make itself felt. This is partly due to the flowing tempo and to phrasing which seems informed more by verbal than by musical meanings.

Very few other singers approach indeed the sweet spontaneity of expression achieved by Björling in this Lied. The manuscript of the score, which came to light in Hungary nine years after the tenor's death, suggests that the music itself emerged in its definitive form practically from the very first draft; it seems likely that Björling in his 1931 recital in Copenhagen caught the spirit of this immortal song right from his first public performance: the reviewer Axel Kjerulf wrote of a tenor who "sings so your heart melts, sings with a voice fresh and strong, a glowing lyric tenor with the most beautiful timbre."[17]

"Ständchen" (*Schwanengesang*, D. 957)

January 14, 1940: New York, Manhattan Center
Harry Ebert, pf.
Naxos 8.110789

April 4, 1949: New York, Rockefeller Center
Bell Telephone Orchestra, cond. Donald Voorhees
Naxos 8.111083

April 11, 1952: New York, Manhattan Center
Frederick Schauwecker, pf.
Testament SBT 1427

September 24, 1955: New York, Carnegie Hall
Frederick Schauwecker, pf.
RCA 88697748922

December 14, 1955: New Orleans, Municipal Auditorium
Frederick Schauwecker, pf.
Premiere Opera 122

March 8, 1958: New York, Carnegie Hall
Frederick Schauwecker, pf.
RCA GD 60520

April 13, 1959: Atlanta, Glenn Memorial Auditorium
Frederick Schauwecker, pf.
Bluebell ABCD 020

It was enough for Björling to say "Schubert's Serenade," when announcing the first surprise encore during his 1958 Carnegie Hall recital, for the audience to understand exactly what he meant (and respond with a round of applause). Although the composer wrote two solo Lieder titled "Ständchen," the Ludwig Rellstab poem he set to music in the final months of his life (included in the posthumous *Schwanengesang*) had long been the more the popular of the two. In the central decades of the last century it was probably the world's most famous serenade, and since being used as the theme tune in Tauber's 1934 film *Blossom Time* (a sentimentalized account of the composer's life) it had been sung in an infinite variety of languages and arrangements. Björling himself, who must have known this Lied since his childhood, for it was in his father's repertoire, is recorded singing it only in German and in the original key (a D minor that shifts intermittently, and then conclusively, into D major) but was not above performing the piece with the sort of syrupy orchestral accompaniment that can also be heard in discs by Tauber (1925)[18] and Beniamino Gigli (1938).[19]

Being a nocturnal love song of great melodic charm, at once yearning and affectionate, sensitive and bold, it is naturally enhanced by a beautiful voice, and it works best when sung by a tenor. Björling's was unequivocally the voice of an attractive young man in love: even when comparing the 1940 New York studio recording with the live performance from Atlanta in 1959, it is hard to pinpoint any dimming of luster, for in a piece like this—which sits largely in the middle of the voice and calls for no extremes of dynamics or virtuosity—the Björling sound maintained its integrity right to the end. If anything one appreciates, in the later recording, the warmer grounding of the lower register (the Ds of "rauschen" and "Lauschen" flow more easily), without any loss of luminescence in the upper octave. At the same time one notes a greater refinement of detail and overall expressive cogency.

There is no doubting, however, the pristine loveliness of the first recording, a model of the sort of seamless legato (enriched by graceful portamentos) that contemporary Lieder singers such as Werner Güra (2007)[20] seem to lack: Güra's shallowly-supported phrasing is carefully thought-out intellectually but ultimately unmoving. Even a more technically solid singer like Peter Anders (1954)[21] sounds strident in comparison with Björling in those upward leaps (encompassing intervals as wide as a minor sixth) that lend an irresistible momentum to the vocal line, their ascent propelled by seductive triplets. There is an appreciable amount of dynamic variety in this early performance: Björling uses a bolder tone to launch the third stanza, which is musically identical to the opening, while the final measures are magically spun out. Nevertheless, as certain phrases—"mit der Töne süßen Klagen" and "mit den Sibertönen"—would seem on paper to be perfectly suited to Björling's voice, we register a slight disappointment at his matter-of-fact reference to the "silver tones" in this first recording, particularly since it is preceded by a pronunciation error ("Röhren" instead of "Rühren"). If we compare this interpretation with Tauber's acoustic recording we cannot but notice how much more crisply the Austrian tenor articulates the text. Although Björling captures well the melancholy of "Liebesschmerz," he fails to suggest, as Tauber does, the colloquial quality of "Ach! sie fliehen dich" or the affectionate warmth of "Liebchen, komm zu mir!" The serenader evoked by Rellstab and Schubert has quite a specific, likeable, character, but Björling's singing undeniably lacks face.

During the *Bell Telephone Hour* nine years later, the tenor—accompanied this time by an orchestra—projects the melody with an almost operatic fullness of tone and more prominent portamentos. The words this time are ardently delivered and there are no pronunciation errors. In its own way this is a highly engaging performance, even though the use of a fairly constant *mezzo forte* dulls the dynamic contrasts, undermining the meaning of the opening line, "Liese flehen meine Lieder" (*softly* my songs implore), and reducing the impact of the crescendo in the final verse, where the serenader entreats his beloved to be moved by his song and make him happy.

A subtler expressive balance begins to emerge in the 1952 studio recording. Schauwecker makes the opening measures sound more interesting, adjusting the tempo and dynamics to the shifting harmonies, and Björling sings more thoughtfully throughout (the pace is slightly slower), combining the soft nocturnal coloring of the earlier reading with a stronger awareness of word-meanings. For the first time "Hörst die Nachtigallen schlagen?" has a questioning quality to it and "Silbertöne" is sung with a certain caress. Nevertheless, he still proves less persuasive than Tauber in his ability to make each phrase flow naturally from the one that precedes it. This quality also distinguishes the recording by Schlusnus[22] (who takes the Lied down a tone but proves exceptionally eloquent), while Fischer-Dieskau,[23] who sings in the same key as Schlusnus, adopts an artful *mezza voce* that would have proved more convincing if he had been capable of making the sound really float (as it must if the serenade is to work its magic). A handsomer half-voice is displayed by another baritone, Gérard Souzay, who lends the song a languorous sensuality in his 1954 recording,[24] while the American tenor Richard Crooks, singing in English (and in the original key) to Schauwecker's accompaniment in 1941,[25] achieves a singularly poetic effect by combining a rich range of dynamic nuance with a more than usually leisurely pace.

Björling's 1955 New Orleans performance reveals greater inspiration in the opening measures, "in der stillen" sung in a genuine *piano*. The tenor's imagination seems fully engaged, as it does in his 1958 Carnegie Hall recital, where the colloquial "Ach! sie flehen dich" is savored more than ever before. The somber coloring of the voice here tends to shift the expressive balance: this time the "heart's yearning" and "pain of love" described in the fourth stanza seem to impregnate the whole song, lending the harmonic modulations of the concluding line a more uncertain meaning (is the serenader rightly optimistic or merely deceiving himself?).

A more serene mood invests Björling's final recording in Atlanta: the hushed leaps to the F at the top of the staff on "stillen" and "Töne" and the seductive melodic curve of "Rühren mit den Silbertönen" create a sense of time suspended. The meaning of the whole song seems in a state of suspension too, poised between optimism and suffering.

SIBELIUS

We think of Björling as being quintessentially Swedish, but his paternal grandmother Henrika Mathilda Lönnquist came from Pori in Finland and it was she who gave her grandson Johan the typically Finnish nickname Jussi. Until 1809 Finland had been under Swedish jurisdiction and even at the time of Björling's birth in 1911 the mother-tongue of most Finnish intellectuals was still Swedish. This was true of Sibelius himself, and although the composer was closely identified with the reawakening of a Finnish national identity, nearly all his songs were set to Swedish texts. Sibelius died in 1957, just two and a half years before Björling, and was the tenor's favorite living composer.[1] As Anna-Lisa Björling wrote, it was "as if Sibelius's music and Jussi's singing sprang from the same source of inspiration."[2] The composer often sent Björling congratulatory telegrams after concerts and when the two finally met, in Ainola on Sibelius's eighty-sixth birthday in 1951, the tenor was given a photograph dedicated to "the genius, the great singer, Jussi Björling."[3]

"Svarta rosor" (op. 36 no. 1)

January 30, 1940: New York, Manhattan Center
Harry Ebert, pf.
Naxos 8.110789

June 20, 1951: Helsinki, University Auditorium
Finnish Radio Orchestra, cond. Nils-Eric Fougstedt

April 11, 1952: New York, Manhattan Center
Frederick Schauwecker, pf.
Testament SBT 1427

October 3, 1952: Stockholm, Concert Hall
Swedish Radio Orchestra, cond. Sten Frykberg
Naxos 8.111083-85

September 24, 1955: New York, Carnegie Hall
Frederick Schauwecker, pf.
RCA 88697748922

December 14, 1955: New Orleans, Municipal Auditorium
Frederick Schauwecker, pf.
Premiere Opera 122

December 8, 1957: New York, Carnegie Hall
New York Philharmonic Orchestra, cond. Martti Similä
Bluebell ABCD 050

July 18, 1958: Stockholm, Concert Hall
Swedish Radio Orchestra, Stockholm Philharmonic Orchestra, cond. Georg Ludwig Jochum
Bluebell ABCD 036

August 5, 1960: Gothenburg, Concert Hall
Gothenburg Symphony Orchestra, cond. Nils Grevillius
Bluebell ABCD 092

Five of the seven Sibelius songs featured in the tenor's concert repertoire were recorded (the two exceptions were "Den första kyssen" and "Jubal") and in no other music does Björling seem to have such easy access to deep emotion. This is certainly true of "Svarta rosor," the most famous of all Sibelius's songs, which brings us face to face with the dark underside of both the composer's psyche and the tenor's. The song, based on a text by Ernst Josephson, was dedicated to the soprano Ida Ekman, who first performed it in September 1899 and went on to record it, aged thirty-one, in 1906.[4] Twelve years later the composer wrote in his diary:

> They—our female singers—they "make too much" of every phrase. The absolute music which I write is so exclusively musical and strictly independent of the words that reciting them is not a good idea. Ida Ekman has understood this, which is why she is incomparable.[5]

In Björling Sibelius found another singer who was profoundly musical in inspiration and there is no doubt that the tenor's approach to verbal coloring, inspired as much by the harmonies and accompanying instruments as by the meaning of the words, was ideally suited to a song like "Svarta rosor," which had been in David Björling's repertoire and which Jussi had sung in public as early as 1931. His emotional understanding of the image of the black-petalled rosebush rooted in a human heart is immediately clear in his 1940 studio recording. Since the song has a low tessitura, he sings it not in C major (easier for a soprano or mezzo with a strong chest register), but in the alternative key of D major, although it is the sharply contrasting refrain in D sharp minor ("ty sorgen har nattsvarta rosor") that clings to the memory, particularly when repeated a final time in the upper register, giving the tenor a chance to rise to a penetrating *fortissimo* A-sharp. At the same time there is no sense of any weakness (as emerges in Nicolai Gedda's 1971 recording)[6] when the voice descends repeatedly to D and D sharp below the staff.

There were no tenors among the singers who recorded this song in the first decade of the twentieth century, but Björling's mentor John Forsell recorded it twice (in the original key). In the 1908 recording[7] we hear a handsome timbre and a solid line, but the wide range of the song compels him to employ his head voice at climaxes, dulling the impact of the G-sharp, and the baritone sounds less willing to expose himself emotionally than his pupil. Interestingly, neither Forsell nor Ida Ekman attempt to distinguish in color between the opening question and the subsequent answer. This is difficult to achieve because the shape and range of the two phrases are similar: Björling himself, in his first studio recording, fails to differentiate between the two "characters" in the song, though his phrasing throughout is winning in its candor and builds up relentlessly to the climax, where he reinforces with a bold portamento the descending interval on "sorgen."

When next recorded in this music, during Finland's Sibelius Week in June 1951, Björling managed a more skillfully nuanced opening, inspired here by the caressing sonorities of the harp in the orchestral accompaniment. He is also more attentive to the *pianissimo* marking at the beginning of the refrain, and his delivery of words such as "döden," "röda," and "blod" suggests an imaginative grasp of their meanings that almost shocks the listener. All in all this is a uniquely atmospheric performance, and although the song does not invite identification with a specific character, the searing pain of the suffering heart is conveyed with unflinching immediacy.

The second studio recording with piano accompaniment, made in 1952, shows no loss of freshness and an even more ringing delivery of the final measures (with a crescendo on the top A-sharp). The Stockholm radio concert from the same year offers nothing new, but the New Orleans recital in 1955, transposed down a semitone, reveals an impressively rich lower register, which can also be heard in the 1957 Sibelius Memorial Concert at the Carnegie Hall (also transposed). While this transposition may seem surprising if one considers that A-sharp is the highest note in the song when sung in D major, Björling's objective was not to simply reach that note (which was always easily within his compass), but to produce an emotionally overwhelming *fortissimo* that included the preceding F-sharp as well: he preferred to transpose rather than risk dulling the effect of that climax.

The finest of the later recordings is the 1958 Swedish concert performance, in D major, which again demonstrates how an orchestral accompaniment could release a wider spectrum of colors in the tenor's voice. His singing here is slightly less atmospheric, but no less intense, than in Helsinki, and his timing in the stringendo passages (which sound like dramatic recitatives) is impeccable. In his final concert in Gothenberg, recorded a month before he died, Björling transposes downward once again and sings with a warmth and beauty of tone that soften the painfulness of the song without reducing its poignancy: as in the other music sung on that occasion, we sense the ripeness of a soul ready to abandon the fray.

"Säv, säv, susa" (op. 36 no. 4)

March 1, 1940: New York, Manhattan Center
Harry Ebert, pf.
Bluebell ABCD 050

June 20, 1951: Helsinki, University Auditorium
Finnish Radio Orchestra, cond. Nils-Eric Fougstedt

October 3, 1952: Stockholm, Concert Hall
Swedish Radio Orchestra, cond. Sten Frykberg
Naxos 8.111083-85

June 9, 1954: Bergen, Concert Palace
Bergen Philharmonic Orchestra, cond. Carl Garaguly
Bluebell ABCD 006

January 18, 1955: Helsinki, B-Messuhalli
Harry Ebert, pf.

September 24, 1955: New York, Carnegie Hall
Frederick Schauwecker, pf.
RCA 88697748922

December 8, 1957: New York, Carnegie Hall
New York Philharmonic Orchestra, cond. Martti Similä
Bluebell ABCD 050

July 18, 1958: Stockholm, Concert Hall
Swedish Radio Orchestra, Stockholm Philharmonic Orchestra, cond. Georg Ludwig Jochum
Bluebell ABCD 036

February 8, 1959: Stockholm, Concert Hall
Royal Court Orchestra, cond. Nils Grevillius
Swedish Society Discofil SCD 1100

August 5, 1960: Gothenburg, Concert Hall
Gothenburg Symphony Orchestra, cond. Nils Grevillius
Bluebell ABCD 092

This song demonstrates, as well as any other piece of music his repertoire, the eloquence Björling could achieve when singing in his mother tongue. Gustaf Fröding's poem is striking enough on its own terms, haunting in atmosphere and painful in its account of the victimization and drowning of a young woman called Ingallil, and in Sibelius's setting (and Björling's voice) it is hard to separate the meaning of the words from the duration and pitches of the notes. The tenor brings the words alive entirely through the music, and by means of the sheer transparency with which each vowel is exposed to the listener's ears. If one compares for example the live recording made in Helsinki by Gérard Souzay (singing in G-flat major) in October 1956[8] with Björling's own recital performance recorded in the same city the year before, one notices how dull by comparison the French baritone's vowels sound, how limited his expressive range seems. This is not simply a matter of idiomatic pronunciation, but of the inner vitality of the voice itself.

Björling was undoubtedly helped by the higher tessitura (he generally chose B-flat major for this song, though he sometimes sang it a semitone lower), for the middle register of the tenor voice is arguably better suited than that of the baritone to evoking both the rustling of the reeds (referred to in the title) and the numbing horror of Ingallil's being blinded by thorns. It is remarkable how the tenor manages to convey, in each of his recorded performances, both the immediacy of that suffering and the infinite tenderness of the narration.

Björling's first studio recording, made when he was barely twenty-nine, reveals already a total understanding of the song's meaning combined with a youthful freshness of sound that lends the narration a singular poignancy. The gently descending lines of the soft opening, bound by the portamento of the breath, show his skill in making the listener visualize the lakeside setting where Ingallil's drowning is recalled. As the narrator goes on to tell his horrifying story we notice how inevitable and spontaneous he makes each harmonic modulation sound, as if this was the only way those words could reveal their full meaning. When the line crests on the top A of "kärleks skull" the effect is potent indeed, but registers entirely as a manifestation of feeling rather than as pure sound. The return of the descending melody, *Molto tranquillo*, at the end of the song is remarkable for the sensitiveness and beauty with which Björling, working within a *piano* dynamic, caresses and modulates each tone in accordance with the inner resonance of the word itself, right up to the dying close on "slå!"

The tenor never entirely surpassed this early version, but if one turns to his final recording in Gothenburg, sung in the same key, the greater ripeness of the voice lends a different perspective to the narration. The orchestral accompaniment does not influence Björling's phrasing as strikingly as in "Svarta rosor," but the drama of Ingallil's death undeniably unfolds on a larger scale here and the top A is released with stunning fullness. His soft singing is no less sensitive than before, but is permeated this time with a truly adult awareness, confirming the extra degree of psychological maturity the tenor attained in his final recordings.

"Demanten på marssnön" (op. 36 no. 6)

January 18, 1955: Helsinki, B-Messuhalli
Harry Ebert, pf.

September 24, 1955: New York, Carnegie Hall
Frederick Schauwecker, pf.
RCA 88697748922

December 14, 1955: New Orleans, Municipal Auditorium
Frederick Schauwecker, pf.
Premiere Opera 122

July 19, 1956: Stockholm, Gröna Lund
Harry Ebert, pf.
Bluebell ABCD 114

December 8, 1957: New York, Carnegie Hall
New York Philharmonic Orchestra, cond. Martti Similä
Bluebell ABCD 050

February 8, 1959: Stockholm, Concert Hall
Royal Court Orchestra, cond. Nils Grevillius
Swedish Society Discofil SCD 1100

In the 1957 Memorial Concert for Sibelius at the Carnegie Hall, Björling announced this song (an encore) as "The Diamond Snow in March." A more accurate translation would be "A Diamond in the March Snow," but both English titles give us an idea of the typically Nordic imagery that imbues this poem about love written by the very young Finnish poet Josef Julius Wecksell in the 1850s (the song itself, like "Säv, säv, susa," was composed at the turn of the century). As in the other two songs he performed from the op.

36 group, Björling arguably surpasses all other male singers on disc in his evocation of the wintry landscape and the dazzling impact of sun on snow. His Helsinki performance in 1955 is as good as any, with the opening lines descending slowly and seamlessly to create an illusion of breathless stillness. Although the range of the song (he takes it up a tone, to C major) offers no particular challenges, the perfection of his line and unfailing luminescence of tone represent a formidable demonstration of technique, even more than does Kirsten Flagstad's studio recording,[9] which is taken a little too fast to savor the timelessness of the moment.

The tenor recaptures the same magical atmosphere in New Orleans in December 1955, while the Carnegie Hall recital recorded three months earlier displays his voice without its usual aura and the Gröna Lund rendition the following July finds him in a more outgoing mood that fits the setting of the concert but makes the song unduly literal in meaning.

The orchestral accompaniment (Sibelius's own arrangement) heard in the 1957 Memorial Concert (Björling's only surviving recording with the New York Philharmonic) encourages him to phrase on a bigger scale, turning the piece into a more conventional romantic song and depriving it of its contemplative intensity. This intensity is recaptured in his studio recording of the orchestral version made with Grevillius in 1959. Once again the phrasing is rapt, suggesting not only the physical reality of the scene described but also the symbolic focus of the poet's line of thought.

"Var det en dröm?" (op. 37 no. 4)

June 20, 1951: Helsinki, University Auditorium
Finnish Radio Orchestra, cond. Nils-Eric Fougstedt

October 3, 1952: Stockholm, Concert Hall
Swedish Radio Orchestra, cond. Sten Frykberg
Naxos 8.111083-85

December 8, 1957: New York, Carnegie Hall
New York Philharmonic Orchestra, cond. Martti Similä
Bluebell ABCD 050

This through-composed song, inspired by another Wecksell love poem, is dominated by the subjective viewpoint of the poet who recalls a brief love-affair as if it had been a mere dream. It is the tone of voice here that counts more than the images evoked, and in his 1951 performance Björling—encouraged by the densely-textured orchestral accompaniment—invests the melody with an extra degree of warmth and fullness, rising stirringly to the As above the staff and pensively to the Cs below, which take on a truly baritonal quality (the song is transposed upward from B-flat major to C major).

The line is just as seamlessly sustained as in his other Sibelius recordings (he shows great dexterity in "stealing" breaths), but the emotion here is much closer to the surface.

A similar effect is achieved in the 1957 concert (where no loss of luster can be perceived), while in Stockholm in 1952 the phrasing is slightly less impulsive, acquiring a wistful hue even on the stronger notes below the staff.

"Flickan kom ifrån sin älsklings möte" (op. 37 no. 5)

June 20, 1951, Helsinki, University Auditorium
Finnish Radio Orchestra, cond. Nils-Eric Fougstedt

December 8, 1957: New York, Carnegie Hall
New York Philharmonic Orchestra, cond. Martti Similä
Bluebell ABCD 050

This troubling ballad of lost innocence—typically nineteenth-century in spirit, but first published in 1901—is commonly known as "The Tryst" and is inspired by a text by Johan Ludvig Runeberg, Finland's national poet (who happened to share Björling's birthday, February 5). In the tenor's 1951 performance (heard by the composer over the radio) he does not invent different voices in the dialogue between the trysting girl and her mother any more than Sibelius distinguishes between the two in the vocal writing, nor does he capture as vividly as Irina Arkhipova[10] (singing in Russian) the artifice with which the girl explains away her red fingers and lips. But although his phrasing is less overtly emotional, Björling displays a capacity for feeling as highly-developed as that of the Russian mezzo in this narrative, and unlike her he makes us share not only the girl's bleak longing for the grave after her lover's betrayal, but also the deep compassion of the narrator who reports her words. Throughout the song the lush string accompaniment draws a tensile yet liquid line from the tenor, who seems to nourish every syllable with human understanding.

The voice sounds slightly drier in New York six years later, but the sense of drama is even more vivid. Björling (who as in Helsinki transposes from D-flat to E-flat major) stretches the phrasing with a more daring sense of rubato and captures with particular intensity the ominous minor-mode opening of the final section of impersonal narrative, leading up to the daughter's bleak confession.

RICHARD STRAUSS

"Zueignung" (op. 10 no. 1)

October 7, 1945: Detroit, Masonic Temple Auditorium
Ford Symphony Orchestra, cond. Dimitri Mitropoulos

October 23, 1950: New York, Rockefeller Center
Bell Telephone Orchestra, cond. Donald Voorhees
WHRA-6036

December 14, 1955: New Orleans, Municipal Auditorium
Frederick Schauwecker, pf.
Premiere Opera 122

March 8, 1958: New York, Carnegie Hall
Frederick Schauwecker, pf.
RCA GD 60520

April 13, 1959: Atlanta, Glenn Memorial Auditorium
Frederick Schauwecker, pf.
Bluebell ABCD 020

The English critic Alan Blyth, writing in *Song on Record*, dismissed "Zueignung" as a "somewhat paltry piece," its interpretation requiring "no great insights."[1] It is true that Richard Strauss set Hermann von Gilm's text (with a tenor voice in mind) when he was just eighteen, but it is impossible to imagine a finer setting of those simple words, with the accompanying triplets lending an undercurrent of youthful buoyancy to the lover's outpouring of gratitude and devotion. Björling captures this buoyancy best in his own most youthful recording (made when he was thirty-four), where he is further inspired by Dimitri Mitropoulos's sweepingly romantic accompaniment. The performance lasts nine seconds longer (1:55) than the disc in which Strauss himself accompanies Heinrich Schlusnus at the piano,[2] but a number of the features found in that disc are also included here, such as the softening of tone and slowing of pace in "und du segnetest den Trank" and the mighty *allargando* on the climax of "heilig" (here a heart-warming top A). It is true that Björling's German diction is not as crisp as Schlusnus's, or Richard Tauber's in his more leisurely 1919 recording (2:06),[3] but there is a hint of squareness in the phrasing of the two German-speaking singers that the Swede avoids here. He seems indeed to be totally alive to the broad emotional gestures the music is making, singing with ever-engaging freshness of tone.

The later recordings are largely similar in phrasing (another feature is the *mezza voce* delivery of "Herzen krank") and even closer to Strauss's own tempo, yet there is a definite loss of immediacy. This is particularly true of the routinely accompanied *Bell Telephone Hour* version, but even the recital performances—though warmly delivered (the Carnegie Hall rendition is a final encore)—fail to recapture the impression of a lover communicating with intense immediacy.

"Ständchen" (op. 17 no. 2)

January 13, 1946: Detroit, Masonic Temple Auditorium
Ford Symphony Orchestra, cond. Eugene Ormandy

November 7, 1949: New York, Rockefeller Center
Bell Telephone Orchestra, cond. Donald Voorhees
WHRA-6036

July 6, 1950: Stockholm, Gröna Lund
Harry Ebert, pf.
Bluebell ABCD 114

November 19, 1951: New York, Rockefeller Center
Firestone Orchestra, cond. Howard Barlow
Kultur DVD D2424

April 11, 1952: New York, Manhattan Center
Frederick Schauwecker, pf.
Testament SBT 1427

July 19, 1956: Stockholm, Gröna Lund
Harry Ebert, pf.
Bluebell ABCD 114

July 18, 1958: Stockholm, Concert Hall
Swedish Radio Orchestra, Stockholm Philharmonic Orchestra, cond. Georg Ludwig Jochum
Bluebell ABCD 036

August 20, 1959: Stockholm, Gröna Lund
Bertil Bokstedt, pf.
Bluebell ABCD 114

This is another young man's song, composed when Strauss was still in his early twenties, and Björling is at his best when he can be seen as well as heard. In the 1951 *Voice of Firestone* telecast he acts out the serenade before a lighted window, where the silhouette of his loved-one appears during the third verse. The staging is ingenuous but the tenor sings with a disarming half-smile and his acting is never less than plausible, his face revealing intense concentration on the meaning of every word. His delivery of much of the song perfectly reflects Strauss's *Vivace e dolce*: the phrasing conveys the urgency of a real lover (the tempo is similar to the composer's own in his 1942 recording with Julius Patzak),[4] but with an appropriate blend of head voice in the upper register to maintain the atmosphere of moonlit intimacy. The words, moreover, are delivered with a certain *sprezzatura*, acquiring an extra density in the sharply contrasting third verse, which soars to a warm (but not overweighted) A-natural.

Björling's phrasing is admittedly less varied in tempo and subtly inflected than Patzak's in his classic 1931 recording,[5] but he exudes a degree of virility that his Viennese colleague cannot match. Both tenors are accompanied by an orchestra (in Felix Mottl's arrangement), but Patzak transposes down a semitone from the original key of F-sharp major and Björling's greater ease in the upper register adds an extra lift to certain phrases.

The televised broadcast is very similar in phrasing to Björling's earlier recordings of the Lied, and later versions maintain a similar overall profile. From the 1952 studio recording onward, however, the tenor increasingly favors a more muscular approach that contrasts with Strauss's *dolce* marking, and he tends to make much less of the traditional rallentando (which Strauss himself adds in his 1942 recording) in "Drum leise, mein Mädchen." By the time we get to the piano-accompanied 1959 recording, the singing is overloud from beginning to end, and the decidedly Wagnerian final cadence sounds exaggerated in its portentousness.

"Cäcilie" (op. 27 no. 3)

November 13, 1938: Detroit, Masonic Temple Auditorium
Ford Symphony Orchestra, cond. José Iturbi
VAIA 1118

July 15, 1939: Stockholm, Concert Hall
Harry Ebert, pf.
EMI 5 75900 2

September 24, 1955: New York, Carnegie Hall
Frederick Schauwecker, pf.
RCA 88697748922

August 5, 1957: Stockholm, Gröna Lund
Bertil Bokstedt, pf.
Bluebell ABCD 114

February 8, 1958: Stockholm, Cirkus
Bertil Bokstedt, pf.
Bluebell ABCD 050

Richard Strauss's operatic roles for tenors are seldom vocally ingratiating, and Björling sang only a handful of performances as Narraboth in *Salome* and Count Elemer in *Arabella* in 1931–34. The composer's Lieder, on the other hand offer unique expressive opportunities for a beautiful and well-trained tenor voice, and no song illustrates this as well as "Cäcilie." In his first recording we hear the orchestral version in E-flat major superbly conducted by José Iturbi, and the solo voice bounds through the music like a young athlete. Phrases leap off the page and the final ascent to B-flat is negotiated with perfect legato and soaring ease. Free from technical preoccupations, the twenty-six-year-old Björling adheres spontaneously to the expressiveness of the music, conveying the contagious enthusiasm, burning passion, anguished loneliness and rising ecstasy that are evoked in turn in Heinrich Hart's poem. The voice is so perfectly poised on the breath that it is sufficient for the tenor to pronounce the words clearly and mirror the orchestral timbres—something he does entirely spontaneously—in order to obtain the ideal coloring for every phrase.

Two years later, in 1939, Björling made a studio recording of the Lied in the original key of E major, but although he has no difficulty with the final ascent to top B, the performance sounds relatively earthbound, as if the studio setting (and routine accompaniment) had blunted his capacity for imaginative identification. The tenor's other truly treasurable performance of "Cäcilie" was captured at his Gröna Lund recital in 1957. Here Bertil Bokstedt's piano accompaniment (in E-flat) helps him enter the spirit of the music with genuine fervor. His darker tone here is reminiscent of Lauritz Melchior's classic 1926 recording,[6] more declamatory in emphasis than Björling's, but no less at ease when riding the crest of Strauss's impetuous melody.

"Morgen" (op. 27 no. 4)

July 15, 1939: Stockholm, Concert Hall
Harry Ebert, pf.
EMI 5 75900 2

April 11, 1952: New York, Manhattan Center
Frederick Schauwecker, pf.
Testament SBT 1427

August 5, 1957: Stockholm, Gröna Lund
Bertil Bokstedt, pf.
Bluebell ABCD 114

July 18, 1958: Stockholm, Concert Hall
Swedish Radio Orchestra, Stockholm Philharmonic Orchestra, cond. Georg Ludwig Jochum
Bluebell ABCD 036

This piece is more closely associated with sopranos than with tenors, even though there is nothing in John Henry Mackay's poem that suggests a specifically female point of view. The truth is that few male voices command the sheer beauty and refinement of tone needed to convey the spiritual serenity of this much-loved song. Indeed Björling's achievement in his 1939 studio recording (in the original key of F major) is unmatched by any other tenor on disc. His purity of sound lends the music a transcendental meaning that is missing in even the finest performances by other tenors. Comparing this version with Patzak's tellingly-inflected interpretation recorded five years later with Strauss himself on the podium,[7] we notice how the Austrian tenor focuses our attention on the personality of the man who is singing, while with Björling it is the vision of "tomorrow" that counts. The Swede's voice—which boasts a rarer, fresher beauty and is grounded on a firmer foundation of breath support—proves deeply reassuring right from the tranquil opening (*sehr ruhig*) and sustains the slowly unfolding melody (*Langsam*) with a simplicity of phrasing that proves directly evocative, in contrast with Patzak's more consciously "artistic" approach. Both tenors employ a pure head voice when ascending to the F and G at the top of the staff, but arguably only Björling conveys, in "Wogenblauen," a sense of infinity, a dimension that goes beyond the literal meaning of the word. Even Tauber, in his fine acoustic disc,[8] fails to conjure up such a persuasive image of future union with the poet's loved-one, although he lends a singularly pensive tone to the Lied's dying close.

Björling's 1952 studio remake is something of a disappointment. The phrasing is beautifully sculpted and words are more scrupulously projected than before, but the fuller tone employed suggests a blunting of the singer's imagination. The 1957 Gröna Lund performance, on the other hand, is gratifyingly alive, darker in coloration but rich in contrasts (the head voice in "Wogenblauen" is reinstated), and the tenor is well-matched at the keyboard by Bertil Bokstedt, the most emotionally sensitive of his accompanists. After Björling's death this fine musician recalled how the tenor would "put his personal stamp" on the accompaniment: "He would say, for example: 'Bertil, when we come to that piano interlude, let the phrase flow in the same spirit as I have sung, let it ring out, don't be slow, feel the music intensely.'"

Almost equally captivating is Björling's only performance of the Lied with orchestral accompaniment, where the prominent solo violin inspires him to employ his sweetest, most finished tones and to recapture much of the magic heard in the 1939 and 1957 recordings.

"Traum durch die Dämmerung" (op. 29 no. 1)

September 24, 1955: New York, Carnegie Hall
Frederick Schauwecker, pf.
RCA 88697748922

December 14, 1955: New Orleans, Municipal Auditorium
Frederick Schauwecker, pf.
Premiere Opera 122

April 13, 1959: Atlanta, Glenn Memorial Auditorium
Frederick Schauwecker, pf.
Bluebell ABCD 020

June 16, 1959: Stockholm, Gröna Lund
Harry Ebert, pf.
ABCD 114

There is little aural evidence that Björling modelled his Lieder singing on that of any earlier singer, but we know that he had a chance to hear Richard Tauber in recital when he was still a student at the Royal Academy in Stockholm and that these two outstandingly musical tenors spent a lot of time together when Björling made his 1936 debut at the Vienna Staatsoper. Of all the Lieder that were common to both their repertoires, "Traum durch die Dämmerung" is the one in which Björling—particularly in his finest performance, recorded in Atlanta in 1959—seems to echo the acoustic disc[9] made by Tauber in the early twenties. Tauber's dynamics are even more hushed than Björling's (who prefers a crescendo to a *mezza voce* on "blaues") and some of his breath spans are even longer (in "nun geh' ich hin zu der schönsten Frau," for example), but the same serene nocturnal spirit takes possession of both tenors in these performances and Björling proves almost as skillful as Tauber in coloring the words. The smoothness of their legato and the perfect integration of their head voices are other shared qualities that have yet to be surpassed. Tauber sings in the original key of F-sharp while Björling takes the Lied up a semitone in his first three recordings, which are similar in approach, although the voice boasts a uniquely golden hue in Atlanta. His final performance in Gröna Lund is transposed upward by a whole tone and can be frankly ignored, for the singing is consistently overloud (he even ignores the *pianissimo* marking on "schönsten") and the right atmosphere is established only in the final measures.

VERDI

Only six of the fifty-three theatrical works Björling sang during his three-decade adult career were composed by Verdi, but these half-dozen roles account for a quarter (222) of all his operatic performances. He was in his early twenties when he made his debut in *Rigoletto, Il trovatore, La traviata, Un ballo in maschera,* and *Aida,* and with the exception of *Traviata* these works were still in his repertoire twenty years later. By the 1950s indeed these four operas, along with *Don Carlo,* represented nearly half his active stage repertoire. Yet in spite of his progressive specialization in the roles he found most congenial, Björling is seldom the first name that springs to mind when making a list of Verdi tenors. This has much to do with the fact that he was neither Italian by birth nor professionally based in Italy, where performing traditions were naturally more idiomatic than elsewhere. Although Björling was engaged for an epoch-making revival of *Don Carlo* at the Met in 1950, he was never actively involved in rediscovering neglected works by Verdi: he performed no music from any of the operas composed before 1850 and had no part in the Stockholm production of the rarely-heard *Simon Boccanegra* in the early 1940s. Nor did he make a point of reinstating traditionally-cut cabalettas or opening up internal excisions in the music he did sing. This is not really surprising, for interest in "neglected masterpieces" and the integrity of the score only gained real momentum after Björling's death, when it became quite clear that no Italian composer born since 1900 could match the audience appeal of the great masters of romantic opera and *verismo.* Repertoire renewal would thus depend much more on rediscoveries and freshly-conceived revivals than on new works. Björling's career developed too soon (and was cut short too early) for him to be involved in this, and there is little doubt that he saw himself not as a Verdi specialist but simply as part of an ongoing performing tradition centered on those canonical works that had long proved most popular with audiences. In this respect he was closer in mentality to Enrico Caruso (who also sang six Verdi roles), Aureliano Pertile (who sang seven), and Giovanni Martinelli (who sang nine) than to Carlo Bergonzi (nineteen) and Placido Domingo (twenty-three).[1]

Perhaps the first tenor, in an Italian context, to see himself as a restorer of lost values was Giacomo Lauri Volpi, who sang eight Verdi operas between 1919 and 1959. Although hardly interested in most aspects of performance practice, he considered himself heir to the tradition embodied by late-nineteenth century singers such as Francesco Marconi, and was often cited by postwar Italian critics[2] as an example of pre-veristic technique and sensibility. Unfortunately a good number of Lauri Volpi's recordings were made when his voice was in decline and when his style had degenerated into mannerism, but he was right in believing that the influence of Caruso—resulting in a less subtly-inflected melodic line and an overweighted middle register—had altered the expressive emphasis of Verdi tenor singing.

Björling would never have reasoned in these terms, and his respect for Lauri Volpi[3] was insignificant compared to the adoration he felt for Caruso. Yet in a very real sense he unconsciously put into practice some of the ideals that Lauri Volpi promoted fervently in his books on singing.[4] This was possible partly because of his physical remoteness, during his musical training, from the nerve centres of the Italian operatic tradition, where the *verismo* aesthetic had a powerful impact on the way the earlier operas were presented. In Stockholm most of the older singers engaged by the Royal Opera in the 1930s conserved many aspects of nineteenth century style, with the director of the company, John Forsell, much closer in spirit to the *bel canto* pedagogue Manuel García than to Pietro Mascagni.

The compelling quality of Björling's singing in mid-nineteenth-century operas owes even more, however, to his musical sensibility and to the unclouded beauty of his timbre, reminiscent perhaps of the quintessentially Verdian tones of Gaetano Fraschini (1816–87). Fraschini's voice was likened by Gino Monaldi to the sound of a silver plate struck by a silver hammer,[5] and though unremarkable as an actor he proved, like Björling, highly successful in the contrasting but complementary parts of Manrico, Alfredo, and the Duke of Mantua. Fraschini created five Verdi roles in all, including Riccardo in *Un ballo in maschera*, and for many years was the composer's favorite tenor.

Unlike the majority of their nineteenth century predecessors (including Fraschini and Francesco Tamagno, the first Otello), most twentieth century "Verdi tenors" (including Caruso, Pertile, Franco Corelli, Bergonzi, and Domingo) tended to favor a covered, almost baritonal, sound; Bergonzi, perhaps the most critically acclaimed of them all, made a point of claiming "you need a dark voice for Verdi."[6] In some cases this is true: an exclusively sunny timbre would be inappropriate for such tormented heroes as Don Alvaro and Otello, who also need, like Manrico and Radamès, to sound sufficiently adult and soldierly to make their military achievements credible. But Verdi's music requires above all a sure command of chiaroscuro—a constant interplay of bright and dark colors—and Björling was supremely well-equipped from this point of view: his voice was so responsive that he could open or cover the sound at will across a range of two octaves. A dark sound, moreover, is certainly not indispensable for the Duke of Mantua or for the Fraschini role of Riccardo, which was one of Björling's most satisfying portrayals. This *melodramma*—which in Verdi's original conception had a Swedish setting—was coincidentally the last opera he sang in Italy, both live (at La Scala in 1951) and in the studio (the ill-fated recording at the Teatro dell'Opera in Rome with Solti, left unfinished in July 1960). The Scala performances were well-received by audiences; Toscanini was present during one of them and was sufficiently impressed by what he heard to engage Björling three years later for his NBC broadcast of the opera (the tenor's poor health would, however, compel him to withdraw from the engagement after rehearsals had started). Nevertheless, the performances disappointed two of the most influential Italian critics of that era, Eugenio Gara (author of a biography of Caruso) and Rodolfo Celletti (author of a guide to recorded operas).[7] This lack of enthusiasm, although based on limited direct experience, had a considerable influence on Björling's subsequent reputation in Italy. This was not helped by some of the complete recordings of Verdi operas that appeared in the following years, where studio microphones dulled the ring in the tenor's upper register and the spontaneity of his projection of the text. Verbal eloquence, reinforced by a fiery, energetic delivery, is an expressive priority for Verdi, whose almost untranslatable term *parola scenica*—used in his correspondence to stimulate the theatrical instincts of his librettists—reminds us of how a few vivid words set to music can focalize the emotional conflicts of an entire scene. One of the male singers the composer most admired, the French baritone Victor Maurel, was appreciated above all for his ability to project verbal nuance with startling immediacy, an admiration that was apparently undiminished by his French accent, clearly audible in his "creator" recordings from *Otello* and *Falstaff*.

Björling's foreign accent was by comparison barely perceptible most of the time, but he never really cultivated (at least in Italian) the sort of eloquence achieved by Maurel or his tenor colleague Francesco Tamagno, who succeeded in making the words come vibrantly alive in his recordings of the final scene from *Otello* (the conductor Tullio Serafin, who heard Tamagno sing that scene on the stage, stressed how uniquely moving his phrasing was).[8] This helps us understand why the baritone Paolo Silveri, who performed with Björling in the Met *Don Carlo* and the Scala *Ballo in maschera*, described him as "a complete artist" of undeniable stage presence but stressed that "the quality of his voice was superior to his interpretative renditions."[9]

On disc, however, the Swedish tenor's sheer musical refinement offers rich compensation. In spite of the relatively limited range of roles he sang, few Verdi tenors have demonstrated such genuine expressive versatility. In

1951 Björling made a hugely effective recording of Otello's most muscular duet, "Sì, pel ciel marmoreo giuro," yet he proved equally adept at negotiating the cadenza attributed to Angelo Masini in the Duke of Mantua's Canzone and the *staccato e leggerissimo* passage in Riccardo's Barcarola. While in the more slowly unfolding lyrical melodies that take us to the heart of Verdi's characters, Björling often surpasses both Caruso and Bergonzi (not to mention Lauri Volpi) in the inspired musical balance he achieves between clear articulation, beauty of tone and an exquisite—yet ever unaffected—shaping of the melody. His instrument was so finely tuned that he was able to reveal the formal architecture of Verdi's set pieces—both arias and ensembles—with incomparable grace, highlighting symmetries and dynamic contrasts, building up climaxes with uncanny rhythmic awareness, and maintaining throughout that elevated nobility of expression that distinguishes the aristocratic heroes of romantic opera, however fallible, from their more earthbound counterparts in *verismo* works. This sensitivity to the shape of the music he was singing was if anything even more indispensable in the seventh Verdi masterpiece he performed, the *Messa da Requiem.* In this monumental work, indeed, the qualities that made him unique as a singer emerge even more conclusively.

Rigoletto
Complete Recordings

December 29, 1945: New York, Metropolitan Opera House
Jussi Björling (Duca di Mantova), Leonard Warren (Rigoletto), Bidú Sayão (Gilda), Norman Cordon (Sparafucile), Martha Lipton (Maddalena), William Hargrave (Monterone); Metropolitan Opera Chorus and Orchestra, cond. Cesare Sodero
Music & Arts CD-636

June 16–28, 1956: Rome, Teatro dell'Opera
Jussi Björling (Duca di Mantova), Robert Merrill (Rigoletto), Roberta Peters (Gilda), Giorgio Tozzi (Sparafucile), Anna Maria Rota (Maddalena), Vittorio Tatozzi (Monterone); Rome Opera Chorus and Orchestra, cond. Jonel Perlea
RCA Victor 60172-2-RG

January 5, 1957: Stockholm, Royal Opera House
Jussi Björling (Duca di Mantova), Erik Sunquist (Rigoletto), Eva Prytz (Gilda), Sven-Erik Jacobsson (Sparafucile), Kerstin Meyer (Maddalena), Georg Svedenbrant (Monterone); Royal Swedish Opera Chorus, Royal Court Orchestra, cond. Kurt Bendix
Bluebell ABCD 044

"Questa o quella"

May 12, 1930: Stockholm, Concert Hall
Unspecified orchestra, cond. Nils Grevillius
Naxos 8.110722

June 16, 1941: Stockholm, Concert Hall
Unspecified orchestra, cond. Nils Grevillius
EMI 5 66306 2

March 27–30, 1944: Stockholm, Concert Hall
Unspecified orchestra, cond. Nils Grevillius
EMI 5 75900 2

April 7, 1951: Stockholm, Royal Academy of Music
Swedish Radio Orchestra, cond. Sten Frykberg
Bluebell ABCD 103

"È il sol dell'anima"

June 17, 1941: Stockholm, Concert Hall
Jussi Björling (Duca), Hjördis Schymberg (Gilda); unspecified orchestra, cond. Nils Grevillius
EMI 5 66306 2 (take 1); Bluebell ABCD 016

February 17, 1957: New York, CBS Studio
Jussi Björling (Duca), Hilde Güden (Gilda), Thelma Votipka (Giovanna), Metropolitan Opera Orchestra, cond. Fausto Cleva

"La donna è mobile"

December 20, 1933: Stockholm, Concert Hall
Unspecified orchestra, cond. Nils Grevillius
Naxos 8.110722

December 3, 1936: Stockholm, Concert Hall
Unspecified orchestra, cond. Nils Grevillius
EMI 5 75900 2

December 5, 1937: New York, Carnegie Hall
General Motors Symphony Orchestra, cond. Erno Rapee
VAI VAIA 1189

August 10, 1951: Stockholm, Gröna Lund
Harry Ebert, pf.
Bluebell ABCD 114

June 4, 1954: Stockholm, Royal Opera House
Royal Opera Orchestra, cond. Lamberto Gardelli
Bluebell ABCD 080

October 20, 1955: Seattle, Civic Auditorium
Frederick Schauwecker, pf.
VRCS-2001

July 19, 1956: Stockholm, Gröna Lund
Harry Ebert, pf.
Bluebell ABCD 114

February 17, 1957: New York, CBS studio
Metropolitan Opera Orchestra, cond. Fausto Cleva
Premiere Opera DVD

March 2, 1958: New York, Carnegie Hall
Frederick Schauwecker, pf.
RCA 60520-2-RG

Rigoletto was not only the earliest (and first) Verdi opera that Björling sang on stage, but also the earliest complete opera by any composer that he continued to sing regularly throughout his career. He interpreted the Duke of Mantua fifty-six times in all, making his debut at the Royal Opera in Stockholm in February 1932 and giving his last performance in Chicago on November 19, 1958. Stockholm and Chicago, along with New York, were the cities where he was heard most often as the Duke, but he also performed the part in Dresden, Vienna, Copenhagen, Milan, Cleveland, Detroit, San Francisco, Los Angeles, and Helsinki, sharing the stage with some of the best-loved sopranos of his era (including Maria Cebotari, Lily Pons, Bidú Sayão, Teresa Stich-Randall, Roberta Peters, Hilde Güden, and Anna Moffo) and a number of the most charismatic baritones (Lawrence Tibbett, Leonard Warren, Carlo Tagliabue, Tito Gobbi, Hugo Hasslo, and Cornell MacNeil). It was, by a short margin, the role that remained longest in his active repertoire.

The Duke is one of Verdi's most original creations, an amoral Renaissance aristocrat, completely and justifiably self-confident (considering the good fortune that accompanies him). Like Don Giovanni he has made an art of seduction, but unlike Mozart's character he invariably succeeds in his conquests. Light-hearted and hedonistic, he seems to inhabit a world of comedy rather than tragedy. In the third act, for example, he is the only character who is intent on enjoying himself, quite unaware of the tragic irony of the situation, and on one level at least we cannot help admiring him for this (the audience, as well as Maddalena, should be swept away by his singing in the quartet). The Duke's mood is less than carefree only in the opening scene of act 2, which Verdi's librettist Piave added to preempt censorship by mitigating the character's immorality. Yet although the agitation and empathy expressed in that scene contrast with the cynical exuberance displayed in the first-act Ballata and third-act Canzone, these feelings do not undermine the credibility of the character: we merely witness another mood of a voluble personality who changes chameleon-like according to the situations in which he finds himself. Believing momentarily that he has lost Gilda, his imaginative sympathy with her distress is largely a product of self-pity.

Most tenors would agree that this is one of Verdi's most difficult roles to sing: not because of its range or length but because of the punishingly high tessitura that exposes the slightest weakness in the singer's voice production, particularly in the sustained lines of "Parmi veder le lagrime," which move up and down across the register break (the problem here lies in the correct placement of the repeated Fs and G-flats at the top of the staff). Few singers on record have dealt with these difficulties as effortlessly as Björling, and rarely have the more technically accomplished of his colleagues also possessed the beauty and brilliance of tone required to delineate a dashingly handsome young man. Recorded evidence nevertheless suggests that Björling's identification with the role was by no means immediate, and that it was only in his full artistic maturity that he marshalled all the details of his portrayal (which never included the second-act cabaletta "Possente amor") into proper balance.

The Ballata "Questa o quella" (sung in Swedish as "O, I kvinnor") featured in one of Björling's earliest adult recording sessions, in September 1930. He was only nineteen at the time and his lack of experience is clearly evident in this performance. His timbre delights the ear, however, and the voice rings out boldly on the first high A-flat, in a manner that later readings could not match. His execution is also impressively accurate (the intermittently florid style of this mid-nineteenth-century work in no way fazes him) and ample in its breath-spans, although some details—such as the triplet followed by an acciaccatura on the word "infiora," which invites embellishment—are dulled by the Swedish vowels.

Rigoletto was the first Verdi work to find a permanent place in the international operatic repertoire, and it is rich in performing traditions. One of these is to introduce a short laugh after "derido" in the second verse, but Björling's attempt at it here sounds forced. He also embellishes the repeat of "se mi punge," rising by means of a mordent to a shining high B-flat. Yet despite these decorative features his performance as a whole is tame, limited in its rhythmic flexibility (he does not even observe the fermata on "forse" in the first verse) and dynamic shading. This aria is the Duke's calling card, in which the character proclaims his sexual freedom with a *sprezzatura* that should be reflected in a play of rubato that bends the jaunty 6/8 rhythm without breaking it. The teenage Björling, though he was by no means as sexually naive as he appears here, is too timid in approach, and his often enchanting sounds end up signifying less than they promise.

Much the same is true of his recording of the third-act Canzone "La donna è mobile," made in December 1933, twenty months after his theatrical debut in the role (the critic William Seymer described his singing on that occasion as "sober" and "neat," but lacking in abandon).[10] Once again he performs in Swedish ("Ack, som ett fjun så lätt"), and he takes the aria down a semitone to B-flat major. His voice however has such a dazzling sheen to it throughout the range that this transposition is hardly noticeable, and the traditional cadenza attributed to Masini and made popular by Caruso—which ends here on a top B-flat—is quite stunning, with every note clearly projected and in perfect balance with the others. It provides us with further evidence of Björling's natural ease in coloratura. Other embellishments too—such as the four-note *gruppetto* that replaces the triplet in the phrase "muta d'accento e di pensier" in the second verse—reflect Caruso's 1908 recording.[11] Yet although this is a more sophisticated performance than the 1930 "Questa o quella," it too is rather cautious and metronomic. Björling fails to relish a number of the characteristic details, such as the recurrent alternation of a dotted sixteenth note and thirty-second note which lends the song its insolent propulsion: he too often gives these notes equal value (Caruso was also slipshod in this respect; perhaps the Swedish tenor was following his aural memory rather than the score here). He equally fails to distinguish clearly between *legato*, *legato-sforzando*, and *sforzando*, and offers little dynamic shading: although he prolongs the Gs of "muta d'accento" he makes no attempt at the traditional diminuendo, an effect eschewed by Caruso but favored for example by Beniamino Gigli.[12]

Three years later he recorded the aria again, this time in Italian and in the original key of B major. The sound stage is very different and the voice, though handsome, is less forward and bright in tone. A number of details are executed more precisely, however, and the cadenza is once again very fluent. Yet Björling still fails to achieve the required insouciance of expression, partly owing to his very approximate command of the Italian text: the *t* in "accento" is too softly pronounced and in the second verse he resorts to gibberish in the six measures beginning "felice appieno." Such defects inevitably undermine the credibility of his Duke, for verbal eloquence is one of the ways in which this character establishes his mastery over others. One is not surprised to discover that Björling had given no further stage performances of the role since 1932.

By the time he was next recorded in this aria, in a *General Motors* broadcast live from the Carnegie Hall in November 1937 (his American debut as a tenor), he had acquired valuable stage experience, singing performances of the opera in Dresden, Vienna, and Stockholm again (where he shared the stage for the first time with the outstanding Rigoletto of Lawrence Tibbett).[13] The recording is distorted but captures the startling resonance of his youthful voice, and for the first time he really conveys the spirit of the Duke, playing with the rhythm and making expressive sense of the notation. He sings in Italian with a strong Swedish accent and makes repeated verbal errors in the second verse, which end up unnerving him and curbing the spontaneity of his phrasing. He compensates, however, with a prolonged B-natural at the end.

Björling's first Italian recording of "Questa o quella" was made in Stockholm in 1941, a year and a half after his Metropolitan debut in the role (which was probably the first occasion on which he sang it entirely in Italian). The progress made since his first recording is evident: the sound is richer and more virile and the triplet on "infiora" more elegant. He neglects—as on the earlier disc—a couple of the acciaccaturas, but adds, like Caruso,[14] an extra one on "meglio ad una" and respects the fermata on "forse," prolonging the note. Immediately afterward, however, he sings "un'*u*altra" instead of "un'altra," an error that will prove recurrent. In the second verse he eschews the laughter after "derido" and this time reproduces exactly the embellishments used by Caruso—a rapid ascent to a B-flat followed by a *gruppetto* and a short scale—on the repeat of "se mi punge." He has difficulty, as on later recordings, in pronouncing this last word correctly (the *g* becomes a *y*), but corrects himself the second time. This cadenza can also be heard in the 1903 disc made by Francesco Marconi[15] at the end of his career, confirming its nineteenth-century origins.

A later war-time reading (March 1944) seems less alive than the 1941 performance, the upper register less fresh and ringing. He makes the same pronunciation errors as before, but sings all the acciaccaturas and reintroduces the laugh—this time before "derido"—which sounds more spontaneous on this occasion (Tito Schipa was a master of this effect).[16] Overall, however, Björling is still far from approaching the mastery of innuendo achieved by tenors with a more complete command of the idiom. Fernando De Lucia (who in his complete recording of the opera made in 1917–18 proves uniquely imaginative in his phrasing),[17] Schipa (1916) and Giuseppe di Stefano (live in Mexico City in 1948)[18] are paragons of eloquence in this piece, while Antonio Cortis (1930)[19] and Gigli (in a Detroit concert in 1938)[20] prove almost equally irresistible.

In spite of the mixed results obtained so far in "Questa o quella" and "La donna è mobile," Björling was almost invariably a highly successful Duke on stage: as early as 1937 he triumphed in the role at the Dresden Semperoper and was praised for his "aura of bravado."[21] It should be stressed that these two short arias, though eagerly awaited, represent a relatively small portion of the role, and that very few tenors on disc prove equally convincing in all the Duke's music (Schipa and Cortis are less persuasive in "La donna è mobile," while Lauri Volpi, who triumphed in *Rigoletto* on many of the world's stages, often disappoints on disc). Björling's 1941 recording of the act 1 duet with Gilda, "È il sol dell'anima," does much, moreover, to redress the critical balance. In both of the takes recorded his phrasing of the solo that opens the duet is youthful and sunny in timbre, with a liquid legato and close attention to dynamics. The rising phrase beginning "Adunque amiamoci" demonstrates the ease with which he traverses the register break, the voice expanding warmly as it rises above the staff. The turns are exquisitely voiced, and he adds an extra one on a repeat of "sarò (per te)." His Gilda, Hjördis Schymberg, who first sang the opera with him in 1937, cannot match the tenor's purity of line and diction, but their joint execution of the shortened cadenza is exceptionally musical in effect. This performance is not only as beautifully sung as any on record, but also notably ardent in expression (the second take perhaps even more so). Björling's diction is both clear and eloquent—one regrets only his hardening of the *g* in "angelo" (always a problematic word for him)—and he proves here an expert seducer, an important quality in an opera in which the Duke woos three different women (the Contessa di Ceprano, Gilda and Maddalena), twice in disguise and adopting a different strategy each time.

Full confirmation of this quality is to be found in his first complete recording of the role, broadcast from the Met in December 1945 (these performances were his first alongside the Rigoletto of Leonard Warren, who offers a strongly-etched if unsubtle portrayal here). Conducted by Cesare Sodero, a Naples-born musician of formidable experience, the performance immediately exudes a degree of vitality that is difficult to reproduce in the studio. From the opening dialogue with Borsa one is struck by Björling's virile timbre (he seems quite unrelated to the effete, self-regarding Dukes of light-lyric tenors such as Dino Borgioli),[22] rhythmic precision, and verbal alertness. He clearly has no difficulty in identifying with this extrovert character, although "Questa o quella"—much darker in color than in earlier performances—is rather weightily voiced: sexually threatening perhaps, but still not ideally fatuous or cynical (Sodero's slowish tempo does not help).

Reviewing the first performance in the series a month earlier, Irving Kolodin found that Björling's "exceptional voice" had lost "some of its youthful bloom."[23] That may be true (the sound is much punchier but no longer wears the silvery sheen of the early recordings), but he retains an ideally limpid tone and fluid emission, which allow for an easy command of chiaroscuro. The gracefully flirtatious manner he adopts in the Minuet with the Contessa di Ceprano contrasts markedly with the macho posturing of the Ballata and proves decidely apt. He does not distinguish—as Luciano Pavarotti does[24]—between the words "inebria," "conquide," and "distrugge," all employed half-ironically, but he is perfectly at ease in the *dramma giocoso*

Figure 16. The Duke in *Rigoletto.* Photograph by Louis Melançon. Courtesy of the Metropolitan Opera Archive.

atmosphere evoked in this scene. The subsequent exchanges with Rigoletto are equally pertinent and his contribution to the first ensemble ("Ah sempre tu spingi lo scherzo all'estremo") is admirable for its rhythmic precision and clarity of articulation. Björling's voice cannot be detected in the ensemble that follows Monterone's curse; probably he was saving himself here (like most tenors), for the low tessitura makes it difficult for the Duke to make himself heard.

In the second scene, where the Duke reappears disguised as Gualtier Maldè, Björling proves even more persuasive. One is struck by the sheer beauty of the short phrase "Sua figlia," sung while observing Rigoletto and his daughter from his hiding place: it is typical of this fine musician to make something special of three notes of equal duration just a semitone apart. When he finally joins Gilda, his declaration of love is irresistible. Warm, impassioned and expansive, "È il sol dell'anima" combines ardor and delicacy in ideal proportions. Bidú Sayão proves a touching Gilda, singing with appreciable purity of tone and diction, although she banalizes some phrases by attacking them staccato rather than staccato-legato. The cadenza is fine, if a little less finished and sweet-toned than in the studio recording. The subsequent dialogue confirms that by this stage of his career Björling was quite at ease singing Italian recitative, though he fails to convey any change in tone when forced to invent a false name on the spur of the moment. The *stretta* (*Vivacissimo*) is performed with fleetness and grace, and after the traditional cut, he sings the written ending while Sayão ascends to a D-flat (when he felt in the right mood, he would join the soprano on the top note here, as happened when he sang the opera with Lily Pons in San Francisco in October 1951).[25]

The recitative "Ella mi fu rapita," at the beginning of the second act, gives Björling the chance to truly show his metal as a Verdi tenor. Apart from a minor verbal error ("Ne' brev*e* istanti"), his declamation here is supremely eloquent, the purity of his vowels lending the diction a noble transparency even at full volume. In the contrasting cantabile sections his legato conveys genuine pathos without sacrificing virility. Typical of his technical assurance is the soft attack on the awkward G-flat of "lo chiede il pianto," while the cadenza that follows is perfectly weighted and resolved in every detail. "Parmi veder le lagrime" is an equally magnificent piece of singing. Although some tenors—notably De Lucia, Schipa,[26] and Alfredo Kraus[27]—have sung it with similar ease and still subtler command of inflection, none have combined these qualities with such beauty of tone (both Caruso[28] and Pavarotti are slightly less smooth in line and refined in detail here, although the Neapolitan's final cadenza is closer to what Verdi wrote than Björling's traditionally simplified ascending scale). One is struck throughout by the facility with which he negotiates the *passaggio*—covering the sounds without tightening them—while maintaining a seamless flow. He interpolates an effortless B-flat on the final repeat of "le sfere agli angeli" (again hardening the pronunciation of the last *g*) and ends the aria on a G-flat attacked *piano* and then reinforced. The rest of this scene is a disappointment, for Björling's questioning of the Courtiers ("dite, dite, come fu?") lacks urgency, and the Duke's phrases during and after the chorus are omitted, as is the entire cabaletta.

Act 3 begins most convincingly for the tenor, his vibrant, forward production and incisive diction contrasting conspicuously with the throatier sounds of the lower voices (Warren as Rigoletto and Norman Cordon as Sparafucile). "La donna è mobile" is sung with golden tone and vivid diction, but the phrasing is less varied than in the 1937 Carnegie Hall concert and the dynamic level remains constant at *mezzo forte*. He omits the extra *gruppetto* on "e di pensier," but the cadenza brings the piece to a warmly applauded close.

Björling continues to sing rather loudly—perhaps he has Caruso's famous recordings[29] in mind—in the Quartet ("le mie pene consolar!" is closer to *mezzo forte* than *pianissimo*), but his phrasing is undeniably seductive, capturing the tongue-in-cheek quality implicit in the Duke's elaborate wooing of a prostitute. The climactic B-flats are glorious, but the release on the final note (where Sayão rises to the high D-flat) is uneven, with Björling holding on longer than the other singers. As the scene proceeds the tenor's voice remains responsive and his diction electric, and in the sleepy reprise of "La donna è mobile" he introduces for the first time a diminuendo on the G-sharp of "accento." However, his final repeat of the aria (offstage) is rhythmically square, lacking the mocking quality required to underline the irony of the situation.

In the 1951 broadcast of the Ballata from Stockholm's Royal Academy of Music, Björling makes the usual pronunciation errors and his Swedish accent is fairly conspicuous, but Sten Frykberg's lively tempo is more appropriate than Sodero's, encouraging the tenor to adopt a lighter tone and gait, better suited to the worldly philosophy of the Duke. The Canzone captured four months later in an open-air recital also benefits from the fleeter tempo, within which Björling makes free use of rubato and dynamic contrasts. The result is his most detailed performance of "La donna è mobile" so far, enhanced by a brilliant cadenza. A June 1954 recording of the aria, drawn from a complete performance in Stockholm, is no less persuasive. The phrasing is rhythmically taut but varied in coloring, and the text (thanks perhaps to the supervision of Lamberto Gardelli) is projected with uncommon accuracy. The real surprise here, however, comes in the encore (the only one recorded in an opera performance with this tenor), where Björling includes this time in the second verse the traditional diminuendo on the G-sharp of "accento." This recording also contains most of the Quartet, where the tenor's phrasing is no less insinuating than before and more respectful of Verdi's dynamic markings. There is a gap after the Duke's solo, however, and Schymberg's Gilda is not at her best.

Another live recording of "La donna è mobile" was made at a Seattle recital in October 1955. This time the voice is kept even lighter, lending an unusual intimacy to the performance, and the piano accompaniment encourages a considerable freedom of phrasing. In the second verse "accento" is attacked *mezzo piano* and then fined away and followed by the *gruppetto* already heard in the studio recordings. It must be said however that the voice is not at its freshest here—one notes a certain sagging of energy—and the downward transposition (to B-flat major) and a slightly labored cadenza rob the piece of some of its brilliance.

In June 1956 Björling made a complete recording of *Rigoletto* in Rome under the leadership of Jonel Perlea, who had already conducted him in this opera in Chicago in 1950. Of all the tenor's complete studio recordings, this is the one that has garnered least praise over the decades. It is certainly disappointing that the two-week recording period was not exploited to restore some of the music usually cut in stage performances (the recent Cetra and Decca recordings with Ferruccio Tagliavini and Mario Del Monaco had both reinstated one verse of the Duke's cabaletta). Still more baffling is the fact that three such gifted singers, who knew each other very well (Björling and Robert Merrill were old friends, and the baritone had been married to his Gilda, Roberta Peters, for a few years), were unable to generate much theatrical tension, in spite of their healthy voices and expert techniques. In truth, Björling is not at his vocal best. The voice does not sound worn or tired, but is less juicy in timbre than usual, and one senses a tightness from the register break upward that is uncharacteristic of him.

One does note some progress in the role since the Met broadcast, and this can be partly attributed to Perlea's conducting, which—while hardly galvanizing in effect—is at all times musically sensitive. He shapes the brief orchestral introduction to "Questa o quella" with considerable care and his lively tempo (♩ = 112 as opposed to Sodero's ♩ = 104) encourages the tenor to lighten his tone and phrase with airier elegance (one appreciates the way he sings "derido" with a chuckle, rather than adding a separate laugh). He courts the Contessa di Ceprano with as much grace (but less ardor) than before and leaves his incisive mark once again on the first ensemble. In the second scene the Duke's opening phrases are less strikingly uttered than at the Met, and although he sounds suitably impassioned when he bursts in on Gilda, his voice fails to open up warmly on the key word "schiudimi." "È il sol dell'anima" is moulded once again with the greatest aplomb and the joint cadenza is immaculate, as is the *stretta*, although Peters's conclusive top D-flat covers the tenor's note two octaves below.

"Ella mi fu rapita" is similar in conception to the Met recording, but Perlea encourages greater contrasts between the *Allegro*, *Andante*, and *Adagio* sections of the recitative, and "Parmi veder le lagrime" is still more expansive than before: the long legato lines are sustained with remarkable repose.

The word "angeli" is pronounced correctly this time, but the interpolated B-flat is less refulgent than in New York and in the final rising scale Björling stresses the wrong syllable of "invidiò." His subsequent exchanges with the chorus are much more alive than before.

"La donna è mobile," like the Ballata, is lighter and more buoyant than the 1945 performance, though less varied in phrasing than the live performances recorded in the meantime. No diminuendo or added *gruppetto* are included in the second verse, and there is a hint of strain on the final B-natural. In the dialogue between the Duke and Maddalena that introduces the Quartet the tempo is faster than at the Met, closer to Verdi's *Allegro* marking, but allowing less time for Björling to capture the insinuating quality of the phrases. In the Quartet itself he mispronounces "sol" as "suol," but adds an extra mordant on "consolar" and once again gives a very fine performance.

The subsequent exchanges with Sparafucile and Maddalena are notably spontaneous and the tenor's voice is extraordinarily limpid in the phrase "Stanco son io." The sleepy reprise of the Canzone is sung in a meltingly beautiful *mezza voce*, with "accento" attacked in a pure head tone. The final repeat unfolds much as it did at the Met, but sounds more appropriately distant.

The Duke's Canzone featured once again—it was an ideal encore piece—in an open air recital just a few weeks after the RCA recording was made. Note-values are more approximate here and the final B terminates uncleanly, but the phrasing sounds much more spontaneous, the voice richer, darker, and more natural in color. The diminuendo on "accento" and the extra flourish on "e di pensier" are both reinstated, and Björling adopts a singularly insinuating, confidential tone in the phrase "chi su quel seno non liba amore." He had already tried out this effect in Seattle, and Borgioli had employed it with considerable panache.

The third and final complete recording of Björling's Duke, made live in Stockholm in January 1957, contains his most satisfying and detailed portrayal of the character. Although the voice is less effortlessly produced than in the Met broadcast, it is in healthy shape, handsome and flexible in all registers. The intimate acoustic of the Royal Opera creates a particularly theatrical atmosphere and both Erik Sundquist (Rigoletto) and the Norwegian soprano Eva Prytz (Gilda), though less expert in Italian than Björling, sound genuinely involved.

After a persuasive prelude (Kurt Bendix proves a sensitive conductor), Björling makes his best entrance so far as the Duke, his phrasing suitably arrogant. Bendix keeps the basic pace lively during "Questa o quella," but at the same time allows the tenor some generous allargandos, thus enabling him to combine an ideal nimbleness of gait with a manly amplitude of tone. The singer sounds totally relaxed and seems to be enjoying himself as much as the Duke himself, adding an extra chuckle during the orchestral postlude. Equally persuasive is his courting of the Contessa: the melody is as suavely sustained as before and the words are more vividly inflected than ever. While the repeated descending lines of "Ah sempre tu spingi lo scherzo all'estremo" are less easily delivered than in the Rome recording, the Duke's refusal to listen to Monterone ("No!") is his most convincing yet, as is the beautiful phrase "sua figlia" in the second scene, where he expresses genuine wonder. In addressing Gilda, his ascent to the A-flat of "schiudimi" is free of the constriction heard in the studio version. The same is true of the soaring melody in the duet that follows, where Bendix allows him to linger lovingly over phrase after phrase, always to exceptionally musical effect (witness the diminuendo on the word "avvicina"). The cadenza is once again immaculate, the dialogue that follows urgent and persuasive, and the *stretta* still fluent, although the tenor's sound is less sparkling here than that of the soprano.

The recitative that opens act 2 is once again phrased with great nobility—under Bendix the shifts of tempo are less marked than with Perlea—and the first note of "Parmi veder le lagrime" (which draws us into the private world of the Duke's emotional imagination) is fully savored. This caressing of the opening note is a feature of De Lucia's performance of this aria, recorded in F major in 1917, and represents a neglected aspect of nineteenth-century performance practice. When compared with the subtly inflected version of the Neapolitan tenor (who also sings the original cadenza with delightful dexterity) Björling's performance may sound unadorned, but apart from a couple of pronunciation errors, his singing is once again supremely musical in overall design, though he ends here in a more extrovert manner than before, building a crescendo on the final G-flat after attacking it *mezzo forte.*

At the beginning of act 3 the request to Sparafucile is uttered sotto voce, sounding strangely timid. In the Canzone Björling offers much more dynamic and rhythmic variety than in the New York and Rome performances, and captures better than ever the insinuating tone of the second verse. His voice falters momentarily after the leisurely diminuendo on "accento," but he compensates with a showy flourish on "e di pensier." The cadenza has less energy behind it than in most earlier performances, but his technique carries him through. The Quartet is more sensually voiced than in the RCA recording and is deliciously spontaneous in phrasing (he adds a number of embellishments), although he continues to pronounce "sol" as "suol." The set piece ends as written, but Björling substitutes a simple crescendo for the *messa di voce* on the final F. The reprise of "La donna è mobile" is once again sung in a melting *mezza voce* (unmatched by any other tenor in this music), and the final offstage repeat is this time appropriately mocking in tone.

A month and a half after the Stockholm broadcast, two scenes from this opera—the duet with Gilda and "La donna è mobile"—were staged with Björling and Hilde Güden (plus Thelma Votipka's Giovanna) on the *Ed Sullivan Show.* The tenor here is not only in golden voice but also a youthful, good-looking and agile actor. One is struck not only by his ardor in addressing Gilda but also by his subtlety in reminding us that the Duke is here in disguise (a delighful half-smile accompanies "Gualtier Maldè"). In "È il sol dell'anima" boisterousness is favored over dynamic shading, but the line is as gleamingly drawn as ever and the rapid figurations of the *stretta* are dispatched with ease. Björling's spontaneity contrasts with Güden's self-conscious coyness, although she certainly has the voice and looks for the part.

In the Canzone, teasingly sung while holding Maddalena's hand, there are at least a couple of verbal slips, but in no other performance do we find such a happy combination of energy, vocal radiance and subtle inflection, particularly in the second verse. The impression gained here, which belies Björling's reputation for indifferent acting, is confirmed by reviews of his stage performances in this opera in the 1950s. Claudia Cassidy, commenting on his final Chicago *Rigoletto* in 1958, wrote that

> his is the most beautiful tenor of them all, a gleaming tenor of quality, range and color, used with a skill so polished that he can toss off "La donna è mobile" as if it were a game, though not a game of chance. Add to this a new ease of stage presence, a patrician sense of style, and there was a performance . . . not easily matched in contemporary opera."[30]

The final sound clip of Björling's Duke is the Canzone recorded at his Carnegie Hall recital eight months before the performance reviewed by Cassidy. Here too he exudes vocal ease and playfulness, although he transposes the piece down a semitone and is casual about note values. One cannot but marvel nonetheless at how supple his singing is at the end of a long recital (he had already sung eighteen Lieder and arias). In a way this encore has as much to do with the shared rituals of the great singer and his loyal audience as with Verdi's opera: it is not so much the Duke who is singing here as Jussi Björling reassuring his public that he can still deliver the goods with immense panache.

The Duke of Mantua may not have been Björling's greatest role but it surely represented his biggest interpretative challenge in the Verdi repertoire, as well as being the part in which he made the most progress over the years, developing from his first timid approaches in Swedish to a supremely confident—if verbally fallible—portrayal in the original language. Verdi's egocentric, licentious aristocrat could hardly be more unlike the real life Björling we (think we) know, and possibly for this very reason the words and music seem to have had a liberating effect on the actor, allowing him perhaps to explore hidden aspects of his own inner nature. The character never becomes an out-and-out villain (as he has sometimes been presented in recent decades): we should not forget that whereas Rigoletto's life is poisoned by hatred and fear, the Duke—however short-lived his emotions—spends much of his time proffering expressions of love. And perhaps no tenor has conveyed better than Björling the real tenderness that accompanies this compulsive courting. His portrayal is cynical without being brutal, stylish without becoming mannered, and graced throughout with the instincts of a great musician.

Il trovatore
Complete Recordings

May 12, 1939: London, Royal Opera House
Jussi Björling (Manrico), Gina Cigna (Leonora), Mario Basiola (Di Luna), Gertrud Pålson-Wettergren (Azucena), Corrado Zimbelli (Ferrando); London Philharmonic Chorus and Orchestra, cond. Vittorio Gui
Urania URN 22.115

January 11, 1941: New York, Metropolitan Opera House
Jussi Björling (Manrico), Norina Greco (Leonora), Francesco Valentino (Di Luna), Bruna Castagna (Azucena), Nicola Moscona (Ferrando); Metropolitan Opera Chorus and Orchestra, cond. Ferruccio Calusio
Arkadia GA 2014

December 27, 1947: New York, Metropolitan Opera House
Jussi Björling (Manrico), Stella Roman (Leonora), Leonard Warren (Di Luna), Margaret Harshaw (Azucena), Giacomo Vaghi (Ferrando); Metropolitan Opera Chorus and Orchestra, cond. Emil Cooper
Opera Live OL

February–March 1952: New York, Manhattan Center
Jussi Björling (Manrico), Zinka Milanov (Leonora), Leonard Warren (Di Luna), Fedora Barbieri (Azucena), Nicola Moscona (Ferrando); Robert Shaw Chorale, RCA Victor Orchestra, cond. Renato Cellini
RCA Victor GD 86643

January 26, 1957: Stockholm, Royal Opera House
Jussi Björling (Manrico), Aase Nordmo-Løvberg (Leonora), Hugo Hasslo (Di Luna), Margareta Bergström (Azucena), Erik Saedén (Ferrando); Royal Swedish Opera Chorus, Royal Court Orchestra, cond. Herbert Sandberg
Caprice CAP 22051

March 6, 1960: Stockholm, Royal Opera House
Jussi Björling (Manrico), Hjördis Schymberg (Leonora), Hugo Hasslo (Di Luna), Kerstin Meyer (Azucena), Erik Saedén (Ferrando); Royal Swedish Opera Chorus, Royal Court Orchestra, cond. Herbert Sandberg
Bluebell ABCD 045

"Ah sì, ben mio"

October 12, 1938: Stockholm, Concert Hall
Unspecified orchestra, cond. Nils Grevillius
Bluebell ABCD 016

July 15, 1939: Stockholm, Concert Hall
Unspecified orchestra, cond. Nils Grevillius
Naxos 8.110701

"Di quella pira"

March 3, 1934: Stockholm
Unspecified orchestra, cond. Nils Grevillius
Naxos 8.110722

October 12, 1938: Stockholm, Concert Hall
Unspecified orchestra, cond. Nils Grevillius
Bluebell ABCD 016

July 15, 1939: Stockholm, Concert Hall
Unspecified orchestra, cond. Nils Grevillius
Naxos 8.110701

"Miserere"

January 2, 1946: New York, Rockefeller Center
Jussi Björling (Manrico), Eleonor Steber (Leonora), Voice of Firestone Orchestra, cond. Howard Barlow
VAIA 1189

Il trovatore is one of the most evocative dramas ever set to music. The distancing effect of the fifteenth-century Spanish setting is an integral part of its appeal. Manrico, Leonora, Azucena and Di Luna are not contemporaries of Verdi disguised in period costumes but romanticized figures who should seem to reemerge from a remote past. The very title suggests nostalgia for the expressive spontaneity of a bygone age. Yet stage performances rarely remind us of the fact that this is the only Verdi opera in which the protagonist is a singer and poet, as well as a soldier. More often than not the chivalric grace of Manrico's melancholy songs is obscured by an excessive muscularity of phrasing and gesture. Rather than drawing listeners back through time into the character's imaginative world, tenors have tended to simplify and update the composer's expressive formulas, tarnishing Manrico's idealized emotions with veristic emphasis.

There have however been a number of exceptions, and few have proven more revelatory than Jussi Björling: from his first performance in Stockholm, aged twenty-four, in August 1935, he gave the impression that "he had known this role long and well."[31] He was to sing the part sixty-seven times in all, right up to the last year of his life. Other Manricos may have appeared more dashing on stage, but recorded evidence suggests that none has made music on such an exalted level, or succeeded in capturing so entirely—through purely vocal means—the character's aura of romance.

Manrico is also the best documented of Björling's roles: there are six more or less complete recordings made over a period of twenty-two years, which give us a unique opportunity to assess the evolution of the tenor's voice during his international career. All these performances are in Italian, but Björling's first encounters with the part were in Swedish, as was his recording of "Di quella pira" ("Skyhögt mot himlen") made in March 1934, a year and a half before his stage debut in *Trovatore.* This cabaletta is the most eagerly awaited number in the score, and the hefty top Cs that are traditionally added at climaxes (the highest written note is an A-natural, but Verdi did not disapprove of the interpolation) can have an incendiary effect, although they are also indirectly responsible for the macho posing adopted by many tenors in this role. Here Björling sings the aria a tone down, in B-flat major: a surprising decision if we consider the high-lying parts he performed in the early thirties. He had also made a downward transposition in his recording of "La donna è mobile" three months earlier, however, while a review of his Viennese debut in *Trovatore* (May 1936) comments on the choice of B major for the cabaletta. There is plenty of indirect evidence that Björling sang high Cs in the theater in the early thirties, but recordings suggest that he became more assured in the highest register in the latter half of the decade.

In some cases the use of a different key may have been determined by the coloristic requirements of the music performed or by the singer's vocal estate on that particular day. Björling's approach to transposition was always pragmatic. Verdi himself—in spite of declarations to the contrary—was often willing to transpose upward or downward in order to accommodate singers: an example can be found in the original version of *La forza del destino,* in which the composer permitted downward transposition of the tenor's solo "Qual sangue sparsi," which is modelled to a certain extent on "Di quella pira" and climaxes on a top C.

This early recording, conducted by Nils Grevillius, is in any case a notable achievement for a twenty-three-year-old. Although the voice is not of heroic proportions, the timbre is virile and each four-note group of sixteenth notes (based on tricky semitone intervals) is dispatched to coruscating effect. There are thirteen of these quadruplets in each verse, most of them marked staccato-legato, an expressive notation that Verdi often used to convey the tension created by conflicting impulses (Manrico here abandons Leonora just as they are about to marry), and that in this case also functions as an evocation of the flickering flames of the pyre that awaits Azucena. Many tenors on record offer only an approximation of these quadruplets, but Caruso's 1906 B major performance[32] demonstrates how even a voice of considerable density need not sacrifice precision of execution, albeit at an unhurried tempo. Like Caruso, Björling softens his tone in Manrico's aside to Leonora ("Era già figlio, prima d'amarti," marked *piano* in the score), where his uniquely melancholy timbre comes to the fore, reminding us that this explosion of frantic energy is motivated purely by love for the woman he believes to be his mother. Only one verse of the cabaletta is performed, without chorus, and interpolated B-flats are heard both on "O teco almeno" and on the final "morir" (the last note is taken up an octave). Both notes are ringing and easily produced, although the sustained cry at the end sharpens in pitch. While in the heat of a live performance this would matter little, in the ascetic studio setting it registers (to some ears) as a defect. And it must be admitted that the performance as a whole is admirable rather than truly stirring. The young Björling seems more intent on showing off his potential as a spinto than on conveying the almost unhinged desperation of man ready to die with his mother if he is unable to save her.

A couple of months before his Met debut in the opera (which took place in December 1938) the tenor recorded, in Italian, both the cabaletta and the preceding *Adagio*, "Ah sì, ben mio." Although these recordings were not issued at the time they are quite remarkable, especially the *Adagio*, an expansive lyrical effusion which sounds as if it had been written with Björling's voice in mind. It showcases not only the poise of his legato and dynamic control—even when the line hovers around the register break—but also the luminous overtones of the timbre itself, which lend the music a unique poetic glow. The aria is a love song impregnated with premonitions of mortality.[33] The minor-major modulation halfway through reinforces the feeling that Manrico is destined to be reunited with Leonora only after death. No other tenor on disc has made as much of this music, and although Björling's eight recordings of the aria differ in a number of ways, they all arguably stand head and shoulders above the efforts of rival singers. This first performance is as lovely as any of them, the timbre singularly fresh and the dynamics regulated with the mastery of a great instrumentalist (the *fortissimo* in the eighth measure is perfectly bound within the broadly arching phrase). Grevillius's tempo is slightly faster than the metronome indication, but he allows the tenor plenty of flexibility. The vowel sounds are ideally pure, combining great tenderness with a chivalric nobility of expression. One is struck by the inwardness with which the tenor observes the *con dolore* marking in "Ma pur, se nella pagina" (the feeling is one of sad resignation to destiny rather than acute suffering), and by the painful beauty of the G-flat of "trafitto," attacked *piano* and then diminished, so as to suggest the waning life of someone pierced by a blade in battle. The performance includes the traditional interpolation of a high B-flat on the repeat of "e solo in ciel precederti," which blooms without interrupting the flow toward the cadential phrases, which are beautifully proportioned and effortlessly intoned (many tenors sound strained or over-vehement here), and end with a magical dying close on the final D-flat. Björling omits in this performance the first trill on the word "parrà," but makes an attempt at the second one, combining it with a diminuendo that creates an illusion of suspended time. This embellishment was usually ignored by Italian tenors in this aria,[34] but Hermann Jadlowker makes a feature of it in his acoustic recording,[35] Franz Völker includes it in his long-breathed and impeccably musical German-language rendition,[36] and Helge Rosvænge incorporates it in his sturdy reading,[37] also in German, committed to disc the same year as Björling's.

"Di quella pira," recorded on the same day, is also very fine, although one regrets not only the elimination of the second verse (this cut was customary, although singers as diverse as Giovanni Martinelli, Richard Tauber, and César Vezzani had sung both verses for the gramophone) and the chorus, but also the fact that the tenor drops out for a few measures in the *più vivo* section of the first verse to prepare himself for the top C on "morir." This time he sings the *stretta* in the original key, and although the higher tessitura makes it impossible to reproduce the dramatically dark coloring of the earlier recording, there is more tension in the sound itself and the top notes have a thrilling attack. The final note again tends toward sharpness, a not infrequent licence when Björling was seeking the maximum spinto resonance in his upper register. After a performance of *Trovatore* at the Met ten years later Jerome D. Bohm commented in the *Herald Tribune* that "Di quella pira" was "topped by a ringingly resonant high C which unfortunately when repeated at the conclusion of the aria was sharpened to a C sharp, which lent an unexpectedly modern touch to Verdi's conventional harmonic scheme."[38] Sensitivity to pitch varies greatly in listeners, but few would find anything grating in the slight dissonance caused by sharpness in this recording, partly because the tone itself is solidly anchored and free from stridency.

Seven months later, the tenor made his Covent Garden debut in *Trovatore* and the first performance was recorded on film (using the Philips-Miller system). The cast was a prestigious one and the audience no less illustrious (spectators included Toscanini, who would conduct Björling in Lucerne later that year, and Gigli, who was singing *Traviata* and *Aida* during the same season). Vittorio Gui offered an intelligently-conceived reading of the score, strongly theatrical, with richly contrasting tempos and dynamics and some vibrant string playing from the London Philharmonic Orchestra. Unfortunately, the recording is unbalanced, favoring the orchestra over the singers, and the performance as a whole is uneven in quality. As Azucena, Gertrud Pålson-Wettergren's recollection of Cammarano's original text is intermittent

Figure 17. Manrico in *Il trovatore,* New York, 1947. Photograph by Louis Melançon. Courtesy of the Metropolitan Opera Archive.

and the unforced purity of her middle register only partially compensates for a whitish top. As Leonora, Gina Cigna's bitingly dark dramatic soprano seems both ill-matched to Björling's more lyrical instrument and ill-equipped to sustain the rapid pace of some of the music.

Yet this remains a recording to treasure for the remarkable performance of the tenor and for the way in which the conductor encourages him to make the most of his unique qualities. The character's calling-card is his offstage serenade in act 1, "Deserto sulla terra," a solo that would have to be sung even if the libretto were performed as a straight play. For this reason it was traditionally approached with particular freedom in the nineteenth century, and Tamagno's almost stately 1903 recording[39] gives us an idea of the effect the aria can have when the singer savors every phrase. Although Björling takes fewer rhythmic liberties than his illustrious predecessor, Gui allows him plenty of time to make his mark as an authentic troubadour: in no other recording of this music does the singing correspond so perfectly to Leonora's romantic description of Manrico in "Tacea la notte placida." He caresses the opening phrases, building up gently to the *tutta forza* climax of the first verse, where he substitutes the written trill with a mordent (this substitution was traditional, though Josef Schmidt sings the original ornament beautifully in a 1930 recording in German).[40] Right from the beginning the voice is limpid and poised and transitions are beautifully managed. In the second verse, sung with slightly more emphasis, he encompasses "bello e casta fede, e d'ogni re maggiore" in a single breath. At the end he interpolates a potent B-flat followed by a *gruppetto*, a traditional variant employed by nearly all tenors, but rarely executed with such aplomb.

The starlit sounds we hear in this serenade, a poetic declaration of love by a man at war with fate, might have surprised the 1939 audience, used to the heroic approach exemplified in the finest acoustic recordings of Manrico's music (by singers such as Tamagno, Caruso, and Martinelli) and in the two earliest complete recordings of the opera in Italian (both made in Milan in 1930),[41] featuring the spinto tenors Pertile and Francesco Merli in the title role. Of course Manrico is not just a youthful troubadour but also a valiant military leader, who in spite of his aristocratic birth has been brought up as a gypsy. The agitated exchanges with Leonora and Di Luna that follow "Deserto sulla terra" are no less important than the serenade itself in establishing his identity. Here it must be admitted that Björling sounds somewhat underpowered, particularly in the defiant phrase "Ravvisami, Manrico io son," although what really diminishes the impact of this episode is the soprano's inability to follow Gui's beat. She shows further signs of waywardness in the trio that follows (boldly attacked by Basiola), but after a few measures her voice and the tenor's come together to incisive effect. They both sustain the top B-flat (on the words "per te suonò") in the second strophe—an unwritten fermata that is featured in the earliest recordings of this trio—and after an equally traditional cut in the *Poco più mosso* section, they drop out for a few measures to prepare for a final top D-flat. This is the only *Trovatore* recording in which Björling attempts this unwritten high note, and the sound that emerges has too much head resonance in it to be able to compete with Cigna's overwhelming show of force (though she sags below him in pitch).

If in addressing Leonora Björling makes the ideal romantic lover, in his duets with Azucena he appears a model of filial devotion. The silvery resonance that invests not only his upper voice but also his middle register lends an adolescent candor to some of his exchanges with his mother. In a legato phrase such as "O madre! . . . non saprei dirlo a me stesso!" the purity of the vowels is such that the words do not require any particular emphasis to register movingly with the listener.

"Mal reggendo" (Manrico's account of his duel with Di Luna and his inability to kill his enemy and rival when the opportunity arose) is the character's second solo, occasionally recorded as a separate number during the first half of the twentieth century. The poetic intensity of the text, with its powerful use of assonance underlying the graphic description of physical conflict, offers several examples of what Verdi himself described as *parole sceniche*: words that, set to music, sum up the emotional experience of a character. The great Italian tenor Pertile, who was chosen by Toscanini for the Scala production in 1925 and recorded a singularly anguished reading of this solo[42] a couple of years later, makes one aware here of the inner resonance of every word. Björling's diction sounds neutral by contrast, his dynamic range modest. Yet the sound portrait he offers of Manrico is no less persuasive overall than Pertile's, for his very timbre conjurs up the image of a handsome and valiant young warrior who at the same time is sufficiently sensitive to make his sudden compassion for Di Luna credible. In describing the "moto arcano" that motivates him from within, Björling does not attempt to darken the color of the voice (as Verdi's *agitato e cupo* suggests), but succeeds in conveying the otherness of this mystical experience by reducing the pressure on the tone and reinforcing the legato. At the end of the solo he demonstrates his technical accomplishment in alternating the ringing A-natural of "cielo" with the purest of pianissimos on "non ferir."

The duet with Azucena that follows is beautifully sung by both tenor and mezzo, with exemplary observance of Verdi's markings. Björling's reading of Ruiz's missive is blurred here by the singer's rapid delivery and distance from the microphone, and his Swedish accent is more noticeable than in purely sung passages. Manrico's contribution to the final part of the duet ("Un momento può involarmi"), with its traditional cut and simplification of the final measures, demonstrates how rhythmic exactness and crisp diction can go a long way toward compensating for a lack of sheer volume. The same could be said of the act 2 finale. The sound the tenor makes is never overwhelming, but always perfectly focused and audible, even in the rising phrases of the ensemble ("Ma gli empi un Dio confonde!"), and when he pulls out all the stops, joining Cigna (as tradition dictates) in the reprise of "Sei tu dal ciel disceso," he sounds no less impassioned than the soprano.

The dialogue that leads up to "Ah sì, ben mio" in act 3 is a classic example of Verdi recitative at its most varied, alternating the infinite tenderness of the lover with the resolution of the man of arms. In this performance it is the former who captures our imagination. If Manrico's instructions to Ruiz sound slightly half-hearted, his reassurance of Leonora is expressed in dulcet tones, making inspired use of Verdi's dynamic markings. No other tenor on record has dared sing these phrases with such unforced lyricism and musical refinement, and as a result Manrico has never seemed so vulnerable in love as he does here, and so capable of expressing that love with the eloquence of a true poet. Even more than in earlier scenes, the head resonance in the middle register lends the voice a rare bloom, and the dynamics are modulated with virtuosic ease, making magic of the final *messa di voce* on "core" (a difficult note on the register break).

The aria that follows is on the same exalted level, and although the voice is more distant from the microphone than in 1938 the tenor's phrasing is even more intimate in expression. Gui's tempo is a real *Adagio,* faithful to Verdi's metronome marking, and it was surely the conductor who persuaded Björling to play down the first crescendo and eschew the unwritten B-flat on the repeat of "in ciel precederti." He may also have encouraged him to articulate both the trills clearly, an effect that the tenor is unable to match on any other recording. In spite of the leisurely pace the voice is poised in every phrase and the music flows beguilingly, the legato reinforced by an occasional portamento (the octave leap in "E solo il ciel" is particularly graceful). But in the end it is not so much the detail as the beauty and emotional truthfulness of the whole that is memorable. Arguably Bergonzi[43] came closest here to matching Björling in his fidelity to the letter and spirit of the score, as well as offering a more complete command of every inflection of the text, but not even he could equal the silvery caress of the Swede's timbre.

The organ-accompanied duet with Leonora is cut, but the dramatic exchanges that follow Ruiz's entrance are appropriately urgent and the cabaletta sacrifices none of the rhythmic precision heard in the two studio recordings, while conveying all the excitement of a live performance at its thrilling climax. Gui respects Verdi's *Allegro* marking, even exceeding the ♩ = 100 indication in the score, and this results in a more sketchy legato in "Era già figlio," but the top C on "O teco almeno" is more prolonged and spectacular than in the 1938 disc and the same is true of the added C at the end of the scene, where Björling joins the chorus only on the final "All'armi!" The second C has less body to it than the first, but there is no doubting its effect on the audience, which responds with an ovation.

We next hear Manrico in the "Miserere" scene, where the song from the tower is bewitchingly phrased, reminding us again of Leonora's rapt remembrance of the troubadour's "versi melanconici." Gui's spacious tempo allows every detail to tell: the crescendos and descrescendos, the crisp acciaccaturas, the featherweight portamentos. Björling's singing is at once enchantingly buoyant and infinitely sad in this farewell to love and life. Cigna too is at her most involved in this scene, projecting the words vividly.

Gui's lyrical approach—Verdi's initial *Largo* indication is taken literally—allows for an equally unforgettable performance of the duet with Azucena in the final scene. This duet is so well-written that most singers are heard at their best here. In his sustained *mezza voce* phrasing this Manrico reveals nonetheless a degree of emotional sensitivity from which other tenors instinctively shy. The harmonic modulations of the phrase "oblia cerca nel sonno, e posa e calma" are thrown into relief by the almost vibrato-free tone. The only flaws here are verbal ones: in "Riposa o madre" we hear the words of the second verse in the opening statement, while in the repeat we are offered a garbled version of the first verse.

Although the imbalance of the recording does not help Björling in the rest of the scene, there is no doubting the impact of his vehement exchanges with Leonora, and in "Ha quest'infame l'amor venduto" he makes a powerful emotional statement without shouting (in spite of the prominent trumpet doubling the vocal line). Here, as in the rest of the opera, his use of dynamics is based on judicious contrasts and a keen respect for the score: he attacks "ed a qual prezzo" *piano*, as required, and conveys the dismay of "Donna, svelami . . . narra" in suffocated tones that are more psychologically revealing than the usual stentorian approach.

Just two months after his London debut, Björling made a second studio recording of Manrico's aria and cabaletta with Grevillius. "Ah sì, ben mio" is not as slow as at Covent Garden, but it is once again beautifully phrased and closer to Verdi's *Adagio* marking than the 1938 performance (3:22 against 3:04). He reinstates the unwritten top B-flat, a traditional interpolation which (according to Toscanini) Verdi considered entirely acceptable;[44] Björling may well been told of this by his Italian opera coach Tullio Voghera, who had worked with Toscanini. Both trills are observed, although they are not as cleanly executed as in London, and the cadential phrase doesn't quite match the poise and freshness of the two earlier readings. The decision to publish these performances rather than those made nine months earlier was probably due to the superiority of the cabaletta. As in 1938, its overall impact is blunted by cuts and the absence of a chorus, but the tenor's tone is darker and more heroic this time and the two top Cs are glorious. The second one in particular is even more ringing than in London, though less prolonged. Grevillius's tempo is calmer than Gui's, and although this lowers the adrenalin level, it allows for a stronger legato binding.

Most admirers of Björling's art would agree that his London *Trovatore* offers uniquely evocative vocalism, but the critical reception of the premiere was not unanimously ecstatic. Some writers acknowledged the lyrical purity of the singing while lamenting a certain lack of dramatic thrust, a criticism that may owe something to the traditional association of Manrico with heavy spinto voices. Whether the critics were right or wrong, Björling's next complete recording of the role sounds like a response to their reservations: the 1941 Met broadcast is in many ways his most dramatic reading of the role on disc (even though he commanded greater volume later in his career), and the one that contrasts most markedly with the Covent Garden performance. The difference in approach also reflects the strong forward momentum and vibrant phrasing imposed by conductor Ferruccio Calusio, whose reading of the score is less original than Gui's but more fully realized in terms of stylistic cohesion and musical discipline, aided by the extensive experience in this repertoire of the Metropolitan Chorus and Orchestra. The Argentinian conductor spent only one season at the Met but had acquired valuable experience as Toscanini's assistant at La Scala in the 1920s (where he had prepared Pertile and other singers for the epoch-making 1925 production of *Trovatore*), and here he inspires an equally strong cast to give of its best in a performance of unflagging theatricality.

The Toscanini influence (Björling had sung Verdi's Requiem with the maestro just six weeks earlier) can arguably be felt right from "Deserto sulla terra," immaculately sung, but taken at a quicker pace than in London, allowing less space for dynamic shading. The voice is in pristine condition and the tone more urgent and authoritative. The conductor gives him time to make a real feature of the climax, with a crescendo on the interpolated B-flat. In the exchanges that follow both Norina Greco (Leonora) and Frank Valentino (Di Luna) are rhythmically and verbally alive and the tenor too projects both words and tone more vividly than before, helped by the closer miking and better balance with the orchestra. The trio too is much more exciting than in London: Valentino is impressive and Greco's impassioned phrasing encourages Björling to respond with equal vibrancy and warmth. They both sing a lusty B-flat in the reprise, but the tenor does not join the soprano on the top D-flat, sticking this time to the written F.

The Italian mezzo Bruna Castagna is possibly the most searing Azucena ever recorded, totally involved in the part and compelling us to share her harrowing memories of the accidental murder of her son. Björling employs weightier tones on this occasion for Manrico's dazed comments and the effect is less psychologically interesting: the softer dynamics employed in London had tellingly underlined the character's dependence on his surrogate mother. But the darker coloring and incisive projection of words when recounting his adventures in battle bring Manrico the warrior more convincingly to life. "Mal reggendo" is once again beautifully sculpted, with each episode of the narration convincingly evoked. The reading of the letter goes much as before, but the text is clearer thanks to the proximity of the microphone. In the final part of the duet with Azucena (*Velocissimo*) Björling's voice matches Castagna's no less effectively than it had blended with Wettergren's in the earlier performance and the overall effect is more stirring this time, even though he mixes up the words. The act 2 finale also proves more involving. Björling is golden-toned throughout and Greco's Leonora conveys real warmth of feeling for Manrico.

When the two appear again in act 3, the tenor shows his increasing confidence in Italian recitative (he seems to have been particularly well-rehearsed for this new production by Herbert Graf) and rightly adopts a contrasting tone for his aside to Ruiz. In accordance with his more adult conception of the role, he makes less poetic use of *piano* dynamics than in London, although the difficult *messa di voce* on "core" is once again exemplary. In the aria Calusio adopts a slightly faster gait than Gui and Björling's tone is fuller and more heroic (there is much less head resonance on the F of "coll'essere"), while the phrasing retains its freshness and finish. As in all subsequent performances, Björling includes the interpolated B-flat on "ciel," accompanied by a generous allargando. A unique feature of this version of the aria is the modification of the cadential phrase to include a startling reiteration of the words "la morte" in the upper octave (A-flat, B-double-flat, A-flat). This interpolation shifts the expressive balance of the whole aria: what begins as a love song turns into a pessimistic vision of death. It can also be heard in recordings by Mario Gilion (1906)[45] and Cortis (1930)[46] and it was later adopted by Pavarotti (1990).[47] Björling makes striking use of it here, without persuading us that it is musically preferable to the more affectionate written ending, which requires a subtler weighting of every note.

In this performance we hear Björling for the first time in the *duettino* that follows the *Adagio*: he sings it most gracefully, but Greco is ungainly. He transposes "Di quella pira" down a semitone, a common solution at the Met and consistent with the darker coloring he adopts for the role on this occasion. His singing is no less thrilling than in London, however, and the excitement is increased by the much finer recording and the vibrant contributions of orchestra and chorus. The tenor himself projects the words as vividly as in any of his performances of the cabaletta and sustains the final B for a good ten seconds.

Manrico's offstage singing during the "Miserere" scene is too distantly recorded to make a memorable effect, his phrasing full-throated and less poetic in detail. The same could be said of the duet with Azucena, but it would nevertheless be a mistake to underestimate this very fine performance. Castagna dominates the stage with her richly-colored voice and imaginative understanding, while Björling once again conveys the infinite tenderness of a son unable to understand the ravings of his mother:

his legato and *mezza voce* (here golden rather than silvery) give enormous pleasure, and his vowels are purer than those of the mezzo, who affects the artificially theatrical diction often heard in female Italian singers trained in the early twentieth century. The rest of the scene works much better than in London, thanks to the fine balance of the recording and superior cohesion of stage and pit. When addressing Leonora Björling employs a narrower range of dynamics but never degenerates into bluster. Indeed his denunciation achieves an exceptional degree of vehemence without any loss of musical aplomb, and the precipitous events of the final pages of the score are given their full emotional weight. Every phrase breathes, however rapid the tempo.

The subsequent Met broadcast with Björling as Manrico took place in December 1947. In the meantime the tenor had made his highly-praised Italian debut in a production of *Il trovatore* at Florence's Maggio Musicale in 1943 (where the great baritone Titta Ruffo was much struck by his portrayal)[48] and had sung further performances of the opera in Stockholm, New York, San Francisco, and Los Angeles. He had also recorded, for the *Voice of Firestone,* a curious version of the "Miserere" scene where the choral part is played by the orchestra and Manrico sounds as if he is standing alongside Leonora (which may well have been the case). This radio broadcast took place in January 1946, with the soprano Eleonor Steber. It is the only occasion on which she was recorded with Björling (although they later performed *Faust, Don Carlo,* and *Tosca* together) and the professionalism of her singing is impressive: every note is clearly articulated, the rhythms are scrupulously respected, and she inserts the traditional high C in the closing measures. She fails, however, to draw us imaginatively into the hallucinatory atmosphere of this scene, or make us share the physical dimension of the horror felt by Leonora. Björling too is not at his most involved, but his singing is warm and generous, less melancholy than in London but as accurate as the soprano's.

The 1947 complete recording documents his first performance with Emil Cooper, a seventy-year-old Russian conductor of remarkable experience who was on the Met's roster from 1944 to 1950. Cooper had obviously studied the score carefully and his respect for Verdi's markings sometimes pays off, but he rarely matches the dramatic tension generated by Calusio in 1941, and his lack of familiarity with Italian performing traditions is sometimes evident. One appreciates, however, his spacious tempo in "Deserto sulla terra," which allows Björling to shape the phrases beautifully (though with less dynamic modulation than at Covent Garden). The rest of the act sounds a little tame, but once again the unhurried tempo allows words to register clearly and Björling phrases very incisively, his voice revealing here a more solid grounding in the lower middle register. Warren (Di Luna) is clumsy at times in recitative, but combines ample volume, beauty of sound, and reasonable precision in the solo opening of the trio. The voice of Stella Roman (Leonora), though not without luster in the upper register, lacks a solid core in her opening scene and her diction is often affected, but she sounds more collected and purposeful when singing in unison with the tenor in the trio (Cooper does not allow them the traditional fermata on the B-flat) and manages a reasonably confident top D-flat at the end of the act.

Margaret Harshaw (Azucena) is no match dramatically for Castagna, but the voice is fresh and the phrasing musically gratifying. Björling interacts with her well, adopting initially a more lyrical stance than in 1941, although his middle voice has a new richness to it here. "Mal reggendo" is as burnished as ever and the reading of Ruiz's letter his best yet, clear and convincing. Further progress is revealed in act 2, where the opening section of recitative in the scene with Leonora is more authoritative than before, with no sacrifice of lyrical poise when Manrico makes his declaration of love. "Ah sì, ben mio" is once again masterly, and more affectionate than in 1941, thanks to Cooper's respect for Verdi's tempo indication. One notices in particular the leisurely diminuendo on the G-flat of "trafitto," revealing rare technical ease and poetic inspiration. Björling does not really attempt to sing the trills this time, but offers *gruppetti* in their place. The concluding phrases are sung as written, as in all subsequent performances, with the final F and D-flat particularly prolonged. In the *duettino* Roman makes a greater effect than Greco, but she too sounds ill-tuned alongside Björling (Cooper's funereal pace in this *Allegro* is perhaps adopted to make things more comfortable for her). The exchanges leading up to the cabaletta are excitingly delivered and there is no downward transposition. The top Cs in the *Allegro* are perfectly placed and without strain but are less spectacular and ringing than in London. The doleful tone of "Era già figlio prima d'amarti" once again reminds us of the complex emotional situation in which Manrico finds himself.

The "Miserere" benefits from Cooper's unhurried tempo, although the soprano isn't entirely at ease and the tenor—more clearly audible than in the 1941 recording—mixes the words of the two strophes. There is more to enjoy in the duet with Azucena, sustained with a purity of tone and legato that comes close to the perfection of the Covent Garden performance (although the tenor's *piano* is now fuller-bodied), and there is much beauty in Harshaw's singing, as well as a generous dose of rubato. Björling's contribution to the final scene is once again emotionally alive and vocally resplendent. The musical context, however, is less thrilling than in 1941 and at times Roman recalls Cigna in her rhythmic imprecision.

Il trovatore was the first complete opera Björling recorded in the studio: the sessions were set up at the Manhattan Center in the early months of 1952, while the tenor was engaged at the Met for a revival of *Don Carlo*. This set made his Manrico famous the world over and won critical acclaim for its starry cast. The four principal singers are indeed remarkable: splendid voices in their prime, technically expert and stylistically aware, with considerable stage experience in their respective roles (Zinka Milanov had sung her first Met Leonora alongside Björling fourteen years earlier, in December 1938). Renato Cellini's conducting guarantees the sort of musical discipline that is hard to achieve in live performance. At the same time he never comes close to creating the sort of sustained narrative tension that this opera thrives on in the theater. Björling's performance too, though superior to those of other tenors who made studio recordings in the 1950s, is less emotionally charged than his live portrayals. It is good, however, to be able to hear him so clearly in "Deserto sulla terra," where the simple harp accompaniment shows off the lyrical sweep of his phrasing, although his upper voice sounds drier here than in the opera house and he anticipates the interpolated B-flat in the second verse, which now coincides (less felicitously) with the word "maggior" rather than "Trovator." In subsequent performances he would maintain this solution, which has a precedent in the first ever recording of this serenade, sung in German by Hermann Winkelmann (the creator of Parsifal) in 1900.[49] In the rest of the scene the rhythmic precision of all three singers proves gratifying, but Warren's clumsy pronunciation is a liability, and one senses a lack of passionate involvement in Milanov's aristocratic Leonora. The soprano and tenor voices are well balanced in the trio, but Cellini does not allow them to linger on the B-flat and there are no added high notes at the end.

In act 2 Fedora Barbieri, whom Björling had first encountered in Florence in 1943, proves a fine Azucena, less moving than Castagna but more natural in diction. The tenor delivers some effective stretches of recitative, offering his best version yet of the awkwardly low phrase "però da forte io caddi." "Mal reggendo," on the other hand, is less varied and alive than his broadcast performances, and one notices a certain tightness on the register break. The act 2 finale reveals Cellini at his least persuasive, rapid, superficial, and unmoving.

The third-act dialogue with Leonora is generally excellent, and although Björling's head voice has less caress than when recorded live, the *messa di voce* on "core" is captivating. Cellini's tempo for "Ah sì, ben mio" is closer to an *Andante* than an *Adagio*, but in spite of some sacrifice of detail (no diminuendo on "trafitto" this time and the trills are only hinted at), Björling never sounds hurried, maintaining the tender lyrical approach of the 1939 and 1947 performances. The organ-accompanied duet is fluent (Luchino Visconti used this excerpt in the soundtrack of his film *Senso*) and the cabaletta is the prize of the RCA recording: although only one verse is sung, it is Björling's most complete rendition of this stirring music, and the relatively close miking enables his voice to dominate the sound stage in a manner that would perhaps have been beyond him in a large opera house. Cellini's tempo is sufficiently rapid to maintain a high degree of tension but not so fast as to sacrifice expressive detail or legato: eighteen years after his first recording of the cabaletta, Björling dispatches the four-note semiquaver groups with as much precision as ever. The two top Cs are not as effortless as in 1938–39, but they are more ringing than in the 1947 broadcast, and truly convey the feeling of a man possessed. In a letter sent to his wife in early 1952 the tenor wrote: "I've had two recording sessions of *Il trovatore.* 'Di quella pira,' in the correct key of course. I've never sung it this well."[50] His pride in his achievement was fully justified. Of the tenors who have made complete studio recordings of this opera only the clarion-voiced Del Monaco[51] approaches his combination of theatrical excitement and musical precision.

As with the act 1 serenade, the studio recording allows us to appreciate every inflection of Manrico's "Ah che la morte ognora" in act 4, and the duet with Azucena is also a highlight. No other tenor has approached Björling in the yearning feeling that fills the phrase "Oh madre! Oh madre!" In the rest of the scene his occasional verbal slips (such as a momentary hardening of the *g* in "angelo") are highlighted by the closeness of the microphone. The final pages of the opera are magnificently sung by all four principal singers, but the tenor's phrasing here is less impassioned than in 1941 and the atmosphere remains studio-bound.

We have the mezzo-soprano Margareta Bergström to thank for the first Stockolm recording of Björling's Manrico (1957): an in-house tape was made in the wings by a chorus member for the production's Azucena.[52] The first scene of the opera is missing, but the sound quality is fine and the unusual positioning of the microphone offers us a different perspective on the tenor's voice: it is thrilling, for example, to hear "Deserto sulla terra" at such close quarters. It is a handsome rendition, unhurried in tempo, and the microphone picks up no impurities in the Björling sound, which if anything acquires an extra warmth in this context. The exchanges that follow the serenade are a bit messy, but conductor Herbert Sandberg—who had led the tenor's first-ever performance as Manrico twenty-two years earlier—generates more excitement than Cellini in the pit and allows the two higher voices (the Norwegian soprano Aase Nordmo-Løvberg is a very musical Leonora) to pause briefly on the top B-flat in the trio.

In the second act we have many opportunities to appreciate Bergström's Azucena, who articulates the trills in "Stride la vampa" better than any other mezzo encountered here and offers a strongly emotional account of "Condotta ell'era in ceppi." Björling phrases much as before, but his voice sounds weightier and darker in the middle register and "Mal reggendo" proves much more stirring than in the RCA recording. In the final part of the duet with Azucena ("Un momento può involarmi") there is a certain amount of friction with Sandberg: the tenor tries to impose a quicker tempo, but the conductor makes only minimal concessions. In the third-act dialogue between Manrico and Leonora (the orchestral introduction here is missing), Björling makes less use of his half-voice than before and transforms the *messa di voce* on "core" into a simple diminuendo (he will do the same two years later). In "Ah sì, ben mio" the voice combines full-bodied emission with amber overtones: the tenor's timbral plenitude is reminiscent of Caruso here and this special quality makes the performance treasurable, especially since Sandberg's spacious tempo enables him to caress the phrases. Both the diminuendo on "trafitto" and the trills are convincingly reinstated and the final measures are masterfully shaped, with a strong crescendo followed by a fading away on the final note. The *duettino* functions well enough, but it is cut short and Nordmo-Løvberg cannot match Milanov, while in the cabaletta Björling transposes down to B-flat major. His diction is particularly incisive and the weighty volume compensates in part for the lower tessitura, but although the final top B-flat is considerably prolonged (the conclusive section of the chorus is cut so that the tenor can sail up to this note without excessive delay), the performance cannot compete in excitement with the RCA recording. This scene gives us the chance to appreciate the incisive Ruiz of Björling's brother Gösta, who was to die, aged forty-five, in October that year.

During the musically excellent "Miserere" Manrico for once sounds much closer to us than Leonora, and although this inverts Verdi's imagined spatial perspective it is a delight to witness the elegance and breadth of the tenor's phrasing at such close quarters. The final scene is equally special: no other *Trovatore* recording captures the overtones of his voice so effectively, although his denunciation of Leonora is almost excessively loud in comparison with the soprano's responses (this is probably due to the microphone placement). Certainly there are no signs here of the heart disease that would manifest itself alarmingly in the following months.

Björling's final recorded *Trovatore,* taped in March 1960, was made when he was already very ill. Yet signs of weakness in the recording are rare: the top B-flats in "Di quella pira" are slightly labored and a handful of notes on the *passaggio* slip back into the throat. Otherwise there is much to prize here. "Deserto sulla terra" is more distant this time (it is a radio broadcast), but once again suavely sung. The more lyrical inflections adopted in the duet with Azucena reveal the ailing tenor's ability to make intelligent expressive use of limited energy, and "Ah sì, ben mio," though slightly faster than in 1957 (Sandberg conducts once again), has plenty of caress, plus a yearning quality that is particularly moving. The rest of the opera continues much as before (there is a surprise in the "Miserere" scene, where Hjördis Schymberg—not the smoothest or most idiomatic of Leonoras—interpolates a top C), and the final duet with Azucena is once again a particular delight (Björling is well matched here by Kerstin Meyer, who earlier in the opera sounds a little over-parted). Generally one is struck by how consistently this performance adheres to the interpretative choices of the Covent Garden production twenty-one years earlier. It suggests that the tenor's intuitive understanding of this role, with its decidedly lyrical emphasis, was complete from the start, and that his vocal mechanism was so well-oiled that it continued to function even when his heart was close to collapse.

Manrico was not only Björling's most frequently performed Verdi role but also his most strikingly original contribution to our understanding of the Italian composer's works. Although some critics (particularly in America) continued to find his voice too small for the role, his portrayal proved extraordinarily successful in the opera house for a quarter of a century. With the aid of hindsight and repeated listening, it appears still more exceptional on disc, where the immaculate finish of his phrasing registers all the more tellingly. Björling's mastery of the role was both technical and musical: no other tenor has performed this part with a comparable feeling for the subtleties of Verdi's rhythms and harmonies, for the arcane beauty of his melodies. Yet beyond that Björling possessed a sixth sense which enabled him to penetrate to the heart of a character whose identity often appears uncertain: "chi son io?" Manrico asks his mother at one point. It is almost as if the experience of several existences were contentrated within a brief lifespan. Yet there is no doubting what the character feels in any given moment, however much his loyalties seem to shift between Leonora, Azucena and the claims of an ongoing civil war. Many tenors interpret Manrico's impetuous arrivals and departures as a sign of soldierly dynamism; Björling more cogently highlights the underlying vulnerability of a character who has difficulty in controlling his destiny and whose activism is largely motivated by love. The essence of the troubadour's character can be heard in his melancholy songs, and it was surely this singular quality of feeling that struck a deep chord within the soul of the singer.

Although six complete *Trovatore* recordings with Björling represent a rich legacy, opera lovers continue to fantasize about a tape of the 1955 Chicago production alongside Maria Callas as Leonora (it was the only time they sang together). It seems unlikely this recording will now resurface, but there are very good reasons for its mythical status, for Callas's singing in this opera had the same sort of evocative force that sets Björling apart from other tenors here. In both cases we seem to hear "a voice from another century" (as the Italian critic Teodoro Celli once wrote of the Greek soprano):[53] imagining the interaction of these two instruments and musical intelligences in a work of this potency is a heady experience.[54]

La traviata
Complete Recording

August 29, 1939: Stockholm, Royal Opera House
Jussi Björling (Alfredo), Hjördis Schymberg (Violetta), Conny Molin (Germont); Royal Swedish Opera Chorus, Royal Court Orchestra, cond. Herbert Sandberg
Grammofono 2000 AB 78640; Bluebell ABCD 103 (highlights)

If 1939 was a disastrous year in world history, it was a highly successful one in the life of Jussi Björling. His son Lars was born in April, and in May he became for the first time an independent artist, no longer bound by contract to the Royal Opera in Stockholm (although he was to remain extremely loyal to this house until the end of his career). It was the year of his Covent Garden debut, his first collaboration with Toscanini, and a series of studio and live recordings that have never been surpassed. These recordings document not only the disarming splendor of one of the century's most beautiful tenor voices, but also the inspired musicality of an artist anxious to demonstrate his expressive potential and endowed with the technical means to do so.

His final performance of *La traviata* (sung in Swedish as *Den vilseförda*), recorded at the Royal Opera just five days before the outbreak of World War II (during which Sweden was to remain neutral), is on the same level of excellence as his other recordings from that year. Although some listeners may be discouraged by the translation (Björling never sang this opera in any other language), the performance as a whole is an involving one. It was the tenor's fourteenth appearance in a role he had sung for the first time on January 5, 1933. At his debut—conducted by Leo Blech, a leading figure in Germany's Verdi renaissance—he had been criticized by the composer William Seymer for the "lack of sensual charm in his singing."[55] Six and a half years later, in one of his first performances at the Royal Opera as a guest artist, the same critic praised the "brilliance and bravura of his interpretation, which combines youthful freshness with strength and maturity of tone and delivery."[56] This is exactly the impression we get from the recording, which also documents Swedish performance practice at that time. The opera is heavily cut, the excisions including Alfredo's crucial dialogue with Annina and the cabaletta in act 2, several exchanges with Germont later in that act and substantial chunks from his duet with Violetta in act 3. It might be more appropriate however to place the duet in act 4, for the division of the opera into four acts (commonly adopted in opera houses) was made official in the Paris version of the score published by Benois in 1864, which seems to have been at least partly the source of the performing edition used in Stockholm. The clearest evidence of this is the full orchestral repeat of Violetta's impassioned outburst "Amami Alfredo" in act 2 (which can also be heard in the complete French-language recording of the opera made by Pathé in 1912).[57] Other curiosities, probably related to the specific needs of the Stockholm production, include the assignation of a handful of choral lines to solo singers and a simplified version of the orchestral parts in the final eight measures of the opera. Yet there is nothing alienatingly eccentric about this performance of *Traviata.* Schymberg, who was making her debut here in a role she would continue to sing for several decades, brings unmistakable conviction to the role of Violetta, and Sandberg's conducting combines close attention to detail with theatrical awareness and ideal flexibility in accompaniment.

What strikes one most in Alfredo's opening phrases is the Nordic coloring of the voice, highlighted by the vowel sounds, which seems to accentuate the shyness and reserve of the character. In "Libiamo ne' lieti calici," which here becomes "Slå i och drick ur!" the tenor's voice is a liquid blend of oboe and clarinet timbres and his breath span formidable. The notation—which includes mordents, acciaccaturas, staccatos, and sforzandos—is observed impeccably, as are the indications *con grazia* and *leggerissimo.*

"Un dì, felice, eterea" is also gracefully limned, combining a generous use of rubato with close attention to relative note values. The expansive "Di quell'amor" is intense but inward in expression, and does not break the continuity of line. The final cadenza is delicately drawn, with all the intervals registering clearly thanks to the tenor's firmly sustained *mezza voce* and perfect intonation. Schymberg does her best here, but she is limited by what her voice can and cannot do, and her phrasing loses some of its poise in rapid passages. As a result, she fails to capture Violetta's feeling of increasing closeness to Alfredo, for the music here contradicts her verbal insistence that he should forget her.

Björling's measured enthusiasm might be exchanged for coolness when Violetta hands him the flower, yet if one listens carefully one realizes that he is simply letting the words and music speak for themselves within a scene in which the tension builds slowly but progressively. He delivers the climactic notes above the staff with increasing intensity, and in Alfredo's offstage *Andantino* (taken at a leasurely pace) after the first verse of "Sempre libera" he rises effortlessly to an unwritten top C in the phrase "croce e delizia." This interpolation is a tradition that dates back to the nineteenth century and was first recorded by Carlo Dani on a 1903 Mapleson Cylinder live from the Met,[58] while in the final decades of the twentieth century it was much favored by Kraus.

At the beginning of the second act, while Sandberg respects Verdi's *Allegro vivace* in the orchestral introduction, Björling adopts a more pensive pace in his recitative, although he later varies the tempo considerably. The freedom of his phrasing and firmness of line (the last note in each musical paragraph is always as beautifully poised as the first) are worthy of a great instrumentalist, and the inwardness of expression suggests a character thinking aloud rather than confiding openly in the audience. The aria "De' miei bollenti spiriti" ("Brännande blodets känsla") is equally remarkable for its purity of tone, free from the veristic highlighting indulged in here by some tenors (such as Gigli, in his live recordings from Covent Garden made a few months earlier).[59] Nevertheless, it must be admitted that the melancholy hue of Björling's voice, thrown into relief by the Swedish vowels, contrasts with the exuberant happiness expressed by Alfredo: his singing is well-sprung, but not really smiling. The cadential phrases are simply and accurately sung, with a potent top A-flat, but he doesn't attempt the prescribed *messa di voce* on the G of "quasi," which would have lent greater finish to the final measure. A very definite full stop is necessary in this case, for the rest of the scene is cut. This was standard practice at the time and had been since the nineteenth century, but one cannot help feeling that "O mio rimorso" would have suited Björling's voice at least as well as those of Helge Rosvænge and Ivan Kozlovsky, both of whom recorded the cabaletta in the 1940s.

We next hear Alfredo in his exchanges with Violetta after she has written the letter. His approach remains understated, but he achieves an admirable variety of expression in the recitative beginning "Giunse mio padre." The latter part of the act is mutilated by cuts, but Björling makes the most of what remains. He does not raise his voice while reading the opening lines of Violetta's letter, but releases all his dismay in the concentrated energy of the A-flat that follows. Equally striking is the vehemence of feeling—suggested not through sheer volume but through density of tone—that he conveys at the end of the act, where he adds a ringing B-flat for good measure.

In the central section of the next act, set in Flora's Paris home, Sandberg conveys the impression of an *Allegro agitato* within a spacious framework so as to allow all details to tell (especially Violetta's asides). Alfredo's curt comments thus register more strongly than usual, and Björling continues to make music both in the card scene and in his subsequent denunciation of Violetta, his voice equally beautiful in *piano* and *forte* passages. The denunciation is developed across a highly effective crescendo, the tone properly supported until after the climactic A-flat. In the great ensemble that follows Germont's entrance Alfredo's asides are sung limpidly, without exaggerated emphasis. Once again the line is clearly audible throughout, even in the quieter and lower passages, a tribute to the excellent acoustics of the Royal Opera but also to the tenor's superbly equalized voice.

Björling's most bewitching singing in this performance comes in "Parigi, o cara" ("Fråm stadens vimmel") in act 4, where he follows Verdi's indication *dolcissimo a mezza voce* right to the end of the solo section, creating an atmosphere of sustained intimacy with Violetta (although this entails ignoring Verdi's subsequent *forte* markings). One is reminded here of his equally poetic half-voice singing three months earlier in the duet "Ai nostri monti" from *Il trovatore*, which has a similar rhythmic structure. Björling never lost his ease in soft singing, but he was rarely more generous in his use of it than during this seminal year in his artistic progress. Once again, his breath span is phenomenal: the four-measure phrases are uninterrupted in their flow, without any hint of the unsteadiness or uncertainty of pitch that regularly afflict other tenors here.

His contribution to the *stretta*, "O mio sospiro e palpito," has once again an almost instrumental quality: he undeniably sounds less involved here than some, but few singers have come so close to maintaining a legato while respecting the dynamic nuances and Verdi's *Allegro* marking. In the finale, the beauty of Alfredo's desperate plea to Violetta ("No, non morrai, non dirmelo") is highlighted by its becoming a solo, for Germont's phrases are omitted, as are those of both father and son after Violetta's death.

In 1939 Björling had an ideal voice for Alfredo, and arguably no other tenor on record offers such diverse musical pleasure in this opera. Although Cesare Valletti, Bergonzi, Kraus, and Nicolai Gedda sang the part in complete recordings with refined musicianship and considerable dramatic involvement, none of them match the young Björling's lustrous tone and sheer vocal facility. At the same time the latter's approach to the role was in a number of ways unconventional: music that sounds sunny and extrovert in other voices here conveys shyness and reserve to a degree that some may find disconcerting. In dramatic terms, however, this approach is not without logic, for only a deeply shy man would have admired Violetta from a distance for a whole year before declaring his love for her. Even Alfredo's most public gesture, his embarrassingly boorish denunciation of Violetta at Flora's party, can be interpreted (as it is by Björling) as the typically exaggerated outburst of someone who usually keeps his emotions bottled up.

Un ballo in maschera
Complete Recordings

December 14, 1940: New York, Metropolitan Opera House
Jussi Björling (Riccardo), Zinka Milanov (Amelia), Stella Andreva (Oscar), Alexander Svéd (Renato), Bruna Castagna (Ulrica), Norman Cordon (Samuel), Nicola Moscona (Tom); Metropolitan Opera Chorus and Orchestra, cond. Ettore Panizza
Myto H008

April 20 or 22, 1950: New Orleans, Municipal Auditorium
Jussi Björling (Riccardo), Suzy Morris (Amelia), Audrey Schuh (Oscar), Marko Rothmüller (Renato), Martha Larrimore (Ulrica), Norman Treigle (Samuel), Jack Dabdoub (Tom); New Orleans Opera House Association Chorus and Orchestra, cond. Walter Herbert
VAIA 11692

Extract from act 2
October 23, 1940: San Francisco, War Memorial Opera House
Jussi Björling (Riccardo), Elisabeth Rethberg (Amelia), Richard Bonelli (Renato); San Francisco Opera Orchestra, cond. Gennaro Papi
Guild GHCD 2238/40

"Di' tu se fedele"

August–September 1937: Stockholm
Svensk Filmindustri Orchestra, cond. Nils Grevillius
Bluebell ABCD 092

June 16, 1941: Stockholm, Concert Hall
Unspecified orchestra, cond. Nils Grevillius
HMV DA 1818

March 1944: Stockholm, Concert Hall
Unspecified orchestra, cond. Nils Grevillius
Naxos 8.10754

August 5, 1957: Stockholm, Gröna Lund
Bertil Bokstedt, pf.
Bluebell ABCD 114

September 1957, Florence, Teatro Comunale
Orchestra of the Maggio Musicale Fiorentino, cond. Albert Erede
Decca 443 930-2

Two months before he died, Björling was prevented from finishing a complete recording of *Un ballo in maschera* by a combination of poor health and artistic divergences with the conductor Georg Solti, which were amplified by the ambiguous attitude of the producer John Culshaw.[60] Just a few pages of the first act seem to have been recorded during those sessions in Rome in July 1960, and nothing survived in Decca's archives. In 1961, after Björling's death, Solti recorded the work with Bergonzi as Riccardo. This was the second time that the tenor had lost an opportunity to leave full sound documentation of one of his favorite roles: in 1954 a prolonged bout of laryngitis had made it impossibile for him to participate in the NBC broadcast of the work which took place on January 17 and 24 under Toscanini's leadership. He had, however, been coached in the role by the conductor, and took part in an orchestral rehearsal (singing "half-voice") before having to give up.[61] He was replaced by Jan Peerce.

These disappointments proved all the more acute because Riccardo was one of Björling's most successful stage roles. He sang it thirty-eight times in all, making his debut at the Royal Opera in Stockholm in April 1934 (in a single performance in Swedish conducted by Sandberg) and performing it for the last time (with Solti on the podium) at the Chicago Lyric Opera in November 1957. Twenty-three is an exceptionally young age at which to attempt the part of Riccardo (Caruso was twenty-six when he first sang it, Pavarotti thirty-six), for no other Verdi tenor role requires such a broad range of expression.

Yet there is little doubt that right from the beginning Björling's voice and technique were well-suited to the challenges of the music, and the opera's original setting (before the censors' intervention) in Sweden, with King Gustav III as protagonist, was an obvious extra attraction for him. Three of the productions in which he took part—in New York, Copenhagen, and New

Figure 18. Riccardo in *Un ballo in maschera,* Milan, 1951. Photograph by Erio Piccagliani. © Photographic Archive of the Teatro alla Scala.

Orleans—re-created that setting (the one in Copenhagen, originally staged in 1935 and revived for Björling in 1945, was the first ever to do this). In his autobiography, the tenor recalled with enthusiasm the Swedish sets designed by Mstislav Dobujinsky for Herbert Graf's new production at the Metropolitan Opera in 1940.[62] Twelve days after the season-opening premiere of that production the opera was broadcast. The surviving recording is the earliest complete documentation in sound of a performance of this opera. Its easy availability on CD goes some way toward making posthumous amends to Björling for the bitter experience in Rome, which may well have shortened his life.

The Met performance was not, however, his first recording of music from *Un ballo in maschera.* The earliest extract is part of the soundtrack of the movie *Fram för framgång,* made three years earlier in 1937. He sings the Canzone (or Barcarola) "Di' tu se fedele" (which here becomes "O säg, när på skummande vågor"), not in a reconstruction of the scene with Ulrica from the first act of the opera, but as the Swedish singer Tore Nilsson speeding across the waves on a sailing boat in the archipelago near Stockholm. This decontextualisation explains perhaps why the performance (without chorus) is less respectful of Verdi's dynamic markings than Björling's later recordings. The volume of his voice never really dips below a *mezzo piano*, in spite of the ***ppp*** indicated in the opening section of each verse. At the same time, the exuberance and nimbleness of his singing enable him to express a greater degree of *brio* (as the composer requests) than any other tenor on record, and Grevillius's respect for the tempo indication (*Allegro giusto*) ensures that the characteristic 6/8 rhythm makes its full effect. Here Riccardo, disguised as a sea-roving fisherman, declares his fearlessness in the face of whatever future Ulrica may predict for him; not even in later performances by Björling himself are all the notes so brimming with vitality as they are here. The pristine tone, crisp diction, and precision of phrasing (clear alternation of legato and staccato, respect for note values, and the exceptionally musical execution of the multiple embellishments) lend his singing an infectious buoyancy. Björling is one of the few twentieth century tenors who sings all the written notes here, including the arduous downward leaps from top A-flat to C below the staff, and he manages the effect with remarkable ease and evenness of tone. The lower C belongs more to the bass than to the tenor register, and even the cello-toned Caruso did not attempt it in his excellent 1911 disc.[63] The Swedish tenor David Stockman did span the full interval—with admirable *souplesse*—in his 1910 recording in translation[64] (he was later to perform the role of Riccardo in the new production at the Royal Opera in 1927). In an HMV recording made a year before Björling's Rosvænge did likewise,[65] but in his case the singing (in German) is so graceless that comparison simply augments our admiration for his younger colleague.

The second sound document of Björling's Riccardo consists of the entire love duet (and the beginning of the scene that follows) from a live performance at the War Memorial Opera House in San Francisco in October 1940. In this twenty-four-minute broadcast the tenor is heard alongside the Amelia of Elisabeth Rethberg (it was the only opera they sang together) under Gennaro Papi's idiomatic leadership. This was Björling's third performance of the role of Riccardo after the Stockholm debut and an appearance at the Vienna Staatsoper in 1937, and the second in which he sang Antonio Somma's Italian text.

The lyricism, repose, and tonal purity of Björling's singing is striking from his first entrance, contrasting with the initially rather unfocused agitation of Rethberg's Amelia. No other tenor on record (not even Björling himself in subsequent performances) begins the duet so gently, even shyly—an approach that, however unconventional, is both musically and psychologically persuasive and enables him to prepare the climax slowly. Since he avoids thickening the sound in the middle register, the voice is free to bloom every time a phrase soars above the staff, an effect reinforced by a liberal dose of fermatas. This, combined with the limpidity of his diction and the caress of his legato (not to mention Papi's impassioned accompaniment, warmed by string portamentos), lends an appropriate degree of rapture to an unhurried "Non sai tu." It must be admitted, however, that in certain phrases—in particular "Quante notti ho vegliato anelante"—he fails to capture the erotic yearning implicit in the text. Nor does he convey the *entusiasmo* requested by Verdi in "La mia vita, l'universo": Di Stefano[66] and Pavarotti[67] come closer here to the required effect, although, as elsewhere, Björling's melancholy tone exerts a fascination all of its own. Few tenors have shaped the descending phrase (from A-natural) "M'ami, Amelia!" so beautifully, and when the tempo changes (*Allegro come prima*) he shows his mastery of musical proportions by building the opening phrase from a quiet beginning ("M'ami!") to an overwhelming climax on the B-flat of "estinto tutto." This is achieved without the slightest unevenness of line, although he does switch round the text, displacing the key word "rimorso."

In "Oh qual soave brivido" Björling seems to want a brisker tempo than that set by Papi, and the conductor quickly adjusts. The difficulty here is to sing *mezzavoce dolcissimo* at a rapid pace, without sacrificing legato or clarity of diction. Björling has the technical means to do this better than most, although the words here are slightly lacking in vitality and he fails to observe (as in later performances) the big portamento leading to the top A of "Astro di queste tenebre." This portamento is convincingly executed in the earliest recordings of this duet, such as the one made by Giovanni Zenatello and Eugenia Burzio in 1906,[68] as well as in many later versions. He does, however, make expressive use of the syncopated rhythm in the passage that follows, investing the music with an extra spurt of energy. Rethberg is not quite able to equal this effect, for her voice is at this stage of her career is less responsive than his, although overall her Amelia is admirable both for musical precision and emotional involvement. Both sail effortlessly to a prolonged top C (unwritten for the tenor), which Björling uncharacteristically holds a couple of seconds longer than the soprano.

Björling was fortunate in being able to sing this opera with many of the finest conductors of his era. In his single Viennese performance he was led by Josef Krips and a revival in Stockholm in 1942 saw Vittorio Gui at the helm, while later performances at the Metropolitan were conducted by Bruno Walter, Fritz Busch, and Dimitri Mitropoulos. The Argentinian Ettore Panizza, who had worked alongside Toscanini at La Scala in the 1920s, was arguably inferior to none of these in the Italian repertoire, and the performance broadcast from the Met in 1940, though less original in conception than Mitropoulos's readings of the 1950s, nonetheless achieves a close to ideal combination of dramatic momentum, courtly elegance and expansive lyricism.

In the opening scene we hear for the first time Björling as the king addressing his court (although his regal status is somewhat undermined by Oscar's announcing him as the "Conte": the names remain unvaried in spite of the Swedish setting). In recitative he cannot match the eloquence of Caruso,[69] Pertile,[70] or later Bergonzi,[71] but his diction is clear and the coloring suitably authoritative, while the phrasing matches in springiness the tripping rhythms of the accompaniment. The noble beauty of his timbre not only gives musical pleasure, but lends credibility to a monarch who, however irresponsible in affairs of the heart, proves capable of supreme magnanimity. The lighter hue of "Avresti alcune beltà" reminds us of Björling's easy mastery of chiaroscuro (although he fails to capture the libertine innuendo in the words), and the long aside in which Riccardo reveals his love for Amelia is delivered in a manner that is at once more inward and more impassioned. The phrase beginning "Anima mia" is typical in its youthful warmth, sustained on two ample breaths with golden tone. The opening of the aria, "La rivedrà in estasi," is no less bewitching in sound but overloud, a *mezzo forte* that contrasts unnecessarily with the ***ppp*** of the accompaniment. Pertile, who recorded the aria in the same year (1926) in which he sang the role with Toscanini (and later with Panizza) at La Scala, is more specific in expression here, although his tone is less ingratiating and his voice less perfectly controlled than Björling's: the latter scrupulously observes the *dolcissimo* marking on the words "la sua parola udrà." Once again the extra sheen his voice acquires above the staff lends finish to the soaring phrases, and the climactic A-sharp springs from his throat with stunning brilliance.

Björling doesn't imitate the baritonal colors employed by Caruso in his recordings from this opera, but shows no signs of discomfort in the lower range. Although in this Met performance he does not attempt the lower C in "Di' tu se fedele," he guarantees a sonorous D-flat in the recitative leading up to Renato's first aria ("Alla vita che t'arride"), where once again the asides contrast effectively with the main dialogue.

It is Oscar who sets the mood at the end of the first scene, and it is rare for the tenor to match the soprano (on this occasion a sweet-toned Stella Andreva) in elegance and precision. Here, however, every accent and grace note is in place, the vowels are impeccably pure, and the rhythm is sustained with ease. It is true that his voice does not convey the smiling warmth that Pavarotti achieves here, but the suppleness of his execution (even when Panizza accelerates) is such that the high spirited music works its magic irresistibly.

In the second scene too, Björling's Riccardo lacks the carefree playfulness that some tenors have achieved (sometimes at the expense of elegance), but he maintains a constant lightness of touch and of step. In the Canzone the tempo is rather more spacious than in the film soundtrack, as is emphasized by the ritardandos on the words "tradir l'amor mio" and their equivalent in the second verse. This results in a more sober tone, but enables the tenor to respect all the dynamic markings and to phrase with greater variety (Panizza's tempo is in fact the conventional one for this piece). The voice remains responsive, although the G-flat above the staff on "canzoni" in the second verse sounds congested.

Björling does not attempt to insert laughter between the notes in "È scherzo od è follia," as Caruso,[72] Bergonzi, and Gigli[73] do to delightful effect (as of course does Alessandro Bonci, whose famous 1926 recording[74] of this quintet was later given to Björling by Toscanini), but his crystalline tone and elegant phrasing (with note values scupulously observed) create an appropriately insouciant impression, and the harmonic modulations of the final measures are exquisitely voiced.

In the second act, his interpretation differs considerably from that in San Francisco: this Riccardo is much more adult and virile in sound, and never emotionally detached. No doubt Panizza's influence was decisive here, for the conductor would have carefully rehearsed this new production. "Non sai tu" is no less beautiful than before, but more is made of the words (though Martinelli, in a 1942 broadcast of the same production,[75] better reveals the moral anguish that accompanies Riccardo's love for Amelia) and the generosity of his phrasing is such that he practically omits to take a breath before "Ma per questo ho potuto un istante," rising to a B-flat. The young Zinka Milanov equals Björling in freshness and beauty of tone: perhaps in no other recording of this scene are two voices matched to such musical effect. The descending phrase "M'ami Amelia" is less expansive than before, but the section beginning "M'ami, m'ami" is no less compelling, with the initial consonant more idiomatically stressed. Throughout the scene Björling's lower register is impressive in its resonance, and the text of "Oh qual soave brivido," with its erotic overtones, is projected tellingly, although again tenor and conductor take a few measures to find a mutually acceptable tempo. The final part of the duet is sung with inspired and enthralling ease by both singers, although Milanov, like Rethberg, cannot quite match Björling in rhythmic precision.

The tenor captures effectively the darker mood of the scene that follows and continues to make music compellingly in the trio, although he is sometimes covered by the generous outpourings of Milanov and Alexander Svéd (a rather rough-hewn Renato, who had already appeared with Björling in Vienna): there is no doubt that the weight of his voice at this stage is closer to a lyric tenor than a *lirico-spinto.* Panizza makes the traditional cut of eight measures in the coda of the trio, which rather spoils the proportions of the piece. A much more compromising cut, however, is that of Riccardo's aria "Ma se m'è forza perderti" in act 3, where Björling passes abruptly from the opening recitative—very beautifully sung and pensive in expression even at the climax of "Ah l'ho segnato"—to the conclusive episode beginning "Ah, dessa è là," where his diction lacks urgency at first but the voice blossoms magnificently in "Sì, rivederti, Amelia." The cut, though not uncommon at the time, is both conspicuous and lamentable, for it eliminates one of Verdi's most inspired tenor arias, surely well-suited to Björling's voice. He had sung it on the first night of the Met production[76] and may have rehearsed it with Toscanini in 1954, but there is no proof of his ever singing it in public after 1940. The decision seems to have been entirely his own: the aria was reinstated by the veteran Martinelli when he performed the opera with Panizza the following season.

Some compensation for this omission is provided by Björling's superb traversal of the final scene of the opera. His plaintive half voice—free from any constriction, with every word poised on the breath—is used generously in the duet with Amelia, marred only by a conspicuous pronunciation error ("perché piagni?" instead of "perché piangi?"). The death scene is sung with exceptional nobility of tone and exemplary breath control. The phrase "rispettato ho il suo candor" shows how eloquent he could be in matching verbal inflections and vocal production. There is little attempt to convey realistically, as Jon Vickers does in a 1962 broadcast from Covent Garden,[77] the physical pain of the character: this Riccardo immediately lifts us onto the higher plane of experience suggested here by the music. No other character in Björling's repertoire faces death more nobly, and his voice rises sublimely to the expressive challenge.

In June 1941 Björling made a commercial recording of "Di' tu se fedele" which has never been officially released. Grevillius conducts, and the tempo is once again sprightlier than the 1940 Met performance, but the tenor finds time to introduce a few extra details, such as a neat diminuendo on the word "l'amor mio" and an acciaccatura when passing from the top B-flat to the A-flat in the final cadence. It is generally a more persuasive performance than the published recording made with the same conductor in 1944. Here the tempo is closer to Panizza's, but the ritardandos are less pronounced and the overall atmosphere is less theatrical (the lower C is avoided once more, as in 1941). The close miking highlights the smooth homogeneity of the voice production, yet this very suavity, combined with the lack of energizing verbal accents, neutralizes the mocking impertinence with which Riccardo addresses Ulrica, and the barcarolle rhythm tends to have a lulling rather than a provocative effect.

The second complete *Ballo* with Björling, solidly conducted by Walter Herbert, was broadcast from New Orleans in April 1950. The sound quality is variable and the rest of the cast ordinary, but the recording reveals an evolution in Björling's voice and interpretative stance. He was by then an established star in the United States (as one can tell from the applause that greets him at his entrance) and his phrasing reflects the self-confidence of a great singer at the peak of his career. This Riccardo has lost almost every trace of youthful ingenuousness and his words are projected much more vividly (although occasional pronunciation errors still emerge). In the opening recitative the timbre is less glowingly fresh than in New York, but the musicality of the phrasing is no less winning and this time the aria begins introspectively. The culminating A-sharp falls victim to distortion, but there is no mistaking the brilliance of the note itself. The dialogue that follows captures Riccardo's rapid mood changes more vividly than previously, revealing both a deeper understanding of the character's feelings of guilt—"Segreta acerba cura m'opprime" conveys genuine perturbation—and a more infectious sense of playfulness: his top notes here have a thrilling impact. The operetta-like ensemble that brings the scene to an end also suffers from the murky recording, but Björling once again takes the lead with ideal elasticity.

His superior musicality is still more conspicuous in the trio with Amelia and Ulrica: Riccardo's asides emerge as models of aplomb amid the poorly controlled lurches of soprano Suzy Morris and mezzo Martha Larrimore. In "Di' tu se fedele" he cannot match the liquid fluency of the 1937 recording, but he throws the music into stronger theatrical relief than ever before, reinstating the spectacular downward leaps to C below the staff (in the second verse the effect is particularly successful) and highlighting dynamic contrasts. His top voice has genuine *squillo* here, and he brings the Barcarola to a dazzling close with demonstrative fermatas on the B-flat and A-flat. Björling probably felt freer to take a few liberties in New Orleans, where he was under less rigorous critical scrutiny. Significantly, for the first time he introduces a mordent to accompany the allargando and diminuendo on the words "le dolci canzoni" in the second verse. This embellishment is entirely idiomatic and can be found in very early recordings by Giovanni Zenatello (1905)[78] and Leo Slezak (1907).[79] Björling may however have introduced it unthinkingly, revealing his instinctive feeling for the style of mid-nineteenth-century Italian opera.

Another surprise in this scene is his decision to take an upward turn in the recitative "se sul campo d'onor ti son grado," ending on a sustained top B. This hyperbolic gesture (unprecedented on disc) highlights Riccardo's reluctance to accept the full significance of Ulrica's prophecy. The effect is spectacular and demonstrates how at ease Björling feels by now with the more ebullient side of Riccardo's personality. In this performance he even attempts some interpolated laughter in the reprise of "È scherzo od è follia," without at any time compromising the elegance of the phrasing: this traditional expressive device is mentioned disapprovingly in a letter Verdi wrote as early as 1865,[80] but Toscanini would encourage Björling to cultivate the embellishment during his coaching sessions in 1954. His tone has less spring to it than at the Met, however, and the musical context is less refined. Curiously, ten measures of this quintet are repeated in the available recordings: no doubt an error made in transferral.

The love duet is intermittently compromised by Suzy Morris's squally Amelia: she has difficulty in dealing accurately with rapid passages, offers little dynamic modulation and her diction is cloudy at best. Björling, however, has never sounded so boldly Italianate at the opening of the scene, so daring in laying bare his emotions. His voice is much darker than before, and accents are more biting. "M'ami Amelia" is as meltingly expansive as in San Francisco, and the more robust vocal approach involves no sacrifice of musicality, although he makes a late entry in one phrase and appears slightly less responsive rhythmically in "Oh qual soave brivido" (the recording is particularly distorted here). Once again a magnificent unison top C brings the duet to a close.

In the following scene there is no risk of his being overpowered on this occasion by the soprano and baritone (Marko Rothmüller's Renato sounds lightweight alongside the tenor). In the trio Herbert includes the first four measures of the coda (omitted by Panizza). This a remarkable staccato passage that in some ways looks forward to the idiom of *Falstaff,* and Björling's dextrous execution makes us regret that he was not allowed to sing the last four measures as well, as he probably did a few years later with Mitropoulos at the Met.[81]

Riccardo's opening recitative in act 3 reveals a deepening of interpretative insights, facilitated by the weightier sonorities of a fully developed voice. The tone is appropriately reflective and the somber coloring of the words matches the gravity of the decision taken (to send Amelia back to England with her husband). Björling here makes a typical pronunciation error, transforming "separi" into "separe," perhaps because he instinctively felt the need for an exact rhyme with "core" at the end of the phrase (this is the sort of trick a musical ear can play on a singer who does not speak the language in which he sings). At the end of the recitative he highlights the final cadence by elaborating on the embellishment (an acciaccatura) on the words "sacrificio mio": this probably had something to do with his need to compensate for the omission of "Ma se m'è forza perderti" (Walter Herbert had tried hard to persuade him to sing the aria). It is surely the same compensatory urge that encouraged him to compound the difficulties of "Sì, rivederti, Amelia" by vaulting to a top C on the words "d'amor" at the end of a phrase in which the B-flat and A have already been ringingly sustained (this interpolation, like that in act 1 scene 2, is clearly marked in the tenor's score).

In the duet with Amelia (where Suzy Morris sounds more vocally collected and copes easily with the sustained phrases above the staff), Björling makes even more continuous use of his *mezza voce* than before, while in the tragic denouement of the opera his tone assimilates more realistically the colors of death, without sacrificing the noble contour of the melody. The phrase "Addio diletta patria," marked by a sudden crescendo, is particularly striking.

No complete recording of *Un ballo in maschera* survives from the last ten years of Björling's career, although he continued to sing the opera fairly frequently. Two recordings of "Di' tu se fedele," however, were made in 1957, which was the year in which he gave his last public performances in the role. The first, taped during an open air recital in Gröna Lund, finds him in excellent shape, and the informal setting favors the sort of expressive spontaneity on which the Barcarola thrives. The voice has darkened still further and Björling tends to favor louder dynamics, as in the Swedish soundtrack twenty years earlier. The top notes are densely weighted, the leaps to C below the staff are executed even more effortlessly than in New Orleans, and once again an embellishment is inserted on the words "dolci canzoni." Björling also adds an extra mordent when passing from the climactic B-flat to the A-flat that follows, a feature that can be found in a 1908 recording by Augusto Scampini.[82] The effect is entirely stylish, and would be included (this time as an acciaccatura, as in the 1941 studio version) in the Decca recording with Alberto Erede made a month later. Here the words are more alive than ever before and the voice is in pristine condition, making it hard to believe that this opera had been in his repertoire for twenty-three years. As in Gröna Lund he sacrifices the pianissimos at the opening of each verse, but the descending intervals are once again negotiated with bravura, the high notes ring out splendidly, and the undulating *staccato e leggerissimo* passages are executed with teasing precision.

It is interesting to compare this performance of the forty-six-year-old Björling with that of the forty-seven-year-old Pavarotti in 1982 (in Solti's second complete recording of the opera). Pavarotti, along with Bergonzi, was one of Björling's two great successors in this role, and of the two he is the one who more closely resembles the Swede in timbre and who makes the more brilliant effect in this piece. He does not attempt the wide descending intervals (as Domingo—generally a less memorable Riccardo—did in some performances), but otherwise exploits all the expressive devices of the aria, and introduces an extra contrast by beginning the second verse more softly than the first. The overall effect is highly engaging, the tone sunnier than the Swedish tenor's, the words more tellingly highlighted. In terms of purity of line, vocal smoothness and general musical refinement, however, Björling remains superior, avoiding the jerky accents and shallowly supported sounds that Pavarotti introduces in his quest for expressive immediacy.

In spite of his stubborn reluctance to sing "Ma se m'è forza perderti" (an aria that Gigli and Bergonzi actually encored on some occasions), Björling's Riccardo is an exceptionally satisfying portrayal. His vision of the character evolved as his voice matured, yet recordings prove that his earlier performances had a unique vocal radiance and were in no way dramatically unresolved. Later on he captured more vividly the mental imbalance that leads Riccardo to dismiss Renato's and Ulrica's warnings and risk everything for the sake of love. There is something suicidal about the way in which this character defies fate right to the end, and there is no doubt that Björling—

himself inclined to burn the candle at both ends[83]—found this demon-driven personality particularly congenial. Although his Riccardo is less light-hearted and hedonistic than others (both Caruso and Gigli convey an irresistible warmth of feeling in their recordings), the compulsive nature of his desire to live dangerously is vividly suggested, as is the generosity of spirit that enables him to face death with inspiring humanity and wisdom.

La forza del destino
"Solenne in quest'ora"

December 5, 1937: New York, Carnegie Hall
Jussi Björling (Alvaro), Donald Dickson (Vargas); General Motors Symphony Orchestra, cond. Erno Rapee
VAIA 1189

January 3, 1951: New York, Manhattan Center
Jussi Björling (Alvaro), Robert Merrill (Vargas); RCA Victor Orchestra, cond. Renato Cellini
RCA 88697748922; Naxos 8.110788

Of all the Verdi tenor roles Björling never sang on stage—and there are over twenty of them—Don Alvaro in *La forza del destino* was perhaps the best suited to his voice and temperament. The reason he did not sing the entire opera probably has something to do with its marginal position in the repertoire in Stockholm: it was performed there just twice between 1930 and 1940 and was not revived at all in the two successive decades. He may well have seen the two performances in the 1933–34 season, when the leading role was assigned to David Stockman, and the part of Alvaro was included provisionally in his Met contract for the 1950–51 season, but in the event the opera was not staged in New York that year and Anna-Lisa Björling had no memory of her husband studying the score.[84]

Björling's recordings of the famous duet "Solenne in quest'ora," during which a severely injured Alvaro entrusts Carlo di Vargas with the key to the cask containing the portrait of Leonora, were probably inspired by repeated playing of the famous disc[85] with Caruso and Antonio Scotti. In this classic interpretation the voices blend impressively (when it was first published Victor felt the need to specify that it is Caruso who sings the opening line) and maintain a striking nobility of tone and diction from beginning to end. Indeed the two Neapolitans sometimes seem more interested in the sculpted perfection of the arching melody than in the subtle interplay of what proves to be a fundamental turning point—striking in its dramatic irony—in Piave's plot. As it happens, in the year that disc was made Björling's father David had heard Caruso and Scotti sing the second tenor-baritone duet from the opera ("Invan Alvaro ti celasti dal mondo") during the third-act finale of a special gala performance of Johann Strauss's *The Gypsy Baron*, in which he himself performed as one of the "Pupils of the School of Opera."[86]

Björling first sang "Solenne in quest'ora" in translation, during a Swedish concert tour with baritone Einar Larson in April 1935. No recording was made of those performances, but the 1937 radio broadcast in Italian with the American baritone Donald Dickson demonstrates that the influence of Caruso can be heard in almost every measure. In some respects the tenor's interpretation sounds as if it has been learned from the recording rather than from the score. Shared qualities include the appropriately somber, almost transfixed, solemnity of diction in the opening *Andante sostenuto* (where the repeated low Gs convey both Alvaro's physically weakened state and his firm inner resolve); the constant, and entirely stylish, use of portamentos on words divided between two notes or more on different pitches ("cercate," "trarrete," "celate," "l'onore") and the generous (unwritten) fermatas on the top As in the *Andante* "Or muoio tranquillo." When Björling deviates from the score, he tends to do so in exactly the same places as Caruso: neither of the tenors makes much of the *morendo* in the phrase "Colà v'ha un mistero che meco morrà" and both pause briefly on the B ("al *cor* mio") in the ninth measure of the *Andante*, which functions as a harmonically crucial leading note (the second half of the duet is in C major). This unwritten fermata is a feature of a number of early recordings, including another made in 1906 with Mario Gilion and Domenico Viglione Borghese,[87] and a noble performance (much influenced by Caruso) in Danish on a 1914 disc with Niels Hansen and Albert Høeberg.[88]

Björling also stands out for the adult richness of his timbre and for a legato that is even more impeccable than his model's. Yet not all goes well in this first performance: his partner (known primarily as a radio artist) is unsubtle in phrasing and unrefined in tone and Björling himself mispronounces the key word "muoio," once omitting the final letter completely. He also proves careless with his double consonants (all-important in Italian) in the final phrase.

These slips are avoided in the RCA recording made in 1951, where the tenor's phrasing is if anything even closer to Caruso's. Here both Björling and Merrill are in magnificent voice, enabling us to relish the long-breathed luxuriance of their phrasing, their ability to highlight the upward curves of the melody in the *Andante* (where the solid harmonic underpinning of the baritone is as important as the glowing expansion of the tenor's voice). Björling's two top As are perfectly bound into the line and while the first is slightly less ringing than in 1937, the second is free and impressively reinforced (once again following Caruso's example). Although words are not as idiomatically projected as by the two Italians, the diction of neither Björling nor Merrill betrays a marked foreign accent, as one hears for example in the intermittently impressive disc made by Hermann Jadlowker and Josef Schwarz in 1918.[89] Their phrasing, however, is less individual than that of Di Stefano and Ettore Bastianini (recorded in 1960 with Mitropoulos);[90] although Di Stefano's open top As blare somewhat gratingly, he shows a more imaginative grasp of Alvaro's dramatic situation than does Björling. In the opening *Andante sostenuto* his sensitive dynamic shading (tending toward *piano* rather than *forte*) and subtle verbal stresses make the scene much more emotionally precise. Del Monaco is almost equally striking in a live performance with Aldo Protti (also under Mitropoulos) in 1953,[91] where he employs a rare *mezza voce* even when ascending above the staff. This performance of the duet is possibly the one that best establishes the contrast in tempo between the declamatory opening section and the burgeoning melody that follows. Gigli also offers some unique qualities in his 1927 version with Giuseppe De Luca,[92] including a glorious top A and a sweetly intoned dying close that translates to perfection Verdi's *pianissimo* marking, but his phrasing is sentimental rather than truly noble and cracks emerge in his legato. Corelli too, alongside Bastianini in Naples in 1958, indulges in lachrymose effects that weaken the line, although he displays some impressive diminuendos.[93] And while Merrill is once again magnificent as Carlo di Vargas in the complete 1964 recording with Thomas Schippers,[94] his Alvaro (Richard Tucker) cannot match Björling's spiritual elevation of sound and feeling, and is not permitted to let the voice bloom on the high As (there is no written fermata on these notes).

Don Alvaro does not die at the end of this opera (at least in the revised version of the score) but eventually kills the very man who claims here to be his friend. Yet this subsequent development of the plot in no way lessens the impact of this scene. The rare beauty that Björling brings to the words "O muoio tranquillo" and to the poignant melody that sustains them conveys a deep understanding of what it feels like to leave this life with an unburdened conscience. Few of his discs prove as spiritually enriching as this one.

Don Carlo
Complete Recordings

November 6, 1950: New York, Metropolitan Opera House
Jussi Björling (Don Carlo), Delia Rigal (Elisabetta di Valois), Cesare Siepi (Filippo II), Robert Merrill (Rodrigo), Fedora Barbieri (Eboli), Jerome Hines (Il Grande Inquisitore), Lubomir Vichegonov (Un Frate), Lucine Amara (Voce dal Cielo); Metropolitan Opera Chorus and Orchestra, cond. Fritz Stiedry
WHRA-6021 (excerpts)

November 11, 1950: New York, Metropolitan Opera House
Jussi Björling (Don Carlo), Delia Rigal (Elisabetta di Valois), Cesare Siepi (Filippo II), Robert Merrill (Rodrigo), Fedora Barbieri (Eboli), Jerome

Hines (Il Grande Inquisitore), Lubomir Vichegonov (Un Frate), Lucine Amara (Voce dal Cielo); Metropolitan Opera Chorus and Orchestra, cond. Fritz Stiedry
WHRA-6021

"Io la vidi e il suo sorriso"

November 30, 1950: New York, Manhattan Center
RCA Victor Chorus and Orchestra, cond. Renato Cellini
RCA 88697748922; Naxos 8.110788

"Qual pallor! . . . Dio che nell'alma infondere"

November 30, 1950: New York, Manhattan Center
Jussi Björling (Don Carlo) Robert Merrill (Posa); RCA Victor Chorus and Orchestra, cond. Renato Cellini
RCA 88697748922; Naxos 8.110788

Today we take it for granted that tenors specializing in the mainstream Italian repertoire will sooner or later take on the role of Don Carlo, Infante di Spagna. In the past sixty years it has been performed by nearly all the most popular Latin tenors with (more or less) sufficient vocal heft for the part: Bergonzi, Corelli, Vanzo, Domingo, Pavarotti, Giacomini, Carreras, Aragall, Alagna, and Villazón. This contrasts with the situation in the first half of the twentieth century, when relatively few great tenors interpreted the title role between the retirement of Francesco Tamagno (who had "created" the part in the four-act version and performed it for the last time in 1890) and the early 1950s. *Don Carlo* was absent, for example, from the stage repertoires of Caruso, Zenatello, Slezak, Gigli, Pertile, Lauri Volpi, Fleta, Masini, Del Monaco, and Di Stefano. For at least some of these singers this was probably as much a matter of choice as of lack of opportunity: the role was widely considered an ungrateful one, with only a brief opening aria that often goes unapplauded. It was for this reason that Bergonzi stopped singing the part on stage in 1956, after just a couple of seasons.

How does Jussi Björling fit into this? Quite simply, his first performance in the role on November 6, 1950—the opening night of the Metropolitan's first new season in the second half of the twentieth century and the official inauguration of the Bing era—marked a decisive turning point in the reception of this opera and in tenors' attitudes to it. He sang the part eighteen times in all during the last decade of his career, not only in New York but also in Philadelphia, Los Angeles, and Chicago. The Met production was revived frequently over the twenty-one seasons that followed, often featuring other high-profile tenors such as Tucker, Corelli, and Domingo in the title role.

Figure 19. Björling's last theatrical debut: Don Carlos at the Met, 1950. Photograph by Louis Melançon. Courtesy of the Metropolitan Opera Archive.

In 1950 Björling was already familiar with the opera, for it had been regularly staged (in a much-modified five-act version) in Stockholm during the 1930s, with sixteen performances in the 1933–34 season alone. The Royal Swedish Opera fell to a certain extent within the orbit of the Verdi renaissance that had originated in Germany in the 1920s; an influence reinforced by the regular guest appearances of the conductor Leo Blech in the early thirties.

The Austrian Rudolf Bing had himself worked closely with some of the artists who contributed to that resurgence of interest in Verdi's operas, notably the director Carl Ebert and the conductor Fritz Stiedry (who mounted the podium for the 1950 *Don Carlo*). Although the opera had not been a success when staged for the first time at the Met across 1920–23 (in spite of a cast headed by Martinelli), Bing was confident of its potential impact:

> During the late 1920s in Central Europe we had learned how to do these late Verdi operas so that they made their proper effect. But part of the approach was the quality of the staging: I would need a first-class director for *Don Carlo*, and I would need the entire cast in New York working at the task for three weeks before opening night.[95]

For a singer who had served an apprenticeship at the Royal Opera in Stockholm, where theatrical cogency and a strong company spirit had always been appreciated, such an approach should not have proved uncongenial. However, Björling never really hit it off with the new general manager, whom he found less approachable than his predecessor Edward Johnson. Bing's two books of memoirs reveal a notable lack of sympathy for the Swedish tenor, and he was justifiably irritated when the tenor failed to turn up for the first rehearsals of *Don Carlo*. On October 21 Bing complained to him that the Italian artists were present "for every rehearsal on the dot and have to rehearse ensembles, duos and everything without a tenor."[96]

This was the only time Björling made a role-debut at the Met, and it was the last new part he tackled on stage. The recording made during the live telecast on November 6 is the only one that exists of his first performance in any opera: the combination of a season-opening, television coverage, and a new role must have made that evening a particularly stressful one.

The work was performed in the four-act Italian version prepared by Verdi for a new production at La Scala in 1884. Stiedry was forced to make a number of cuts (none of which involved the tenor role), but the only significant departure from the score was the reintroduction of the brief chorus of monks included in the final measures of the original Paris edition. This had been a feature of a number of German-language productions in the 1930s, which often took liberties with Verdi's original dramaturgy: in Fritz Werfel and Lothar Wallerstein's Viennese staging in 1932 Carlos actually stabbed himself at the end of the opera. Nothing like that happens here, however, and the production by Margaret Webster and Rolf Gérard was Shakespearian rather than Schillerian in inspiration, providing a dignified framework for a group of unusually youthful singers. At thirty-nine Björling was the oldest, twelve years senior to his on-stage father, Cesare Siepi. In the *Philadelphia Evening Bulletin*, Max de Schauensee was dismissive of the tenor's acting—"Neither Mr Björling nor Mr Merrill were more than mere stage puppets as far as characterizations went"—and claimed that he sang "with a voice much too lyric for a role which was once sung by the iron-lunged Tamagno."[97] A review by Cecil Smith in *Musical America* makes a similar point:

> His is not an ideal voice for the music, since a darker and harder timbre would make some of the climactic passages sound less petulant. Yet as his voice opened up during the progress of the opera and after some pinched singing at the outset, he contributed much that was beautiful. He had not fully investigated the stylistic possibilities of the music, however, since a good many blandishing colorations that would have benefited the melodic line did not occur to him. As competent, straight singing by a good tenor, Mr Björling's Don Carlo was unexceptional, but there is more in the role than that.[98]

Smith was a discriminating critic and it is interesting to compare his immediate impressions of the performance with those aroused by the audio recording of the telecast (no video seems to have survived). This recording is not quite complete and very erratic in quality, but Ward Marston's restoration of lengthy excerpts (including most of the title role) has made at least part of it accessible to all. This is in fact the first recording of the whole opera in Italian: it was preceded only by a 1948 German-language broadcast from Berlin with Boris Greverus as Carlos. And at times we get the impression that Björling was still feeling his way into a role for which no well-established performing tradition existed.

There is nothing tentative, however, about the beginning of Carlo's opening recitative: "Io l'ho perduta!" is attacked with an exceptional variety of tonal coloring and unusual incisiveness of diction. The Infante appears close here to Schiller's tragic hero, an attractive young man of uncommon sensibility, oppressed by fate. The timbre is both youthful and noble (this Carlo never alienates us by becoming simply neurotic); and the intensity of the key words—"padre," "re," "rapita"—highlighted by Stiedry's urgent accompaniment, reveals both a deep involvement in the part and an ability to exploit the harmonic instability of the vocal line to expose the psychological vulnerability of the character. No other tenor has made the words "la sposa a me promessa!" sound so achingly melancholy, although Bernardo De Muro in his slower-paced 1914 recording[99] also proves eloquent here, and a number of tenors (including De Muro) have made more of the reminiscences that follow ("quanto puro e bello fu il dì"). Here the clumsiness of the Italian translation, with words and notes often awkwardly matched, exposes Björling's limited command of the language: only a singer who speaks Italian can easily make the subtle adjustments in verbal and musical stresses that are necessary here to compensate for the ineptitude of the word-setting. This is very evident if one compares this recording with later ones by Domingo (at La Scala in 1970 with Claudio Abbado)[100] and Carreras (with Herbert von Karajan in 1978),[101] where words are projected more caressingly and the conductors appear perfectly attuned to the expressive needs of the singers. Stiedry had conducted quite a lot of Verdi in the course of his career, but he was not as sensitive to the nuances of the Italian language as Abbado and Karajan (or Tullio Serafin, in a compelling studio recording[102] of the scene made with Vickers in 1961). As a result Björling's voice sounds less well-anchored to the accompaniment than the above-mentioned singers in much of the recitative. While this does effectively convey the feeling of a soul adrift, it proves less conducive to those "blandishing colorations" to which Smith referred in his review, and may also explain the "pinched" quality the critic noted. The staccato-legato of "nel dolce suol di Francia" is a little too rushed to suggest Carlo's mental absorption in a happier past, and the prescribed *messa di voce* on the sustained F of "Fontainebleau"—persuasively executed by De Muro, Vickers, and Carreras—is ignored.

Although vocally simplified—the tessitura is lowered by the transposition from C to B-flat major and the melodic line is shorn of its characteristic *gruppetti*—the revised version of Carlo's aria, "Io la vidi e il suo sorriso," is emotionally much more complex than the equivalent piece in the five-act version of the score. Rather than expressing the straightforward happiness of a young man who has just fallen in love, Carlo communicates a combination of intense nostalgia and bitter frustration at having been robbed by his father of the woman he loves. In this psychologically revealing solo, devoid of repetition, Björling proves less suavely fluent than Domingo and less conscientiously attentive than Carreras to the many *piano* markings. He offers no extra embellishments like the mordent Hermann Jadlowker adds to the final phrase in his 1913 recording[103] (the first ever made of this version of the aria) and does not match the delicate inwardness of De Muro's *mezza voce* in the opening measure and the elegance of his tapered phrase endings. Yet in its way this is a disarmingly spontaneous reading, generous in rubato, in which the occasional rhythmic tension created by the contrast with the accompaniment reinforces our sense of the character's unpredictability; our feeling that his experiences are real and present (the phrase "e cor e speme e sogni e amor" is projected with particular vividness) and not simply part of a well-rehearsed routine. Björling's deviations from the letter of the score are often persuasive, such as when he ignores the *dolcissimo* marking to lend emphasis to "un padre, un re!" or when he opens his voice thrillingly on the high As and B-flat to a degree that few tenors—perhaps only Corelli (in Vienna in 1970)[104]—are able to match. But while Corelli's wayward phrasing, however fascinating, often sounds self-serving, Björling remains unostentatiously faithful to the character he is playing.

No applause greets the quiet close of the aria, which enables the bass Lubomir Vichegonov (il Frate) to startle the listener as well as Carlo with his reflection on the prince's monologue, "del core sol la guerra in ciel si calmerà." This comment reinforces our perception of the otherwordly dimension that accompanies the unfolding of the plot, and will lend Carlo's mysterious disappearance in that very cloister at the end of the opera a special significance. In the recitative that follows, Björling's diction maintains its vitality and he makes good use of his skill in chiaroscuro, employing an appropriately dark coloration for "È voce che nel chiostro appaia ancor!" a phrase that makes it doubly clear that the prince has recognized the monk's voice as being that of his late grandfather, Carlo V.

The substantial scene with Rodrigo that follows was the most important duet for tenor and baritone in Björling's stage repertoire, and it is fitting that his colleague here should be the thirty-three-year-old New Yorker Robert Merrill, who had already sung with him in *Faust* and *Il trovatore* and who was to prove a loyal colleague throughout the 1950s. There is thus no simulation of the friendship celebrated in this scene, and although Merrill was not the most imaginative of singers, his command of the basics of tone production was as solid as Björling's and his musical discipline no less impeccable. Both voices were capable of alternating lyrical effusions with intensely dramatic declamation, and of spinning out a legato across an ample range in which a burnished top register in no way compromised the tonal balance of the lower octave.

In the first of their three recorded performances of the duet Merrill's strong vocal presence is immediately apparent, although his instrument sounds initially a little unresponsive to the emotional demands of the character. It is Björling who really brings the scene to life with his buoyant voicing of "Mio salvator, mio fratel," which speaks eloquently of tender friendship and of Carlo's desire to open up his heart. His confession of his love for Elisabetta is convincingly uttered (although he cannot match the psychological insight achieved by Corelli here) and the exchanges leading up to the final *Allegro assai moderato* are urgently delivered.

The two singers offer a vigorous account of "Dio, che nell'alma infondere," where tenor and baritone sing in thirds of their eternal friendship and desire for political freedom. This popular, marchlike tune represents a key moment in the development of the protagonist, for it shows us a Carlo no longer obsessed exclusively with his own misfortunes and capable of aspiring to higher ideals. To this end the performance functions admirably, the two voices blending to rousing effect and with ideal rhythmic aplomb. The singers however offer little dynamic modulation (they ignore the *piano* marking in the first measure) and do nothing to vary the phrasing in the repeat (with identical words) of the opening theme. Stiedry respects Verdi's metronome marking (♩ = 84), rather than adopting the often-heard slower tempo that makes it possible to savor the words and highlight the traditional *stringendo* and *più mosso* effects. Caruso and Scotti (in a 1912 recording[105] with which Björling must have been familiar) sing the cabaletta at a markedly slower pace, and Martinelli and De Luca (1921)[106] adopt an even more leisurely gait. In both recordings we also hear a portamento leading from the joint cadenza to the reprise of the opening melody, an ornament that Björling and Merrill eschew. Their performance is also less musically varied than Domingo and Cappuccilli's rendition at La Scala in 1970, where Verdi's tempo is respected but the second verse is sung more softly than the first. Mario Filippeschi and Tito Gobbi, in their complete recording with Gabriele Santini,[107] maintain the slower tempo and softer dynamics for both verses; Carreras and Cappuccilli (under Karajan) also reinstate the portamento linking the two verses.

This duet may have been one of the episodes the veteran soprano Geraldine Farrar was thinking of when, after following both the telecast and the subsequent radio broadcast, she commented that "the conductor, Fritz Stiedry, had impossible tempos and no clear understanding of Italianate feeling."[108] Yet it would be unfair not to recognize the Viennese conductor's ability to invest the score with an appreciable breadth of vision and to exploit the psychological potential of the orchestral accompaniments.

The woodwind soloists highlight the harmonic tensions of the orchestral melody that anticipates—almost as if he were rehearsing it mentally—Carlo's opening statement in his long duet with the queen, "Io vengo a domandar grazia alla mia Regina." Björling's voice, seeming to synthesize the timbres of the instruments, creates an uncommonly beautiful effect here, suggesting the emotional tension that Carlo attempts to conceal behind his excessively formal discourse. This unease surfaces in the ensuing *Allegro agitato* "Quest'aura m'è fatale." Although his command of the text is occasionally uncertain (he adds an unwritten "pietà" at one point), Björling's phrasing is wrenching in effect (we follow this scene from Carlo's rather than Elisabetta's point of view), thanks to the rhythmic alertness of his singing and the constant play of chiaroscuro, which enables him to alternate the most dramatically forthright utterances with moments of adolescent vulnerability. What makes Björling's chiaroscuro doubly effective is the forward placement that informs both bright and dark-hued sounds, without allowing the "covered" tone of the latter to obscure the projection of words.

Elisabetta's formal reply to Carlo's outburst ("Prence, se vuol Filippo / Udire la mia preghiera") is indicated *con emozione assai frenata.* Yet this hardly justifies Rigal's sluggish phrasing: her voice seems incapable of moving at the necessary pace, and devoid of the radiance that would make the queen a credibly attractive object of Carlo's adoration. Although the Argentinian soprano was good-looking and her instrument possessed an imposing weightiness that suited the character's regal status, it must have been difficult for Björling—whose voice possessed in abundance the easy flow that Rigal's was lacking—to connect emotionally with such an unresponsive Elisabetta. He continues, however, to sing with notable animation, rising impetuously to the climaxes above the staff, lending singular pathos to the descending duplets on the words "alma," "oppressa," "core," and "gel," and spinning the melody "Perduto ben, mio sol tesor" on silvery thread of melancholy tone (accomodating even the awkward octave drop on the word "vita"). The soprano's ungainly attack of "Clemente Iddio" hardly augurs well, but there is an interruption in the broadcast after a couple of measures and the next line we hear is Carlo's ecstatic "il sovvenir del dolor s'invola." The sound here is particularly poor (this section was not included in the commercially released excerpts), but Björling is at his most inspired, reinforcing his head voice to suggest the spiritual exaltation felt by the prince on realizing that the queen still loves him. The trance-like phrases uttered when he emerges from his swoon ("Qual voce a me dal ciel") are moulded in spellbinding fashion. There is less sensual ardor than we hear from Corelli, but in Björling's voice the poetic imagery ("il ciel s'illuminò, la selva rifiorì") comes breathtakingly alive: the listener has the impression of sharing the prince's heightened state of consciousness. The voice is equally attuned to the music's expressive needs in the premonitory "Alla mia tomba, al sonno dell'avel," in the almost ferocious desperation of Carlo's final embrace with Elisabetta, and in the horror felt when the queen reveals to her "son" the full implications of his oedipal fantasies.

Before Carlo reappears at the beginning of the second act, the audience acquires a fuller understanding of the political implications of the drama and observes, in the long duet between Posa and Filippo, two psychologically mature men exchanging opinions with unusual frankness. Although we perceive a clear difference between the idealistic distinterestedness of the marquis and the emotional fossilization of the king, Verdi wants us to understand both points of view. This in turn distances us temporarily from the relatively immature and impulsive Carlo, who in the garden scene makes a foolish blunder, confusing Eboli with Elisabetta and sparking off a chain of events that will lead to Rodrigo's death and the definitive rupturing of the precarious triangular relationship between Filippo, his wife and son.

Björling's voice is in magnificent shape in this scene and the ingenuous quality of his timbre lends extra credibility to Carlo's failure to recognize Eboli, although the words he utters are sometimes less eloquent than the sounds he makes and the ardor he expresses in the opening *Allegro* is not as erotically charged ("Ebbro d'amor, ebbro di gioia il core") as Domingo's. Like most tenors here he does not fully respect the *sottovoce* indication when first addressing Eboli. This is difficult to bring off on stage without Carlo seeming excessively muted, but José Carreras, in his recording with Karajan, does sing softly, and the dynamic contrast naturally adds an extra degree of psychological credibility to the scene: Carlo fully releases his pent-up feelings only when he is sure that his love is reciprocated.

Fedora Barbieri is hardly the most aristocratic of Ebolis in her opening Veil Song and she later has difficulties with the high tessitura of "O don fatale," but she throws herself into this scene with notable abandon and provokes a lively response from the tenor. Björling is at his most expressive not when engrossed in the somewhat contrived psychological interplay but when he can take refuge in pure lyricism. He shapes "noi facemmo ambedue un sogno strano" with caressing tone and really makes us feel for Carlo when he floats the poignant line "Stolto fui! O destin spietato!" in the subsequent trio. In the *Allegro agitato* that follows ("Trema per te falso figliolo") Barbieri and Merrill tend to dominate. The final exchange between Rodrigo and Carlo begins promisingly but is truncated by an interruption in the recording thirty measures before the end of the scene.

In the second-act finale, the healthy glow of Björling's voice illuminates both vigorous declamation and the plaintively arching phrases of the great ensemble (where his melodic line significantly mirrors that of Elisabetta), making it difficult for us not to share Carlo's idealistic hopes, even when we recognize the foolhardiness of his public defiance of his father. The sudden hyperbolic leap to a top B in the phrase "sarò tuo salvator, popol fiammingo, io sol!" symbolizes the rashness of Carlo's gesture. Björling invests the note with considerable energy, although the sound itself is not entirely free from the petulance Cecil Smith noted "in climactic passages." The tenor also allows himself an overlong pause for breath before the upward leap, uncharacteristically sacrificing musical cogency to his own vocal comfort. He is however by no means the only tenor to seek a compromise solution here (Corelli too introduces a lengthy pause and Bergonzi injects a strong dose of head voice into the high note), and one can understand his anxiety in approaching this exposed B before such a large audience (forty-two years later Pavarotti would falter on that very note during a telecast of La Scala's opening night). The confrontation with the king—Siepi is superbly authoritative here—has in any case a lacerating effect on the listener, for Verdi forces us to share the point of view not only of Carlo but also of Filippo and Posa, who intercedes to ask the prince to hand over his sword. Carlo's response—"O ciel! Tu! . . . Rodrigo!"—is often barely audible in the opera house because few spinto tenors can really project a *pianissimo*, but Björling makes every word tell, allowing us us to empathize entirely with Carlo's dismay at his friend's apparent betrayal.

The prison scene is dominated by Rodrigo, but it is Björling who offers the most memorable singing, shaping the welcoming phrase "O Rodrigo, io ti son ben grato / Di venir di Carlo alla prigion" with disarming purity of tone and nobility of diction. Here the prince appears oppressed by the awareness of his own emotional vulnerability ("più valor non ho per i viventi"), yet we warm to the character here as in no earlier scene. Listening to Björling sing we can understand exactly why Carlo has won not only the devotion of Elisabetta, Eboli, and Rodrigo (who here sacrifices his life for his friend), but also of the Spanish people in general, who stage an uprising in his defence later in the scene.

The cut of "Per me giunto è il dì supremo" forces Carlo into an egregious *non sequitur,* "Che parli tu di morte?" for no mention of death has been made up to this point. Björling makes up for this in the final part of the scene, where he vividly communicates Carlo's shock and outrage after witnessing the murder of his closest friend. All pretence seems stripped away, and despite Max de Schauensee's observation that the tenor's instrument was too lyrical for the role, the recording demonstrates a formidable mastery of dramatic declamation.

Björling reserves some of his finest singing for the last act, and of all recorded tenors perhaps only Franz Völker (captured live in Vienna in 1937)[109] comes close to matching the unearthly beauty of his *mezza voce* in "Vago sogno m'arrise." In the rest of this monologue, however, the German tenor, though exceptionally intense in utterance, cannot equal the burnished tones of his Swedish colleague, whose magnificent crescendo is based more on the concentration of tone than on the projection of words. His singing is ideally responsive in the subsequent Marziale, combining timbral luster and rhythmic buoyancy, and he surpasses himself in the final section of the duet (*assai sostenuto*), "Ma lassù ci vedremo in un mondo migliore." Here the words of the translation sit comfortably on the notes and Björling has plenty of time to articulate each syllable clearly without disturbing the legato or deviating more than momentarily from an exquisitely sustained *mezzo piano.*

The serenity expressed by Carlo in this duet (his belief in an after-life in which he will be reunited with the woman he loves) makes it clear how much the character has developed since the opening scene in that same monastery. This symmetry contributes notably to the dramaturgical cogency of the four-act version of the opera, particularly if the performers help us believe in the supernatural events that take place in the opening and closing scenes (as well as during the auto-da-fé, where Lucine Amara sings sweetly as the Heavenly Voice). While it is hard to deny that there is something disconcertingly abrupt in the appearance of the ghost(?) of Charles V, who draws his grandson into the cloister at the end of the opera, Björling makes us understand, as well as any other interpreter of the role, Carlo's spiritual readiness for divine intervention.

The radio broadcast of the second performance at the Met on November 11, in much better sound than the telecast, enables us to appreciate the eloquent performance of the orchestra and the impressive vocal solidity of the male singers in particular. The differences between the two performances by Björling may seem negligible, but one does become aware of a greater degree of fluency and stability in his phrasing, even though a number of passages had been more imaginatively projected five days earlier. This is true, for example, of the beginning of Carlo's opening recitative in act 1, which is less urgently delivered, while there is greater repose in Björling's singing in the measures that follow and the nostalgia for Fontainebleau is expressed more persuasively, although the tenor does not attempt the prescribed *messa di voce.* In "Io la vidi" the vocal line and the accompaniment are more tightly meshed and the legato is if anything even more fluid (one notes as before the judicious employment of portamentos), but overall there is a slight loss of spontaneity and excitement and the voice sounds less incandescent at both ends of the range.

In the first part of the duet with Rodrigo, Björling alternates moments of relative inertia ("O terror!") with some lovingly shaped snatches of melody. The two singers' approach to "Dio che nell'alma infondere" remains substantially unchanged: this version is just slightly faster and a little less incisive. As on November 6, the second verse is attacked not by means of the once-traditional portamento, but by adding an acciaccatura that enables the two voices to kick up to the opening note, a well-established device used here to elegant effect. After the entrance of the king we can appreciate much better this time the combined splendor of the three male voices singing together above the chants of the chorus.

The long duet with Elisabetta finds Björling at his very best: the voice is magnificent in color, more responsive to verbal meanings, and impressive in its command of the ever-changing rhythmic patterns. Rigal remains a rather distant and awkward queen, but here seems less unworthy of her partner, whose singing is consistently "emotion-charged, dramatically alive."[110] Although the tenor is this time rather too generous in his outpouring of tone to capture the *voce morente* ideally needed for "Perduto ben, mio sol tesor," his blandishing timbre is hard to resist and Rigal's repeat of the phrase is relatively graceful. One misses here the ecstatic atmosphere he had created in the first performance for the phrases leading up to Carlo's swoon (he sings rather loudly and makes a few verbal slips). He also employs more volume than before when Carlo regains consciousness ("Qual voce a me dal ciel"), but the tone is so disarmingly pure that the words continue to ring in our ears long after hearing them. The precipitous close to the duet is memorable above all for Carlo's final phrase ("Ah! maledetto io son!"), culminating in a magnificent B-flat.

The prelude to act 2—based thematically on the opening six measures of Carlo's aria—benefits once again from the atmospheric playing of the Met woodwinds. This nocturnal atmosphere of uneasy suspense is well sustained by Björling in his reading of the letter (more confident than in the first performance) and impulsive opening statements. Once again he does not attempt to address *sottovoce* the woman he believes to be Elisabetta, but displays his skill by negotiating the fast moving and sharply accented "Sei tu, sei tu, bell'adorata" without breaking the legato. The expressive balance between words and rhythm is more complete this time, although occasional verbal errors emerge. As on the opening night his top voice is exceptionally responsive during the duet with Eboli: all the B-flats are effortlessly ringing and the prolonged one on the crest of the phrase "Rodrigo! qual mistero a me si rivelò?" is impressively reinforced. "Noi facemmo ambedue un sogno strano" is less softly sung than before but no less persuasive, with Björling's portamentos highlighting the slippery harmonies that betray Carlo's evasiveness.

The tenor's lyrical contribution to the first part of the trio once again gives enormous pleasure and the short scene for Carlo and Rodrigo that follows the exit of Eboli is completely concentrated in expression. Björling achieves a uniquely moving effect in the phrase "del mio cor sei la speranza": his timbre alone speaks of unambiguous trust and friendship, which is as much the subject of this opera as romantic love. Of all tenors on record it is indeed Björling—whose vocal personality seems foreign to cynicism or mistrust—who best succeeds in involving us in the spiritual bond that unites Carlo and Rodrigo.

In the auto-da-fé scene we can appreciate even better Stiedry's confident shaping of the the big central ensemble, where Björling's voice is not always perfectly audible but emerges beautifully in the passage where Carlo, Elisabetta, Rodrigo, and Tebaldo (Anne Bollinger) sing alone without the chorus. Carlo's public appeal to Filippo is very incisively phrased and the climactic B of "sarò tuo salvator" better integrated this time.

In the prison scene Björling duplicates his fine performance on the opening night, and while Carlo's brief confrontation with Filippo after Posa's death is less electrifying than before the final scene is once again mightily impressive, with Rigal's voice under better control even in the exacting Marziale. Björling confirms his increasing familiarity with the libretto, although when describing the tomb he will erect for Rodrigo in Flanders he fails to stress sufficiently the key word "re." He makes less use of his head voice in "Vago sogno m'arrise" and "Ma lassù ci vedremo in un mondo migliore," but his tone loses none of its purity and one marvels at the way he invests even the simplest of phrases—the repeated quarter notes on D-sharp and C-sharp in the middle register—with surpassing beauty. This quality derives not only from his ability to float the tones evenly on the breath but also from the contrasting vowel sounds, which banish any sense of monotony. In his voice—if not entirely in that of the soprano, whose vowels are too "covered" for her to move the listener—this duet emerges as one of the most spiritually intense pieces of music Verdi ever composed (more uplifting than anything in the Requiem). When Carlo sings the words "suonan per noi già l'ore" we feel that he is in that rare state of grace which enables people to see clearly into the future. Rigal cannot match this kind of eloquence, but the sweet radiance of her top B in the phrase "sospirato ben" demonstrates that she too can generate a sense of suspended time. As on the first night, her magnificent, full-voiced B at the end of the act helps bring the opera to a suitably impressive conclusion. Even though we may wonder what exactly is happening, we can sense that it is something of great import.

After six performances Björling entered the RCA studio at the Manhattan Center and recorded the first ten minutes of his new Verdi role (up to the coda of the duet) with Merrill as Rodrigo and Emil Markow doubling as the Frate and Filippo. That the tenor was able to immortalize part of his new role so soon after opening night was a sign of his hard-earned prestige as a singer and popularity with record-buyers.[111] Cellini, who was to conduct a revival of the Met *Don Carlo* with Björling in 1952, was on the podium and dispatched the music at a rather more rapid pace than Stiedry, influenced perhaps by the limited duration of the 78 discs on which the recording was first released. It is a credit to the tenor that he seldom sounds rushed: his performance of the recitative and aria is well-defined in every detail and, in spite of an occasionally clipped delivery, his mastery of words is now more complete. His upper register rings out resplendently and both his voice and Merrill's are better recorded in studio conditions, thus redoubling the listeners' pleasure during "Dio che nell'alma infondere." Bruce Burroughs wrote of this duet that "The superb, youthful, utterly unvexed voices of these two great singers meet every requirement of this stirring music without stint or strain or a single sound less than fully polished, rounded, and free."[112]

Cellini's hasty tempo mars somewhat the dialogue that precedes the *Allegro assai moderato*: when Carlo confesses to Rodrigo his love for Elisabetta the tenor is unable to make the sense of what he is saying really register. And although the aria is remarkable for tonal seductiveness, one misses Stiedry's willingness to let the music breathe, leaving space for a rhythmic flexibility that gives the impression Björling is truly experiencing what it feels like to be Carlo, rather than simply turning in an accomplished performance.

Cecil Smith's final comment on Björling's first performance as Don Carlo—"there is more to the role than that"—is not necessarily unjust: apart from the stiffness of the actor, the tenor's phrasing during that opening night suggests that he was just beginning to explore the possibilities of this multifaceted character. Yet the description of his performance simply as "competent, straight singing by a good tenor," surely understates the case. Björling's was possibly the most beautiful tenor voice ever heard in this part up to that moment in the work's performance history: without wishing to diminish the exceptional qualities of Tamagno, De Muro, Martinelli, Mazaroff, and Francesco Merli (who sang the role regularly between 1926 and 1947), none of these singers possessed such an exquisitely musical timbre. And although it is possible to create a plausible portrait of Carlo even with a less ingratiating voice (witness the intelligence of Mirto Picchi's phrasing in the first complete studio recording of the opera in 1951),[113] an excessive emphasis on the character's less attractive traits, his neuroses and obsessions, tends to throw the dramaturgy out of balance. If the character becomes little more than a clinical case (as if Verdi had sought inspiration in history rather than in Schiller), one is left wondering how the prince has succeeded in winning the love of three of the other four main figures in the drama.

Many recent tenors have proved more expert in the projection of the text than Björling in his first performances of the role, but none of them has possessed the deep-rooted innocence that was such a singular feature of the Swede's vocal personality. Even a tenor of acute psychological awareness such as Vickers lacked the purity of tone needed to convince us of Carlo's access to experiences that take him beyond physical reality. "Qual voce a me dal ciel" the prince sings while rousing from his swoon in act 1, unconsciously anticipating the intervention of the Heavenly Voice in the following act. Most commentators interpret this trance-like statement simply as a sign of Carlo's psychological weakness, a form of self-delusion, but nothing in the music invites us to distance ourselves from the character here. Although it has become a critical commonplace to describe both Carlo and Filippo as deeply flawed characters (as if there were no fundamental difference in the audience's attitude to them), there is no doubting with whom we side at the end of the opera. And of all tenors it is surely Björling who best prepares us for the mysterious, otherworldly conclusion.

Aida
Complete Recording

July 2–13, 1955: Rome, Teatro dell'Opera
Jussi Björling (Radamès), Zinka Milanov (Aida), Fedora Barbieri (Amneris), Leonard Warren (Amonasro), Boris Christoff (Ramfis), Plinio Clabassi (il Re); Rome Opera Chorus and Orchestra, cond. Jonel Perlea
RCA Victor GD86652; Naxos 8.111042-44

Extracts from acts 1–3
June 7, 1936: Vienna, Staatsoper
Jussi Björling (Radamès), Mária Németh (Aida), Kerstin Thorborg (Amneris), Alexander Svéd (Amonasro), Ludwig Hofmann (Ramfis); Vienna State Opera Chorus and Orchestra, cond. Victor de Sabata
Koch Schwann 3-1454-2

Act 1
March 29, 1940: Stockholm, Royal Opera
Jussi Björling (Radamès), Inez Köhler (Aida), Gertrud Pålson-Wettergren (Amneris), Folke Jonsson (Ramfis), Leon Björker (il Re), Inez Wassner (Sacerdotessa); Royal Swedish Opera Chorus and Royal Court Orchestra, cond. Kurt Bendix
Bluebell ABCD 103

"Celeste Aida"

December 1 and 3, 1936: Stockholm, Concert Hall
Unspecified orchestra, cond. Nils Grevillius
Naxos 8.110701

December 19, 1937: New York, Carnegie Hall
General Motors Symphony Orchestra, cond. Erno Rapee

January 13, 1951: New York, Manhattan Center
RCA Victor Orchestra, cond. Renato Cellini
Naxos 8.110788

March 12, 1951: New York, Carnegie Hall
Bell Telephone Orchestra, cond. Donald Voorhees
WHRA-6036

April 17, 1951: Stockholm, Royal Academy of Music
Swedish Radio Orchestra, cond. Sten Frykberg
Bluebell ABCD 103

September 27, 1953: Stockholm, Oscar Theater
Royal Court Orchestra, cond. Sune Engström
Bluebell ABCD 092

July 19, 1956: Stockholm, Gröna Lund
Harry Ebert, pf.
Bluebell ABCD 114

When Björling made his debut as Radamès in *Aida* on October 12, 1935, he was twenty-four years old, just like the character he was playing (the age is specified in production notes prepared by Ricordi for the Italian premiere in 1872). The notion of assigning this soldierly part to such a youthful lyric tenor might seem hazardous, but this assignment did no apparent damage to his voice. As the Italian periodical *La rassegna melodrammatica* commented after Enrico Caruso's debut in the role in 1900:

> where is it written that the part of Radamès can only be sung by a *tenore di forza?* Masini was never considered as such, and yet he was one of its most widely acclaimed exponents. And what effects he could produce with that beautiful, manly voice that he colored with such enchanting nuances! Such effects are within Caruso's means as well. He endows Radamès with sensitivity and vulnerability, along with the heroic aspects of the warrior.[114]

Angelo Masini was a lyric tenor who at the age of thirty (1875) sang Radamès successfully under Verdi's baton in Vienna, while the twenty-six-year-old Caruso—though darker in timbre than Björling—was still in an early phase of his vocal evolution when he first performed the role in St. Petersburg. Reviews of Björling's Stockholm debut in *Aida,* though not unconditional in their praise, acknowledge the singer's ability to combine effortless high notes with uncommon sensitivity of phrasing, particularly in the later acts.[115] The first recording of his Radamès, made at the Vienna Staatsoper eight months later and comprising extracts from the first three acts, confirms Björling's assurance in the role. It was the sixth of his thirty-one complete performances of *Aida* and is the earliest live documentation of his singing in any Verdi opera. He sings in Swedish, while the rest of the cast performs in German, and the use of his mother tongue seems to enhance his sensitivity to character and situation. His phrasing is arresting right from the opening of the recitative "Se quel guerrier io fossi," sung introspectively as if to draw the audience into the atmosphere of a soliloquy. It is rare to hear a Radamès use so much pure head resonance here, and the high placement also lends a particular brilliance to the heroic declamation that follows ("un esercito di prodi da me guidato"), which is announced with a brass fanfare. This is one of those places where the tenor needs to display what the Italians call *squillo,* clarion tones that match the martial glitter of the trumpets (an instrument that plays a key role in defining the character of Radamès). Björling commanded a ringing upper register throughout his career, but recordings suggest that his voice was never more brilliant in overtones than in the 1930s. This explains why he was able to bring off parts that comparably gifted lyric tenors such as Gigli and Pavarotti left to the latter half of their careers. Although the twenty-five-year-old Björling's voice is hardly overwhelming in volume, we never have the uneasy impression of a lyric singer simulating heroic accents he only half believes in: only the awkward low D of "e la vittoria" sounds underprojected. At the same time one is struck by the magical *piano* attack and legato caress of "E a te, mia dolce Aida": few tenors reveal such a vulnerable contrast here between the ambitions of the warrior and the emotional abandon of the lover (a vulnerability that will later prove fatal). No less impressive is the final phrase with its sturdy octave descent from the high A-flat: there is no overt portamento here but the two notes are well bound together, as is the whole recitative. Throughout the scene one senses the expressive tension of the orchestral playing under Victor de Sabata, and the tempo adopted for "Celeste Aida" ("Ljuva Aida") is daringly spacious (slower than Verdi's metronome marking), inspiring one of the tenor's most poetic performances on record.

Eight months earlier, after Björling's debut in the role, Moses Pergament had criticised the tenor for seeking brilliance at the cost of subtlety in this Romanza—"every ascending phrase represented a crescendo up to a *forte*, and that doesn't accord with the mood of the aria"[116]—and the criticism had clearly been heeded, for here, in spite of a certain amount of nervous tension (his vibrato is more prominent than usual), he approaches the opening phrases with the utmost gentleness. Few tenors attempt this, as singing these phrases *piano* (as marked) adds to the difficulty of negotiating the awkward upward intervals, graced here with portamentos. The whole aria can be seen indeed as an exercise in portamento, which Björling employs with ideal dexterity and taste, making us aware of the intermediate notes but never indulging in lazy upward slurs in the hope of hitting the right pitch. He is also one of the few singers to respect the full dynamic range Verdi prescribes in this aria, from ***pppp*** to *forte*. Like most of his colleagues, however, he does not attempt the biggest technical challenge of all, the *morendo* on the final top B-flat: here it is sung *forte*, although it is attacked cleanly and with purity of tone. Yet it is rare to hear a tenor observe, as Björling does here, the *sempre dolcissimo* marking in the minor key section of the first verse ("Il tuo bel cielo vorrei ridarti") or contrast the full-throated top B-flat of "ergerti un trono" in the second verse with a dreamy head voice on the top A that immediately follows it.

Hermann May, the Staatsoper's sound engineer, was only able to record a few minutes of music at a time and as a consequence there are four measures missing at the beginning of the second verse. Yet the interruption cannot destroy the magical mood that Björling and De Sabata create here: other tenors have proved more ardent and expansive in this aria, but arguably none have combined such a high degree of musical refinement with such radiant sounds.

The next extract from the Viennese performance is part of the second-act finale, beginning with the King's question "Dunque . . . tu sei?" Svéd's response as Amonasro is characteristically generous in tone but he fails to match the rhythmic subtleties of the orchestral accompaniment, and here as elsewhere in the opera Mária Németh, though technically secure, lacks psychological allure as Aida. Björling exploits his natural melancholy timbre to telling effect in Radamès's aside "Il dolor che in quel volto favella," but he is only intermittently audible in the rest of the great ensemble, which suffers from considerable distortion. De Sabata's conducting, however, is masterly in his exploitation of ever-changing tempos (including some striking allargandos) to create an inexorable buildup of tension. The same quality is evident in the Nile scene: the recorded extracts intermittently follow Radamès's progress from a bold entrance to his final defiant "Io resto a te." Apart from a slight overloading of the sound on those three climactic top As (probably attributable to the recording), Björling sounds magnificent throughout, his glittering timbre used with exemplary rhythmic precision. In spite of De Sabata's free use of rubato, the tenor is at one with the orchestra in every phase. His singing is full of ardor at Radamès's entrance ("Pur ti riveggo, mia dolce Aida"), where the voice expands thrillingly above the staff and every expressive marking (legato, staccato-legato) is scrupulously observed. His phrasing in "Nel fiero anelito" is beautifully set off by the trumpet accompaniment and manages to combine heroic accents with intimacy of expression (De Sabata's pace is appropriately unhurried here): this Radamès seems to be thinking only of Aida, not of the effect he is making on the audience. In the tricky *Allegro assai vivo* "Sì fuggiam da queste mura," Björling is one of the few tenors whose voices are sufficiently responsive to alternate *piano* and *forte* phrases at a rapid pace (Verdi indicates ***ppp*** for "al deserto insiem fuggiamo"). The duet develops all the more excitingly thanks to this dynamic variety and the performers exploit the full expressive potential of the *molto ritardando* in the final measures, where tenor and soprano sing the same notes an octave apart. The brief extracts from the rest of the act are no less involving and overall this Viennese *Aida* emerges as one of the tenor's finest achievements, unsurpassed in his studio recordings of the same music. One is hardly surprised to read in Björling's autobiography: "Maestro de Sabata was so fascinated by my singing that he wanted me to go immediately with him to Italy." He then adds: "I had engagements with the Stockholm Opera and couldn't accept his invitation."[117] He never worked again with this Italian musician, who had inspired him to give one of his most exciting performances of a Verdi role.

Six months after the Viennese *Aida* Björling recorded Radamès's Romanza in Italian for the first time. The voice sounds drier in the studio but this is a very fine performance, and the pronunciation is less fallible than in "Che gelida manina" and "La donna è mobile" recorded during the same sessions (here the most conspicuous error is his tendency to confuse "suol" [soil] with "sol" [sun]). In his survey of *Aida* recordings in *Opera on Record,* John Steane rightly describes this as the finest studio rendition of the aria "in the late 78 period":

> We can take joy in the legato, the ring, the youthfulness and maturity of that sound . . . in recent years the young Placido Domingo made a comparably striking impression with a richer, rounder tone and with considerable dignity in his enunciation. It is doubtful whether either of these tenors improved on his earlier recording."[118]

If we compare these two versions, we can understand why Domingo became more widely associated with this role than Björling, for although he was only twenty-seven in 1968, his sound is riper and more sensual in the middle register. The richness of sound is partly due to an artificially resonant recording[119] that dulls the projection of the words (it is significant that Steane refers to the "dignity" rather than the "vividness" of his enunciation). Yet this is undeniably the sort of sound that most people associate with Radamès: the twenty-five-year-old Swede sounds almost adolescent by comparison. Domingo is also in excellent vocal shape, although his limited dynamic range shows up some technical limitations. Unlike Björling he rarely drops below a *mezzo forte*, creating an impression of generic ardor rather than an emotional outpouring shaped by the development of individual thoughts. His singing is clean to the point of blandness, a style much favored in those years: he eschews even the traditional rising portamentos in the first verse (as do Tucker, in the Toscanini recording,[120] and Vickers with Solti[121]). Björling too sounds less emotionally focused in the studio than singers such as Bergonzi (particularly accomplished in his recorded overview of Verdi tenor arias)[122] or Pertile (eloquent in the complete 1928 recording with Sabajno),[123] but he employs all the traditional portamentos to stylish effect and offers an abundance of musical variety in his phrasing. The words are projected with more feeling than Domingo conveys, even though his pronunciation is less correct. His head voice is used less extensively than in Vienna, both in the recitative and aria, but his breath spans are more generous and he manages an exquisite *piano* transition between the two verses. It is a pity, however, that he didn't take advantage of the studio setting to attempt the final note as written: other Björling recordings made in those years reveal a rare facility in executing diminuendos in the upper register.

There is no *morendo* on the final note when Björling sings the scene in Italian once again at the Carnegie Hall in December 1937, nor will there be on any later recording. The recording is somewhat crackly, but the performance is more exciting than the HMV version. In some ways his phrasing here is reminiscent of Caruso's 1911 disc with orchestral accompaniment:[124] no real head voice is heard in the recitative (or aria) this time, but expressive contrasts are well established. For the first time on record he accompanies the downward leap from the prolonged A-flat of "vinto" with a portamento, adding a note on the lower pitch: this special feature of Caruso's only recording of this recitive is an entirely classical expressive device, illustrated in the second volume of García's treatise on singing,[125] although it is but sketchily realized by Björling on this occasion. The aria itself is beautifully sung, the suave shaping of the melody helped by the unhurried tempo. There are again a few verbal slips, one of which (the singular "serto" rendered as the plural "serti") is grammatically disconcerting, but every phrase, including the transition between the two verses, is elegantly managed and the virile stance of the singer never compromises the lyrical breadth of the music.

Toward the end of March 1940 the Swedish Broadcasting Corporation recorded Björling live in Stockholm in the first act of *Aida.* The performance, conducted by Kurt Bendix, who had accompanied Björling in his role-debut five years earlier, contains quite a lot of music not included in the extracts from the Vienna, including the opening scene between Ramfis and Radamès. The bass Folke Jonsson makes an imposing impression here, and Björling immediately draws a convincing sound portrait of Radamès as the ambitious young soldier, tensely eager to seize his opportunity for fame and glory. This time we can fully appreciate the contrast of tone he establishes when the high priest leaves the stage: as in Vienna, the soliloquy begins introspectively (the Swedish language seems to encourage his use of the head voice), but the declamation resounds all the more blazingly in the martial phrases that follow. If the caress of "E a te mia dolce Aida" is less persuasive than in Vienna (a slightly gutteral attack hints that the voice has not entirely warmed up), the ascent to a prolonged A-flat on "vinto" is Björling's most thrilling ever: the Swedish vowel (the *e* of "segrat") makes it easier for him to amplify the tone without forcing than the Italian *i* vowel. Once again he accompanies the downward leap with a portamento; this time the effect is more finished, suggesting an apt homage to the tenor (Caruso) who did most to establish the popularity of a Romanza, which was sometimes omitted in the late nineteenth century, even by singers as eminent as Jean de Reszke. The aria itself is sung with a fluency and richness of sound at the climaxes (the three B-flats are all attacked *fortissimo* and the last one is produced with excessive vehemence) that is reminiscent of Caruso, although the coloring of the voice suggests Nordic melancholy rather than Mediterranean warmth and the relatively fast tempo allows for less repose and dynamic nuance.

In the scene that follows Gertrud Pålson-Wettergren hardly suggests Amneris's arrogant wilfulness and erotic yearning, but the tenor's line is beautifully highlighted against hers, and Björling distinguishes appropriately between his responses to the princess and his aside to the audience. The scene becomes theatrically alive with the entrance of Inez Köhler's Aida. The soprano—who also partnered the tenor in *Tosca, Fidelio, Un ballo in maschera,* and *Trovatore*—is completely involved in the part right from the opening measures, her voice capable of mirroring a wide range of feeling. The trio that concludes the scene works very well both as music and drama, vividly conveying the sense of three characters possessed by sharply differing emotions.

Köhler's emotional alertness is equally evident in the scene that follows, where the two bass voices (Leon Björker's King and Jonsson's Ramfis) are well contrasted. Björling's Radamès greets the announcement that he will be "condottier supremo" in the war against the Ethiopians with typical inwardness of expression: a generous use of head voice in "Ah! Sien grazie ai Numi!" combined with a real savoring of every word.

The first-act finale, the "Gran scena della consacrazione," proves less spectacular than it can be (the voices being on a relatively small scale), but musical values are upheld throughout, with some particularly fine choral singing. Radamès's statements have an unusually prayerful quality to them—which doesn't diminish the ring of the four final high B-flats of "immenso Fthà"—and Inez Wassner's Sacerdotessa phrases with a plaintive tone that clings to the memory.

Björling sang (in translation) single performances of *Aida* in Stockholm every year until 1945, but then—apart from a gala staging of the fourth act for the King of Denmark in October 1947—dropped the role of Radamès from his repertoire for a whole decade (Toscanini would have liked to engage him for his 1949 broadcast of the opera, but the tenor was not free to take part). He did occasionally air the Romanza in recital, however, and in January 1951 he rerecorded "Celeste Aida" in the studio, this time with Cellini on the podium. In purely musical terms he does not surpass the results achieved a decade and a half earlier, but for many listeners the weightier *spinto* tone displayed right from the opening line of the recitative may sound better suited to a character of Radamès's military aspirations. Words are projected more confidently than in 1936, although a surprising number of verbal errors remain in the Romanza, where—not for the last time—the first syllable of the first word, "Celeste," is held too long, distracting the listener momentarily from the perfectly drawn line. Nor does he bind the tenth and eleventh measures of the aria ("del mio pensiero tu sei regina") into one unit, as he did in 1936, although he proves more generous in the second verse.

Just a couple of months after the RCA recording, Björling sang the aria (complete with recitative) on the *Bell Telephone Hour.* The voice is similar in color to that heard in the studio recording and Björling duplicates the overlong stress in the opening word, yet his phrasing is much more varied and alive. The opening of the recitative is uncommonly lyrical, while the phrases that follow contrast vividly in their heroic amplitude. In the aria everything remains in perfect expressive balance and the tenor is consistently sensitive to dynamic shadings and word meanings: listen to the caress with which he evokes "le dolci brezze del patrio suol" (getting this last word right this time).

There is not so much to enthuse about in another version of the aria broadcast from Sweden a month later: here Björling sounds less idiomatic, and although he makes greater use of head voice than in the other two recordings from that year, his tone in the aria is self-pitying rather than rapt. The second verse of "Celeste Aida" recorded in September 1953 comes from the soundtrack of the film *Resan till dej* (The journey to you), in which

Björling plays himself as a guest on a radio program. He was in a particularly expansive mood on this occasion and the performance culminates in a magnificently ringing, if slightly sharp, final note.

Björling sang the role of Radamès in Italian for the first time in the complete recording made at the Rome Opera in the summer of 1955. The cast was essentially the same as that of the successful 1952 *Il trovatore*, with the added attractions of one of the great twentieth century basses, Boris Christoff, in the role of Ramfis and a musician of considerable refinement, Jonel Perlea, on the podium. The Rumanian conductor's spacious reading was well-suited to Björling's lyrical approach to the role of Radamès, but if one compares his leadership with that of Serafin, who recorded *Aida* (with Barbieri as Amneris, as here) at La Scala just a month later,[126] one cannot help noticing the relative lack of theatrical tension. The excitement in the RCA *Aida* must be generated in large part by the singers themselves, and in this respect it is the mezzo-soprano—the only Italian in a leading role—who responds most vividly to verbal meanings and dramatic situations. Björling, by contrast, can sound somewhat neutral if not prompted by a galvanizing presence on the podium. This is evident right from the opening encounter with Christoff's Ramfis—although it is fascinating to hear these two very individual timbres in proximity—and in Radamès's recitative, which proves less warm and impulsive than the March 1951 radio broadcast and less striking in its expressive contrasts than the 1936 Vienna performance. Yet in many ways his singing and phrasing here are hard to fault: Björling conveys both the caress of the lover and the ambition of the warrior. Only the sustained top A-flat of "vinto"—followed by the customary downward portamento—shows signs of strain. His phrasing in the Romanza is very fine indeed: he takes full advantage of studio conditions, lengthening his breath spans—he conceives "del mio pensiero tu sei regina" in a single arc—and observing Verdi's dynamics more closely than in his other post-1936 recordings. His phrasing is cast in a caressing *mezzo piano* rather than an extrovert *mezzo forte*, and this delicacy of approach is beautifully set off by the evocative woodwind accompaniment. The final note is attacked *mezzo forte* and then tapered away slightly (it lasts about eight seconds). This slight concession toward a *morendo* effect is curiously more pronounced in the RCA recording based on the original master tapes than in the Naxos issue derived from the LPs. Overall this performance is as poetically inspired as any in a complete recording of the opera, a more lyrical alternative to similarly effective interpretations by Bergonzi, Corelli[127] (both of whom respect Verdi's dynamic marking in the final measure) and Pertile.

The scene that follows is slow to catch fire and reveals one of the main difficulties for tenors performing the role of Radamès on stage or on disc: the relative passivity of the character. This man of action, the inspiring military commander who leads the Egyptian army to victory, remains almost paralyzed in his private life and is easily manipulated by the two women who vie for his affections. His only dynamic gesture on stage during the course of the opera is when he prevents Amonasro from murdering Amneris in act 3, a gesture that is often blurred by the ineptitude of the staging and the rapid pace of the music. If this passivity is accentuated by lyrically understated phrasing, as it sometimes is here, then Radamès loses credibility as a hero and risks appearing simply insipid. It is not simply a matter of volume: Bergonzi, a highly effective Radamès who first sang the role at the Met in 1956, hardly commanded greater power than his Swedish colleague. Nor is it merely a question of timbre: Lauri Volpi, whose 1929–30 Victor recordings of act 3[128] have long been acclaimed, was no darker in timbre than Björling. What is lacking here in the Swedish tenor (who was singing Ghislanzoni's libretto in the original language for the first time) is rhetorical conviction in declamatory passages, a quality that develops only with thorough mastery of the text. This is particularly evident in Di Stefano's live recording of the role in a performance at La Scala in 1956:[129] phrase after phrase comes to life as if newly composed, and the Sicilian tenor's lyric voice responds surprisingly well to the expressive needs of the music.

What Di Stefano cannot guarantee at all times is the vocal aplomb that delights us in Björling's Radamès, even when the character appears emotionally withdrawn. In the "Gran scena della consacrazione" he doesn't cast the phrases in bronze, as Del Monaco was capable of doing, but he sings with manly dignity and a confident ring in the upper register. In the second-act finale this Radamès sounds somewhat half-hearted when asking for the Ethiopian prisoners to be released (an important gesture that underlines the moral superiority of the character), though he touchingly conveys his feelings for Aida when he observes her pleading for the release of the soldiers: in "ogni stilla del pianto adorato" his lyrical tones cut through the ensemble to memorable effect. Yet although Björling transposes some notes up an octave in this scene, the voice only dominates intermittently at climaxes, and Radamès's distress on hearing of the plan to marry him to Amneris registers much more mildly than Aida's.

By the end of the second act it is indeed the opera's protagonist who has become the central focus of the audience's attention, as she has had repeated opportunities to reveal her innermost feelings. We also share her point of view (rather than Radamès's) in the third act, during the crucial duet that represents the turning point in the drama. The complexity of the heroine's emotional dilemma here contrasts with the straightforward candor of the hero. In "Celeste Aida," the character's daydream of crowning Aida as queen in her own land (without realizing that she is in fact the king's daughter) gains our undivided attention. By contrast, our response to Radamès's second solo, the trumpet-like "Nel fiero anelito" that illustrates his plan to win Aida's hand openly by means of another victory over the Ethiopians, is conditioned by our awareness of how unrealistic that dream is. Yet Radamès should appear neither half-hearted nor foolish here; he should rather make us believe that love can make the impossible come true (it is Di Stefano who offers the most striking account of this solo). The more persuasive he sounds, the more wrenching the subsequent duet with Aida will prove.

Björling was proud of his recording of this scene. In the more lyrical passages, where Radamès expresses his dismay at Aida's proposal to escape together to her homeland, the tenor's *piano* singing—notably the floated B-flat of "Il ciel de' nostri amori"—has a radiance unmatched by any other singer on disc, although Bergonzi is equally attentive to Verdi's dynamic markings. When Radamès finally allows himself to be persuaded by Aida ("Ah no! fuggiamo"), his singing is no less generous than Milanov's, and unlike the soprano, he does not need to cheat in the soaring phrase of the *Allegro assai vivo* ("su noi gli astri brilleranno") by eliminating the words in the upper register. One misses however the sharp definition of consonants offered not only by Di Stefano but also by an earlier and less poetic Swedish tenor, Aroldo Lindi (stage name for Harald Lindau), in his complete recording with Giannina Arangi-Lombardi (1928).[130] A comparison between Björling's Vienna and Rome recordings of both "Nel fiero anelito" and the repeat of the same melody in "Vieni meco, insieme fuggiamo" confirms the greater emotional sweep of the performance conducted by De Sabata: in Vienna the young Björling seems capable of doing whatever he wants with his voice and colors words with genuine abandon; with Perlea he sounds relatively cautious.

In the judgement scene that follows we can sense the tenor responding in his own understated fashion to Barbieri's dynamic personality, and we note the poise of his singing even in the lowest register (the repeated E-flats of "svanita ogni speranza, sol bramo di morir"). Yet the desire for death expressed here comes across relatively weakly, owing once again to an insufficient vividness of articulation. Björling proves most memorable in this scene when defending Radamès's honor ("puro il mio pensiero") and imagining Aida's escape to her homeland.

The tomb scene, on the other hand, finds both Björling and Milanov—who had only sung this opera together once on stage, eighteen years earlier—at their most expressive. Here one is thankful for Perlea's deliberate, spacious accompaniment and for the opportunities offered by the recording studio to perfect every detail. No other singers have caught so well the serenity of two lovers whose readiness for death and anticipation of the "estasi d'un immortal amor" is articulated in phrasing of constant refinement and beauty, mirroring the shimmering harmonics of the violins. *Pianissimo* singing in the upper register was a Milanov speciality, but the tenor equals the soprano here in every phrase and surpasses her in the penultimate ascent to B-flat ("volano al raggio dell'eterno dì") where, unlike his partner, he adheres to Verdi's dynamic markings in introducing a blossoming crescendo after the *piano* attack. Equally remarkable, in "O terra addio," is the perfection of his legato sustained across the repeated wide intervals, immaculately sculpting one of Verdi's most inspired melodies. While he does not convey the pain of Pertile or Di Stefano in "Morir! sì pura e bella!" or attempt the *voce cupa* achieved by Vickers and Caruso[131] in "La fatal pietra," the purity of the repeated B-flats in the opening recitative lends Radamès's opening words an appropriate solemnity.

There could hardly be a greater contrast between the distilled refinement of the final scene in the Perlea recording and the frank spontaneity of Björling's rendition of "Celeste Aida" at an open air recital with Harry Ebert a year later. A piano accompaniment will show up any weaknesses in a tenor's technique in this difficult aria, but none emerge here. His singing is ardent, free (the top A-flat of "vinto" is more ringing than in Rome), yet admirable in repose. All in all it is an impressive final souvenir of a role he would sing just five more times in all: two performances were given in Stockholm in June 1957 and a Chicago staging in Italian followed in November 1958 with an all-star cast—Leonie Rysanek (Aida), Giulietta Simionato (Amneris), and Tito Gobbi (Amonasro)—under the leadership of Georges Sébastian.

Radamès is one of Verdi's hardest and most tiring tenor roles and the ambivalent nature of the character—the great war hero who gives up everything for the sake of a slave girl—reflects the expressive dualities of the work as a whole: a spectacular grand opera whose emotional core is singularly intimate. Both Aida and Radamès are expected to combine power and lyricism, brilliance of sound and subtlety of nuance to an almost impossible degree. Björling came close to finding an ideal balance in the part when inspired by De Sabata in 1936, while in the official recording made twenty years later he proves less persuasive. This complete Radamès is a nobler conception than Tucker's sturdy but sentimental portrayal, recorded with Serafin a month later, but it is not as involving a performance as those offered by Pertile, Bergonzi, or Corelli at their best and has to face respectable competition also from Del Monaco, Di Stefano, Vickers, Domingo, and Pavarotti. None of these, however, surpass the Swedish tenor's supreme musical refinement in the opening Romanza and final duet, and these two moments remain touchstones of excellence in the history of operatic recordings.

Messa da Requiem
Complete Recordings

August 16, 1939: Lucerne, Jesuitenkirche
Jussi Björling (tenor), Zinka Milanov (soprano), Kerstin Thorborg (mezzo-soprano), Nicola Moscona (bass); Lucerne Festival Chorus and Orchestra, cond. Arturo Toscanini

November 23, 1940: New York, Carnegie Hall
Jussi Björling (tenor), Zinka Milanov (soprano), Bruna Castagna (mezzo-soprano), Nicola Moscona (bass); Westminster Choir, NBC Symphony Orchestra, cond. Arturo Toscanini
Music & Arts 4240

June 12–19, 1960: Vienna, Sofiensaal
Jussi Björling (tenor), Leontyne Price (soprano), Rosalind Elias (mezzo-soprano), Giorgio Tozzi (bass); Singverein der Gesellschaft der Musikfreunde Wien, Vienna Philharmonic Orchestra, cond. Fritz Reiner
Decca 467119-2

"Ingemisco"

October 12, 1938: Concert Hall, Stockholm
Unspecified orchestra, cond. Nils Grevillius
EMI 5 66306 2

June 8, 1939: Hilversum, AVRO Studio
AVRO Hilversum Orchestra, cond. Frieder Weissmann
Bluebell ABCD 006

April 17, 1951: Stockholm, Royal Academy of Music
Swedish Radio Orchestra, cond. Sten Frykberg
Bluebell ABCD 103

June 9, 1954: Bergen, Concert Palace
Bergen Philharmonic Orchestra, cond. Carl Garaguly
Bluebell ABCD 006

March 2, 1958: New York, Carnegie Hall
Frederick Schauwecker, pf.
RCA 88697748922; Naxos 8.110788

In the first decade of his career as an adult singer Jussi Björling sang five large-scale nonoperatic works, all of them masterpieces based on religious texts. He appeared as a soloist in eight performances of Beethoven's *Missa Solemnis* and Handel's *Messiah*, four of Verdi's *Messa da Requiem*, two of Mozart's Requiem and one alone—his first high-profile engagement as a professional adult singer—of the rather shorter *Te Deum* by Bruckner.

Although a mere four live performances, concentrated in the years between 1937 and 1940, suggest that the work held a more marginal place in his repertoire than the great operas, Björling's lasting fondness for Verdi's

Requiem is demonstrated by his regular inclusion of the "Ingemisco" in his concert programs from the late thirties onward. His first studio recording of the "Ingemisco" was made in October 1938, eighteen months after his debut in the Requiem, under Fritz Busch at the Stockholm Concert Hall. The shellac disc contains Björling's finest interpretation of this solo, and has never been surpassed. The opening phrase is captivating, built on two *messe di voce* that are sustained in tones of breathtaking translucency and bound together with an impeccable legato, reinforced by featherweight portamentos. Grevillius rightly observes the leisurely tempo marking (*Adagio maestoso*), which remains unchanged from the preceding "Rex tremendae majestasis." The words of the "Ingemisco" express deep shame, yet nothing in the score suggests that they should be uttered with undue emphasis: we know that Verdi favored singers who could guarantee above all beauty of tone. He rejected Roberto Stagno for the part on the grounds that his voice was "extremely bad," concluding that "his good qualities" were therefore "useless for the *Mass*."[132] It is perhaps no coincidence that Pertile, another great tenor of intermittently ungrateful timbre, sang the work only twice at the beginning of his career (1913). And Björling's superiority in the Requiem to the 1964 performance of Nicolai Gedda (under Carlo Maria Giulini),[133] with its remarkably sensitive phrasing, is largely due to the extra dimension of tonal beauty that he commands in every measure of the tenor part.

With his limpid emission of tone, Björling allows the words to speak for themselves in the "Ingemisco," whilst making us feel that no deity could reject such a melting supplication. The transition to the second stanza (in E-flat major) is typically masterful: he highlights the attack on the E-flat of "Qui Mariam" by making a slight crescendo on the C that precedes it, drawing on a dynamic marking found in the string parts rather than the vocal line. Unlike most Italian tenors he does not approach the phrase with extrovert warmth but respects Verdi's indication of *dolce con calma*, reinforced by the *poco meno mosso* indication. This phrase also demonstrates the disarming purity of Björling's head voice in this early phase of his career. The *morendo* effect on the final E-flats of "absolvisti" and "exordisti" is achieved with extraordinary delicacy, employing an almost disembodied sound that emerges seamlessly from the notes that precede it. In "Mihi quoque spem dedisti" one appreciates the smoothness of his crescendo (during which he carefully avoids over-aspirating the "h" of "Mihi") and the clean contrast between the unforced and radiant top B-flat and the dying close that follows an octave below.

The third stanza, "Preces meæ non sunt dignæ," is more declamatory, with a lower tessitura. The well-balanced sonority of Björling's voice in the lower octave enables him to make the required crescendo on the low F of "cremer igne": he is one of the few lyric tenors capable of modulating the voice expressively in the baritonal range.

The fourth and final stanza, beginning "Inter oves locum præsta," has the longest and most varied musical setting (twenty-one measures in all) and finds Björling at his most inspired. He starts in the sweetest of head voices (Verdi indicates *dolce*) and builds up slowly to the double climax of "Statuens in parte dextra." Within this gradual crescendo, which covers fifteen measures of music leading to the first climax, he introduces a series of smaller crescendos and decrescendos. We are thus reminded that the *messa di voce* lies at the foundation of the Italian school of singing, not simply as a means of technical display but above all as an expressive resource.

Björling ignores Verdi's *morendo* indication on the first "dextra," however, sustaining the *gruppetto* that accompanies the return to the tonic (E-flat) in a bold *forte*. He may have been influenced here by Caruso's 1915 recording[134] (much more overtly emotional), where the *gruppetto* is delivered with equal frankness. Francesco Marconi, whose career began two years after the world premiere of the Requiem and who had won considerable acclaim performing it, does likewise in his 1903 disc[135] (the first ever of this music). This is in any case Björling's only significant departure from the score, and it in no way detracts from the soaring crescendo in the final phrase, where once again he rises to a gleaming B-flat.

Björling quickly realized how effective the "Ingemisco" was in showing off the qualities of his voice, and frequently included it in his concert programs. It was the opening number, for example, in the June 1939 broadcast from Hilversum. Here his tone has a darker quality, the pace is slightly quicker and dynamic contrasts are even more marked. There is greater drama in his phrasing but less spiritual repose; and his command of the head voice is once again magisterial. The influence of Caruso seems more perceptible here, but the Swedish tenor's breath spans are longer and he allows no hint of emotional overlay to disturb the perfection of the melodic line. He cannot match the organ-like fullness Caruso achieved in the stanza beginning "Preces meae," but his first live recording of this music offers again a rare combination of prayerful inwardness and rapt beauty. The words are less fervently delivered than by Gigli in the complete recording under Tullio Serafin made that same year,[136] or by Pavarotti in his quiveringly urgent 1967 version with Solti;[137] and those who expect in this solo a more extrovert, Italian style (Gigli in particular sings the Latin text as if it were his native tongue), may find greater satisfaction in these recordings (along with Caruso's) than in Björling's. Nevertheless, Verdi himself observed that "one mustn't sing this Mass in the way one sings an opera, and therefore phrasing and dynamics that may be fine in the theater won't satisfy me at all, not at all."[138]

A couple of weeks before the Dutch broadcast Björling had been heard by Toscanini in *Il trovatore* at Covent Garden. The two men were introduced by Tullio Voghera, who enjoyed a friendly relationship with the conductor (whose assistant he had been at the Metropolitan thirty years earlier), and who coached Björling regularly in the Italian repertoire until his sudden death in 1943. Voghera, born in Padua in 1879 but based in Sweden from the year of Björling's birth (1911),[139] had himself conducted a broadcast performance of the Verdi Requiem in Stockholm in 1934, with David Stockman in the tenor role. Having accompanied Caruso on many occasions, both in Italy and America, he provided a constructive link between the greatest tenor of the early twentieth century and the singer who was considered by many his most worthy successor.

Toscanini was so impressed with Björling's Manrico that he decided to engage him for two performances of the Requiem at the Lucerne Festival in August 1939. Although the festival was of very recent foundation it succeeded in attracting some of the greatest musicians of the twentieth century, including Sergei Rachmaninov, Vladimir Horowitz, Pablo Casals, Bronislaw Huberman, and the Busch Quartet. Taking place just two weeks before the outbreak of World War II, the Lucerne concerts were the conductor's last European appearances until 1946. The tension we perceive in the music-making is perhaps heightened by a sense of impending disaster, although the heavy distortion of the short-wave NBC broadcast makes critical evaluation of this Requiem (Toscanini's twenty-first, but only the second of them to be recorded) an arduous task.

The recording is also incomplete. Most of the opening "Requiem" and "Kyrie" is missing: all we hear is the final "Christe, Christe eleison" sung *pianissimo* by all four soloists and the chorus. Yet even these few measures convey something of the spiritual concentration of the performance, enhanced by the perfect blending of the soprano and tenor voices, with their gently placed head tones floating in the resonant acoustic of the baroque Jesuitenkirche. Björling and Milanov, his partner here, were to be linked in future decades through their complete studio recordings of four operas. Their association covered practically the entire span of Björling's international career: twenty-two years separated an *Aida* in Prague in March 1937 from a *Tosca* at the Met in December 1959. Nevertheless, they sang together in only fifteen performances of five different operas, plus five concerts (four of which were conducted by Toscanini). The Verdi Requiem is the only single work in which they can be heard together in two more or less complete performances, and the stunning beauty of sound they both command in this Lucerne recording is a source of wonder and delight. The soprano's voice has a silvery glow throughout the range and her ascents above the staff are effortless. While she is clearly a more impulsive singer than Björling, occasionally turning rhythmically wayward or shooting above the written note, the sound never loses its honeyed core and is consistently matched in purity by both the tenor and the mezzo-soprano. Kirsten Thorborg (an eminent Swedish singer who had already sung with Björling in *I cavalieri di Ekebù,*

Aida, Il trovatore, and *Un ballo in maschera*) does not bring much depth of expression to the opening phrase of "Quid sum miser tunc dicturus," where the tenor makes his second "appearance" in the Requiem, but her timbre is impressively limpid: she makes greater use of pure head resonance than do most Italian mezzos. The tenor is equally flexible in technique and his tone acquires here a touchingly plaintive quality, while blending easily with the other voices.

"Rex tremendae majestasis" shows Toscanini at his most inspired, in a reading of stark *terribilità* in which the contrast between the choral and solo parts could hardly be more intense. Here the bass Nicola Moscona has a prominent role and he fills it impressively, although his voice is less refined in timbre and technique than those of the other soloists. Björling is at his very best: every ascent above the staff is gleaming in tone and in the final "Salva, salva me," where his line duplicates the soprano's an octave above, he matches Milanov in vocal splendor.

The "Ingemisco," although slightly brisker than Björling's earlier performances, is nothing like as rapid as Toscanini's official 1951 recording,[140] where the conductor turns Verdi's *Adagio* into a flowing *Andante.* This approach suits the lively phrasing of Di Stefano who, although compelling on his own terms, never comes close to achieving the spiritual concentration Björling conveys here.

Björling told his wife that he saw Toscanini put down his baton at one point while he was rehearsing the Requiem in Lucerne. "What's the matter, maestro?" he asked. "Nothing," Toscanini replied. "Sing, Björling. Just sing! I'll follow you."[141] The tenor's head voice is once again iridescent in its beauty, and although the transition to "Qui Mariam" is less gentle than with Grevillius, the second stanza is phrased with vibrant *morbidezza.* In the final stanza the crescendo is more gradual than in the Hilversum concert, and although the climax of the solo falls victim to distortion, for the first time Björling respects the diminuendo on "dextra." Nevertheless, he does not equal the effect Giacinto Prandelli achieves in the 1950 live recording of the Requiem from La Scala,[142] Toscanini's other supremely moving account of this work.

In the "Lacrymosa" Björling's voice comes into his own in "Pie Jesu domine," where his soft attack on the high G of "Jesu Dona eis" is appropriately ethereal, although the tuning of the four voices in these ten unaccompanied measures is occasionally suspect. The opening of the "Offertorio" is disturbed by the American radio announcer speaking over the music, but "Domine Jesu Christe" demonstrates the fine musical understanding between the tenor and mezzo. Once again we feel the tension in the phrasing, in spite of the distortion. In "Quam obim Abramae promisisti" the long solo phrases sung by soprano and tenor—spanning an octave and a half—reveal the exemplary equalization of Björling's voice; he sustains the tone sturdily when the line dips below the staff, where Milanov's weakens notably.

In a note to his mistress Ada Mainardi sent on August 16, Toscanini wrote, "This evening during the Offertorio at the Hostias think of me and I will be all yours—inside your very soul."[143] Listening to Björling's inspired singing, one can entirely understand why the conductor chose that moment to commune with the woman he had loved secretly for many years. The refinement of the voice matches that of the instrumental accompaniment (the tremolo of the second violins and violas), and not even Gigli can approach Björling here in his combination of gently floated tone and seamless legato (though his voice is no less beautiful in texture and he makes a more honest attempt at the cadential trill). In the "Lux aeterna" Thorborg proves admirable in the opening statement and Björling blends his timbre with the others in masterly fashion. The two unaccompanied sections are occasionally affected by distortion, but the tenor line is immaculately drawn. In her biography Anna-Lisa Björling regretted that "none of Jussi's recordings were made in a church: the acoustics gave an almost unearthly beauty to his voice that elevated the simplest music to a higher plane."[144] When she wrote those words she was unaware of this broadcast from the Jesuitenkirche, which in spite of the poor recording captures the unique aura of the Björling sound in a reverberant acoustic.

A much-respected American biographer of Toscanini, Harvey Sachs, considers the live New York performance of the Requiem, broadcast in November 1940, the "most extraordinary"[145] of the maestro's recordings of Verdi's masterpiece. The highly experienced English critic Alan Blyth, on the other hand, wrote that "Björling apart, this is the most dispensable of the Toscanini sets."[146] The truth perhaps lies somewhere in between. The American broadcast is undoubtedly much easier to listen to than the Lucerne performance, with most details more clearly in focus (the recording is vastly superior in quality), but cannot match it in terms of spiritual inwardness or awe-inspiring drama. The occasion, a charity concert inaugurating the 1940–41 season of the NBC Symphony Orchestra, was less emotionally charged for the conductor, but although the American orchestra and chorus sound relatively detached in comparison with the Lucerne Festival musicians, the solo singing is once again on an exalted level. The tenor's entrance in the "Kyrie eleison"—which Toscanini prepares with a highly theatrical crescendo on "luceat eis"—would seem to justify Sachs's enthusiasm. The soaring ease with which Björling negotiates the electrifying ascending phrase, which rises by a seventh to the leading tone, but then falls back rather than resolving on the tonic, could hardly be surpassed. The other three soloists also make strong entrances, with Castagna immediately standing out for the typically Italian incisiveness of her word projection. Nearly all this opening movement is missing from the Lucerne performance, but when direct comparison becomes possible, in the hushed final measures, the atmosphere in New York seems more earthbound.

The tenor is next heard in "Quid sum miser," where Castagna proves more overtly expressive than Thorborg and Björling's phrasing is so disarmingly pure that his contributions are in no way overshadowed by the mezzo's. In the "Rex tremendae," on the other hand, Toscanini's leadership is much less awe-inspiring than in Lucerne. This undeniably affects the response of the soloists, although the tenor sounds notably ardent in his opening "Salva me, fons pietatis." The "Ingemisco" also disappoints if heard after the Lucerne performance. The tempo Toscanini set is for faster than any of Björling's other recordings of this music (though not nearly as fast as in the conductor's official RCA version). "Qui Mariam" is less sensitively phrased and the first ascent to B-flat less ringing. Overall the tenor's phrasing retains its poise and finish—he once again respects the diminuendo on "dextra"—but his voice is not at its freshest.

In the "Lacrymosa" Björling is less in evidence—the solo tenor often the doubles the line of the bass (solidly drawn by Moscona) or that of the tenors in the chorus—and when he finally has a chance to shine, in the unaccompanied measures of "Pie Jesu Domine," the voice sounds attractive but hardly as limpid as in Lucerne. The same is true of the "Offertorio," where Toscanini again seems less emotionally involved. The tenor and mezzo voices blend beautifully, however, and Milanov sounds as radiant as ever above the staff. Björling's attack in the "Hostias" is immaculate, but one notices a slight catch on the D of "Domine." In the final measures of the solo the voice expands less freely than before and his attempt at a trill remains feeble. The tenor's singing in "Lux aeterna" is ideally poised, and although his *mezza voce* is less liquid than on other occasions, the unaccompanied passages for the three soloists are ideally cohesive.

Twenty years separated Björling's last Requiem with Toscanini from his final recording of Verdi's score. Over those years he continued to sing the "Ingemisco" in concert and recital. The Stockholm radio performance recorded in 1951 is fresh and spontaneous, the sound brighter than in Hilversum and free from the veiled quality occasionally heard in New York. The voice is now a more robust instrument and *piano* dynamics are emphasized less than before. In the absence of Toscanini Björling once again ignores the *morendo* on the first "dextra," but a highlight of this recording is the brilliant first ascent to the top B-flat. The same note unfurls impressively at the end of the solo, although the tenor breaks the ascending phrase with two breaths (rather than one), after "sequestra" and "statuens."

In Bergen in 1954 we can almost sense the voice resounding within the warm acoustic of the Concert Palace. Björling's dynamics are similar to those heard in 1951 (no real head voice here), but there is a trace of constriction on the Gs above the staff and overall this proves to be his least finished recording of the solo. The final note (a B-flat) of "dedisti" in the second stanza is inexplicably omitted, and in "non sunt digne" the tenor replaces a

C with a D-flat, imitating (owing no doubt to a lapse in memory) the almost exact repetition of the phrase on the words "fac benigne." The first "dextra" is marked by a slight diminuendo, but the tone is then quickly reinforced and the final phrase is broken up even more conspicuously than in 1951.

We only have one recording of Björling singing the "Ingemisco" with piano accompaniment: it is daringly presented as the opening number in his 1958 Carnegie Hall recital, with Frederick Schauwecker at the keyboard (he plays the conclusion of the preceding 'Ricordare' to give the tenor his first note). Björling is in conspicuously better voice here: the opening phrase has more repose to it, the top Gs are freely produced, and the final phrases are not only stirringly sonorous but also perfectly bound together.

The Verdi Requiem committed to disc in June 1960 was Björling's last published studio recording, and in a very real sense he was singing a requiem for himself (the recording was released after his death). He certainly surpasses himself, vocally and spiritually, in this performance immortalized in the Vienna Sofiensaal (the only time he sang there), as if conscious of the fact that he was the setting the final seal on a recording career of exceptional duration and distinction. The voice is very well reproduced and sounds splendid in the resonant acoustic of the hall, even though—as in other Decca recordings made in that period—the soloists are sometimes overpowered by the orchestra and chorus.

Björling seems to have got on well with Reiner: they had already collaborated on two of the *Ford Sunday Evening Hours*, broadcast in 1939 and 1946. The conductor had long wanted to make a recording of the Requiem, and in spite of the last minute defections of Leonie Rysanek and Giulietta Simionato he could boast a strong cast, coached carefully in his hotel suite before recording began. Although this edition has seldom won unconditional acclaim, there is no denying the excellent rapport Reiner establishes with the principal singers. His approach is strikingly different to Toscanini's, particularly in the choice of tempos. And while his expansive pace does occasionally sound lethargic, it inspires Björling to phrase with a long-breathed lyricism that works magic in the more introspective episodes (where Reiner himself is at his best).

In the opening "Kyrie eleison" his voice blooms in the airy acoustic, as do those of the other soloists. Leontyne Price, with whom the tenor had sung *Il trovatore* in San Francisco in September 1958, approaches the luxuriant ease of the young Milanov in the upper register, and both Rosalind Elias and Giorgio Tozzi—though less remarkable in purely vocal terms—perform with singular nobility of phrasing and diction. In the G minor *Adagio* "Quid sum miser" Björling sings with a freshness and beauty and command of the *mezza voce* that seem to defy the passing years, while in the "Rex tremendae" the stereo recording allows for an impressive dynamic range, although Reiner never approaches the fervor and expressive tension Toscanini achieved in Lucerne. In the a cappella section of the "Lacrymosa" the tenor's *piano* singing floats as beautifully as ever. The "Ingemisco" is the slowest Björling ever recorded, at 4:13—a full forty seconds longer than the second Toscanini performance (1940). This is indeed his most lyrical performance of the solo since the disc made with Grevillius: he lingers raptly over "reus" in the opening line and once again—as in 1938—makes a slight crescendo on the final C of "Deus." "Qui Mariam" is lovingly phrased, although the *morendo* effect is less breathtaking than in his first two recordings. Studio conditions make it possible for Björling to emphasize again the crescendo on the low F of "igne." The first "dextra" is sung in a generous *forte* and the final phrase is impressively dispatched. Throughout the solo the strings and woodwinds of the Vienna Philharmonic set off Björling's timbre to captivating effect. Fellow tenor Nigel Douglas was present in the Singverein that day and remembers that

> Reiner said he would like to take the passage through, just for the orchestra. While he did so, Björling sang along, marking the whole piece in rehearsal voice, which in his case meant a sustained *mezza voce* of such beauty and technical perfection that it seemed almost a crime to let it disappear into the morning air. Then came the take, for which he simply did the same thing again, but opening his mouth a bit wider and bringing in his effortless chest voice.[147]

Reiner's spacious long-breathed approach pays considerable dividends in the "Offertorio" too: in the attack of "Quam olim Abramae" the conductor gets the singers to observe the *piano* marking, which Toscanini had ignored. The relatively light accompaniment allows us to appreciate here the full beauty of Björling's timbre, and Price's *messa di voce* on her entrance is even more finished than Milanov's. The "Hostias" is much more glowing than in New York, and Björling compensates for the lack of a trill by introducing a mordent in its place (he comes closer to articulating a shake on the repeat).

The tenor makes his final appearance in the ethereal "Lux aeterna," where Reiner is at his best, maintaining a degree of intensity that even Toscanini could not surpass, and Elias and Tozzi respond with the right sort of spiritual inwardness. Björling has never sounded so moving in this music and the a cappella passages are immaculately intoned.

The Verdi Requiem is one of the least consoling of sacred works, the supplicating solo voices seeming threatened to the very end by the wrath of God, yet the surpassing loveliness of the Björling sound evokes an inner stillness and serenity that transcend the unquiet mood of much of the music.

Otello
"O mostruosa colpa . . . Sì, pel ciel marmoreo giuro"

January 3, 1951: New York, Manhattan Center
Jussi Björling (Otello), Robert Merrill (Jago); RCA Victor Orchestra, cond. Renato Cellini
RCA 88697748922; Naxos 8.110788 (first take); OASI 7006 (second take)

In his autobiography, Björling expressed his desire to sing Verdi's *Otello* one day, while making it clear that he wished to preserve his "lyric tone as long as possible" and had no intention of "hurting" his voice by taking on such a dramatic role "too soon."[148] His timbre still possessed a surprisingly youthful bloom when, fifteen years later, death robbed him of any chance to perform the most heroically muscular and starkly tragic of Verdi's tenor roles. Caruso, too, had died in his late forties, before getting round to singing Otello on stage. In January 1914 (seven years before his death) the forty-year-old Neapolitan tenor had, however, entered the Victor studios in New Jersey to record an overwhelming performance of the duet with Jago that brings act 2 to a close.[149] It was this recording above all—in which Caruso sings alongside the most phenomenally endowed of his baritone partners, Titta Ruffo—that nurtured Björling's interest in the role of Otello. He himself sang this duet in concert in Sweden in the early 1930s and recorded it for RCA Victor in New York in 1951, just a few weeks before his fortieth birthday. Merrill, who sung Jago in that recording, recalls their listening several times to the old Victor disc before heading for the Manhattan Center: "I want to sound like Caruso. I want it to sound like a Caruso and Titta Ruffo record," said Björling.[150]

"Wanting to sound like Caruso" was an aspiration shared by many twentieth-century tenors, sometimes with mixed results. Björling never heard Caruso live: he and his brothers Olle and Gösta had rejected their father's pressing offer to take them to a performance at the Met in 1919, when the family was touring the States as a vocal quartet (they chose to see a movie instead). But David Björling had heard Caruso live when studying in New York at the beginning of the century, and Jussi's intensive coaching with Tullio Voghera, who had been the Neapolitan's accompanist three decades earlier, established a very real link between the two singers.

The most potent influence, however, came through the gramophone. Caruso's recordings had a profound effect on the evolution of singing, and it is easy to understand their appeal to the young Björling. The Swedish tenor's natural sound, however, remained that of a lyric tenor throughout his career: the darker, Caruso-like timbre with which he occasionally experimented was used primarily as a coloristic device in phrases of exceptional dramatic import, rather than being adopted for the entire duration of a performance. This was probably just as well, for the muscular, covered tone that represented Björling's version of the Caruso sound sometimes led the voice to slip back into the throat (particularly on the register break) and to sharpen on climactic high notes. This sound was a constant temptation for Björling, but one he was right to resist most of the time. The history of singing in the twentieth century shows how many tenors were led astray by the desire to match the soulful density, virility, and emotional truthfulness of Caruso's phrasing. It is no coincidence that three of the most famous interpreters of the role of Otello—Martinelli, Del Monaco, and Domingo—all reduced their expressive ranges in their attempts to reproduce in part the effect of that unique instrument. The two Italian tenors, in spite of their sharply differing vocal personalities, both achieved a Caruso-like expansiveness of phrasing at the cost of a certain rigidity of emission (their diction is clearly articulated but the words do not float freely on the breath). Domingo, by comparison, exploited to profitable effect the rich sensual coloring of his lower-middle range, but only occasionally succeeded (as Caruso did) in carrying that full-bodied sound into the upper register, where his voice was neither truly ringing nor easily modulated.

Björling, on the other hand, in this, his most explicit imitation of Caruso, manages to maintain an admirable fluidity of phrasing (although the words are generally less alive than when he sings lyrically) while displaying a dense, burnished sound in both the middle and upper registers. Regina Resnik recalled how his voice acquired an extra dimension of resonance as it moved seamlessly into the upper register, an effect that she had otherwise heard only in Caruso's recordings,[151] and which may have had something to do with similarities in the bone structure of the two tenors (P. Mario Marafioti's observations on the relationship between bone structure and resonance, quoted in chapter 9, are relevant here).

For much of the twentieth century it seemed natural for a tenor—even one with a spontaneously brilliant timbre, such as Martinelli—to darken his tone markedly when singing the role of Otello. A number of famous Otellos, including Zenatello, Renato Zanelli, and Domingo, started out as baritones, while the most vocally exciting interpreter of the role in recent decades, Giacomini, sounded even more baritonal than Caruso. Yet attitudes were different in the early 1900s, when opera-lovers still had vivid recollections of the bright and vibrant timbre of the role's creator Tamagno, whose performances had overwhelmed audiences in Milan, New York, London, and Paris. Tamagno possessed what was probably the most powerful tenor voice of his era, and the exceptional completeness of his portrayal probably explains Caruso's continual postponement of his own stage debut in the opera—but there was nothing baritonal about his sound. In his 1903 recording of "Sì, pel ciel"[152] (where he sings alongside an elderly baritone, possibly his brother), he transposes the repeated descents to C below the staff (on the word "sterminator") up by a third, while conserving a brazen ease in the upper register. These transpositions, together with the uncertainties of his partner, may explain why the recording was never published, yet the tenor's repeated takes of "Esultate!" "Ora e per sempre addio," and the death scene made during the same sessions leave no doubts as to the exceptional eloquence of his Otello. In more recent decades Pavarotti reminded us of how expressive a relatively open and vibrant sound, combined with outstandingly crisp diction, can prove in this music.

In some ways the differing conceptions of what may be the right timbre for Otello reflect the continuing debate about the color of his skin. Verdi and Boito seem to have imagined the character as a black African, and it is tempting to consider the dark timbre adopted by the majority of twentieth century tenors as a result of the increasing insistence on dramatic realism imposed subsequently by the *verismo* aesthetic. Nevertheless, the expressive potential of baritonal tenors had already been exploited in the early nineteenth century: the contrast between dark and light timbres in the same range is equally a feature of Rossini's *Otello,* composed in 1816, where the roles of Otello, Rodrigo and Jago are all assigned to tenors. Manuel García's treatise on singing (1840–47) also makes it clear what a wide range of coloristic effects was expected of singers in the Romantic era. Nor should one forget how persuasively, in the mid-twentieth century, Maria Callas demonstrated that it was possible to identify a distinct vocal color for each character portrayed without seeking any extra-musical inspiration.

Caruso's recorded Otello, like Callas's Gilda or Lady Macbeth, owes its distinctive coloration and expressive cogency to the purely musical instincts of a great singer. The scene he recorded with Ruffo begins with the final measures of Jago's "Sogno," performed by the orchestra alone, where the horns and strings end on a low-lying C minor chord. The repeated Cs of Otello's unaccompanied opening line, "O mostruosa colpa," lead Caruso to echo the dark coloring of the preceding chord (the repetition of the *o* vowel encourages a covered sound here), appropriately setting the mood for the whole scene.

Björling declaims the words in a similarly ominous manner, and the success of his performance derives not simply from his gift for imitation but also from his instinctive understanding of the musical logic of Caruso's interpretative choices. The Swedish tenor's sensitivity to verbal nuance was, however, more limited when singing in Italian and his clipped delivery of Otello's second line ("Un sogno che rivela un fatto") suggests that his performance is based more closely on his aural memory of the 1914 Victor recording than on an attentive reading of the score. Here, following Caruso's example, he reduces the duration of the dotted eighth note on the stressed second syllable of "rivela." While the spontaneity of the Neapolitan's delivery helps him get away with this liberty, with Björling the main result is to make the meaning of the word less clear. The tense concentration of his tone, which remains almost vibrato-free throughout the scene, is nonetheless immediately arresting and contrasts effectively with the more relaxed and vibrant emission of Merrill. As with Caruso and Ruffo, the two voices are distinguishable more in terms of texture than of color, and although Merrill is less precise in his verbal inflexions than the great Tuscan baritone (and less generous in his use of portamento), his delivery has a bluff directness that fits Verdi's conception of Jago rather well (much better than the artificially "evil" timbre he would employ in a televised rendition of this duet with James McCracken in 1964).[153]

While Otello's first two phrases in the dialogue are largely limited to a single note, suggesting the increasingly obsessive focus of the character's mind, the third phrase, "È il fazzoletto ch'io le diedi, pegno primo d'amor," modulates across an interval of a fourth and allows us a brief backward glimpse of the noble, loving Otello of the opening scenes. Although Björling does not allow his tone to soften here, the beauty of his sound and the purity of his vowels make it clear (even within this brief scene) that Otello cannot be considered an entirely evil character. The long recitative that follows, leading up to the attack of the *Molto sostenuto* "Sì, pel ciel," reveals a man who has quite lost his bearings and is totally possessed by a destructive desire for revenge. No other passage in Björling's repertoire exposes negative feelings so devastatingly, and the tenor enters the spirit of the music with unfailing honesty, strongly supported by Cellini. In "Tutto il mio vano amor esalo al cielo," where Otello banishes definitively any remnant of love for Desdemona, Björling fails to bring the words as vividly to life as Lauri Volpi, in his 1941 recording with Mario Basiola.[154] This is due to the Italian tenor's adoption of a less compressed tone, which allows each syllable to float freely on the breath. The Swede almost equals him, however, in the vehemence and perfect timing of the repeated cries of "Sangue!" where the dense focus of his sound highlights the audacity of the harmonic progressions; and throughout the recitative and cabaletta he binds the phrases together with a legato (and an exactness of intonation) that the Italian is unable to match.

In the magniloquent repetition of "Sì, pel ciel marmoreo giuro," where Otello and Jago formally swear to take revenge, singing first alone and then together, the tempo of Björling's opening statement is less stately than those adopted by Tamagno or Lauri Volpi, who articulate each word with exemplary incisiveness, but he compensates by creating an irresistible sense of forward momentum: we can feel Otello being drawn into a spiral of violence and hatred that can end only in tragedy. Once again the tenor's voice—now extended over a range stretching from top B-flat to C below the staff—loses none of its wrenching beauty. It is precisely this innate nobility of tone that preserves Otello from appearing utterly degraded here, even though this joint oath is nothing less than a ghastly parody of his former heroism. If one excepts the final F-sharp (on the register break) of "folgori," where the sound slips backward, the opening statement of this cabaletta is the most impressive piece of solo heroic singing Björling ever committed to disc. When Merrill joins him in the repeat of the melody (the voices start an octave apart but end up increasingly in unison, with the two timbres blending excitingly), the proximity of the baritone, whose voice was by nature more voluminous than the tenor's, inspires the latter to maintain his prominence through an ever-increasing concentration of tone, lending a searing splendor to the repeated ascents above the staff. At the close of the duet Björling does not follow the example of Tamagno in inserting an appoggiatura on "stendo" (an interesting remnant of nineteenth-century performance practice), but he projects the final phrase ("Dio! vendicator!") superbly, with a generous portamento up to the final top A. There is a second take of this recording, where the final F-sharp of "folgori" has more forward placement and the interaction between the tenor and baritone seems slightly more spontaneous, but otherwise the performance is practically identical.

According to Anna-Lisa Björling, "what mattered most to Jussi," after recording this extract from *Otello*, was "that the duet had shown that the role, in time, would not be beyond his scope."[155] There is no doubt that the demonstration was a highly successful one, for the recording is one of the three or four finest performances of this music on disc, surpassing the efforts of such experienced Otellos as Martinelli and Ramón Vinay. It is a success not only in purely vocal terms but also from a dramatic or even psychological point of view: in this brief extract he proves capable of making us understand what it feels like to be possessed by the demon of (self-)destruction.

However impressive Björling's voice may sound here, it cannot match—in terms of sheer volume—that of the greatest Otello of the 1950s, Mario Del Monaco (whose overwhelming effect on the audience in this scene is attested to by his Met broadcast with Warren in 1958).[156] Yet there is a degree of unbridled violence in Del Monaco's reading that undermines the nobility of the tragic hero: we are made to feel that the character is showing here his real face for the first time. Björling's conception, like Caruso's, is more authentically Shakespearian: he never lets us forget the character's potential for greatness.

WAGNER

Lohengrin
"In fernem Land"

October 3, 1952: Stockholm, Concert Hall
Swedish Radio Orchestra, cond. Sten Frykberg
Naxos 8.111083

December 20, 1954: Stockholm, Södersjukjuset
Harry Ebert, pf.
WHRA-6036

January 8, 1955: Helsinki, B-Messuhalli
Harry Ebert, pf.

August 5, 1960: Gothenburg, Concert Hall
Gothenburg Symphony Orchestra, cond. Nils Grevillius
WHRA-6036

On a number of occasions, particularly in the final decade of his career, Björling expressed the desire to sing, at least on record, the title role in *Lohengrin.* Of all the projects that never came to fruition, this—together with the concert performance of Bellini's *Il pirata* he was asked to sing in 1959 (at the Carnegie Hall with Maria Callas)—was surely the one that would have proved most revelatory. As his regular accompanist Harry Ebert pointed out, Björling was "the eternally pure one."[1] No tenor voice on record is as well-equipped to convey the spiritual otherness of the *Gralserzählung* (narrative of the Grail) in which Lohengrin describes, with sublime gentleness and authority, the mystical domain of Montsalvat whence he came forth to rescue Elsa.

Of his four recordings of this solo, it is the first and last that really count, for with piano accompaniment the build-up of tension that accompanies the narration—characterized by a progressive increase in volume and density and by a gradual speeding up of the initially slow tempo (*Langsam*)—inevitably proves more limited in its expressive impact. While the 1955 Helsinki performance impressively demonstrates what a brilliant effect Björling could make in a number of phrases even with this skimpy accompaniment (this was not the only occasion on which he chose this solo to open a recital), the 1954 Stockholm recording shows the voice in relatively dull condition, prone even to a slight throatiness in certain attacks.

Two years earlier, on the other hand, the tenor was recorded in a performance as unique in its virtues as any on disc, for the surpassing beauty of his tone—in the lambent opening as in the clarion climaxes above the staff (where the whole body of the singer seems to be projecting the sound)—and for the spiritual elevation of his diction, set off by the refined string playing of the Swedish Radio Orchestra. As in later recordings, he sings the piece in translation ("I fjärran land"), but the Swedish words fit the line well and the singer's attention to note values (often a problem with Wagnerian tenors) is exemplary. When the trombones and bass tubas join the accompaniment one notes the additional weight of the voice, which is then sustained right through to the end in a mesmerizing combination of incisive diction and implicit legato (although portamentos are kept at a minimum, being used almost only where specific slur-markings are to be found in the score).

No other recorded performance offers similar qualities in such ideal balance. The Hungarian tenor Sándor Kónya (recorded live in Bayreuth in 1958)[2] was the finest Lohengrin of that era, and his dreamily lyrical start to the narrative, as silvery in its way as Björling's, is attractive indeed; but he lacks tonal density when the volume increases, and his ascents above the staff are relatively strident and constricted. The finest Bayreuth Lohengrin of the interwar years, Franz Völker, offers stronger competition in his 1927 recording,[3] but his forthright yet sensitive phrasing (much freer than Kónya's above the staff) remains that of a noble knight, without any of the transcending radiance that Björling exudes. The other great Lohengrin of those years, Lauritz Melchior, heard in his classic 1939 recording,[4] did have something superhuman about him: a sensation of immense power in reserve, reinforced by a reassuring springiness of tone sustained on a firm cushion of air. The virile timbre, while possessing none of the ethereal beauty Björling conveys, commands an enormous authority, as does the declamatory style. Melchior separates his words more distinctly than do the other three tenors, a testament to his training in 1920s Bayreuth under the supervision of Cosima Wagner, who famously favored verbal emphasis over legato during her long reign over the Festspielhaus. The opposite approach, closer perhaps to the *bel canto* style favored by Richard Wagner himself,[5] can be heard in Aureliano Pertile's finest recording,[6] in Italian, which makes generous use of portamentos and builds the phrasing around a series of *messe di voce* (not unjustified if one considers the hairpin dynamics in the orchestral accompaniment). His timbre, however, is relatively earthbound and his phrasing, though compelling in its fervor, lacks the sort of finish we associate with the nineteenth-century school of Italian singing.

From this point of view Björling himself represents a purer stylistic model, particularly in his second recording with orchestra. In Gothenburg the narration is gentler in contour (there are a number of extra portamentos), and slightly darker and less brilliant in color, as if filtered through a veil of melancholy. This suits the dramatic context rather well, as Lohengrin reveals his origins only at the end of the opera, after Elsa has broken her vow and relinquished her right to him as a husband. The narrative of self-presentation thus becomes implicitly a song of imminent farewell. It is doubly appropriate therefore that Björling should have chosen "In fernem Land"—a swansong indeed—as the final number in his last-ever concert with orchestra, just over a month before he died.

BJÖRLING'S REMAINING RECORDINGS

A Survey of the Best (1920–60)

Traditional: "Sommarglädje"
February 1920: New York, Columbia Studio
Jussi, Olle, and Gösta Björling; unattributed violin and piano accompaniment
Bluebell ABCD 0166

Wennerberg: "Psalm IV"
February 1920: New York, Columbia Studio
Jussi, Olle, and Gösta Björling; unattributed organ accompaniment
Bluebell ABCD 016

Geehl: "For You Alone" ("För dig allein")
September 4, 1929: Stockholm, Concert Hall
Unknown pianist
Testament SBT 1427

Peterson-Berger: "Bland skogens höga furustammar"
September 29, 1930: Stockholm, Concert Hall
Unspecified orchestra, cond. Nils Grevillius
Naxos 8.110791

Kálmán: "Heut' Nacht hab' ich geträumt von dir" ("Jag drömmer varje natt om dig"), *Das Veilchen von Montmartre*
September 9, 1932: Copenhagen
Unspecified orchestra, cond. Jens Warny
Naxos 8.110722

Laparra: "Mélancolique tombe le soir" ("Fylld av vemod sänker sig natten"), *L'illustre Fregona*

March 1933: Stockholm, Concert Hall
Unspecified orchestra, cond. Nils Grevillius
Naxos 8.110722

Traditional: "Ack Värmeland du sköna"
October 7, 1936: Stockholm, Concert Hall
Unspecified orchestra, cond. Nils Grevillius
Naxos 8.110722

Pérez-Freire: "Ay, ay, ay"
October 8, 1936: Stockholm, Concert Hall
Unspecified orchestra, cond. Nils Grevillius
Naxos 8.110740

Rimsky-Korsakov: "Ne shchest' almazov" ("I söderns hav"), *Sadko*
October 8, 1936: Stockholm, Concert Hall
Unspecified orchestra, cond. Nils Grevillius
Naxos 8.110722

Stenhammar: "Sverige"
January 26, 1937: Stockholm, Concert Hall
Unspecified orchestra, cond. Nils Grevillius
Naxos 8.110791

Althén: "Land, du välsignade"
January 26, 1937: Stockholm, Concert Hall
Unspecified orchestra, cond. Nils Grevillius
Naxos 8.110791

Traditional: "Hej dunkom"
October 1937: Stockholm
Bluebell ABCD 092

Johann Strauss II: "Wer uns getraut?" ("Vem oss har vigt"), *Der Zigeunerbaron*
May 30, 1938: Stockholm, Concert Hall
Hjördis Schymberg (soprano); unspecified orchestra, cond. Nils Grevillius
Naxos 8.110722

Millöcker: "Ich hab kein Geld" ("Nu är jag pank och fågelfri"), *Der Bettelstudent*
May 30, 1938: Stockholm, Concert Hall
Unspecified orchestra, cond. Nils Grevillius
Naxos 8.110722

Offenbach: "Au Mont Ida trois déesses" ("Uti en skog på berget Ida"), *La belle Hélène*
May 31, 1938: Stockholm, Concert Hall
Unspecified orchestra, cond. Nils Grevillius
Naxos 8.110722

Denza: "Funiculì, funiculà"
December 8, 1940: Detroit, Masonic Temple Auditorium
Ford Symphony Orchestra, cond. Eugene Ormandy
VAIA 1189

Godard: "Oh! ne t'éveille pas encor" ("Oh! wake not yet"), *Jocelyn*
March 25, 1946: New York, Rockefeller Center
Firestone Orchestra, cond. Howard Barlow
WHRA-6036

Morgan: "Clorinda"
March 25, 1948: New York, Rockefeller Center
Bell Telephone Orchestra, cond. Donald Voorhees
WHRA-6036

Tosti: "L'alba separa dalla luce l'ombra"
August 11, 1949: Stockholm, Concert Hall
Stockholm Concert Association Orchestra, cond. Nils Grevillius
Naxos 8.110792S

Herbert: "Neapolitan Love Song," *The Princess Pat*
November 20, 1950: New York, Rockefeller Center
Firestone Orchestra, cond. Howard Barlow
Kultur DVD D2424

Liszt: "Es muss ein Wunderbares sein"
April 11, 1952: New York, Manhattan Center
Frederick Schauwecker, pf.
Testament SBT 1427

Beach: "Ah, Love, but a Day"
November 21, 1952: London, HMV Studio
Ivor Newton, pf.
EMI 5 66306 2

Fétis: "Se i miei sospiri"
June 9, 1954: Bergen, Concert Palace

Bergen Philharmonic Orchestra, cond. Carl Garaguly
Bluebell ABCD 006

Sjöberg: "Tonerna"
March 15, 1955: Helsinki, B-Mässhallen
Harry Ebert, pf.
So Entertainment (CD attached to Forsell, *Jussi: Sången, människan, bilderna*; see Bibliography)

Foster: "Jeanie with the Light Brown Hair"
September 24, 1955: New York, Carnegie Hall
Frederick Schauwecker, pf.
RCA 88697748922

Rachmaninoff: "V molchan 'i nochi taynoy" ("In the Silence of the Night")
December 14, 1955: New Orleans, Municipal Auditorium
Frederick Schauwecker, pf.
Premiere Opera 122

Flotow: "Ach, so fromm" ("M'apparì"), *Martha*
January 23, 1957: Stockholm, Concert Hall
Royal Court Orchestra, cond. Nils Grevillius
RCA 88697748922

Thomas: "Elle ne croyait pas" ("Hon kunde icke tro"), *Mignon*
August 5, 1957: Stockholm, Gröna Lund
Bertil Bokstedt, pf.
Bluebell ABCD 114

Nordqvist: "Till havs"
August 5, 1957: Stockholm, Gröna Lund
Bertil Bokstedt, pf.
Bluebell ABCD 114

Giordano: "Amor ti vieta," *Fedora*
September 1957: Florence, Teatro Comunale
Orchestra of the Maggio Musicale, cond. Albert Erede
Decca 433 930-2

Cilea: "È la solita storia del pastore," *L'Arlesiana*
September 1957: Florence, Teatro Comunale
Orchestra of the Maggio Musicale, cond. Albert Erede
Decca 433 930-2

Ponchielli: "Cielo e mar," *La Gioconda*
September 1957: Florence, Teatro Comunale
Orchestra of the Maggio Musicale, cond. Albert Erede
Decca 443 930-2

Peterson-Berger: "När jag för mig själv i mörka skogen går"
September 25, 1957: Stockholm, Europafilm Studio
Royal Court Orchestra, cond. Nils Grevillius
Swedish Society Discofil SCD 1100

Söderman: "Trollsjön"
February 8, 1959: Stockholm, Concert Hall
Royal Court Orchestra, cond. Nils Grevillius
Swedish Society Discofil SCD 1100

Wolf: "Verborgenheit"
August 20, 1959: Stockholm, Gröna Lund
Bertil Bokstedt, pf.
Bluebell ABCD 114

Tchaikovsky: "Kuda, kuda" ("Förbi, förbi"), *Eugene Onegin*
August 5, 1960: Gothenburg, Concert Hall
Gothenburg Symphony Orchestra, cond. Nils Grevillius
WHRA-6036

This survey of the most significant of Björling's remaining recordings begins with the finest of the six songs performed in front of the acoustic horn alongside his brothers Olle and Gösta in February 1920. These discs were made during the Björling Quartet's American tour (in concerts they were joined on the platform by their father David), which lasted from November 1919 to March 1921. They serve both as a souvenir of the intense professional singing activity Jussi and his brothers undertook between 1915 and 1927 (over 950 concerts have been documented)[1] and as a demonstration of how closely their singing reflected the pedagogical principles outlined by David Björling in his bilingual pamphlet *How to Sing*.

The music itself, chosen entirely for Swedish-speaking Americans, is of limited appeal today, but the traditional song translatable as "Summer Joy" has a naïve C major jauntiness that the trio clearly enjoy: one of the boys can't help chuckling at the end, an effect repeated when the adult Björling brothers rerecorded the song for Swedish Radio in 1952.[2] While Gunnar Wennerberg's nineteenth century setting of the opening verses of the fourth Psalm captures the spirit of the Old Testament text rather well and gives the boys a chance for some solo singing.

"Children must not sing *pianissimo*," wrote David Björling in his pamphlet, "because that contracts the throat and affects the voice. Nor must children sing too loud so that it sounds like screaming; but let them produce a rich and powerful tone with open throat cavity and chest high and deep breathing, and you will soon obtain results."[3] The colorful, open-throated emission that can be heard in "Sommarglädje" contrasts strongly with the headtone-based approach, typically associated with English cathedral choirs and often advocated by teachers[4] as it facilitates correct intonation and purity of sound. This is not, however, the method used in Italy (where both Enrico Caruso and Beniamino Gigli sang as boys in church choirs) and indeed seems less conducive to subsequent development into a golden-toned operatic tenor.

The open chest voice the boys employ in "Sommarglädje" would not, however, have been suited to a sacred text: in Wennerberg's Psalm we hear a blending of head and chest tones to produce a sound combining characterful purity with impressive power. The initial solo passages were probably assigned to Olle, who was then almost eleven years old and possessed the strongest of the three voices. After two and a half minutes, however, we hear another soloist, with a less powerful but sweeter instrument: this is almost certainly Jussi. His father wrote that "by opening the throat you also open the canals of the nasal cavities, and the tone places itself . . . and thereby becomes soft and beautiful."[5] This is exactly what we hear in this brief extract of unaccompanied singing, where Björling switches easily from a *voix mixte* in the upper-middle register to a chest voice on the low B. This skillful blending and alternation of head and chest resonance at the age of nine helps us understand why Björling never had to stop singing when his voice later descended into the tenor range (it never "broke," in the usual sense) and why his instrument remained so well-integrated throughout his career.

The next documentation of that instrument is the test recording made nine years later of an eighteen-year-old tenor singing Henry Geehl's Edwardian love song "For You Alone," which had been composed in 1909 and recorded by Caruso the year after, just two months before Björling's birth. Björling seems to have listened intently to that disc, for both tenors perform the song in G major, with a ringing climax on the A natural, and their phrasing is very similar in profile. The Swede's youthful voice has a fresh brilliance in the upper octave that is in no way dulled by comparison with the thirty-seven-year-old Caruso's richly expert singing in the original language. We have a sense of the tone placing itself spontaneously, as David Björling had taught, which counts for much in expressive terms. At the same time we are aware of the relative weakness of Jussi's lower octave, and a certain caution in dealing with dynamic contrasts. When, in the first verse, he tries to lighten the attack on one of the Gs above the staff, we hear a throaty catch to the sound, a not infrequent occurrence in his earliest recordings. He himself later admitted that it took him some time to achieve an ideally sweet attack at all dynamic levels, a skill he probably learnt from Joseph Hislop (who continued to give him advice right up to their last meeting in March 1960).[6]

No hint of throatiness can be heard in Björling's first version of Wilhelm Peterson-Berger's "Bland skogens höga furustammar," recorded just a year later, and the lower register has also gained in solidity, while the top Gs have lost none of their incandescence. The Swedish composer, then nearing the end of his life but still active as a critic, was one of the more colorful characters Björling encountered in his early years in Stockholm. He told the tenor that "everything you do is fine because you are an extremely musical singer,"[7] and the latter repaid the compliment by singing six of the composer's songs in concert and recording four of them. He never bettered this early version of the serene folk-like melody, although the more introspective, G minor "När jag för mig själv i mörka skogen går," which deals with unrequited love, works better in the performance recorded some twenty-nine years later: the tenor's phrasing is more finished and spacious, and the deep sadness of the penultimate line ("allting gåfve jag för vännen som jag mist") acquires a quite different poignancy from the perspective of middle age.

Björling tells us in his autobiography how his early Peterson-Berger recordings attracted the attention of the director of Copenhagen's Tivoli amusement park, Richard Rydberg,[8] who engaged him for his first (highly successful) recital abroad. It was in Denmark that the tenor made the best of his early operetta recordings, some three years before he attempted *Die Fledermaus* on stage. His rendition in Swedish of the tango "Heut Nacht hab ich geträumt von dir" from Kálmán's *Das Veilchen vom Montmartre* (which had been premiered only two years earlier) is relatively plodding in rhythm compared with Nicolai Gedda's suavely idiomatic 1970 performance,[9] but it does reveal real progress in the twenty-one-year-old Björling's mastery of legato, and an increasing ease in dynamic modulation. This progress is confirmed (apart from an occasional hint of throatiness) in the recording made six months later of an aria ("Mélancolique tombe le soir") from Raoul Laparra's "zarzuela" *L'Illustre Fregona,* which the tenor sang in Stockholm twenty-two times, including the Swedish premiere in January 1932. In this serenade he conjures up the nocturnal atmosphere rather well and makes a skillful slow crescendo on the culminating A-flat, but the melody, despite its cloying string and harp accompaniment, fails to cling to the memory.

Björling waited until his technique was fully developed (in 1936) before recording some of the patriotic songs that form a significant part of Sweden's musical heritage, and which came to be uniquely associated with his voice. There is no doubting his deep love for his native land, which he knew much better than most fellow-Swedes, having toured the country innumerable times as both child and adult. He is eloquent in extolling the beauties of the western province of Värmland, where his maternal grandmother had her roots. "Ack Värmeland du sköna" is a simple melody of ancient origin and disarming beauty that presents a young man's view of the world, with a sturdy optimism that invests the first verse and a serene melancholy that softens the second, where death suddenly comes into view. Images of death also infuse Stenhammar's "Sverige" and Althén's "Land, du välsignade," two contrasting expressions of patriotic feeling. The latter, which opens like a late-romantic piano concerto in the 1937 studio recording and closes with equal fervor, was a more suitable encore piece for Björling's concerts and this performance brings out beautifully, and without bluster, the diversified dynamics of each verse. It is the more pensive and poetic Stenhammar song, however, that arouses the deepest response in listeners. It is a through-composed work without an instantly hummable melody, but its expressive scope is all-comprehending, dealing as it does with the past and the future, with nature and the changing seasons and those who "sleep under the churchyard stone." That final line undoubtedly resonated with Björling, who at the age of twenty-six had long since buried both his mother and his father in the churchyard of Stora Tuna in Dalarna. He too would be laid to rest there some twenty-three years later, and "Sverige" was sung by the choir at his Stockholm funeral.

Björling never sang anything in Spanish, but that did not prevent him from making much of the Chilean composer Osman Pérez-Freire's aubade "Ay, ay, ay." This song had been famously recorded by Miguel Fleta,[10] and Björling—who by 1936 had acquired total mastery of the *messa di voce*—was probably anxious to demonstrate that he could deliver it with equal virtuosity. The tempo adopted is faster than Fleta's, but the diminuendos (including a spectacular one on the final top A) are just as deftly executed. While Fleta offers a more explicitly sensual timbre in the original Spanish, Björling in Swedish sounds both engagingly youthful and remarkably insinuating.

He was indeed particularly generous with hairpin dynamics in the late 1930s, as we hear in Rimsky-Korsakov's "Song of India" from *Sadko,* where he first softens an E at the top of the staff and then reinforces an E-flat, while recurrent top Gs are attacked with decreasing intensity. This effect can also be found in Fleta's 1931 recording[11] (in Spanish), which Björling may have heard, although he doesn't follow his example in interpolating an extra *pianissimo* high note at the end (a solution favored also by Beniamino Gigli). The Swede, unlike the Spaniard and Italian, actually sang this cameo role of the Indian Merchant on stage—the last of his eleven performances took place six months before the recording was made—and in the disc every note is as polished as the precious stones evoked in the text. The melismas are delightfully musical and only Gigli (singing in French) equals Björling's beauty of tone here. Nevertheless, the Italian tenor's vocalization is ruffled by aspirates, a defect that is absent from Ivan Kozlovsky's performance in the original Russian (1949),[12] where he compensates for a lack of timbral luster with a mesmeric combination of rubato and dynamic shading.

Still more virtuosic in its way is Björling's unaccompanied rendition of the traditional festive song "Hej, dunkom!"—a carefree invitation to make merry as long as one has money in one's pocket—that featured in the film *Fram för framgång* a year later. The character he plays, Tore Nilsson, stands at a table, glass in hand, and bursts into song, attacking a top B-flat which, when repeated in the brief reprise, is momentarily lifted a semitone to B-natural. The voice exudes here a degree of vitality that the tenor will never entirely equal in later years and displays astonishing flexibility in the high tessitura as well as impeccable intonation. The climactic top C—held for seven seconds—is a liberating sound that sets the seal on one of the most remarkable examples of tenorial showmanship on record.

High spirits naturally predominate in the three operetta excerpts (all of them in Swedish) that follow. While Björling's earlier operetta recordings functioned above all as dance tunes, he projects a real sense of character here, having in the meantime made his debuts as Alfred in *Die Fledermaus* and Sándor Barinkay in *Der Zigeunerbaron.* The recording of the duet from the latter work was made just a few weeks after his first stage appearance in Johann Strauss's operetta, although Hjördis Schymberg, his Saffi on disc, was not his partner in the Stockholm production. The recording was initially intended for the Swedish market alone (and Björling playfully switches round the words in the opening exchange), but as the best-sung performance ever recorded of this duet—with Schymberg at her freshest and most appealing, a real sense of theatrical interaction in the dialogue, and a breathtaking joint diminuendo on the top B-flat in the final measure—it didn't take long to win admiration abroad.

Even more astounding is the combination of full-throated exuberance and exquisite vocal finish in "Ich hab kein Geld" from Millöcker's *Der Bettelstudent,* a work Björling never sang on stage. The way he accelerates each time into the *Allegro moderato* after the opening couplet is a model of how to make this music swing, and he caps the performance with a stunning top D-flat—his finest recorded note above top C—at the close. A similar interpolation, a C this time, lends extra glamor to "Au Mont Ida" from Offenbach's *La belle Hélène.* This is rather a low-lying piece, but one would never think so hearing Björling's delivery, for the sweet, high placement of his voice lends a rare sparkle and lift to the line.

All three operetta recordings have a smiling charm that was very much a part of Björling's personality,[13] and that surfaces again both in his 1940 rendition in Italian translation of Denza's "Funiculì, funiculà"—an unsurpassed demonstration of the youthful tenor's *joie de vivre* (and ease of harmonization when singing above the chorus in the second verse)—and in the two versions of the "Neapolitan Love Song," from Victor Herbert's 1915 "comic opera" *The Princess Pat*, performed on the televised *Voice of Firestone* in March and November 1950. The latter performance, with its cooing female chorus, is perhaps more visually engaging, but Björling is at his very best in the former, his smile opening up with the melody itself. The English-Italian lyrics by Henry Blossom are so embarrassingly jejune that one doesn't mind their being partly camouflaged by his Swedish accent.

Another *Firestone Hour* broadcast four years earlier (radio only this time), includes the "Berceuse" from Benjamin Godard's long-neglected opera *Jocelyn* (premiered in Brussels in 1888). Björling performs it in Nathan Haskell Dole's English translation and takes the music down a tone. The second recitative is cut and the reprise of the aria is "sung" initially by the strings alone, until the tenor takes over in the last seven measures. In spite of these textual liberties, this is the most atmospheric of Björling's recorded performances of this scene and compares well with two earlier recordings in the original keys (F major in the *Andante*): the 1930 French version (one verse only) by André D'Arkor[14] and the uncut 1914 performance in English by John McCormack[15] (who uses a different English translation). These two tenors offer a command of the head voice no less remarkable than Björling's, but the effect of their phrasing is less moving and direct, partly because they cannot equal the caressing beauty of the Swede's middle register. One notices in particular how easily Björling amplifies the vibrato on his sustained *piano* tones in order to increase their expressive intensity, just as a violinist would do.

Two years later, on the *Bell Telephone Hour*, Björling performed a song by the Welsh composer Robert Orlando Morgan, who was still alive (aged eighty-eight) at the time of this broadcast. The title of this playful A minor melody, "Clorinda," clearly advertises its pastiche-like character, and John Bledlowe's lyrics, like the music itself, parody the idiom of an earlier era. It is a delight to hear Björling's liquid phrasing here, rhythmically alert and fluent in the triplets. The words are disarmingly delivered, with the vowels "coloring" the tune with an emotional honesty that transcends the derivative nature of the composition.

Much more regular items on Björling's concert programs were the two Tosti songs he had in his repertoire. He sang the first of these, "Ideale" (1882), with polished tones, but never came close to suggesting the perfumed intimacy of a *fin de siècle* drawing-room that both the words and music should conjure up (Fernando De Lucia is unmatched in his 1902[16] recording). The d'Annunzio-inspired "L'alba separa dalla luce l'ombra" is another matter. The decadent feeling evoked here is closer to the open spaces of Wagner's *Tristan und Isolde* than to a Victorian salon and the song acquires an almost transcendental scope in Caruso's 1917 recording,[17] which was first played to Björling by his American agent Frederick Schang in the fall of 1948. Björling apparently listened intently and asked for the disc to be played another two times, unbuttoning his shirt and singing along with Caruso the third time round.[18] The following summer he made the studio recording that still stands as his most moving tribute to the Neapolitan tenor. Singing in the same key of E-flat major—with an all-enveloping B-flat interpolated at the climax ("Il sole eterno!")—his phrasing closely matches the expansive breadth and dark, virile coloring of Caruso's, and his diction is both clear and idiomatic (in later performances he will transform "dalla luce" into a paradoxical "della luce"). Overall he cannot entirely match the full-throated baritonal magnificence of his predecessor, but there is nothing second-hand about the generosity of feeling with which he projects every legato phrase, lingering warmly over "Chiudimi, o Notte." No later tenors have surpassed the Björling sound here.

He has more competition in Liszt's "Es muss ein Wunderbares sein." For this intensely spiritual song of love (Oscar von Redwitz-Smölz's poem imagines two souls locked together "from the first kiss until death") Björling chooses A-flat major (rather than Liszt's E-flat), which means that the tessitura straddles the register break rather than remaining comfortably in the lower-middle register. The effect is rather like hearing high notes played on the lower strings of a viola, with a tightly drawn legato matching the intensity of the words. Björling makes very limited use of his pure head tones, and when he does—on the D and E-flat of "sagen"—a slight catch in the voice distracts momentarily from the ethereal atmosphere generated by the very spacious tempo (the performance, one of the slowest ever recorded, lasts 2:32). However interesting, his performance pales alongside that of Richard Tauber, who sings in G major in his 1928 recording,[19] varying the tempo and dynamics with singular imagination and lending an inimitable flavor to the poetic text.

During the same one-day session Björling recorded his only Wolf Lied, "Verborgenheit." Paradoxically, this very intimate song rang truer when he faced a mass open-air audience in Gröna Lund seven years later. In 1959 his frank, unfussy, yet deeply romantic delivery of this Mörike text demonstrates not only how impermeable he remained to the more coolly analytic approach to Lieder interpretation that was then fashionable in some quarters, but also how much more moving his singing was as a result.

Björling leaves a rather indeterminate impression in "Ah, Love, but a Day," composed in 1900 by Amy Beach. Although the composer was American (she died eight years before Björling's record was made) the words themselves are by Robert Browning, so it is appropriate that Björling should have included this song in his sole recording session in London, which he undertook with his regular English accompanist Ivor Newton in November 1952. Only the first two verses of the poem were set to music, but the words are sufficiently revealing psychologically to merit thoughtful delivery. Björling comes closer to achieving this in London than he had on the televised

Figure 20. Rehearsing with Ivor Newton, London, 1937. Courtesy of the Jussi Björling Museum.

Voice of Firestone a year earlier, where he was hampered by a bloated orchestral accompaniment and erratic pronunciation. The relative complexity of the poem, dealing with a wife's distress on realizing that her marriage has gone stale, leaves him looking somewhat perplexed in front of the TV cameras, although his melancholy timbre demonstrates its all-purpose usefulness. In the EMI studio a number of vowels are still distorted, but meanings seem more focused and the piano accompaniment helps. The relative sophistication of the line "Should I fear surprise?" seems to escape the tenor, however, who curiously chose to record this piece the very year in which his own marriage had been most dangerously on the rocks.

The pseudo-baroque aria "Se i miei sospiri," by François-Joseph Fétis, was first performed in Paris in 1833. The famous musicologist claimed it was by Stradella, but it now seems certain that Fétis himself was responsible for the music. The piece is better-known with an alternative religious text, "Pietà Signore," and it was this version that De Lucia sang at Caruso's funeral in August 1921. Both Neapolitans had recorded the aria to moving and stylish effect in 1918,[20] and it is strange that Björling did not adopt the same text, which fits the music more closely than the alternative lyrics, evoking a hero's sense of guilt and desire for punishment. He also mispronounces "l'empio" and changes the tense of "m'allettò," spoiling the rhyme. Yet his Norwegian concert performance (his only recording of this aria) is well worth hearing, for the candor of his timbre and his instinctive feeling for the musical idiom that Fétis is counterfeiting prove so persuasive that this interpretation sounds more emotionally revealing than many "authentic" renditions of authentic baroque music, even though his trills are sketchier than Caruso's.

With Carl Sjöberg's "Tonerna" we return to the heart of Björling's concert repertoire (he had sung the song since the age of twelve and was recorded in it twelve times in all), for this is the song that lays bare more revealingly than any other his relationship with music itself. Music is in fact the subject of Erik Gustaf Geijer's poem, where it is presented as a medium offering spiritual repose to a troubled heart. The six lines of the poem are sung twice, with an almost identical setting (the only difference being an octave transposition of the A-flat on "Till er" in the repeat), and the 1955 Helsinki performance is remarkable for the way it makes every word and every note tell, generating an extra degree of intimacy in the repeat by means of softer dynamics and a pure head voice drawn out on the top A-flat. This sound—though arguably less virtuosic than the diminuendo heard in the 1936 studio recording[21] with orchestra—reveals the increasing willingness of the mature singer to expose himself emotionally in this late nineteenth-century melody (as beautiful in its way as Schubert's "An die Musik," which Björling never sang).

Sjöberg was a physician by profession and when he died aged thirty-eight in 1900 he was little-known as a composer, yet today this music may speak to us more directly (even across language barriers) than Stephen Foster's much more famous "Jeanie with the Light Brown Hair." This too is best heard with a piano accompaniment; in the 1955 Carnegie Hall recital Björling employs a textual variant ("zephyr" rather than "vapor" in the second line) which is not heard in his earlier readings with orchestra. It is not difficult to find recordings of this song—by Richard Crooks[22] in particular—that project the text more crisply, but Björling's more "horizontal" approach, favoring a long-breathed unfolding of the melody over verbal meanings (and including some wide-spanning upward portamentos), proves no less persuasive, for unlike Beach's "Ah, Love, but a Day" (the other American art song in his repertoire), this poetic text has aged more quickly than the music.

While the 1955 New York recital, like the 1954 concert in Bergen, was one of those occasions on which Björling's voice was not at its most responsive, he was on top form for his New Orleans recital in December 1955, where offered perhaps his finest recorded performance of a Rachmaninoff song. "In the Silence of the Night" is in truth more commonly associated with baritones and is usually sung much more slowly than it is here, for Björling transforms the composer's *Lento* into an *Andante*. He also sings the song in

F major (a third above the original key) and prefers a soft opening to Rachmaninoff's *forte.* Yet he succeeds in making this nostalgic lament for lost love entirely his own, phrasing with consistent poignancy and abundant use of portamento (entirely appropriate in this late-Romantic piece), and making as much of the *fff* climax as of the ***ppp*** conclusion. He projects the words less eloquently than Cesare Valletti[23] (who uses the same English translation), but his voice takes on something of the atmosphere of the night itself, and no other singer rivals his graceful ascent to a sustained head-voice F in the final measures.

The tenor was in equally splendid voice for his recording session in Stockholm in January 1957: the interpretation of Flotow's "M'appari" is deeply satisfying, the still-youthful timbre perfectly framed by the prominent woodwinds in the introductory measures. Even by Björling's standards this performance is remarkable for the smoothness with which he negotiates the phrases that circle awkwardly around the top of the staff, and for the elegance with which he employs the alternation of dotted eighth notes and sixteenth notes to lend an extra lift to the melody. Apart from an insignificant omission in the *Più animato* section his diction is exemplary and in perfect balance with the tone production: both retain that liquid quality which is one of the most attractive features of his singing, contrasting with the more biting emphasis lent to the phrases by Mario Lanza,[24] who thereby undermines the atmosphere of ecstatic contemplation. Equally admirable is Björling's free play of rubato in the repeat of the opening melody and neat execution of the traditional extra embellishments that help maintain a sense of improvisatory freedom at a fairly rapid pace (*Allegro moderato*). He was taught this aria by his father David, who suggested singing it initially a tone below score pitch; this he did, much to John Forsell's surprise, at his first audition with the Opera House director in 1928. In 1933 he was assigned three performances of the role of Lyonel at the Royal Swedish Opera: although he never performed the part again the music sounds as if it were written with his voice in mind, and the climactic B-flat projects with real freedom—without making the character seeming more heroic than he really is (as inevitably happens with Caruso in 1917).[25]

Björling performed the role of Wilhelm Meister in Thomas's *Mignon* more often (1932–37) than Flotow's Lyonel, but his sole recording of "Elle ne croyait pas" occupies a much less important place in his discography. The difference derives not so much from the Swedish translation ("Hon kunde icke tro") as from his inability to exploit fully the expressive potential of the music. Perhaps it was the open-air setting of the recital that discouraged him from respecting Thomas's *dolce* marking at the beginning of the two couplets, and if one excepts the *forte* climax of the refrain there is little dynamic variety to his singing here. As a result he proves much less interesting than Gianni Raimondi[26]—who employed his *mezza voce* to poetic effect in a concert performance in Italian recorded eleven months earlier—and sounds frankly insignificant alongside the exquisitely-moulded version of another Italian, De Lucia,[27] who turns every phrase into a work of art.

Much better suited to the outdoor setting was one of Björling's favorite songs, Gustaf Nordqvist's "Till havs," which was sung at the same recital. In a stuffy concert hall this extrovert call to the sea can sound rather forced in its blustery rhetoric, but in the open air on an August night it conveys a sense of shared adventure that is keenly felt here. This song gave Björling a chance to show off his tone at its most trumpet-like. He once admitted that he could never have sustained this emission for the whole duration of an opera,[28] but the sound projects impressively in this song, winning over an audience of some fifteen thousand people without recourse to amplification.

Giordano's Andrea Chénier was one of the heroic roles that Björling avoided in the opera house. He did, however, sing "Come un bel dì di maggio" in recital and on disc,[29] lending a degree of spiritual refinement to the opening *Andantino*, where the delicate harp accompaniment highlights the elegance of his grace notes (dealt with crudely in recordings by such celebrated Chéniers as Aureliano Pertile and Franco Corelli). At the same time he makes recurrent verbal slips—a serious limitation in an aria sung by a poet—and the climactic B-flat tends to sharpen in pitch. "Amor ti vieta" from *Fedora* proved, on the other hand, to be one of the tenor's most effective recital "numbers," even though he never had a chance to perform the entire role of Loris. This brief *Andante cantabile*, in C major and 4/4 time, lasts less than two minutes and unfolds within the range of a single octave, but it is one of the most infectious melodies in Italian opera, as well as being a vocal test piece that sorts the great from the good and the merely ordinary. Nothing like a simple cantabile revolving around the tenor's register break (F and G at the top of the staff) demonstrates the evenness of a singer's emission, the smoothness of his legato, and the ease with which he passes from *piano* to *forte* and back again. Björling overcomes the test impressively in all his recordings, obtaining the finest results in the 1957 studio version. This performance is free from verbal errors, and enhanced by a magnificent climax (the top A opens up impressively) and a resolute conclusion (he embellishes the final note with an acciaccatura to lend it extra finish). In a very real sense he transforms this aria into a genuine expression of *bel canto*, for the effect of his phrasing is to create the illusion of a suspension of time, in which the often convulsive movement of the second act of the opera suddenly switches to slow motion. The words, which play on Fedora's emotional ambivalence, are savored as fully as the notes.

Björling employs more portamentos in this music than either De Lucia[30] or Caruso[31] (both of whom made outstanding recordings of the aria), demonstrating how gracefully this embellishment can be used to regulate the rubato by slowing the pace before the attack: we are reminded that great musical phrasing is often simply a matter of finding the most logical way of passing from one note to another. Björling invests his tone with a striking melancholy in "che mi respinge" and his intakes of breath are imperceptible throughout.

In the seventh chapter of his autobiography the tenor wrote, "I never learn the words without the music. For me the words and music are a single unit."[32] This statement helps us understand the predominantly musical nature of his expressive imagination. Few would quarrel with his working method—he would start by writing the words of the translated libretto into the piano score, then he would go through the opera phrase by phrase with a répétiteur—but recordings reveal that the process of assimilation was not always complete when he first came to record arias in a foreign language; one sometimes feels that he would have benefitted from a more exclusive focus on the text alone. The Italian conductor Tullio Serafin, with whom Björling worked in the mid-fifties in Chicago, always advised reciting the texts aloud in order to find the right stresses in relatively free musical settings. This is particularly appropriate in arias such as Federico's Lament from *L'Arlesiana*, which has a bewitching melody—both Beniamino Gigli and Tito Schipa thought it was the "loveliest"[33] of all tenor arias—that seems to grow from the rhythms of speech. Yet only in his final recording of this aria does Björling seem to have assimilated the full meaning of Leopoldo Marenco's text. Here, although he cannot rival the heartbreaking eloquence of Schipa,[34] his delivery of the words is deeply moving and he is more attentive than before to Cilea's dynamic markings, employing a delicate *mezzo piano* in his first ascents above the staff. This, combined with a melting legato, not only allows for a more gradual buildup to the climax, but also makes us fully aware of the emotional instability of a character who ultimately commits suicide. His B-natural (an interpolation introduced by Gigli and frowned upon by the composer himself) is a truly thrilling sound, filled with genuine sorrow.

As with Federico's Lament, it took Björling some years to get the words of Enzo's "Cielo e mar" right, and even in his last—and finest—recording, made during the same sessions as the Cilea aria, he omits the *r* from the word "ombra." Yet from his first attempt in the studio twenty years earlier this very difficult piece of music proved highly congenial to him, even though he never sang *La Gioconda* on stage. Alternating between rapt contemplation of the sea and sky at night and an impatient desire to embrace Laura, Enzo's aria requires singing of uncommon elegance and imagination to reveal its full expressive impact. Björling caught both moods to perfection, moulding the phrases with rare lyricism and consistently golden tone, and achieving striking urgency in the *Poco più mosso* section. The head voice employed for "O sogni d'or" is as perfectly poised as the final ascent to the B-flat, the portamentos are executed with a dexterity that makes the melody seem suspended in air, and every phrase is bound satisfyingly into the whole. This performance is one of the finest ever recorded, and after hearing Björling deal so effortlessly with the aria's multiple difficulties, it comes as something of a shock to realize how clumsy many of his colleagues sound in this music: only Caruso[35] and Carlo Bergonzi[36] at their best achieve a similar degree of expressive balance here.

Björling's voice sounds as much at ease in the Venetian lagoon as it does in the timeless world of Nordic legend evoked in Söderman's "Trollsjön," where the tenor's evident involvement lends fascination and credibility to the story of the magic lake: he clearly distinguishes between the voice of the narrator and that of the mysterious being with a "swan-white hand" who tries to lure the shepherd-boy into the waters. This unsettling tale is told with uncontrived simplicity and a vocal ease that allows Björling access to a prolonged top C. If he was reluctant to sing this note in public by 1959, he still enjoyed letting loose in his summer studio on the island of Siarö. As Bertil Bokstedt recalled, "Notwithstanding all his wonderful concerts at which I accompanied him, it was there in that studio that I experienced Jussi's most beautiful tones; there, even during the later years, he gave his high C free expression with an exhilaration and a joy which were absolutely incomparable."[37]

There are no high Cs in the second-act aria from *Eugene Onegin*, but Björling's voice was at its most responsive in his concert in Gothenburg. It is curious that the tenor should have programmed—for the last occasion on which his voice was recorded—an aria in which the character reflects on the inevitability of fate and reveals total readiness for death.

He had sung eight performances as Lensky between January 1933 and December 1935, and he again uses the Swedish translation in this, his most intimate recording of the aria. His ability to convey acutely painful experience (the opening phrase tells all) through sheer beauty of tone (the low Es are as rounded and mellow as the notes above the staff) is surely unique. Although he employs less variety of nuance than Sergei Lemeshev[38] and proves less daring in rubato than Ivan Kozlovsky,[39] his singing is just as emotionally charged as theirs, and his range of dynamics as wide as anyone's. The Russian tenors make us more aware of the physiognomy of Lensky, suggesting (in a very twentieth-century manner) the psychological impulses that lead him to challenge Onegin to a duel. Björling's character is more transparent, timeless, and universal, the voice inviting us to share feelings as uncomplicated as they are deep.

EVOLUTION AND INFLUENCE

In what ways did Jussi Björling evolve as an interpreter during his three-decade career? To what extent was he influenced by earlier singers? To what degree did he himself exert an influence over later generations of performers? These three questions are necessary to an overview of the tenor's artistic progress and his role in the history of music. The first two have been at least partly addressed in many of the preceding chapters. Addressed, but not perhaps entirely answered, for if we try to fit Björling into an evolutionary theory of musical interpretation we seriously risk losing sight of what made (and makes) him unique as a musical artist.

If we base our assessment on recordings and chronology, a case could be made for claiming that any five-year period between 1930 and 1960—with the arguable exception of the war years, when Björling was intermittently depressed, sometimes distracted, and afflicted by a series of physical ailments (including pneumonia and appendicitis)—could be seen as the highpoint of his career in artistic terms. In the first period we see him singing a stunning range of roles with a voice of unique fragrance and bloom. In the late 1930s we hear that voice achieving its fullest technical development, broadening the imaginative scope of his phrasing. In the postwar years we admire the weightier sound of a genuine spinto tenor combined with an increasingly idiomatic command of the foreign languages in which he now performed regularly. In the early fifties we recognize an artist of truly international renown, taking part in the some of the first LP recordings of complete operas with prestigious casts. And in the final years we observe how he continued to mature as an interpreter, acquiring an extra degree of sensuality and spiritual awareness, and refining his phrasing to compensate for the lower energy levels caused by increasing ill-health.

If we return moreover to his interpretation of single works, we recall that different qualities seem to emerge in different periods, and that sometimes Björling seems at his most inspired in his twenties (*Il trovatore*, "Adelaide," *Aida*), while in other works he offers greater satisfaction in his forties (*Rigoletto*, "Frühlingsglaube," *Tosca*). At times his development seems to follow a cyclical pattern: his last complete *Bohème* (1956) and *Faust* (1959) echo excerpts from the same operas recorded in 1940 and 1937. Yet "seem" is the right verb, for the tenor may well have phrased with similar sensitivity on any number of (unrecorded) occasions between those dates. The conductor Gianandrea Gavazzeni, with whom Björling sang *La bohème* in Chicago in 1957, always insisted that it was a mistake to generalize about interpretation rather than focusing on the specific musical and theatrical tensions generated (by an infinity of factors) on particular occasions in the opera house or concert hall. The differences between Björling's studio *Rigoletto* made in June 1956 and the live performance of the same opera recorded seven months later; between the Helsinki recital in January 1955 and the one in New York in September that year; or even between the two performances of *Un ballo in maschera* in the fall of 1940, should warn us of the risks of glibly labelling different phases of a career. Björling was ever-sensitive to the musical and psychological environment in which he was performing and thrived on spontaneity. Bertil Bokstedt recalls that in recital he

> did not always sing to a predetermined program. He preferred to decide, as he stood on the concert platform, what he would sing a few moments later. Therefore I always had to be ready to find immediately and play any of the seventy or so arias and songs which Jussi could choose from his repertory.[1]

One of the chapters in his wife's biography is entitled "Vocal Problems" and deals with the multiple cancellations the tenor was forced to make in the winter and spring of 1953–54. Those problems were all too real, but were caused not—as is usually the case—by an ill-used or over-stressed vocal mechanism, but by a persistent laryngitis that affected the throat for several months. Björling's difficulty in recovering from that illness was a warning signal, and in the years that followed his weakening health made him increasingly vulnerable both on stage and in the recording studio. In spite of this, the pathos of vocal (and artistic) decline is not really part of the Björling story, for he was in outstanding form on a number of occasions during the last five years of his career (examples include the recording sessions in September 1957 and February 1959, the Atlanta recital in April 1959, the Stockholm *Manon Lescaut* in November that year, the Verdi Requiem with Reiner, and the Gothenburg concert in 1960), and was in any case careful not to let audiences perceive any sign of vocal failing. Right from the early years of his career he would transpose songs and arias whenever he felt it necessary, and he also regulated the use of head and chest resonance in accordance with how his body was responding (sometimes a *mezza voce* was his salvation, on other occasions it was best avoided). Having lived with it professionally since the age of four, he knew his singing voice supremely well (he did not even have to do any serious vocalizing before going on stage), and that self-knowledge is one of the keys to both his greatness as a singer and to his ever-changing responsiveness as an interpreter.

One of the clearest things that emerges from this study is how strongly Björling was affected by the recordings of Enrico Caruso, while the innumerable other tenors he listened to live and on record had little perceptible influence on him. In this he had much in common with tens of other tenors who focused on the Italian repertoire and were born between the 1880s (Giovanni Martinelli) and the 1940s (Placido Domingo). Björling, however, distinguishes himself from his colleagues by the quality of his imitation: he only intermittently drew inspiration from the color of Caruso' voice and ignored the tearful inflections that had been turned into a mannerism by Gigli, focusing rather on the equalization of the registers, the noble diction, the cello-like legato, and a number of typically nineteenth-century stylistic traits, including a subtle use of portamento and a deft way with embellishment. If Björling had concentrated exclusively on the Italian repertoire he might have ended up sacrificing flexibility by cultivating a tensely drawn heroic line (like Martinelli) or a sensually dark timbre (like Domingo), and thereby reducing (as they did) the dynamic flexibility of his phrasing. By continuing to sing regularly in his native tongue (which facilitated the use of head resonance and freed him from external influence), he maintained his vocal equilibrium much better than Caruso himself, who underwent several throat operations, which limited his ability to sing softly in the upper register after 1907.

If ever Björling's phrasing in the Italian repertoire seems to us bland, this may be due to the fact that Caruso's all-surpassing vocal splendor and emotional honesty had effectively neutralized the influence (if one excepts Ivan Kozlovsky's isolated recordings from the Soviet Union) of earlier, and more individual, styles of tenor singing. This is the reason why this book refers so regularly to another Neapolitan, Fernando De Lucia, whose recordings offer an alternative vision of how a remarkable musical imagination can be applied to the great operatic masterpieces of the nineteenth century.

The complex nature of influence is further clarified if we look at the singers who learnt from Björling. In Sweden his impact was deep and not limited to tenor voices[2] or to the operatic repertoire. His most immediate and talented successor, Nicolai Gedda, demonstrated in early recordings that he was capable of matching Björling's musicality in phrase after phrase. If his Faust and Rodolfo fail to enchant the listener to the same degree, that is largely because Gedda started out with a less exceptional musical instrument. This disadvantage led him rightly to diversify his repertoire as much as possible and to seek vocal and linguistic challenges that were beyond Björling's scope: Gedda became an increasingly individual artist across the thirty years that followed his predecessor's death.

A more limited natural endowment, however, is not the only factor conditioning influence. No one admired Björling more than his eldest son Rolf, who from 1967 to 1985 was a leading tenor at the Royal Swedish Opera, and who possessed a colorful Italianate voice of spinto potential. His recordings[3] deserve serious critical evaluation, but his phrasing rarely approaches the quality of his father's (the same can be said for Jussi's younger brother Gösta, who came to specialize in character roles). The reason for this lies in the ways different degrees of musicality inevitably regulate both timbre and technique. The sheer refinement of sound that Jussi achieved and maintained throughout his career should not be seen simply as a gift of nature, but as a result of the instinctive need to mould the musical line with a purity that satisfied his own inborn standards: sounds have to be imagined before they can be emitted.

No tenor since Björling has maintained such exacting standards, not even Luciano Pavarotti, who sensibly studied the Swede's recordings (owing to the similar weight and color of their voices) and who undoubtedly surpassed him in his idiomatic familiarity with a number of roles. Like Gedda, however, the Italian tenor came to sound increasingly unlike Björling as the decades passed by and his own personality came to the fore.

The tenor who at the time of writing comes closest to offering, live in the opera house and concert hall, the sort of rich musical pleasure Björling guaranteed is Juan Diego Flórez. This is not because of any similarity in repertoire (although both Björling and Flórez enjoyed great success in *Il barbiere di Siviglia, L'elisir d'amore, La fille du régiment* and *Rigoletto*), timbre, or even technique, but because the Peruvian singer's musical ear protects him from even the slightest risk of stylistic solecism, and reveals a rare sensitivity to the textures and colors of accompanying instruments. This awareness was, as we have seen, one of the secrets of Björling's expressiveness. His uncanny ability to blend his voice with those timbres—which went beyond what Flórez has thus far achieved—explains why his phrasing was at once so haunting and so apt in so many different contexts. Björling's was not, however, an intellectualized art, but simply the result of an uncommonly limpid voice responding to the instinctive promptings of a unique musical sensibility.

NOTES

Preface

1. The Jussi Björling Museum (Borlange), accessed November 27, 2011, http://www.borlange.se/templates/BlgUnitStartPage____6972.aspx.
2. Forsell, *Jussi* (CD-ROM).
3. The cause of death was purportedly a heart attack, but the autopsy report has mysteriously disappeared. For the official version of his death, see Björling and Farkas, *Jussi*, 352. For a present-day medical perspective, see Rosenqvist, "Jussi Björlings hjärta," 874–76. For an alternative interpretation of events, see Stenius, *Tills vingen brister*, 405–13.
4. For examples of Sundberg's spectograms, see Potter, *Cambridge Companion to Singing*, 231–47.

A Biographical Note

1. Springer, "On the Road with Jussi," 31.
2. This is one of several names used for an ensemble that consisted initially of David Björling and his three eldest sons, Olle, Jussi, and Gösta.
3. Hagman, *Minnesbok*, 64. See also Stenius, *Tills vingen brister*, 258–64.

Introduction

1. Björling, *Med bagaget*, 111.
2. Björling, *Med bagaget*, 116.
3. De Lucia, "Che gelida manina," Phonotype C 1767.
4. Hagman, *Minnesbok*, 98–99.
5. Steane, *Singers of the Century*, 69.
6. See interview with Söderström in the video documentary by Schmidt-Garre, *Belcanto: Tenors of the 78 era*, TDK Euroarts DVD 2050217.
7. *The Dawn of Recording: The Julius Block Cylinders*, Marston 53011-2, compact disc, 2008.
8. An explanation is offered in Leech-Wilkinson, *The Changing Sound of Music*, chapter 1.
9. See Harald Henrysson's chronology for the first three months of 1935, Forsell et al., *Jussi* (CD-ROM).

10. Gedda, *My Life and Art*, 114.
11. The use of his first name even on the posters announcing Björling's death on the streets of Stockholm on the morning of September 9, 1960—"Jussi död i morse"—speaks eloquently of the Swedish people's uniquely close relationship with this classical singer.

Chapter One

1. Caruso, "Cantique de Noël," Victor 88561.
2. Thill, "Cantique de Noël," French Columbia LFX 275.
3. This recording was made in the Large Auditorium of the Concert Hall. In earlier periods of his career Björling had made recordings in the Small Auditorium (now called the Grünewaldsalen) and the Attic Auditorium (now known as the Aulinsalen).
4. Hagman, *Minnesbok*, 75.

Chapter Two

1. Steane, *Singers of the Century*, 36.
2. Alfvén to Björling, June 11, June 1957, letter in the collection of the Jussi Björling Museum, Borlänge.
3. Newton, *At the Piano*, 199–201.
4. One rare exception is the 1938 performance of Gounod's "Sanctus" from the *Messe Solennelle de Sainte Cécile.*
5. Nävermyr, "Song of Sweden," 44.

Chapter Three

1. Björling, "Advice from Jussi Björling."

Chapter Four

1. Beethoven to Matthesson, August 4, 1800, see Beethoven, *Letters*, 1: 33.
2. Steane, *The Grand Tradition*, 374.
3. Björling, "Advice from Jussi Björling."
4. Gedda, "Adelaide," EMI 5 85090 2.
5. Wunderlich, "Adelaide," DG 9806790.
6. Schlusnus, "Adelaide," Grammophon 95391.
7. Anders, "Adelaide," Membran 232116.
8. Blyth, *Song on Record 1*, 20.
9. Schlusnus, "Die Ehre Gottes aus der Natur," Grammophon 95421.

10. Fischer-Dieskau, "Die Ehre Gottes aus der Natur," DG 463 507-2.
11. Blyth, *Choral Music on Record*, 149.
12. Sachs, *Toscanini*, 304–5.
13. Björling, *Med bagaget*, 74–75.
14. Wunderlich, *Missa Solemnis*, DG 423 913-2.

Chapter Five

1. *Stockholms Tidningen*, September 6, 1933.
2. He initially agreed to record the opera with Fritz Reiner for RCA in 1951, but backed out because he didn't have time to learn the part. Jan Peerce replaced him.
3. Among the tenors who sang Don José in Stockholm in the 1930s and 1940s were Set Svanholm and Torsten Ralf.
4. Björling and Farkas, *Jussi*, 211.
5. Kaplan, "Bits and Pieces," 5.
6. Gösta Björling, "Au fond du temple saint," Bluebell ABCD 066.
7. Luccioni, "Au fond du temple saint," Columbia BFX 16.
8. Clément, "Au fond du temple saint," HMV DK 105.
9. Vanzo, "Au fond du temple saint," Gala GL 100.504.
10. Caruso, "Del tempio al limitar," Victor 89007.
11. Gigli, "Del tempio al limitar," Victor 8084.
12. Gigli, "Mi par d'udir ancora," Victor AGSB 56.
13. Caruso, "Je crois entendre encore," Victor 88580.
14. Gedda, *Les pêcheurs de perles*, EMI 6406782.
15. Dalmorès, "La fleur que tu m'avais jetée," Victor 85122.
16. Friant, "La fleur que tu m'avais jetée," Odéon 171.028.
17. Caruso, "La fleur que tu m'avais jetée, "Victor 88208.
18. Fleta, "Il fior che avevi a me tu dato," HMV DB 524.

Chapter Six

1. Björling and Farkas, *Jussi*, 182–83.
2. Smirnov, "Medlenno den' ugasal," HMV 2-022025.
3. Lemeshev, "Medlenno den' ugasal," Grammplasrest 03800-1.
4. Kozlovsky, *Prince Igor*, Melodiya M10-46279/84.

Chapter Seven

1. Fischer-Dieskau, "Die Mainacht," EMI 5 75922 2.
2. Wunderlich, "Die Mainacht," DG 476 5244.
3. McCormack, "Die Mainacht," HMV DA 628.

4. Leisner, “Die Mainacht,” Membran 223073-303.
5. Slezak, “Ständchen,” Grammophon B 42752.

Chapter Eight

1. Steane, *The Grand Tradition*, 32.
2. De Lucia, “Una furtiva lagrima,” Phonotype 1754-2.
3. Caruso, “Una furtiva lagrima,” G&T 52346, Zonophone x 1552, Victor 81027, Victor 88339.
4. Bonci, “Una furtiva lagrima,” Columbia D 17533; McCormack, “Una furtiva lagrima,” Victor 6204; Anselmi, “Una furtiva lagrima,” Fonotipia 62272.
5. Björling sang six performances in Stockholm between November 1932 and February 1933.
6. Di Stefano, “Una furtiva lagrima, Bongiovanni GB 1141-2.
7. Goldberg, “A Charmless Jussi?,” 18–19.
8. Schipa, “Una furtiva lagrima,” Victor 6570 B.
9. Flórez, “Una furtiva lagrima,” Decca 473 440-2.
10. Bergonzi, *L'elisir d'amore*, Hardy Classic Video HR 4129/30.
11. Pavarotti, *L'elisir d'amore*, Decca 475 7514.
12. Ricci, *Variazioni*, 2:16.
13. See Henrysson, *Phonography*, 171.

Chapter Nine

1. J. Cook, “Jussi Bjoerling: The Supreme Operatic Tenor,” 7.
2. Discussed in Joseph Horowitz, *Understanding Toscanini*, 231.
3. Stolze, *Messe solennelle de Sainte Cécile*, DG 477 7114.
4. Hahn, *Du chant*, 104.
5. Drake, “Kipnis Speaks,” 88.
6. Crooks, *Faust*, Naxos 8.110016-7.
7. Lee, *First Intermissions*, 145.
8. Clampton, “Salut! demeure,” 205.
9. Alagna, *Faust*, EMI 6 31611 9.
10. Condé, “Faust: Guide d'Écoute,” 26.
11. The other two arias were “Che gelida manina” (*Bohème*) and “Di quella pira” (*Il trovatore*).
12. Domingo, *Faust*, EMI CDS7 47493.
13. Hislop, *Faust*, Pearl GEM 0203.
14. Lemeshev, “Salut! demeure,” Grammplasrest 0495.
15. Rosvænge, *Faust*, Preiser 90040.
16. New York: Dover, 1994.
17. Caruso, “Salut! demeure,” Victor 88003.
18. Thill, “Salut! demeure,” Columbia 25-LF 17.
19. Hagman, *Minnesbok*, 77.

20. Kraus, *Faust,* VAI 4417.
21. Kraus's speaking voice can be heard in Kraus, *Una lezione di canto,* Bongiovanni GB550/51-2; Björling's in *Jussi Björling Live,* WHRA-6036.
22. Marafioti, *Caruso's Method,* 102–3. See also Tomatis, *The Ear and the Voice,* 89–96.
23. Jackson, *Sign-Off for the Old Met,* 30.
24. Di Stefano, *Faust,* Arkadia 78065.
25. Vezzani, *Faust,* Malibran CDRG 104.
26. Ansseau, "Mais ce Dieu," HMV DB 1364.
27. Björling and Farkas, *Jussi,* 85.
28. Noré, *Faust,* Naxos 8.110117-18.
29. Kozlovsky, *Faust,* LYS 301-303.
30. Caruso, "Il se fait tard," Victor 89031.
31. Gigli, "Dammi ancor," HMV DB 268.
32. Caruso, "Mon cœur est penetré d'épouvante," Victor 89033.
33. Gedda, *Faust,* Brilliant 93964.
34. Caruso, "Que voulez-vous, messieurs?," Victor 95206.
35. Beecham, "The Question of Faust."
36. Björling and Farkas, *Jussi,* 102.
37. Björling, *Med bagaget,* 126.
38. Hagman, *Minnesbok,* 42.
39. Björling, *Med bagaget,* 64.
40. David Björling, *Hur man skall sjunga,* 7.
41. Hagman, *Minnesbok,* 77.
42. Gigli, "Ange Adorable," HMV 2-034033.
43. Gigli, "Ah sorgi alfin," Immortal Performances IPCD 1003-2.
44. Gigli, "Ah! ne fuis pas encore," Victor 87581.
45. Björling and Farkas, *Jussi,* 70.
46. Kozlovsky, *Roméo et Juliette,* Guild GHCD 2264/5.
47. Björling, *Med bagaget,* 84.
48. Corelli, *Roméo et Juliette,* EMI 5 65290 2.
49. Steane, *The Grand Tradition,* 373.
50. Thill, "Ah! Lève-toi, soleil!" Columbia 30-L 1985.
51. Clément, "Ah! lève-toi, soleil!" Odeon 56000.
52. Scaremberg, "Ah! lève-toi, soleil!" Fonotipia 39172.
53. Muratore, "Ah! lève-toi, soleil!" Zonophone X 82577.
54. Gedda, "Ah! lève-toi, soleil!" EMI 85090 2.
55. Kraus, *Roméo et Juliette,* EMI 7 47365 8.
56. Alagna, *Roméo et Juliette,* EMI 5 56123 2.
57. Osborne, "Roméo et Juliette," 32–33.
58. Hackett, *Roméo et Juliette,* Naxos 8.110140-41.
59. Osborne, "Roméo et Juliette," 32–33.
60. Scott, "Not Yet the Fourth Tenor," 54.
61. Björling and Farkas, *Jussi,* 228.

Chapter Ten

1. Melchior, "Jeg elsker dig," Victor 1882.
2. Richard Crooks, "I love thee," Victor 2175-9.
3. Tauber, "Ich liebe dich," Odeon xxB 6966.
4. Flagstad, "En svane," BBC Legends BBCL 4190-2.
5. Gedda, "En svane," Arkadia GI 806.1.
6. Tauber, "Ein Traum," Odeon RXxx 76205.

Chapter Eleven

1. Giacomini, "O mio Signor," Phoenix PH95105.
2. Caruso, "Ombra mai fu," Victor 88617.
3. Gigli, "Ombra mai fu," HMV DB 1901.
4. Domingo, "Ombra mai fu," EMI 54266.
5. Del Monaco, "Ombra mai fu," Decca 475 7269.
6. Schipa, "Ombra mai fu," Victor 6753.

Chapter Twelve

1. Pertile, "Vesti la giubba," Fonotipia R-20012; Pertile, "Un grande spettacolo," Fonotipia R-20026.
2. Gigli, *Pagliacci,* Naxos 8.110155.
3. Del Monaco, *Pagliacci,* VAI 4421.
4. Cura, *Pagliacci,* Arthaus 101 489.
5. De Lucia, "No! Pagliaccio non son," Phonotype M 1803.
6. Caruso, "Vesti la giubba," Victor 88061.
7. Paoli, *Pagliacci,* Bongiovanni GB 1120-2.
8. De Lucia, "Vesti la giubba," Phonotype C 2560.
9. Anselmi, "Vesti la giubba," Fonotipia 62160.
10. Martinelli, "Vesti la giubba," Victor 6754.
11. Gigli, "Il prologo," HMV DB 05353.
12. Del Monaco, "Il prologo," Decca 475 7269.
13. Schipa, "O Colombina," Pathé 59009.
14. Kozlovsky, "O Colombina," Myto MCD921.55.
15. At the Met on February 3, 1953, Del Monaco's performance as Canio was preceded by Björling's Turiddu in *Cavalleria rusticana.*
16. The costume was for the Duke of Mantua in *Rigoletto.* See Björling and Farkas, *Jussi,* 212.
17. Melchior, "Vesti la giubba," VAI 69124.
18. Di Stefano, "Vesti la giubba." Warner 0630-15898-2.
19. Alagna, *Pagliacci,* DG 983 926-6.
20. Bergonzi, "Vesti la giubba," Bongiovanni GB1100-2.

21. Masini, *Pagliacci*, Fimvelstar FR033.
22. Corelli, *Pagliacci*, EMI CMS 763967 2.
23. Henrysson, "Jussi Björling's Canio," 17.
24. Björling and Farkas, *Jussi*, 86.
25. Caruso, "Mattinata," G&T 52034.
26. Di Stefano, "Mattinata," Testament SBT 1097.
27. Pavarotti, "Mattinata," Decca 475 8386.
28. De Lucia, "Mattinata," Fonotipia 29695.

Chapter Thirteen

1. Björling and Farkas, *Jussi*, 179.
2. Patzak, "Siciliana," Grammophon 24327.
3. Piccaver, "Siciliana," Odeon 99937.
4. De Lucia, "Siciliana," G&T 52652.
5. Caruso, "Siciliana," Victor 81030.
6. Garbin, "Siciliana," Fonotipia 39039.
7. Valero, "Siciliana," G&T 52717.
8. Schipa, "Siciliana," Pathé 54034.
9. Melandri, *Cavalleria rusticana*, Bongiovanni GB 1050-2; Gigli, *Cavalleria rusticana*, Naxos 8.110714-15.
10. Caruso, "Addio alla madre," Victor 88458.
11. Di Stefano, *Cavalleria rusticana*, EMI 6407222.
12. Carreras, *Cavalleria rusticana*, EMI 6365022.
13. Caruso, "Viva il vino spumeggiante," Victor 81062.
14. Valero, "Viva il vino spumeggiante," G&T 52718.
15. Garbin, "Viva il vino spumeggiante," Fonotipia 71129.
16. Domingo, "Addio alla madre," Telarc 3984-23292-2.

Chapter Fourteen

1. Thill, "Élégie," Columbia 25-LF 104.
2. Chaliapin, "Élégie," HMV DB 1525.
3. Caruso, "Élégie," Victor 89066.
4. Tauber, "Élégie," Eklipse EKR CD5.
5. Kraus, "Élégie," CD Amedeo 429 557-2.
6. Gigli, "Chiudo gli occhi," HMV DA 1216; Fleta, "Chiudo gli occhi," HMV DB 986.
7. Clément, "En fermant les yeux," Victor 74258.
8. Devriès, "En fermant les yeux," Odéon 188-505.
9. Gedda, "En fermant les yeux," EMI 5 85080 2.
10. Valletti, *Manon*, Bongiovanni HOC 013/14.
11. Alagna, *Manon*, EMI 5 57005 2.
12. Patzak, "Ich schloss die Augen," Grammophon 90062.

13. Campagnola, "En fermant les yeux," Gramophone 432244.
14. Caruso, "Ah! fuyez, douce image," Victor 88348.
15. Alagna, *Manon*, EMI 5 57005 2.

Chapter Fifteen

1. Caruso, "O paradiso," Victor 88054.
2. Gigli, "O paradiso," HMV DB1382.
3. Melchior, "Land so wunderbar," Polydor 66439.
4. Bergonzi, "O paradiso," Decca 440 417-2.
5. Raimondi, "O paradiso," Bongiovanni GB 1187-2.
6. De Lucia, "O paradiso," Phonotype 1766/2.
7. De Reszke, "Ô paradis," Symposium 1284.
8. Muratore, "Ô paradis," Pathé 63012.
9. Domingo, "Ô paradis" EMI 5 75906 2.

Chapter Sixteen

1. Björling, *Med Bagaget*, 38.
2. See Björling and Farkas, *Jussi*, 61.
3. Jussi Björling, "Good Singing is Natural," 655.
4. Schipa, *Don Giovanni*, Andromeda ANDRCD 9026.
5. Jackson, *Saturday Afternoons*, 65.
6. McCormack, "Il mio tesoro," Victor 74484.
7. Anders, "Folget der Heissgeliebten," Telefunken E1796.
8. Valletti, "Il mio tesoro," Urania 22.236.
9. Domingo, "Il mio tesoro," EMI 5 75909 2.
10. Recent research suggests that this may have been related to his heart condition: see Rosenqvist, "Jussi Björlings hjärta," 874–76.
11. Wunderlich, "Dies Bildnis," EMI 5 75915 2.
12. Urlus, "Dies Bildnis," Gramophone 042339.
13. Tauber, "Dies Bildnis," Parlophone PMB1011.
14. Rosvænge, *Don Giovanni*, EMI CHS 7 61034 2.

Chapter Seventeen

1. An exception to this may have been the role of Ramerrez, which seems made to measure for the voice of Enrico Caruso, who was engaged for the world première of *La fanciulla del West* at the Metropolitan in December 1910.
2. Gara, *Carteggi Pucciniani*, 548.
3. Kurt Atterberg, *Stockholms-Tidningen*, October 21, 1934.

4. Ludovico Ariosto, *Orlando Furioso,* canto XII, verse 41 (Turin: Società Editrice Internazionale, 1939), 176.
5. Gigli, "Donna non vidi mai," Victor 1213.
6. Di Stefano, *Manon Lescaut,* EMI CDS 7 47393 8.
7. Anselmi, "Donna non vidi mai," Fonotipia 62398.
8. De Lucia, "Donna non vidi mai," Phonotype 1793.
9. Garbin, "Donna non vidi mai," Fonotipia 39116.
10. Pertile, "Donna non vidi mai," Columbia 15625.
11. Gara, *Carteggi Pucciniani,* 535.
12. Caruso, "Donna non vidi mai," Victor 87138.
13. Martinelli, "Donna non vidi mai," Victor 64410.
14. Hislop, "Aldrig jag hennes like," HMV DA 1083.
15. Hislop, "Bland er alla, nätta, blona och brunetta," HMV DA 1084.
16. Francesco Merli, *Manon Lescaut,* Phonographe PH 5006/07.
17. Review available through *Metopera Database: The Metropolitan Opera Archives,* accessed September 18, 2011, http://archives.metoperafamily.org/archives/frame.htm.
18. Frankenstein, *San Francisco Chronicle,* October 3, 1949.
19. Lauri Volpi, "No, pazzo son," HMV DA 1385.
20. Hope-Wallace, "Manon Lescaut," *Gramophone,* February 1956, 64.
21. Prévost, *Manon Lescaut,* 286.
22. Del Monaco, *Manon Lescaut,* Decca 475 9385.
23. Seymour Raven, *Chicago Tribune,* October 22, 1957.
24. Björling and Farkas, *Jussi,* 299.
25. An in-house recording, using a different microphone, has been published in part by Caprice (CAP 22051, 2010, compact disc).
26. Björling and Farkas, *Jussi,* 321.
27. This aria is missing from the radio broadcast; the Opera Depot OD 10190-2 release replaces it with the performance from the 1954 RCA recording. The original version of the aria can be heard on Caprice CAP 22051, as cited in note 26 above).
28. See Elisabeth Söderström's comment on page 145.
29. See Stenius, *Tills vingen brister,* 405–13.
30. Porter, *Music of Three Seasons,* 96.
31. Moses Pergament, *Svenska Daglbladet,* October 14, 1934.
32. Desmond Shawe-Taylor, *Sunday Times,* March 13, 1960.
33. This performance, on December 15, was the first occasion on which Björling sang this music in Italian.
34. Gara, *Carteggi Pucciniani,* 128.
35. Gigli, "Che gelida manina," HMV DB 1538.
36. Alagna, *La bohème,* Decca 466 070-2.
37. De Lucia, "Che gelida manina," Phonotype 1767.
38. Douglas, *Legendary Voices,* 6.
39. Lugo, "Que cette main est froide," Polydor 566139.
40. Fleta, "Che gelida manina," HMV DB1034.
41. Bergonzi, "Che gelida manina," Decca 440 417-2.
42. Amis, "Elisabeth Söderström," 49.

43. Caruso, "Che gelida manina," Victor 88002.
44. Schipa, "Che gelida manina," Grammofono 052422.
45. Peerce, *La bohème,* RCA GD60288.
46. Groos and Parker, *La Bohème,* 71.
47. Björling and Farkas, *Jussi,* 113.
48. Gigli, *La bohème,* Naxos 8.110072-73.
49. Pavarotti, *La bohème,* Decca 421 049-2.
50. See Jackson, *Saturday Afternoons,* 389.
51. Ardoin, *Callas at Juilliard,* 269.
52. Di Stefano, "Che gelida manina," Bongiovanni GB 1141-2.
53. Di Stefano, *La bohème,* EMI CDS 7 47475 8.
54. Raimondi, *La bohème,* DG B0004767-09.
55. Gigli, "O soave fanciulla," HMV DB 271.
56. All the surviving extracts from the scene have been restored and will be released on CD by Immortal Performances.
57. Bruce Burroughs, liner notes to *Producer's Showcase, vol. 1,* VAI 4244.
58. Kolodin, "Beecham on *Bohème,*" 27.
59. Raimondi, "Che gelida manina," Elsa Music ELM 203.
60. Harald Henrysson, liner note to *Jussi Björling Sings Puccini,* Bluebell ABCD 078.
61. Hope-Wallace, *Opera,* May 1960, 363.
62. Baxter, "Jussi Björling (1911–1960)," 188.
63. Björling and Farkas, *Jussi,* 101.
64. Nyblom, "Jussi Björling," 34.
65. De Lucia, "Recondita armonia," Phonotype 2157.
66. Anselmi, "Recondita armonia," Fonotipia XPh 2604.
67. Vickers, "Recondita armonia," VAIA 1016.
68. Caruso, "Recondita armonia," Victor 87043.
69. Domingo, *Tosca,* EMI 5 66504 2.
70. De Lucia, "E lucevan le stelle," Phonotype 2233.
71. Fleta, "E lucevan le stelle," Victor 950.
72. Caruso, "E lucevano le stelle," Victor 81028.
73. Ricci, *Puccini,* 89–90.
74. Di Stefano, *Tosca,* EMI CDS 7 47175 8.
75. Bergonzi, "E lucevano le stelle," Decca 440 417-2.
76. Björling and Farkas, *Jussi,* 284.
77. Burroughs, "Milanov and Floria Tosca," 710.
78. Ibid.
79. Bergonzi, "Qual occhio al mondo," Bongiovanni GB 1106-2.
80. Gigli, *Tosca,* Grammofono 2000 AB 78591/92.
81. Corelli, *Tosca,* Urania URN 221.314.
82. De Marchi, "Vittoria! Vittoria!," Symposium 1284.
83. Ricci, *Puccini,* 105.
84. Burroughs, "Milanov and Floria Tosca," 726–28.
85. Osborne, "Tosca," 417.
86. Burroughs, "Milanov and Floria Tosca."
87. Ricci, *Puccini,* 112.
88. Björling, Farkas, *Jussi,* 309.

89. Gigli, *Madama Butterfly*, Naxos 8.110183-84.
90. Pavarotti, *Madama Butterfly*, Decca 417 577-2.
91. Di Stefano, *Madama Butterfly*, EMI CDS 7 49575 2.
92. Caruso, "O quanti occhi fisi," Victor 89017.
93. Bergonzi, *Madama Butterfly*, EMI 56788855.
94. Gedda, *Madama Butterfly*, EMI 7479598.
95. Björling and Farkas, *Jussi*, 110.
96. Bassi, "Ch'ella mi creda," Pathé 86390.
97. Zenatello, "Ch'ella mi creda," Fonotipia 92851.
98. Pertile, "Ch'ella mi creda," Pathé 88413.
99. Patzak, "Lasset sie glauben," Grammophon 90182.
100. Celli, Pugliese, *Tullio Serafin*, 86.
101. Öhman, "Ch'ella mi creda," Bluebell ABCD 080.
102. Ricci, *Puccini*, 150.
103. The others are "Questa o quella," "Di quella pira,""Di' tu se fedele," "Vesti la giubba."
104. Del Monaco, *La fanciulla del West*, Decca 475 9385.
105. Giacomini, "Ch'ella mi creda," Bongiovanni GB 2526-2.
106. Di Stefano, "Ch'ella mi creda," EMI 7 63105 2.
107. Padoan and Tiberi, *Giovanni Martinelli*, 75.
108. Gara, *Carteggi pucciniani*, 556.
109. Ibid.
110. HMV made a live recording of the world premiere production, but it was technically defective and never released. See Greenfield, "Turandot," 618.
111. Lázaro, "Nessun dorma!," Columbia D 18000.
112. Cortis, "Nessun dorma!," HMV DA 1075.
113. Valente, "Nessun dorma!," HMV B 2458.
114. Pertile, "Nessun dorma!," Fonotipia 6024.
115. Thill, "Nessun dorma!," Columbia 14544.
116. Merli, "Nessun dorma!," Columbia 1139.
117. Pavarotti, *Turandot*, Decca 414 2742.
118. Martinelli, "Nessun dorma!," Dutton SJB 1032.
119. Gigli, "Nessun dorma!," HMV DB 21138.
120. De Palma, *Turandot*, Naxos 8.111334-35.
121. Nilsson, *La Nilsson*, 226.
122. Di Stefano, *Turandot*, Orfeo C 757 0821.
123. Douglas, *Legendary Voices*, 3.
124. Corelli, *Turandot*, Myto MCD 982 181.
125. Pavarotti, *Turandot*, Legato LCD 188-2.

Chapter Eighteen

1. Björling and Farkas, *Jussi*, 144.
2. The three songs were dedicated to the baritone Sven-Olof Sandberg.

Chapter Nineteen

1. A copy of Björling's *Barbiere* score is to be found in the Jussi Björling Museum in Borlänge.
2. Björling, *Med bagaget*, 84.
3. Björling and Farkas, *Jussi*, 66.
4. Pavarotti, "La danza," Decca 000320809.
5. Caruso, "La danza," Victor 88355.
6. Gigli, "La danza," HMV DA 1650.
7. Björling, *Med bagaget*, 84.
8. Caruso, "Cuius animam," Victor 88460.
9. Gigli, "Cuius animam," HMV DB 1831.
10. Pavarotti, *Stabat Mater*, Hunt LSMH 34026.
11. Grigolo, "Cuius animam," Youtube, accessed September 18, 2011, http://www.youtube.com/watch?v=Ft3PUVNrWd0.

Chapter Twenty

1. Porter, "Björling at Carnegie Hall," 20.
2. The baritone Hermann Prey recalled this cultural climate in his autobiography: "I remember that in those early years I would do anything to avoid appearing emotional or sentimental." See Prey, *First Night Fever*, 77–78.
3. Björling and Farkas, *Jussi*, 264.
4. Schlusnus, "Die Forelle," Grammophon 62855.
5. Wunderlich, "Die Forelle," DG 9806790.
6. Hugo Riemann, in his *Musik-Lexicon* (1882), was typical in suggesting that "a slight urging, pressing forward is in place when the musical development becomes more intense." See Philip, *Early Recordings and Musical Style*, 7.
7. Schlusnus, "Frühlingsglaube," Grammophon 62795.
8. Wunderlich, "Frühlingsglaube," DG 447 452-2.
9. Fischer-Dieskau, "An die Leier," DG 463 504-2.
10. Schiøtz, *Die schöne Müllerin*, Danacord DACOCD 452.
11. Horowitz, *Understanding Toscanini*, 244.
12. Virgil Thompson, "This Side Perfection," *New York Herald Tribune*, March 22, 1948.
13. Gedda, "Die Allmacht," Orfeo C 508 011B.
14. Scheppan, "Die Allmacht," Membran 223210303.
15. David Björling, *Hjur man skall sjunga*, 6.
16. Wunderlich, "An Sylvia," DG 9806790.
17. Björling and Farkas, *Jussi*, 65.
18. Tauber, "Ständchen," Odeon 0-8160.
19. Gigli, "Ständchen," HMV DA 1657/1658.
20. Güra, "Ständchen," Harmonia Mundi HMC 901931.
21. Anders, "Ständchen," Membran 232166.
22. Schlusnus, "Ständchen," Grammophon 67181.

23. Fischer-Dieskau, "Ständchen," EMI 5 75922 2.
24. Souzay, "Ständchen," Testament SBT 1313.
25. Crooks, "Serenade," Victor 2175-9.

Chapter Twenty-One

1. Björling, *Med bagaget*, 153.
2. Björling and Farkas, *Jussi*, 215.
3. Ibid.
4. Ekman, "Svarta rosor," Gramophone 83623.
5. Quoted on Vesa Sirén, ed., *The Jean Sibelius Website*, "The Singers," accessed September 18, 2011, http://www.sibelius.fi/english/musiikki/laulut_7.htm.
6. Gedda, "Svarta rosor," Arkadia GI 806.1.
7. Forsell, "Svarta rosor," Gramophone 2-82720.
8. Souzay, "Säv, säv, susa," Youtube, accessed September 18, 2011, http://www.youtube.com/watch?v=eLnM4Hle-sg&playnext=1&list=PL8F6BA019367001B3.
9. Flagstad, "Demanten på marssnön," Australian Eloquence 4801804.
10. Arkhipova, "The Tryst," Youtube, accessed September 18, 2011, http://www.youtube.com/watch?v=SqW34AfIGZA.

Chapter Twenty-Two

1. Blyth, *Song on Record 1*, 300.
2. Schlusnus, "Zueignung," Grammophon 14120r.
3. Tauber, "Zueignung," Odeon Rxx 76755.
4. Patzak, "Ständchen," Rococo 5348.
5. Patzak, "Ständchen," Grammophon 23923.
6. Melchior, "Cäcilie," Polydor 66440.
7. Patzak, "Morgen," BASF 10.22055-9.
8. Tauber, "Morgen," Odeon 80082.
9. Tauber, "Traum durch die Dämmerung," Odeon Rxx 80451.

Chapter Twenty-Three

1. All these totals include secondary roles and baritone parts.
2. Celletti, *Le grandi voci*, 454–57.
3. Kaplan, "Bits and Pieces about Jussi," 5.
4. The most famous of these is *Voci parallele*, in which Lauri Volpi compares some of the greatest voices of the nineteenth and twentieth centuries, relegating Jussi Björling to a mere footnote.
5. Monaldi, *Cantanti celebri del secolo XIX*, 120.
6. Bergonzi, in conversation with the author, January 2009.

7. Celletti, *Il Teatro d'Opera in Disco.*
8. Celli and Pugliese, *Tullio Serafin,* 74.
9. Björling and Farkas, *Jussi,* 215.
10. *Nya Dagligt Allehanda,* February 26, 1932.
11. Caruso, "La donna è mobile," Victor 87017.
12. Gigli, "La donna è mobile," HMV DA 1372.
13. Björling considered Tibbett the finest American singer he ever performed with (Kaplan, "Bits and Pieces about Jussi," 5).
14. Caruso, "Questa o quella," Victor 87018.
15. Marconi, "Questa o quella,"G&T 52788.
16. Schipa, "Questa o quella," Pathé 10242.
17. De Lucia, *Rigoletto,* Phonotype 1911-1931.
18. Di Stefano, "Questa o quella," Fono Enterprise FONO 063.
19. Cortis, "Questa o quella," HMV DA 1153.
20. Gigli, "Questa o quella," Bongiovanni GB 1189/91-2.
21. See Björling and Farkas, *Jussi,* 97.
22. Borgioli, *Rigoletto,* Phonographe PH5036/37.
23. *The Sun,* November 30, 1945.
24. Pavarotti, *Rigoletto,* Decca 414 269-2.
25. *San Francisco Examiner,* September 29, 1951.
26. Schipa, "Parmi veder le lagrime," Gramophone 252143/4.
27. Kraus, *Rigoletto,* Ricordi ACDOC 264.
28. Caruso, "Parmi vedere la lagrime," Victor 88429.
29. The Neapolitan tenor's most famous recording of the Quartet was made in 1917 (Caruso, "Bella figlia dell'amore," Victor 95100).
30. *Chicago Tribune,* November 16, 1958.
31. Atterberg, *Stockholms Tidningen,* August 18, 1935.
32. Caruso, "Di quella pira," Victor 87001.
33. The words Björling, and most other twentieth-century tenors, sang in this aria were less logical than those originally set to music by Verdi: see Gossett, *Divas and Scholars,* 365–67.
34. A rare exception was Francesco Signorini (1861–1927). See Signorini, "Ah sì, ben mio," Gramophone 2-52669.
35. Jadlowker, "Ah si, ben mio,"Gramophone 042482.
36. Völker, "Das nur für mich dein Herz erlebt," Grammophon 95377.
37. Rosvænge, "Das nur für mich dein Herz erlebt," HMV DB 4524.
38. Bohm, *Herald Tribune,* December 4, 1949.
39. Tamagno, "Deserto sulla terra," G&T 7-52277.
40. Schmidt, "Einsam steh ich und verlassen," BelAge BLA 103.004.
41. Pertile, *Il trovatore,* Deltadischi DPR 2002; Merli, *Il trovatore,* Arkadia 78033.
42. Pertile, "Mal reggendo all'aspro assalto," Fonotipia R.20047.
43. Bergonzi, *Il trovatore,* DG 435 055-2.
44. Padoan and Tiberi, *Giovanni Martinelli,* 188.
45. Gilion, "Ah sì, ben mio," Fontipia 39653.
46. Cortis, "Ah sì, ben mio," HMV DA 1155.
47. Pavarotti, *Il trovatore,* Decca 430 694-2.
48. Björling and Farkas, *Jussi,* 150.

49. Winkelmann, "Einsam steh ich und verlassen," Berliner 1528A.
50. Björling and Farkas, *Jussi*, 230.
51. Del Monaco, "Di quella pira," Decca 480 0150.
52. See Stefan Johansson's booklet notes accompanying Caprice CAP 22051.
53. This was the title of Celli's article as translated by Herbert Weinstock in *The Saturday Review*, January 31, 1959.
54. Three years later Björling's memory of the soprano's singing was so vivid that "mention of Callas brought from him a burst of song, to demonstrate how precisely and beautifully she sang opposite Jussi in *Trovatore*." *Chicago Daily News*, March 15, 1958.
55. *Nya Dagligt Allehanda*, January 7, 1933.
56. *Nya Dagligt Allehanda*, August 30, 1939.
57. Verdi, *La traviata*, Marston 52043-2.
58. Dani, "Amor è palpito dell'universo," Romophone 81027.
59. Gigli, *La traviata*, Arkadia GA 2019.
60. See Björling and Farkas, *Jussi*, 339–48, for a full account of events.
61. Ibid., 247.
62. Björling, *Med bagaget*, 165.
63. Caruso, "Dì tu se fedele," Victor 87091.
64. Stockman, "O säg, när på skummande vågor," HMV V162.
65. Rosvænge, "O sag, wenn ich fahr," HMV DB 4445.
66. Di Stefano, *Un ballo in maschera*, EMI 5 67981 2.
67. Pavarotti, *Un ballo in maschera*, Decca 410 210-2.
68. Zenatello, "Oh qual soave brivido," Fonotipia 39665/66.
69. Caruso, "Forse la soglia," Victor 89077.
70. Pertile, "Forse la soglia," Fonotipia 74974.
71. Bergonzi, *Un ballo in maschera*, RCA CD86645.
72. Caruso, "È scherzo od è follia," Victor 89076.
73. Gigli, *Un ballo in maschera*, Naxos 8.110178-79.
74. Bonci, "È scherzo od è follia," Columbia GQX 1048.
75. Martinelli, *Un ballo in maschera*, Eklipse EKR CD 12.
76. Farkas, "Björling and Ballo," 190–203.
77. Vickers, *Un ballo in maschera*, Royal Opera House ROHS009.
78. Zenatello, "Dì tu se fedele," Odeon 40250.
79. Slezak, "O sag, wenn ich fahr," Gramophone 3-42930.
80. See Gossett, "Verdi's Ideas on Interpreting his Operas," 403.
81. This passage can be heard in Tucker, *Un ballo in maschera*, GOP 66.326.
82. Scampini, "Dì tu se fedele," Gramophone 2-52616.
83. Björling himself used this expression to describe his lifestyle (Björling and Farkas, *Jussi*, 314).
84. Ibid., 201.
85. Caruso, "Solenne in quest'ora," Victor 89001.
86. Harald Henrysson, "David Björling: Swedish Tenor," 1: 17.
87. Gilion, "Solenne in quest'ora," Fonotipia 92663.
88. Hansen, "Solenne in quest'ora," Odeon X118031.
89. Jadlowker, "Solenne in quest'ora," Grammophon 2-054056.
90. Di Stefano, *La forza del destino*, Orfeo C681 0621.

91. Del Monaco, *La forza del destino*, Aura LRC 1124-2.
92. Gigli, "Solenne in quest'ora," Victor 8069.
93. Corelli, *La forza del destino*, Golden Age of Opera GAO 151/52/53.
94. Richard Tucker, *La forza del destino*, RCA GD8971.
95. Bing, *5000 Nights*, 148.
96. Ibid., 167–68.
97. Review available through *Metopera Database: The Metropolitan Opera Archives*, accessed September 18, 2011, http://archives.metoperafamily.org/Imgs/DonCarlo1950.htm.
98. Ibid.
99. De Muro, "Io l'ho perduta," HMV 052429.
100. Domingo, *Don Carlo*, Hunt 582.
101. Carreras, *Don Carlo*, EMI 7 69304 2.
102. Vickers, "Io la vidi," VAIA 1016.
103. Jadlowker, "Io l'ho perduta,"Gramophone 13199.
104. Corelli, *Don Carlo*, Myto MCD 983.189.
105. Caruso, "Dio, che nell'alma infondere," Victor 89064.
106. Martinelli, "Dio, che nell'alma infondere," Victor 89160.
107. Filippeschi, *Don Carlo*, Naxos 8.111132-34.
108. Farrar, *All Good Greetings*, 141.
109. Völker, "Süsse Bilder des Glückes entschwanden," Koch Schwann 3-1460-2.
110. Jackson, *Sign-Off for the Old Met*, 10.
111. That year he had also received the *Musical America* Award of Achievement as "Radio's Foremost Man Singer."
112. Bruce Burroughs, "In Review: Met Stars Sing Verdi," 172.
113. Picchi, *Don Carlo*, Fonit Cetra CDO 25.
114. *Rassegna Melodrammatica*, January 7, 1900.
115. Moses Pergament, *Svenska Dagbladet*, 13 October 1935.
116. Ibid.
117. Björling, *Med bagaget*, 77.
118. See Blyth, *Opera on Record*, 312.
119. Domingo, "Celeste Aida," Teldec 3984-23292-2.
120. Tucker, *Aida*, Urania 22.244.
121. Vickers, "Celeste Aida," Decca 460 765-2.
122. Bergonzi, "Celeste Aida," Philips 432 486-2.
123. Pertile, *Aida*, Deltadischi DPR 2004.
124. Caruso, "Celeste Aida," Victor 88127.
125. See examples from Cimarosa's *Sacrificio d'Adamo* in Garcia, *Trattato completo dell'arte del canto*, 86.
126. See Tucker, *Aida*, Naxos 8.111240-41.
127. Corelli, *Aida*, EMI 58645.
128. Lauri Volpi, "Pur ti riveggo," Victor 8160/8206.
129. Di Stefano, *Aida*, IDIS 6565/66.
130. Lindi, *Aida*, VAIA 1083-2.
131. Caruso, "La fatal pietra," Victor 89028.
132. See Rosen, *Verdi: Requiem*, 16.
133. Gedda, *Messa da Requiem*, EMI 5 67560 2.

134. Caruso, "Ingemisco,"Victor 88514.
135. Marconi, "Ingemisco," G&T 052057.
136. Gigli, *Messa da Requiem,* Pearl GEMM 9162.
137. Pavarotti, *Messa da Requiem,* Decca 475 7735.
138. Rosen, *Verdi: Requiem,* 16.
139. See Voghera, *Tullio Voghera,* my father."
140. Di Stefano, *Messa da Requiem,* RCA GD 60326.
141. Björling and Farkas, *Jussi,* 127.
142. Prandelli, *Messa da Requiem,* IDIS 345/46.
143. Sachs, ed., *Lettere di Arturo Toscanini,* 494.
144. Björling and Farkas, *Jussi,* 69.
145. Sachs, *Toscanini,* 304.
146. Blyth, *Choral Music on Record,* 188.
147. Douglas, *Legendary Voices,* 17.
148. Björling, *Med bagaget,* 84–85.
149. Caruso, "Sì, pel ciel marmoreo giuro," Victor 89075.
150. Björling and Farkas, *Jussi,* 210.
151. Ibid., 357–58.
152. Tamagno, "Sì, pel ciel marmoreo giuro,"G&T Matrix 19.
153. McCracken, "Sì, pel ciel marmoreo giuro," VAI 4280.
154. Lauri Volpi, "Sì, per ciel marmoreo giuro," HMV DB 5416.
155. Björling and Farkas, *Jussi,* 210.
156. Del Monaco, *Otello,* Myto MCD 944.107.

Chapter Twenty-Four

1. Björling and Farkas, *Jussi,* 132.
2. Kónya, *Lohengrin,* Myto MCD 890.02.
3. Völker, "In fernem Land," Grammophon 19711.
4. Melchior, "In fernem Land," Victor 17726.
5. After hearing the baritone Mattia Battistini—arguably Italy's finest male exponent of *bel canto* in that era—sing the Herald in *Lohengrin* in Rome in 1880, the composer was eager for him to take on the roles of Wolfram in *Tannhäuser* and the Dutchman.
6. Pertile, "Da voi lontan," Fonotipia 120.000.

Chapter Twenty-Five

1. Henrysson, "Chronology," in Forsell et al., *Jussi,* 228–36.
2. Björling, "Sommarglädje," Bluebell ABCD 066.
3. David Björling, *Hur man skall sjunga,* 7.
4. Lawrence, "Children's Singing," 222–23.
5. David Björling, *Hur man skall sjunga,* 8.
6. Meyer, "Björling's Vocal Training," 7.

7. Björling, *Med bagaget*, 154.
8. Ibid., 125.
9. Gedda, "Heut' Nacht hab' ich geträumt von dir," EMI 56095.
10. Fleta, "Ay, ay, ay,"Gramophone Co. DB 1483.
11. Fleta, "De grandes perlas," Gramophone Co. DB 1518.
12. Kozlovsky, "Ne shchest' almazov," Melodiya D 01480/87.
13. Björling was also a brilliant mimic, offering once a hilarious parody of the great soprano Luisa Tetrazzini (Marguerite Wenner-Gren, *Minnesbok*, 151).
14. D'Arkor, "Oh! ne t'éveille pas encor," Columbia LB 160-2.
15. McCormack, "Angels guard thee," Victor 88483.
16. De Lucia, "Ideale," G&T 52410.
17. Caruso, "L'alba separa dalla luce l'ombra," Victor 87272.
18. Björling and Farkas, *Jussi*, 190.
19. Tauber, "Es muss ein Wunderbares sein," Odeon 8353.
20. De Lucia, "Pietà Signore," Phonotype 1879; Caruso, "Pietà Signore," Victor 88599.
21. Björling, "Tonerna." Naxos 8.110791, compact disc.
22. Crooks, "Jeanie With the Light Brown Hair," HMV DA 1599.
23. Valletti, "In the Silence of the Night," Testament SBT2-1413.
24. Lanza, "M'apparì," Naxos 8.120547.
25. Caruso, "M'apparì," Victor 88001.
26. Raimondi, "Ah! non credevi tu," Bongiovanni GB 1187-2.
27. De Lucia, "Ah! non credevi tu," G&T 2-52518.
28. In an interview with Jay S. Harrison in the *New York Herald Tribune* on March 15, 1958, Björling recalls the effect created by Giovanni Martinelli in *Otello*: "He sang like a trumpet from the beginning of the opera to the end. And always the sound was beautiful. I could never do that."
29. His finest recording of the aria (Stockholm, 1957) can be heard in the box set *Jussi Björling: The Complete RCA Album Collection*, RCA 88697748922.
30. De Lucia, "Amor ti vieta," G&T 52436.
31. Caruso, "Amor ti vieta," G&T 52439.
32. Björling, *Med bagaget*, 69.
33. Ferraro et al., *Francesco Cilea*, 38.
34. Schipa, "È la solita storia del pastore," Victor 1362.
35. Caruso, "Cielo e mar," Victor 85055.
36. Bergonzi, "Cielo e mar," Decca 430 042 2.
37. Hagman, *Minnesbok*, 144–45.
38. Lemeshev, "Kuda, kuda," LYS 0010.
39. Kozlovsky, "Kuda, kuda," Arkadia 78064.

Chapter Twenty-Six

1. Hagman, *Minnesbok*, 144–45.
2. One hears clear echoes of Björling in the recordings of the baritone Håkan Hagegård.
3. See Rolf Björling, Bluebell ABCD 111.

DISCOGRAPHY

A complete and continually updated discography of Jussi Björling's live and studio recordings—the result of a lifetime's research by Harald Henrysson—is accessible on the website of the Jussi Björling Museum in Borlänge, Sweden: http://www.borlange.se/templates/BlgUnitStartPage____6972.aspx. The discography below gives further information on all the recordings cited in the notes and is divided into two sections. The first lists recordings of singers who are compared with Björling in the course of this study. The second lists other cited recordings, including two of the principal compendiums of songs, arias, and duets performed by Björling.. For pre-1950 studio recordings (with the exception of complete operas) I give the catalogue number of the original shellac discs. For all other recordings I indicate the CD or DVD release that I used for my comparisons.

Recordings of Other Singers

Alagna, Roberto. Gounod, *Faust.* With Angela Gheorghiu, Bryn Terfel, Simon Keenlyside. Chorus and Orchestra of the Royal Opera House, cond. Antonio Pappano. EMI 6 31611 9, DVD. Recorded 2004.

———. Gounod, *Roméo et Juliette.* With Angela Gheorghiu, Simon Keenlyside. Chorus and Orchestra of the Théâtre du Capitole, cond. Michel Plasson. EMI 7 47365 8, compact disc. Recorded 1995.

———. Leoncavallo, *Pagliacci.* With Svetla Vassileva, Alberto Mastromarino, Enrico Marrucci. Chorus and Orchestra of the Verona Arena, cond. Viekoslav Sutej. DG 983 926-6, DVD. Recorded 2002.

———. Massenet, *Manon.* With Angela Gheorghiu. Chorus and Orchestra of the Monnaie, cond. Antonio Pappano. EMI 5 57005 2, compact disc. Recorded 1999.

———. Puccini, *La bohème.* With Angela Gheorghiu. La Scala Chorus and Orchestra, cond. Riccardo Chailly. Decca 466 070-2, compact disc. Recorded 1998.

Anders, Peter. Beethoven, "Adelaide." Pf. Michael Raucheisen. Membran 232116, compact disc. Recorded 1942.

———. Mozart, *Don Giovanni*, "Folget der Heissgeliebten." Orchestra of the Deutsche Oper, cond. Hans Schmidt-Issertedt. Telefunken E1796, shellac disc. Recorded 1935.

———. Schubert, "Standchen." Pf. Günther Weissenborn. Membran 232166, compact disc. Recorded 1954.

Anselmi, Giuseppe. Donizetti, *L'elisir d'amore*, "Una furtiva lagrima." Fonotipia 62272, shellac disc. Recorded 1907.

———. Leoncavallo, *Pagliacci*, "Vesti la giubba." Fonotipia 62160, shellac disc. Recorded 1907.

———. Puccini, *Manon Lescaut*, "Donna non vidi mai." Pf. Vincenzo Bellezza. Fonotipia 62398, shellac disc. Recorded 1909.

———. Puccini, *Tosca*, "Recondita armonia." Fonotipia 62185, shellac disc. Recorded 1907.

Ansseau, Fernand. Gounod, *Faust*, "Mais ce Dieu." With Marcel Journet. HMV DB 136 shellac disc. Recorded 1929.

Arkhipova, Irina. Sibelius, "The Tryst." Youtube, accessed September 18, 2011. http://www.youtube.com/watch?v=SqW34AfIGZA. Recording date unknown.

Bassi, Amedeo. Puccini, *La fanciulla del West*, "Ch'ella mi creda." Pathé 86390, shellac disc. Recorded 1912.

Bergonzi, Carlo. Donizetti, *L'elisir d'amore*. With Renata Scotto, Giuseppe Taddei, Carlo Cava. Chorus and Orchestra of the Maggio Musicale, cond. Gianandrea Gavazzeni. Hardy Classic Video HR 4129/30, DVD. Recorded 1967.

———. Leoncavallo, *Pagliacci*, "Vesti la giubba." Bavarian Radio Orchestra, cond. Kurt Eickhorn. Bongiovanni GB1100-2, compact disc. Recorded 1970.

———. Meyerbeer, *L'Africaine*, "Ô paradis" ("O paradiso"). Orchestra of the Accademia di Santa Cecilia, cond. Gianandrea Gavazzeni. Decca 440 417-2, compact disc. Recorded 1957.

———. Puccini, *La bohème*, "Che gelida manina." Orchestra of the Accademia di Santa Cecilia, cond. Gianandrea Gavazzeni. Decca 440 417-2. Recorded 1957.

———. Puccini, *Tosca*, "E lucevano le stelle." Orchestra of the Accademia di Santa Cecilia, cond. Gianandrea Gavazzeni. Decca 440 417-2, compact disc. Recorded 1957.

———. Puccini, *Tosca*, "Qual occhio al mondo." With Eleonor Steber. Metropolitan Opera Orchestra, cond. Kurt Adler. Bongiovanni GB 1106-2, compact disc. Recorded 1959.

———. Puccini, *Madama Butterfly*. With Renata Scotto. Rome Opera Chorus and Orchestra, cond. John Barbirolli. EMI 56788855, compact disc. Recorded 1966.

———. Verdi, *Il trovatore*. With Antonietta Stella, Fiorenza Cossotto, Ettore Bastianini. La Scala Chorus and Orchestra, cond. Tullio Serafin. DG 435 055-2, compact disc. Recorded 1962.

———. Verdi, *Un ballo in maschera*. With Leontyne Price, Robert Merrill. RCA Italiana Opera Chorus and Orchestra, cond. Erich Leinsdorf. RCA CD86645, compact disc. Recorded 1966.

———. Verdi, *Aida*, "Celeste Aida." Royal Philharmonic Orchestra, cond. Lamberto Gardelli. Philips 432 486-2, compact disc. Recorded 1974.

———. Ponchielli, *La Gioconda*, "Cielo e mar." Orchestra of the Accademia di Santa Cecilia, cond. Lamberto Gardelli. Decca 430 042 2. Recorded 1967.

Björling, Gösta. Bizet, *Les pêcheurs de perles*, "Au fond du temple saint." With Erik Saedén. Swedish Radio Orchestra, cond. Stig Rybrant. Bluebell ABCD 066, compact disc. Recorded 1952.

Björling, Rolf. Extracts from *Il trovatore*, *Aida*, *Rigoletto*, *Turandot*, *Bohème*, *Pagliacci*. Royal Court Orchestra. Bluebell ABCD 111, compact disc. Recorded 1964–81.

Bonci, Alessandro. Donizetti, *L'elisir d'amore*, "Una furtiva lagrima." Columbia D 17533, shellac disc. Recorded 1913.

———. Verdi, *Un ballo in maschera*, "È scherzo od è follia." Columbia GQX 1048, shellac disc. Recorded 1926.

Borgioli, Dino. Verdi, *Rigoletto*. With Riccardo Stracciari, Mercedes Capsir. La Scala Chorus and Orchestra, cond. Lorenzo Molajoli. Phonographe PH5036/37, compact disc. Recorded 1930.

Campagnola, Leon. Massenet, *Manon*, "En fermant les yeux." Gramophone 432244, shellac disc. Recorded 1908.

Carreras, José. Mascagni, *Cavalleria rusticana*. With Montserrat Caballé, Matteo Manuguerra. Ambrosian Opera Chorus, Philharmonia Orchestra, cond. Riccardo Muti. EMI 6365022, compact disc. Recorded 1979.

———. Verdi, *Don Carlo*. With Mirella Freni, Piero Cappuccilli, Agnes Baltsa. Chorus of the Deutsche Oper, Berlin Philharmonic Orchestra, cond. Herbert von Karajan. EMI 7 69304. 2, compact disc. Recorded 1978.

Caruso, Enrico. Adam, "Cantique de Noël." Cond. Walter B. Rogers. Victor 88561, shellac disc. Recorded 1916.

———. Bizet, *Les pêcheurs de perles*, "Au fond du temple saint" ("Del tempio al limitar"). With Mario Ancona. Victor 89007, shellac disc. Recorded 1907.

———. Bizet, *Les pêcheurs de perles*, "Je crois d'entendre encore." Cond. Josef Pasternack. Victor 88580, shellac disc. Recorded 1916.

———. Bizet, *Carmen*, "La fleur que tu m'avais jetée." Victor 88208, shellac disc. Recorded 1909.

———. Donizetti, *L'elisir d'amore*, "Una furtiva lagrima." Pf. Salvatore Cottone. G&T 52346, shellac disc. Recorded 1902.

———. Donizetti, *L'elisir d'amore*, "Una furtiva lagrima." Zonophone x 1552, shellac disc. Recorded 1903.

———. Donizetti, *L'elisir d'amore*, "Una furtiva lagrima." Pf. C. H. H. Booth. Victor 81027, shellac disc. Recorded 1904.

———. Donizetti, *L'elisir d'amore*, "Una furtiva lagrima." Victor 88339, shellac disc. Recorded 1911.

———. Gounod, *Faust*, "Salut! demeure." Victor 88003, shellac disc. Recorded 1906.

———. Gounod, *Faust*, "Il se fait tard." With Geraldine Farrar. Cond. Walter B. Rogers. Victor 89031, shellac disc. Recorded 1910.

———. Gounod, *Faust*, "Mon cœur est penetré d'épouvante." Cond. Walter B. Rogers. Victor 89033, shellac disc. Recorded 1909.

———. Gounod, *Faust*, "Que voulez-vous, messieurs?" With Marcel Journet and Antonio Scotti. Cond. Walter B. Rogers. Victor 95206, shellac disc. Recorded 1910.

———. Handel, "Ombra mai fu." Cond. Josef Pasternack. Victor 88617, shellac disc. Recorded 1920.

———. Leoncavallo, *Pagliacci*. "Vesti la giubba." Victor 88061, shellac disc. Recorded 1907.

———. Leoncavallo, "Mattinata." Pf. Ruggero Leoncavallo. G&T 52034, shellac disc. Recorded 1904.

———. Mascagni, *Cavalleria rusticana*, "Siciliana." Pf. C. H. H. Booth. Victor 81030, shellac disc. Recorded 1904.

———. Mascagni, *Cavalleria rusticana*, "Addio alla madre." Victor 88458, shellac disc. Recorded 1913.

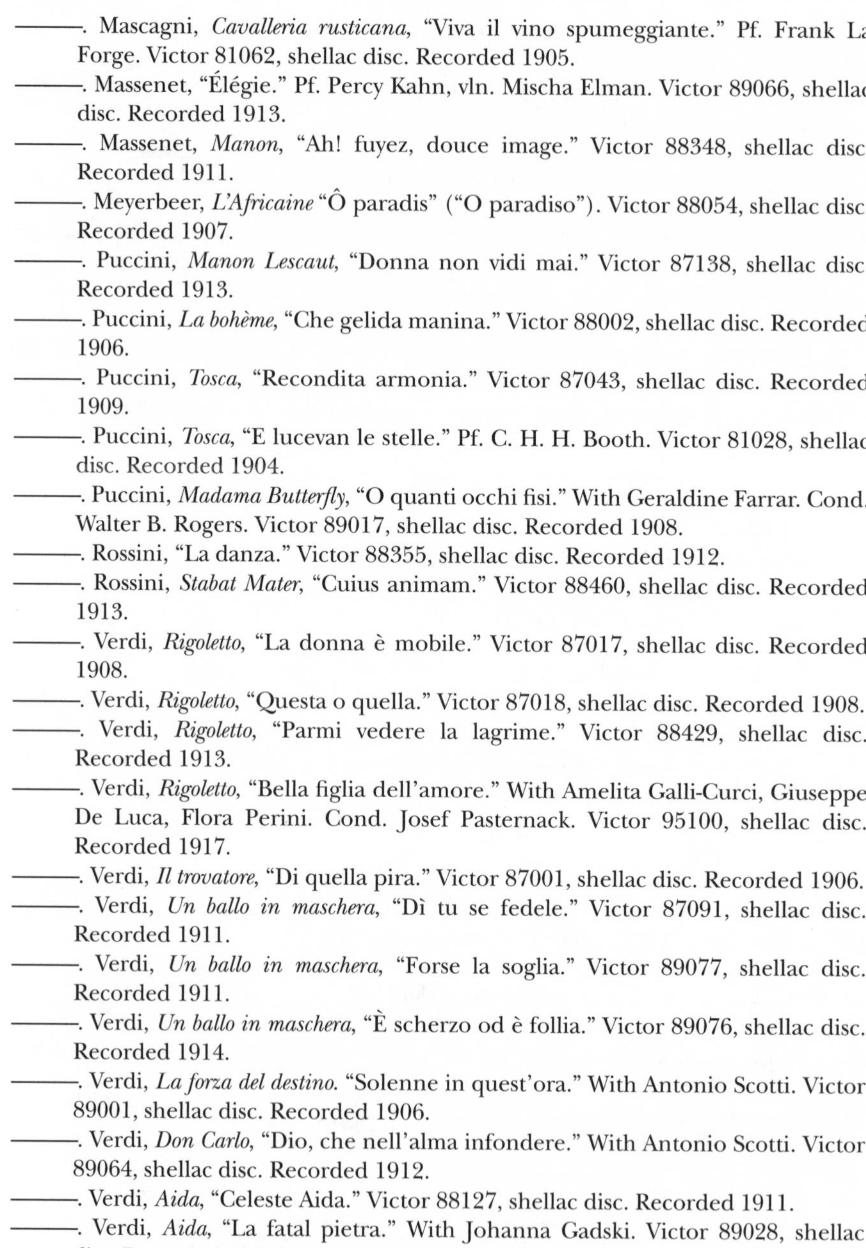

———. Mascagni, *Cavalleria rusticana,* "Viva il vino spumeggiante." Pf. Frank La Forge. Victor 81062, shellac disc. Recorded 1905.

———. Massenet, "Élégie." Pf. Percy Kahn, vln. Mischa Elman. Victor 89066, shellac disc. Recorded 1913.

———. Massenet, *Manon,* "Ah! fuyez, douce image." Victor 88348, shellac disc. Recorded 1911.

———. Meyerbeer, *L'Africaine* "Ô paradis" ("O paradiso"). Victor 88054, shellac disc. Recorded 1907.

———. Puccini, *Manon Lescaut,* "Donna non vidi mai." Victor 87138, shellac disc. Recorded 1913.

———. Puccini, *La bohème,* "Che gelida manina." Victor 88002, shellac disc. Recorded 1906.

———. Puccini, *Tosca,* "Recondita armonia." Victor 87043, shellac disc. Recorded 1909.

———. Puccini, *Tosca,* "E lucevan le stelle." Pf. C. H. H. Booth. Victor 81028, shellac disc. Recorded 1904.

———. Puccini, *Madama Butterfly,* "O quanti occhi fisi." With Geraldine Farrar. Cond. Walter B. Rogers. Victor 89017, shellac disc. Recorded 1908.

———. Rossini, "La danza." Victor 88355, shellac disc. Recorded 1912.

———. Rossini, *Stabat Mater,* "Cuius animam." Victor 88460, shellac disc. Recorded 1913.

———. Verdi, *Rigoletto,* "La donna è mobile." Victor 87017, shellac disc. Recorded 1908.

———. Verdi, *Rigoletto,* "Questa o quella." Victor 87018, shellac disc. Recorded 1908.

———. Verdi, *Rigoletto,* "Parmi vedere la lagrime." Victor 88429, shellac disc. Recorded 1913.

———. Verdi, *Rigoletto,* "Bella figlia dell'amore." With Amelita Galli-Curci, Giuseppe De Luca, Flora Perini. Cond. Josef Pasternack. Victor 95100, shellac disc. Recorded 1917.

———. Verdi, *Il trovatore,* "Di quella pira." Victor 87001, shellac disc. Recorded 1906.

———. Verdi, *Un ballo in maschera,* "Dì tu se fedele." Victor 87091, shellac disc. Recorded 1911.

———. Verdi, *Un ballo in maschera,* "Forse la soglia." Victor 89077, shellac disc. Recorded 1911.

———. Verdi, *Un ballo in maschera,* "È scherzo od è follia." Victor 89076, shellac disc. Recorded 1914.

———. Verdi, *La forza del destino.* "Solenne in quest'ora." With Antonio Scotti. Victor 89001, shellac disc. Recorded 1906.

———. Verdi, *Don Carlo,* "Dio, che nell'alma infondere." With Antonio Scotti. Victor 89064, shellac disc. Recorded 1912.

———. Verdi, *Aida,* "Celeste Aida." Victor 88127, shellac disc. Recorded 1911.

———. Verdi, *Aida,* "La fatal pietra." With Johanna Gadski. Victor 89028, shellac disc. Recorded 1909.

———. Verdi, *Messa da Requiem,* "Ingemisco." Cond. Walter B. Rogers. Victor 88514, shellac disc. Recorded 1915.

———. Verdi, *Otello,* "O mostruosa colpa!" With Titta Ruffo. Victor 89075, shellac disc. Recorded 1914.

———. Tosti, "L'alba separa dalla luce l'ombra." Victor 87272, shellac disc. Recorded 1917.

———. Giordano, *Fedora*, "Amor ti vieta." Pf. Salvatore Cottone. G&T 52439, shellac disc. Recorded 1902.

———. Flotow, *Martha*, "Ach, so fromm" ("M'apparì"). Victor 88001, shellac disc. Recorded 1917.

———. Ponchielli, *La Gioconda*, "Cielo e mar." Pf. Frank La Forge. Victor 85055, shellac disc. Recorded 1905.

———. Fétis, "Pietà Signore," Victor 88599, shellac disc. Recorded 1919.

Chaliapin, Feodor. Massenet, "Élégie." Pf. Ivor Newton, vc. Cecil Sharpe. HMV DB 1525, shellac disc. Recorded 1931.

Clément, Edmond. Bizet, *Les pêcheurs de perles*, "Au fond du temple saint." With Marcel Journet. HMV DK 105, shellac disc. Recorded 1912.

———. Gounod, *Roméo et Juliette*, "Ah! lève-toi, soleil!" Odeon 56000, shellac disc. Recorded 1905.

———, Massenet, *Manon*, "En fermant les yeux." Pf. Frank La Forge. Victor 74258, shellac disc. Recorded 1911.

Corelli, Franco. Gounod, *Roméo et Juliette*. With Mirella Freni, Henri Gui. Paris Opéra Chorus and Orchestra, cond. Alain Lombard. EMI 5 65290 2. Recorded 1968.

———. Leoncavallo, *Pagliacci*. With Lucine Amara, Tito Gobbi, Mario Zanasi. La Scala Chorus and Orchestra, cond. Lovro von Matačić. EMI CMS 763967 2, compact disc. Recorded 1960.

———. Puccini, *Tosca*. With Zinka Milanov, Giangiacomo Guelfi. Chorus and Orchestra of the Royal Opera House, cond. Alexander Gibson. Urania URN 221.314, compact disc. Recorded 1957.

———. Puccini, *Turandot*. With Birgit Nilsson, Galina Vishnevskaya. La Scala Chorus and Orchestra, cond. Gianandrea Gavazzeni. Myto MCD 982 181. Recorded 1964.

———. Verdi, *La forza del destino*. With Renata Tebaldi, Ettore Bastianini. Chorus and Orchestra of the Teatro San Carlo, cond. Francesco Molinari Pradelli. Golden Age of Opera GAO 151/52/53, compact disc. Recorded 1958.

———. Verdi, *Don Carlo*. With Gundula Janowitz, Eberhard Waechter, Shirley Verrett. Vienna State Opera Chorus and Orchestra, cond. Horst Stein. Myto MCD 983.189, compact disc. Recorded 1970.

———. Verdi, *Aida*. With Birgit Nilsson, Mario Sereni, Grace Bumbry. Rome Opera Chorus and Orchestra, cond. Zubin Mehta. EMI 58645, compact disc. Recorded 1967.

Cortis, Antonio. Puccini, *Turandot*, "Nessun dorma!" HMV DA 1075, shellac disc. Recorded 1929.

———. Verdi, *Rigoletto*, "Questa o quella." HMV DA 1153, shellac disc. Recorded 1930.

———. Verdi, *Il trovatore*, "Ah sì, ben mio." HMV DA 1155, shellac disc. Recorded 1930.

Crooks, Richard. Gounod, *Faust*. With Helen Jepson, Ezio Pinza, Leonard Warren. Metropolitan Opera Chorus and Orchestra, cond. Wilfred Pelletier. Naxos 8.110016-7, compact disc. Recorded 1940.

———. Grieg, "Jeg elsker dig" ("I love thee"). Pf. Frederick Schauwecker. Victor 2175-9, shellac disc. Recorded 1941.

———. Schubert “Ständchen” (“Serenade”). Pf. Frederick Schauwecker. Victor 2175-9. Recorded 1941.

———. Foster, “Jeanie With the Light Brown Hair.” Pf. Frank La Forge. HMV DA 1599, shellac disc. Recorded 1937.

Cura, José. Leoncavallo, *Pagliacci*. With Fiorenza Cedolins, Carlo Guelfi, Gabriel Bermudez. Chorus and Orchestra of the Zurich Opera House, cond. Stefano Ranzani. Arthaus 101 489, DVD. Recorded 2009.

Dalmorès, Charles. Bizet, *Carmen*, “La fleur que tu m’avais jetée.” Victor 85122, shellac disc. Recorded 1912.

Dani, Carlo. Verdi, *La traviata*, “Amor è palpito dell’universo.” With Marcella Sembrich. Metropolitan Opera Orchestra, cond. Luigi Mancinelli. Romophone 81027, compact disc. Recorded 1903.

D’Arkor, André. Godard, *Jocelyn*, “Oh! ne t’éveille pas encor.” Columbia LB 160-2, shellac disc. Recorded 1930.

Del Monaco, Mario. Handel, *Serse*, “Ombra mai fu.” Org. Brian Runnett. Decca 475 7269, compact disc. Recorded 1965.

———. Leoncavallo, *Pagliacci*. With Gabriella Tucci, Aldo Protti, Attilio D’Orazi. NHK Symphony Orchestra, cond. Giuseppe Morelli. VAI 4421, DVD. Recorded 1961.

———. Leoncavallo, *Pagliacci*, “Il prologo.” Orchestra of the Accademia di Santa Cecilia, cond. Albert Erede. Decca 475 7269, compact disc. Recorded 1953.

———. Puccini, *Manon Lescaut*. With Renata Tebaldi, Mario Borriello, Fernando Corena. Chorus and Orchestra of the Accademia di Santa Cecilia, cond. Francesco Molinari-Pradelli. Decca 475 9385. Recorded 1954.

———. Puccini, *La fanciulla del West*. With Renata Tebaldi, Cornell MacNeil. Chorus and Orchestra of the Accademia of Santa Cecilia, cond. Franco Capuana. Decca 475 9385. Recorded 1958.

———. Verdi, *Il trovatore*, “Di quella pira.” Chorus of the Maggio Musicale, and Orchestra of the Grand Théâtre, Geneva, cond. Alberto Erede. Decca 480 0150, compact disc. Recorded 1956.

———. Verdi, *La forza del destino*. With Renata Tebaldi, Aldo Protti. Chorus and Orchestra of the Maggio Musicale, cond. Dimitri Mitropoulos. Aura LRC 1124-2, compact disc. Recorded 1953.

———. Verdi, *Otello*. With Victoria de los Angeles, Leonard Warren. Metropolitan Opera Chorus and Orchestra of the Metropolitan Opera, cond. Fausto Cleva. Myto MCD 944.107, compact disc. Recorded 1958.

De Lucia, Fernando. Puccini, *La bohème*, “Che gelida manina.” Cond. Salvatore Sassano. Phonotype C 1767, shellac disc. Recorded 1917.

———. Donizetti, *L’elisir d’amore*, “Una furtiva lagrima.” Cond. Salvatore Sassano. Phonotype 1754-2, shellac disc. Recorded 1917.

———. Leoncavallo, *Pagliacci*, “No! Pagliaccio non son.” Cond. Salvatore Sassano. Phonotype M 1803, shellac disc. Recorded 1917.

———. Leoncavallo, *Pagliacci*, “Vesti la giubba.” Cond. Salvatore Sassano. Phonotype C 2560, shellac disc. Recorded 1921.

———. Leoncavallo, “Mattinata.” Fonotipia 29695, shellac disc. Recorded 1911.

———. Mascagni, *Cavalleria rusticana*, “Siciliana.” Pf. Salvatore Cottone. G&T 52652, shellac disc. Recorded 1902.

———. Meyerbeer, *L'Africaine,* "Ô paradis" ("O paradiso"). Cond. Salvatore Sassano. Phonotype 1766/2, shellac disc. Recorded 1917.

———. Puccini, *Manon Lescaut,* "Donna non vidi mai." Cond. Salvatore Sassano. Phonotype 1793, shellac disc. Recorded 1921.

———. Puccini, *Tosca,* "Recondita armonia." Cond. Salvatore Sassano. Phonotype 2157, shellac disc. Recorded 1919.

———. Puccini, *Tosca,* "E lucevan le stelle." Cond. Salvatore Sassano. Phonotype 2233, shellac disc. Recorded 1920.

———. Verdi, *Rigoletto.* With Antonio Armentano Anticorona, Angela De Angelis. San Carlo Chorus and Orchestra, cond. Salvatore Sassano. Phonotype 1795-1919, shellac disc. Recorded 1915–20.

———. Tosti, "Ideale." Pf. Salvatore Cottone. G&T 52410, shellac disc. Recorded 1902.

———. Thomas, *Mignon,* "Elle ne croyait pas" ("Ah! non credevi tu"). Pf. Carlo Sabajno. G&T 2-52518, shellac disc. Recorded 1906.

———. Giordano, *Fedora,* "Amor ti vieta." Pf. Salvatore Cottone. G&T 52436. Recorded 1902.

———. Fétis, "Pietà Signore." Phonotype 1879, shellac disc. Recorded 1918.

De Marchi, Emilio. Puccini, *Tosca,* "Vittoria! Vittoria!" With Emma Eames, Antonio Scotti. Metropolitan Opera Orchestra, cond. Luigi Mancinelli. Symposium 1284, compact disc. Recorded 1903.

De Muro, Bernardo. Verdi, *Don Carlo,* "Io l'ho perduta." HMV 052429, shellac disc. Recorded 1914.

De Reszke, Jean. Meyerbeer, *L'Africaine,* "Ô paradis." Metropolitan Opera Orchestra, cond. Philippe Flon. Symposium 1284, compact disc. Recorded 1901.

Devriès, David. Massenet, *Manon,* "En fermant les yeux." Odéon 188.505, shellac disc. Recorded 1927.

Di Stefano, Giuseppe. Donizetti, *L'elisir d'amore,* "Una furtiva lagrima." Bongiovanni GB 1141-2, compact disc. Recorded 1944.

———. Gounod, *Faust.* With Dorothy Kirsten, Italo Tajo, Leonard Warren. Metropolitan Opera Chorus and Orchestra, cond. Wilfred Pelletier. Arkadia 78065, compact disc. Recorded 1949.

———. Leoncavallo, *Pagliacci,* "Vesti la giubba." Royal Philharmonic Orchestra, cond. Eric Robinson. Warner 0630-15898-2, DVD. Recorded 1958.

———. Leoncavallo "Mattinata." Cond. Gian Mario Guarino. Testament SBT 1097, compact disc. Recorded 1961.

———. Mascagni, *Cavalleria rusticana.* With Maria Callas, Rolando Panerai. La Scala Chorus and Orchestra, cond. Tullio Serafin. EMI 6407222, compact disc. Recorded 1953.

———. Puccini, *Manon Lescaut.* With Maria Callas, Giulio Fioravanti, Franco Calabrese. La Scala Chorus and Orchestra, cond. Tullio Serafin. EMI CDS 7 47393 8, compact disc. Recorded 1957.

———. Puccini, *La bohème,* "Che gelida manina." Bongiovanni GB 1141-2, compact disc. Recorded 1944.

———. Puccini, *La bohème.* With Maria Callas, Rolando Panerai. La Scala Chorus and Orchestra, cond. Antonino Votto. EMI CDS 7 47475 8, compact disc. Recorded 1956.

———. Puccini, *Tosca.* With Maria Callas, Tito Gobbi. La Scala Chorus and Orchestra, cond. Victor de Sabata. EMI CDS 7 47175 8, compact disc. Recorded 1953.

———. Puccini, *Madama Butterfly.* With Victoria de los Angeles, Tito Gobbi. Rome Opera Chorus and Orchestra, cond. Gianandrea Gavazzeni. EMI CDS 7 49575 2, compact disc. Recorded 1954.

———. Puccini, *La fanciulla del West,* "Ch'ella mi creda." La Scala Orchestra, cond. Antonino Votto. EMI CDM 7 63105 2, compact disc. Recorded 1955.

———. Puccini, *Turandot.* With Birgit Nilsson, Leontyne Price. Vienna State Opera Chorus and Orchestra, cond. Francesco Molinari-Pradelli. Orfeo C 7570821, compact disc. Recorded 1961.

———. Verdi, *Rigoletto,* "Questa o quella." Chorus and Orchestra of the Palacio de Bellas Artes, cond. Renato Cellini. Fono Enterprise FONO 063, compact disc. Recorded 1948.

———. Verdi, *Un ballo in maschera.* With Maria Callas, Ettore Bastianini. La Scala Chorus and Orchestra, cond. Gianandrea Gavazzeni. EMI 5 67981 2, compact disc. Recorded 1957.

———. Verdi, *La forza del destino.* With Antonietta Stella, Ettore Bastianini. Vienna State Opera Chorus and Orchestra, cond. Dimitri Mitropoulos. Orfeo C681 0621, compact disc. Recorded 1960.

———. Verdi, *Aida.* With Antonietta Stella, Giangiacomo Guelfi, Giulietta Simionato. La Scala Chorus and Orchestra, cond. Antonino Votto. IDIS 6565/66, compact disc. Recorded 1956.

———. Verdi, *Messa da Requiem.* With Herva Nelli, Fedora Barbieri, Cesare Siepi. Robert Shaw Chorale, NBC Symphony Orchestra, cond. Arturo Toscanini. RCA GD 60326, compact disc. Recorded 1951.

Domingo, Placido. Gounod, *Faust.* With Mirella Freni, Nicolai Ghiaurov, Thomas Allen. Paris Opéra Chorus and Orchestra, cond. Georges Prêtre. EMI CDS7 47493, compact disc. Recorded 1978.

———. Handel "Ombra mai fu." Vln. Itzhak Perlman. New York Studio Orchestra, cond. Jonathan Tunick. EMI 54266, compact disc. Recorded 1991.

———. Mascagni, *Cavalleria rusticana,* "Addio alla madre." Orchestra of the Deutsche Oper, cond. Nello Santi. Telarc 3984-23292-2, compact disc. Recorded 1968.

———. Meyerbeer, *L'Africaine,* "Ô paradis." Orchestra of the Royal Opera House, cond. John Barker. EMI 5 75906 2. Recorded 1989.

———. Mozart, *Don Giovanni,* "Il mio tesoro." Bavarian Radio Orchestra, cond. Eugene Kohn. EMI 5 75909 2. Recorded 1991.

———. Puccini, *Tosca.* With Renata Scotto, Renato Bruson. Ambrosian Opera Chorus, Philharmonia Orchestra, cond. James Levine. EMI 5 66504 2, compact disc. Recorded 1980.

———. Verdi, *Don Carlo.* With Rita Orlandi Malaspina, Piero Cappuccilli, Shirley Verrett. La Scala Chorus and Orchestra, cond. Claudio Abbado. Hunt 582, compact disc. Recorded 1970.

———. Verdi, *Aida,* "Celeste Aida." Orchestra of the Deutsche Oper, cond. Nello Santi. Teldec 3984-23292-2, compact disc. Recorded 1968.

Ekman, Ida. Sibelius, "Svarta rosor." Pf. Karl Ekman. Gramophone 83623, shellac disc. Recorded 1906.

Filippeschi, Mario. Verdi, *Don Carlo.* With Antonietta Stella, Tito Gobbi, Elena Nicolai. Rome Opera Chorus and Orchestra, cond. Gabriele Santini. Naxos 8.111132-34. Recorded 1954.

Fischer-Dieskau, Dietrich. Beethoven, "Die Ehre Gottes aus der Natur." Pf. Jörg Demus. DG 463 507-2, compact disc. Recorded 1966.

———. Brahms, "Die Mainacht." Pf. Wolfgang Sawallisch. EMI 5 75922 2, compact disc. Recorded 1974.

———. Schubert, "An die Leier." Pf. Jörg Demus. DG 463 504-2, compact disc. Recorded 1961.

———. Schubert, "Ständchen." Pf. Gerald Moore. EMI 5 75922 2, compact disc. Recorded 1958.

Flagstad, Kirsten. Grieg, "En svane." BBC Symphony Orchestra, cond. Sir Malcolm Sargent. BBC Legends BBCL 4190-2. Recorded 1957.

———. Sibelius, "Demanten på marssnön." London Symphony Orchestra, cond. Øivin Fjeldstad. Australia Eloquence 4801804, compact disc. Recorded 1958.

Fleta, Miguel. Bizet, *Carmen,* "La fleur que tu m'avais jetée" ("Il fior che avevi a me tu dato"). HMV DB 524, shellac disc. Recorded 1922.

———. Massenet, *Manon,* "En fermant les yeux" ("Chiudo gli occhi"). HMV DB 986, shellac disc. Recorded 1927.

———. Puccini, *La bohème,* "Che gelida manina." Cond. Gelabert. HMV B1034, shellac disc. Recorded 1927.

———. Puccini, *Tosca,* "E lucevan le stelle." Cond. Rosario Bourdon. Victor 950, shellac disc. Recorded 1924.

———. Pérez-Freire, "Ay, ay, ay."Gramophone Co. DB 1483, shellac disc. Recorded 1930.

———. Rimsky-Korsakov, *Sadko,* "Ne shchest' almazov" ("De grandes perlas"). Gramophone Co. DB 1518, shellac disc. Recorded 1931.

Flórez, Juan Diego. Donizetti, *L'elisir d'amore,* "Una furtiva lagrima." Orchestra Verdi, Milan, cond. Riccardo Frizza. Decca 473 44025, compact disc. Recorded 2002.

Forsell, John. Sibelius, "Svarta rosor." Gramophone 2-82720, shellac disc. Recorded 1908.

Friant, Charles. Bizet, *Carmen,* "La fleur que tu m'avais jetée." Odéon 171.028, shellac disc. Recorded 1927.

Garbin, Edoardo. Mascagni, *Cavalleria rusticana,* "Siciliana." Fonotipia 39039, shellac disc. Recorded 1904.

———. Mascagni, *Cavalleria rusticana,* "Viva il vino spumeggiante." Fonotipia 71129, shellac disc. Recorded 1904.

———. Puccini, *Manon Lescaut,* "Donna non vidi mai." Fonotipia 39116, shellac disc. Recorded 1905.

Gedda, Nicolai. Beethoven, "Adelaide." Pf. Jan Eyron. EMI 5 85090 2, compact disc. Recorded 1969.

———. Bizet, *Les pêcheurs de perles.* With Ernest Blanc, Janine Micheau. Chorus and Orchestra of the Opéra Comique, cond. Pierre Dervaux. EMI 566020, compact disc. Recorded 1960.

———. Gounod, *Faust.* With Victoria de los Angeles, Jean Borthayre, Boris Christoff. Chorus and Orchestra of the Paris Opéra, cond. André Cluytens. EMI 565256, compact disc. Recorded 1953.

———. Gounod, *Roméo et Juliette*, "Ah! lève-toi, soleil!" Philharmonia Orchestra, cond. Alceo Galliera. EMI 85090 2, compact disc. Recorded 1954.

———. Grieg, "En svane." Pf. Geoffrey Parsons. "Northern and Russian Songs." Arkadia GI 806.1, compact disc. Recorded 1971.

———. Massenet, *Manon*, "En fermant les yeux." Philharmonia Orchestra, cond. Alceo Galliera. EMI 5 85090 2, compact disc. Recorded 1954.

———. Puccini, *Madama Butterfly*. With Maria Callas. La Scala Chorus and Orchestra, cond. Herbert von Karajan. EMI 7479598, compact disc. Recorded 1955.

———. Schubert, "Die Allmacht." Pf. Hermann Reutter. Orfeo C 508 011B. Recorded 1964.

———. Sibelius, "Svarta rosor." Pf. Geoffrey Parsons. Arkadia GI 806.1, compact disc. Recorded 1971.

———. Verdi, *Messa da Requiem*. With Elisabeth Schwarzkopf, Christa Ludwig, Nicolai Ghaiurov. Philharmonia Chorus and Orchestra, cond. Carlo Maria Giulini. EMI 5 67560 2, compact disc. Recorded 1963–64.

———. Kálmán, *Das Veilchen vom Montmartre*, "Heut' Nacht hab' ich geträumt von Cond. Willy Mattes. EMI 56095, compact disc. Recorded 1970.

Giacomini, Giuseppe. Handel, *Serse*, "Ombra mai fu" ("O mio signor"). Accademia Venezia, cond. Roberto Padoin. Phoenix PH 95105, compact disc. Recorded 1995.

———. Puccini, *La fanciulla del West*, "Ch'ella mi creda." Symphonia Perusina, cond. Guido Maria Guida. Bongiovanni GB 2526-2. Recorded 1997.

Gigli, Beniamino. Bizet, *Les pêcheurs de perles*, "Au fond du temple saint" ("Del tempio al limitar"). With Giuseppe De Luca. Cond. Rosario Bourdon. Victor 8084, shellac disc. Recorded 1927.

———. Bizet, *Les pêcheurs de perles*, "Je crois d'entendre encore" ("Mi par d'udir ancora"). Cond. Rosario Bourdon. Victor AGSB 56, shellac disc. Recorded 1929.

———. Gounod, *Faust*, "Laisse-moi" ("Dammi ancor"). With Maria Zamboni. Cond. Carlo Sabajno. HMV DB 268, shellac disc. Recorded 1919.

———. Gounod, *Roméo et Juliette*, "Ange adorable." With Lucrezia Bori. HMV 2-034033. Recorded 1923.

———. Gounod, *Roméo et Juliette*, "Ah! lève-toi soleil!" ("Ah, sorgi alfin"). La Scala Orchestra, cond. Gabriele Santini. Immortal Performances IPCD 1003-2, compact disc. Recorded 1934.

———. Gounod, *Roméo et Juliette*, "Ah! ne fui pas encore." With Lucrezia Bori. Victor 87581, shellac disc. Recorded 1923.

———. Handel, *Serse*, "Ombra mai fu." Cond. John Barbirolli. HMV DB 1901, shellac disc. Recorded 1933.

———. Leoncavallo, *Pagliacci*. With Iva Pacetti, Mario Basiola, Leone Paci. La Scala Chorus and Orchestra, cond. Franco Ghione. Naxos 8.110155, shellac disc. Recorded 1934.

———. Leoncavallo, *Pagliacci*, "Il prologo." HMV DB 05353, shellac disc. Recorded 1943.

———. Mascagni, *Cavalleria rusticana*. With Lina Bruna Rosa, Gino Bechi. La Scala Chorus and Orchestra, cond. Pietro Mascagni. Naxos 8.110714-15, compact disc. Recorded 1940.

———. Massenet, *Manon*, "En fermant les yeux" ("Chiudo gli occhi"). HMV DA 1216, shellac disc. Recorded 1931.

———. Meyerbeer, *L'Africaine*, "Ô paradis" ("O paradiso"). HMV DB1382, shellac disc. Recorded 1928.

———. Puccini, *Manon Lescaut*, "Donna non vidi mai." Victor 1213, shellac disc. Recorded 1926.

———. Puccini, *La bohème*, "Che gelida manina." HMV DB 1538, shellac disc. Recorded 1931.

———. Puccini, *La bohème*. With Licia Albanese, Afro Poli. La Scala Chorus and Orchestra, cond. Umberto Berrettoni. Naxos 8.110072-73, compact disc. Recorded 1938.

———. Puccini, *La bohème*, "O soave fanciulla." With Maria Zamboni. HMV DB 271, shellac disc. Recorded 1919.

———. Puccini, *Tosca*. With Maria Caniglia, Armando Borgioli. Rome Opera Chorus and Orchestra, cond. Oliviero de Fabritiis. Grammofono 2000 AB 78591/92, compact disc. Recorded 1938.

———. Puccini, *Madama Butterfly*. With Toti Dal Monte. Rome Opera Chorus and Orchestra, cond. Oliviero de Fabritiis. Naxos 8.110183-84, compact disc. Recorded 1939.

———. Puccini, *Turandot*, "Nessun dorma!" HMV DB 21138, shellac disc. Recorded 1949.

———. Rossini, "La danza." HMV DA 1650, shellac disc. Recorded 1938.

———. Rossini, *Stabat Mater*, "Cuius animam." HMV DB 1831, shellac disc. Recorded 1932.

———. Schubert, "Ständchen." HMV DA 1657/1658, shellac disc. Recorded 1938.

———. Verdi, *Rigoletto*, "La donna è mobile." HMV DA 1372, shellac disc. Recorded 1934.

———. Verdi, *Rigoletto*, "Questa o quella." Bongiovanni GB 1189/91-2, compact disc. Recorded 1938.

———. Verdi, *La traviata*. With Maria Caniglia, Mario Basiola. Chorus and Orchestra of the Royal Opera House, cond. Vittorio Gui. Arkadia GA 2019, compact disc. Recorded 1939.

———. Verdi, *Un ballo in maschera*. With Maria Caniglia, Gino Bechi. Rome Opera Chorus and Orchestra, cond. Tullio Serafin. Naxos 8.110178-79. Recorded 1943.

———. Verdi, *La forza del destino*, "Solenne in quest'ora." With Giuseppe De Luca. Victor 8069, shellac disc. Recorded 1927.

———. Verdi, *Messa da Requiem*. With Maria Caniglia, Ebe Stignani, Ezio Pinza. Rome Opera Chorus and Orchestra, cond. Tullio Serafin. Pearl GEMM 9162, compact disc. Recorded 1939.

Gilion, Mario. Verdi, *Il trovatore*, "Ah sì, ben mio." Fontipia 39653, shellac disc. Recorded 1906.

———. Verdi, *La forza del destino*, "Solenne in quest'ora." With Domenico Viglione Borghese. Fonotipia 926, shellac disc. Recorded 1906.

Grigolo, Vittorio. Rossini, *Stabat Mater*, "Cuius animam." Rome Opera Orchestra, cond. Gianluigi Gelmetti. Youtube, accessed September 18, 2011. http://www.youtube.com/watch?v=Ft3PUVNrWd0. Recorded 2004.

Güra, Werner. Schubert, "Ständchen." Pf. Christoph Berner. Harmonia Mundi HMC 901931. Recorded 2007.

Hackett, Charles. Gounod, *Roméo et Juliette.* With Eidé Norena, Giuseppe De Luca. Metropolitan Opera Chorus and Orchestra, cond. Louis Hasselmans. Naxos 8.110140-41, compact disc. Recorded 1935.

Hansen, Niels. Verdi, *La forza del destino,* "Solenne in quest'ora" (in Danish). With Albert Høeberg. Odeon X118031, shellac disc. Recorded 1914.

Hislop, Joseph. Gounod, *Faust* (excerpts). With Feodor Chaliapin. Orchestra of the Royal Opera House, cond. Sir Eugene Goossens. Pearl GEM 0203, compact disc. Recorded 1928.

———. Puccini, *Manon Lescaut,* "Donna non vidi mai" ("Aldrig jag hennes like"). Cond. Nils Grevillius. HMV DA 1083, shellac disc. Recorded 1929.

———. Puccini, *Manon Lescaut,* "Tra voi belle" ("Bland er alla"). Cond. Nils Grevillius. HMV DA 1084, shellac disc. Recorded 1929.

Jadlowker, Hermann. Verdi, *Il trovatore,* "Ah si, ben mio." Gramophone 042482, shellac disc. Recorded 1915.

———. Verdi, *La forza del destino,* "Solenne in quest'ora." With Joseph Schwarz. Grammophon 2-054056, shellac disc. Recorded 1918.

———. Verdi, *Don Carlo,* "Io l'ho perduta." Grammophon 13199, shellac disc. Recorded 1913.

Kónya, Sándor. Wagner, *Lohengrin.* With Leonie Rysanek, Ernest Blanc, Astrid Varnay. Bayreuth Festival Chorus and Orchestra, cond. André Cluytens. Myto MCD 890.02, compact disc. Recorded 1958.

Kozlovsky, Ivan. Borodin, *Prince Igor.* With Alexander Baturin, Sofia Panova, Alexander Pirogov, Maxim Mikjailov, Nadezhda Obukhova. Bolshoi Chorus and Orchestra, cond. Alexander Melik-Pashayev. Melodiya M10-46279/84. Recorded 1941.

———. Gounod, *Faust.* With Yelizaveta Shumskaya, Mark Reizen, Ivan Burlak. Bolshoi Chorus and Orchestra, cond. Vassily Nebolsin. LYS 301-303, compact disc. Recorded 1948.

———. Gounod, *Roméo et Juliette.* With Yelizaveta Shumskaya, Ivan Burlak. Bolshoi Chorus and Orchestra, cond. Alexander Orlov. Guild GHCD 2264/5, compact disc. Recorded 1947.

———. Leoncavallo, *Pagliacci,* "O Colombina" (in Russian). Cond. Samuil Samosud. Myto MCD 921.55, compact disc. Recorded 1952.

———. Tchaikovsky, *Eugene Onegin.* With Elena Kruglikova, Andrei Ivanov. Bolshoi Chorus and Orchestra, cond. Alexander Orlov. Arkadia 78064, compact disc. Recorded 1948.

Kraus, Alfredo. Gounod, *Faust.* With Renata Scotto, Nicolai Ghiaurov, Lorenzo Saccomani. NHK Italian Opera Chorus and Symphony Orchestra, cond. Paul Ethuin. VAI 4417. DVD. Recorded 1973.

———. "Una lezione di canto." Bongiovanni GB 550/51-2, compact disc. Recorded 1990.

———. Gounod, *Roméo et Juliette.* With Catherine Malfitano, Gino Quilico. Chorus and Orchestra of the Théâtre du Capitole, cond. Michel Plasson. EMI 7 47365 8, compact disc. Recorded 1984.

———. Massenet, "Élégie." Pf. Edelmiro Arnaltes. Amadeo 429 557-2. Recorded 1990.

———. Verdi, *Rigoletto*. With Renata Scotto, Ettore Bastianini. Chorus and Orchestra of the Maggio Musicale, cond. Gianandrea Gavazzeni. Ricordi ACDOC 264. Recorded 1959.

Lanza, Mario. Flotow, *Martha*, "Ach, so fromm" ("M'apparì"). Naxos 8.120547. Recorded 1950.

Lauri Volpi, Giacomo. Puccini, *Manon Lescaut*, "No, pazzo son." HMV DA 1385, shellac disc. Recorded 1934.

———. Verdi, *Aida*, "Pur ti riveggo." With Elisabeth Rethberg, Giuseppe De Luca. Victor 8160/8206, shellac disc. Recorded 1929.

———. Verdi, *Otello*, "Sì, per ciel marmoreo giuro." With Mario Basiola. La Scala Orchestra, cond. Gino Marinuzzi. HMV DB 5416, shellac disc. Recorded 1941.

Lázaro, Hipólito. Puccini, *Turandot*, "Nessun dorma!" Columbia D 18000, shellac disc. Recorded 1926.

Leisner, Emmi. Brahms, "Die Mainacht." Pf. Michael Raucheisen. Membran 223073-303, compact disc. Recorded 1942.

Lemeshev, Sergei. Borodin, *Prince Igor*, "Medlenno den' ugasal." Grammplasrest 03800-1, shellac disc. Recorded 1937.

———. Gounod, *Faust*, "Salut! demeure" (in Russian). Cond. Alexander Melik-Pashayev. Grammplasttrest 0495, shellac disc. Recorded 1933.

———. Tchaikovsky, *Eugene Onegin*. With Glacier Zhukovskaya, Panteleimon Nortzov. Bolshoi Chorus and Orchestra, cond. Vasily Nebolsin. LYS 0010. Recorded 1936.

Lindi, Aroldo. Verdi, *Aida*. With Giannina Arangi-Lombardi, Armando Borgioli, Maria Capuana. La Scala Chorus and Orchestra, cond. Lorenzo Molajoli. VAIA 1083-2, compact disc. Recorded 1928.

Luccioni, José. Bizet, *Les pêcheurs de perles*, "Au fond du temple saint." With Pierre Deldi. Columbia BFX 16, shellac disc. Recorded 1935.

Lugo, Giuseppe. Puccini, *La bohème*, "Che gelida manina" ("Que cette main est froide"). Polydor 566139, shellac disc. Recorded 1932.

Marconi, Francesco. Verdi, *Rigoletto*, "Questa o quella." Pf. Salvatore Cottone. G&T 52788, shellac disc. Recorded 1903.

———. Verdi, *Messa da Requiem*, "Ingemisco." G&T 052057, shellac disc. Recorded 1903.

Martinelli, Giovanni. Leoncavallo, *Pagliacci*, "Vesti la giubba." Cond. Rosario Bourdon. Victor 6754, shellac disc. Recorded 1927.

———. Puccini, *Manon Lescaut*, "Donna non vidi mai." Victor 64410, shellac disc. Recorded 1914.

———. Puccini, *Turandot*, "Nessun dorma!" Orchestra of the Royal Opera House, cond. John Barbirolli. Dutton SJB 1032, compact disc. Recorded 1937.

———. Verdi, *Un ballo in maschera*. With Stella Roman, Richard Bonelli. Chorus and Orchestra of the Metropolitan Opera, cond. Ettore Panizza. Eklipse EKR CD 12, compact disc. Recorded 1942.

———. Verdi, *Don Carlo*, "Dio, che nell'alma infondere." With Giuseppe De Luca. Cond. Joseph Pasternack. Victor 89160, shellac disc. Recorded 1921.

Masini, Galliano. Leoncavallo, *Pagliacci*. With Onelia Fineschi, Tito Gobbi. Roma Opera Chorus and Orchestra, cond. Giuseppe Morelli. Fimvelstar FR033, compact disc. Recorded 1949.

McCormack, John. Brahms, "Die Mainacht." Pf. Edwin Schneider. HMV DA 628, shellac disc. Recorded 1924.

———. Donizetti, *L'elisir d'amore*, "Una furtiva lagrima." Victor 6204, shellac disc. Recorded 1910.

———. Mozart, *Don Giovanni*, "Il mio tesoro." Cond. Walter B. Rogers. Victor 74484, shellac disc. Recorded 1916.

———. Godard, *Jocelyn*, "Oh! ne t'éveille pas encor" ("Angels guard thee"). Vln. Fritz Kreisler. Cond. Walter B. Rogers. Victor 88483, shellac disc. Recorded 1914.

McCracken, James. Verdi, *Otello*, "Sì, pel ciel marmoreo giuro." With Robert Merrill. Bell Telephone Hour Orchestra, cond. Donald Voorhees. VAI 4280, DVD. Recorded 1964.

Melandri, Antonio. Mascagni, *Cavalleria rusticana*. With Lina Bruna Rasa, Afro Poli. Cond. Pietro Mascagni. Bongiovanni GB 1050-2, compact disc. Recorded 1938.

Melchior, Lauritz. Grieg, "Jeg elsker dig." Pf. Ignace Strasfogel. Victor 1882. Recorded 1937.

———. Leoncavallo, *Pagliacci*, "Vesti la giubba." Firestone Orchestra, cond. Howard Barlow. VAI 69124, VHS. Recorded 1950.

———. Meyerbeer, *L'Africaine*, "Ô paradis" ("Land so wunderbar"). Polydor 66439, shellac disc. Recorded 1926.

———. Strauss, "Căcilie." Polydor 66440, shellac disc. Recorded 1926.

———. Wagner, *Lohengrin*, "In fernem Land." Philadelphia Orchestra, cond. Eugene Ormandy. Victor 17726, shellac disc. Recorded 1939.

Merli, Francesco. Puccini, *Manon Lescaut*. With Maria Zamboni, Lorenzo Contati, Attilio Bardonali. La Scala Chorus and Orchestra, cond. Lorenzo Molajoli. Phonographe PH 5006/07, compact disc. Recorded 1930.

———. Puccini, *Turandot*, "Nessun dorma!" Columbia 1139, shellac disc. Recorded 1930.

———. Verdi, *Il trovatore*. With Bianca Scacciati, Giuseppina Zinetti, Enrico Molinari. La Scala Chorus and Orchestra, cond. Lorenzo Molajoli. Arkadia 78033, compact disc. Recorded 1930.

Muratore, Lucien. Gounod, *Roméo et Juliette*, "Ah! lève-toi, soleil!" Zonophone X 82577, shellac disc. Recorded 1905.

———. Meyerbeer, *L'Africaine*, "Ô paradis." Pathé 63012, shellac disc. Recorded 1916.

Noré, Georges. Gounod, *Faust*. With Geori Boué, Roger Rico, Roger Bourdin. Royal Philharmonic Chorus and Orchestra, cond. Sir Thomas Beecham. Naxos 8.110117-18, compact disc. Recorded 1947–48.

Öhman, Martin. Puccini, *La fanciulla del West*, "Ch'ella mi creda." Swedish Radio Orchestra, cond. Adolf Wiklund. Bluebell ABCD 080, compact disc. Recorded 1935.

Paoli, Antonio. Leoncavallo, *Pagliacci*. With Josefina Huguet, Francesco Cigada, Ernest Badini. La Scala Chorus and Orchestra, cond. Carlo Sabajno. Bongiovanni GB 1120-2, compact disc. Recorded 1907.

Patzak, Julius. Mascagni, *Cavalleria rusticana*, "Siciliana" ("O Lola, rosengleich blüh'n deine Wangen"). Berlin State Opera Orchestra, cond. Alois Melichar. Grammophon 24327, shellac disc. Recorded 1931.

———. Massenet, *Manon*, "En fermant les yeux" ("Ich schloss die Augen"). Grammophon 90062, shellac disc. Recorded 1929.

———. Puccini, *La fanciulla del West* "Ch'ella mi creda" ("Lasset sie glauben"). Grammophon 90182, shellac disc. Recorded 1931.

———. Strauss, "Ständchen." Cond. Richard Strauss. Rococo 5348, LP. Recorded 1944.

———. Strauss, "Ständchen." Pf. Julius Prüwer. Grammophon 23923, shellac disc. Recorded 1931.

———. Strauss, "Morgen." BASF 10.22055-9, tape recording. Recorded 1944.

Pavarotti, Luciano. Donizetti, *L'elisir d'amore.* With Joan Sutherland, Dominic Cossa, Spiro Malas. Ambrosian Chorus, English Chamber Orchestra, cond. Richard Bonynge. Decca 475 7514, compact disc. Recorded 1970.

———. Leoncavallo, "Mattinata." Philharmonia Orchestra, cond. Piero Gamba. Decca 475 8386. Recorded 1977.

———. Puccini, *La bohème.* With Mirella Freni, Rolando Panerai. Chorus of the Deutsche Oper, Berlin Philharmonic Orchestra, cond. Herbert von Karajan. Decca 421049-2, compact disc. Recorded 1972.

———. Puccini, *Madama Butterfly.* With Mirella Freni. Vienna State Opera Chorus, Vienna Philharmonic Orchestra, cond. Herbert von Karajan. Decca 417 577-2, compact disc. Recorded 1974.

———. Puccini, *Turandot.* With Joan Sutherland, Montserrat Caballé. John Alldis Choir, London Philharmonic Orchestra, cond. Zubin Mehta. Decca 414 2742, compact disc. Recorded 1972.

———. Puccini, *Turandot.* With Monserrat Caballé, Leona Mitchell. Chorus and Orchestra of the San Francisco Opera, cond. Riccardo Chailly. Legato LCD 188-2, compact disc. Recorded 1977.

———. Rossini, "La danza." Pf. James Levine. Decca 000320809, DVD. Recorded 1988.

———. Rossini, *Stabat Mater.* With Teresa Zylis-Gara, Shirley Verrett, Nicola Zaccaria. Chorus and Orchestra of the RAI, Milan, cond. Carlo Maria Giulini. Hunt LSMH 34026, compact disc. Recorded 1967.

———. Verdi, *Rigoletto.* With Sherill Milnes, Joan Sutherland. Ambrosian Chorus, London Symphony Orchestra, cond. Richard Bonynge. Decca 414 269-2, compact disc. Recorded 1971.

———. Verdi, *Il trovatore.* With Antonella Banaudi, Shirley Verrett, Leo Nucci. Chorus and Orchestra of the Maggio Musicale, cond. Zubin Mehta. Decca 430 694-2, compact disc. Recorded 1990.

———. Verdi, *Un ballo in maschera.* With Margaret Price, Renato Bruson. London Opera Chorus, National Philharmonic Orchestra, cond. Sir Georg Solti. Decca 410 210-2, compact disc. Recorded 1983.

———. Verdi, *Messa da Requiem.* With Joan Sutherland, Marilyn Horne, Martti Talvela. Vienna State Opera Chorus, Vienna Philharmonic Orchestra, cond. Georg Solti. Decca 4757735, compact disc. Recorded 1967.

Peerce, Jan. Puccini, *La bohème.* With Licia Albanese, Frank Valentino. NBC Symphony Chorus and Orchestra, cond. Arturo Toscanini. RCA GD60288. Recorded 1946.

Pertile, Aureliano. Leoncavallo, *Pagliacci,* "Vesti la giubba." Fonotipia 20012, shellac disc. Recorded 1927.

———. Leoncavallo, *Pagliacci*, "Un grande spettacolo." Fonotipia R-20026, shellac disc. Recorded 1927.

———. Puccini, *Manon Lescaut*, "Donna non vidi mai." Columbia 15625, shellac disc. Recorded 1923.

———. Puccini, *La fanciulla del West*, "Ch'ella mi creda." Pathé 88413, shellac disc. Recorded 1924.

———. Puccini, *Turandot*, "Nessun dorma!" Fonotipia 6024, shellac disc. Recorded 1927.

———. Verdi, *Il trovatore*. With Maria Carena, Irene Minghini-Cattaneo, Apollo Granforte. La Scala Chorus and Orchestra, cond. Gino Nastrucci. Deltadischi DPR 2002, compact disc. Recorded 1930.

———. Verdi, *Il trovatore*, "Mal reggendo all'aspro assalto." Fonotipia R.20047, shellac disc. Recorded 1927.

———. Verdi, *Un ballo in maschera*, "Forse la soglia." Fonotipia 74974, shellac disc. Recorded 1926.

———. Verdi, *Aida*. With Dusolina Giannini, Irene Minghini-Cattaneo, Giovanni Inghilleri. La Scala Chorus and Orchestra, cond. Carlo Sabajno. Deltadischi DPR 2004, compact disc. Recorded 1928.

———. Wagner, *Lohengrin*, "In fernem Land" ("Da voi lontan"). Fonotipia 120.000, shellac disc. Recorded 1926.

Piccaver, Alfred. Mascagni, *Cavalleria rusticana*, "Siciliana." Odeon 99937, shellac disc. Recorded 1923.

Picchi, Mirto. Verdi, *Don Carlo*. With Maria Caniglia, Paolo Silveri, Ebe Stignani. RAI Chorus and Orchestra, cond. Fernando Previtali. Fonit Cetra CDO 25, compact disc. Recorded 1951.

Prandelli, Giacinto. Verdi, *Messa da Requiem*. With Renata Tebaldi, Cloe Elmo, Cesare Siepi. La Scala Chorus and Orchestra, cond. Arturo Toscanini. IDIS 345/46, compact disc. Recorded 1951.

Raimondi, Gianni. Meyerbeer, *L'Africaine*, "Ô paradis" ("O paradiso"). RAI Orchestra, cond. Alfredo Simonetto. Bongiovanni GB 1187-2, compact disc. Recorded 1956.

———. Puccini, *La bohème*. With Mirella Freni, Rolando Panerai. La Scala Chorus and Orchestra, cond. Herbert von Karajan. DG B0004767-09, DVD. Recorded 1965.

———. Puccini, *La bohème*, "Che gelida manina." Cond. Benedetto Ghiglia. Elsa Music ELM 203, compact disc. Recorded 1962.

———. Thomas, *Mignon*, "Ah! non credevi tu." RAI Orchestra, cond. Alfredo Simonetto. Bongiovanni GB 1187-2, compact disc. Recorded 1956.

Rosvænge, Helge. Gounod, *Faust*. With Margarete Teschemacher, Georg Hann, Hans Hermann Nissen. Stuttgart Radio Chorus and Orchestra, cond. Joseph Keilberth. Preiser 90040, compact disc. Recorded 1937.

———. Mozart, *Don Giovanni*. With Tiana Lemnitz, Gerhard Hüsch, Erna Berger, Wilhelm Streinz. Berlin Philharmonic Orchestra, cond. Sir Thomas Beecham. EMI CHS 761034 2, compact disc. Recorded 1937.

———. Verdi, *Il trovatore*, "Ah sì, ben mio" ("Das nur für mich dein Herz erlebt"), HMV DB 4524, shellac disc. Recorded 1938.

———. Verdi, *Il trovatore,* "Dì tu se fedele" ("O sag, wenn ich fahr"). HMV DB 4445, shellac disc. Recorded 1936.

Scampini, Augusto. Verdi, *Un ballo in maschera,* "Di' tu se fedele." Gramophone 2-52616, shellac disc. Recorded 1908.

Scaremberg, Émile. Gounod, *Roméo et Juliette,* "Ah! lève-toi, soleil!" Fonotipia 39172, shellac disc. Recorded 1905.

Scheppan, Hilde. Schubert, "Die Allmacht." Pf. Michael Raucheisen. Membran 223210303. Recorded 1943.

Schiøtz, Axsel. Schubert, *Die schöne Müllerin.* Pf. Gerald Moore. Danacord DACOCD 452. Recorded 1945.

Schipa, Tito. Donizetti, *L'elisir d'amore,* "Una furtiva lagrima." Victor 6570, shellac disc. Recorded 1925.

———. Handel, *Serse,* "Ombra mai fu." Victor 6753, shellac disc. Recorded 1926.

———. Leoncavallo, *Pagliacci,* "O Colombina." Pathé 59009, shellac disc. Recorded 1916.

———. Mascagni, *Cavalleria rusticana,* "Siciliana." Pathé 54034, shellac disc. Recorded 1919.

———. Mozart, *Don Giovanni* (excerpts). With Rosa Ponselle, Ezio Pinza. Orchestra of the Metropolitan Opera, cond. Tullio Serafin. Andromeda ANDRCD 9026, compact disc. Recorded 1934.

———. Puccini, *La bohème,* "Che gelida manina." Cond. Carlo Sabajno. Grammofono 052422. Recorded 1913.

———. Verdi, *Rigoletto,* "Questa o quella." Pathé 10242, shellac disc. Recorded 1916.

———. Cilea, *L'Arlesiana,* "È la solita storia del pastore." Victor 7583, shellac disc. Recorded 1928.

Schlusnus, Heinrich. Beethoven, "Adelaide." Pf. Franz Rupp. Grammophon 95391, shellac disc. Recorded 1930.

———. Beethoven, "Die Ehre Gottes aus der Natur." Cond. Hermann Wiegart. Grammophon 95421, shellac disc. Recorded 1930.

———. Schubert, "Die Forelle." Pf. Sebastian Peschko. Grammophon 62855, shellac disc. Recorded 1943.

———. Schubert, "Frühlingsglaube." Pf. Sebastian Peschko. Grammophon 62795, shellac disc. Recorded 1938.

———. Schubert, "Standchen." Pf. Sebastian Peschko. Grammophon 67181, shellac disc. Recorded 1938.

———. Strauss, "Zueignung." Pf. Richard Strauss. Grammophon 14120, shellac disc. Recorded 1921.

Schmidt, Joseph. Verdi, *Il trovatore,* "Deserto sulla terra" ("Einsam steh ich und verlassen"). BelAge BLA 103.004, compact disc. Recorded 1930.

Signorini, Francesco. Verdi, *Il trovatore,* "Ah sì, ben mio," Gramophone 2-52669, shellac disc. Recorded 1908.

Slezak, Leo. Brahms, "Ständchen." Pf. Heinrich Schacker. Grammophon 42752, shellac disc. Recorded 1928.

———. Verdi, *Un ballo in maschera,* "Dì tu se fedele" ("O sag, wenn ich fahr"). Gramophone 3-42930, shellac disc. Recorded 1907.

Smirnov, Dimitri. Borodin, *Prince Igor,* "Medlenno den' ugasal." Cond. Julius Harrison. HMV 2-022025, shellac disc. Recorded 1923.

Souzay, Gérard. Schubert, "Ständchen." Pf. Dalton Baldwin. Testament SBT 1313, compact disc. Recorded 1954.

———. Sibelius, "Säv, säv, susa." Pf. Dalton Baldwin. Youtube, accessed September 18, 2011. http://www.youtube.com/watch?v=eLnM4Hle-sg&playnext=1&list=PL8F6BA019367001B3. Recorded 1956.

Stockman, David. Verdi, *Un ballo in maschera,* "Dì tu se fedele" ("O säg, när på skummande vågor"). HMV V162, shellac disc. Recorded 1910.

Stolze, Gerhard. Gounod, *Messe solennelle de Sainte Cécile.* With Irmgard Seefried, Hermann Uhede. Czech Philharmonic Chorus and Orchestra, cond. Igor Markevitch. DG 4777114, compact disc. Recorded 1965.

Tamagno, Francesco. Verdi, *Il trovatore,* "Deserto sulla terra." G&T 7-52277, shellac disc. Recorded 1903.

———. Verdi, *Otello,* "Sì, pel ciel marmoreo giuro." Historic Masters HMFT5, vinyl 78 rpm disc. Recorded 1903.

Tauber, Richard. Grieg, "Jeg elsker dig" ("Ich liebe dich"). Odeon Rxx 80867. Recorded 1924.

———. Grieg, "En Drøm" ("Ein Traum"). Odeon RXxx 76205, shellac disc. Recorded 1920.

———. Massenet, "Élégie," Eklipse EKR CD5, compact disc. Recorded 1937.

———. Mozart, *Die Zauberflöte,* "Dies Bildnis." Parlophone PMB1011, shellac disc. Recorded 1922.

———. Schubert, "Ständchen," Odeon 0-8160, shellac disc. Recorded 1925.

———. Strauss, "Zueignung." Odeon Rxx 76755, shellac disc. Recorded 1919.

———. Strauss, "Morgen." Odeon 80082, shellac disc. Recorded 1920.

———. Strauss, "Traum durch die Dämmerung." Odeon Rxx 80451, shellac disc. Recorded 1926.

———. Liszt, "Es muss ein Wunderbares sein," Odeon 8353, shellac disc. Recorded 1928.

Thill, Georges. Adam, "Cantique de Noël." Cond. Armand Bernard. French Columbia LFX 275, shellac disc. Recorded 1932.

———. Gounod, *Faust,* "Salut! demeure." Cond. E. Bigot. Columbia 25-LF 17, shellac disc. Recorded 1931.

———. Gounod, *Roméo et Juliette,* "Ah! lève-toi, soleil!" Cond. P. Gaubert. Columbia 30-L 1985, shellac disc. Recorded 1927.

———. Massenet, "Élégie." Cond. P. Chagnon. Columbia 25-LF 104, shellac disc. Recorded 1932.

———. Puccini, *Turandot,* "Nessun dorma!" Columbia 14544, shellac disc. Recorded 1927.

Tucker, Richard. Verdi, *Un ballo in maschera.* With Zinka Milanov, Josef Metternich. Metropolitan Opera Chorus and Orchestra, cond. Dimitri Mitropoulos. GOP 66.326, compact disc. Recorded 1955.

———. Verdi, *La forza del destino.* With Leontyne Price, Robert Merrill. RCA Italiana Chorus and Orchestra, cond. Thomas Schippers. RCA GD8971. Recorded 1964.

———. Verdi, *Aida.* With Herva Nelli, Giuseppe Valdengo, Eva Gustavson. Robert Shaw Chorale, NBC Symphony Orchestra, cond. Arturo Toscanini. Urania 22.244, compact disc. Recorded 1949.

———. Verdi, *Aida.* With Maria Callas, Tito Gobbi, Fedora Barbieri. La Scala Chorus and Orchestra, cond. Tullio Serafin. Naxos 8.111240-41, compact disc. Recorded 1955.

Urlus, Jacques. Mozart, *Die Zauberflöte,* "Dies Bildnis." Gramophone 042339, shellac disc. Recorded 1911.

Valente, Alessandro. Puccini, *Turandot,* "Nessun dorma!" HMV B 2458, shellac disc. Recorded 1927.

Valero, Fernando. Mascagni, *Cavalleria rusticana,* "Siciliana." G&T 52717, shellac disc. Recorded 1903.

———. Mascagni, *Cavalleria rusticana,* "Viva il vino spumeggiante." G&T 52718, shellac disc. Recorded 1903.

Valletti, Cesare. Massenet, *Manon.* With Victoria de los Angeles. Metropolitan Chorus and Orchestra, cond. Pierre Monteux. Bongiovanni HOC 013/14, compact disc. Recorded 1954.

———. Mozart, *Don Giovanni,* "Il mio tesoro." RAI Orchestra, cond. Arturo Basile. Urania 22.236. Recorded 1949.

———. Rachmaninoff, "v molchan 'i nochi taynoy" ("In the Silence of the Night"). Pf. Leo Taubman. Testament SBT2-1413. Recorded 1960.

Vanzo, Alain. Bizet, *Les pêcheurs de perles.* With Gabriel Bacquier, Janine Micheau. Orchestre Radio-Lyrique, cond. Manuel Rosenthal. Gala GL 100.504, compact disc. Recorded 1959.

Vezzani, César. Gounod, *Faust.* With Mireille Berthon, Marcel Journet, Louis Musy. Chorus and Orchestra of the Paris Opéra, cond. Henri Busser. Malibran CDRG 104, compact disc. Recorded 1930.

Vickers, Jon. Puccini, *Tosca,* "Recondita armonia." Rome Opera Orchestra, cond. Tullio Serafin. VAIA 1016, compact disc. Recorded 1961.

———. Verdi, *Un ballo in maschera.* With Amy Shuard, Ettore Bastianini. Chorus and Orchestra of the Royal Opera House, cond. Edward Downes. Royal Opera House ROHS009, compact disc. Recorded 1962.

———. Verdi, *Don Carlo,* "Io la vidi." Rome Opera Orchestra, cond. Tullio Serafin. VAIA 1016, compact disc. Recorded 1961.

———. Verdi, *Aida.* With Leontyne Price, Rita Gorr, Robert Merrill. Rome Opera Chorus and Orchestra, cond. Georg Solti. Decca 460 765-2, compact disc. Recorded 1962.

Völker, Franz. Verdi, *Il trovatore,* "Ah sì, ben mio" ("Das nur für mich dein Herz erlebt"). Grammophon 95377, shellac disc. Recorded 1928.

———. Verdi. *Don Carlo,* "Vago sogno d'arrise" ("Süsse Bilder des Glückes entschwanden"). With Hilde Konetzni. Vienna State Opera Chorus and Orchestra, cond. Bruno Walter. Koch Schwann 3-1460-2, compact disc. Recorded 1937.

———. Wagner, *Lohengrin,* "In fernem Land." Grammophon 19711, shellac disc. Recorded 1927.

Winkelmann, Hermann. Verdi, *Il trovatore,* "Deserto sulla terra" ("Einsam steh ich und verlassen"). Berliner 1528A, shellac disc. Recorded 1900.

Wunderlich, Fritz. Beethoven, "Adelaide." Pf. Hubert Giesen. DG 9806790, compact disc. Recorded 1966.

———. Beethoven, *Missa Solemnis.* With Gundula Janowitz, Christa Ludwig, Walter Berry. Vienna Singverein, Berlin Philharmonic Orchestra, cond. Herbert von Karajan. DG 423 913-2, compact disc. Recorded 1966.

———. Brahms, "Die Mainacht." DG 476 5244, compact disc. Undated private recording released 2008.

———. Mozart, *Die Zauberflöte,* "Dies Bildnis." Berlin Symphony Orchestra, cond. Berislav Kobucar. EMI 5 75915 2, compact disc. Recorded 1960.

———. Schubert, "Die Forelle." Pf. Hubert Giesen. DG 9806790, compact disc. Recorded 1966.

———. Schubert, "Frühlingsglaube." Pf. Hubert Giesen. DG 447 452-2, compact disc. Recorded 1966.

———. Schubert, "An Sylvia." Pf. Hubert Giesen. DG 9806790, compact disc.

Zenatello, Giovanni. Puccini, *La fanciulla del West,* "Ch'ella mi creda." Fonotipia 92851, shellac disc. Recorded 1911.

———. Verdi, *Un ballo in maschera,* "Oh qual soave brivido." With Eugenia Burzio. Fonotipia 39665/66, shellac disc. Recorded 1906.

———. Verdi, *Un ballo in maschera,* "Dì tu se fedele." Odeon 40250, shellac disc. Recorded 1905.

Other Cited Recordings

Björling, Jussi. *The Björling Family: Four Singing Brothers and Two Ladies.* With Gösta Björling, Olle Björling, Karl Björling, Anna-Lisa Björling, Bette Wermine Björling. Bluebell ABCD 066, compact disc. Recorded 1920–71.

———. *Jussi Björling Collection, vol. 7.* Naxos 8.110792, compact disc. Recorded 1929–53.

———. *Jussi Björling Live: Broadcast Concerts 1937–1960.* West Hill Radio Archives WHRA-6036, compact disc. Recorded 1937–60.

———. *The Complete RCA Album Collection.* RCA 88697748922, compact disc. Recorded 1947–59.

Block, Julius. *The Dawn of Recording: The Julius Block Cylinders.* Marston 53011-2, compact disc. Recorded 1890–1927.

Kraus, Alfredo. *Una Lezione di Canto.* Bongiovanni GB550/51-2, compact disc Recorded 1990.

Puccini, *Turandot.* With Maria Callas, Eugenio Fernandi, Elizabeth Schwarzkopf, Nicola Zaccaria, Mario Borriello, Renato Ercolani, Piero De Palma, Giuseppe Nessi. La Scala Chorus and Orchestra, cond. Tullio Serafin. Naxos 8111334-35, compact disc. Recorded 1957.

Schmidt-Garre, Jan. *Belcanto: Tenors of the 78 Era, Part II.* TDK Euroarts DVD 2050217, DVD. Televised 1997.

Verdi, *La traviata.* With Jane Morlet, Maurizio Troselli, Henri Albers. Cond. Émile Archainbaud. Marston 52043-2, compact disc. Recorded 1912.

BIBLIOGRAPHY

Amis, John. "Elisabeth Söderström." In *Sopranos in Opera.* London: Opera Magazine, 2001.

Ardoin, John. *Callas at Juilliard: The Master Classes.* London: Robson, 1987.

Baxter, Robert. "Jussi Björling (1911–1960)." *Opera Quarterly* 16, no. 2 (2000): 181–89.

Beecham, Thomas. "The Question of Faust as Sir Thomas Beecham put it to the Metropolitan Opera Guild." *Opera News,* January 25, 1943, 6.

Beethoven, Ludwig van. *Letters.* Vol. 1. Edited by A. C. Kalischer. Translated by J. D. Shedlock. New York: Dent; Dutton, 1909.

Bing, Sir Rudolf. *The Memoirs of Sir Rudolph Bing: 5000 Nights at the Opera.* New York: Doubleday, 1972.

Björling, Anna-Lisa, and Andrew Farkas. *Jussi.* Portland: Amadeus, 1996.

Björling, David. *Hur man skall sjunga.* Stockholm: Eriks Förlaget, 1978.

Björling, Jussi. *Med bagaget i strupen.* Stockholm: Wahlström & Widstrand, 1945.

———. "Good Singing is Natural." *Etude* 58, no. 10 (October 1940): 655.

———. "Advice from Jussi Björling: Your Vocal Problem." *Etude* 68, no. 6 (June 1950): 21.

Blyth, Alan, ed. *Opera on Record.* London: Hutchinson, 1979.

———. *Opera on Record 2.* London: Hutchinson, 1983.

———. *Opera on Record 3.* London: Hutchinson, 1984.

———. *Song on Record 1: Lieder.* Cambridge: Cambridge University Press, 1986.

———. *Choral Music on Record.* Cambridge: Cambridge University Press, 1991.

Burroughs, Bruce. "In Review: Met Stars Sing Verdi." *Opera Quarterly* 18, no. 2 (2002): 155–82.

———. "Zinka Milanov and Floria Tosca: Art, Love and Politics" II. *Opera Quarterly* 19, no. 4 (2003): 683–753.

Celletti, Rodolfo. *Il Teatro d'Opera in Disco.* Milan: Rizzoli, 1988.

———, ed. *Le grandi voci.* Rome: Istituto per la Collaborazione Culturale, 1964.

Celli, Teodoro, and Giuseppe Pugliese. *Tullio Serafin: Il patriarca del melodramma.* Venice: Corbo e Fiore, 1985.

Clampton, Denis. "Comparisons of an Aria: "Salut! demeure." *Record Collector* 40, no. 3 (1995): 204–16.

Condé, Gérard. "Faust: Guide d'écoute." *Avant-scène opéra* 231 (2006): 8–70.

Cook, J. Douglas. "Jussi Bjoerling: The Supreme Operatic Tenor." *The Argonaut,* September 21, 1956, 7.

Cook, Nicholas, Eric Clarke, Daniel Leech-Wilkinson, and John Rink, eds. *The Cambridge Companion to Recorded Music.* Cambridge: Cambridge University Press, 2009.

Douglas, Nigel. *Legendary Voices*. London: Andre Deutch, 1992.
Drake, James. "Kipnis Speaks." *Opera Quarterly* 8, no. 2 (1991): 88.
Farkas, Andrew. "Björling and Ballo: The Most Unkindest Cut of All." *Opera Quarterly* 16, no. 2 (2000): 190–203.
Farrar, Geraldine. *All Good Greetings, G. F.: Letters of Geraldine Farrar to Ilka Marie Stotler, 1946–1958*. Edited by Aida Craig Truxall. Pittsburgh: University of Pittsburgh Press, 1991,
Ferraro, Domenico, Nandi Ostali, and Piero Ostali Jr. *Francesco Cilea*. Milano: Casa Musicale Sonzogno, 2000.
Forsell, Jacob, Björn Ranelid, and Harald Henrysson. *Jussi: Sången, människan, bilderna*. Stockholm: Norstedts förlag, 2010.
Gara, Eugenio, ed. *Carteggi pucciniani*. Milan: Ricordi, 1986.
García, Manuel. *Trattato completo dell'arte del canto: Scuola di García*. Milan: Ricordi, 1847.
Gedda, Nicolai. *Nicolai Gedda: My Life and Art*. Portland: Amadeus, 1999.
Goldberg, Don. "A Charmless Jussi?." *Journal of the Jussi Björling Society* 9 (2000): 18–19.
Gossett, Philip. "Verdi's Ideas on Interpreting his Operas." In *Verdi 2001: Atti del Convegno Internazionale, Parma—New York—New Haven*, edited by Fabrizio Della Seta, Roberta Montemorra Marvin, and Marco Marica, 399–407. Florence: Leo S. Olschki, 2003.
———. *Divas and Scholars: Performing Italian Opera*. Chicago: University of Chicago Press, 2006.
Green, London, William Ashbrook, M. Owen Lee, and Robert Baxter. "Jussi Björling (1911–1960): A Remembrance." *Opera Quarterly* 16, no. 2 (2000): 180–89.
Greenfield, Edward."Turandot." In Blyth, *Opera on Record*, 618.
Groos, Arthur, and Roger Parker. *Giacomo Puccini: La Bohème*. Cambridge Opera Handbooks. Cambridge: Cambridge University Press, 1986.
Hagman, Bertil. *Jussi Björling: En minnesbok*. Stockholm: Bonniers, 1960.
Hahn, Reynaldo. *Du chant*. Paris: Gallimard, 1957.
Heckler, Karl, Ed Walter, Don Goldberg, Bill Clayton, and Mati Zeiti. "Memories of Jussi Björling as Turiddu." *Journal of the Jussi Björling Society* 16 (2008): 30–33.
Henrysson, Harald. *A Jussi Björling Phonography*. Stockholm: Svenskt Musikhistoriskt Arkiv, 1993.
———. "Björling's Canio on Stage: A Survey of Reviews." *Journal of the Jussi Björling Society* 16 (2008): 16–19.
———. "David Björling: Swedish Tenor." 2 parts. *Journal of the Jussi Björling Society* 18 (2010): 15–18; 19 (2011): 12–16.
Hope-Wallace, Philip. "Manon Lescaut." *Gramophone*, February 1956, 64.
Horowitz, Joseph. *Understanding Toscanini*. New York: Knopf, 1987.
Jackson, Paul. *Saturday Afternoons at the Old Met*. London: Duckworth, 1992.
———. *Sign-Off for the Old Met*. London: Duckworth, 1997.
Kaplan, Louis. "Bits and Pieces about Jussi: An Interview with Albert White." *Journal of the Jussi Björling Society* 9 (2000): 2–8.
Kolodin, Irving. "Sir Thomas Beecham on *La Bohème* and Puccini." *Gramophone*, January 1957, 27.
Lauri Volpi, Giacomo. *Voci parallele*. Bologna: Bongiovanni, 1977.

Lawrence, Felicity. "Children's Singing." In Potter, *The Cambridge Companion to Singing*, 221–30.

Lee, M. Owen. *First Intermissions*. Oxford: Oxford University Press, 1995.

Leech-Wilkinson, Daniel. *The Changing Sound of Music: Approaches to Studying Recorded Musical Performances*. London: CHARM, 2009. www.charm.kcl.ac.uk.

Marafioti, P. Mario. *Caruso's Method of Voice Production*. New York: Appleton, 1922.

Metopera Database: The Metropolitan Opera Archives. Accessed September 18, 2011. http://archives.metoperafamily.org/archives/frame.htm.

Meyer, Michael. "Jussi Björling's Vocal Training." *Journal of the Jussi Björling Society* 19 (2011): 5–7.

Monaldi, Gino. *Cantanti celebri del secolo XIX*. Rome: Nuova Antologia, 1907.

Nävermyr, Stefan. "Song of Sweden." *Classic Record Collector* 24 (2001): 38–44.

Newton, Ivor. *At the Piano-Ivor Newton: The World of an Accompanist*. London: Hamilton, 1966.

Nilsson, Birgit. *La Nilsson: My Life in Opera*. Boston: Northeastern University Press, 2007.

Nyblom, Teddy. "Jussi Björling." *Scenen* 24 (November 1933): 34.

Osborne, Conrad. "Roméo et Juliette." *Opus* 1, no. 1 (December 1984): 32–33.

———. "Tosca." In *The Metropolitan Opera Guide to Recorded Opera*, edited by Paul Gruber, 411–25. New York: Norton, 1993.

Padoan, Paolo, and Maurizio Tiberi. *Giovanni Martinelli: Un leone al Metropolitan*. Rome: Edizioni del Timaclub, 2007.

Philip, Robert. *Early Recordings and Musical Style*. Cambridge: Cambridge University Press, 1992.

Porter, Andrew. *Music of Three Seasons, 1974–1977*. London: Chatto & Windus, 1979.

———. "Björling at Carnegie Hall." *Gramophone*, February 1958, 20.

Potter, John. *Tenor: History of a Voice*. New Haven: Yale University Press, 1999.

———, ed. *The Cambridge Companion to Singing*. Cambridge: Cambridge University Press, 2000.

Prévost, Antoine François (Abbé). *Manon Lescaut*. New York: Random House, 1940.

Prey, Hermann. *First Night Fever*. Translated by Andrew Shackleton. London: John Calder, 1985.

Ricci, Luigi. *Puccini interprete di se stesso*. Milan: Ricordi, 1954.

———. *Variazioni—cadenze—tradizioni: per canto*. Vol. 2. Milan: Ricordi, 1981.

Rosen, David. *Verdi: Requiem*. Cambridge: Cambridge University Press, 1995.

Rosenqvist, Mårten. "Jussi Björlings hjärta slot 200 slag per munut." *Läkartidningen* 15 (2011): 874–76.

Sachs, Harvey. *Toscanini*. Turin: EDT, 1978.

———, ed. *Nel mio cuore troppo d'assoluto: Lettere di Arturo Toscanini*. Milan: Garzanti, 2003,

Scott, Michael. *The Record of Singing*. 2 vols. London: Duckworth, 1977–79.

Scott, Michael. "Not Yet the Fourth Tenor." *Spectator*, December 2, 1995, 53–54.

Sirén, Vesa, ed. *The Jean Sibelius Website*. Accessed September 18, 2011. http://www.sibelius.fi/english.

Springer, Morris. "On the Road with Jussi." *Opera News*, February 26, 1972, 30–31.

Steane, John, *The Grand Tradition*. London: Duckworth, 1974.

———. *Singers of the Century*. Vol. 2. London: Duckworth, 1998.

Stenius Yrsa. *Tills vingen brister:Utökad Jubileumsutgåva.* Stockholm: Brombergs, 2011.

Tomatis, Alfred. *The Ear and the Voice.* Translated by Roberta Prada. Lanham, MD: Scarecrow, 2005.

Voghera, Giulio. "Tullio Voghera, My Father." *Journal of the Jussi Björling Society* 17 (2009): 5–10.

INDEX

Page numbers in italics indicate illustrations.